ROAD ATLAS

2025 BRITAIN & IRELAND

www.philips-maps.co.uk

First published in 2009 as
Complete Road Atlas Britain and Ireland by Philip's,
a division of Octopus Publishing Group Ltd
www.octopusbooks.co.uk
Carmelite House, 50 Victoria Embankment
London EC4Y 0DZ
An Hachette UK Company
www.hachette.co.uk

Sixteenth edition 2024
First impression 2024

ISBN 978-1-84907-668-5 spiral-bound
ISBN 978-1-84907-667-8 paperback

Cartography by Philip's
Copyright © 2024 Philip's

This product includes mapping data licensed from Ordnance Survey®, with the permission of the Controller of His Majesty's Stationery Office. © Crown copyright 2024. All rights reserved. Licence number AC0000851689.

The map of Ireland on pages XVI–XVII is based upon the Crown Copyright and is reproduced with the permission of Land & Property Services under delegated authority from the Controller of His Majesty's Stationery Office, © Crown Copyright and database right 2023, PMLPA number 100503, and on Ordnance Survey Ireland by permission of the Government © Ordnance Survey Ireland / Government of Ireland Permit number 9296.

While every reasonable effort has been made to ensure that the information compiled in this atlas is accurate, complete and up-to-date at the time of publication, some of this information is subject to change and the Publisher cannot guarantee its correctness or completeness.

The information in this atlas is provided without any representation or warranty, express or implied and the Publisher cannot be held liable for any loss or damage due to any use or reliance on the information in this atlas, nor for any errors, omissions or subsequent changes in such information.

The representation in this atlas of any road, drive or track is no evidence of the existence of a right of way.

Information for National Parks, National Trails and Country Parks in Wales supplied by the Countryside Council for Wales.

Information for National Parks, National Landscapes, National Trails and Country Parks in England supplied by Natural England. Data for Regional Parks, Long Distance Footpaths and Country Parks in Scotland provided by Scottish Natural Heritage.

Gaelic name forms used in the Western Isles provided by Comhairle nan Eilean.

Data for the National Nature Reserves in England provided by Natural England. Data for the National Nature Reserves in Wales provided by Countryside Council for Wales. Darparwyd data'n ymwneud â Gwarchodfeydd Natur Cenedlaethol Cymru gan Gyngor Cefn Gwlad Cymru.

Information on the location of National Nature Reserves in Scotland was provided by Scottish Natural Heritage.

Data for National Scenic Areas in Scotland provided by the Scottish Government. Crown copyright material is reproduced with the permission of the Controller of HMSO and the King's Printer for Scotland. Licence number C02W0003960.

Printed in China

*Data from Nielsen Total Consumer Market 2023 weeks 1–52

CONTENTS

T0299506

II **Key to map symbols**

III **Smart motorways and motorway service areas**

IV **Restricted motorway junctions**

VI **Route planning maps**

XVI **Road map of Ireland**

XVIII **Top tips for better driving**

XIX **The Highway Code**

XX **Distances and journey times**

1 **Key to road map pages**

2 **Road maps of Britain**

161 **Urban approach maps**

161 Bristol *approaches*
162 Birmingham *approaches*
164 Cardiff *approaches*
165 Edinburgh *approaches*
166 Glasgow *approaches*
167 Leeds *approaches*
168 London *approaches*
172 Liverpool *approaches*
173 Manchester *approaches*
174 Newcastle *approaches*

175 **Town plans**

175 Aberdeen, Ayr, Bath
176 Birmingham, Blackpool, Bournemouth
177 Bradford, Brighton, Bristol
178 Bury St Edmunds, Cambridge, Canterbury,Cardiff
179 Carlisle, Chelmsford, Cheltenham, Chester
180 Chichester, Colchester, Coventry, Derby
181 Dorchester, Dumfries, Dundee, Durham
182 Edinburgh, Exeter, Gloucester
183 Glasgow, Grimsby, Harrogate
184 Hull, Inverness, Ipswich, Kendal
185 King's Lynn, Lancaster, Leeds
186 London
188 Leicester, Lincoln, Liverpool
189 Llandudno, Llanelli, Luton, Macclesfield
190 Manchester, Maidstone, Merthyr Tydfil
191 Middlesbrough, Milton Keynes, Newcastle, Newport
192 Newquay, Northampton, Norwich, Nottingham
193 Oxford, Perth, Peterborough, Plymouth
194 Poole, Portsmouth, Preston, Reading
195 St Andrews, Salisbury, Scarborough, Shrewsbury,
196 Sheffield, Stoke-on-Trent (Hanley), Southampton
197 Southend, Stirling, Stratford-upon-Avon, Sunderland
198 Swansea, Swindon, Taunton, Telford
199 Torquay, Truro, Winchester, Windsor
200 Wolverhampton, Worcester, Wrexham, York

201 **Index to town plans**

213 **Index to road maps of Britain**

Inside back cover:
County and unitary authority boundaries

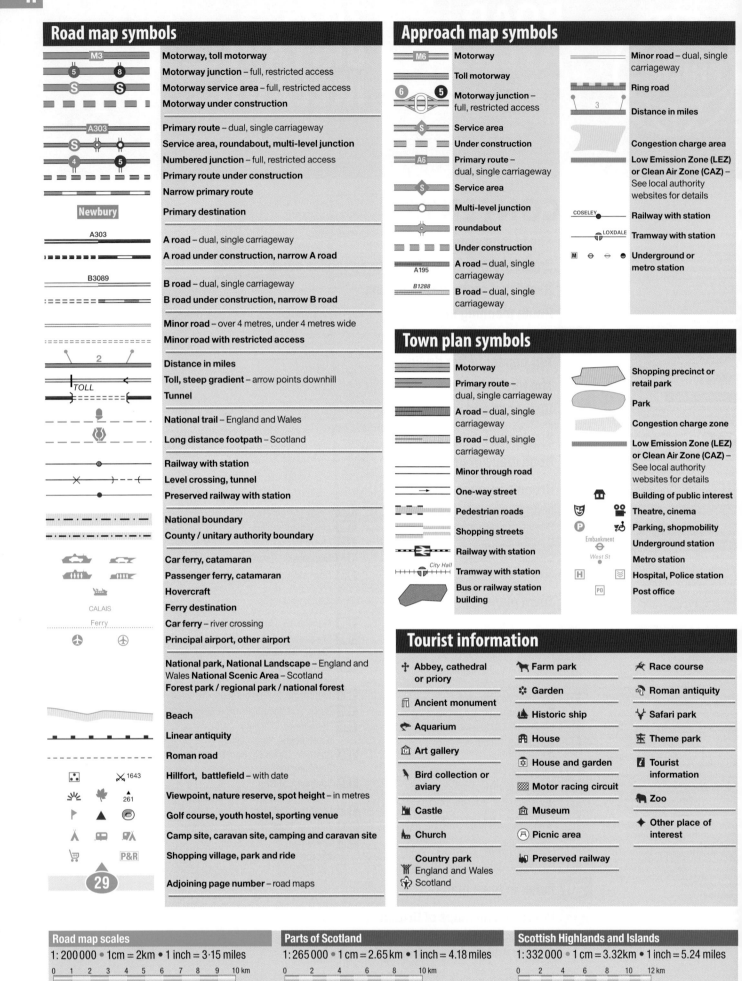

Road map symbols

- Motorway, toll motorway
- Motorway junction – full, restricted access
- Motorway service area – full, restricted access
- Motorway under construction

- Primary route – dual, single carriageway
- Service area, roundabout, multi-level junction
- Numbered junction – full, restricted access
- Primary route under construction
- Narrow primary route
- **Newbury** Primary destination

- A303 A road – dual, single carriageway
- A road under construction, narrow A road
- B3089 B road – dual, single carriageway
- B road under construction, narrow B road
- Minor road – over 4 metres, under 4 metres wide
- Minor road with restricted access
- Distance in miles
- TOLL Toll, steep gradient – arrow points downhill
- Tunnel
- National trail – England and Wales
- Long distance footpath – Scotland
- Railway with station
- Level crossing, tunnel
- Preserved railway with station
- National boundary
- County / unitary authority boundary
- Car ferry, catamaran
- Passenger ferry, catamaran
- Hovercraft
- CALAIS Ferry destination
- Ferry Car ferry – river crossing
- Principal airport, other airport
- National park, National Landscape – England and Wales National Scenic Area – Scotland Forest park / regional park / national forest
- Beach
- Linear antiquity
- Roman road
- Hillfort, battlefield – with date
- Viewpoint, nature reserve, spot height – in metres
- Golf course, youth hostel, sporting venue
- Camp site, caravan site, camping and caravan site
- Shopping village, park and ride
- 29 Adjoining page number – road maps

Approach map symbols

- M6 Motorway
- Toll motorway
- Motorway junction – full, restricted access
- S Service area
- Under construction
- A6 Primary route – dual, single carriageway
- S Service area
- Multi-level junction
- roundabout
- Under construction
- A195 A road – dual, single carriageway
- B1288 B road – dual, single carriageway
- Minor road – dual, single carriageway
- Ring road
- Distance in miles
- Congestion charge area
- Low Emission Zone (LEZ) or Clean Air Zone (CAZ) – See local authority websites for details
- COSELEY Railway with station
- LOXDALE Tramway with station
- Underground or metro station

Town plan symbols

- Motorway
- Primary route – dual, single carriageway
- A road – dual, single carriageway
- B road – dual, single carriageway
- Minor through road
- One-way street
- Pedestrian roads
- Shopping streets
- Railway with station
- City Hall Tramway with station
- Bus or railway station building
- Shopping precinct or retail park
- Park
- Congestion charge zone
- Low Emission Zone (LEZ) or Clean Air Zone (CAZ) – See local authority websites for details
- Building of public interest
- Theatre, cinema
- Parking, shopmobility
- Embankment Underground station
- West St Metro station
- H Hospital, Police station
- PO Post office

Tourist information

- ✝ Abbey, cathedral or priory
- 🏛 Ancient monument
- 🐟 Aquarium
- 🖼 Art gallery
- 🦜 Bird collection or aviary
- 🏰 Castle
- ⛪ Church
- Country park 🎪 England and Wales 🏴󠁧󠁢󠁳󠁣󠁴󠁿 Scotland
- 🐎 Farm park
- ❀ Garden
- ⚓ Historic ship
- 🏫 House
- House and garden
- Motor racing circuit
- 🏛 Museum
- Ⓟ Picnic area
- 🚂 Preserved railway
- 🏇 Race course
- Roman antiquity
- Safari park
- Theme park
- ℹ Tourist information
- 🐘 Zoo
- ✦ Other place of interest

Road map scales
1 : 200 000 • 1cm = 2km • 1 inch = 3·15 miles

0 1 2 3 4 5 6 7 8 9 10 km
0 1 2 3 4 5 6 miles

Parts of Scotland
1 : 265 000 • 1 cm = 2.65 km • 1 inch = 4.18 miles

0 2 4 6 8 10 km
0 1 2 3 4 5 6 miles

Scottish Highlands and Islands
1 : 332 000 • 1 cm = 3.32km • 1 inch = 5.24 miles

0 2 4 6 8 10 12 km
0 1 2 3 4 5 6 7 8 miles

Orkney and Shetland Islands 1:400 000 • 1cm = 4km • 1 inch = 6.31 miles

Smart motorways and motorway service areas

Smart motorways

M1
J6a–J10	Controlled motorway, 4-lane
J10–J13	Dynamic hard shoulder
J16–J13	All lane running
J19–J16	All lane running
J23a–J24	Controlled motorway, 4-lane
J24–J25	All lane running
J25–J28	Controlled motorway, 4-lane
J28–J31	All lane running
J31–J32	Controlled motorway, 4-lane
J32–J35a	All lane running
J 39–J42	All lane running

M3
J2–J4a	All lane running

M4
J3–J12	All lane running

M4–M5 interchange
M4J19–J20	Dynamic hard shoulder
M5J15–J16	Controlled motorway
M5J16–J17	Dynamic hard shoulder

M5
J4a–J6	All lane running

M6
J2–J3a	All lane running
J3a–J4	Controlled motorway, 3-lane
J4–J4a	*Northbound:* Dynamic hard shoulder *Southbound:* Controlled motorway, 3-lane
J4a–J8	Dynamic hard shoulder
J8–J10a	Dynamic hard shoulder
J10a–J11a	Controlled motorway, 3-lane
J11a–J13	All lane running
J13–J15	All lane running
J16–J19	All lane running
J20a–J26	All lane running

M20
J3–J5	All lane running
J5–J6	Controlled motorway, 3-lane
J6–J7	Controlled motorway, 4-lane

M23
J8–J10	All lane running

M25
J2–J3	Controlled motorway, 4-lane
J5–J6	All lane running
J6–J7	*Eastbound:* Controlled motorway, 4-lane *Westbound:* All lane running
J7–J12	Controlled motorway, 4-lane
J12–J14	Controlled motorway, 5-lane
J14–J15	Controlled motorway, 6-lane
J15–J23	All lane running
J23–J27	All lane running
J27–J30	Controlled motorway, 4-lane

M27
J4–J11	All lane running

M42
J3a–J7	Dynamic hard shoulder
J7–J9	Controlled motorway, 4-lane

M56
J6–J8	All lane running

M60
J8–J12	Controlled motorway, 3-lane
J12–J17	Controlled motorway, 4-lane

M62
J10–J12	All lane running
J18–J20	All lane running
J25–J26	All lane running
J 26–J28	Dynamic hard shoulder
J 28–J29	Controlled motorway, 4-lane
J 29–J30	*Eastbound:* Dynamic hard shoulder *Westbound:* All lane running

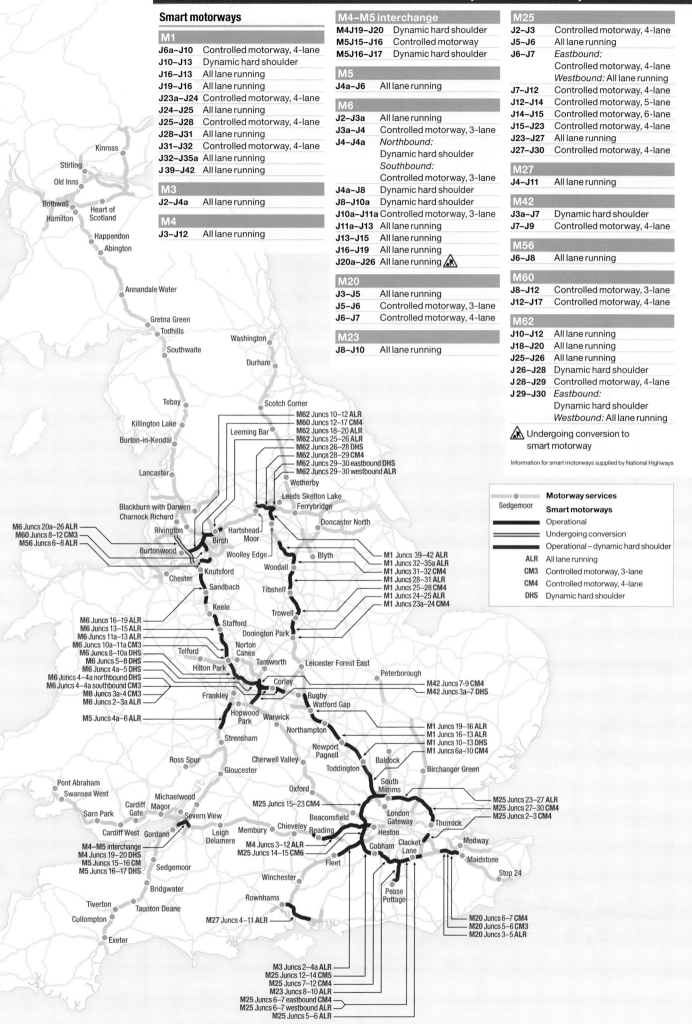

Undergoing conversion to smart motorway

Information for smart motorways supplied by National Highways

Legend:
- Motorway services — Sedgemoor
- Smart motorways
  - Operational
  - Undergoing conversion
  - Operational – dynamic hard shoulder
- ALR — All lane running
- CM3 — Controlled motorway, 3-lane
- CM4 — Controlled motorway, 4-lane
- DHS — Dynamic hard shoulder

Map labels:

Kinross, Stirling, Old Inns, Bothwell, Hamilton, Heart of Scotland, Happendon, Abington, Annandale Water, Gretna Green, Todhills, Southwaite, Washington, Durham, Tebay, Scotch Corner, Killington Lake, Burton-in-Kendal, Leeming Bar, Wetherby, Lancaster, Leeds Skelton Lake, Ferrybridge, Blackburn with Darwen, Charnock Richard, Rivington, Hartshead Moor, Doncaster North, Birch, Woolley Edge, Blyth, Woodall, Chester, Knutsford, Sandbach, Tibshelf, Keele, Stafford, Trowell, Donington Park, Norton Canes, Telford, Tamworth, Leicester Forest East, Hilton Park, Peterborough, Frankley, Corley, Rugby, Watford Gap, Hopwood Park, Warwick, Northampton, Strensham, Newport Pagnell, Baldock, Birchanger Green, Ross Spur, Cherwell Valley, Toddington, Gloucester, South Mimms, Pont Abraham, Swansea West, Oxford, Michaelwood, Cardiff Gate, Magor, Sarn Park, Cardiff West, Gordano, Severn View, Leigh Delamere, Membury, Chieveley, Reading, Beaconsfield, London Gateway, Heston, Cobham, Clacket Lane, Thurrock, Medway, Maidstone, Sedgemoor, Fleet, Winchester, Stop 24, Bridgwater, Tiverton, Taunton Deane, Rownhams, Cullompton, Pease Pottage, Exeter

Annotation callouts:

- M62 Juncs 10–12 ALR
- M60 Juncs 12–17 CM4
- M62 Juncs 18–20 ALR
- M62 Juncs 25–26 ALR
- M62 Juncs 26–28 DHS
- M62 Juncs 28–29 CM4
- M62 Juncs 29–30 eastbound DHS
- M62 Juncs 29–30 westbound ALR
- M6 Juncs 20a–26 ALR
- M60 Juncs 8–12 CM3
- M56 Juncs 6–8 ALR
- M1 Juncs 39–42 ALR
- M1 Juncs 32–35a ALR
- M1 Juncs 31–32 CM4
- M1 Juncs 28–31 ALR
- M1 Juncs 25–28 CM4
- M1 Juncs 24–25 ALR
- M1 Juncs 23a–24 CM4
- M6 Juncs 16–19 ALR
- M6 Juncs 13–15 ALR
- M6 Juncs 11a–13 ALR
- M6 Juncs 10a–11a CM3
- M6 Juncs 8–10a DHS
- M6 Juncs 5–8 DHS
- M6 Juncs 4a–5 DHS
- M6 Juncs 4–4a northbound DHS
- M6 Juncs 4–4a southbound CM3
- M6 Juncs 3a–4 CM3
- M6 Juncs 2–3a ALR
- M5 Juncs 4a–6 ALR
- M42 Juncs 7–9 CM4
- M42 Juncs 3a–7 DHS
- M1 Juncs 19–16 ALR
- M1 Juncs 16–13 ALR
- M1 Juncs 10–13 DHS
- M1 Juncs 6a–10 CM4
- M25 Juncs 15–23 CM4
- M25 Juncs 23–27 ALR
- M25 Juncs 27–30 CM4
- M25 Juncs 2–3 CM4
- M4 Juncs 3–12 ALR
- M25 Juncs 14–15 CM6
- M4–M5 interchange
- M4 Juncs 19–20 DHS
- M5 Juncs 15–16 CM
- M5 Juncs 16–17 DHS
- M27 Juncs 4–11 ALR
- M20 Juncs 6–7 CM4
- M20 Juncs 5–6 CM3
- M20 Juncs 3–5 ALR
- M3 Juncs 2–4a ALR
- M25 Juncs 12–14 CM5
- M25 Juncs 7–12 CM4
- M23 Juncs 8–10 ALR
- M25 Juncs 6–7 eastbound CM4
- M25 Juncs 6–7 westbound ALR
- M25 Juncs 5–6 ALR

Restricted motorway junctions

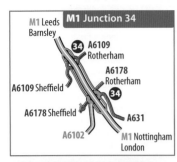

M1 Junction 34
M1 Leeds Barnsley
34 A6109 Rotherham
A6109 Sheffield
A6178 Rotherham
A6178 Sheffield
34 A631
A6102
M1 Nottingham London

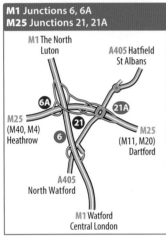

M1 Junctions 6, 6A
M25 Junctions 21, 21A
M1 The North Luton
A405 Hatfield St Albans
6A
21A
M25 (M40, M4) Heathrow
21
6
M25 (M11, M20) Dartford
A405 North Watford
M1 Watford Central London

M4 Junctions 25, 25A, 26
A4042 Abergavenny Cwmbran
A4051 Cwmbran
25A
25 B4596 Caerleon
26
A4042
A4051 Newport B4596
M4 Chepstow London
M4 Cardiff

M5 Junction 11A
A417 Gloucester
M5 Cheltenham (A40)
11A
A417 Cirencester
M5 Bristol B4641

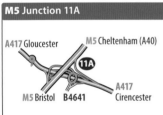

M11 Junctions 13, 14
A14 Huntingdon
A1307 Dry Drayton Oakington
A14 Newmarket
14
A1307 Cambridge
A428 St Neots
A1303 St Neots
13
A1303 Cambridge
M11 London

M8 Junctions 8, 9 ·
M73 Junctions 1, 2
9
M8 Glasgow
8
M73 Stirling
A89 Coatbridge
2
A8 M8 Edinburgh
1/4
M73
B7001
A74 B765 B7058
M74 Glasgow
A74
2A
3
M74
3A
B7071
B758
A721
M74 Carlisle
A763

M1	Northbound	Southbound
2	No exit	No access
4	No exit	No access
6A	No exit. Access from M25 only	No access. Exit to M25 only
7	No exit. Access from A414 only	No access. Exit to A414 only
17	No access. Exit to M45 only	No exit. Access from M45 only
19	No exit to A14	No access from A14
21A	No access	No exit
23A		Exit to A42 only
24A	No exit	No access
35A	No access	No exit
43	No access. Exit to M621 only	No exit. Access from M621 only
48	No exit to A1(M) southbound	

M3	Eastbound	Westbound
8	No exit	No access
10	No access	No exit
13	No access to M27 eastbound	
14	No exit	No access

M4	Eastbound	Westbound
1	Exit to A4 eastbound only	Access from A4 westbound only
2	Access from A4 eastbound only	Access to A4 westbound only
21	No exit	No access
23	No access	No exit
25	No exit	No access
25A	No exit	No access
29	No exit	No access
38		No access
39	No exit or access	No exit
42	Access from A483 only	Exit to A483 only

M5	Northbound	Southbound
10	No exit	No access
11A	No access from A417 eastbound	No exit to A417 westbound

M6	Northbound	Southbound
3A	No access.	No exit. Access from M6 eastbound only
4A	No exit. Access from M42 southbound only	No access. Exit to M42 only
5	No access	No exit
10A	No access. Exit to M54 only	No access. Access from M54 only
11A	No exit. Access from M6 Toll only	No access. Exit to M6 Toll only
20	No exit to M56 eastbound	No access from M56 westbound
20A	No exit	No access
24	No exit	No access
25	No access	No exit
30	No exit. Access from M61 northbound only	No access. Exit to M61 southbound only
31A	No access	No exit
45	No access	No exit

M6 Toll	Northbound	Southbound
T1		No exit
T2	No exit, no access	No access
T5	No exit	No access
T7	No access	No exit
T8	No access	No exit

M8	Eastbound	Westbound
6	No exit	No access
6A	No access	No exit
7	No Access	No exit
7A	No exit. Access from A725 northbound only	No access. Exit to A725 southbound only
8	No exit to M73 northbound	No access from M73 southbound
9	No access	No exit
13	No exit southbound	Access from M73 southbound only
14	No access	No exit
16	No exit	No access
17	No exit	
18		No exit
19	No exit to A814 eastbound	No access from A814 westbound
20	No exit	No access
21	No access from M74	No exit
22	No exit. Access from M77 only	No access. Exit to M77 only
23	No exit	No access
25	Exit to A739 northbound only. Access from A739 southbound only	
25A	No exit	No access
28	No exit	No access
28A	No exit	No access
29A	No exit	No access

M9	Eastbound	Westbound
2	No access	No exit
3	No exit	No access
6	No access	No exit
8	No exit	No access

M11	Northbound	Southbound
4	No exit	No access
5	No access	No exit
8A	No access	No exit
9	No access	No exit
13	No access	No exit
14	No exit to A428 westbound	No exit. Access from A14 westbound only

M20	Eastbound	Westbound
2	No access	No exit
3	No exit. Access from M26 eastbound only	No access. Exit to M26 westbound only
10	No access	No exit
11A	No access	No exit

M23	Northbound	Southbound
7	No exit to A23 southbound	No access from A23 northbound
10A	No exit	No access

M25	Clockwise	Anticlockwise
5	No exit to M26 eastbound	No access from M26 westbound
19	No access	No exit
21	No exit to M1 southbound. Access from M1 southbound only	No exit to M1 southbound. Access from M1 southbound only
31	No access	No exit

M27	Eastbound	Westbound
10	No exit	No access
12	No access	No exit

M40	Eastbound	Westbound
3	No exit	No access
7	No exit	No access
8	No exit	No access
13	No exit	No access
14	No access	No exit
16	No access	No exit

M42	Northbound	Southbound
1	No exit	No access
7	No access Exit to M6 northbound only	No exit. Access from M6 northbound only
7A	No access. Exit to M6 southbound only	No exit
8	No exit. Access from M6 southbound only	Exit to M6 northbound only. Access from M6 southbound only

M45	Eastbound	Westbound
M1 J17	Access to M1 southbound only	No access from M1 southbound
With A45	No access	No exit

M48	Eastbound	Westbound
M4 J21	No exit to M4 westbound	No access from M4 eastbound
M4 J23	No access from M4 westbound	No exit to M4 eastbound

M49	Southbound	Northbound
18A	No exit to M5 northbound	No access from M5 southbound

M53	Northbound	Southbound
11	Exit to M56 eastbound only. Access from M56 westbound only	Exit to M56 eastbnd only. Access from M56 westbound only

M56	Eastbound	Westbound
2	No exit	No access
3	No access	No exit
4	No exit	No access
7		No access
8	No exit or access	No exit
9	No access from M6 northbound	No access to M6 southbound
15	No exit to M53	No access from M53 northbound

M57	Northbound	Southbound
3	No exit	No access
5	No exit	No access

M60	Clockwise	Anticlockwise
2	No exit	No access
3	No exit to A34 northbound	No exit to A34 northbound
4	No access from M56	No exit to M56
5	No exit to A5103 southbound	No exit to A5103 northbound
14	No exit	No access
16	No exit	No access
20	No access	No exit
22		No access
25	No access	
26		No exit or access
27	No exit	No access

M61	Northbound	Southbound
2	No access from A580 eastbound	No exit to A580 westbound
3	No access from A580 eastbound. No access from A666 southbound	No exit to A580 westbound
M6 J30	No exit to M6 southbound	No access from M6 northbound

M62	Eastbound	Westbound
23	No access	No exit

M65	Eastbound	Westbound
9	No access	No exit
11	No exit	No access

M66	Northbound	Southbound
1	No access	No exit

M67	Eastbound	Westbound
1A	No access	No exit
2	No exit	No access

M69	Northbound	Southbound
2	No exit	No access

M73	Northbound	Southbound
2	No access from M8 eastbound	No exit to M8 westbound

M74	Northbound	Southbound
3	No access	No exit
3A	No access	No access
7	No exit	No access
9	No exit or access	No access
10		No access
11	No exit	No access
12	No access	No exit

M77	Northbound	Southbound
4	No exit	No access
6	No exit	No access
7	No exit	
8	No access	No access

M80	Northbound	Southbound
4A	No access	No exit
6A	No access	No access
8	Exit to M876 northbound only. No access	Access from M876 southbound only. No exit

M90	Northbound	Southbound
1	Access from A90 northbound only	No access. Exit to A90 southbound only
2A	No access	No exit
7	No exit	No access
8	No access	No exit
10	No access from A912	No exit to A912

M180	Eastbound	Westbound
1	No access	No exit

M621	Eastbound	Westbound
2A	No exit	No access
4	No exit	
5	No exit	No access
6	No access	No exit

M876	Northbound	Southbound
2	No access	No exit

A1(M)	Northbound	Southbound
2	No access	No exit
3		No access
5	No exit	No exit, no access
14	No exit	No access
40	No access	No access
43	No exit. Access from M1 only	No access. Exit to M1 only
57	No access	No exit
65	No access	No exit

A3(M)	Northbound	Southbound
1	No exit	No access
4	No access	No exit

A38(M) with Victoria Rd, (Park Circus) Birmingham	
Northbound	No exit
Southbound	No access

A48(M)	Northbound	Southbound
M4 Junc 29	Exit to M4 eastbound only	Access from M4 westbound only
29A	Access from A48 eastbound only	Exit to A48 westbound only

A57(M)	Eastbound	Westbound
With A5103	No access	No exit
With A34	No access	No exit

A58(M)	Southbound
With Park Lane and Westgate, Leeds	No access

A64(M)	Eastbound	Westbound
With A58 Clay Pit Lane, Leeds	No access from A58	No exit to A58

A74(M)	Northbound	Southbound
18	No access	No exit
22		No exit to A75

A194(M)	Northbound	Southbound
A1(M) J65 Gateshead Western Bypass	Access from A1(M) northbound only	Exit to A1(M) southbound only

M3 Junctions 13, 14 · M27 Junction 4

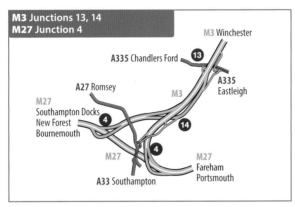

M6 Junctions 3A, 4A · M42 Junctions 7, 7A, 8, 9 · M6 Toll Junctions T1, T2

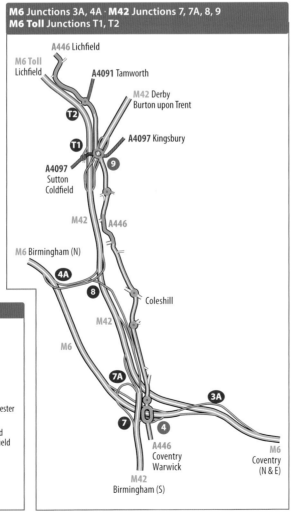

M6 Junction 20 · M56 Junction 9

M62 Junctions 32A, 33 · A1(M) Junctions 40, 41

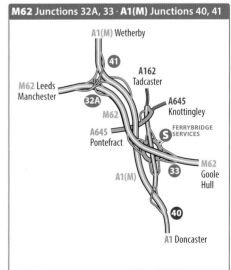

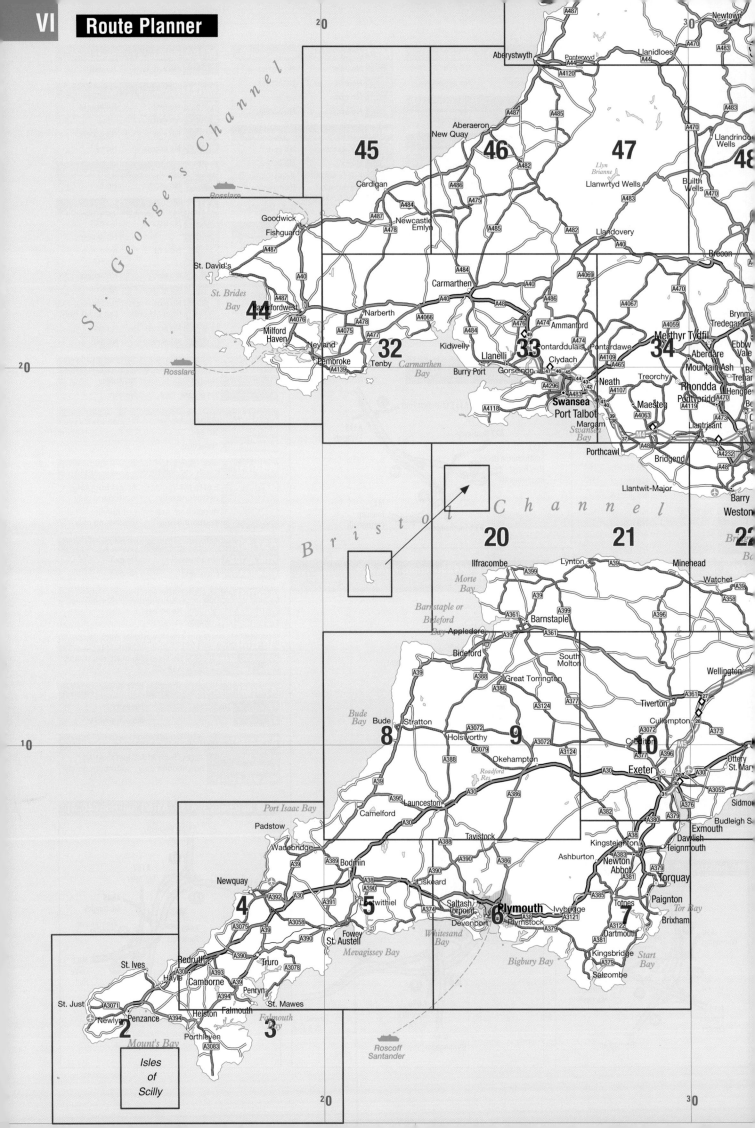

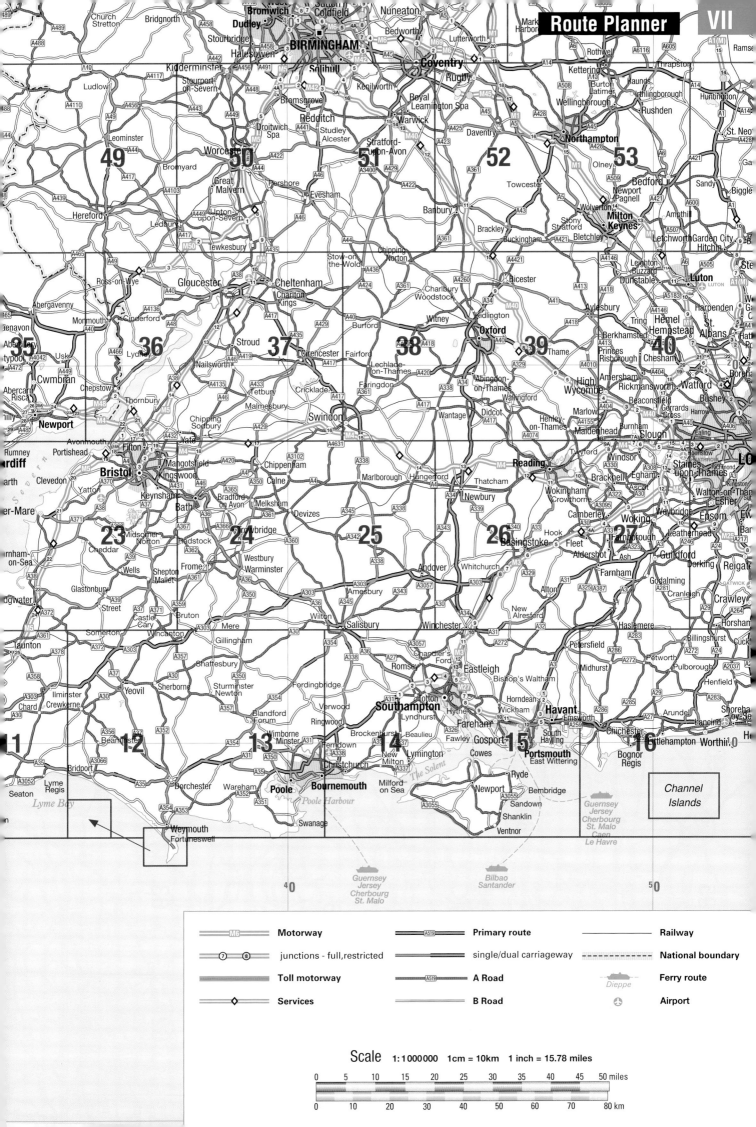

Scale 1:1 000 000   1cm = 10km   1 inch = 15.78 miles

0	5	10	15	20	25	30	35	40	45	50 miles
0	10	20	30	40	50	60	70	80 km

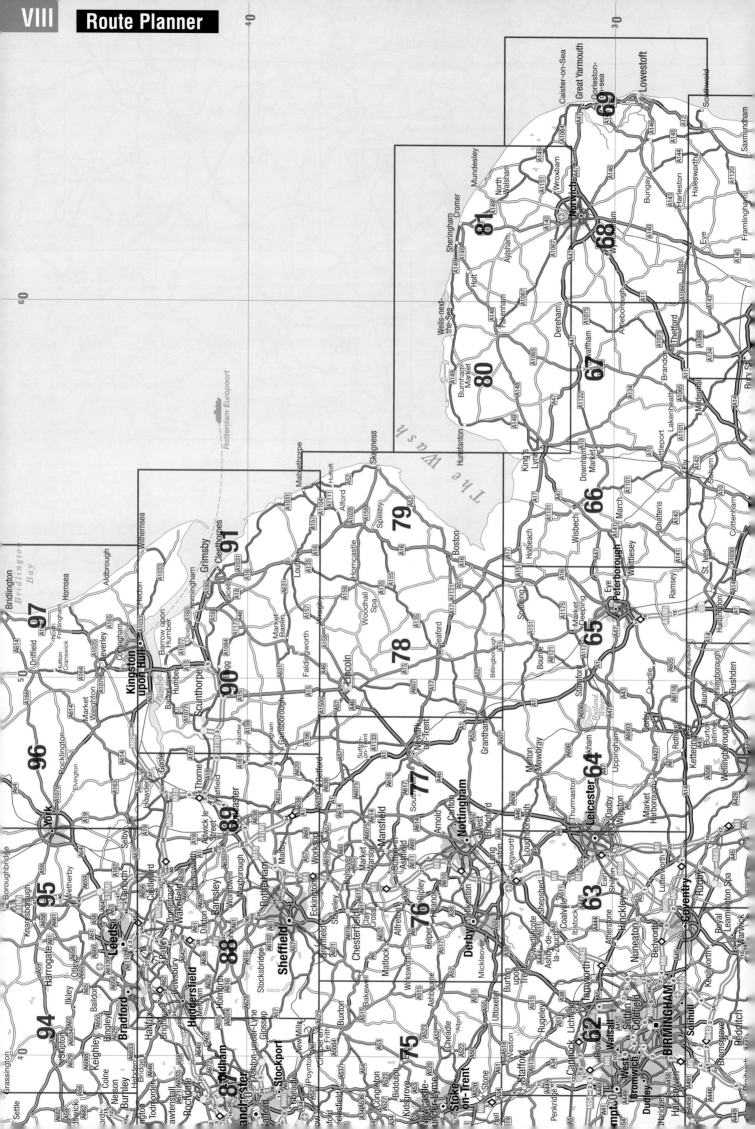

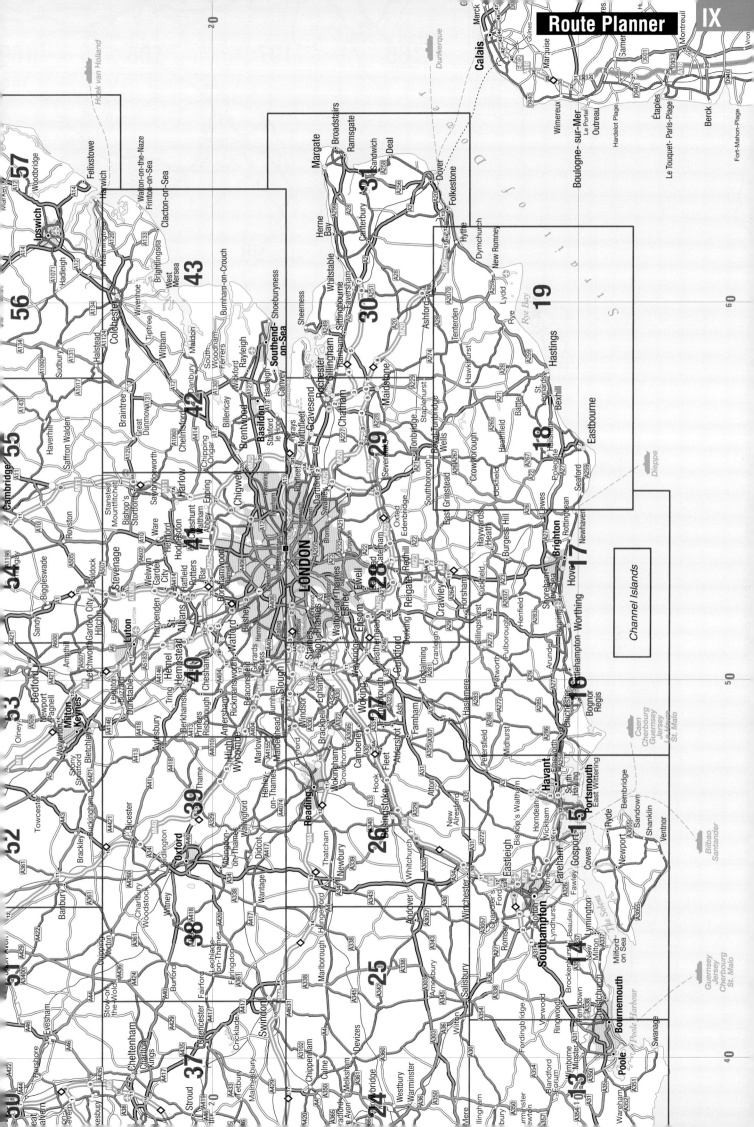

Route Planner

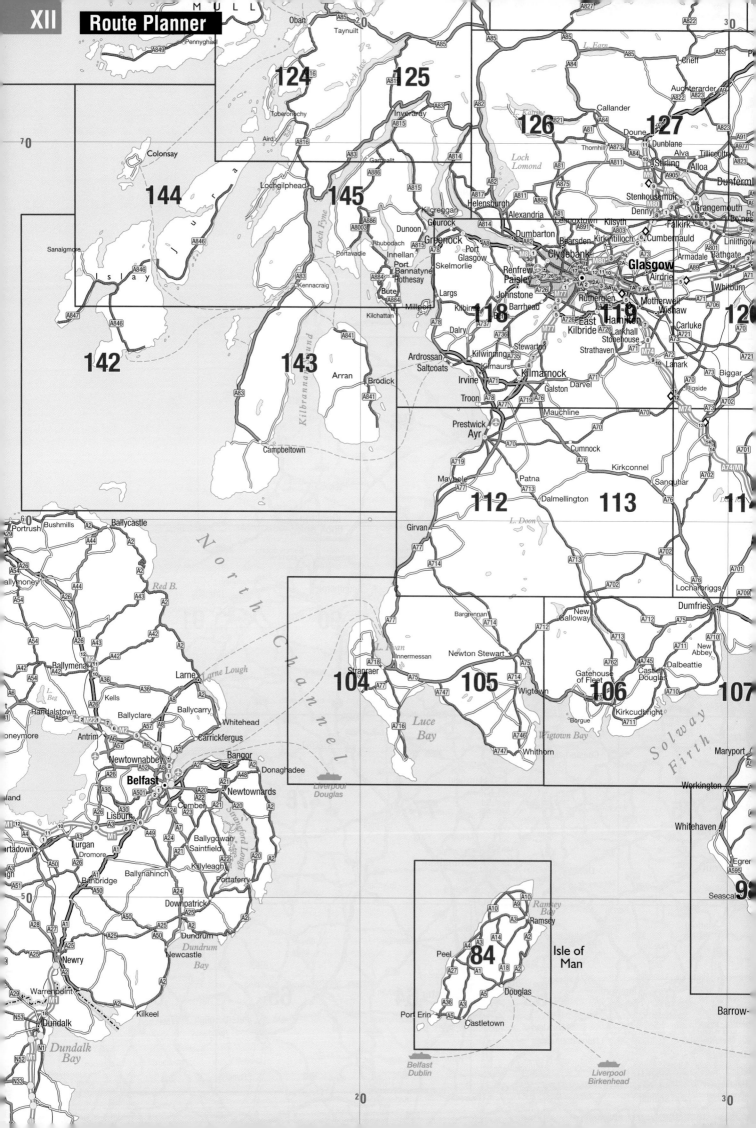

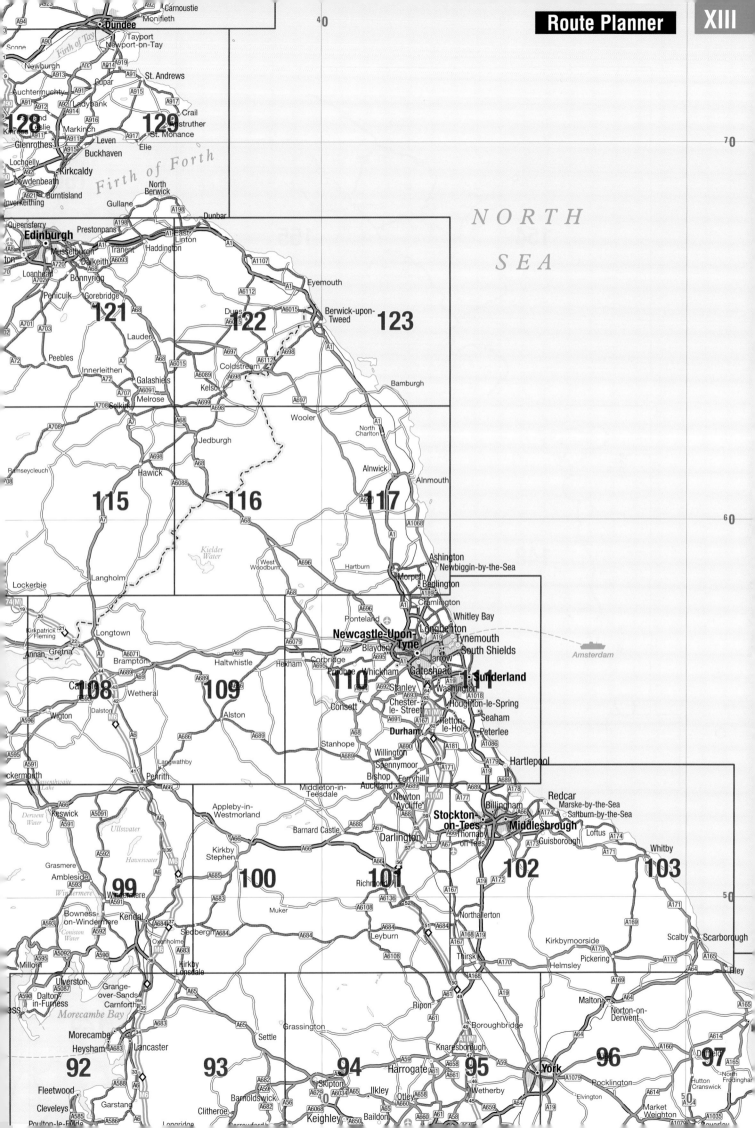

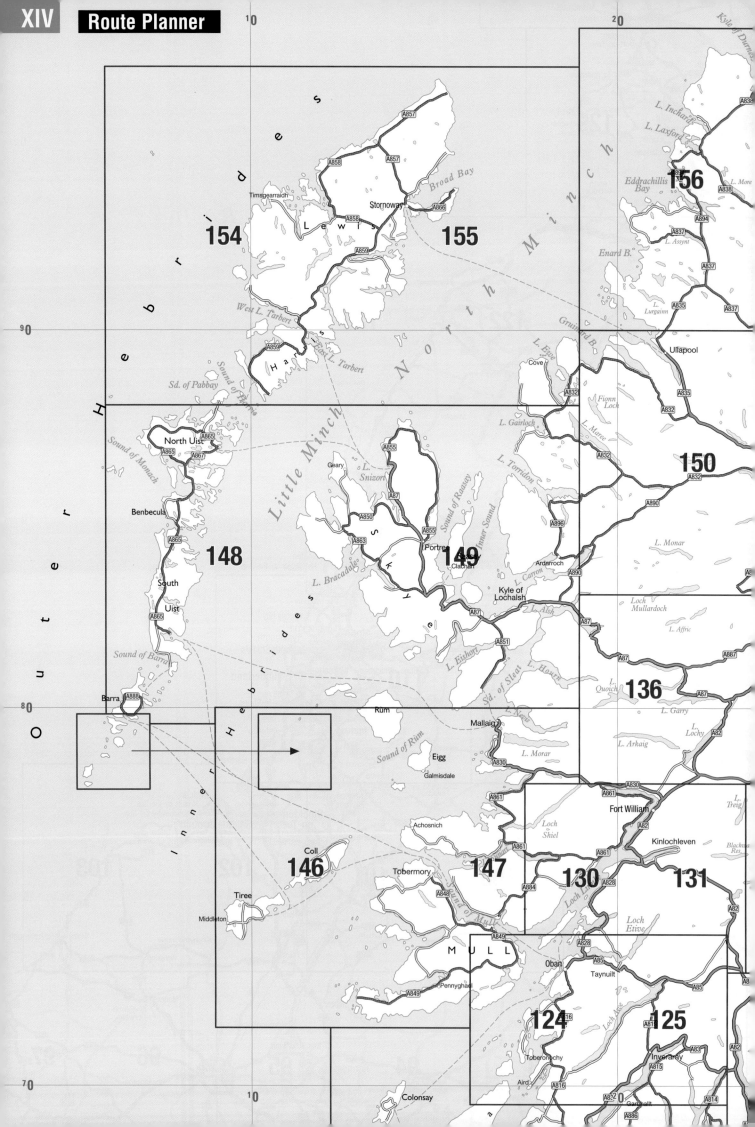

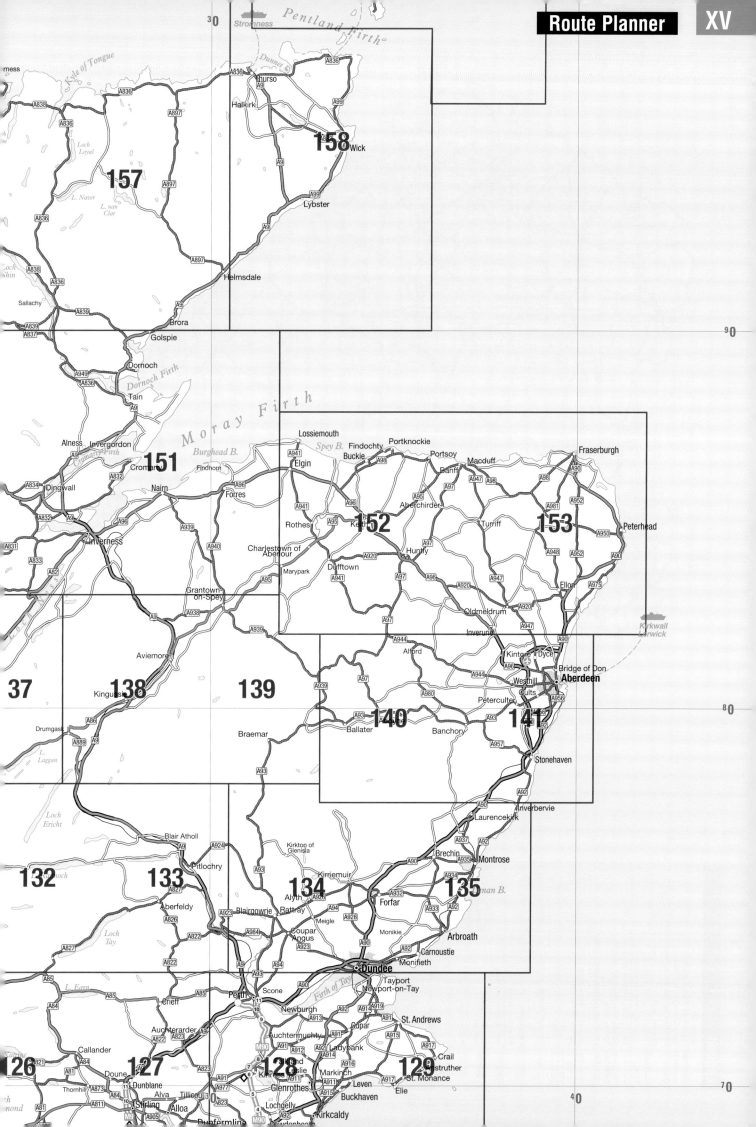

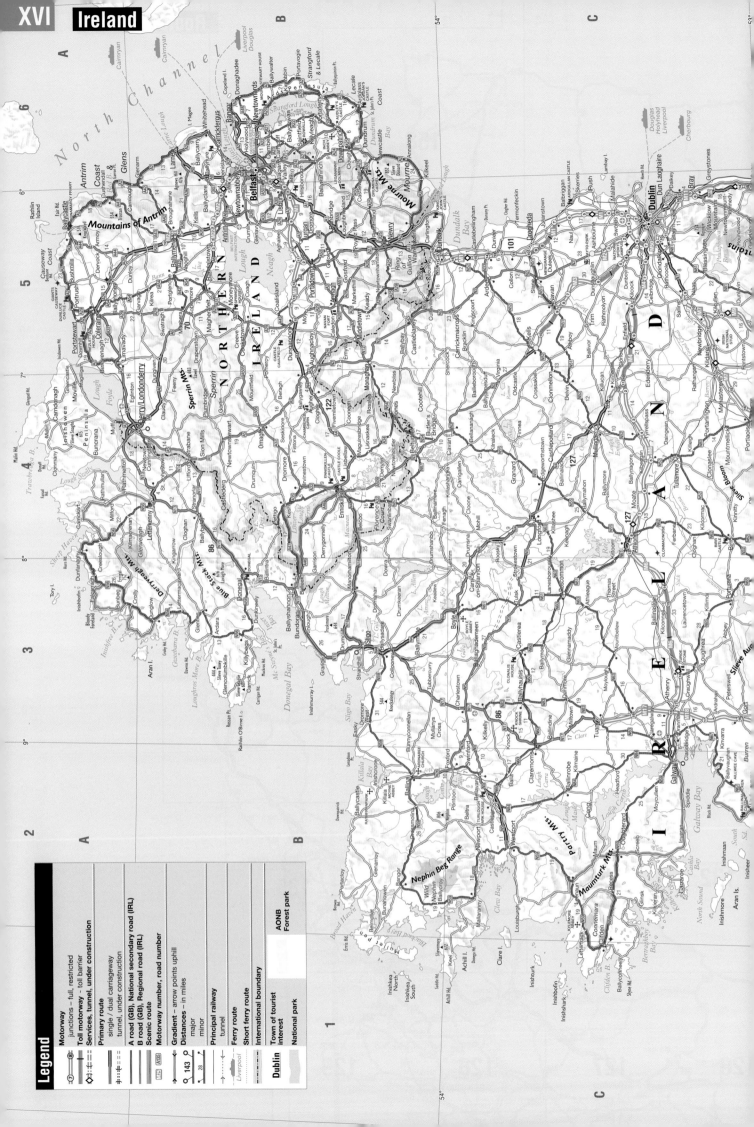

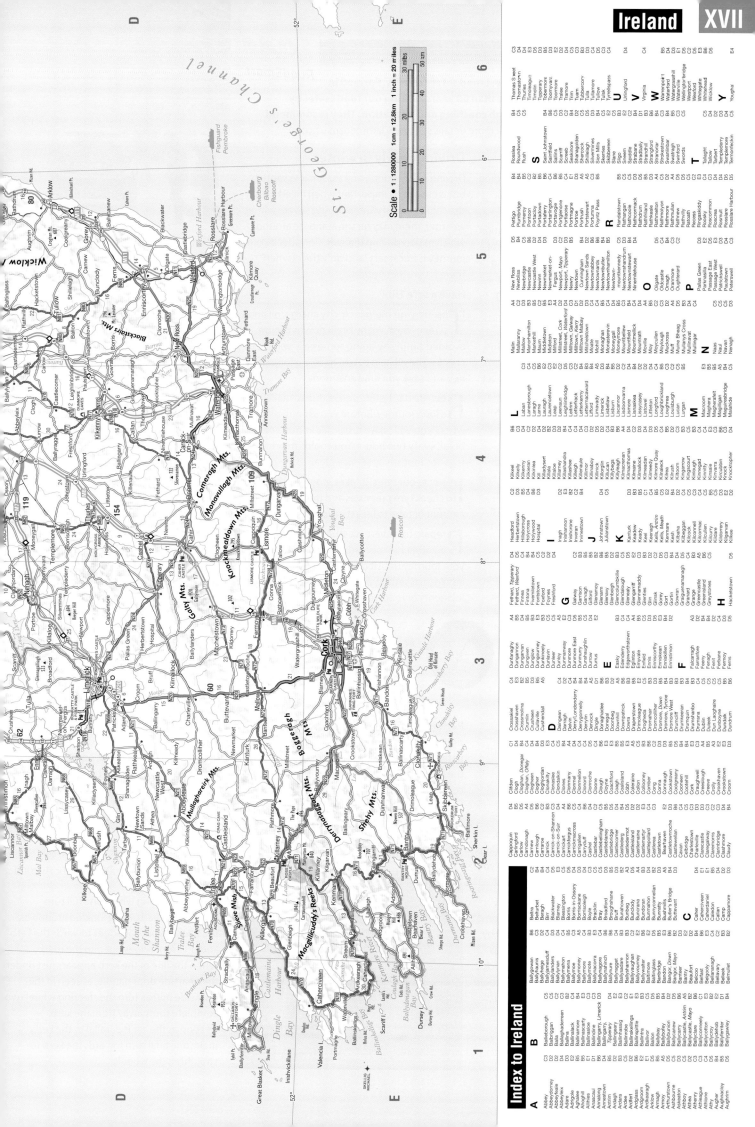

Top tips for better driving

iAM RoadSmart

iAM RoadSmart is the UK's largest road safety charity. Formed in 1956, they have spent more than 60 years making our roads safer by improving driver and rider skills through coaching and education. They recommend the following tips for better driving. For more details see www.iamroadsmart.com

Check your tyres

Tyres play a huge part in road safety, including steering, braking, and acceleration.

Pressure Make sure your tyres have the correct pressure. You can find this information in the vehicle handbook and on the inside of the fuel filler cap or driver's door sill. Having the correct pressure in your tyres will ensure even wear and will also help with handling and fuel efficiency.

Tread Ensure that your tyres have a tread depth of at least 1.6mm. Remember that this is a legal minimum, but a newer tyre with deeper tread will perform much better in wet conditions. Use the wear indicators on the tyre itself, or a tyre tread depth gauge, to check if your tyres are safe. If you're unsure, take them to a specialist.

Condition Cracks and bulges in a tyre's sidewalls indicate damage and this means the tyre should be replaced, even if the tread depth is still within the legal limit. A damaged tyre can be a ticking timebomb; it's best to get it replaced as soon as possible.

Overloading your vehicle can cause excessive heat and wear on your tyres. Ensure that your vehicle's overall weight does not exceed its Gross Vehicle Weight (GVW) rating – this can be found on your VIN plate. Heavy loads can also lead to poor braking and stability, so even if the weight is below the GVW rating, adjust your driving style to match these decreases in vehicle performance.

Driving safely in winter

Driving safely during any season is essential but is especially important when faced with the challenges of winter. During severe winter weather, there may be snow and ice around which makes driving difficult. Consider if your journey is necessary, and only travel when there is no other option.

Have a safe TRIP

Top-up your fuel/electricity charge, oil and screen-wash. Many breakdowns can be avoided simply by doing some easy vehicle checks. They'll help you to have a safer journey and save you time and money.

Rest the day before you're due to make a long journey. Before you set out, plan where you will take a break. It's important to break every two hours. You could stretch your legs at a motorway service area.

Inspect your tyres. It takes around 10 minutes to check tyre pressures and treads – a small amount of time to invest in your big trip.

Prepare for severe weather. If severe weather is expected, consider delaying your journey until it clears. Check your route in advance of setting out to see if there are any incidents or roadworks to be aware of.

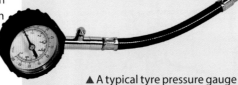

▲ A typical tyre pressure gauge

Pack a winter kit of essentials

Consider carrying a winter kit especially if there's a forecast of severe weather. This should include an ice-scraper, torch, blanket, de-icer and a first aid kit, just in case. Packing water and snacks is also a good idea, should you find yourself waiting for a recovery truck.

When you're on the road

Follow this advice when travelling in winter weather when icy and snowy conditions can be a challenge:

- Stick to main roads where you can and only travel if necessary.
- Slow down – it can take 10 times longer to stop in icy conditions.
- Use a high gear to avoid spinning your wheels.
- Accelerate gently, using low revs. You may need to start in second gear to avoid skidding.
- You may need up to 10 times the normal gap between your car and the car in front.
- Avoid sudden braking, it may lock up your wheels and you could skid further.
- Be extra cautious at road junctions where road markings may not be visible.

Improve your parking

Being able to park well is an essential part of being a responsible and confident driver.

Can I park here? Before choosing a spot make sure it's safe and legal to park there. Can you get in and out of the parking space easily and confidently? If you must drive in, take extra care when reversing out. Adjusting your nearside mirror downwards will help you check the kerb – just remember to adjust it back again.

Concentration Firstly, avoid any distractions. Turn the music down, don't get distracted by the tech in your vehicle. Doing these things mean you're more likely to hear other vehicles and pedestrians, including children who could be running around the area where are you trying to park.

Take your time Don't feel pressured, many drivers feel the watchful eye of other drivers and pedestrians when they try to park.

Parking manoeuvres For those new to driving, and even the most experienced, parallel parking can be a source of anxiety at the best of times. It involves a lot of hand-eye coordination, judgement, and vehicle control.

How to parallel park There is no one correct way, but here are some useful guidelines. Take your time and keep watching and listening throughout all your manoeuvres.

- Select a space that is one and a half times the length of your vehicle or more.
- In your direction of travel, on a two-way street, line up parallel to the kerb, with your near side mirror just past the farthest end of the vehicle you intend parking behind.
- Check, indicate and select reverse gear.
- Reverse until the top of your backseat is in line with the nearest end of the vehicle you intend parking behind before steering towards the kerb.
- Turn the steering wheel one full turn towards the kerb. Keep looking around as the back of your car edges towards the kerb and the front edges out into the road.
- When the line of the kerb appears just under the nearside door handle, as seen in the near side mirror, turn the steering wheel two complete turns away from the kerb.
- As soon as the car is parallel to the kerb, make one final turn towards the kerb to straighten the wheels.

The aim of The Highway Code is to promote safety on the road, whilst also supporting a healthy, sustainable and efficient transport system. The new edition of The Highway Code published in 2022 introduced a new section covering the 'hierarchy of road users'.

Hierarchy of road users

The 'hierarchy of road users' is a concept that places those road users most at risk in the event of a collision at the top of the hierarchy. The hierarchy does not remove the need for everyone to behave responsibly. The road users most likely to be injured in the event of a collision are pedestrians, cyclists, horse riders and motorcyclists, with children, older adults and disabled people being more at risk. The following H rules clarify this concept.

Rule H1

It is important that ALL road users are aware of The Highway Code, are considerate to other road users and understand their responsibility for the safety of others.

Everyone suffers when road collisions occur, whether they are physically injured or not. But those in charge of vehicles that can cause the greatest harm in the event of a collision bear the greatest responsibility to take care and reduce the danger they pose to others. This principle applies most strongly to drivers of large goods and passenger vehicles, vans/minibuses, cars/taxis and motorcycles.

Cyclists, horse riders and drivers of horse-drawn vehicles likewise have a responsibility to reduce danger to pedestrians.

None of this detracts from the responsibility of ALL road users, including pedestrians, cyclists and horse riders, to have regard for their own and other road users' safety.

Always remember that the people you encounter may have impaired sight, hearing or mobility and that this may not be obvious.

Rule H2

Rule for drivers, motorcyclists, horse-drawn vehicles, horse riders and cyclists

At a junction you should give way to pedestrians crossing or waiting to cross a road into which or from which you are turning.

You **MUST** give way to pedestrians on a zebra crossing, and to pedestrians and cyclists on a parallel crossing.

Pedestrians have priority when on a zebra crossing, on a parallel crossing or at light controlled crossings when they have a green signal.

You should give way to pedestrians waiting to cross a zebra crossing, and to pedestrians and cyclists waiting to cross a parallel crossing.

Horse riders should also give way to pedestrians on a zebra crossing, and to pedestrians and cyclists on a parallel crossing.

Cyclists should give way to pedestrians on shared- use cycle tracks and to horse riders on bridleways.

Only pedestrians may use the pavement. Pedestrians include wheelchair and mobility scooter users.

Pedestrians may use any part of the road and use cycle tracks as well as the pavement, unless there are signs prohibiting pedestrians.

Rule H3

Rule for drivers and motorcyclists

You should not cut across cyclists, horse riders or horse-drawn vehicles going ahead when you are turning into or out of a junction or changing direction or lane, just as you would not turn across the path of another motor vehicle. This applies whether they are using a cycle lane, a cycle track, or riding ahead on the road and you should give way to them.

Do not turn at a junction if to do so would cause the cyclist, horse rider or horse-drawn vehicle going straight ahead to stop or swerve.

You should stop and wait for a safe gap in the flow of cyclists if necessary. This includes when cyclists are:

- approaching, passing or moving off from a junction
- moving past or waiting alongside stationary or slow-moving traffic
- travelling around a roundabout

▲ **Rule H2** Wait for the pedestrian to cross the junction before turning. This applies if you are turning right or left into the junction.

▲ **Rule H3** Wait for the cyclist to pass the junction before turning. This also applies if there is a cycle lane or cycle track and if you are turning right or left into the junction.

To access the full Highway Code:

Print The Official Highway Code ISBN 978-0-11-553995-4
Online The Highway Code – Guidance – GOV.UK (www.gov.uk)

Distances and journey times

How to use this table

Distances are shown in miles and kilometres with estimated journey times in hours and minutes.

For example: the distance between Dover and Fishguard is 331 miles or 533 kilometres with an estimated journey time of 6 hours, 20 minutes.

Estimated driving times are based on an average speed of 60mph on Motorways and 40mph on other roads. Drivers should allow extra time when driving at peak periods or through areas likely to be congested.

Supporting

THINK!

**Travel safe –
Don't drive tired**

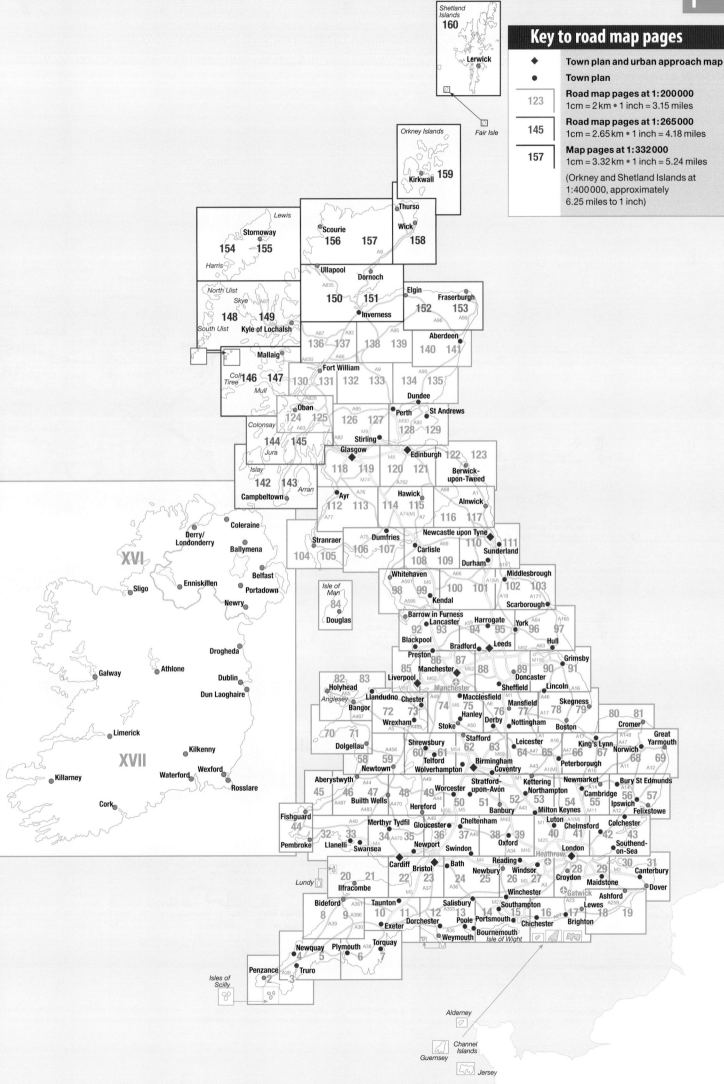

Shetland Islands
160
Lerwick

Fair Isle

Key to road map pages

◆ Town plan and urban approach map

● Town plan

123 Road map pages at 1:200 000
1cm = 2 km • 1 inch = 3.15 miles

145 Road map pages at 1:265 000
1cm = 2.65 km • 1 inch = 4.18 miles

157 Map pages at 1:332 000
1cm = 3.32 km • 1 inch = 5.24 miles

(Orkney and Shetland Islands at 1:400 000, approximately 6.25 miles to 1 inch)

Orkney Islands
Kirkwall **159**

Thurso
Scourie **156** **157** Wick **158**
Stornoway
Lewis
154 **155**
Harris
Ullapool
Dornoch
North Uist
Skye
148 **149**
South Uist Kyle of Lochalsh
A835
Elgin Fraserburgh
150 **151** **152** **153**
Inverness
Aberdeen
136 **137** **138** **139** **140** **141**
Mallaig
Coll Fort William
Tiree **146** **147** **130** **131** **132** **133** **134** **135**
Mull Dundee
Oban Perth St Andrews
Colonsay **124** **125** **126** **127** **128** **129**
Stirling
144 **145** Glasgow Edinburgh **122** **123**
Jura
Islay Berwick-upon-Tweed
142 **143** **118** **119** **120** **121**
Arran Ayr Hawick Alnwick
Campbeltown **112** **113** **114** **115** **116** **117**

Coleraine Newcastle upon Tyne
Derry/ Ballymena Stranraer Dumfries **110** **111**
Londonderry Carlisle Sunderland
XVI Belfast **104** **105** **106** **107** **108** **109** Durham
Sligo Enniskillen Portadown Middlesbrough
Newry Whitehaven **102** **103**
Isle of **98** **99** **100** **101** Scarborough
Man Kendal
84 Barrow in Furness York
Douglas Lancaster Harrogate
92 **93** **94** **95** **96** **97**
Drogheda Blackpool Bradford Leeds Hull
Preston **86** **87** **88** Grimsby
Galway Athlone **85** Manchester **89** **90** **91**
Dublin **82** **83** Liverpool Doncaster
Holyhead Sheffield Lincoln
Dun Laoghaire Anglesey Chester Macclesfield Skegness
Bangor **72** **73** **74** **75** **76** **77** **78** **79** **80** **81**
Limerick Wrexham Hanley Mansfield Cromer
Kilkenny Stoke Derby Nottingham Boston
XVII **70** **71** Great
Dolgellau Shrewsbury Stafford Leicester King's Lynn Norwich Yarmouth
58 **59** **60** **61** **62** **63** **64** **65** **66** **67** **68** **69**
Waterford Telford
Killarney Wexford Aberystwyth Newtown Wolverhampton Coventry Peterborough Newmarket Bury St Edmunds
Rosslare Birmingham Kettering **56** **57**
Cork **45** **46** **47** **48** **49** Worcester Stratford-upon-Avon Northampton Cambridge Ipswich
Builth Wells Hereford **50** **51** **52** **53** **54** **55** Felixstowe
Milton Keynes Colchester
Fishguard Merthyr Tydfil Gloucester Cheltenham Banbury Luton **42** **43**
44 **32** **33** **34** **35** **36** **37** **38** **39** **40** **41** Chelmsford Southend-on-Sea
Pembroke Llanelli Swansea Newport Swindon Oxford London
Heathrow **30** **31**
Cardiff Bristol Bath Reading Windsor Croydon Canterbury
Lundy **20** **21** **22** **23** **24** **25** **26** **27** **28** **29** Dover
Ilfracombe Newbury Maidstone
Taunton Salisbury Winchester Gatwick Ashford
Bideford Southampton Lewes
8 **9** **10** **11** **12** **13** **14** **15** **16** **17** **18** **19**
Dorchester Poole Portsmouth Chichester Brighton
Exeter Bournemouth
Newquay Weymouth Isle of Wight
Torquay
Plymouth
4 **5** **6** **7**
Penzance Truro
2 **3**
Isles of Scilly

Alderney

Channel Islands
Guernsey

Jersey

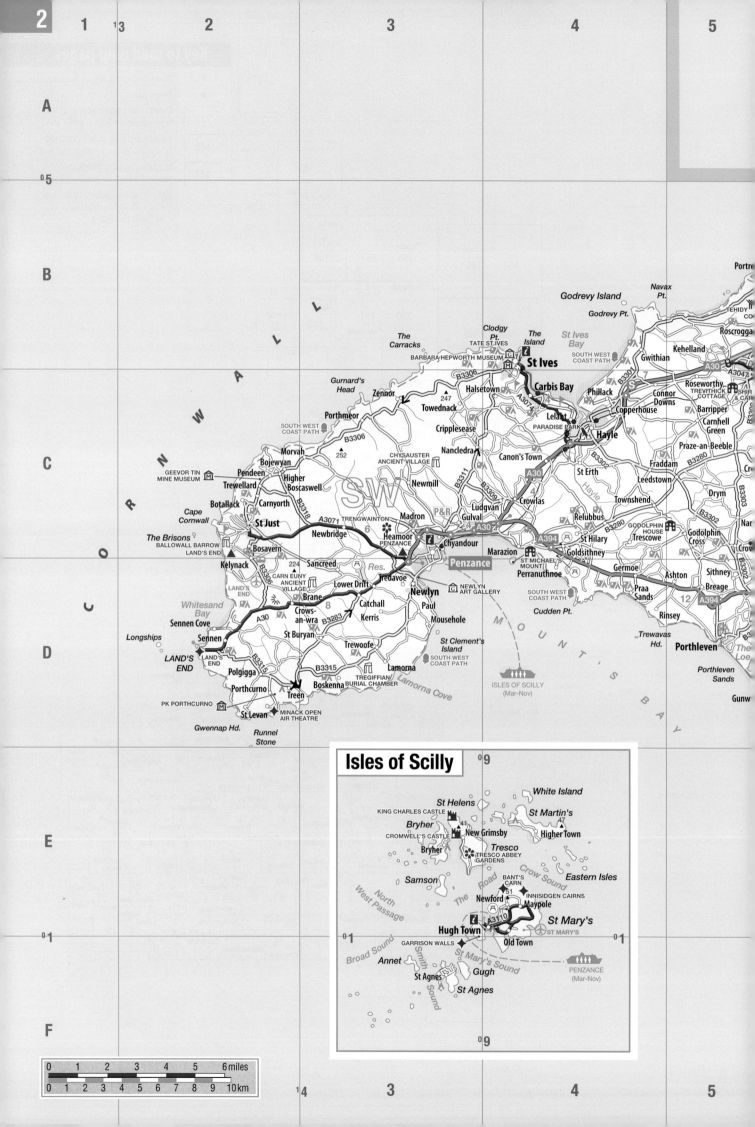

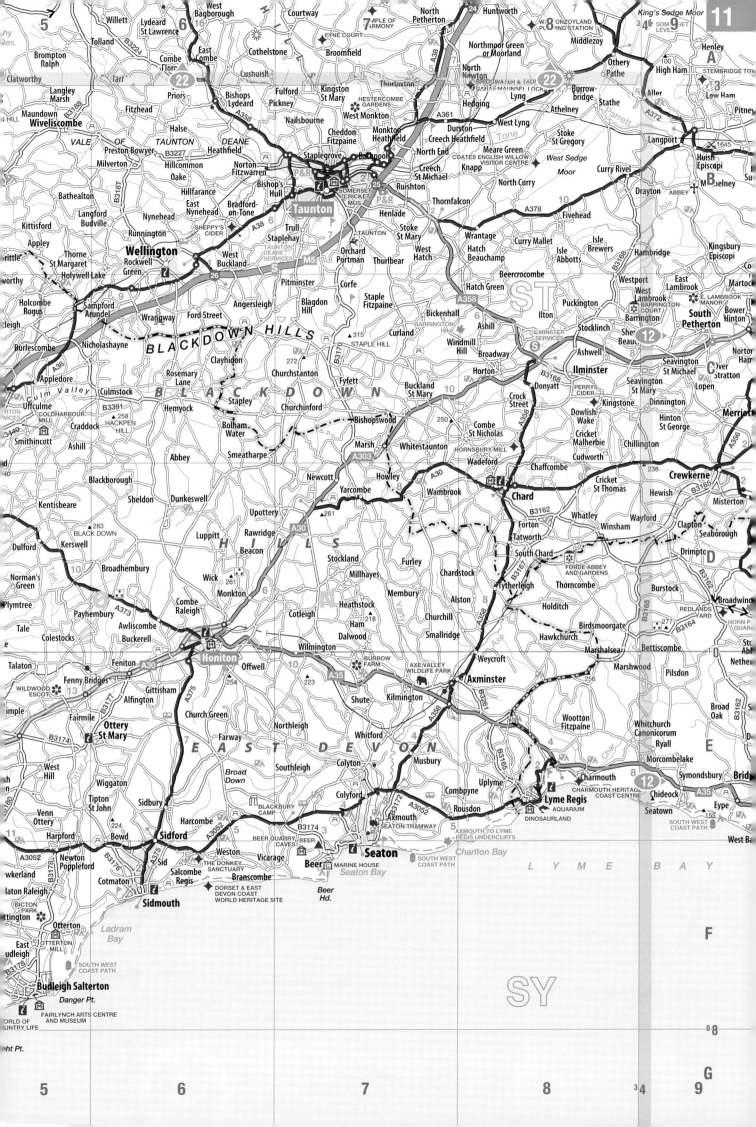

Jersey
3½ miles to 1 inch

JERSEY

1   2   3   4   5

A

¹8

B

C

¹5
²2

North West
Point   North East
Point

LUNDY MARINE
NATURE RESERVE   LUNDY

142

ILFRACOMBE
BIDEFORD
(April-Oct)

South West
Point   Surf
Point

²1
¹4

D   SS

E

LUNDY
(April-Oct)

Rillage Pt.   Combe Martin
Bay   Trentishoe

HELE CORN MILL
ILFRACOMBE   Ilfracombe   ILFRACOMBE
MUSEUM   WATERMOUTH CASTLE.   Girt Down   Heale

Bull Pt.   Hele   349
Rockham Bay   Lee   206   B3230
Whitestone   Berrynarbor   Combe   A10
Mortehoe   Slade   Sterridge   Martin   WILDLIFE & DINOSAUR PARK
Morte Point   A361   A399
Trimstone   269   A3123   Kentisbury
Woolacombe   Cheglinch   Berry   Berry Down   B3229   Kentisbury
MORTE   B3343   Down   Cross   Ford
BAY   210   Dean   West   Bittadon   East Down   EXMOO
Woolacombe Sand   Down   B3230   Churchill   ZC
SOUTH WEST   North   Arlington
Pickwell   COAST PATH   Buckland   Milltown   ARLINGTON
Baggy Pt.   Putsborough   Nethercott   Halsinger   Muddiford   COURT   Loxhore   Knightac
Georgeham   Darracott   Marwood   A39   Shirwell
Croyde Bay   Croyde   Lobb   Knowle   MARWOOD   Guineaford   198   Shirwell   Stoke
B3231   158   HILL GARDENS   Kingsheanton   BROOMHILL   Cross   Rivers
Saunton   Pippacott   Prixford
14   Heanton   Ashford
Braunton   Punchardon   Burridge   Goodleigh   Gunn
ELLIOT GALLERY   Wrafton   Chivenor   A361   Barnstaple
Saunton   TOLL   Pilton   MUSEUM OF BARNSTAPLE
Sands   & NORTH DEVON   Westacott
Braunton   Taw   P&R   Newport
Burrows   Fremington   Bickington   Landkey
Yelland   B3233   Bishops   Swimbridge
LUNDY   Bickleton   Tawton   Newland
(April-Oct)   Instow   A39   Swimbridge

¹3   BIDEFORD BAY   NORTH DEVON   Westward Ho!   TAPELEY   7   10
MARITIME MUSEUM   PARK GDNS
NORTHAM BURROWS   Westleigh
Appledore   Northam   Horwood   Newton
⑨   Northam   Tracey   Ensis
A386   Bideford   Eastleigh
0 1 2 3 4 5 6 miles   THE BIG SHEEP   Orchard   Herner   Col5ton
0 1 2 3 4 5 6 7 8 9 10km   Hill   ⑨   East
Abbotsham   Woodtown   Hiscott   Chapelton
Handy   East-the-   COBBATON
CLOVELLY VILLAGE   A39   Water   COMBAT   Fishleigh

BURTON ART
GALL.& MUS

NORTH   DEVON

MÔR HAFREN CHANNEL

MÔR BRISTOL

SS

5 6 7 8 9

A

B

C

D

E

F

G

Porthcawl

Pyle (Y Pil)

Bridgend (Pen-y-bont ar Ogwr)

Pencoed

Cowbridge (Y Bont-Faen)

Llantwit Major (Llanilltud Fawr)

GLAMORGAN

VALE OF

Nottage
Hutchwns
Clevis
Newton

Kenfig
Mawdlam
North Cornelly
South Cornelly

ROYAL PORTHCAWL
CONEY BEACH
Tusker Rock

MERTHYR MAWR WARREN
Ogmore-by-Sea
OGMORE CASTLE

St Brides Major
Southerndown
Penuchadre
Marcross
Monknash
Wick
Broughton
GLAMORGAN HERITAGE COAST CENTRE

Nash Pt.
Trwyn yr As
St Donat's

Breaksea Pt.
Trwyn Breaksea

Boverton
St Athan
East Aberthaw

BEDFORD
Kenfig Hill
Cefn Cross
Aberkenfig
Sarn
SARN PARK SERVICES

Cefn Cribbwr
Pen-y-fai
Pendre
Coity
COITY CASTLE

Brynna
Llanharan
Talbot Gre
Dolau
Bryncae
Brynsadler
Pontyclu
Miskin

NEWCASTLE
Laleston
Coychurch
St Mary Hill
Treoes
Corntown
Ewenny
B4524
Colwinston
Pentre Meyrick
Penllyn
Llangan
Llansannor
Llanmihangel
Llysworney
Llandow
Llandough
Sigingstone
Llanmaes
Eglwys Brewis
Flemingston

Craig Penllyn
Maendy
Aberthin
Welsh St Donats
St Hilary
OLD BEAUPRE CASTLE
Llanblethian
St Mary Church
Llantrith

BRO MORGANNWG

RHOOS
(Y Rhw)

Ystradowen

Foreland Pt.
Lynmouth Bay
CLIFF RAILWAY
Lynmouth
TOLL
Lynton
Countisbury
Woody Bay
Martinhoe
WATERSMEET HOUSE
Barbrook
East Ilkerton
Cheriton
Furzehill
Shallowford
Malmsmead
Brendon
Oare

Hurlstone Pt.
EXMOOR OWL & HAWK CENTRE
SOUTH WEST COAST PATH
SELWORTHY BEACON 308
Porlock Bay
Bossington
Allerford
Selworthy
Porlock Weir
TOLL
Porlock
CULBONE HILL 413
Woodcombe
Minehead
WEST SOMERSET RAILWAY
BUTLINS
Alcombe
Periton
Marsh Street
Blue Anchor Bay
Blue Anchor
Old Cleeve

MINEHEAD
DOLL COLLECTION
Dunster
DUNSTER CASTLE
Carhampton
Withycombe
Bilbrook
CLEEVE ABBEY
Rodhuish
Roadwater

EXMOOR FOREST
NATIONAL PARK

Blackmoor Gate
Challacombe Common
Martinhoe Cross
Challacombe
B3358
PINKERY CENTRE FOR OUTDOOR LEARNING
Pinkworthy Pond
487
Exe Plain
Shoulsbarrow Common
Simonsbath
Leworthy
Lydcott
Brayford
High Bray
Charles
North Radworthy
North Heasley
Heasley Mill
South Radworthy
East Buckland
Twitchen
Molland
Molland Common

West Luccombe
HAWKCOMBE WOODS
Holnicote Estate
THE DUNKERY & HORNER WOOD
DUNKERY BEACON 519
465
Luccombe
Wootton Courtenay
Cowbridge
Timberscombe
DUNKERY VINEYARD
CROYDON HILL 365
BRENDON FOREST
Luxborough
Treborough
Kingsbridge
LYPE HILL 423
Wheddon Cross
Cutcombe
Luckwell Bridge
Edgcott
Exford
EXFORD
Withypool
Withypool Common
WINSFORD HILL
Winsford
Exton
Bridgetown
Brompton Regis
Withiel Florey
Clatworthy Res.
Wimbleball Lake
Upton
Huish
Champflower

HORSEN HILL 443
TARR STEPS WOODLAND
TARR STEPS
Hawkridge
Liscombe
Dane's Brook
377
Molland
Anstey Common
West Anstey
East Anstey
EXMOOR VISITOR CENTRE
Dulverton
Battleton
Nightcott
Brushford
Morebath
Petton
HADDON HILL 355
Skilgate
Waterrow
Chip Dible
HEYDON HILL 138

QUINCE HONEY FARM
Yeo Mill
B3227

A39 A399 A361 A396 B3222 B3223 B3224 B3225

EXMOOR

BRENDON HILLS

34
22
10
11
13
17

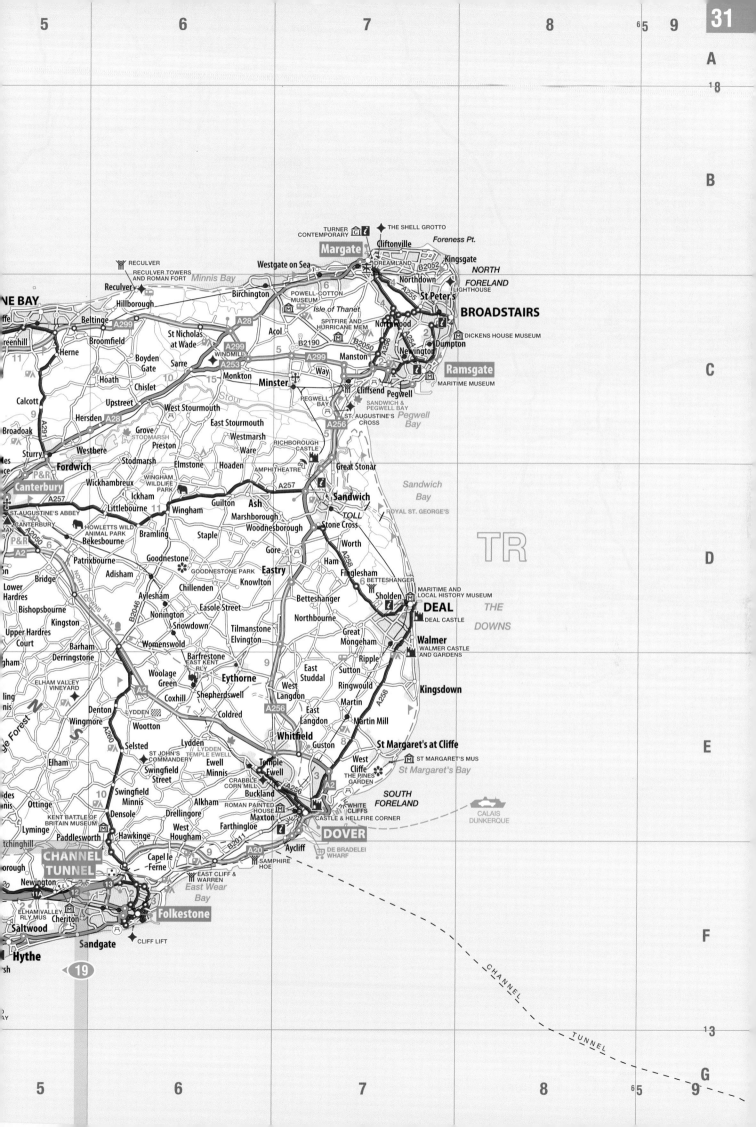

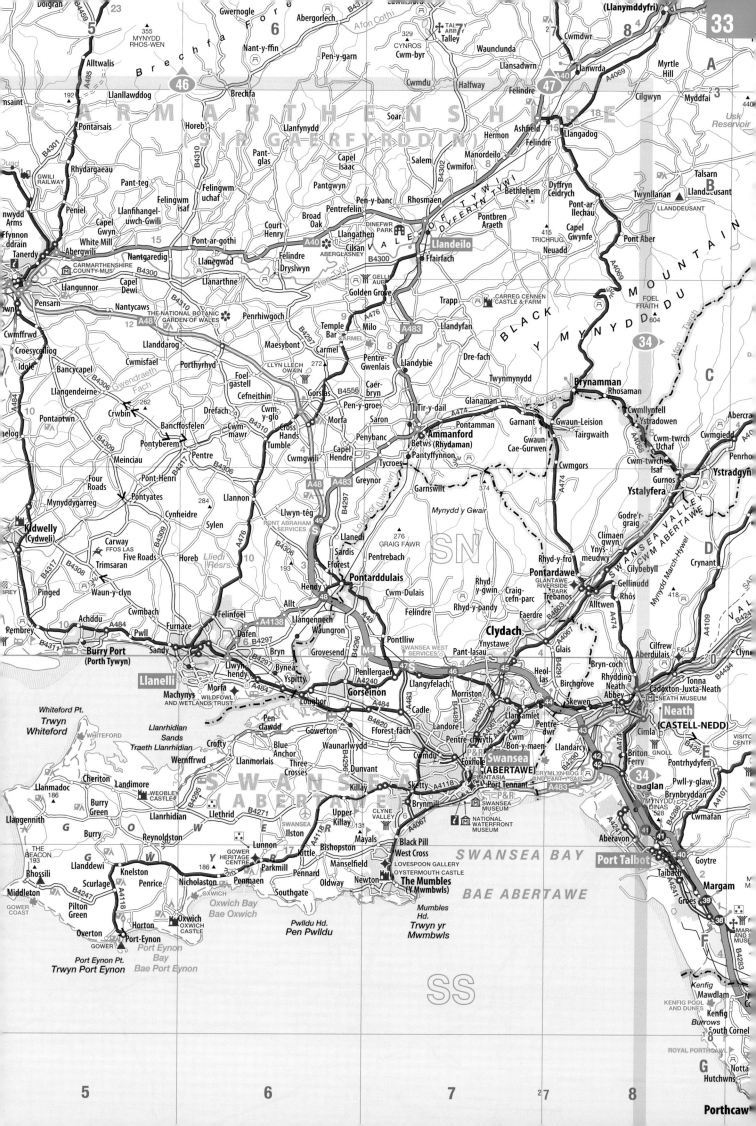

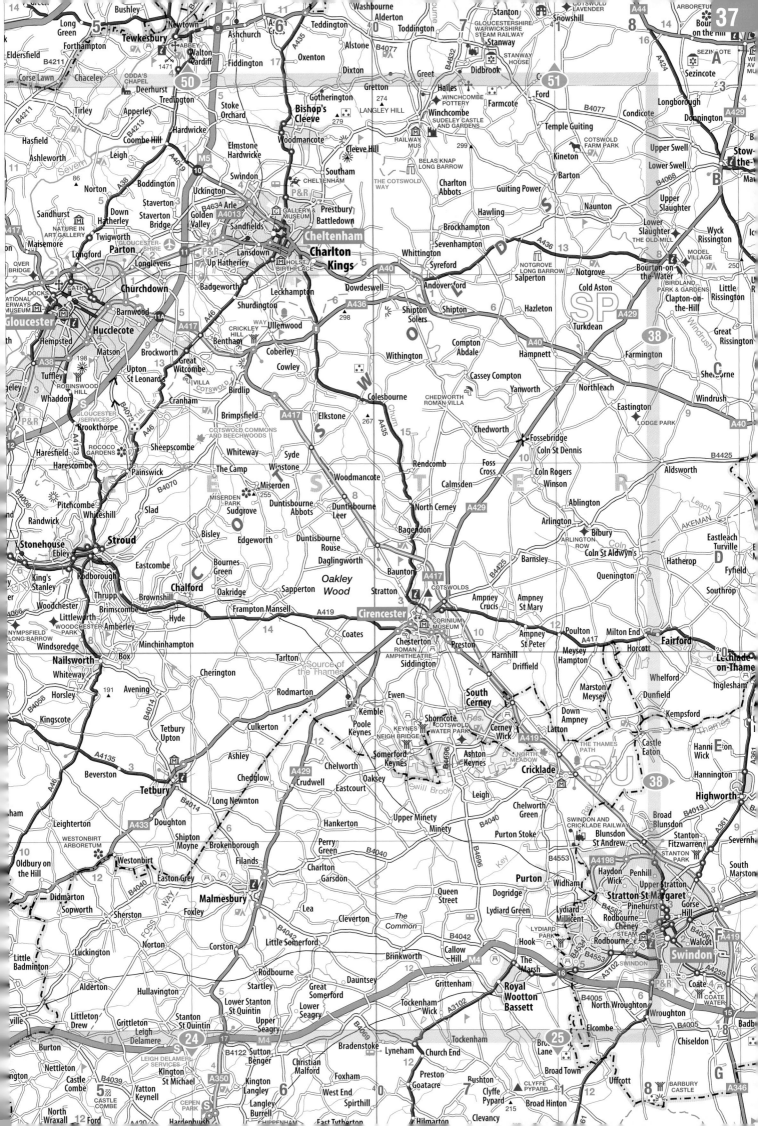

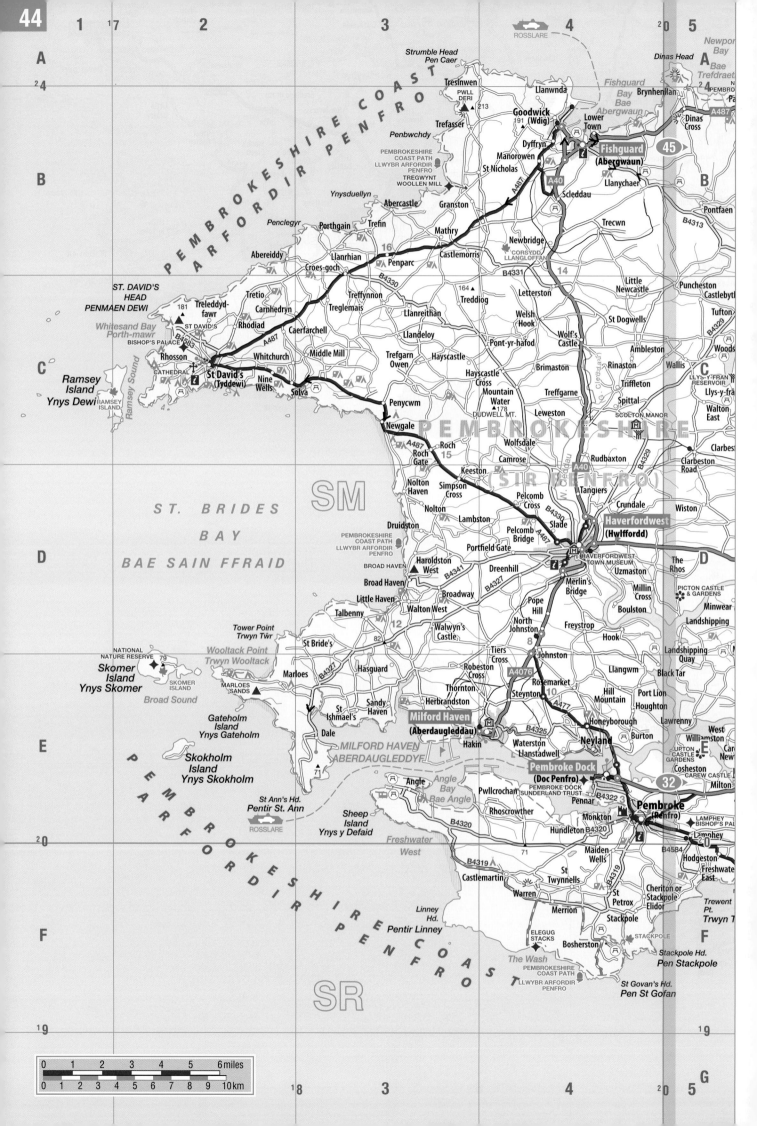

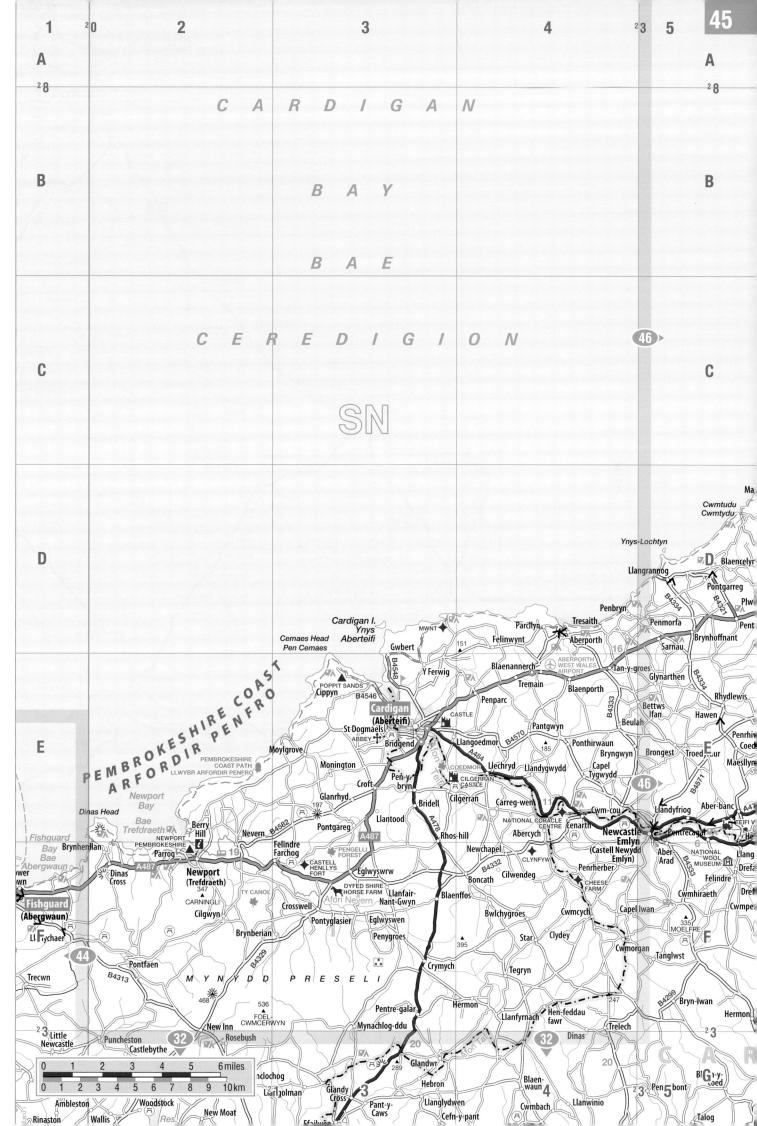

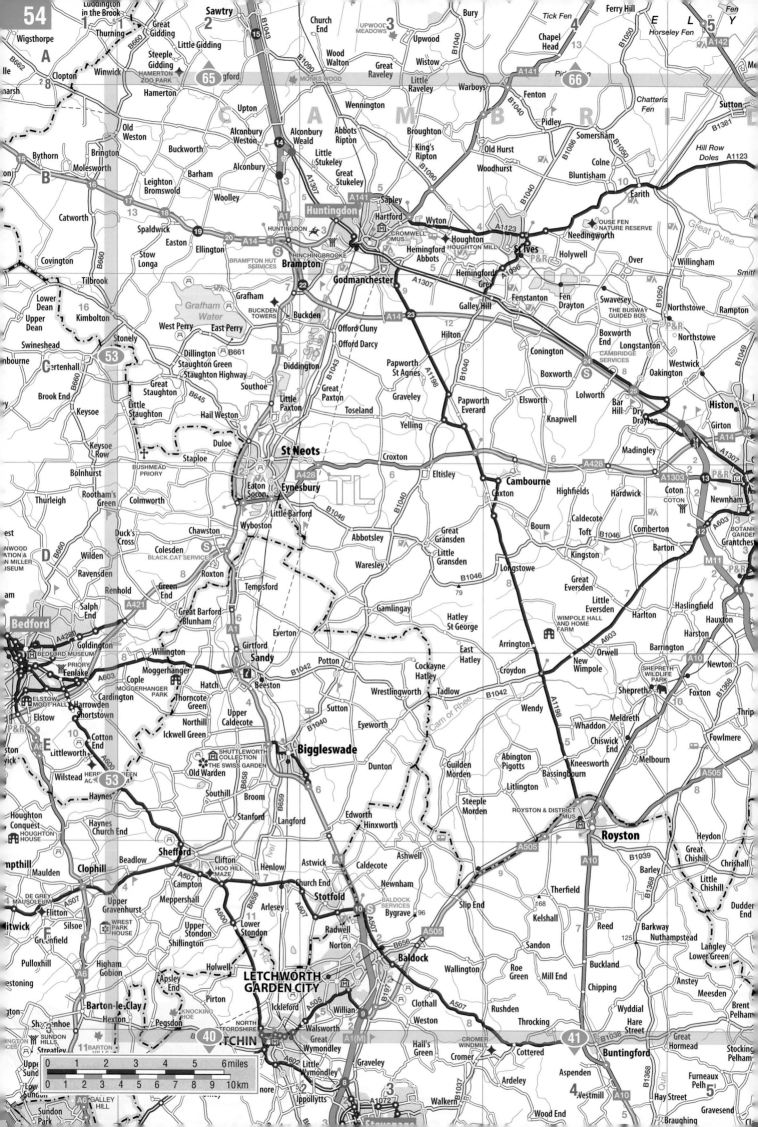

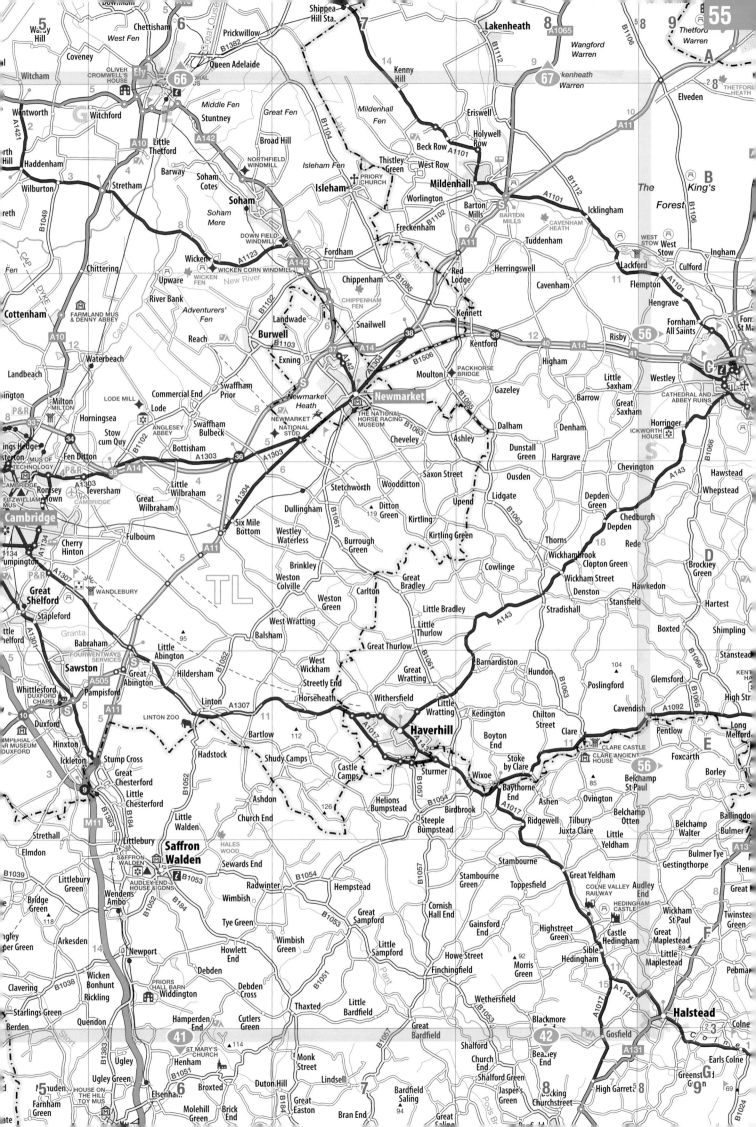

1 ²1 2 3 4 5 CA REGIMENTA

³6

A

Malltraeth Bay
Bae Malltraeth
Newborough
Forest
ANGLESEY
MODEL
VILLAGE

Llanddwyn I.
Ynys Llanddwyn
The Bar
Abermenai
Pt.
Trwyn
Abermenai

AIRWORLD
AVIATION MUSEUM

Morfa Dinlle
Dinas Dinlle
Ffr
Llandwrog
GLYNLLIF

C A E R N A R F O N

B A Y

B A E

C A E R N A R F O N

B

14

Pontllyfni
Aberdesach
Tai
82
Clynnog-fawr

Gyrn-goch
Capel Uchaf
Bryn-yr-eryr

509
BWLCH
MAWR
U
Cly
Trefor
522
GYRN DDU
Llanaelhaearn
Pen-sarn

SH

564
YR EIFL
Llithfaen
B4417
6
Pencaenewydd
Llwyndyrys
Llangybi
Carreg Ddu
Porth
Dinllaen
Pistyll
7
Morfa Nefyn
Nefyn
LLYN MARITIME
MUSEUM
Fron
Llanarmon
Edern
Tan-y-graig
Rhos-fawr
B4354
Y Ffôr
Chwiloc
Porth Ysgadan
B4417
Glanrhyd
Boduan
Llannor
PENARTH FAWR
MEDIEVAL HOUSE
Rhos-y-llan
CORS
GEIRCH
7
Efailnewydd
Abererch
Tudweiliog
Dinas
Rhyd-y-clafdy
Denio
Pwllheli
14
Garnfadryn
Penrhos
Carreg yr Imbill
Porth Golmon
Bryn-mawr
Llaniestyn
B4415
7
South Beach
Pen-y-graig
Rhedyn
Llangwnnadl
Sarn
Meyllteyrn
7
Llanbedrog
Penrhyn Mawr
Botwnnog
Nanhoron
B4413
Trwyn Llanbedrog
Ty-hen
Pen-y-groeslon
Bryncroes
Mynytho
St Tudwal's
Road
Angorfa St Tudwal
Methlem
Rhydlios
Llandegwning
304
MYNYDD
RHIW
PLAS-YN-RHIW
Llawrdref
Bellaf
Llangian
Abersoch
Capel Carmel
Rhoshirwaun
Rhiw
St Tudwal's Island East
Ynys St Tudwal Dwyrain
191
B4413
Llanengan
Sarn Bach
Marchroes
St Tudwal's Island West
Ynys St Tudwal Gorllewin
Uwchmynydd
Aberdaron
Llanfaelrhys
Porth Neigwl or
Hell's Mouth
Bwlchtocyn
Bodermid
Cilan Uchaf
Pen-y-cil
Bardsey Sound
Swnt Enlli
Trwyn Cilan
167
Bardsey
Island
Ynys Enlli
YNYS ENLLI
L L E Y N

D

E

F

³1

²2 3 4 5

0 1 2 3 4 5 6 miles
0 1 2 3 4 5 6 7 8 9 10 km

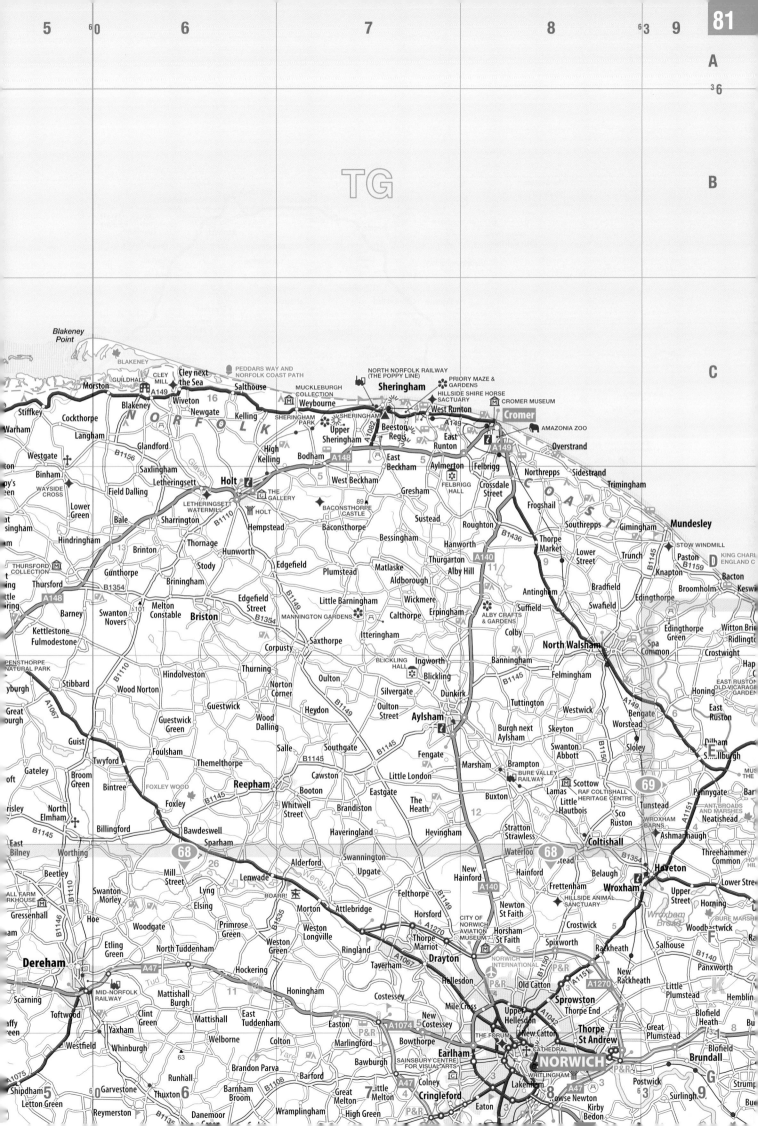

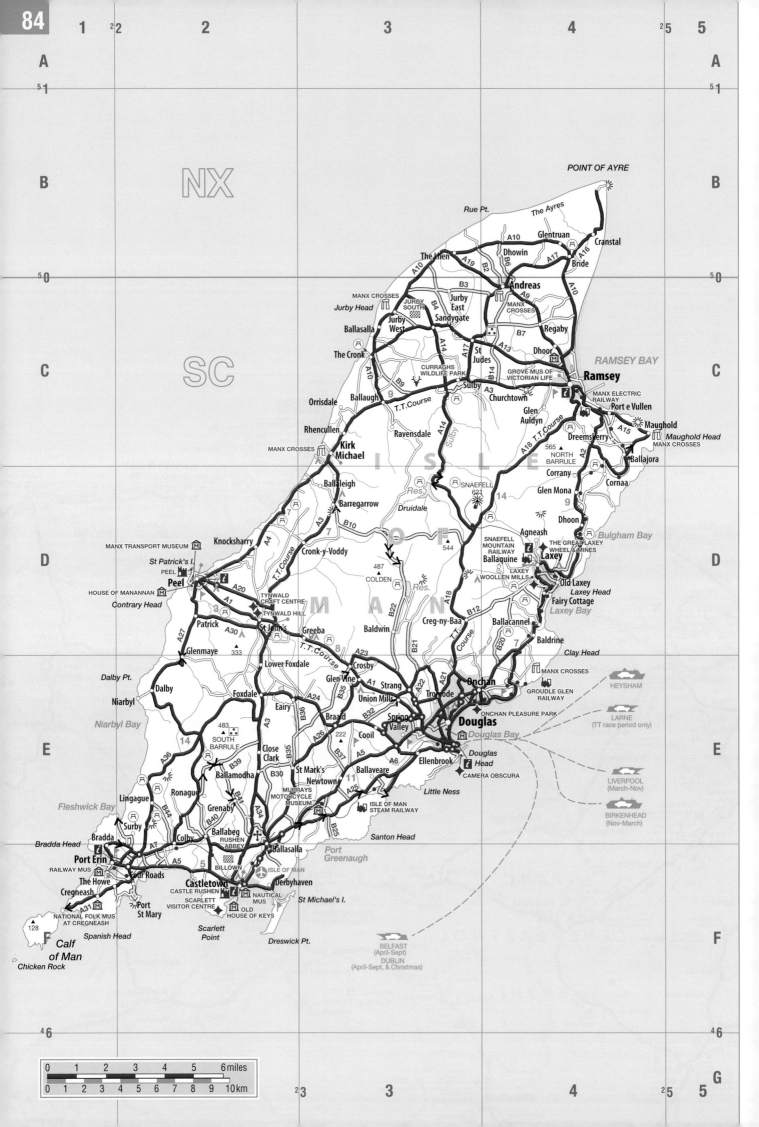

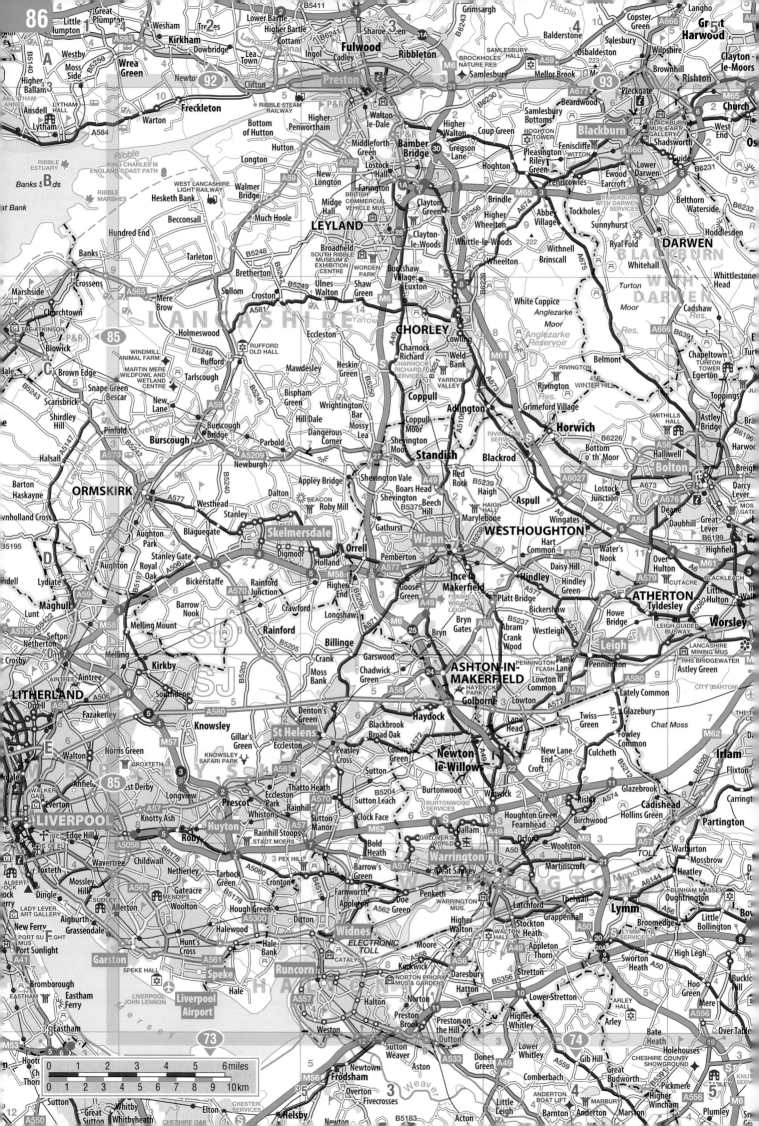

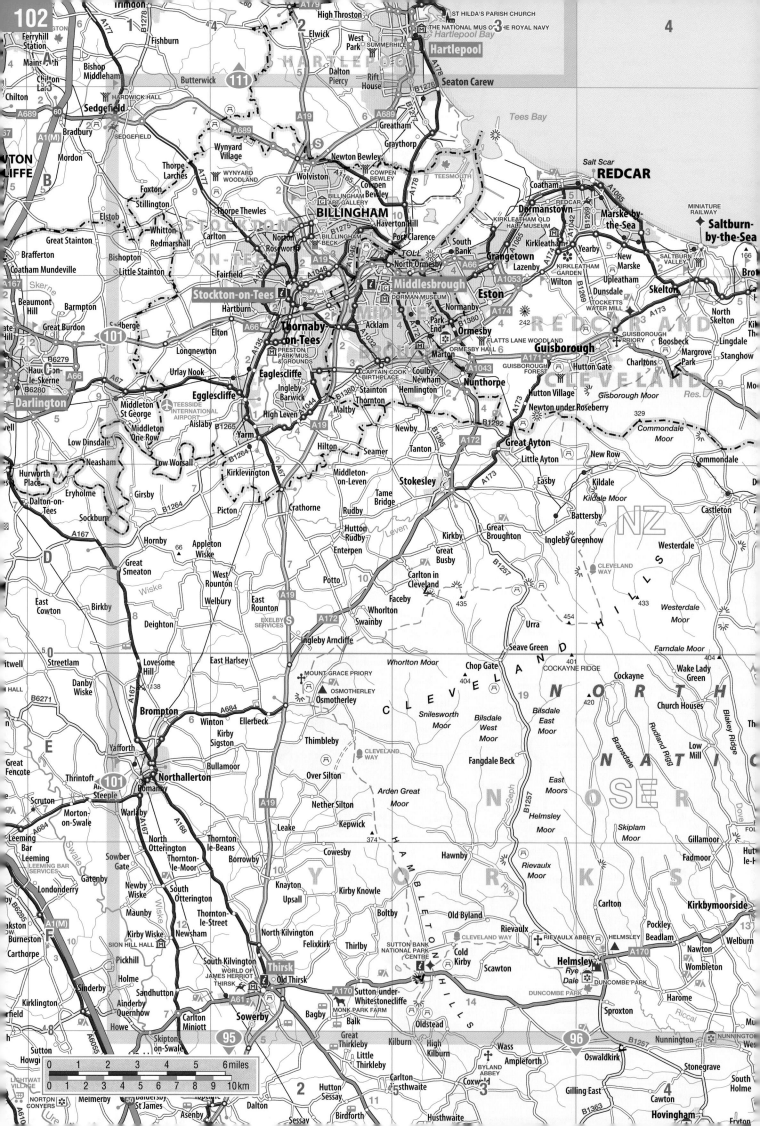

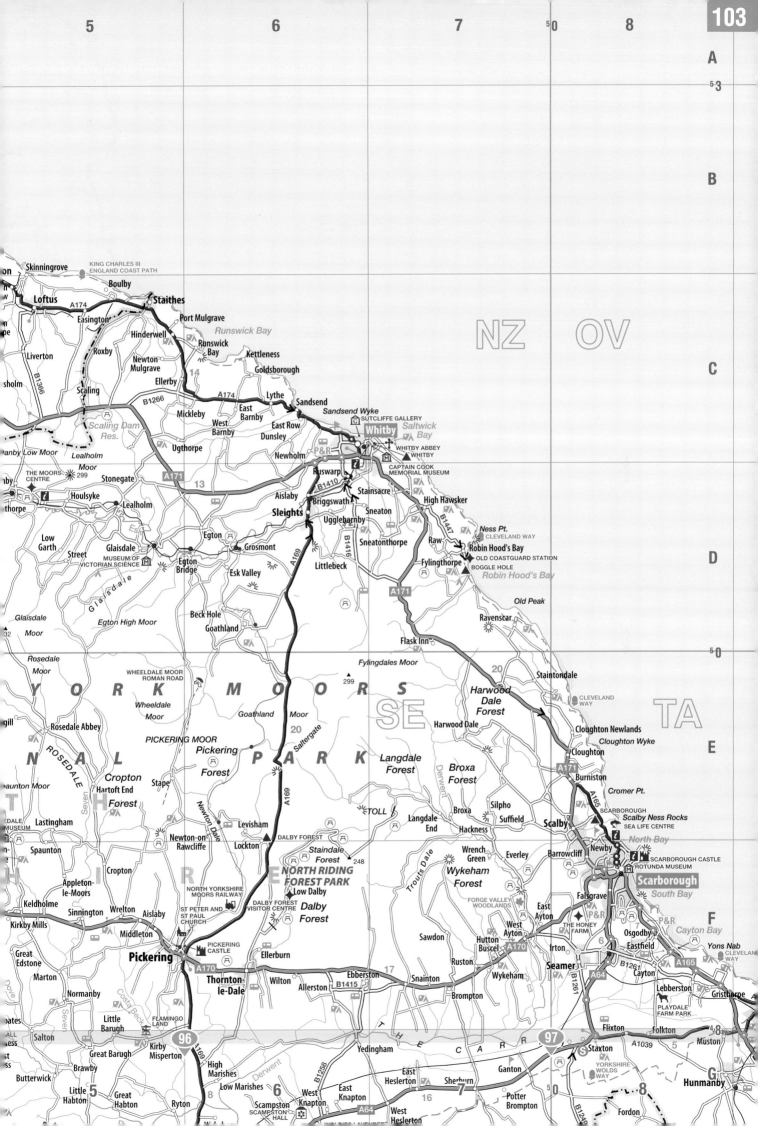

A
B
C
D
E
F
G

5   6   7   8

NZ OV

SE

TA

Skinningrove
KING CHARLES III
ENGLAND COAST PATH
Boulby
Loftus A174
Staithes
Easington
Port Mulgrave
Hinderwell
Runswick Bay
Liverton
Roxby
Runswick
Bay
Newton
Mulgrave
Kettleness
Goldsborough
Scaling
B1266
Ellerby
A174
Lythe
Sandsend
Sandsend Wyke
SUTCLIFFE GALLERY
Mickleby
East
Barnby
East Row
Whitby
Saltwick
Bay
Scaling Dam Res.
West
Barnby
Dunsley
WHITBY ABBEY
WHITBY
nby Low Moor
Lealholm
Ugthorpe
Newholm
P&R
CAPTAIN COOK
MEMORIAL MUSEUM
Moor 299
THE MOORS
CENTRE
A171
Ruswarp
B1410
Stainsacre
High Hawsker
Houlsyke
Lealholm
Aislaby
Briggswath
Sneaton
Ness Pt.
CLEVELAND WAY
Stonegate
13
Sleights
Ugglebarnby
Sneatonthorpe
Raw
Robin Hood's Bay
Low
Garth
Egton
Grosmont
Littlebeck
B1416
A169
Sneaton
OLD COASTGUARD STATION
Glaisdale
Street
MUSEUM OF
VICTORIAN SCIENCE
Egton
Bridge
Esk Valley
B1447
Fylingthorpe
BOGGLE HOLE
Robin Hood's Bay
Glaisdale
Glaisdale Moor
Egton High Moor
Beck Hole
Goathland
A171
Old Peak
Ravenscar
Y O R K   M O O R S
Flask Inn
Fylingdales Moor
WHEELDALE MOOR
ROMAN ROAD
299
20
Staintondale
CLEVELAND WAY
Rosedale
Moor
Wheeldale
Moor
Goathland Moor
20
Saltergate
Harwood
Dale
Forest
ROSEDALE
Rosedale Abbey
PICKERING MOOR
Pickering
Forest
N A L
P A R K
Langdale
Forest
Harwood Dale
Cloughton Newlands
Cloughton Wyke
Cropton
Hartoft End
Forest
Stape
Broxa
Forest
A171
Cloughton
Burniston
Cromer Pt.
Lastingham
Newton
Dale
Levisham
TOLL
Langdale
End
Broxa
Silpho
SCARBOROUGH
A165
Scalby Ness Rocks
SEA LIFE CENTRE
Spaunton
Newton-on-
Rawcliffe
Lockton
DALBY FOREST
Staindale
Forest
Langdale
Hackness
Suffield
Scalby
North Bay
Cropton
248
Wrench
Green
Everley
Barrowcliff
Newby
SCARBOROUGH CASTLE
ROTUNDA MUSEUM
Appleton-
le-Moors
NORTH RIDING
FOREST PARK
*Wykeham
Forest*
Scarborough
Keldholme
NORTH YORKSHIRE
MOORS RAILWAY
Low Dalby
Sawdon
Hutton
Buscel
East
Ayton
THE HONEY
FARM
South Bay
Sinnington
Aislaby
ST PETER AND
ST PAUL CHURCH
DALBY FOREST
VISITOR CENTRE
*Dalby
Forest*
West
Ayton
Falsgrave
P&R
Osgodby
Cayton Bay
Kirkby Mills
Middleton
PICKERING CASTLE
Ellerburn
Ruston
Irton
Seamer
P&R
Eastfield
Yons Nab
CLEVELAND WAY
Great
Edstone
Marton
Pickering
A170
Thornton-
le-Dale
Wilton
Allerston
Ebberston
17
Snainton
Wykeham
A170
A64
B1261
A165
Cayton
Normanby
B1415
Brompton
Lebberston
Gristhorpe
Little
Barugh
FLAMINGO
LAND
96
THE CAR
PLAYDALE
FARM PARK
Salton
Kirby
Misperton
High
Marshes
Yedingham
97
Flixton
Folkton
Muston
Great Barugh
Low Marishes
Staxton
A1039
Butterwick
Little
Habton
Great
Habton
Brawby
Ryton
West
Knapton
East
Knapton
East
Heslerton
Sherburn
16
Ganton
YORKSHIRE
WOLDS WAY
Hunmanby
Scampston
SCAMPSTON
HALL
West
Heslerton
A64
Potter
Brompton
Fordon
B1249

5   6   7   8

A

B

C

D

E

F

NW

CARLETON CASTLE
Bennane Hd.
112
Colmonell
B734 265 Knockdolian
Heronsford
Glen Tig
Ballantrae Bay
Balkis
Ballantrae
Downan Pt.
Auchencrosh

BELFAST
LARNE

439 BENERAIRD

A77
Mark
Glen App
17
257

Milleur Pt.

Corsewall Pt.
Barnhills
Portencalzie
North Cairn
Penwhirn
Res.
South Cairn
B738
Corsewall
Cairnryan
Braid Fell
Dounan Bay
Loch
Connell
Kirkcolm
Mains of Airies
Ervie
Low
Salchrie
The Wig
LOCH RYAN
A77
B798
6
Knocknain
Leswalt
Innermessan
Auchmar
Slouchnawen
Bay
B738
Black Loch
CASTLE KENNEDY
GARDENS
B7043
Craigencross
A751
Glenstockadale
A718
White Loch
Castle Kennedy
Stranraer
Aird
CASTLE OF
3 ST JOHN
VISITOR
CENTRE
R
7
H
Broadsea Bay
T
H
E
R
G
G
Knockglass
STRANRAER
MUSEUM
Soulseat
Loch
Mark
A75
Black Hd.
B738
182
Lochans
B7077
Dunskey Ho.
A77
5
5
6
B7084
6
Torrs Wa
Portpatrick
Awhirk
A716
Luce S
8
Stoneykirk
B7042
Port of Spittal Bay
Cairngarroch
KIRKMADRINE
STONES
Sandhead
Sandhead Bay
Cairngarroch Bay
Money Hd.
Clachanmore
Hole Stone Bay
Ardwell
Ardwell
Mains
Chapel Rossan
Ardwell Pt.
Logan
Mains
10
LOGAN
BOTANIC
GARDEN
Balgowan P
Mull of Logan
Port Nessock or Port Logan Bay
Port Logan
B7065
A716
Cairnywellan Hd.
Clanyard Bay
Low Clanyard
Drumr
Laggantalluch Hd.
Kirkmaiden
164
Damnaglaur
B7041
M
Crammag Hd.
Cairngaan
Port Kemin

0 1 2 3 4 5 6 miles
0 1 2 3 4 5 6 7 8 9 10km

6   7   8   9

A

B

C

D

E

F

G

BLYTH

WHITLEY BAY

AMSTERDAM

Tynemouth
North Shields
South Shields
SOUTH SHIELDS MUSEUM & GALLERY
ARBEIA ROMAN FORT AND MUSEUM

Cullercoats
TYNEMOUTH AQUARIUM
TYNEMOUTH CASTLE & PRIORY

KING CHARLES III
ENGLAND COAST PATH

ST MARY'S LIGHTHOUSE
St Mary's or Bait I.

Seaton Sluice
SEATON DELAVAL HALL
Hartley

Blyth
Newsham
New Delaval
Seaton Delaval
Holywell

East Cramlington
Seghill
Annitsford
Burradon
Backworth
Earsdon
Monkseaton
Shiremoor
Marden

Camperdown
Killingworth
Longbenton
Willington

WALLSEND
Tyne Tunnel
Westoe
Harton
Marsden

Byker
Jarrow
Walker
Hebburn
Hedworth
Whiteleas
Cleadon

THE LEAS AND
MARSDEN ROCK
Marsden Bay

SOUTER
LIGHTHOUSE

Whitburn Colliery

Gateshead
INTERNATIONAL
STADIUM
Pelaw
Boldon Colliery
Whitburn

Felling
Carr Hill
Low Fell
Wrekenton
Springwell
Blackfell

Boldon
FULWELL WINDMILL
Downhill
Hylton Castle
Southwick
Fulwell
Roker
Monkwearmouth
NATIONAL GLASS CENTRE
ST PETER'S CHURCH
SUNDERLAND MINSTER

Castletown
Usworth

WASHINGTON
Lambton
Pennywell
South Hylton
High Barnes
Pallion
Sunderland
Hendon

Birtley
WASHINGTON
SERVICES
Ouston
Barley Mow
Rickleton
Fatfield
Penshaw
THE WILDFOWL &
WETLANDS TRUST
PENSHAW MON
East Herrington
New Silksworth
Tunstall
Ryhope
RYHOPE ENGINES MUS

Shiney Row
New Herrington
Newbottle
Doxford Park
DOWN AT
THE FARM
Burdon
Seaton
Northlea

Chester Moor
Great Lumley
Colliery Row
East Rainton
HOUGHTON-LE-SPRING
Hetton-le-Hole
Murton
DALTON PARK
West Lea
SEAHAM
Dalton-le-Dale
Cold Hesledon

Plawsworth
West Rainton
Leamside
Low Moorsley
Easington Lane
South Hetton
Hawthorn
Beacon Pt

Kimblesworth
Pity Me
Framwellgate Moor
FINCHALE PRIORY
Carrville
Littletown
Haswell
Easington Colliery

DURHAM CITY
DURHAM CATH
DURHAM UNIV
ORIENTAL MUS
Shincliffe
Sherburn
Sherburn Hill
Haswell Plough
Shotton Colliery
Easington
Horden

Shadforth
Ludworth
CASTLE
EDEN DENE
PETERLEE
Shotton
Blackhall Colliery
Blackhall Rocks

Bowburn
Old Cassop
Thornley
Wheatley Hill
Castle Eden
High Hesleden
DURHAM COAST

Quarrington Hill
Kelloe
Coxhoe
CASSOP VALE
Wingate
Deaf Hill
Hesleden

Cornforth
Trimdon Grange
Trimdon Colliery
Station Town
Hart Station
ST HILDA'S PARISH CHURCH

Ferryhill
Ferryhill Station
Trimdon
Hutton Henry
Sheraton
Hart
THE NATIONAL MUS OF THE ROYAL NAVY
Hartlepool Bay

Kirk Merrington
Mainsforth
Fishburn
High Throston
Hartlepool

Middlestone
Chilton
Bishop Middleham
Butterwick
Elwick
West Park
SUMMERHILL

Chilton
Sedgefield
Dalton Piercy
Rift House
Seaton Carew

NEWTON AYCLIFFE
Bradbury
Mordon
Wynyard Village
Newton Bewley
Greatham
Greathorp
Tees Bay
Salt Scar
REDCAR

NZ

HARTLEPOOL

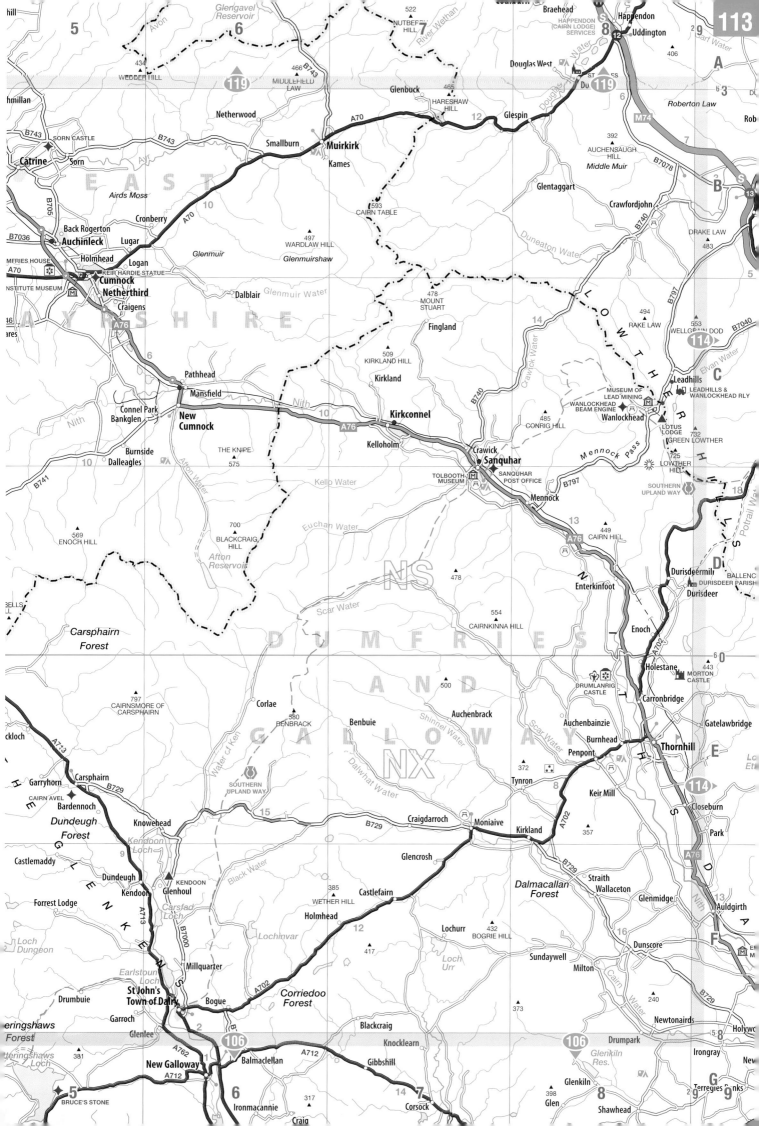

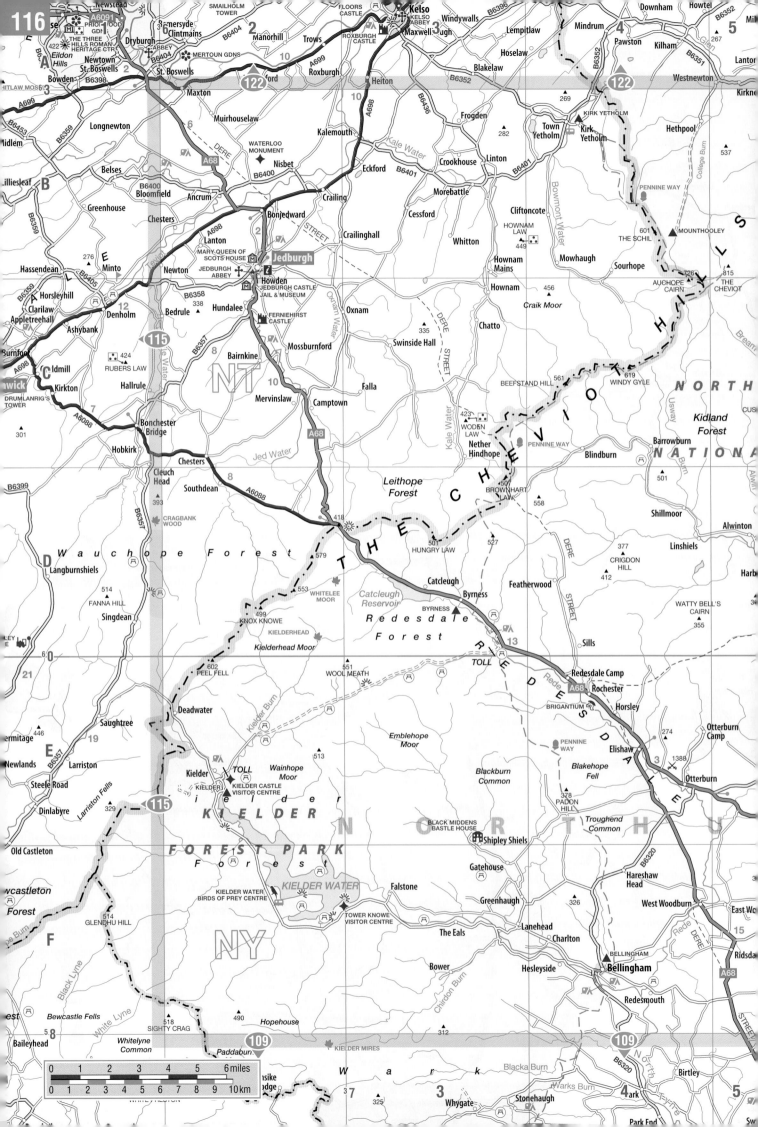

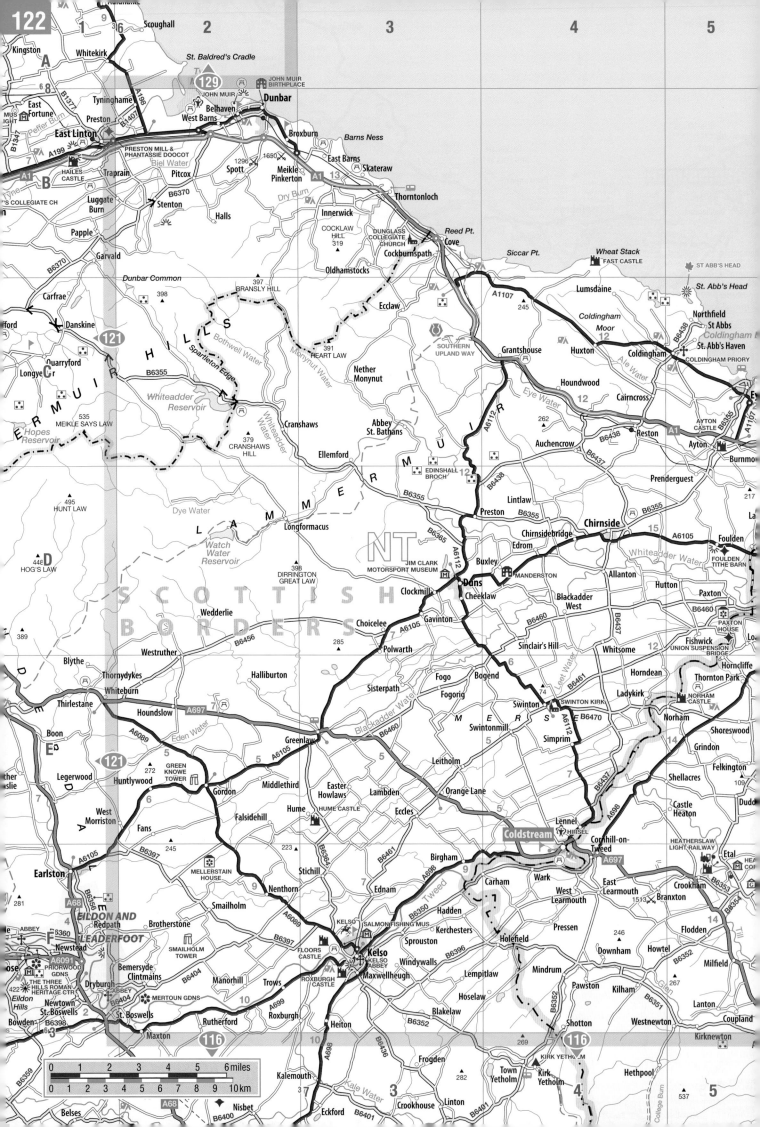

A

B

C

D

E

F

G

5   0   6   7   8   43   9

EYEMOUTH MUSEUM
mouth

Lamberton
Beach
berton

appers

1333

Highfields

Berwick-upon-Tweed
BERWICK-UPON-TWEED
BARRACKS & MAIN GUARD
BERWICK

B6461

East
Ord
Tweedmouth
Spittal

end   A698

Priory
Park
Redshin Cove

108

Murton
Thornton

Scremerston

West Allerdean
Shoresdean

Cheswick

B6554

Ancroft

Goswick

North Low

Haggerston

Berrington

South Low   Beal

A1

Bowsden

82

12

Barmoor
Castle   Barmoor
Lane End   Lowick

West
Kyloe
Fenwick

ERSLAW
MILL
WATERFORD HALL

B6353

Kyloe
Hills
East
Kyloe

Buckton

Elwick   Ross

157

Holburn

Detchant

Middleton

Kimmerston

Nesbit

Hetton
Steads

211

North Hazelrigg

Belford

Fenton
Town

Doddington

200

South
Hazelrigg

Easington

B1342

Mousen

Spindlestone

Newtown

West
Horton
East Horton

10

Warenton

B6525

Weetwood Hall

Humbleton

1402

B6348

166

Wooler

WOOLER

Earle

5   0

Haugh Head

6

Chatton

Greendikes

CHILLINGHAM
CASTLE
Chillingham
WILD CATTLE OF
CHILLINGHAM

Newtown

Middleton Hall

Rosebrough

7

Newstead

NU

NORTHUMBERLAND

LINDISFARNE

Causeway
Holy
Island
Sands

Holy
Island

HERITAGE
CENTRE

Fenham

Emmanuel Hd.

**Holy Island
(Lindisfarne)**

LINDISFARNE CASTLE

Castle Pt.

LINDISFARNE
PRIORY

Guile
Pt.

COAST

Budle
Bay

Farne
Islands

Staple Sound

FARNE ISLANDS

Inner Sound

BAMBURGH
CASTLE

Budle

Bamburgh

Waren Mill

Glororum   Burton

Bradford

Elford

Bellshill

Adderstone

Lucker

ADDERSTONE
SERVICES

117

NEWHAM BOG

Warenford

Newham
Hall

North
Sunderland

Swinhoe

A1

Newham

Fleetham

Chathill

Ellingham   Preston

Brunton

15

Seahouses

Bead

117

Benthall

KING CHARLES III
ENGLAND COAST PATH

Bead   ll Bay

High Newton-
by-the-Sea

8   43   9

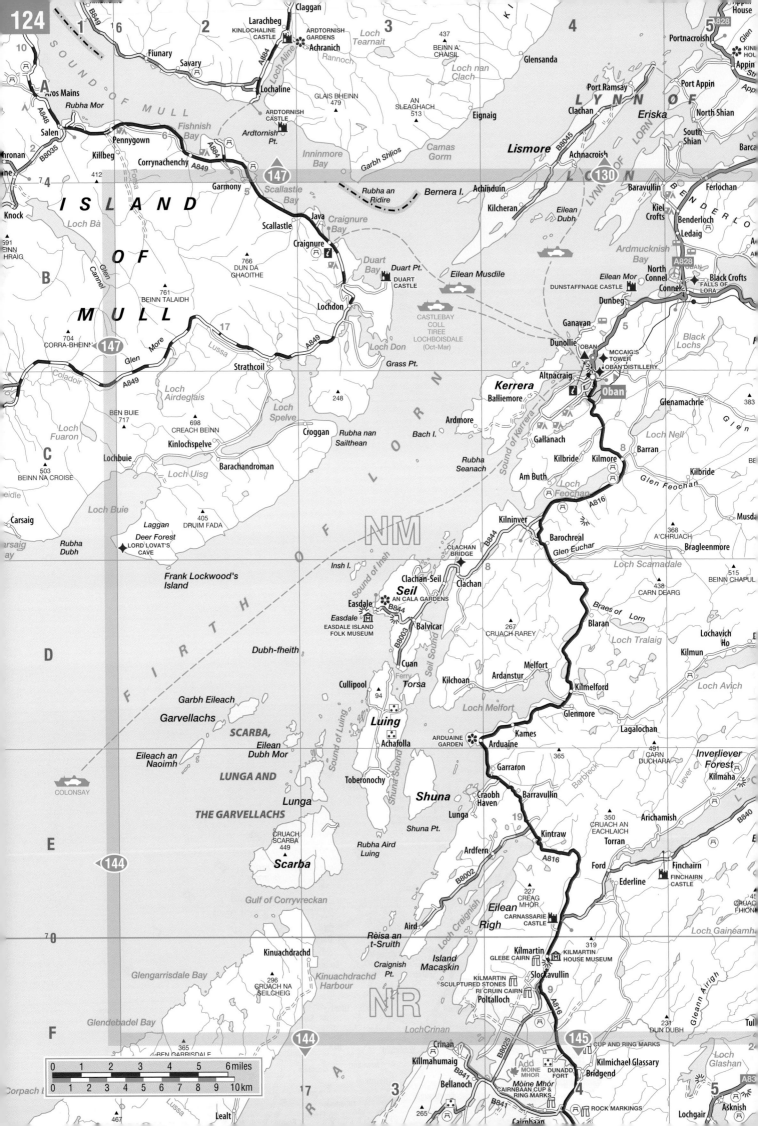

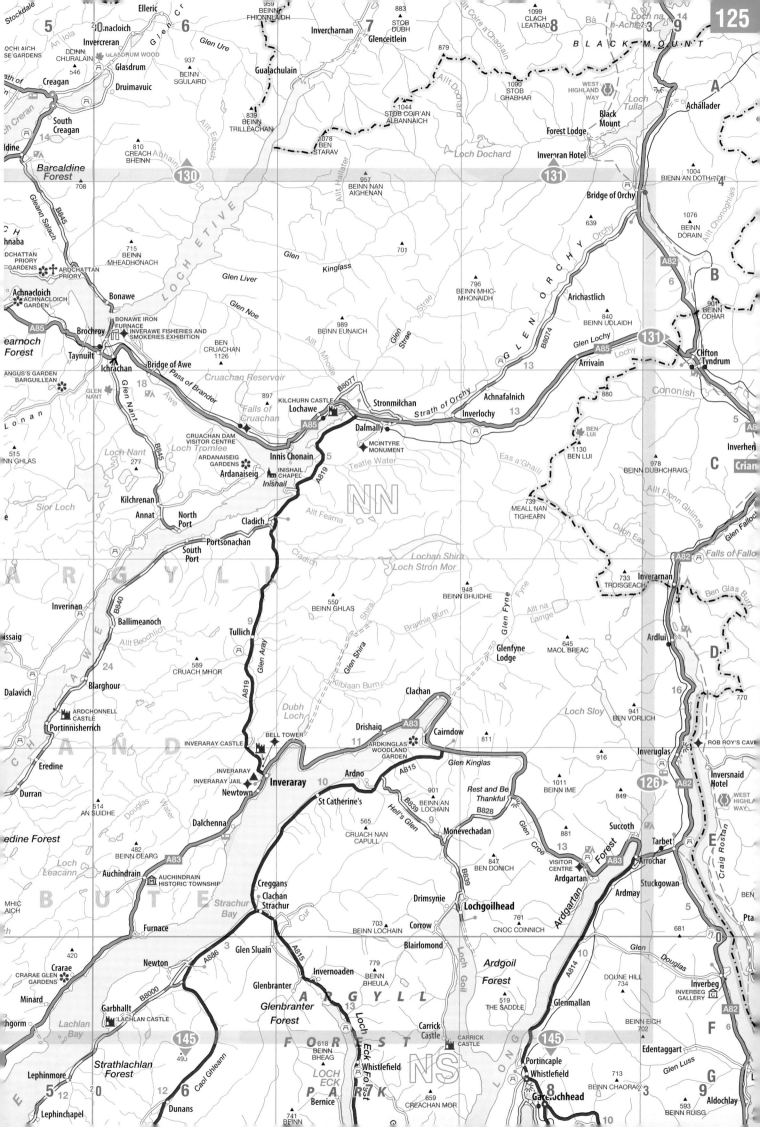

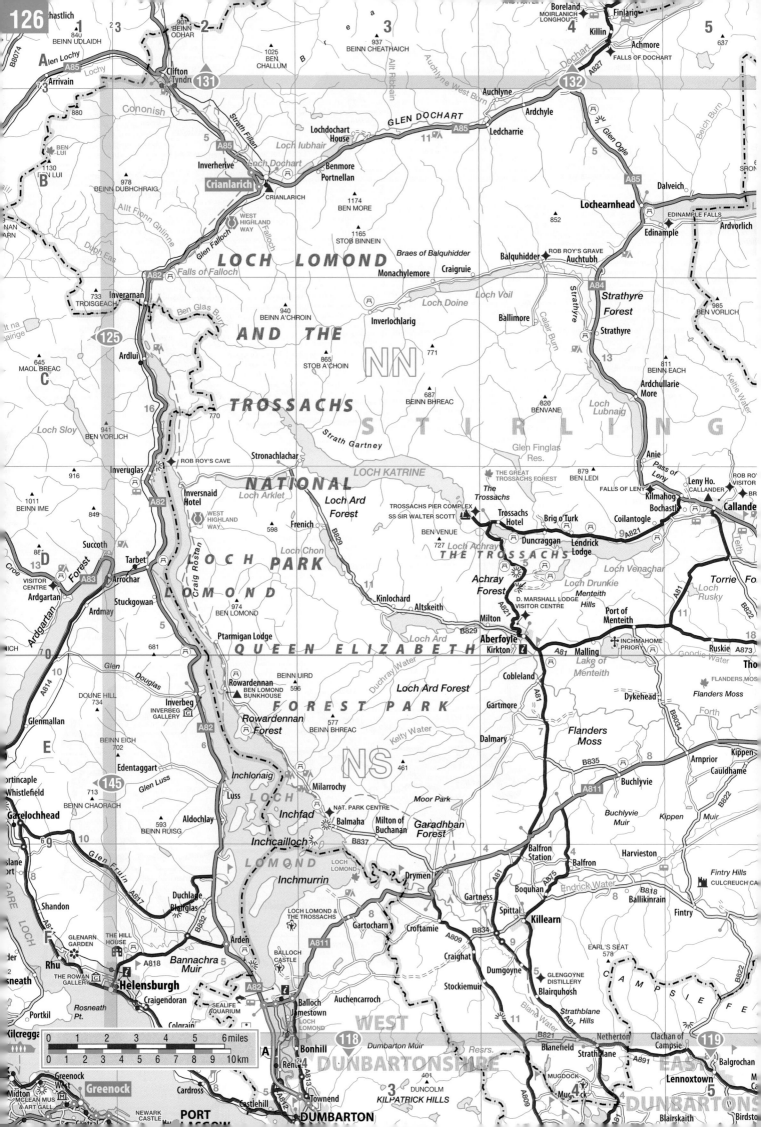

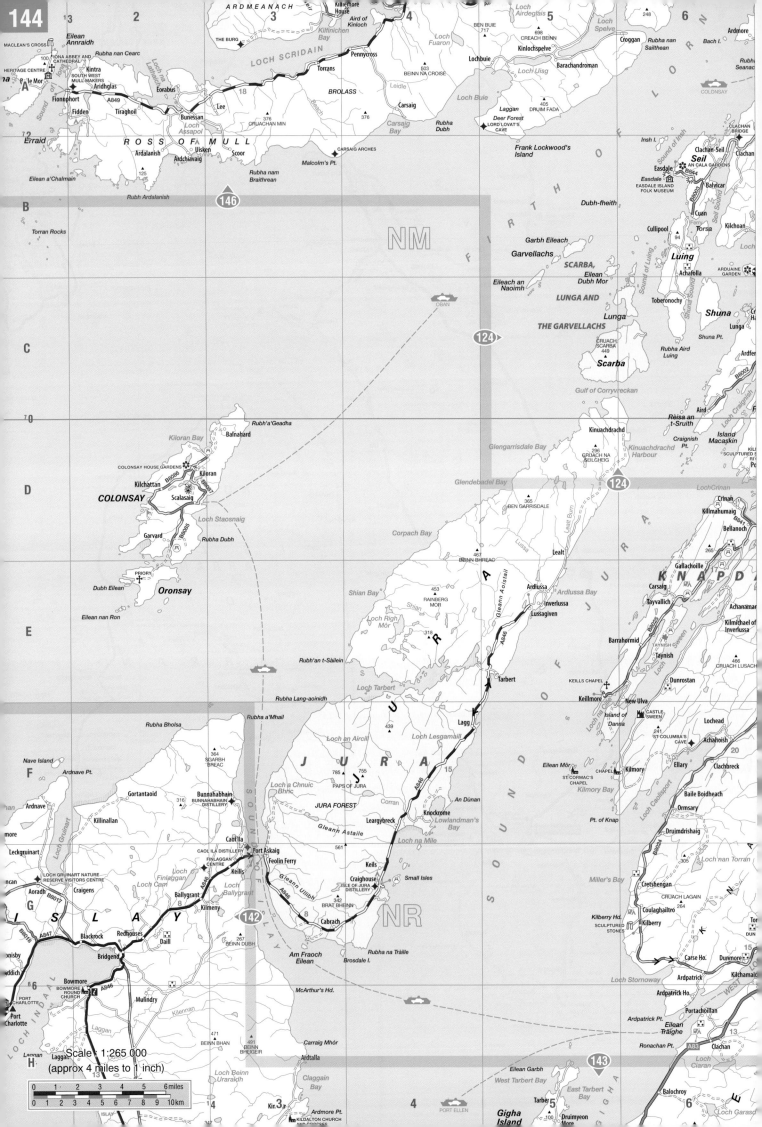

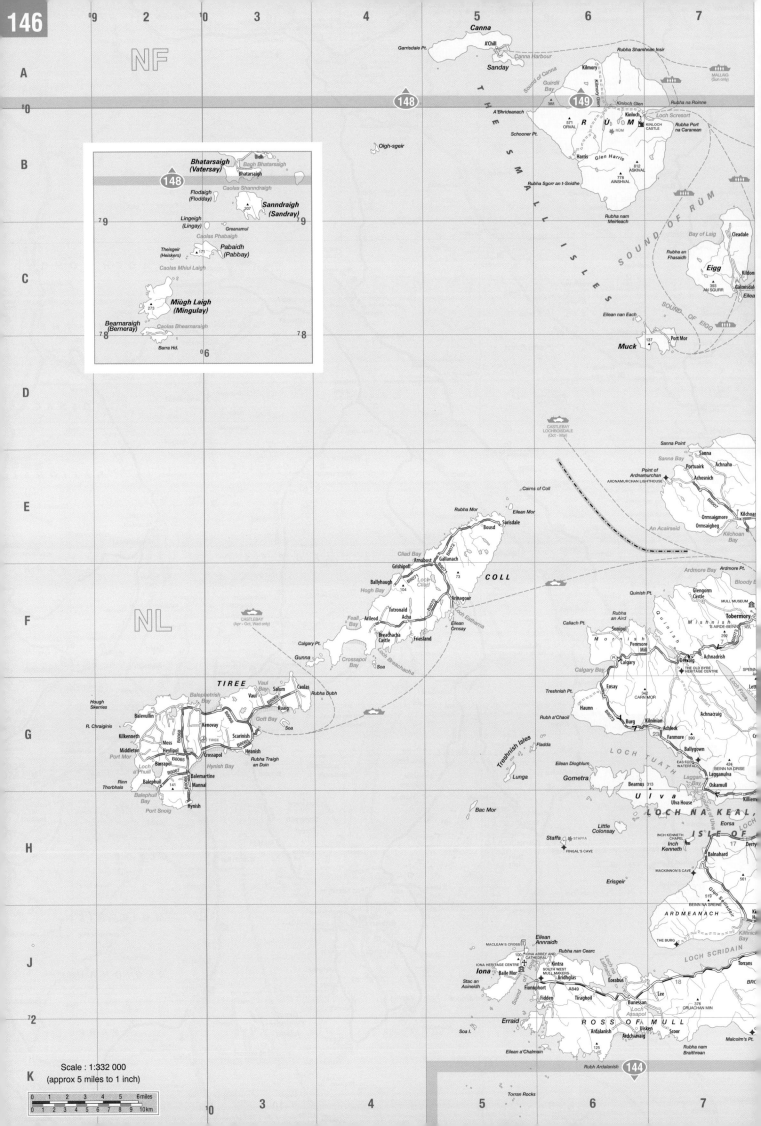

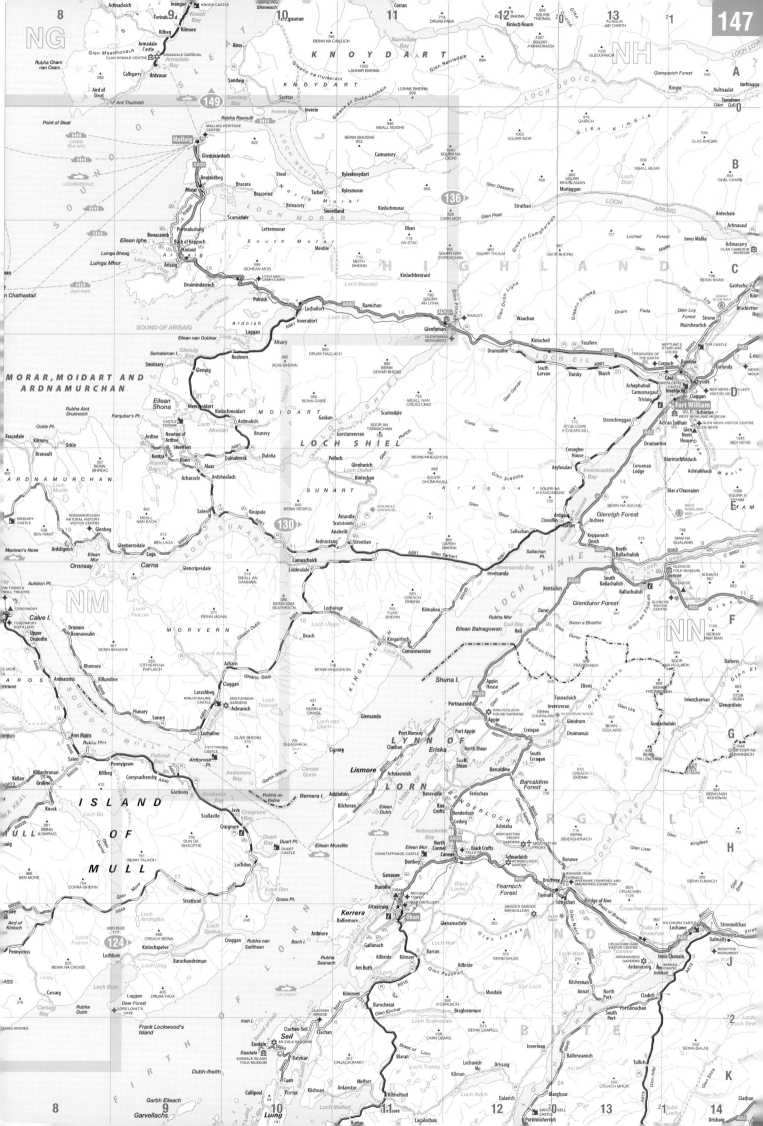

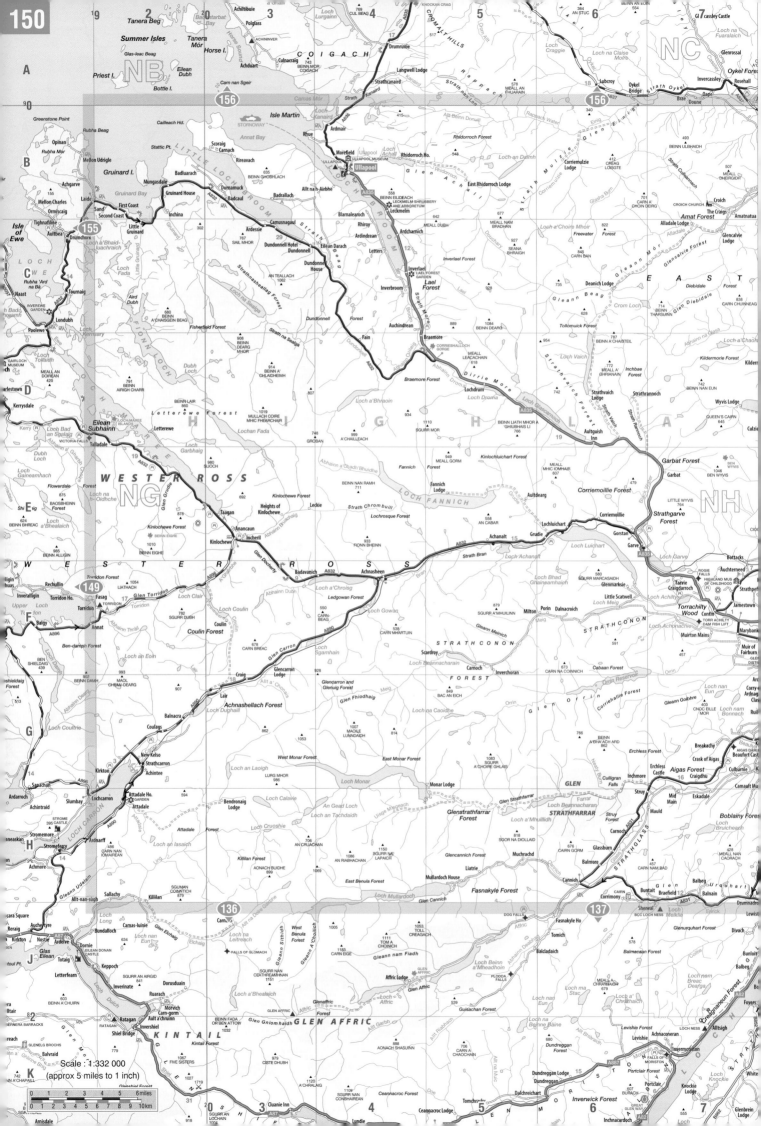

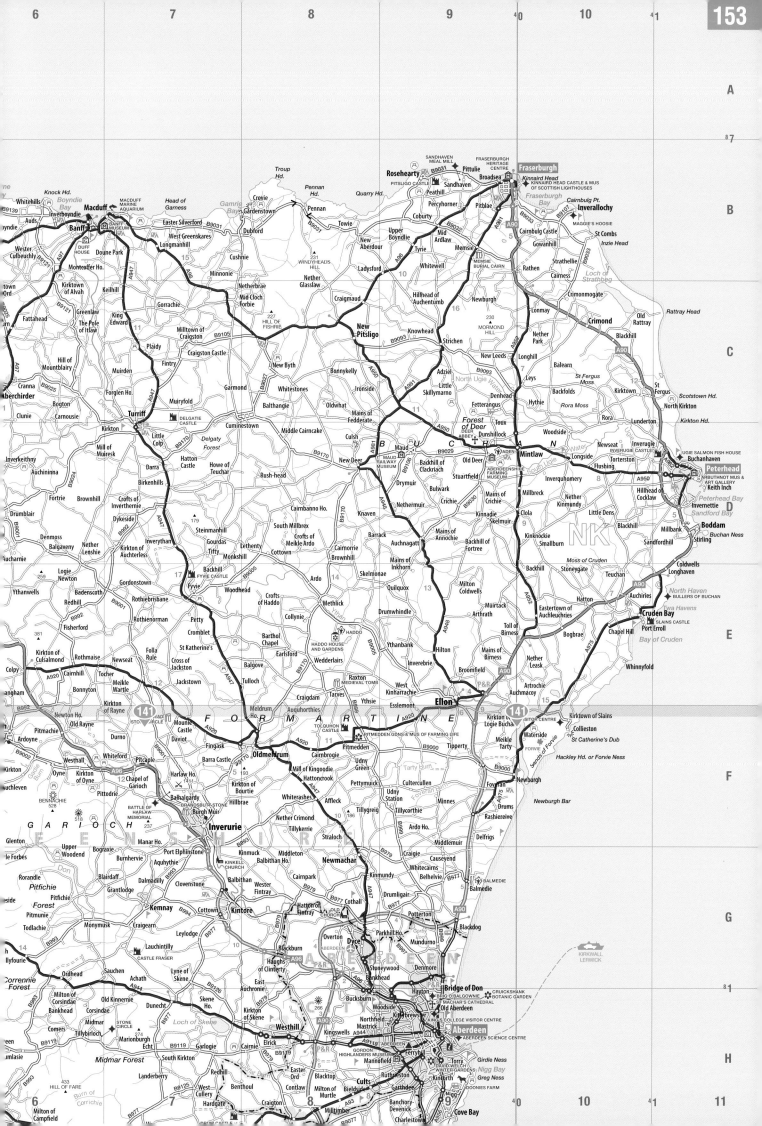

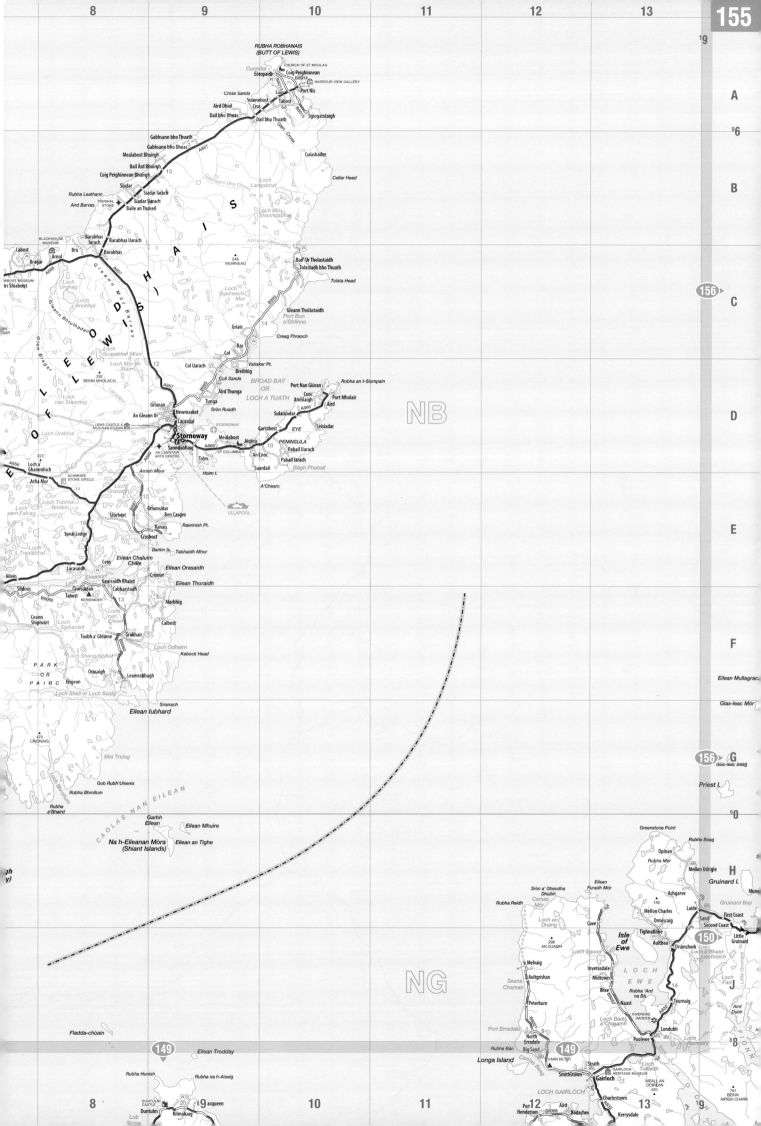

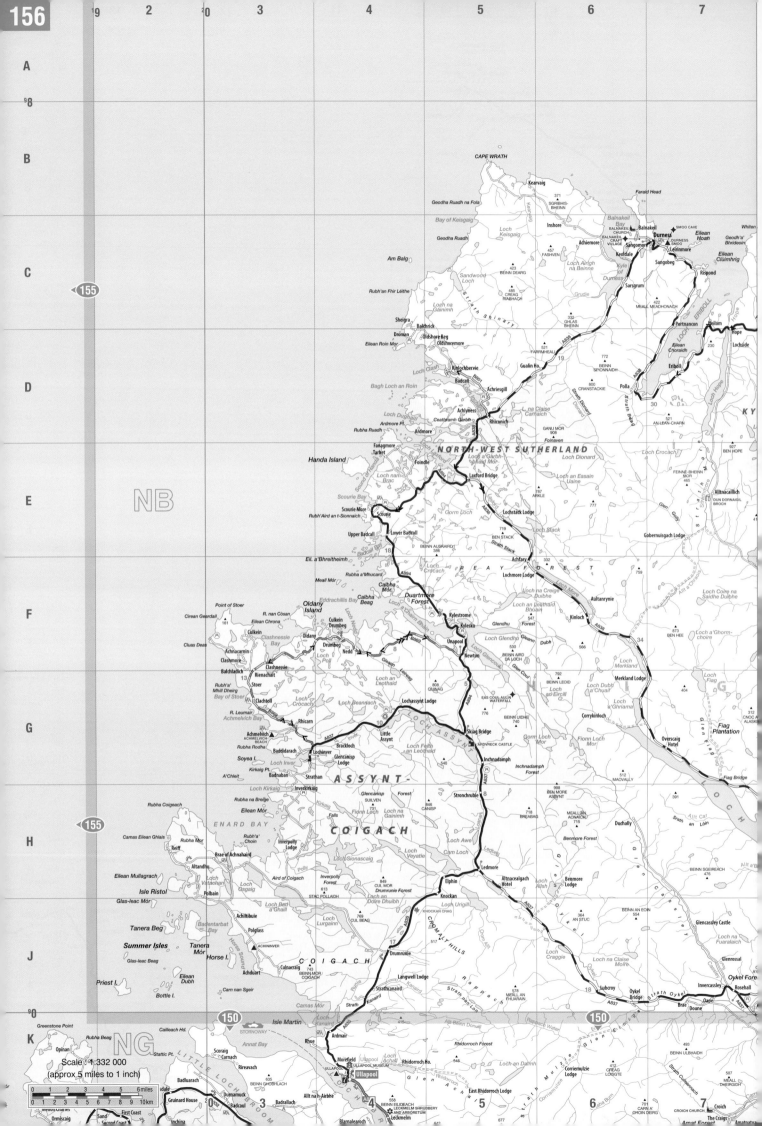

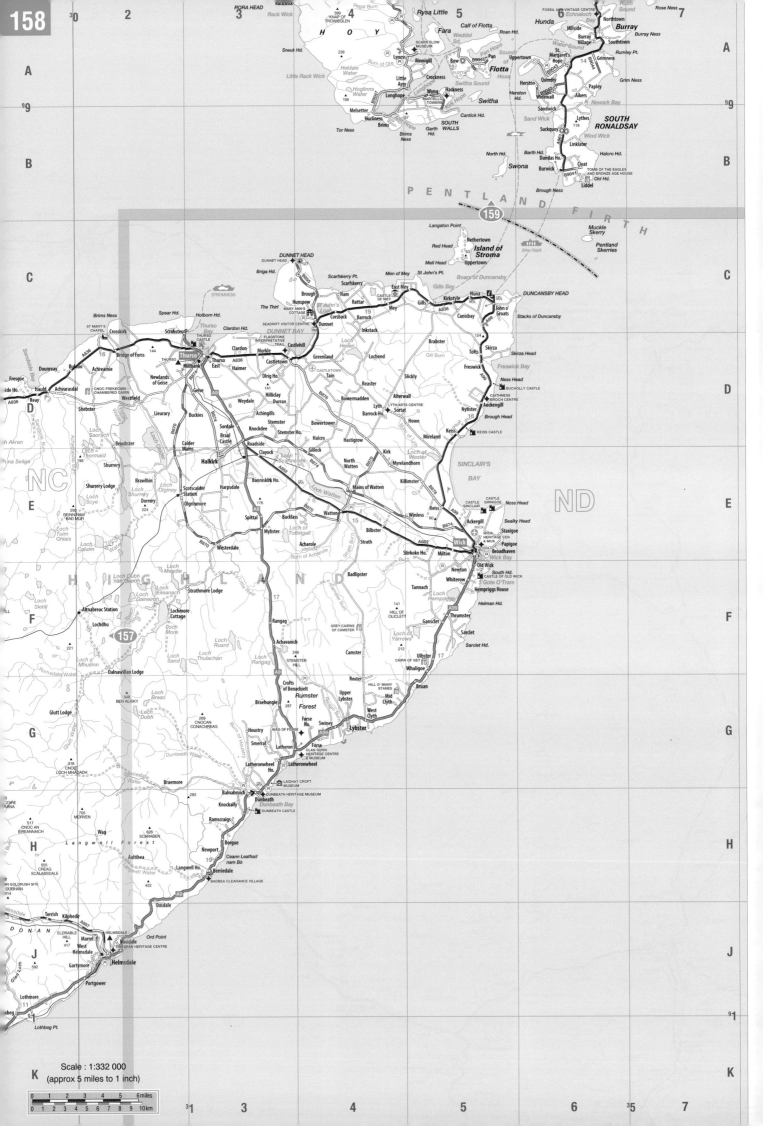

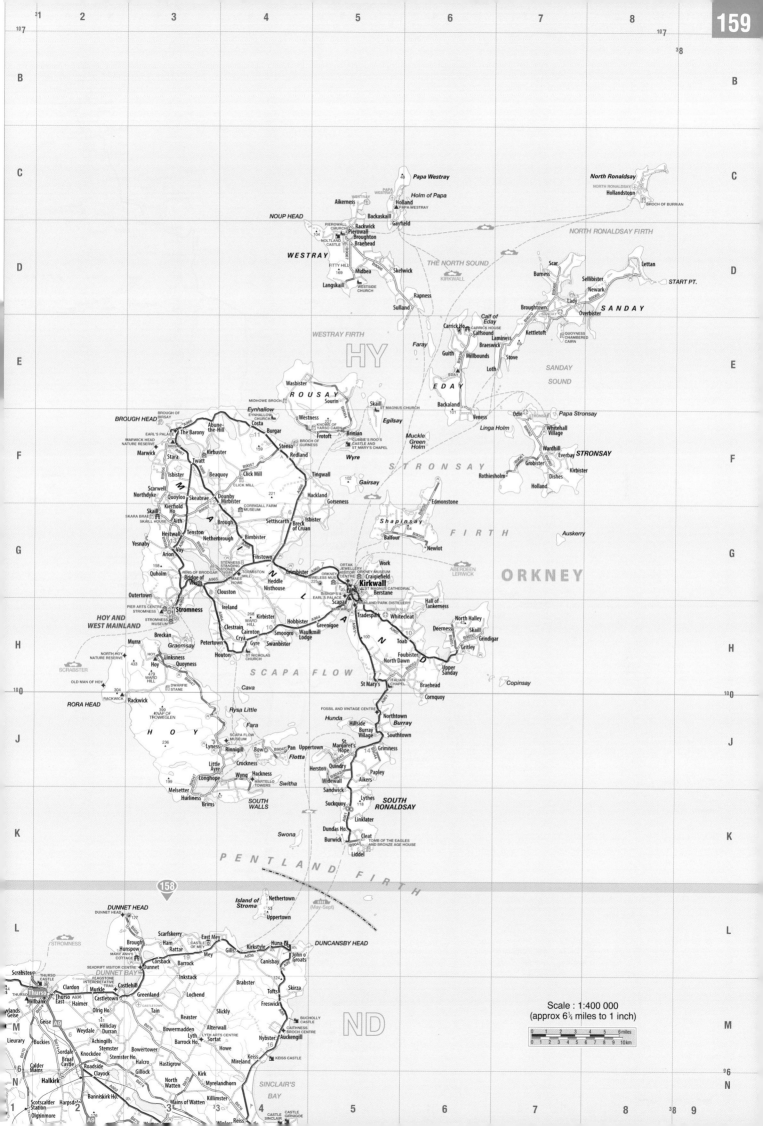

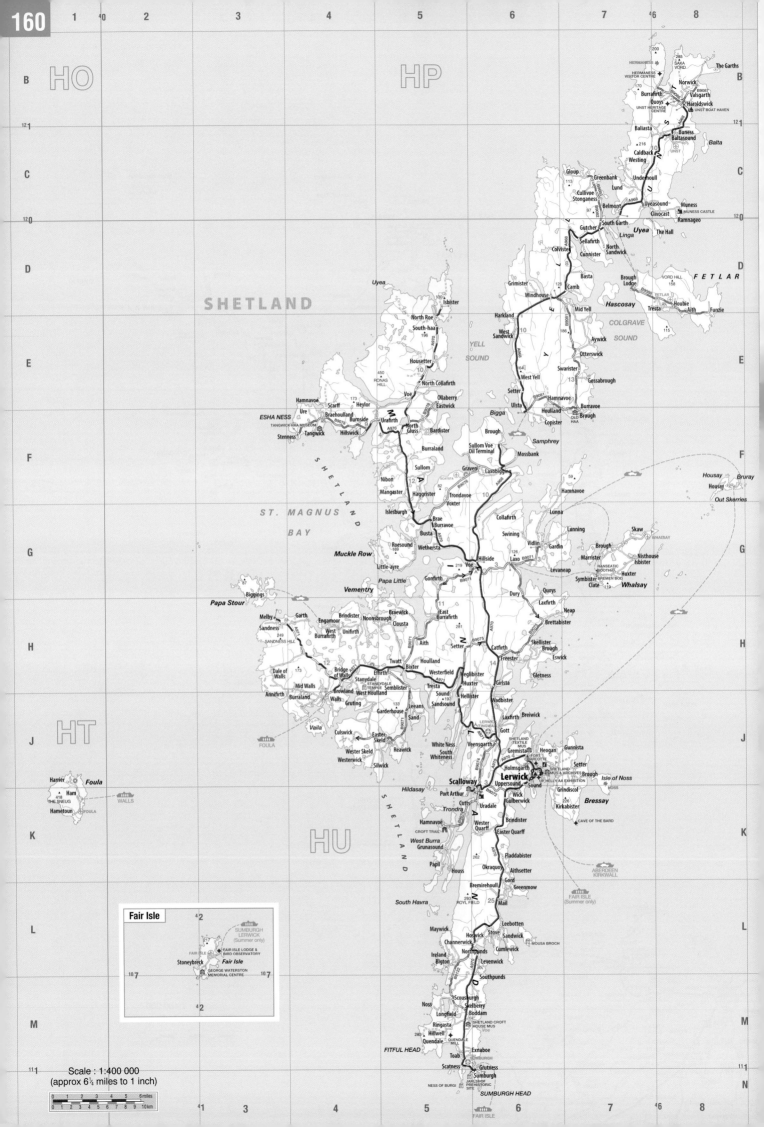

HO

HP

B

HERMANESS
VISITOR CENTRE
200
285
SAXA
VORD
The Garths
Hermaness
170
Norwick
Burrafirth
Valsgarth
Quoys
Haroldswick
UNST HERITAGE
CENTRE
UNST BOAT HAVEN

12 1

Baliasta
Buness
216
Baltasound
Balta
Caldback
Westing
UNST
12 0

SHETLAND

C
Gloup
113
Greenbank
Cullivoe
Stonganess
Lund
Underhoull
Belmont
Uyeasound
Clivocast
Muness
MUNESS CASTLE
Ramnageo

12 0

Uyea
130
Isbister
North Roe
South-haa
196

Grimister
Windhouse
126
Camb
Basta
Mid Yell
Gutcher
Linga
Uyea
The Hall
Sellafirth
Cunnister
North
Sandwick
ColVister

Brough
Lodge
VORD HILL
158
FETLAR

D

Hascosay
Tresta
Houbie
Aith
Funzie
115

Harkland
West
Sandwick
186
Aywick
COLGRAVE
SOUND

450
RONAS
HILL
173
Heylor
Housetter
10
North Collafirth
Voe
Ollaberry
Eastwick
YELL
SOUND
West Yell
Setter
Ulsta
B9081
Hamnavoe
Houlland
Burravoe
OLD
HAA
Brough
13
Otterswick
Swarister
Gossabrough

E

Hamnavoe
Scarff
Ure
Braehoulland
Burnside
ESHA NESS
TANGWICK HAA MUSEUM
Stenness
Tangwick
Hillswick
Urafirth
North
Gluss
A970
Bardister
Bigga
Copister
Samphrey

Housay
Bruray
59
Housay
Out Skerries

F

Burraland
Sullom Voe
Oil Terminal
Mossbank
Nibon
Sullom
A
Graven
Laxobigging
SCATSTA
82
Mangaster
Haggrister
Trondavoe
Voxter
10
Hamnavoe

ST. MAGNUS
BAY
Islesburgh
Brae
Burravoe
Busta
Collafirth
Swining
Lunna
Lunning
Skaw
WHALSAY
Brough
Nisthouse
Isbister
Roesound
169
Wetherial
Vidlin
Gardin
Marrister
HANSEATIC
BOOTH
Symbister
Clate
Huxter
119

G

Muckle Row
Little-ayre
Papa Little
Vementry
Biggings
Papa Stour
Melby
Sandness
87
219
Voe
3
Hillside
Gonfirth
B9071
Laxo
Levaneap
Quoys
Dury
Laxfirth
Neap
Brettabister

H

SANDNESS HILL
249
Garth
Engamoor
Brindister
Noonsbrough
Clousta
Braewick
East
Burrafirth
281
Setter
Catfirth
Skellister
Brough
Eswick
Gletness
Freester
14

Dale of
Walls
173
West
Burrafirth
Unifirth
Aith
Houlland
Bixter
Twatt
Westerfield
Neglibister
Huxter
Girlsta

J

Annifirth
Mid Walls
Bridge
of Walls
Effirth
Stanydale
STANEYDALE
TEMPLE
Semblister
Tresta
Sound
197
Hellister
Wadbister
FOULA
Walls
Browland
West Houlland
Gruting
Garderhouse
Leeans
Sand
Sandsound
Laxfirth
Breiwick
Gott
LERWICK
TINGWALL
SHETLAND
TEXTILE
MUS
Gremista
Heogan
Gunnista
Vaila
Culswick
Easter
Skeld
Reawick
White Ness
South
Whiteness
Veensgarth
Holmsgarth
SHETLAND
MUS & ARCHIVES
UP HELLY AA EXHIBITION
Setter
Brough
Isle of Noss

K

Harrier
Foula
Ham
418
THE SNEUG
Hametoun
FOULA
WALLS
Wester Skeld
Westerwick
Silwick
Scalloway
Uppersound
Sound
FORT
CHARLOTTE
Lerwick
Grindiscol
Kirkabister
Bressay
NOSS
Hildasay
Port Arthur
Cutts
Trondra
Uradale
Wick
Gulberwick
Brindister
CAVE OF THE BARD

HT

HU

SHETLAND

Hamnavoe
CROFT TRAIL
West Burra
Grunasound
Papil
Houss
262
Wester
Quarff
Easter Quarff
Fladdabister
Okraquoy
Aithsetter
Gord
Greenmow

L

South Havra
Maywick
293
ROYL FIELD
25
Mail
Leebotten
Stove
Sandwick
MOUSA BROCH
FAIR ISLE
(Summer only)
ABERDEEN
KIRKWALL

Fair Isle

42
SUMBURGH
LERWICK
(Summer only)
Hoswick
Cumlewick
Channerwick
Ireland
Bigton
Northpunds
Levenwick
Southpunds

Stoneybreck
FAIR ISLE
George Waterston
Memorial Centre
Fair Isle
FAIR ISLE LODGE &
BIRD OBSERVATORY
10 7
42
10 7

M

Noss
Scousburgh
Skelberry
Boddam
Longfield
Ringasta
280
Hillwell
Quendale
QUENDALE
MILL
SHETLAND CROFT
HOUSE MUS
Voe

FITFUL HEAD
Exnaboe
Toab
SUMBURGH
JARLSHOF
PREHISTORIC
SITE
Scatness
Grutness
Sumburgh

11 1

NESS OF BURGI
SUMBURGH HEAD

11 1

FAIR ISLE

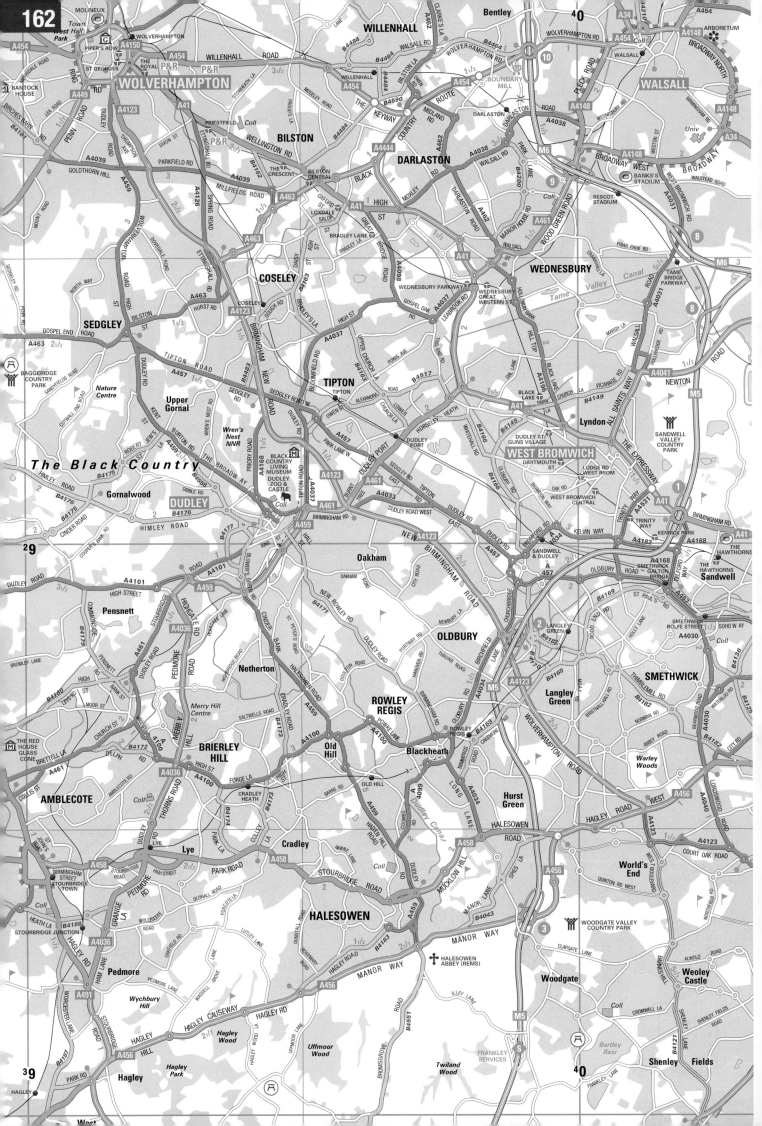

GLASGOW

Low Emission Zone

Ultra Low Emission Zone

Town plan symbols

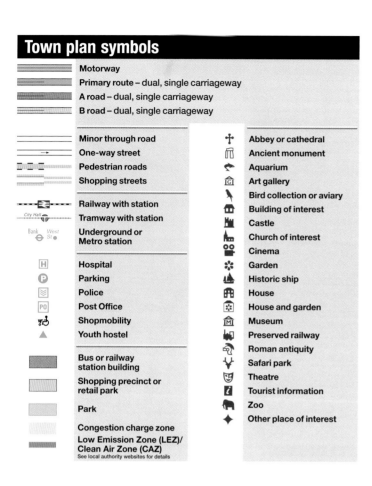

Motorway

Primary route – dual, single carriageway

A road – dual, single carriageway

B road – dual, single carriageway

Minor through road
One-way street
Pedestrian roads
Shopping streets

Railway with station
Tramway with station
Underground or Metro station

Hospital
Parking
Police
Post Office
Shopmobility
Youth hostel

Bus or railway station building
Shopping precinct or retail park
Park
Congestion charge zone
Low Emission Zone (LEZ)/Clean Air Zone (CAZ)
See local authority websites for details

† Abbey or cathedral
Ancient monument
Aquarium
Art gallery
Bird collection or aviary
Building of interest
Castle
Church of interest
Cinema
Garden
Historic ship
House
House and garden
Museum
Preserved railway
Roman antiquity
Safari park
Theatre
Tourist information
Zoo
Other place of interest

Aberdeen

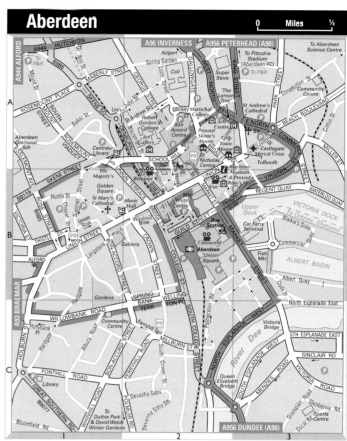

0 Miles ¼

Low Emission Zone (LEZ)/Clean Air Zone (CAZ)

Ayr

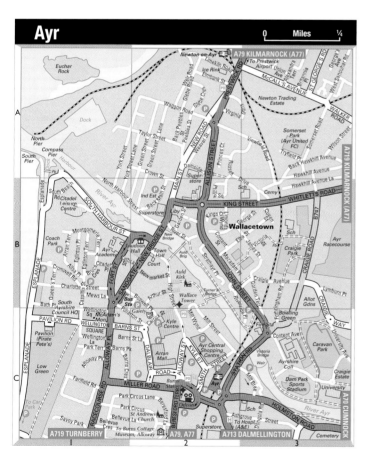

0 Miles ¼

Bath

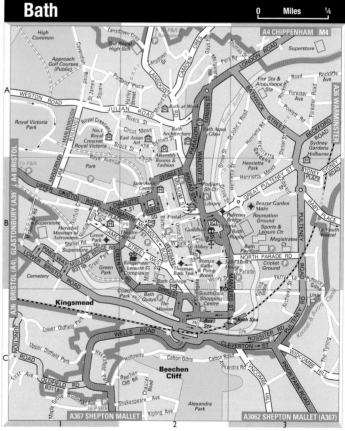

0 Miles ¼

Low Emission Zone (LEZ)/Clean Air Zone (CAZ)

Birmingham

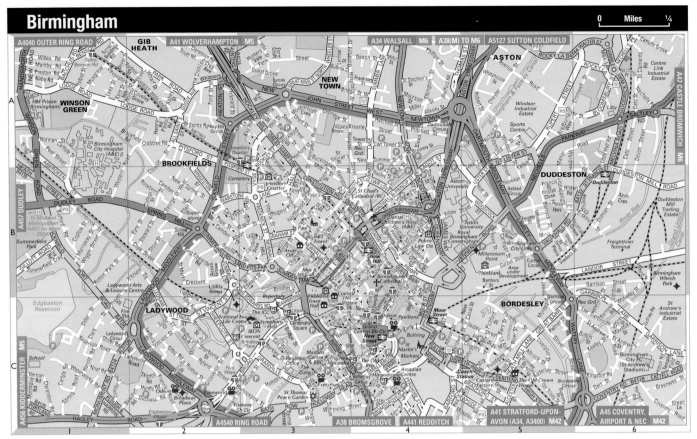

0   Miles   ¼

━━━ Low Emission Zone (LEZ)/Clean Air Zone (CAZ)

Blackpool

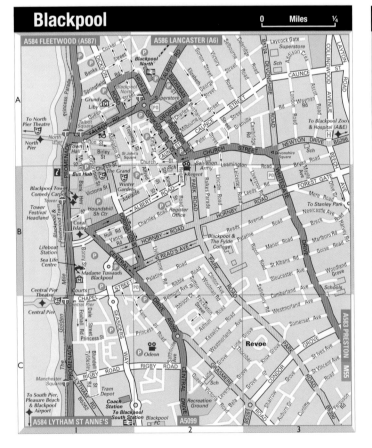

0   Miles   ¼

Bournemouth

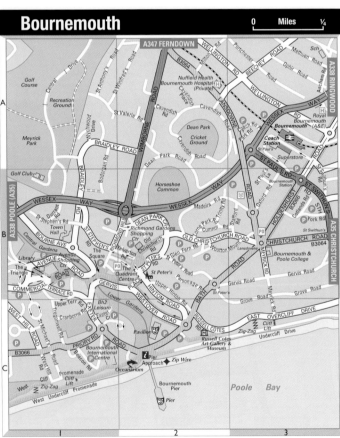

0   Miles   ¼

Bradford
0   Miles   ¼

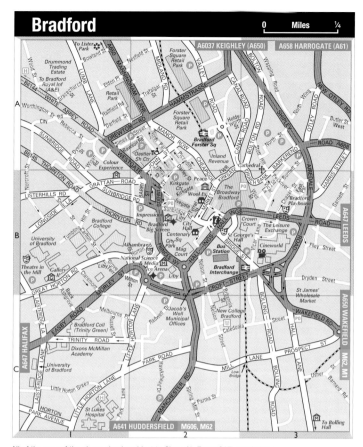

All of the area of the above plan is subject to Clean Air Zone (CAZ) restrictions

Brighton
0   Miles   ¼

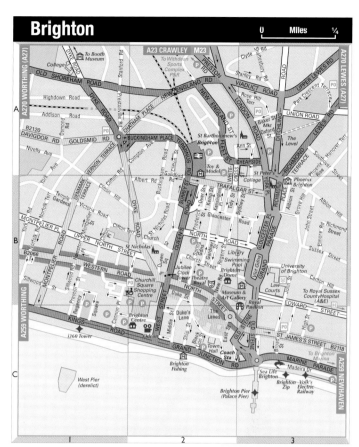

Low Emission Zone (LEZ)/Clean Air Zone (CAZ)

Bristol
0   Miles   ¼

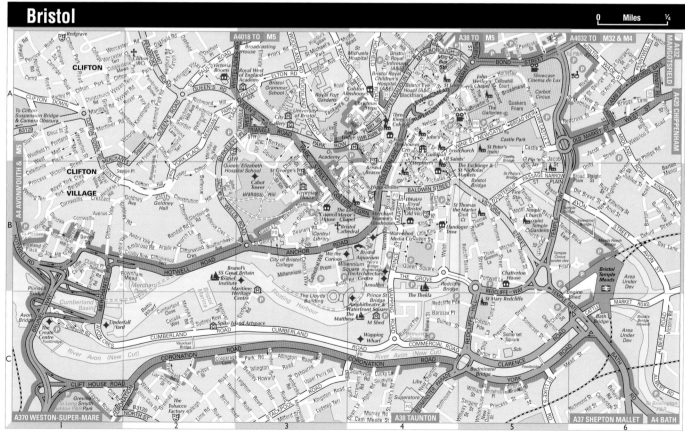

Low Emission Zone (LEZ)/Clean Air Zone (CAZ)

Bury St Edmunds

0 Miles ¼

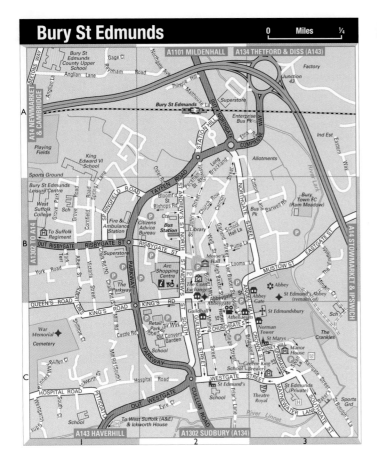

Cambridge

0 Miles ¼

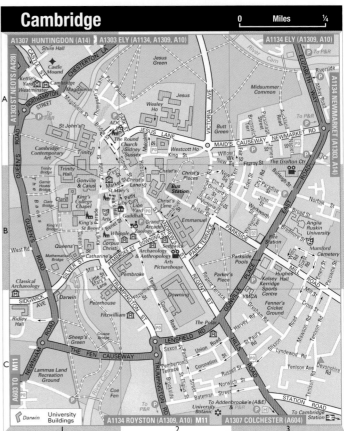

Canterbury

0 Miles ¼

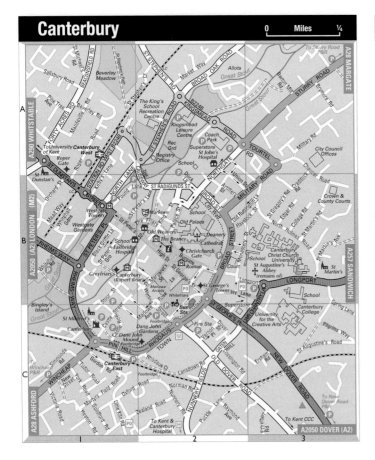

Cardiff / Caerdydd

0 Miles ¼

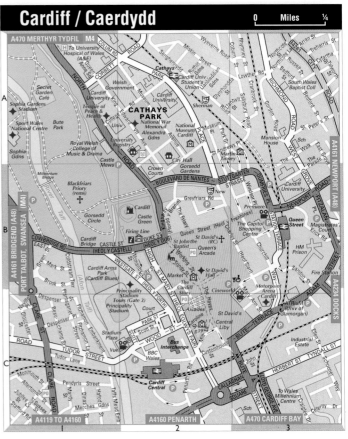

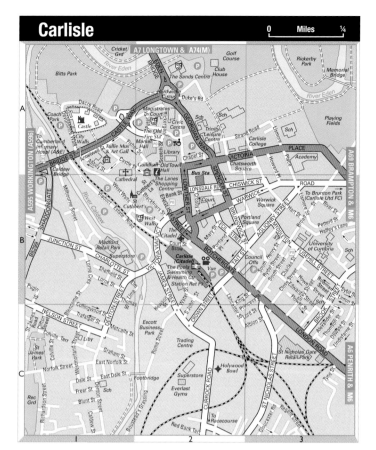

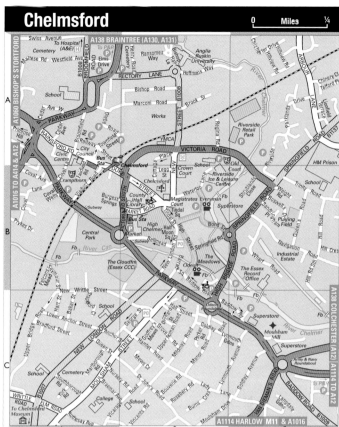

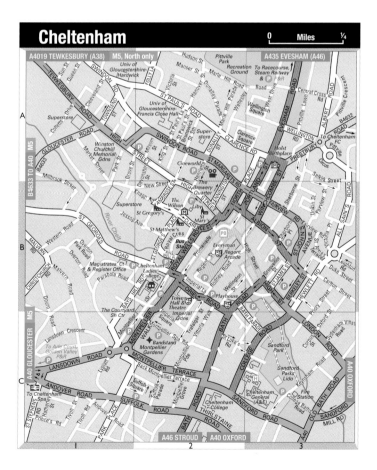

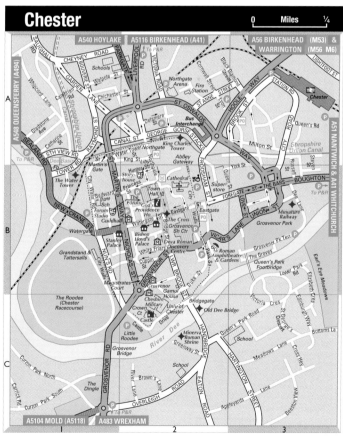

Chichester

0   Miles   ¼

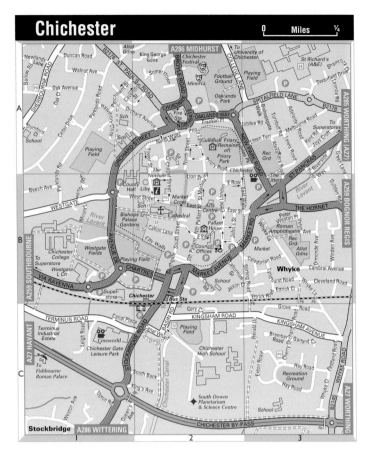

Colchester

0   Miles   ¼

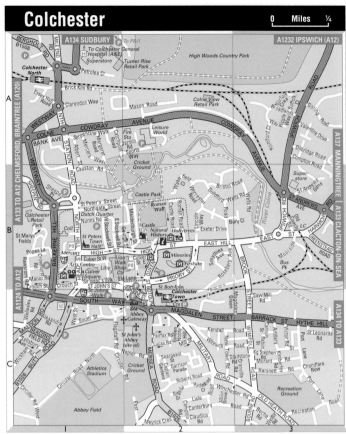

Coventry

0   Miles   ¼

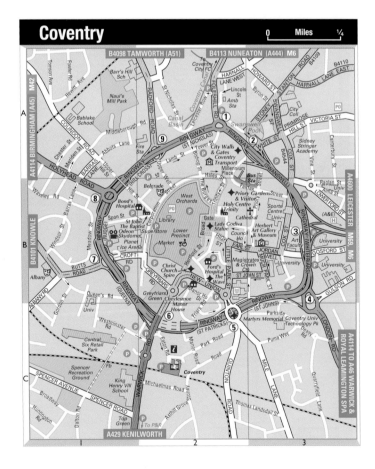

Derby

0   Miles   ¼

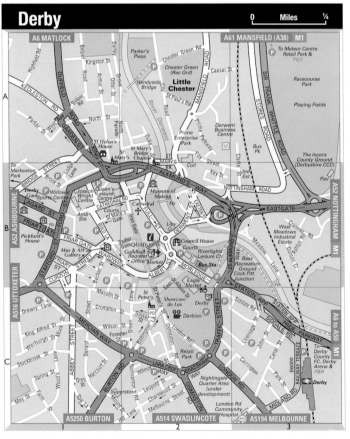

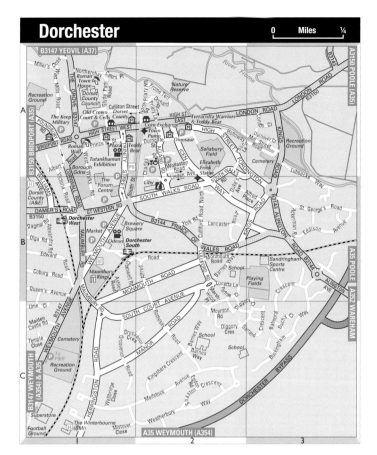

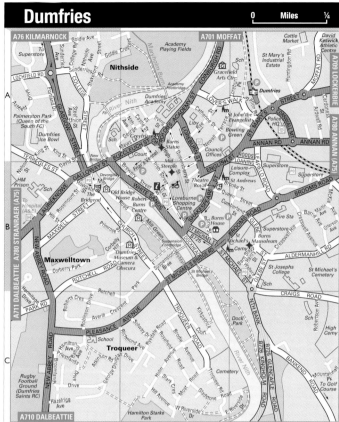

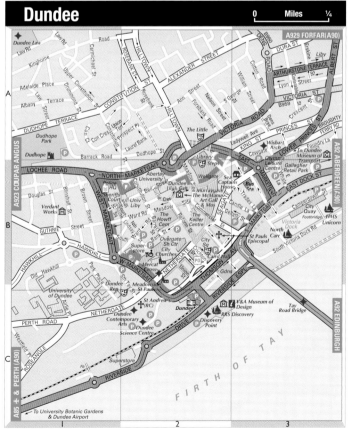

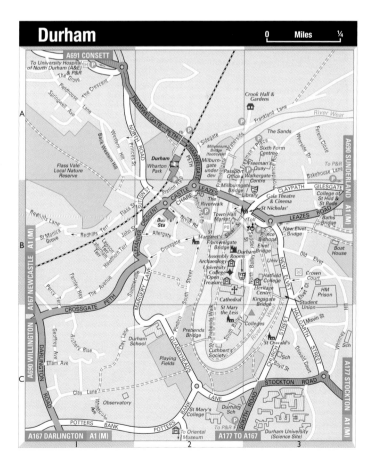

Low Emission Zone (LEZ)/Clean Air Zone (CAZ)

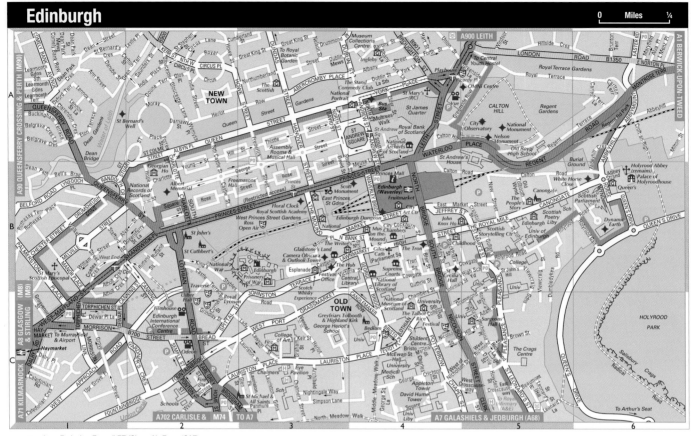

Edinburgh

0 Miles ¼

Low Emission Zone (LEZ)/Clean Air Zone (CAZ)

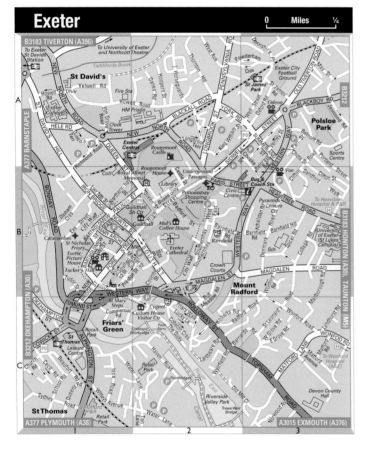

Exeter

0 Miles ¼

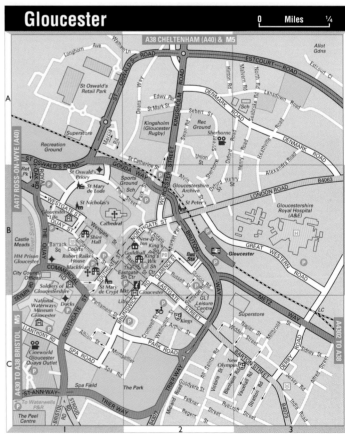

Gloucester

0 Miles ¼

Glasgow

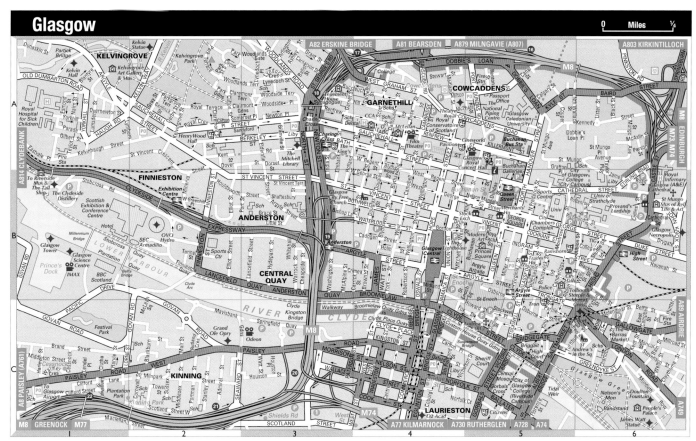

Low Emission Zone (LEZ)/Clean Air Zone (CAZ)

Grimsby

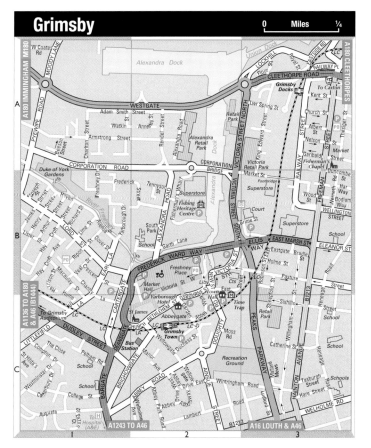

Harrogate

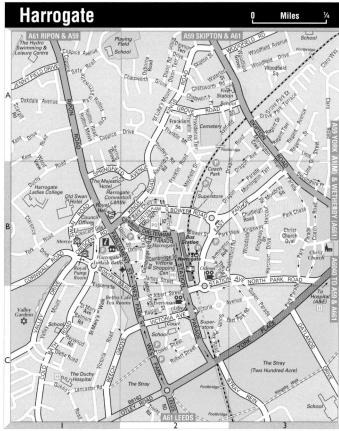

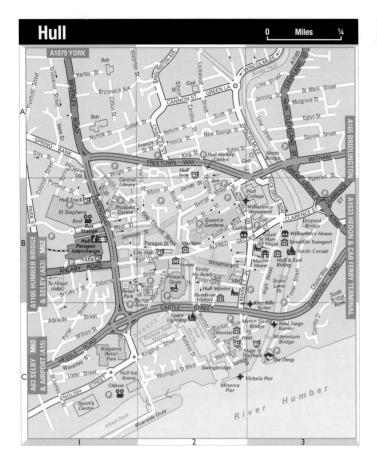

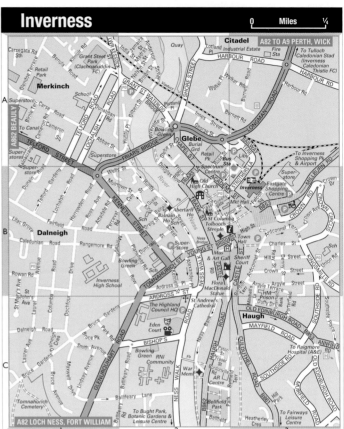

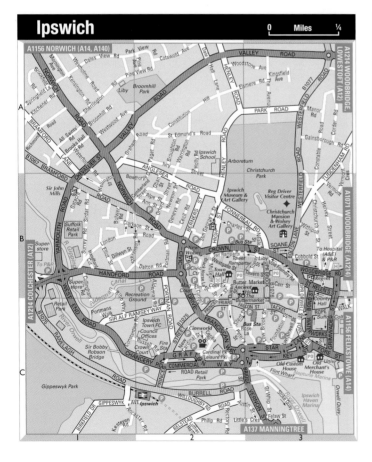

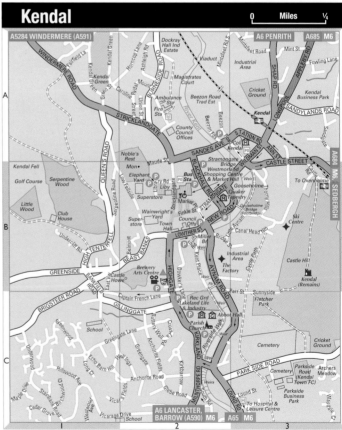

King's Lynn

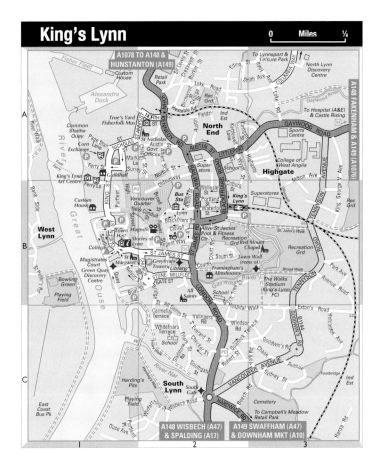

Lancaster

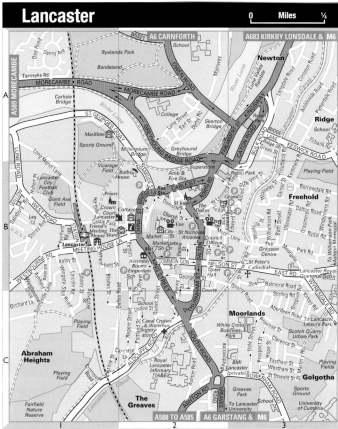

Leeds

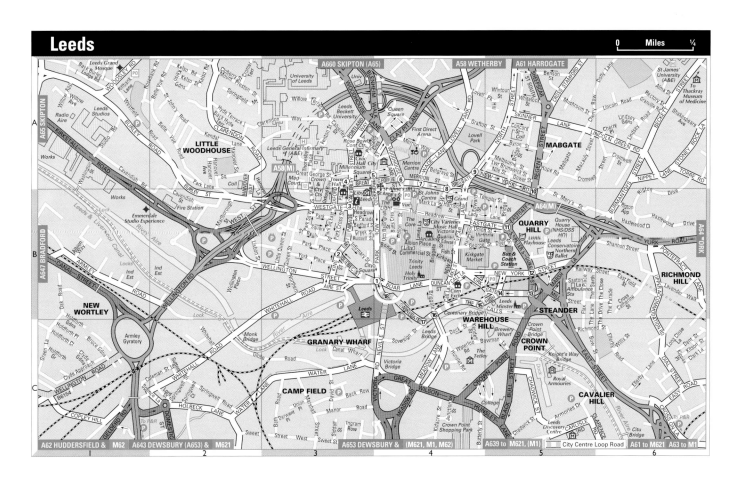

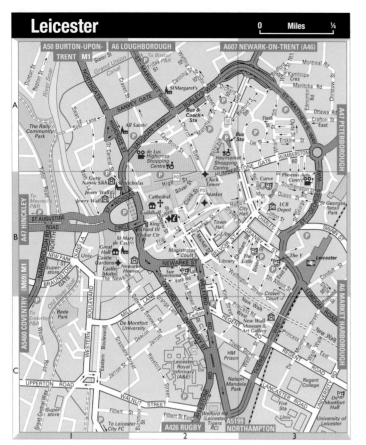

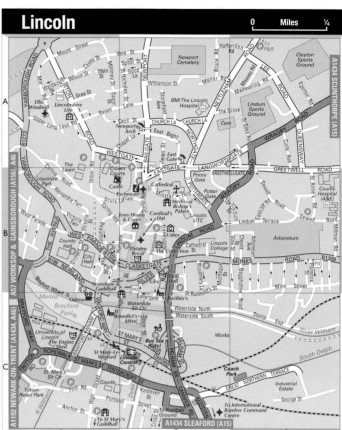

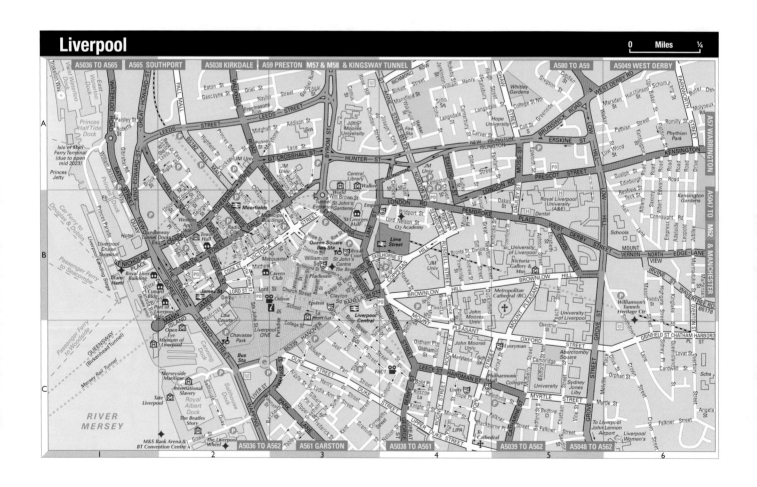

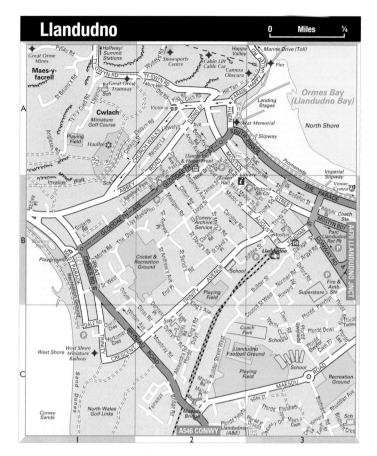

Llandudno

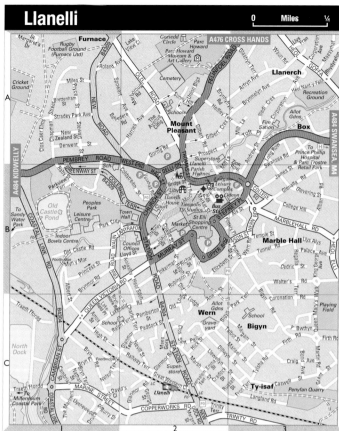

Llanelli

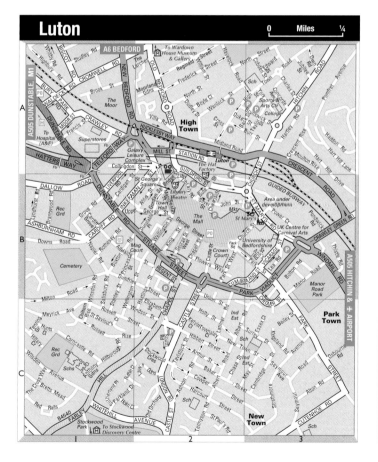

Luton

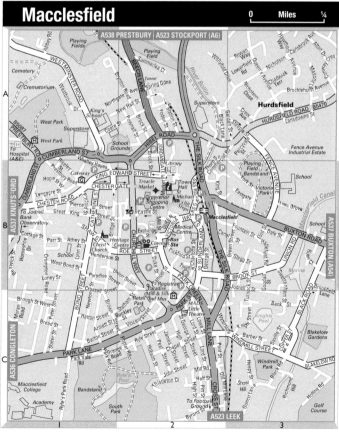

Macclesfield

Manchester

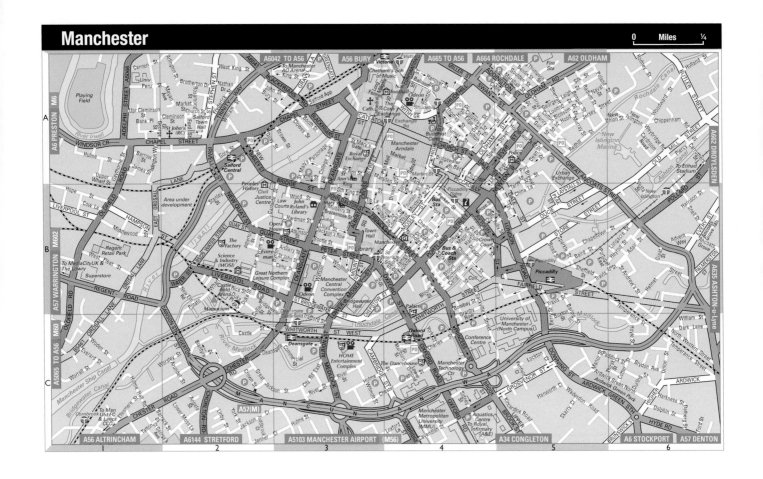

Maidstone

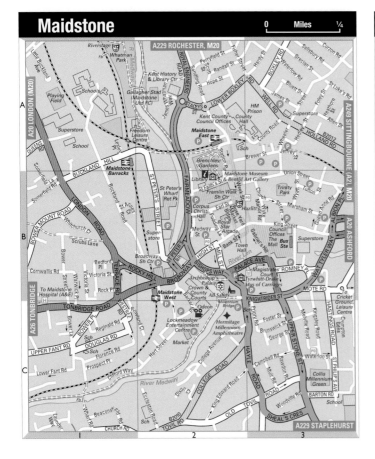

Merthyr Tydfil / Merthyr Tudful

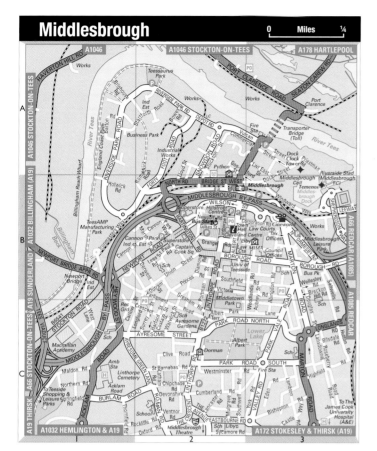

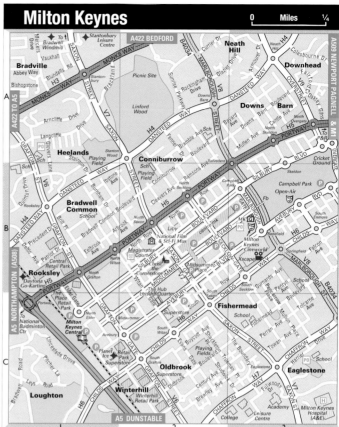

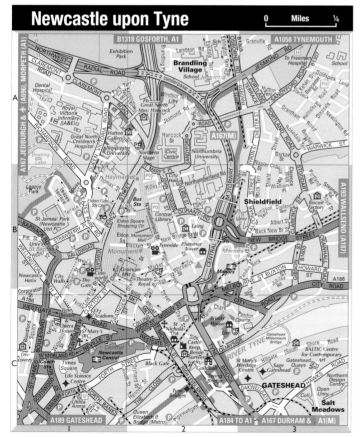

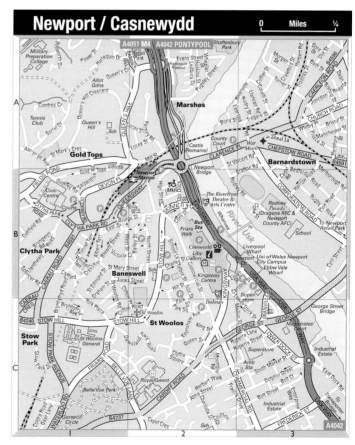

▨▨▨▨ Low Emission Zone (LEZ)/Clean Air Zone (CAZ)

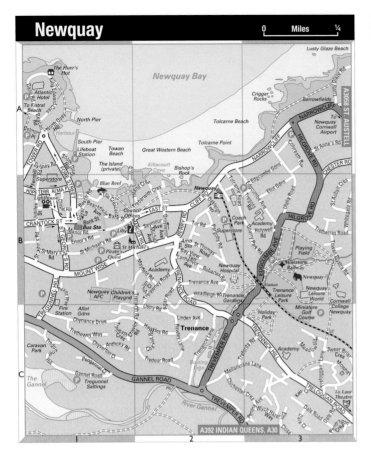

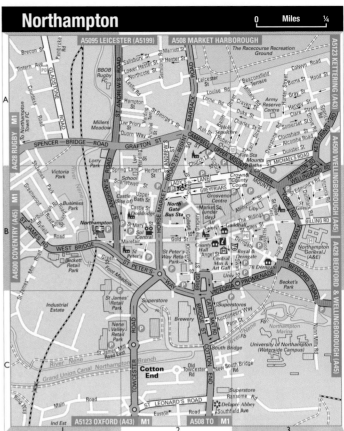

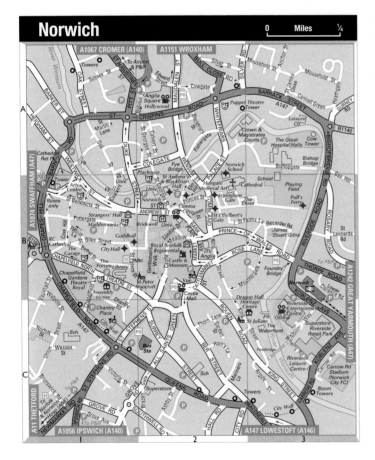

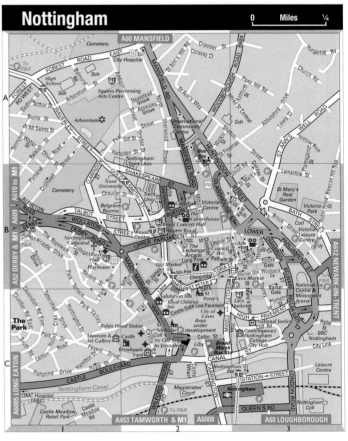

Oxford

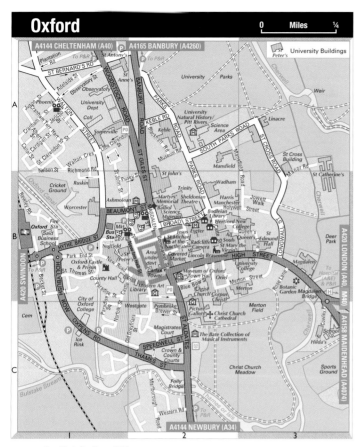

Zero Emission Zone (ZEZ)

Perth

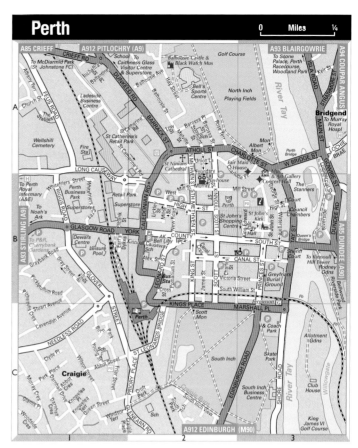

Peterborough

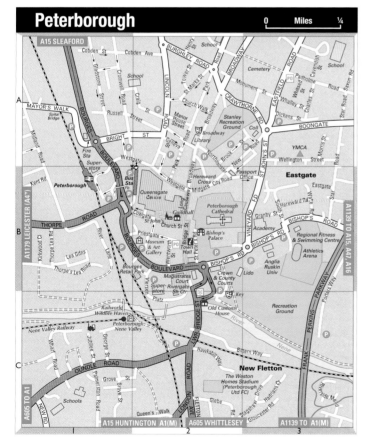

Plymouth

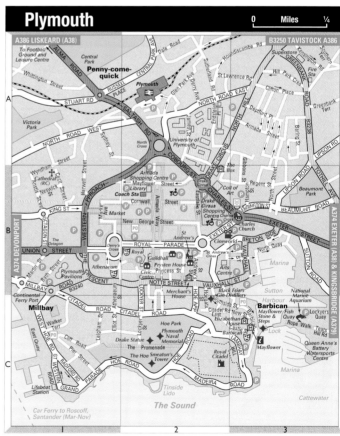

Poole
0 Miles ¼

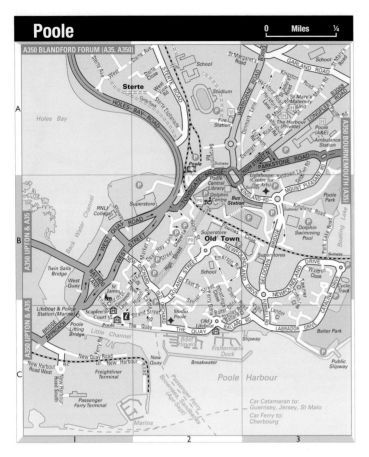

Portsmouth
0 Miles ¼

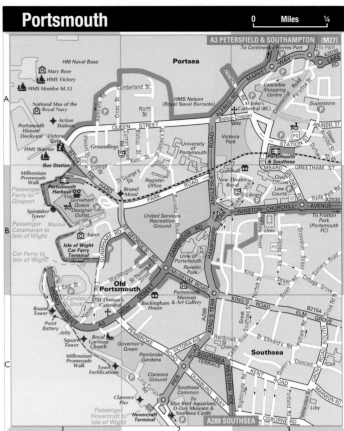

Low Emission Zone (LEZ)/Clean Air Zone (CAZ)

Preston
0 Miles ¼

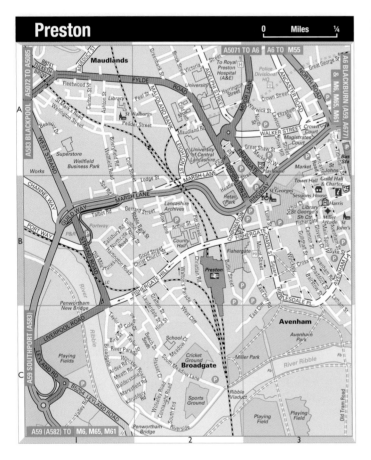

Reading
0 Miles ¼

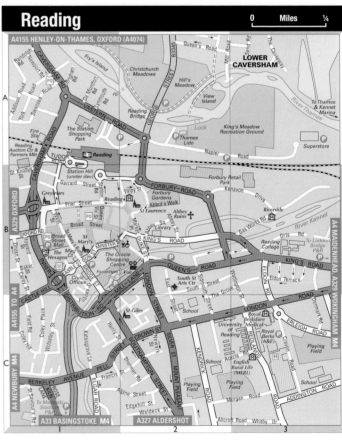

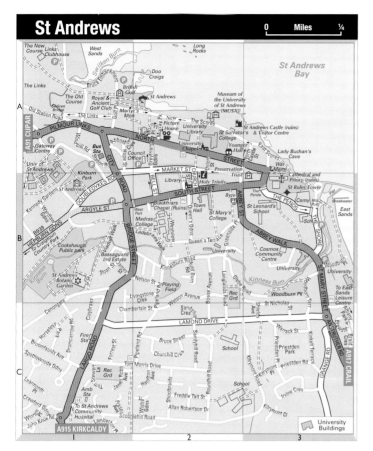

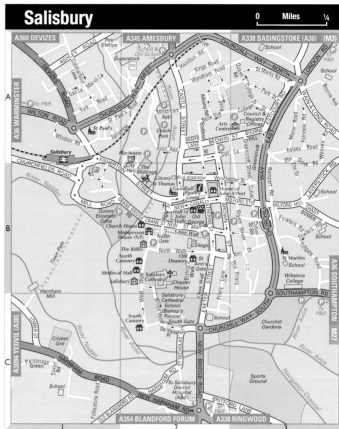

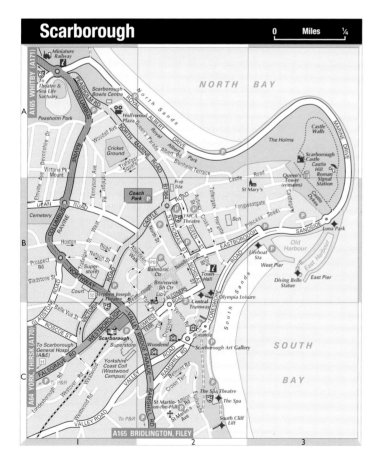

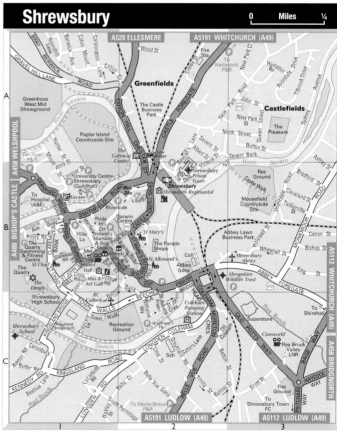

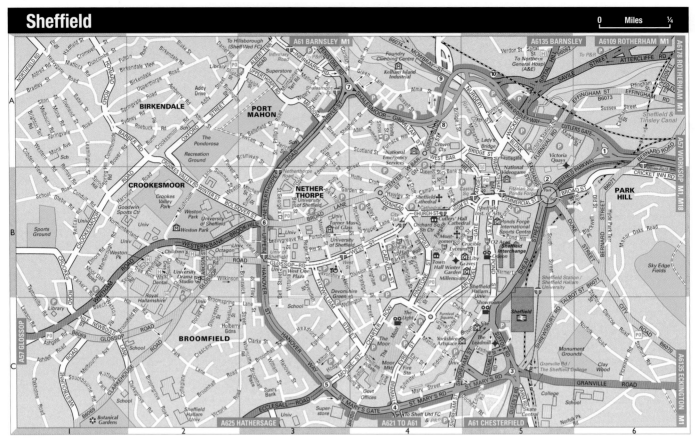

Low Emission Zone (LEZ)/Clean Air Zone (CAZ)

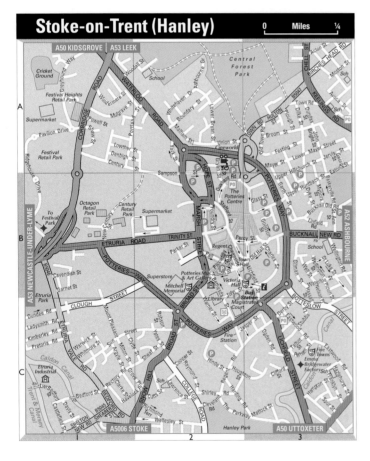

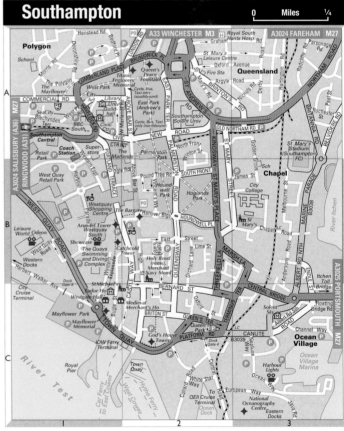

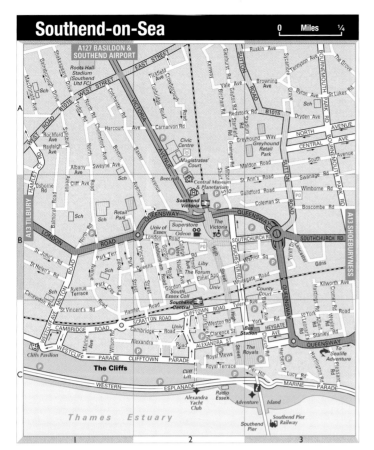

Southend-on-Sea

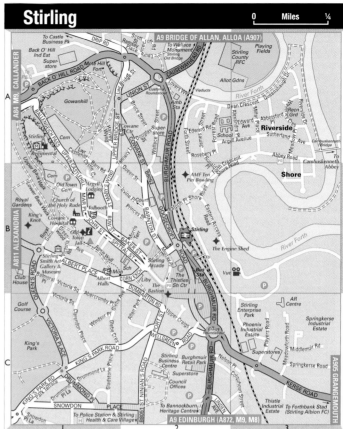

Stirling

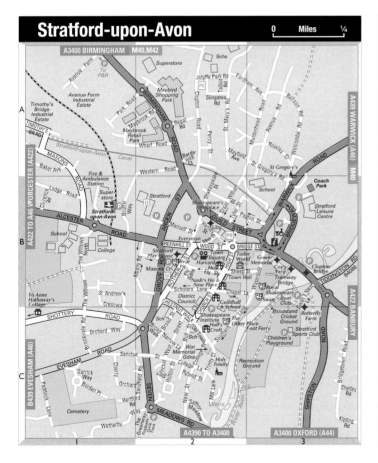

Stratford-upon-Avon

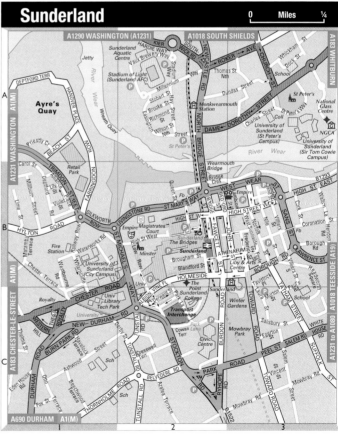

Sunderland

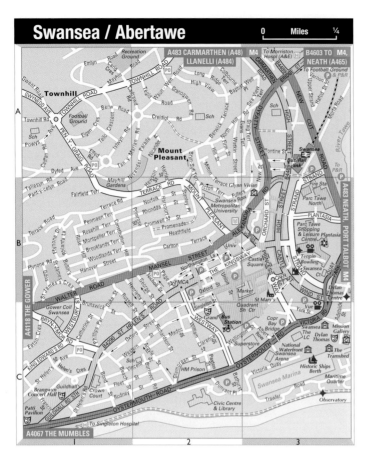

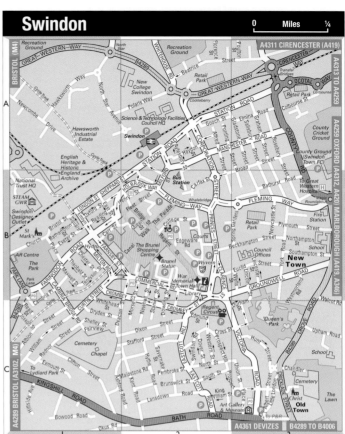

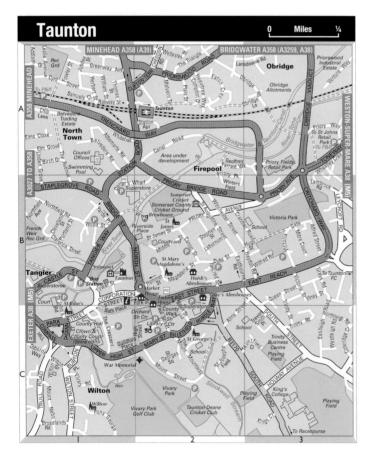

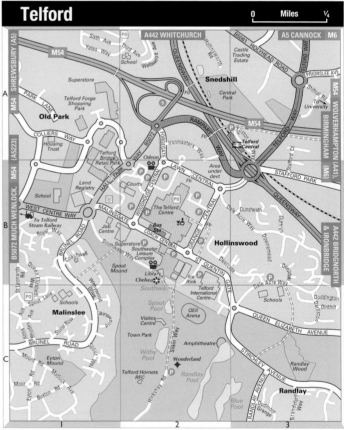

Torquay

0 Miles ¼

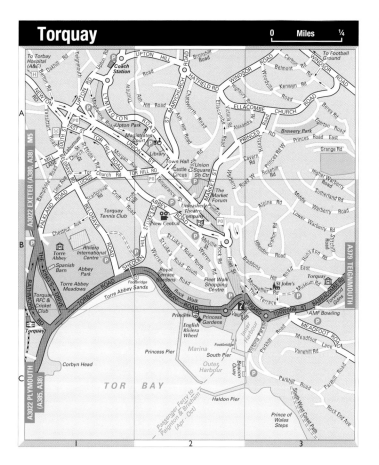

Truro

0 Miles ¼

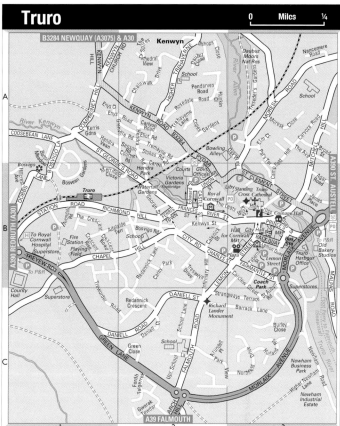

Winchester

0 Miles ¼

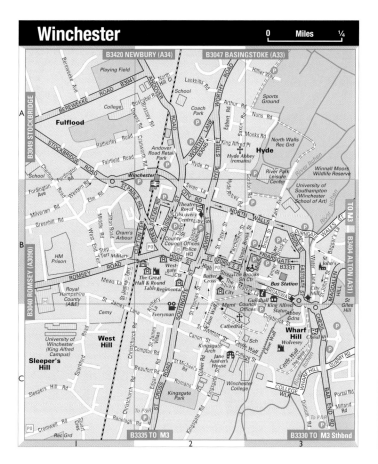

Windsor

0 Miles ¼

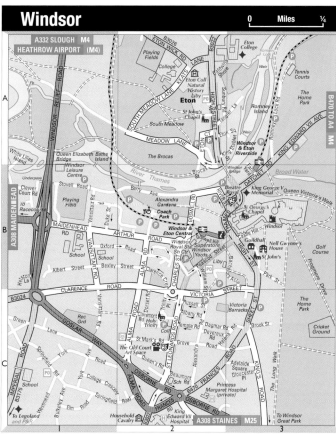

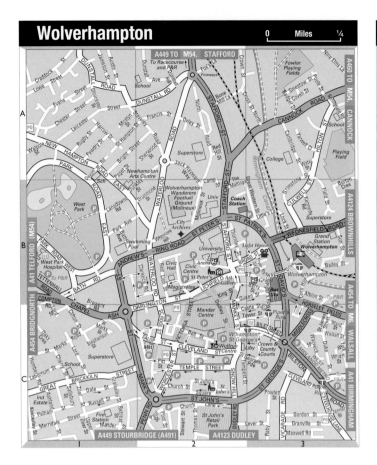

Wolverhampton

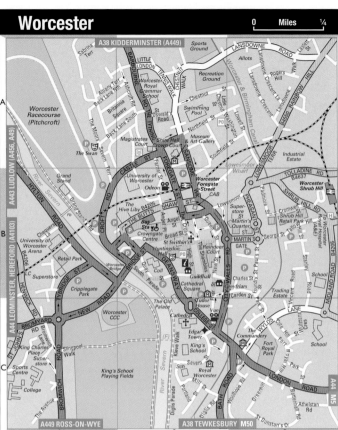

Worcester

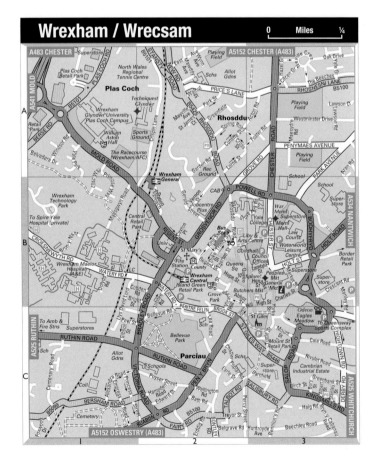

Wrexham / Wrecsam

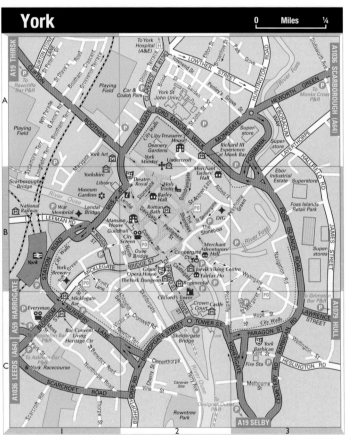

York

Town plan indexes

Aberdeen 175

Aberdeen B2
Aberdeen Grammar School A1
Academy,The B2
Albert Basin B3
Albert Quay B3
Albury Rd C1
Alford Place B1
Ann St A1
Art Gallery A2
Arts Centre A2
Back Wynd A2
Baker St A1
Beach Boulevard A3
Belmont B2
Belmont St B2
Berry St A2
Blackfriars St A2
Blaikie's Quay B3
Bloomfield Rd C1
Bon Accord Centre A2
Bon-Accord St B1/C1
Bridge St B2
Broad St A2
Bus Station B2
Car Ferry Terminal B3
Castlegate A3
Central Library A1
Chapel St B1
Cineworld B2
Clyde St B3
College A2
College St B2
Commerce St A3
Commercial Quay B3
Community Ctr A3/C1
Constitution St A3
Cotton St A3
Crown St B2
Denburn Rd A2
Devanha Gardens C2
Devanha Gardens South C2
East North St A3
Esslemont Avenue A1
Ferryhill Rd C2
Ferryhill Terrace C2
Fish Market B3
Fonthill Rd C1
Galleria B1
Gallowgate A2
George St A2
Glenbervie Rd C3
Golden Square B1
Grampian Rd C3
Great Southern Rd C1
Guild St B2
Hardgate B1/C1
His Majesty's Theatre A1
Holburn St C1
Hollybank Place C1
Huntly St B1
Hutcheon St A1
Information Ctr B2
John St A2
Justice St A3
King St A2
Langstane Place B1
Lemon Tree,The A2
Library C1
Loch St A2
Maberly St A1
Marischal Coll A2
Maritime Museum & Provost Ross's House B2
Market B2
Market St B2/B3
Menzies Rd C3
Mercat Cross A3
Millburn St C2
Miller St A3
Mount St A1
Music Hall B1
North Esp East C3
North Esp West C2
Oscar Rd C3
Palmerston Rd C2
Park St A3
Polmuir Rd C2
Post Office A2/B1/C2
Provost Skene's House A2
Queen Elizabeth Br C2
Queen St A2
Regent Quay B3
Regent Road B3
Robert Gordon's College A2
Rose St B1
Rosemount Place A1
Rosemount Viaduct A1
St Andrew St A2
St Andrew's Cath A3
St Mary's Cath B1
St Nicholas Centre A2
St Nicholas St A2
School Hill A2
Sinclair Rd C3
Skene Square A1
Skene St B1
South College St C2
South Crown St C2
South Esp East C3
South Esp West C3
South Mount St A1
Sports Centre C3
Spring Garden A2
Springbank Terrace C2
Summer St B1
Superstore A2
Thistle St B1
Tolbooth A3
Town House A2
Trinity Centre B2
Union Row B1
Union Square B2
Union St B1/B2
University A2
Upper Dock B3
Upper Kirkgate A2
Victoria Bridge C3
Victoria Dock B3
Victoria Rd C3
Victoria St B2
Virginia St A3
Vue B2
Waterloo Quay B3
Wellington Place B2
West North St A2
Whinhill Rd C1
Willowbank Rd C1
Windmill Brae B2

Ayr 175

Ailsa Place B1
Alexandra Terrace A3
Allison St B2
Alloway Park C1
Alloway Place C1
Alloway St C2
Arran Mall C2
Arran Terrace B1
Arthur St B2
Ashgrove St C2
Auld Brig B2
Auld Kirk B2
Ayr B2
Ayr Academy B1
Ayr Central Shopping Centre C2
Ayr Harbour A1
Ayr Racecourse C3
Ayrshire College C3
Back Hawkhill Ave A3
Back Main St B2
Back Peebles St A2
Barns Crescent C1
Barns Park C1
Barns St C1
Barns Street Lane C1
Bath Place B1
Bellevue Crescent C1
Bellevue Lane C1
Beresford Lane C2
Beresford Terrace C2
Boswell Park B2
Britannia Place A3
Bruce Crescent B1
Burns Statue C2
Bus Station B1
Carrick St C2
Cassillis St B1
Cathcart St B1
Charlotte St B1
Citadel Leisure Ctr B1
Citadel Place B1
Compass Pier A1
Content Avenue C3
Content St B2
Craigie Avenue B3
Craigie Rd B3
Craigie Way B3
Cromwell Rd B1
Crown St A2
Dalblair Rd C2
Dam Park Sports Stadium C3
Damside A2
Dongola Rd C3
Eglinton Place B1
Eglinton Terrace B1
Elba St B2
Elmbank St A3
Esplanade B1
Euchar Rock A1
Farifield Rd C1
Fort St B1
Fothringham Rd C3
Fullarton St C1
Gaiety C2
Garden St B2
George St B2
George's Avenue A3
Glebe Crescent A2
Glebe Rd A2
Gorden Terrace B3
Green St A2
Green Street Lane A2
Hawkhill Avenue A3
Hawkhill Ave Lane B3
High St B2
Holmston Rd C3
Ice Rink A2
James St B3
John St B2
King St B2
Kings Court B2
Kyle Centre C2
Kyle St C2
Library B2
Limekiln Rd A2
Limonds Wynd B2
Loudoun Hall B2
Lymburn Place B3
Macadam Place B2
Main St B2
McAdam's Monument C1
McCall's Avenue A3
Mews Lane B1
Mill Brae C3
Mill St C2
Mill Wynd C2
Miller Rd C1
Montgomerie Terr B1
New Bridge B2
New Bridge St B2
New Rd A2
Newmarket St B2
Newton-on-Ayr A2
North Harbour St B1
North Pier A1
Odeon C2
Park Circus C1
Park Circus Lane C1
Park Terrace C1
Pavilion Rd C1
Peebles St A2
Philip Square B2
Police Station B2
Prestwick Rd B1
Princes Court A2
Queen St C1
Queen's Terrace B1
Racecourse Rd C1
River St B2
Riverside Place B2
Russell Drive A2
St Andrews Church C2
St George's Rd A3
Sandgate B1
Savoy Park C1
Smith St C2
Somerset Park (Ayr United FC) A3
Somerset Rd A3
South Beach Rd B1
South Harbour St B1
South Pier A1
Station Rd C2
Strathayr Place B2
Superstore A2/B2
Taylor St A2
Town Hall B2
Tryfield Place A3
Turner's Bridge B2
Union Avenue A3
University Avenue C3
Victoria Bridge C3
Victoria St B3
Viewfield Rd A3
Virginia Gardens A2
Waggon Rd A2
Walker Rd A3
Wallace Tower B2
Weaver St A2
Weir Rd A2
Wellington Lane C1
Wellington Square C1
West Sanouhar Rd A3
Whitletts Rd B3
Wilson St A3
York St A1
York Street Lane B1

Bath 175

Alexandra Park C2
Alexandra Rd C2
Ambulance Station A3
Approach Golf Courses (Public) A1
Archway St C3
Assembly Rooms & Fashion Mus A2
Avon St B2
Barton St B2
Bath Abbey B2
Bath Aqua Glass A2
Bath at Work Museum A2
Bath College B2
Bath Rugby (The Recreation) B3
Bath Spa Station C3
Bathwick St A3
Beazer Gdn Maze B3
Beckford Road A3
Beechen Cliff Rd C2
Bennett St A2
Bloomfield Avenue C1
Broad Quay C2
Broad St B2
Brock St A1
Bus Station C2
Calton Gardens C2
Calton Rd C2
Camden Crescent A2
Cavendish Rd A1
Cemetery B1
Charlotte St B2
Chaucer Rd C2
Cheap St B2
Circus Mews A2
Claverton St C2
Coach Park C2
Corn St C2
Cricket Ground B3
Daniel St A3
East Asian Art Museum A2
Edward St B3
Ferry Lane B3
Fire Station A3
First Avenue C1
Forester Avenue A3
Forester Rd A3
Gays Hill A2
George St B2
Great Pulteney St B3
Green Park B1
Green Park Rd B2
Green Park Sta B1
Grove St B2
Guildhall B2
Harley St A2
Hayesfield Park C1
Henrietta Gardens A3
Henrietta Mews B3
Henrietta Park B3
Henrietta Rd A3
Henrietta St B3
Henry St B2
Herschel Museum of Astronomy B1
High Common A1
Holburne Mus B3
Holloway C2
James St West B1/B2
Jane Austen Ctr B2
Julian Rd A1
Junction Rd C1
Kingsmead Leisure Complex B2
Kipling Avenue C2
Lansdown Crescent A1
Lansdown Grove A2
Lansdown Rd A2
Library B2
London Rd A3
London St A2
Lower Bristol Rd B1
Lower Oldfield Park C1
Lyncombe Hill C3
Magistrates' Court B3
Manvers St B3
Maple Grove C1
Margaret's Hill A2
Marlborough Bldgs A1
Marlborough Lane B1
Midland Bridge Rd B1
Milk St B2
Milsom St B2
Mission The C2
Monmouth St B2
Morford St A2
Museum of Bath Architecture, The A2
New King St B1
No 1 Royal Cres A1
Norfolk Buildings B1
Norfolk Crescent B1
North Parade Rd B3
Oldfield Rd C1
Paragon A2
Pera Rd A2
Pines Way B1
Podium Shopping Centre B2
Police Station B3
Portland Place A2
Post Office B2/C2
Postal Museum B2
Powlett Rd A3
Prior Park Rd C3
Pulteney Bridge B2
Pulteney Gardens B3
Pulteney Rd B3/C3
Queen Square B2
Raby Place B3
Recreation Ground B3
Rivers St A2
Rockliffe Avenue A3
Rockliffe Rd A3
Roman Baths & Pump Room B2
Rossiter Rd C3
Royal Avenue A1
Royal Crescent A1
Royal High Sch,The A2
Royal Victoria Park A1
St James Square A1
St John's Rd A3
Sally Lunn's Ho B2
Shakespeare Ave C2
Shopmobility B2
South Parade B3
SouthGate Shopping Centre C2
Sports & Leisure Ctr B3
Spring Gardens C3
Stall St B2
Stanier Rd B1
Superstore A3/B1
Sydney Gardens A3
Sydney Place B3
Sydney Rd B3
Theatre Royal B2
Thermae Bath Spa B2
Thomas St A3
Tyning,The C3
Union St B2
University C3
Upper Bristol Rd B1
Upper Oldfield Park C1
Victoria Art Gall B2
Victoria Bridge Rd B1
Walcot St B2
Wells Rd C1
Westgate Buildings B2
Westgate St B2
Weston Rd A1
Widcombe Hill C3

Birmingham 176

Abbey St A2
Aberdeen St A1
Acorn Grove B2
Adams St A5
Adderley St C5
Albert St B4
Albion St B2
Alcester St C5
Aldgate Grove A3
All Saint's St A2
All Saints Rd A2
Allcock St C5
Allesley St A4
Allison St C4
Alma Crescent B6
Alston Rd C1
Arcadian Centre C4
Arthur St C6
Assay Office B3
Ashted Circus B5
Aston Expressway A5
Aston St B4
Aston University B4/B5
Avenue Rd A5
Bacchus Rd A1
Bagot St B4
Banbury St B5
Barford Rd B1
Barford St C4
Barn St C5
Barnwell Rd C6
Barr St A3
Barrack St B5
Barwick St B4
Bath Row C3
Beaufort Rd C1
Belmont Row B5
Benson Rd A1
Berkley St C3
Bexhill Grove C3
Birchall St C5
Birmingham City FC (St Andrew's) C6
Birmingham City Hospital (A&E) A1
Birmingham City University B3
Birmingham Wheels Park B6
Bishopsgate St C3
Blews St B4
Bloomsbury St A6
Blucher St C3
Bordesley St C4
Bowyer St C5
Bradburne Way A5
Bradford St C5
Branston St A3
Brearley St A4
Brewery St A4
Bridge St C3
Bridge St West A4
Brindley Drive B3
Brindley Place C3
Broad St C3
Broadway Plaza C2
Bromley St C5
Bromsgrove St C4
Brookfield Rd A2
Browning St C2
Bryant St A1
BT Tower B3
Buckingham St A3
Bull St B4
Bull St B4
Bullring C4
Cambridge St C3
Camden Drive B3
Camden St B2
Cannon St C4
Cardigan St B5
Carlisle St A1
Carlyle Rd C1
Caroline St B3
Carver St B2
Cato St A6
Cattell Rd C6
Cattells Grove A6
Cawdor Crescent C1
Cecil St B4
Cemetery A2/B2
Cemetery Lane A2
Centenary Square C3
Centre Link Ind Est A6
Charlotte St B3
Cheapside C4
Chester St A5
Children's Hospital (A&E) B4
Church St B4
Cineworld C2
Claremont Rd A2
Clarendon Rd C1
Clark St C1
Clement St B3
Clissold St B2
Cliveland St B4
Coach Station C5
College St B2
Colmore Circus B4
Colmore Row B4
Commercial St C3
Constitution Hill B3
Convention Ctr,The C3
Cope St B2
Coplow St B1
Corporation St C4
Council House B3
County Court B4
Coveley Grove A2
Coventry Rd C6
Coventry St C5
Cox St B3
Crabtree Rd A2
Cregoe St C3
Crescent Avenue A2
Crescent Theatre C3
Crescent,The A2
Cromwell St A6
Cromwell St B3
Cube,The C3
Curzon Circle B5
Curzon St B5
Custard Factory C5
Cuthbert Rd B1
Dale End B4
Dart St C6
Dartmouth Circus A4
Dartmouth Middleway A5
Dental Hospital B4
Deritend C5
Devon St A6
Devonshire St A1
Digbeth High St C4
Dolman St B6
Dover St A1
Duchess Rd C2
Duddeston B6
Duddeston Manor Rd B5
Duddeston Mill Rd B6
Duddeston Mill Trading Estate B6
Dudley Rd B1
Edgbaston Village C2
Edmund St B3
Edward St B3
Elkington St A4
Ellen St B2
Ellis St C3
Erskine St B6
Essex St C4
Everyman C3
Eyre St B2
Farm Croft A3
Farm St A3
Fazeley St B4/C5
Felstead Way B5
Finstall Close B5
Five Ways C2
Five Ways C2
Fiveway Shopping Centre C2
Fleet St B3
Floodgate St C5
Ford St A2
Fore St C4
Forster St B5
Francis Rd C2
Francis St B5
Frankfort St A4
Frederick St B3
Freeth St C1
Freightliner Term. B6
Garrison Circus C5
Garrison Lane C6
Garrison St B6
Gas St C3
Geach St A4
George St B3
George St West B2
Gibb St C5
Gilby Rd C2
Gillott Rd B1
Glover St C5
Goode Avenue A2
Goodrick Way A6
Gordon St B6
Graham St B3
Grand Central Shopping Centre C4
Granville St C3
Gray St C6
Great Barr St C5
Great Charles St Queensway B3
Great Francis St B6
Great Hampton Row A3
Great Hampton St A3
Great King St A3
Great King St North A3
Great Lister St A5
Great Tindal St C2
Green Lane C6
Green St C5
Greenway St C6
Grosvenor St West C2
Guest Grove A3
Guild Close C2
Guildford Drive A4
Guthrie Close A3
Hagley Rd C1
Hall St B3
Hampton St A3
Handsworth New Rd A1
Hanley St B4
Harford St A3
Harmer Rd A2
Harold Rd C1
Hatchett St A4
Heath Mill Lane C5
Heath St B1
Heaton St A2
Heneage St B5
Henrietta St B4
Herbert Rd C6
High St C4
High St C5
Hilden Rd B5
Hill St C3/C4
Hindlow Close B6
Hingeston St B2
Hippodrome C4
HM Prison A1
Hockley Circus A2
Hockley Hill A3
Hockley St A3
Holliday St C3
Holloway Circus C4
Holloway Head C3
Holt St B5
Horse Fair C4
Hospital St A4
Howard St B3
Howe St B5
Hubert St A5
Hunters Rd A2
Hunters Vale A3
Huntly Rd C2
Hurst St C4
Icknield Port Rd B1
Icknield Square B2
Icknield St A2/B2
IKON C3
Inge St C4
Irving St C3
James Watt Queensway B4
Jennens Rd B5
Jewellery Quarter A3
Jewellery Quarter Museum B3
John Bright St C4
Keeley St C6
Kellett Rd B5
Kent St C4
Kent St North A1
Kenyon St B3
Key Hill A3
Key Hill Circus A2
Kilby Avenue C2
King Edwards Rd B2
King Edwards Rd C3
Kingston Rd C6
Kirby Rd A1
Ladywood Arts & Leisure Centre B1
Ladywood Circus C1
Ladywood Middleway C2/C3
Ladywood Rd C1
Lancaster St B4
Landor St B6
Law Courts B4
Lawley Middleway B5
Ledbury Close C2
Ledsam St B2
Lees St A1
Legge Lane B3
Lennox St A3
Library A6/C3
Library C3
Lighthorne Avenue B2
Link Rd B1
Lionel St B3
Lister St B5
Little Ann St C5
Little Hall Rd A6
Liverpool St C5
Livery St B3/B4
Lodge Rd A1
Lord St A5
Love Lane A5
Loveday St B4
Lower Dartmouth St C6
Lower Loveday St B4
Lower Tower St A4
Lower Trinity St C5
Lucus Circus A3
Ludgate Hill B3
Mailbox Ctr & BBC C3
Margaret St B3
Markby Rd A1
Marroway St B1
Maxstoke St C6
Melvina Rd A6
Meriden St C4
Midland St B6
Milk St C5
Mill St A5
Millennium Point B5
Miller St A4
Milton St A4
Moat Lane C4
Montague Rd C1
Montague St C5
Monument Rd C1
Moor St Queensway C4
Moor Street C4
Moorsom St A4
Morville St C2
Mosborough Cres A3
Moseley St C4
Mott St B3
Mus & Art Gallery B3
Musgrave Rd A1
National Sea Life Centre C3
Navigation St C3
Nechell's Park Rd A6
Nechells Parkway B5
Nechells Place A6
New Alexandra C3
New Bartholomew St C4
New Canal St C5
New John St West A3
New Spring St B2
New St C4
New Street C4
New Summer St A4
New Town Row A4
Newhall Hill B3
Newhall St B3
Newton St B4
Newtown A4
Noel Rd C1
Norman St A1
Northbrook St B1
Northwood St B3
Norton St A2
Odeon C2
Old Crown Ho C5
Old Rep Theatre, The C4
Old Snow Hill B4
Oliver Rd C1
Oliver St A5
Osler St C1
Oxford St C5
Palmer St C5
Paradise C3
Paradise St C3
Park Rd A2
Park St C4
Pavilions C4
Paxton Rd A2
Peel St A1
Pershore St C4
Phillips St A4
Pickford St C5
Pinfold St C4
Pitsford St A2
Plough & Harrow Rd C1
Police Museum B4
Police Station A4/A6/B1/C2/C4
Pope St B2
Portland Rd C1
Post Office A5/B1/B3/B5/C3/C5
Preston Rd A1
Price St B4
Princip St B4
Printing House St B4
Priory Queensway B4
Pritchett St A4
Proctor St A5
Radnor St A2
Rea St C4
Regent Place B3
Register Office C3
Repertory Theatre C3
Reservoir Rd C1
Richard St A5
River St C5
Rocky Lane A5/A6
Rodney Close C2
Roseberry St B2
Rotton Park St B1
Royal Birmingham Conservatoire B5
Rupert St A5
Ruston St C2
Ryland St C2
St Andrew's Ind Est C6
St Andrew's Rd C6
St Andrew's St C6
St Bolton St C6
St Chads B4
St Chad's Cathedral (RC) B4
St Chads Queensway B4
St Clements Rd A6
St George's St A3
St James Place B5
St Marks Crescent B2
St Martin's C4
St Paul's B3
St Paul's B3
St Paul's Square B3
St Philip's B4
St Stephen's St A4
St Thomas' Peace Garden C3
St Vincent St C2
Saltley Rd A6
Sand Pits Parade B3
Severn St C3
Shadwell St B4
Sheepcote St C2
Shefford Rd A4
Sherborne St C2
Shylton's Croft C2
Skipton Rd C2
Smallbrook Queensway C4
Smith St A3
Snow Hill B4
Snow Hill Queensway B4
Soho, Benson Rd A1
South Rd A2
Spencer St B3
Spring Hill B2
Staniforth St B4
Station St C4
Steelhouse Lane B4
Stephenson St C4
Steward St B2
Stirling Rd C1
Stour St B2
Suffolk St Queensway C3
Summer Hill Rd B2
Summer Hill St B2
Summer Hill Terr B2
Summer Lane A4
Summer Row B3
Summerfield Cres B1
Summerfield Park B1
Superstore B2
Sutton St C3
Swallow St C3
Sydney Rd C6
Symphony Hall C3
Talbot St A1
Temple Row C4
Temple St C4
Templefield St C6
Tenby St B3
Tenby St North B2
Tennant St C2/C3
Thimble Mill Lane A6
Thinktank (Science & Discovery) B5
Thomas St A4
Thorpe St C4
Tilton Rd C6
Tower St A4
Town Hall C3
Town Hall C3
Trent St C5
Turner's Buildings A1
Unett St A3
Union Terrace B5
Upper Trinity St C5
Utilita Arena C2
Uxbridge St A3
Vauxhall Grove B5
Vauxhall Rd B5
Vernon Rd C1
Vesey St B4
Viaduct St B5
Victoria Square C3
Villa St A3
Vittoria St B3
Vyse St B3
Walter St A6
Wardlow Rd A5
Warstone Lane B2
Washington St C3
Water St B3
Waterworks Rd C1
Watery Lane C5
Western Rd B1
Wharf St A2
Wheeler St A3
Whitehouse St A5
Whitmore St A2
Whittall St B4
Wiggin St B1
Willes Rd A1
Windsor Ind Est A5
Windsor St A5
Windsor St B5
Winson Green Rd A1
Witton St C6
Wolseley St C6
Woodcock St B5

Blackpool 176

Abingdon St A1
Addison Crescent A3
Adelaide St B1
Albert Rd B2
Alfred St B2
Ascot Rd A3
Ashton Rd C2
Auburn Grove C3
Bank Hey St B1
Banks St A1
Beech Avenue A3
Bela Grove C2
Belmont Avenue B2
Birley St A1
Blackpool & Fleetwood Tram B1
Blackpool & the Fylde College B2
Blackpool FC C2
Blackpool North A2
Blackpool North A2
Blackpool Tower B1
Blundell St C1
Bonny St B1
Breck Rd B3
Bryan Rd A3
Buchanan St A2
Bus Hub A2
Cambridge Rd A3
Caunce St A2/A3
Central Drive B1/C2
Central Pier C1
Central Pier C1
Central Pier Theatre C1
Chapel St C1
Charles St A2
Charnley Rd B2
Church St A1/A2
Clinton Avenue B2
Coach Station A2/C1
Cocker St A1
Coleridge Rd A3
Collingwood Ave A3
Comedy Carpet B1
Condor Grove C3
Cookson St A2
Coronation St B1
Corporation St A1
Courts B1
Cumberland Ave B3
Cunliffe Rd C3
Dale St C1
Devonshire Rd A3
Devonshire Square A3
Dickson Rd A1
Elizabeth St A2
Ferguson Rd C3
Forest Gate B3
Foxhall Rd C1
Freckleton St C2
George St A2
Gloucester Avenue B3
Golden Mile,The C1
Gorse Rd B3
Gorton St A2
Grand Theatre B1
Granville Rd A2
Grasmere Rd C2
Grosvenor St A2
Grundy Art Gall A1
Harvey Rd B3
Hornby Rd B2
Houndshill Shopping Centre B1
Hull Rd B1
Ibbison Court C2
Kent Rd C2
Keswick Rd C2
King St A2
Knox Grove C3
Laycock Gate A3
Layton Rd A3
Leamington Rd B2
Leeds Rd B3
Leicester Rd B2
Levens Grove C2
Library A1
Lifeboat Station B1
Lincoln Rd B2
Liverpool Rd B3
Livingstone Rd B2
London Rd A3
Lune Grove C2
Lytham Rd C1
Madame Tussaud's Blackpool B1
Manchester Sq C1
Manor Rd B3
Maple Avenue B3
Market St A1
Marlboro Rd B3
Mere Rd B3
Milbourne St A2
Newcastle Avenue B3
Newton Drive A3
North Pier A1
North Pier A1
North Pier Theatre A1
Odeon C2
Olive Grove B3
Palatine Rd B2
Park Rd B2/C3
Peter St A2
Post Office A2/B2/B3
Princess Parade A1
Princess St C1/C2
Promenade A1/C1
Queen St A1
Queen Victoria Rd C2
Raikes Parade B2
Reads Avenue B2
Regent Cinema B2
Regent Rd B2
Register Office B2
Ribble Rd B2
Rigby Rd C1/C2
Ripon Rd B3
St Albans Rd B3
St Ives Avenue C3
St John's Square A1
St Vincent Avenue C3
Salisbury Rd B3
Salthouse Avenue C2
Salvation Army Ctr A2
Sands Way C2
Sea Life Centre B1
Seasiders Way C1
Selbourne Rd A2
Sharrow Grove C3
Somerset Avenue C3
South King St B2
Springfield Rd A1
Sutton Place B2
Talbot Rd A1/A2
Talbot Square A1
Thornber Grove C2
Topping St A1
Tower B1
Town Hall A1
Tram Depot C1
Tyldesley Rd C1
Vance Rd B1
Victoria St B1
Victory Rd A2
Wayman Rd A3
Westmorland Avenue C2/C3
Whitegate Drive B3
Winter Gardens Theatre B1
Woodland Grove B3
Woolman Rd B2

Bournemouth 176

Ascham Rd A3
Avenue Rd B1
Ave Shopping Ctr B1
Bath Rd C2
Beacon Rd C1
Beechey Rd A3
Bodorgan Rd B1
Bourne Avenue B1
Bournemouth A3
Bh2 Leisure C1
Bournemouth & Poole College B3
Bournemouth International Ctr C1
Bournemouth Pier C2
Bournemouth Station B3
Braidley Rd A1
Cavendish Place A2
Cavendish Rd A2
Central Drive A1
Central Gardens B1
Christchurch Rd B3
Cliff Lift C1/C3
Coach House Place A3
Coach Station A3
Commercial Rd B1
Cotlands Rd B3
Cranborne Rd C1
Cricket Ground A2
Cumnor Rd B2
Dean Park A2
Dean Park Cres B2
Dean Park Rd A2
Durrant Rd B1
East Overcliff Drive C3
Exeter Crescent C1
Exeter Rd C1
Gervis Place B1
Gervis Rd B3
Glen Fern Rd B2
Golf Club B1
Grove Rd B3
Hinton Rd C2
Holdenhurst Rd B3
Horseshoe Common B2
Information Ctr C2
Lansdowne B3
Lansdowne Rd A2
Lorne Park Rd B2
Lower Gardens B1/C2
Madeira Rd B2
Methuen Rd A3
Meyrick Park A1
Meyrick Rd B3
Milton Rd A2
Nuffield Health Bournemouth Hosp (private) A2
Oceanarium C2
Old Christchurch Rd B2
Ophir Rd A3
Oxford Rd B3
Park Rd A3
Parsonage Rd B2
Pavilion C2
Pier Approach C2
Pier Theatre C2
Police Station A3
Portchester Rd A3
Post Office B1/B3
Priory Rd C1
Quadrant,The B2
Recreation Ground A1
Richmond Gardens Shopping Centre B2
Richmond Hill Rd B1
Russell-Cotes Art Gallery & Mus C2
Russell Cotes Rd C2
St Anthony's Rd A1
St Michael's Rd C1
St Paul's A3
St Paul's Lane B3
St Paul's Rd A3
St Peter's B2
St Peter's B2
St Peter's Rd B2
St Stephen's Rd B1/B2
St Swithun's B3
St Swithun's Rd B3
St Swithun's Rd S B3
St Valerie Rd A2
St Winifred's Rd A2
Square,The B1
Stafford Rd B3
Terrace Rd B1
Town Hall B1
Tregonwell Rd C1
Triangle,The B1
Trinity Rd B2
Undercliff Drive C3
Upper Hinton Rd B2
Upper Terrace Rd C1
Wellington Rd A2/A3
Wessex Way A3/B1/B2
West Cliff Prom C1
West Hill Rd C1
West Undercliff Promenade C1
Westover Rd B2
Wimborne Rd A2
Wootton Mount B2
Wychwood Drive A1
Yelverton Rd B2
York Rd B3
Zig-Zag Walks C1/C3
Zip Wire C2

Bradford 177

Alhambra B2
Back Ashgrove B1
Barkerend Rd A3
Barnard Rd C3
Barry St B2
Bolling Rd C3
Bolton Rd A3
Bowland St A1
Bradford Big Screen B2
Bradford College B1
Bradford College (Trinity Green) C1
Bradford Forster Square A2
Bradford Interchange B3
Bradford Playhouse B3
Bridge St B2
Britannia St B2
Broadway Bradford, The B2
Burnett St B3
Bus Station B2
Butler St West A3
Caledonia St C2
Canal Rd A2
Carlton St B1
Cathedral A3
Centenary Square B2
Chapel St B3
Cheapside A2
Church Bank B3
Cineworld B3
City Hall B2
City Rd A1
Claremont B1
Colour Experience B1
Croft St B2
Crown Court B3
Darfield St A1
Darley St A2
Dixons McMillan Academy C1
Drewton Rd A1
Drummond Trading Estate A1
Dryden St B3
Dyson St A1
Easby Rd C1
East Parade B3
Eldon Place A1
Filey St B3
Forster Sq Retail Pk A2
Gallery II B1
Garnett St B3
Godwin St B2
Gracechurch St A1
Grattan Rd B1
Great Horton Rd B1/B2
Grove Terrace B1
Hall Ings B2
Hall Lane C3
Hallfield Rd A1
Hammstrasse A2
Harris St B3
Hawkshead Drive C2
Holdsworth St A2
Ice Arena B2
Impressions B2
Information Ctr B2
Inland Revenue A2
Ivegate B2
Jacob's Well Municipal Offices B2
James St A2
John St A2
Kirkgate B2
Kirkgate Centre B2
Laisteridge Lane C1
Leeds Rd B3
Leisure Exchange, The B3
Library B1/B2
Listerhills Rd B1
Little Horton Green C1
Little Horton Lane C1
Longside Lane B1
Lower Kirkgate B2
Lumb Lane A1
Magistrates Court B2
Manchester Rd C2
Manningham Lane A1
Manor Row A2
Market C3
Market St B2
Melbourne Place C1
Midland Rd A2
Mill Lane C2
Morley St B1
National Science and Media Museum B2
Nelson St B2/C2
Nesfield St A2
New Coll Bradford B1
New Otley Rd A3
Norcroft St B1
North Parade A2
North St A3
North Wing A3
Oastler Shopping Centre A2
Otley Rd A3
Park Avenue C1
Park Lane C1
Park Rd C2
Parma St C2
Peace Museum B2
Peckover St B3
Piccadilly A2
Police Station C2
Post Office B2/B3/C3
Princes Way B2
Prospect St C3
Radwell Drive C2
Rawson Rd A1
Rebecca St A1
Russell St C1
St George's Hall B2
St Lukes Hospital C1
Shipley Airedale Rd A3/B3
Shopmobility A2
Simes St A1
Smith St B1
Spring Mill St C2
Stott Hill A3

202 Brighton • Bristol • Bury St Edmunds • Cambridge • Canterbury • Cardiff • Carlisle

Sunbridge Rd A1/B1/B2
Theatre in the Mill B1
Thornton Rd A1/B1
Trafalgar St A2
Trinity Rd C1
Tumbling Hill St B1
Tyrrel St B2
Univ of Bradford B1/C1
Usher St C3
Valley Rd A2
Vicar Lane B3
Wakefield Rd C3
Wapping Rd A3
Well St B3
Westgate A1
White Abbey Rd A1
Wigan Rd A1
Wilton St B1
Wood St A1
Wool Exchange B2
Worthington St A1

Brighton 177

Addison Rd A1
Albert Rd B2
Albion Hill B3
Albion St B3
Ann St A3
Baker St A3
Black Lion St C2
Brighton ≷ A2
Brighton Centre C2
Brighton Fishing Museum C2
Brighton Pier (Palace Pier) ✦ C3
Brighton Zip ✦ C3
British Airways i360Tower ✦ C1
Broad St C3
Buckingham Place A2
Buckingham Rd B2
Cannon Place C1
Carlton Hill B3
Chatham Place A1
Cheapside A3
Church St B2
Churchill Square Shopping Centre B2
Clifton Hill B1
Clifton Place B1
Clifton Rd B1
Clifton St A2
Clifton Terrace B1
Clyde Rd A3
Coach Station C3
Compton Avenue A2
Davigdor Rd A1
Denmark Terrace B1
Ditchling Rd A3
Dome B2
Duke St B2
Duke's Lane C2
Dyke Rd A1/B2
East St C2
Edward St B3
Elmore Rd B3
Fleet St A2
Frederick St B2
Gardner St B2
Gloucester Place B3
Gloucester Rd B2
Goldsmid Rd A1
Grand Junction Rd C2
Grand Parade B3
Grove Hill B3
Guildford St A2
Hampton Place B1
Hanover Terrace A3
High St C3
Highdown Rd A1
John St B3
Jubilee Clock Tower B2
Kemp St B2
Kensington Place B2
Kings Rd C1
Lanes, The C2
Law Courts B3
Lewes Rd A3
Library B2
London Rd A3
Madeira Drive C3
Marine Parade C3
Middle St C2
Montpelier Place B1
Montpelier Rd B1
Montpelier St B1
Mus & Art Gallery B3
New England Rd A2
New England St A2
New Rd B2
Nizells Avenue A1
Norfolk Rd B1
Norfolk Terrace B1
North Rd B2
North St B2
Odeon C2
Old Shoreham Rd A1
Old Steine C3
Osmond Rd A1
Over St B2
Oxford St A3
Park Cres Terrace A3
Phoenix Brighton B3
Phoenix Rise A3
Police Station B3
Post Office A1/A3/C3
Preston Rd A2
Preston St B1
Prestonville Rd A1
Queen's Rd B2
Queen Square B2
Regency Square C1
Regent St B2
Richmond Place B3
Richmond St B3
Richmond Terrace A3
Rose Hill Terrace A3
Royal Pavilion B2
St Bartholomew's A3
St James's St C3
St Nicholas Rd B2
St Nicholas' B2
St Peter's A3
Sea Life Brighton C3
Shaftesbury Rd A3
Ship St C2
Sillwood Rd B1
Sillwood St B1
Southover St A3
Spring Gardens B2
Stanford Rd A1
Stanley Rd A3
Surrey St B2
Sussex St B3
Swimming Pool B3
Sydney St B3
Temple Gardens B1
Terminus Rd A2
Theatre Royal B2
Tidy St B2
Town Hall C3
Toy & Model Mus A2
Trafalgar St B2
Union Rd A3
Univ of Brighton B3
Upper Lewes Rd A3
Upper North St B1
Viaduct Rd A3
Victoria Gardens B3
Victoria Rd B1
Volk's Electric Railway ✦ C3
West Pier (derelict) C1
West St C2
Western Rd B1
Whitecross St B2
YHA C3
York Place B3
York Rd B1

Bristol 177

Acramans Rd C4
Albert Rd C6
Alfred Hill A4
All Saint's St A4
All Saints' B4
Allington Rd C3
Alpha Rd C4
Ambra Vale B1
Ambra Vale East B2
Ambrose Rd B2
Amphitheatre & Waterfront Sq ✦ C4
Anchor Rd B3
Anvil St B6
Arcade, The A5
Architecture Centre, The ✦ B4
Argyle Place B2
Arlington Villas A2
Arnolfini ✦ B4
Art Gallery A3
Ashton Gate Rd C2
Avon Bridge C1
Avon Crescent C1
Avon St B6
Baldwin St B4
Baltic Wharf C2
Barossa Place C4
Barton Manor B6
Barton Rd B6
Barton Vale B6
Bath Rd C6
Bathurst Basin C4
Bathurst Parade C4
Beauley Rd C3
Bedminster Bridge C5
Bedminster Parade C4
Bellevue B2
Bellevue Crescent B2
Bellevue Rd C6
Berkeley Place A2
Berkeley Square A3
Birch Rd C2
Birdcage Walk B2
Blackfriars A4
Bond St A5
Braggs Lane A6
Brandon Hill B3
Brandon Steep B3
Bristol Aquarium B4
Bristol Beacon B4
Bristol Bridge B5
Bristol Cath (CE) ✝ B3
Bristol Eye Hospital (A&E) A4
Bristol Grammar School A3
Bristol Marina C2
Bristol Royal Children's Hosp A4
Bristol Royal Infirmary (A&E) A4
Bristol Temple Meads Station ≷ B6
Broad Plain B6
Broad Quay B4
Broad St A4
Broad Weir A5
Broadcasting Ho A3
Broadmead A5
Brunel Institute ✦ B3
Brunel's SS Great Britain B2
Brunel Way C1
Brunswick Square A5
Burton Close C5
Bus Station A4
Butts Rd B3
Cabot Circus A5
Cabot Tower ✦ B3
Caledonia Place B1
Callowhill Court A5
Cambridge St C6
Camden Rd C3
Camp Rd A1
Canada Way C2
Cannon St A4
Canon's Way B3
Cantock's Close A3
Canynge Rd A1
Canynge Square A1
Castle Park A5
Castle St A5
Cathedral Walk B3
Catherine Meade St C4
Cattle Market Rd C6
Central Library B3
Charles Place B1
Charlotte St B3
Charlotte St South B3
Chatterton Ho B5
Chatterton Square C5
Chatterton St C5
Cheese Lane B5
Christchurch A4
Christchurch Rd A1
Christmas Steps ✦ A4
Church Lane B2/B5
Church St B5
City Museum A3
City of Bristol Coll B3
Civil and Family Justice Centre B5
Clare St B4
Clarence Rd C5
Cliff Rd C1
Clift House Rd C1
Clifton Cath (RC) ✝ A2
Clifton Down A1
Clifton Down Rd A1
Clifton Hill B2
Clifton Park A1/A2
Clifton Park Rd A1
Clifton Rd A2
Clifton Vale B1
Cliftonwood Cres B2
Cliftonwood Rd B2
Cliftonwood Terrace B2
Cobblestone Mews A1
College Green B3
College Rd A1
College St B3
Colston Almshouses A4
Colston Avenue B4
Colston Parade C5
Colston St A4
Commercial Rd C4
Constitution Hill B2
Cooperage Lane C2
Corn St B4
Cornwallis Avenue B1
Cornwallis Cres B1
Coronation Rd C1/C2/C4
Council House B3
Counterslip B5
Create Ctr, The ✦ C1
Crosby Row B2
Crown Court A4
Culver St B3
Cumberland Basin C1
Cumberland Close C2
Cumberland Rd C2/C3
Dean Lane C4
Deanery Rd B3
Denmark St B4
Dowry Square B1
Eaton Crescent A2
Elmdale Rd A3
Elton Rd A3
Eugene St A4/A6
Exchange and St Nicholas' Mkts, The B4
Fairfax St A4
Fire Station B5
Floating Harbour C3
Fosseway, The A2
Foster Almshouses A4
Frayne Rd C1
Frederick Place A2
Freeland Place B1
Friary B5
Frogmore St B3
Fry's Hill B2
Galleries Shopping Centre, The A5
Gas Lane B6
Gasferry Rd C3
Georgian House B3
Glendale B1
Glentworth Rd B2
Gloucester St A1
Goldney Hall B2
Goldney Rd B1
Gordon Rd A2
Granby Hill B1
Grange Rd A1
Great Ann St A6
Great George Rd B3
Great George St A6/B3
Green St North B1
Green St South B1
Greenay Bush Lane C2
Greenbank Rd C2
Greville Smyth Park C1
Grove, The B4
Guildhall A4
Guinea St C4
Hamilton Rd C3
Hanbury Rd A2
Hanover Place C2
Harley Place A1
Haymarket A5
Hensman's Hill B1
High St B4
Highbury Villas A3
Hill St B3
Hill St C6
Hippodrome B4
Hopechapel Hill B1
Horfield Rd A4
Horsefair, The A5
Horton St B6
Host St A4
Hotwell Rd B1/B2
Houlton St A6
Howard Rd C3
Islington Rd C3
Jacob St A5/A6
Jacob's Wells Rd B2
John Carr's Terrace B2
John Wesley's Chapel A5
Joy Hill B1
Jubilee St B6
Kensington Place A2
Kilkenny St B6
King St B4
Kingsland Rd B6
Kingston Rd C3
Lamb St A6
Lansdown Rd A2
Lawford St A6
Lawfords Gate A6
Leighton Rd C3
Lewins Mead A4
Lime Rd C2
Litfield Rd A1
Little Ann St A6
Little Caroline Pl B1
Little George St A6
Little King St B4
Llandoger Trow B4
Lloyds' Building, The C3
Lodge St A4
Lord Mayor's Chapel, The B4
Lower Castle St A5
Lower Church Lane A4
Lower Clifton Hill B2
Lower Guinea St C4
Lower Lamb St B3
Lower Maudlin St A4
Lower Park Rd A4
Lower Sidney St C2
Lucky Lane C4
Lydstep Terrace C3
M Shed C4
Magistrates' Court A4
Manilla Rd A1
Mardyke Ferry Rd C2
Maritime Heritage Centre B3
Marlborough Hill A4
Marlborough St A4
Marsh St B4
Matthew, The B5
Mead St C5
Merchant Dock B2
Merchant Seamen's Almshouses B4
Merchant St A5
Merchants Rd A1
Merchants Rd C1
Meridian Place A2
Meridian Vale A2
Merrywood Rd C3
Midland Rd A6
Milford St C3
Millennium Prom B3
Millennium Square B3
Mitchell Lane B5
Mortimer Rd A1
Murray Rd C4
Myrtle Rd A3
Narrow Plain B5
Narrow Quay B4
Nelson St A4
New Charlotte St C4
New Kingsley Rd B6
New Queen St C5
New St A6
Newgate A5
Newton St A6
Norland Rd A1
North St C2
O2 Academy B3
Oakfield Grove A2
Oakfield Place A2
Oakfield Rd A2
Old Bread St B6
Old Market St A6
Old Park Hill A4
Oldfield Rd B1
Orchard Avenue B4
Orchard Lane B4
Orchard St B4
Osbourne Rd C3
Oxford St B6
Park Place A2
Park Rd C3
Park Row A3
Park St A3
Passage St B5
Pembroke Grove A2
Pembroke Rd A2
Pembroke Rd C3
Pembroke St A5
Penn St A5
Pennywell Rd A6
Percival Rd A1
Pero's Bridge B4
Perry Rd A4
Phipps St C2
Pip 'n' Jay B5
Plimsoll Bridge B1
Police Station A6
Polygon Rd B1
Portland St A1
Portwall Lane B5
Post Office A1/A3/A5/B3/B4/C4
Prewett St C5
Prince St B4
Prince St Bridge C4
Princess St C5
Princess Victoria St B1
Priory Rd A3
Pump Lane C5
QEH Theatre A2
Quakers Friars A5
Quay St A4
Queen Charlotte St B4
Queen Elizabeth Hospital School B2
Queen Square B4
Queen St A5
Queen's Avenue A3
Queen's Parade B3
Queen's Rd A2/A3
Raleigh Rd C2
Randall Rd B2
Red Lodge A4
Redcliffe Backs B5
Redcliffe Bridge B4
Redcliffe Hill C5
Redcliffe Parade C4
Redcliffe St B5
Redcliffe Way B5
Redcross St A6
Redgrave Theatre A1
Regent St B1
Richmond Hill A2
Richmond Hill Ave A2
Richmond Lane A2
Richmond Park Rd A2
Richmond St C6
Richmond Terrace A2
River St A6
Rownham Mead B2
Royal Fort Rd A3
Royal Park A2
Royal West of England Academy A3
Royal York Crescent B1
Royal York Villas B1
Rupert St A4
Russ St B6
St George's B3
St George's Rd B3
St James A4
St John's A4
St John's Rd C4
St Luke's Rd C5
St Mary Redcliffe C5
St Matthias Park A6
St Michael's Hill A3
St Michael's Hospital A4
St Michael's Park A3
St Nicholas St B4
St Paul St A5
St Paul's Rd A2
St Peter's (ruin) A5
St Philip's Bridge B5
St Philips Rd A6
St Stephen's B4
St Stephen's St B4
St Thomas St B5
St Thomas the Martyr B5
Sandford Rd B1
Sargent St C5
Saville Place B1
Ship Lane C5
Shopmobility A5
Showcase Cinema de Lux A5
Silver St A4
Sion Hill A1
Small St A4
Smeaton Rd C1
Somerset Square C5
Somerset St C5
Southernhay Ave B2
Southville Rd C4
Spike Island Artspace C2
Spring St C5
Superstore C4
Stackpool Rd C3
Staight St B6
Stillhouse Lane C4
Sydney Row C2
Tankard's Close A3
Temple Back B5
Temple Back East B5
Temple Bridge B5
Temple Church B5
Temple Circus B5
Temple Gate C5
Temple St B5
Temple Way B5
Terrell St A4
Theatre Royal (Bristol Old Vic) B4
Thekla B4
Thomas Lane B5
Three Kings of Cologne A4
Three Queens Lane B5
Tobacco Factory, The C2
Tower Hill B5
Tower Lane A4
Trenchard St A4
Triangle South A3
Triangle West A3
Trinity Rd A6
Trinity St A6
Tyndall Avenue A3
Underfall Yard ✦ C1
Union St A5
Union St B6
Unity St A6
Unity St B3
University of Bristol A3
University Rd A3
Upper Byron Place A3
Upper Maudlin St A4
Upper Perry Hill C3
Upton Rd C2
Valentine Bridge B6
Vauxhall Bridge C4
Victoria Grove C5
Victoria Rd C6
Victoria Rooms A2
Victoria Square A2
Victoria St B5
Vyvyan Rd A1
Vyvyan Terrace A1
Wade St A6
Walter St C2
Wapping Rd C4
Wapping Wharf ✦ C4
Water Lane B5
Waterloo Rd A6
Waterloo St A1
Waterloo St A6
Watershed Media Centre ✦ B4
We the Curious ✦ B3
Welling Terrace B1
Welsh Back B4
West Mall A1
West St A6
Westfield Place A1
Wetherell Place A2
Whitehouse Place C5
Whitehouse St C5
Whiteladies Rd A2
Whitson St A4
William St C5
Willway St C5
Windsor Place B1
Wine St A4
Woodland Rd A3
Woodland Rise A3
Worcester Rd A1
Worcester Terrace A1
YHA B4
York Gardens B1
York Place A2
York Rd C5

Bury St Edmunds 178

Abbey Gardens B3
Abbey Gate B3
Abbeygate B2
Abbeygate St B2
Albert Crescent B1
Albert St B1
Angel Hill B2
Angel Lane B2
Anglian Lane A1
Arc Shopping Ctr B2
Athenaeum C2
Baker's Lane C3
Barwell Rd B3
Beetons Way A1
Bishops Rd B2
Bloomfield St B2
Bridewell Lane C2
Bullen Close C1
Bury St Edmunds ≷ A2
Bury St Edmunds County Upper Sch A1
Bury St Edmunds Leisure Centre B1
Bury Town FC (Ram Meadow) B3
Bus Station B2
Business Park B3
Butter Market B2
Cannon St B2
Castle Rd C1
Cemetery C1
Chalk Rd (N) B1
Chalk Rd (S) B1
Church Row B2
Churchgate St C2
Citizens Advice Bureau B2
College St C2
Compiegne Way A3
Corn Exchange, The B2
Cornfield Rd B1
Cotton Lane B3
Courts B2
Covent Garden C2
Crown St C3
Cullum Rd C2
Eastern Way A3
Eastgate St B3
Enterprise Bsns Pk A2
Etna Rd A2
Eyre Close C2
Fire & Ambulance Station B1
Friar's Lane C2
Gage Close A1
Garland St B2
Greene King Brewery C3
Grove Park B1
Grove Rd B1
Guildhall C2
Guildhall St C2
Hatter St C2
High Baxter St B2
Honey Hill C3
Hospital Rd C1/C2
Ickworth Drive C1
Industrial Estate A3
Information Ctr B2
Ipswich St A2
King Edward VI Sch A1
King's Rd C1/B2
Library B2
Long Brackland A2
Looms Lane B2
Lwr Baxter St B2
Malthouse Lane A2
Manor House C3
Maynewater Lane C3
Mill Rd C1
Mill Rd (South) C1
Minden Close B3
Moyse's Hall B2
Mustow St B3
Norman Tower C3
Northgate Avenue A2
Northgate St B2
Osier Rd A2
Out Northgate A2
Out Risbygate B1
Out Westgate C2
Parkway B1/C2
Parkway, The B1
Peckham St B2
Petticoat Lane C1
Phoenix Day Hospital C1
Pinners Way C1
Police Station C3
Post Office B2
Pump Lane B2
Queen's Rd B1
Raingate St C3
Raynham Rd A1
Retail Park C1
Risbygate St B1/B2
Robert Boby Way C2
St Andrew's St North B2
St Andrew's St South B2
St Botolph's Lane C3
St Edmund's C2
St Edmund's Abbey (Remains) ✦ B3
St Edmunds Hospital (Private) C3
St Edmundsbury ✝ C3
St John's St B2
St Marys C3
School Hall Lane B2
Shillitoe Close C1
South Close C1
Southgate St C3
Sparhawk St C3
Spring Lane B1
Springfield Rd B1
Station Hill A2
Swan Lane C3
Tayfen Rd B2
Theatre Royal C3
Thingoe Hill A2
Victoria St B1
Vinefields, The B3
War Memorial ✦ C1
Well St B2
West Suffolk Coll B1
Westgarth Gardens C1
Westgate St C2
Whiting St C2
York Rd B1
York Terrace B1

Cambridge 178

Abbey Rd A3
ADC A2
Anglia Ruskin Univ B3
Archaeology & Anthropology B2
Arts Picturehouse B2
Arts Theatre B1
Auckland Rd A3
Backs, The B1
Bateman St C2
Benet St B1
Bradmore St B3
Bridge St A1
Broad St B3
Brookside C2
Brunswick Terrace A3
Burleigh St B3
Bus Station B2
Butt Green A2
Cambridge Contemporary Art Gallery B1
Castle Mound ✦ A1
Castle St A1
Cemetery B3
Chesterton Lane A1
Christ's (College) B2
Christ's Lane B2
Christ's Pieces B2
City Rd B3
Clare Bridge B1
Clare (College) B1
Clarendon St B2
Coe Fen C2
Coronation St C2
Corpus Christi (College) B1
Court B3
Cross St C3
Crusoe Bridge C1
Darwin (College) C1
Devonshire Rd C3
Downing (College) C2
Downing St B2
Earl St B2
East Rd B3
Eden St B3
Elizabeth Way A3
Elm St B2
Emery St B3
Emmanuel (Coll) B2
Emmanuel Rd B2
Emmanuel St B2
Fair St A3
Fen Causeway, The C1
Fenner's Cricket Gd C3
Fire Station B3
Fitzroy St A3
Fitzwilliam Mus C2
Fitzwilliam St C2
Garrett Hostel Bridge B1
Glisson Rd C3
Gonville & Caius (College) B1
Gonville Place C2
Grafton Centre, The A3
Grand Arcade B2
Green St B1
Gresham Rd C3
Guest Rd B3
Guildhall B2
Harvey Rd C3
Hills Rd C3
Hobson St B2
Hughes Hall (Coll) B3
James St A3
Jesus (College) A2
Jesus Green A2
Jesus Lane A2
Jesus Terrace B3
John St B3
Kelsey Kerridge Sports Centre B3
Kettle's Yard A1
King's Bridge B1
King St A2
King's (College) B1
King's College Chapel B1
King's Parade B1
Lammas Land Recreation Ground C1
Lensfield Rd C2
Library B2
Lion Yard B2
Little St Mary's La B1
Lyndewod Rd C3
Magdalene (Coll) A1
Magdalene St A1
Maid's Causeway A3
Malcolm St A2
Market St B1
Mathematical Bridge B1
Mawson Rd C3
Midsummer Common A3
Mill Lane B1
Mill Rd B3
Mill St C3
Mumford B3
Museum of Cambridge A1
Museum of Classical Archaeology C1
Napier St A3
New Square A2
Newmarket Rd A3
Newnham Rd C1
Norfolk St B3
Northampton St A1
Norwich St C2
Orchard St B2
Panton St C2
Paradise St B3
Park Parade A1
Park St A2
Park Terrace B2
Parker St B2
Parker's Piece B2
Parkside B3
Parkside Pools B3
Parsonage St A3
Pea's Hill B1
Pemberton Terrace C2
Pembroke (College) B2
Pembroke St B1
Perowne St B3
Peterhouse (Coll) C1
Petty Cury B2
Polar Mus, The C2
Police Station B3
Post Office A3/B2/C1/C2/C3
Queen's Lane B1
Queen's Rd B1
Queens' (College) B1
Regent St B2
Regent Terrace B2
Ridley Hall (Coll) C1
Riverside A3
Round Church, The A1
Russell St C2
St Andrew's St B2
St Benet's B1
St Catharine's (Coll) B1
St Eligius St C2
St John's (College) A1
St Mary's B1
St Paul's Rd C3
Saxon St C2
Sedgwick Mus B2
Sheep's Green C1
Shire Hall A1
Sidgwick Avenue C1
Sidney St A2
Sidney Sussex (College) A2
Silver St B1
Station Rd C3
Tenison Avenue C3
Tenison Rd C3
Tennis Court Rd C2
Thompson's Lane A1
Trinity (College) A1
Trinity Bridge B1
Trinity Hall (Coll) B1
Trinity St B1
Trumpington Rd C2
Trumpington St B1
Union Rd C2
University Botanic Gardens C2
Victoria Avenue A2
Victoria St B2
Warkworth St B3
Warkworth Terrace B3
Wesley House (Coll) A2
West Rd B1
Westcott Ho (Coll) A2
Westminster (Coll) A1
Whipple B2
Willis Rd B3
Willow Walk A2
YMCA C3
Zoology B2

Canterbury 178

Artillery St B2
Barton Mill Rd A3
Beaconsfield Rd A1
Beaney, The B2
Beverley Meadow A1
Beverley Rd A1
Bingley's Island B1
Black Griffin Lane B1
Broad Oak Rd A2
Broad St B2
Brymore Rd A3
Burgate B2
Bus Station C2
Canterbury Castle C1
Canterbury Christ Church University B3
Canterbury College C3
Canterbury East ≷ C1
Canterbury West ≷ A1
Castle Row C1
Castle St C1
Cathedral ✝ B2
Causeway, The A2
Chaucer Rd A3
Christchurch Gate ✦ B2
City Council Offices A3
City Wall B2
Coach park A2
College Rd B3
Cossington Rd C2
Court B2
Craddock Rd A3
Crown & County Courts B3
Dane John Gardens C2
Dane John Mound ✦ C1
Deanery B2
Dover St C2
Duck Lane B2
Eastbridge Hosp B1
Edgar Rd B3
Ersham Rd C3
Ethelbert Rd C3
Fire Station C2
Forty Acres Rd A1
Friars, The B2
Gordon Rd C1
Greyfriars ✦ B1
Guildford Rd C1
Havelock St B2
Heaton Rd C1
High St B2
Information Centre A2/B2
Ivy Lane B2
New St C1
King St B2
King's School B2/B3
King's School Rec Ctr, The A2
Kingsmead Leisure Centre A2
Kingsmead Rd A2
Kirby's Lane B1
Lansdown Rd C2
Lime Kiln Rd C1
Longport B3
Lower Chantry La C3
Mandeville Rd A1
Market Way A2
Marlowe Arcade B2
Marlowe Avenue C2
Marlowe Theatre B2
Martyrs Field Rd C1
Mead Way B1
Military Rd B2
Monastery St B2
Museum of Canterbury (Rupert Bear Museum) B1
New Dover Rd C3
New St C1
Norman Rd C2
North Holmes Rd B3
North Lane B1
Northgate A2
Nunnery Fields C2
Nunnery Rd C2
Oaten Hill C2
Old Dover Rd C2
Old Palace B2
Old Ruttington La B2
Old Weavers B2
Orchard St B1
Oxford Rd C1
Palace St B2
Pilgrims Way C3
Pin Hill C1
Pine Tree Avenue A1
Police Station C2
Post Office B2, C1
Pound Lane B1
Puckle Lane C2
Raymond Avenue C2
Recreation Ground A2
Registry Office A2
Rheims Way B1
Rhodaus Close C2
Rhodaus Town C2
Roman Museum B2
Roper Gateway A1
Roper Rd A1
Rose Lane B2
Shopmobility B2
St Augustine's Abbey (remains) ✝ B3
St Augustine's Rd C3
St Dunstan's A1
St Dunstan's St A1
St George's Place C2
St George's St B2
St George's Tower ✦ B2
St Gregory's Rd B3
St John's Hosp A2
St Margaret's St B2
St Martin's B3
St Martin's Avenue B3
St Martin's Rd B3
St Michael's Rd A1
St Mildred's C1
St Peter's Grove B1
St Peter's Lane B2
St Peter's Place B1
St Peter's St B1
St Radigunds St B2
St Stephen's Court A1
St Stephen's Path A1
St Stephen's Rd A2
Salisbury Rd A1
Simmonds Rd C1
Spring Lane C3
Station Rd West B1
Stour St B1
Sturry Rd A3
Tourtel Rd A3
Tudor Rd C1
Union St B2
Univ for the Creative Arts (UCA) C3
Vernon Place C2
Victoria Rd C1
Watling St B2
Westgate Gardens B1
Westgate Towers B1
Whitefriars B2
Whitehall Gardens B1
Whitehall Rd B1
Wincheap C1
York Rd C1
Zealand Rd C2

Cardiff Caerdydd 178

Adam St B3
Alexandra Gardens A2
Allerton St C1
Arran St A3
ATRiuM (University of Glamorgan) C3
BBC Wales C2
Beauchamp St C1
Bedford St A3
Blackfriars Priory (rems) ✝ B1
Bvd De Nantes B2
Brains Brewery C2
Brook St B1
Bute Park A1
Bute St C2
Bute Terrace C3
Callaghan Sq C2/C3
Capitol Shopping Centre, The B3
Cardiff Arms Park (Cardiff Blues) B1
Cardiff Bridge B1
Cardiff Castle B2
Cardiff Central Station ≷ C2
Cardiff Story, The B2
Cardiff University A1/A2/B3
Cardiff University Student's Union A2
Caroline St C2
Castle Green B2
Castle Mews A1
Castle St (Heol y Castell) B1
Cathays Station ≷ A2
Celerity Drive C3
Central Library C2
Charles St (Heol Siarl) B3
Churchill Way B3
City Hall A2
City Rd A3
Clare Rd C1
Clare St C1
Coburn St A3
Coldstream Terrace B1
College Rd A1
Colum Rd A1
Court C2
Court Rd C1
Craiglee Drive C3
Cranbrook St A3
Crown Courts A2
Customhouse St C2
Cyfartha St A3
Despenser Place C1
Despenser St C1
Dinas St C1
Duke St (Heol y Dug) B2
Dumfries Place B3
East Grove A3
Ellen St C3
Firing Line B2
Fire Station B3
Fitzalan Place B3
Fitzhamon Embankment C1
Fitzhamon Lane C1
Friary, The B2
g39 . . . . B2
Gloucester St C1
Glynrhondda St A2
Gordon Rd A3
Gorsedd Gardens B2
Green St B1
Greyfriars Rd B2
Hafod St C1
Hayes, The B2
Herbert St C3
High St B2
HM Prison B3
Industrial Estate C3
Information Ctr B2
John St C3
Jubilee St C1
King Edward VII Ave A1
Kingsway (Ffordd y Brenin) B2
Knox Rd B3
Llanbleddian Gardens A2
Llantwit St A2
Lloyd George Ave C3
Lower Cathedral Rd B1
Lowther Rd A3
Magistrates Court B3
Mansion House A3
Mardy St C1
Mark St B1
Market B2
Mary Ann St C3
Merches Gardens C1
Mill Lane C2
Millennium Bridge B1
Miskin St A2
Monmouth St C1
Motorpoint Arena Cardiff ✦ C3
Museum Avenue A2
Museum Place A2
National Museum Cardiff A2
National War Memorial ✦ A2
Neville Place C1
New Theatre B2
Newport Rd B3
Northcote Lane A3
Northcote St A3
Parade, The A3
Park Grove A4
Park Place A2
Park St C2
Penarth Rd C2
Pendyris St C1
Plantaganet St C1
Post Office B2/C1/C2
Premiere Cinema B3
Principality Stadium C1
Principality Stadium Tours (Gate 3) ✦ B2
Quay St B2
Queen's Arcade B2
Queen Anne Sq A1
Queen St (Heol y Frenhines) B2
Queen St Station ≷ B3
Rhymney St A3
Richmond Rd A3
Royal Welsh College of Music and Drama A1
Russell St A3
Ruthin Gardens A2
St Andrews Place A2
St David's B2/C2
St David's ✝ B2
St David's Hall ✦ B2
St John the Baptist B2
St Mary St (Heol Eglwys Fair) B2
St Peter's St A3
Salisbury Rd A3
Sandon St B3
Schooner Way C3
Scott Rd C2
Scott St C2
Senghennydd Rd A2
Sherman Theatre A2
Sophia Gardens A1
Sophia Gardens Stadium ✦ A1
South Wales Baptist College A3
Sport Wales National Centre ✦ A1
Stafford Rd C1
Stadium Plaza C1
Station Terrace B3
Stuttgarter Strasse B2
Sussex St C1
Taffs Mead Emb C1
Talworth St A3
Temple of Peace & Health ✦ A1
Treharris St A3
Trinity St B2
Tudor Lane C1
Tudor St C1
Tyndall St C3
Vue C1
Walk, The A3
Welsh Government A1
West Grove A3
Westgate St (Heol y Porth) B2
Windsor Place B3
Womanby St B2
Wood St C2
Working St B2
Wyeverne Rd A2

Carlisle 179

Abbey St A1
Aglionby St B3
Albion St C3
Alexander St C3
Annetwell St A1
Bank St B2
Bitts Park A1
Blackfriars St B2
Blencome St C1
Blunt St C1
Botchergate B2
Boustead's Grassing C2
Bowman St B3
Bridge St A1
Broad St B3
Brook St C3
Brunswick St B2
Bus Station B2
Caldew Bridge A1
Caldew St C1
Carlisle (Citadel) Station ≷ B2
Carlisle College A2
Castle A1
Castle St A1
Castle Way A1
Cathedral ✝ A1
Cecil St B2
Chapel St A2
Charles St B3
Charlotte St B1
Chatsworth Square A2
Chiswick St B2
Citadel, The ✦ B2
City Walls A1
Civic Centre A2
Clifton St C1
Close St B3
Collingwood St C1
Colville St C1
Colville Terrace C1
Council Offices B3
Court B2
Court St Brow B2
Crosby St B2
Crown St C2
Currock Rd C2
Dacre Rd A1
Dale St C1
Denton St C1
Devonshire Walk A1
Duke's Rd A2
Escott Bsns Park C2
East Dale St C1
East Norfolk St C1
Eden Bridge A2
Edward St B3
Elm St B1
English St B2
Everlast Gyms C2
Fire Station A2

Fisher St A1
Flower St B3
Freer St C1
Fusehill St B3
Georgian Way A2
Gloucester Rd C3
Golf Course A2
Graham St C1
Grey St B3
Guildhall Mus 🏛 A2
Halfey's Lane B3
Hardwicke Circus A2
Hart St B3
Hewson St C2
Holywood Bowl ✦ C2
Howard Place A3
Howe St B3
Information Ctr ℹ A2
James St B2
Junction St B1
King St B2
Lancaster St B2
Lanes Shopping Centre,The B2
Library C1
Lime St B1
Lindisfarne St C3
Linton St B3
Lismore Place A3
Lismore St B3
London Rd C3
Lonsdale Rd B2
Lord St C3
Lorne Crescent B1
Lorne St B1
Lowther St B2
Madford Retail Pk B1
Magistrates' Court A2
Market Hall A2
Mary St B2
Memorial Bridge A3
Metcalfe St C1
Milbourne St B1
Myddleton St B3
Nelson St C1
Norfolk St C1
Old Fire Sta,The 🎭 A2
Old Town Hall A2
Oswald St C3
Peter St A2
Petteril St B3
Pools B2
Portland Place B2
Portland Square B2
Post Office ✉ A2/B2/B3
Princess St C2
Pugin St B1
Red Bank Terrace C2
Regent St C3
Richardson St C1
Rickerby Park A3
Rickergate A2
River St B3
Rome St C2
Rydal St B3
St Cuthbert's ⛪ B2
St Cuthbert's Lane B2
St James' Park C1
St James' Rd C1
St Nicholas Gate Retail Park C3
St Nicholas St C3
Sands Centre,The A2
Scotch St A2
Shaddongate B1
Sheffield St B1
Shopmobility A2
South Henry St B3
South John St C2
South St B3
Spencer St B2
Station Retail Park B2
Strand Rd A2
Superstore B1/C2
Sybil St B3
Tait St B2
Thomas St B1
Thomson St C3
Trafalgar St C1
Trinity Leisure Ctr A2
Tullie Museum & Art Gallery 🏛 A1
Tyne St C3
Univ of Cumbria B3
Viaduct Estate Rd B1
Victoria Place A2
Victoria Viaduct B2
Vue 🎦 B2
Warwick Rd B2
Warwick Square B3
Water St B2
West Walls B1
West Walls 🎭 B2
Westmorland St C1

Chelmsford 179

Anchor St C1
Anglia Ruskin Univ A2
Arbour Lane A3
Baddow Rd B2/C3
Baker St C1
Barrack Square B2
Bellmead B2
Bishop Hall Lane A2
Bishop Rd A2
Bond St B2
Boswells Drive B3
Bouverie Rd C2
Bradford St C1
Braemar Avenue C1
Brook St A2
Broomfield Rd A1
Burgess Springs B1
Burns Crescent C2
Bus Station B1/B2
Cedar Avenue A1
Cedar Avenue West A1
Cemetery A1
Cemetery A2
Cemetery C1
Central Park B1
Chelmsford ✝ B2
Chelmsford ⇌ A1
Chichester Drive A3
Chinery Close A3
City Council A1
Civic Centre A1
Crampthorn 🎭 B1
Cloudfm Ground (Essex CCC),The B2
College C1
Cottage Place A2
County Hall B2
Coval Avenue B1
Coval Lane B1
Coval Wells B1
Cricket Ground A1
Crown Court B2
Duke St B2
Elm Rd C1
Elms Drive A1
Essex Record Office,The B3
Everyman 🎦 B2
Fairfield Rd B1
Falcons Mead B1
George St C2
Glebe Rd A1
Godfrey's Mews C2
Goldlay Avenue C3
Goldlay Rd C2
Grove Rd C2
Half Moon Square B2
Hall St C2
Hamlet Rd C2
Hart St C1
Henry Rd A2
High Bridge Rd B2
High Chelmer Shopping Centre B2
High St B2
Hill Crescent B3
Hill Rd B3
Hill Rd Sth B3
Hillview Rd A3
HM Prison A3
Hoffmans Way A2
Hospital Ⓗ B2
Lady Lane C2
Langdale Gardens C3
Legg St B2
Library B2
Lionfield Terrace A3
Lower Anchor St C1
Lynmouth Avenue C2
Lynmouth Gardens C3
Magistrates Court B2
Maltese Rd A1
Manor Rd C2
Marconi Rd A2
Market B2
Market Rd B2
Marlborough Rd C1
Meadows Shopping Centre,The B2
Mews Court C2
Mildmay Rd C2
Moulsham Drive C2
Moulsham Mill ✦ C3
Moulsham St C1/C2
Navigation Rd B3
New London Rd B2/C1
New St A2/B2
New Writtle St C1
Nursery Rd C2
Old Court 🎭 A3
Orchard St C2
Odeon 🎦 B2
Parker Rd C2
Parklands Drive A3
Parkway A1/B1/B2
Police Station 🚓 A2
Post Office ✉ B2/B3/C2
Primrose Hill A1
Prykes Drive B1
Queen St C1
Queen's Rd B3
Railway St A1
Rainsford Rd A1
Ransomes Way A2
Rectory Lane A2
Regina Rd A2
Riverside A3
Riverside Ice & Leisure Centre B2
Riverside Retail Park A3
Rosebery Rd C2
Rothesay Avenue C1
St John's Rd C2
Sandringham Place B3
Seymour St B1
Shopmobility B2
Shrublands Close B3
Southborough Rd C1
Springfield Rd A3/B2/B3
Stapleford Close C1
Superstore B2/C3
Swiss Avenue A1
Telford Place A3
Tindal Square B2
Tindal St B2
Townfield St A1
Trinity Rd B3
University B1
Upper Bridge Rd C1
Upper Roman Rd C2
Van Dieman's Rd C3
Viaduct Rd B1
Vicarage Rd C1
Victoria Rd A2
Victoria Rd South B2
Vincents Rd C2
Waterloo Lane B2
Weight Rd B3
Westfield Avenue A1
Wharf Rd B3
Writtle Rd C1
YMCA A2
York Rd C1

Cheltenham 179

Albert Rd A3
Albion St B3
All Saints Rd B3
Ambrose St B2
Andover Rd C1
Back Montpellier Terrace C2
Bandstand ✦ C2
Bath Parade B2
Bath Rd C2
Bays Hill Rd C1
Bennington St B2
Berkeley St B3
Brewery Quarter, The A2
Brunswick St South A2
Bus Station B2
Carlton St B3
Central Cross Road A3
Cheltenham Coll C2
Cheltenham FC A3
Cheltenham General (A&E) Ⓗ C3
Cheltenham Ladies' College ⌂ B2
Christchurch Rd B1
Cineworld 🎦 A2
Clarence Rd A2
Clarence Square A2
Clarence St B2
Cleeveland St A1
College Baths Road C3
College Rd C2
Colletts Drive A1
Corpus St C3
Devonshire St A2
Douro Rd B1
Duke St B3
Dunalley Parade A2
Dunalley St A2
Everyman 🎭 B2
Evesham Rd A3
Fairview Rd B3
Fairview St B3
Fire Station C3
Folly Lane A2
Gloucester Rd A1
Grosvenor St B3
Grove St A1
Hanover St A2
Hatherley St C1
Henrietta St A2
Hewlett Rd B3
High St B2/B3
Holst Birthplace Museum 🏛 A3
Hudson St A2
Imperial Gardens C2
Imperial Lane B2
Imperial Square C2
Keynsham Rd C3
King St A2
Knapp Rd B2
Lansdown Crescent C1
Lansdown Rd C1
Leighton Rd B3
Library B2
London Rd C3
Lypiatt Rd C1
Magistrates' Court & Register Office B1
Malvern Rd B1
Manser St A2
Market St A1
Marle Hill Parade A2
Marle Hill Rd A2
Millbrook St A1
Milsom St A2
Montpellier Gardens C2
Montpellier Grove C2
Montpellier Parade C2
Montpellier Spa Rd C2
Montpellier St C1
Montpellier Terrace C2
Montpellier Walk C2
New St B2
North Place B2
Old Bath Rd C3
Oriel Rd B2
Overton Park Rd B1
Overton Rd B1
Oxford St C3
Parabola Rd B1
Park Place C1
Park St A1
Pittville Circus A3
Pittville Crescent A3
Pittville Lawn A3
Pittville Park A2
Playhouse 🎭 B2
Portland St B3
Prestbury Rd A3
Prince's Rd C1
Priory St B3
Promenade B2
Queen St A1
Recreation Ground A2
Regent Arcade B2
Regent St B2
Rodney Rd B2
Royal Crescent B2
Royal Well Place B2
Royal Wells Rd B2
St George's Place B2
St Georges Rd B1
St Gregory's ⛪ B2
St James St B3
St John's Avenue B3
St Luke's Rd C2
St Margarets Rd A2
St Mary's ⛪ B2
St Matthew's ⛪ B2
St Paul's Lane A2
St Paul's Rd A2
St Paul's St A2
St Stephen's Rd C1
Sandford Parks Lido C3
Sandford Mill Road C3
Sandford Park C3
Sandford Rd C2
Selkirk St A3
Sherborne Place B3
Sherborne St B3
Suffolk Parade C2
Suffolk Rd C1
Suffolk Square C1
Sun St A1
Swindon Rd B2
Sydenham Villas Rd C3
Tewkesbury Rd A1
The Courtyard B1
Thirlstaine Rd C2
Tivoli Rd C1
Tivoli St C1
Town Hall & Theatre 🎭 B2
Townsend St A1
Trafalgar St C2
Union St B3
University of Gloucestershire (Francis Cl Hall) A2
University of Gloucestershire (Hardwick) A1
Victoria Place B3
Victoria St A2
Vittoria Walk C2
Wellesley Rd A2
Wellington Rd A3
Wellington Square A3
Wellington St B2
West Drive A3
Western Rd B1
Wilson,The 🏛 B2
Winchcombe St B3
Winston Churchill Meml Gardens ❀ A1

Chester 179

Abbey Gateway A2
Appleyards Lane C3
Bars,The B3
Bedward Row B1
Beeston View C3
Bishop Lloyd's Palace ⌂ B2
Black Diamond St A2
Bottoms Lane C3
Boughton B3
Bouverie St A1
Bus Interchange A2
Bridge St B2
Bridgegate C2
Brook St A3
Brown's Lane C2
Cambrian Rd A1
Canal St A2
Carrick Rd C1
Castle ♜ C2
Castle Drive C2
Cathedral ✝ B2
Catherine St A1
Cheshire Military Museum 🏛 C2
Chester ⇌ A3
Cheyney Rd A1
Chichester St A1
City Rd A3
City Walls B1/B2
City Walls Rd B1
Cornwall St A2
Cross Hey C3
Cross,The ✦ B2
Crown Court C2
Cuppin St B2
Curzon Park North C1
Curzon Park South C1
Dee Basin A1
Dee Lane B3
Delamere St A2
Deva Roman Discovery Ctr 🏛 B2
Dingle,The C1
Duke St B2
Eastgate B2
Eastgate St B2
Eaton Rd C2
Edinburgh Way C3
Elizabeth Crescent B3
Fire Station A2
Foregate St B2
Forum Studio 🎭 B2
Forum,The B2
Frodsham St B2
Gamul House B2
Garden Lane A1
George St A2
Gladstone Avenue A1
God's Providence House ⌂ B2
Gorse Stacks A2
Greenway St C2
Grosvenor Bridge C1
Grosvenor Mus 🏛 B2
Grosvenor Park B3
Grosvenor Pk Terr C1
Grosvenor Shopping Centre B2
Grosvenor St B2
Groves Rd B3
Groves,The B3
Guildhall Mus 🏛 B1
Handbridge C2
Hartington St C3
Hoole Way A2
Hunter St B2
Information Ctr ℹ B2
King Charles' Tower ✦ A2
King St A2
Library B2
Lightfoot St A3
Little Roodee C2
Liverpool Rd A2
Love St B3
Lower Bridge St B2
Lower Park Rd B3
Lyon St A2
Magistrates Court B2
Meadows Lane C3
Meadows,The B3
Milton St A3
Minerva Roman Shrine ✦ C2
Miniature Railway ✦ B3
New Crane St B1
Nicholas St B2
Northgate A2
Northgate Arena A2
Northgate St A2
Nun's Rd B1
Old Dee Bridge ✦ C2
Overleigh Rd C2
Park St B2
Police Station 🚓 B2
Post Office ✉ A2/A3
Princess St B2
Queen St B2
Queen's Park Rd C3
Queen's Rd A3
Race Course B1
Raymond St A1
River Lane C2
Roman Amphitheatre & Gardens 🏺 B2
Roodee (Chester Racecourse),The B1
Russell St A3
St Anne St A2
St George's Cres C3
St Martin's Gate A1
St Martin's Way B1
St Oswalds Way A2
Saughall Rd A1
Sealand Rd A1
South View Rd A1
Stanley Palace ⌂ B1
Station Rd A3
Steven St A3
Storyhouse 🎭 B2
Superstore B2
Tower Rd B1
Town Hall B2
Union St B3
Univ of Chester C2
Vicar's Lane B2
Victoria Crescent C3
Victoria Rd A2
Walpole St A1
Water Tower St A1
Water Tower,The ✦ B1
Watergate B1
Watergate St B2
Whipcord Lane A1
White Friars B2
York St B3

Chichester 180

Adelaide Rd A3
Alexandra Rd A3
Arts Centre B2
Ave de Chartres B1/B2
Barlow Rd A1
Basin Rd C2
Beech Avenue B1
Bishops Palace Gardens B2
Bishopsgate Walk A3
Bramber Rd C3
Broyle Rd A2
Bus Station B2
Caledonian Rd B3
Cambrai Avenue B3
Canal Place C1
Canal Wharf C2
Canon Lane B2
Cathedral ✝ B2
Cavendish St A1
Cawley Rd B2
Cedar Drive A1
Chapel St A2
Cherry Orchard Rd C3
Chichester ⇌ B2
Chichester By-Pass C2/C3
Chichester College B1
Chichester Cinema 🎦 B3
Chichester Festival 🎭 A2
Chichester Gate Leisure Park C1
Chichester High School C2
Churchside A2
Cineworld 🎦 C1
City Walls B2
Cleveland Rd B3
College Lane A2
Cory Close C2
Council Offices B2
County Hall B2
Duncan Rd A1
Durnford Close A1
East Pallant B2
East Row B2
East St B2
East Walls B3
Eastland Rd C3
Ettrick Close B3
Ettrick Rd B3
Exton Rd C3
Fire Station A2
Football Ground A2
Franklin Place A2
Friary (Rems of) A2
Garland Close C3
Green Lane A3
Grove Rd C3
Guilden Rd B3
Guildhall 🏛 A2
Hawthorn Close A1
Hay Rd C3
Henty Gardens B1
Herald Drive C3
Hornet,The B3
Information Ctr ℹ B2
John's St B2
Joys Croft A3
Jubilee Park A3
Jubilee Rd A3
Juxon Close B2
Kent Rd A3
King George Gardens A2
King's Avenue C2
Kingsham Avenue C3
Kingsham Rd C2
Laburnum Grove B2
Leigh Rd C1
Lennox Rd A3
Lewis Rd A3
Library B2
Lion St B2
Litten Terrace A3
Litten,The A3
Little London B2
Lyndhurst Rd B3
Market B3
Market Avenue B2
Market Cross B2
Market Rd B3
Melbourne Rd A3
Minerva 🎭 A2
Mount Lane B1
New Park Rd A3
Newlands Lane A1
North Pallant B2
North St A2
North Walls A2
Northgate A2
Novium,The 🏛 B2
Oak Avenue A1
Oak Close A1
Oaklands Park A2
Oaklands Way A2
Orchard Avenue A1
Orchard St A1
Ormonde Avenue B3
Pallant House 🏛 B2
Parchment St A1
Parklands Rd A1/B1
Peter Weston Place B3
Police Station 🚓 C2
Post Office ✉ A1/B2/C3
Priory Lane A2
Priory Park A2
Priory Rd A2
Queen's Avenue C1
Riverside A3
Roman Amphitheatre B3
St Cyriacs A2
St Martins' St B2
St Pancras A3
St Paul's Rd A2
St Richard's Hospital (A&E) Ⓗ A3
Shamrock Close A3
Sherbourne Rd A1
Somerstown A2
South Bank C2
South Downs Planetarium & Science Centre ✦ C2
South Pallant B2
South St B2
Southgate B2
Spitalfield Lane A3
Stirling Rd B3
Stockbridge Rd C1/C2
Swanfield Drive A3
Terminus Ind Est C1
Tower St A2
Tozer Way A3
Turnbull Rd A3
Upton Rd C1
Velyn Avenue B3
Via Ravenna B1
Walnut Avenue A1
West St B2
Westgate B1
Westgate Fields B1
Westgate Leisure Centre B1
Weston Avenue C1
Whyke Close C3
Whyke Lane B3
Whyke Rd C3
Winden Avenue B3

Colchester 180

Abbey Gateway ✝ C2
Albert St A1
Albion Grove C2
Alexandra Rd C1
Artillery St C3
Arts Centre 🏛 B1
Balkerne Hill B1
Barrack St C3
Beaconsfield Rd C1
Beche Rd C3
Bergholt Rd A1
Bourne Rd C3
Brick Kiln Rd A1
Brigade Grove C2
Bristol Rd B2
Broadlands Way A3
Brook St B3
Bury Close B2
Bus Station C2
Butt Rd C1
Campion Rd C2
Cannon St C3
Canterbury Rd C2
Captain Gardens C2
Castle ♜ B2
Castle Park B2
Castle Rd B2
Catchpool Rd A1
Causton Rd B1
Chandlers Row C3
Circular Rd East C2
Circular Rd North C1
Circular Rd West C1
Clarendon Way A1
Claudius Rd C2
Colchester ⇌ A1
Colchester Camp Abbey Field C1
Colchester Retail Park B1
Colchester Town ⇌ C2
Colne Bank Avenue A1
Colne View Retail Park A2
Compton Rd A3
Cowdray Ave A1/A2
Crouch St B1
Crowhurst Rd B1
Culver Square Shopping Centre B1
Culver St East B2
Culver St West B1
Dilbridge Rd A3
East Hill B2
East St B3
East Stockwell St B1
Eld Lane B1
Essex Hall Rd A1
Exeter Drive B2
Fairfax Rd C2
Fire Station A2
Firstsite 🏛 B2
Flagstaff Rd C1
Garrison Parade C2
George St B2
Gladstone Rd C2
Golden Noble Hill C2
Goring Rd A3
Granville Rd C3
Greenstead Rd B3
Guildford Rd B2
Harsnett Rd C3
Harwich Rd B3
Head St B1
High St B1/B2
High Woods Ctry Pk A2
Hollytrees 🏛 B2
Hyderabad Close C2
Hythe Hill C3
Information Ctr ℹ B2
Jarmin Rd A2
Kendall Rd C2
Kimberley Rd C3
King Stephen Rd C3
Leisure World A2
Library B1
Lincoln Way B2
Lion Walk Shopping Centre B1
Lisle Rd C2
Lucas Rd C2
Magdalen Green C3
Magdalen St C2
Maidenburgh St B2
Maldon Rd C1
Manor Rd B1
Margaret Rd A1
Mason Rd A2
Mercers Way A1
Mercury 🎭 B1
Mersea Rd C2
Meyrick Crescent C2
Mile End Rd A1
Military Rd C2
Mill St C2
Minories 🏛 B2
Moorside B3
Morant Rd C3
Napier Rd C2
Natural History 🏛 B2
New Town Rd C2
Norfolk Crescent A3
North Hill B1
North Station Rd A1
Northgate St B1
Nunns Rd B1
Odeon 🎦 B1
Old Coach Rd B3
Old Heath Rd C3
Osborne St B2
Petrolea Close A1
Police Station 🚓 C1
Popes Lane B1
Port Lane C3
Post Office ✉ B1/B2
Priory St B2
Queen St B2
Rawstorn Rd B1
Rebon St C3
Recreation Rd C3
Ripple Way A3
Roberts Rd C2
Roman Rd B2
Roman Wall B2
Romford Close A3
Rosebery Avenue B2
St Andrews Avenue B3
St Andrews Gdns B3
St Botolph St B2
St Botolphs ⛪ B2
St John's Abbey (site of) ✝ C2
St John's St B1
St Johns Walk Shopping Centre B1
St Leonards Rd C3
St Marys Fields B1
St Peter's St B1
St Peters ⛪ B1
Salisbury Avenue C1
Saw Mill Rd C3
Sergeant St C2
Serpentine Walk A1
Sheepen Place B1
Sheepen Rd B1
Shopmobility B2
Sir Isaac's Walk B1
Smythies Avenue B2
South St C1
South Way C1
Sports Way A2
Suffolk Close A3
Superstore A1
Town Hall B1
Turner Rise Retail Park A2
Valentine Drive A3
Victor Rd C3
Wakefield Close B2
Wellesley Rd C1
Wells Rd B2/B3
West St C1
West Stockwell St B1
Weston Rd C3
Westway A1
Wickham Rd C1
Wimpole Rd C3
Winchester Rd C2
Winnock Rd C2
Worcester Rd B2

Coventry 180

Abbots Lane A1
Albany 🎭 B1
Albany Rd B1
Alma St B3
Ambulance Station A2
Art Faculty B3
Asthill Grove C2
Bablake School A1
Barras Lane A1/B1
Barr's Hill School A1
Belgrade 🎭 B2
Bishop St A2
Bond's Hospital ⌂ B1
Broad Gate B2
Broadway C1
Burges,The B2
Bus Station A3
Butts Radial B1
Byron St A3
Canterbury St A3
Cathedral ✝ B3
Central Six Retail Park C1
Chester St A1
Cheylesmore Manor House ⌂ B2
Christ Church Spire ✦ B2
City College A3
City Walls & Gates ✦ A2
Corporation St B2
Council House B2
Coundon Rd A1
Coventry Station ⇌ C2
Coventry Transport Museum 🏛 A2
Coventry University Technology Park C3
Cox St A3
Croft Rd B1
Dalton Rd C1
Deasy Rd C3
Earl St B2
Eaton Rd C2
Fairfax St B2
Fire Station A2
Foleshill Rd A2
Ford's Hospital ⌂ B2
Fowler Rd A1
Friars Rd C2
Gordon St C1
Gosford St B3
Greyfriars Green B2
Greyfriars Rd B2
Gulson Rd B3
Hales St A2
Harnall Lane East A3
Harnall Lane West A2
Herbert Art Gallery & Museum 🏛 B3
Hertford St B2
Hewitt Avenue A1
High St B2
Hill St B1
Holy Trinity ⛪ B2
Holyhead Rd A1
Howard St A3
Huntingdon Rd C1
Information Ctr ℹ C2
Jordan Well B3
King Henry VIII School C1
Lady Godiva Statue ✦ B2
Lamb St A2
Leicester Row A2
Library B2
Lincoln St A2
Little Park St B2
London Rd C3
Lower Ford St B3
Lower Precinct Shopping Centre B2
Magistrates & Crown Courts B2
Manor House Drive B2
Manor Rd C2
Market B2
Martyrs Meml ✦ C2
Meadow St B1
Meriden St A1
Michaelmas Rd C2
Middleborough Rd A1
Mile Lane C3
Millennium Place A2
Much Park St B3
Naul's Mill Park A1
New Union B2
Odeon 🎦 B1
Park Rd C2
Parkside C3
Planet Ice Arena B1
Post Office ✉ A3,B2
Primrose Hill St A3
Priory Gardens & Visitor Centre ✦ B2
Priory St B3
Puma Way C3
Quarryfield Lane C3
Queen's Rd B1
Quinton Rd C2
Radford Rd A2
Raglan St B3
Ringway (Hill Cross) A1
Ringway (Queens) B1
Ringway (Rudge) B1
Ringway (St Johns) B3
Ringway (St Nicholas) A2
Ringway (St Patricks) C2
Ringway (Swanswell) A2
Ringway (Whitefriars) B3
St John St B2
St John the Baptist ⛪ B2
St Nicholas St A2
Sidney Stringer Academy A3
Skydome B1
Spencer Avenue C1
Spencer Rec Gnd C1
Spencer Rd C1
Spon St B1
Sports Centre B3
Stoney Rd C2
Stoney Stanton Rd A3
Superstore B2
Swanswell Pool A3
Thomas Landsdail St C2
Tomson Avenue A1
Top Green C1
Tower St A2
Trinity St B2
University B3
Univ Sports Ctr B3
Upper Hill St A1
Upper Well St A2
Victoria St A3
Vine St A3
Wave,The ✦ B2
Warwick Rd C2
Waveley Rd B1
West Orchards Shopping Centre B2
Westminster Rd C1
White St A3
Windsor St B1

Derby 180

Abbey St C1
Agard St B1
Albert St B2
Albion St B2
Ambulance Station B1
Arthur St A1
Ashlyn Rd B3
Assembly Rooms 🏢 B2
Babington Lane C2
Bass Recreation Ground B3
Becket St B1
Belper Rd A1
Bold Lane B1
Bradshaw Way C2
Bradshaw Way Retail Park C2
Bridge St B1
Brook St B1
Burton Rd C1
Bus Station B2
Business Park A3
Caesar St A2
Canal St C3
Carrington St C3
Cathedral ✝ B2
Cathedral Rd B1
Charnwood St C2
Chester Green Rd A2
City Rd A2
Clarke St A3
Cock Pitt Junction B3
Council House 🏢 B2
Courts B1
Cranmer Rd B3
Crompton St C1
Crown & County Courts B2
Curzon St B1
Darley Grove A1
Derbion C2
Derby ⇌ C3
Derby 🎭 C2
Derby Gaol 🏛 B1
Derwent Bsns Ctr A2
Derwent St B2
Drewry Lane C1
Duffield Rd A1
Duke St A2
Dunton Close B3
Eagle Market C2
East St B2
Eastgate B3
Exeter St B2
Farm St C1
Ford St B1
Forester St C1
Fox St A2
Friar Gate B1
Friary St B1
Full St B2
Garden St A1
Gerard St C1
Gower St C2
Green Lane C2
Grey St C1
Guildhall 🏢 B2
Handyside Bridge A2
Harcourt St C1
Highfield Rd A1
Hill Lane C2
Incora County Ground (Derbyshire CCC), The B3
Information Ctr ℹ B2
Iron Gate B2
John St C3
Joseph Wright Ctr B1
Kedleston Rd A1
Key St B2
King Alfred St C1
King St A1
Kingston St A1
Lara Croft Way C2
Leopold St C2
Liversage St C3
Lodge Lane B1
London Rd C2
London Rd Community Hospital Ⓗ C2
Macklin St C1
Mansfield Rd A2
Market B2
Market Place B2
May St C1
Meadow Lane B3
Melbourne St C2
Mercian Way C1
Midland Rd C3
Monk St C1
Morledge B2
Mount St C1
Museum & Art Gallery 🏛 B1
Museum of Making 🏛 B2
North Parade A1
North St A1
Nottingham Rd B3
Osmaston Rd C2
Otter St A1
Park St C3
Parker St A1
Pickford's House 🏛 B1
Police Station 🚓 A2, B2
Post Office ✉ A1/A2/B1/C2/C3
Pride Parkway C3
Prime Enterprise Pk A2
Prime Parkway A2
QUAD ✦ B2
Queens Leisure Ctr B1
Racecourse Park A3
Railway Terrace C3
Register Office B2
Riverlights Leisure Centre B2
Sadler Gate B1
St Alkmund's Way B1/B2
St Helens House ✦ A1
St Mary's ⛪ A1
St Mary's Bridge A2
St Mary's Bridge Chapel ⛪ A2
St Mary's Gate B1
St Paul's Rd A2
St Peter's ⛪ C2
St Peter's St C2
Showcase De Lux 🎦 C2
Siddals Rd C3
Sir Frank Whittle Rd A3
Spa Lane C1
Spring St C1
Stafford St B1
Station Approach C3
Stockbrook St C1
Stores Rd A3
Traffic St C2
Wardwick B1
Werburgh St C1
West Avenue A1
West Meadows Industrial Estate B3
Wharf Rd A2
Wilmot St C2
Wilson St C1
Wood's Lane C1

Dorchester 181

Ackerman Rd B3
Acland Rd A2
Albert Rd A1
Alexandra Rd B1
Alfred Place B3
Alfred Rd B2
Alington Avenue B3
Alington Rd B3
Ashley Rd B1
Balmoral Crescent C3
Barnes Way B2/C2
Borough Gardens A1
Brewery Square B1
Bridport Rd A1
Buckingham Way C3
Caters Place A1
Cemetery A3/C1
Charles St A2
Coburg Rd B1
Colliton St A1
Cornwall Rd A1
Cromwell Rd B1
Culliford Rd B2
Culliford Rd North B2
Dagmar Rd B1
Damer's Rd B1
Diggory Crescent C2
Dinosaur Mus 🏛 A2
Dorchester Bypass C2
Dorchester South Station ⇌ B1
Dorchester West Station ⇌ B1
Dorset County (A&E) Ⓗ B1
Dorset County Council Offices A1
Dorset County Museum 🏛 A1
Duchy Close C3
Duke's Avenue B2
Durngate St A2
Durnover Court A3
Eddison Avenue B3
Edward Rd B1
Egdon Rd C2
Elizabeth Frink Statue ✦ B2
Farfrae Crescent B2
Forum Centre,The B1
Friary Hill A2
Friary Lane A2
Frome Terrace A2
Garland Crescent C3
Glyde Path Rd A1
Grosvenor Crescent C1
Grosvenor Rd C1
Grove,The A1
Gt Western Rd B1
Herringston Rd C1
High St East A2
High St Fordington A2
High Street West A1
Holloway Rd A2
Icen Way A2
Information Ctr ℹ B2
Keep Military Museum,The 🏛 A1
Kings Rd A3/B3
Kingsbere Crescent C2
Lancaster Rd B2
Library B1
Lime Close C1
Linden Avenue B2
London Close A3
London Rd A2/A3
Lubbecke Way A3
Lucetta Lane B2
Maiden Castle Rd C1
Manor Rd C2
Market B1
Marshwood Place B2
Maumbury Rd B1
Maumbury Rings 🏺 B1
Mellstock Avenue C2
Mill St A3
Miller's Close A1
Mistover Close C1
Monmouth Rd B1/B2
Moynton Rd C2
Nature Reserve A2
North Square A2
Northernhay A1
Odeon 🎦 B1
Old Crown Court & Cells ⌂ A1
Olga Rd B1
Orchard St A2
Plaza 🎦 A1
Police Station 🚓 B1
Post Office ✉ A1
Pound Lane A2
Poundbury Rd A1
Prince of Wales Rd B2
Prince's St A1
Queen's Avenue B1
Roman Town Ho 🏺 A1
Roman Wall 🏺 A1
Rothesay Rd C2
St George's Rd B3
Salisbury Field A2
Sandringham Sports Centre B3
Shaston Crescent C2
Smokey Hole Lane B3
South Court Ave C1
South St B1
South Walks Rd B2
Superstore C3
Teddy Bear Mus 🏛 A1
Temple Close C1
Terracotta Warriors & Teddy Bear Mus 🏛 A2
Town Hall ⌂ A2
Town Pump ✦ A2
Trinity St A1
Tutankhamun Exhibition 🏛 A1
Victoria Rd B1
Weatherbury Way C2
Wellbridge Close C1
West Mills Rd A1
West Walks Rd A1
Weymouth Avenue C1
Williams Avenue B1
Winterbourne (BMI) Ⓗ C1
Wollaston Rd A2
York Rd B2

Dumfries 181

Academy St A2
Aldermanhill Rd B3
Annan Rd A3
Ardwall Rd A3
Ashfield Drive A1
Atkinson Rd C1
Averill Crescent C1
Balliol Avenue C1
Bank St B2
Bankend Rd C3
Barn Slaps B3
Barrie Avenue B3
Beech Avenue A1
Bowling Green A3
Brewery St B2
Bridgend Theatre 🎭 B1
Brodie Avenue C2
Brooke St B2
Broomlands Drive C1
Brooms Rd B3
Buccleuch St A2
Burns House ⌂ B2
Burns Mausoleum ✦ B3
Burns St B2
Burns Statue ✦ A2
Cardoness St A3
Castle St A2
Catherine St A2
Cattle Market A3
Cemetery B3
Cemetery C2
Church Crescent A2
Church St B2
College Rd A1
College St A1
Corbelly Hill B1
Corberry Park B1
Cornwall Mt A3
Council Offices A2
Court A2
Craigs Rd C3
Cresswell Avenue B3
Cresswell Hill B3
Cumberland St B3
David Keswick Athletic Centre A3
David St B1
Dock Park C3
Dockhead B2
Dumfries ⇌ A3
Dumfries Academy A2
Dumfries Ice Bowl A1

Dumfries Museum & Camera Obscura ... B2
East Riverside Dr ... C3
Edinburgh Rd ... B2
English St ... B3
Fire Station ... B3
Friar's Vennel ... A2
Galloway St ... B3
George Douglas Dr ... C1
George St ... A2
Gladstone Rd ... C2
Glasgow St ... A1
Glebe St ... A1
Glencaple Rd ... C3
Goldie Avenue ... C1
Goldie Crescent ... C1
Golf Course ... A1
Gracefield Arts Centre ... A2
Greyfriars ... B2
Grierson Avenue ... B3
Hamilton Avenue ... C1
Hamilton Starke Pk ... C2
Hazelrigg Avenue ... C1
Henry St ... B3
Hermitage Drive ... C1
High Cemetery ... A1
High St ... A2
Hill Avenue ... C2
Hill St ... B1
HM Prison ... B1
Holm Avenue ... C2
Hoods Loaning ... A3
Howgate St ... B1
Huntingdon Rd ... A3
Information Ctr ... B2
Irish St ... B2
Irving St ... B2
King St ... A1
Kingholm Rd ... B2
Kirkpatrick Court ... C2
Laurieknowe ... A2
Leafield Rd ... B3
Leisure Complex ... B3
Library ... B2
Lochfield Rd ... A2
Loreburn Park ... A3
Loreburn St ... A3
Loreburne Shopping Centre ... B2
Lover's Walk ... B2
Martin Avenue ... B3
Maxwell St ... B1
McKie Avenue ... B3
Mews Lane ... A2
Mid Steeple ◆ ... B2
Mill Green ... B1
Mill Rd ... B1
Moat Rd ... C2
Moffat St ... B2
Mountainhall Park ... C3
Nelson St ... B3
New Abbey Rd ... B1/C1
New Bridge ... A2
Newall Terrace ... A2
Nith Avenue ... C2
Nith Bank ... C3
Nithside Avenue ... B1
Old Bridge ... A2
Old Bridge Ho ... B1
Palmerston Pk (Queen of the South FC) ... A1
Park Rd ... A2
Pleasance Avenue ... C1
Police HQ ... A3
Police Sta ... A2/A3
Portland Drive ... B1
Post Office ... B1/B2/B3
Priestlands Drive ... C1
Primrose St ... A2
Queen St ... B2
Queensberry St ... A2
Rae St ... A2
Richmond Avenue ... C2
Robert Burns Ctr ... B2
Roberts Crescent ... B1
Robertson Avenue ... C1
Robinson Drive ... C1
Rosefield Rd ... A2
Rosemount St ... B1
Rotchell Park ... C1
Rotchell Rd ... C1
Rugby Football Gd ... C1
Ryedale Rd ... C2
St Andrews St ... B2
St John the Evangelist ... A2
St Josephs College ... B3
St Mary's Ind Est ... A3
St Mary's St ... A3
St Michael St ... B2
St Michael's ... B2
St Michael's Bridge ... B2
St Michael's Bridge Rd ... B2
St Michael's Cemetery ... B2
Shakespeare St ... B2
Solway Drive ... C2
Stakeford St ... A1
Stark Crescent ... A3
Station Rd ... A3
Steel Avenue ... A1
Sunderries Avenue ... A1
Sunderries Rd ... A1
Superstore ... B3
Suspension Brae ... B2
Terregles St ... B1
Theatre Royal ... B2
Troqueer Rd ... C2
Union St ... B3
Wallace St ... B3
Welldale ... C2
West Riverside Dr ... C2
White Sands ... B2

Dundee 181
Abertay University ... A1
Adelaide Place ... A1
Airlie Place ... C1
Albany Terrace ... A1
Albert St ... A2
Alexander St ... A2
Ann St ... A2
Arthurstone Terr ... A3
Bank St ... B1
Barrack Rd ... A1
Barrack St ... B2
Bell St ... B2
Blinshall St ... B1
Broughty Ferry Rd ... B3
Brown St ... B1
Bus Station ... B1
Caird Hall ... B2

Camperdown St ... B3
Candle Lane ... B3
Carmichael St ... A1
City Churches ... B2
City Quay ... B3
City Square ... B2
Commercial St ... B2
Constable St ... A3
Constitution Cres ... A1
Constitution Court ... A1
Constitution Rd ... A1/B2
Cotton Rd ... A3
Courthouse Square ... B1
Cowgate ... A3
Crescent St ... A2
Crichton St ... B2
Dens Brae ... A3
Dens Rd ... A3
Discovery Point ◆ ... B1
Douglas St ... B1
Drummond St ... A1
Dudhope Castle ... A1
Dudhope St ... A2
Dudhope Terrace ... A1
Dundee ... B3
Dundee Contemporary Arts ◆ ... C2
Dundee High School ... B2
Dundee Law ◆ ... A1
Dundee Rep ... C2
Dundee Science Centre ◆ ... C2
Dunhope Park ... A1
Dura St ... A3
East Dock St ... B3
East Marketgait ... B3
East Whale Lane ... B3
Erskine St ... A3
Euclid Crescent ... B2
Forebank Rd ... A2
Foundry Lane ... A3
Gallagher Retail Pk ... B3
Gellatly St ... B3
Guthrie St ... B1
Hawkhill ... B1
Hilltown ... A2
HMS Unicorn ◆ ... B3
Howff Cemetery, The ... B1
Information Ctr ... C2
Keiller Shopping Ctr B2
Keiller Centre, The ... B2
King St ... B2
Kinghorne Rd ... A1
Ladywell Avenue ... A3
Laurel Bank ... A2
Law Rd ... A1
Law St ... A1
Library ... A2/A3
Library and Steps Theatre ... A2
Little Theatre ... A2
Lochee Rd ... B1
Lower Princes St ... A3
Lyon St ... A3
McManus Art Gallery & Museum, The ... B2
Meadow Side ... B2
Meadowside St Pauls ... B2
Mercat Cross ◆ ... B2
Murraygate ... B2
Nelson St ... A2
Nethergate ... B2/C1
North Carr ◆ ... B3
North Lindsay St ... B1
North Marketgait ... B2
Old Hawkhill ... B1
Olympia Leisure Ctr ... B3
Overgate Shopping Centre ... B1
Park Place ... B1
Perth Rd ... C1
Police Station ... B2
Post Office ... B1
Princes St ... A3
Prospect Place ... A2
Reform St ... B2
Riverside Drive ... C1
Riverside Esplanade ... C1
Roseangle ... C1
RRS Discovery ... C2
St Andrew's St ... B2
St Pauls Episcopal † ... B2
Seagate ... B2
Sheriffs Court ... B1
Shopmobility ... B2
Sidegate ... A2
Silver St ... B2
Sixth Form College ... B2
South George St ... B2
South Marketgait ... B3
South Tay St ... B2
South Victoria Dock Road ... B2
South Ward Rd ... B2
Tay Road Bridge ◆ ... C3
Thomson Avenue ... B1
Trades Lane ... B3
Union St ... B2
Union Terrace ... A1
University Library ... C1
Univ of Dundee ... C1
Upper Constitution St ... A1
V&A ... B1
Verdant Works ◆ ... B1
V&A Museum of Design ... C2
Victoria Dock ... B3
Victoria Rd ... A2
Victoria St ... A3
Ward Rd ... B1
Wellgate ... B2
West Bell St ... B1
West Marketgait B1/B2
Westfield Place ... C1
William St ... A3
Wishart Arch ◆ ... A3

Durham 181
Alexander Crescent B2
Allergate ... B2
Archery Rise ... C1
Assembly Rooms ... B2
Avenue, The ... B1
Back Western Hill ... A1
Bakehouse Lane ... B3
Baths Bridge ... B3
Boat House ... B3
Boyd St ... C3
Bus Station ... B2
Castle Chare ... B2
Cathedral † ... B2
Church St ... C3

Clay Lane ... C1
Claypath ... B3
College of St Hild & St Bede ... B3
County Hospital ... A1
Crescent, The ... A1
Crook Hall & Gardens ◆ ... A3
Crossgate ... B2
Crossgate Peth ... C1
Crown Court ... B2
Darlington Rd ... C1
Durham ... B2
Durham Castle ... B2
Durham School ... C2
Durham University (Science Site) ... C3
Ellam Avenue ... C1
Elvet Bridge ... B3
Elvet Court ... B3
Farnley Hey ... C1
Ferens Close ... A3
Fieldhouse Lane ... A1
Flass St ... B1
Flass Vale Local Nature Reserve ... A1
Framwellgate Bridge ... B2
Framwelgate ... A2
Framwellgate Peth ... A2
Framwellgate Waterside ... A2
Frankland Lane ... A3
Freeman's Place ... A3
Freeman's Quay Leisure Centre ... A3
GalaTheatre & Cinema ... B3
Geoffrey Avenue ... C1
Gilesgate ... B3
Grey College ... C2
Grove, The ... A1
Hallgarth St ... C3
Hatfield College ... B2
Hawthorn Terrace ... B1
Heritage Centre ... B3
HM Prison ... B3
John St ... B1
Kingsgate Bridge ... B3
Laburnum Terrace ... B1
Lawson Terrace ... B1
Leazes Rd ... B2/3
Library ... B2
Margery Lane ... B2
Market ... B2
Mavin St ... C3
Millburngate ... B2
Millburngate Bridge ... B2
Millennium Bridge (foot/cycle) ... B2
Mountjoy Research Centre ... C3
Museum of Archaeology ... B2
New Elvet ... B3
New Elvet Bridge ... B3
North Bailey ... B3
North End ... A1
Observatory ... C1
Old Elvet ... B3
OpenTreasure ... B2
Oriental Mus ... C2
Oswald Court ... C3
Passport Office ... B1
PercyTerrace ... B1
Pimlico ... C2
Police Station ... B2
Potters Bank ... C1/C2
Prebends Bridge ... C2
Prebends Walk ... C2
Prince Bishops Shopping Centre ... B3
Princes St ... A1
Providence Row ... A3
Quarryheads Lane ... C2
Redhills Lane ... B1
Redhills Terrace ... B1
Riverwalk, The ... B2
Saddler St ... B3
St Cuthbert's Society ... C2
St Margaret's ... B2
St Mary the Less ... C2
St Mary's College ... C2
St Monica Grove ... C1
St Nicholas' ... B3
St Oswald's † ... C3
Sands, The ... B3
Shopmobility ... B3
South Bailey ... C2
South Rd ... C3
South St ... B2
Springwell Avenue ... A1
Station Approach ... B2
Stockton St ... C3
Student Union ... B1
Summerville ... B1
Sutton St ... B1
Town Hall ... B2
Univ Arts Block ... C3
University Coll ◆ ... B2
Walkergate Centre ... B3
Wearside Drive ... C1
Western Hill ... A1
Wharton Park ... A2
Whinney Hill ... C3
Whitehouse Ave ... C1
YHA ... A3

Edinburgh 182
Abbey Strand ... C6
Abbeyhill ... A6
Abbeyhill Crescent ... B6
Abbeymount ... A6
Abercromby Place ... A4
Adam St ... C5
Albany Lane ... A4
Albany St ... A4
Albert Memorial ◆ ... B2
Albyn Place ... A3
Alva St ... B2
Alva St ... B2
Ann St ... A2
Appleton Tower ... C4
Archibald Place ... C3
Assembly Rooms & Musical Hall ... A4
Atholl Crescent ... B2
Atholl Cres Lane ... B2
Bank St ... B4
Barony St ... A4

Beaumont Place ... C5
Bedlam ... C4
Belford Rd ... B1
Belgrave Crescent ... A1
Belgrave Cres Lane ... A1
Bell's Brae ... B1
Blackfriars St ... B4
Blair St ... B4
Bread St ... C2
Bristo Place ... C4
Bristo St ... C4
Brougham St ... C2
Broughton St ... A4
Brown St ... C5
Brunton Terrace ... A6
Buckingham Terr ... A1
Burial Ground ... A6
Bus Station ... A4
Caledonian Cres ... C1
Caledonian Rd ... C1
Calton Hill ... A5
Calton Hill ... A5
Calton Rd ... B4
Camera Obscura & OutlookTower ◆ ... B4
Candlemaker Row ... C4
Canning St ... B2
Canongate ... B5
Canongate ... B5
Carlton St ... A1
CarltonTerrace ... A6
CarltonTerrace La ... A6
Castle St ... B2
Castle Terrace ... B2
Castlehill ... B4
Central Library ... B4
Chalmers Hosp ... C3
Chalmers St ... C3
Chambers St ... C4
Chapel St ... C4
Charles St ... C4
Charlotte Square ... B2
Chester St ... B1
Circus Lane ... A2
Circus Place ... A3
City Art Centre ... B4
City Chambers ◆ ... B4
City Observatory ◆ ... A5
Clarendon Cres ... A1
Clerk St ... C5
Coates Crescent ... B1
Cockburn St ... B4
College of Art ... C3
Comely Bank Ave ... A1
Comely Bank Row ... A1
Cornwall St ... C2
Cowgate ... B4
Cranston St ... B5
Crichton St ... C4
Croft-An-Righ ... A6
Cumberland St ... A3
Dalry Place ... C1
Dalry Rd ... C1
Danube St ... A2
Darnaway St ... A3
David Hume Tower ... C4
Davie St ... C5
Dean Bridge ... A1
Dean Gardens ... A1
Dean Park Cres ... A1
Dean Park Mews ... A1
Dean Path ... B1
Dean St ... A2
Dean Terrace ... A2
Dewar Place ... C1
Dewar Place Lane ... C1
Doune Terrace ... A3
Drummond Place ... A4
Drummond St ... C5
Drumsheugh Gdns ... B1
Dublin Mews ... A4
Dublin St ... A4
Dublin St La South ... A4
Dumbiedykes Rd ... C5
Dundas St ... A3
Dynamic Earth ◆ ... B6
Earl Grey St ... C2
East Crosscauseway ... C5
East Market St ... B4
East Norton Place ... A6
East Princes St Gardens ... B3
Easter Rd ... A6
Edinburgh (Waverley) ... B4
Edinburgh Castle ... B3
Edinburgh Dungeon ◆ ... B4
Edinburgh International Conference Ctr ... C2
Elder St ... A4
Esplanade ... B4
EtonTerrace ... A1
Eye Pavilion ... C4
Festival Office ... B3
Festival Theatre Edinburgh ... C4
Filmhouse ... C2
Fire Station ... C2
Floral Clock ◆ ... B3
Forres St ... A3
Forth St ... A4
Fountainbridge ... C2
Frederick St ... A3
Freemasons' Hall ... B3
Fruitmarket ... B4
Gardner's Cres ... C2
George Heriot's School ... C3
George IV Bridge ... B4
George Square ... C4
George Square La ... C4
George St ... B3
Georgian House ... B2
Gladstone's Land ◆ ... B4
Glen St ... C3
Gloucester Lane ... A2
Gloucester Place ... A2
Gloucester St ... A2
Graham St ... C1
Grassmarket ... B3
Great King St ... A3
Great Stuart ... A3
Greenside Lane ... A5
Greenside Row ... A5
Grindlay St ... C2
Grosvenor St ... B1
Grove St ... C1
Gullan's Close ... B5
Guthrie St ... C4
Hanover St ... A3
Hart St ... A4
Haymarket ... C1

Haymarket Sta ... C1
Heriot Place ... C3
Heriot Row ... A3
High School Yard ... B5
High St ... B4
Hill Place ... C5
Hill St ... B3
Hillside Crescent ... A5
Holyrood Abbey (Remains) † ... A6
Holyrood Gait ... B6
Holyrood Park ... C6
Holyrood Rd ... B5
Home St ... C2
Hope St ... B2
Horse Wynd ... B6
Howden St ... C5
Howe St ... A3
Hub, The ◆ ... B3
India Place ... A2
India St ... A3
Infirmary St ... B4
Ingleby ... A4
Information Ctr ... B4
Jeffrey St ... B4
John Knox House ... B5
Johnston Terrace ... B3
Keir St ... C3
Kerr St ... A2
King's Stables Rd ... B3
Lady Lawson St ... C3
Lauriston Gardens ... C3
Lauriston Park ... C3
Lauriston Place ... C3
Lauriston St ... C3
Lawnmarket ... B3
Learmonth Gdns ... A1
LearmonthTerrace ... A1
Leith St ... A4
Lennox St ... A1
Lennox St Lane ... A1
Leslie Place ... A2
London Rd ... A5
Lothian Rd ... B2
Lothian St ... C4
Lower Menz Place ... A6
Lynedoch Place ... B1
Manor Place ... B1
Market St ... B4
Marshall St ... C4
Maryfield ... A6
McEwan Hall ... C4
Medical School ... C4
Melville St ... B1
Meuse Lane ... B3
Middle Mdw Walk ... C4
Milton St ... A6
MontroseTerrace ... A6
Moray Place ... A2
Morrison Link ... C1
Morrison St ... C1
Mound Place ... B3
Mound, The ... B3
Multrees Walk ... A4
Mus Collections Ctr ... A4
Museum of Childhood ... B5
Museum of Edinburgh ... B5
Museum of Fire ... C3
Museum on the Mound ◆ ... B4
National Archives of Scotland ... A4
National Museum of Scotland ... C4
National Gallery ◆ ... B3
National Library of Scotland ... B4
National Monument ◆ ... A5
National Portrait Gallery ... A4
National War Museum ◆ ... B3
Nelson Monument ◆ ... A5
Nelson St ... A3
New St ... B5
Nicolson Square ... C5
Nicolson St ... C5
Niddry St ... B4
Nightingale Way ... C5
North Bank St ... B4
North Bridge ... B4
North Castle St ... A3
North Charlotte St ... B2
North Mdw Walk ... C4
North St Andrew St ... A4
North St David St ... A4
North West Circus Place ... A2
Northumberland St ... A4
Odeon ... C5
Old Royal High School ... A5
Old Tolbooth Wynd ... B5
OMNi Centre ◆ ... A5
OxfordTerrace ... A1
Palace of Holyroodhouse ... B6
Palmerston Place ... B1
Panmure Place ... C3
Parliament Square ... B4
People's Story, The ... B5
Picardy Place ... A4
Playhouse ... A5
Pleasance ... C5
Police Station ... C5
Ponton St ... C2
Post Office ... A3/B4/B5/C1/C2/C4
Potterrow ... C4
Princes Mall ... B4
Princes St ... B3
Princes St ... B3
Prisoners of War ... B3
Queen's Gallery ◆ ... B6
Queen St ... A3
Queen's Drive ... B6/C6
Queensferry Rd ... A1
Queensferry St ... B2
Queensferry St La ... B2
Radical Rd ... C6
Randolph Crescent ... B1
Regent Gardens ... A6
Regent Rd ... A5
Regent Rd Park ... A6
RegentTerrace ... A5
Richmond Lane ... C5
Richmond Place ... C5
Rose St ... B3
Ross Open Air Theatre ... B3
Rothesay Place ... B1

Rothesay Terrace ... B1
Roxburgh Place ... C5
Roxburgh St ... C5
Royal Bank of Scotland ... A4
Royal Circus ... A3
Royal Lyceum ... C2
Royal Mile, The ◆ ... B4
Royal Scottish Academy ... B3
RoyalTerrace ... A5
RoyalTerr Gardens ... A5
Rutland Square ... B2
Rutland St ... B2
St Andrew Sq ... A4
St Andrew Sq ... A4
St Andrew's House ... A5
St Bernard's Cres ... A1
St Bernard's Well ◆ ... A1
St Cecilia's Hall ◆ ... B4
St Colme St ... A2
St Cuthbert's ... B2
St Giles' † ... B4
St James Quarter Shopping Centre ... A4
St John St ... B5
St John's ... B2
St John's Hill ... C5
St Leonard's Hill ... C5
St Leonard's Lane ... C5
St Leonard's St ... C5
St Mary's ... A4
St Mary's Scottish Episcopal † ... B1
St Mary's St ... B5
St Michael & All Saints ... C3
St Stephen St ... A3
Salisbury Crags ... C6
Saunders St ... A2
Scotch Whisky Experience ◆ ... B4
Scott Monument ◆ ... B4
Scottish, The ◆ ... A4
Scottish Parliament ◆ ... B6
Scottish Storytelling Centre ◆ ... B5
Semple St ... C2
Shandwick Place ... B2
Simpson Lane ... C3
South Bridge ... B4
South Charlotte St ... B2
South College St ... C4
South Learmonth Gardens ... A1
South St Andrew St ... A4
South St David St ... A4
Spittal St ... C2
Stafford St ... B2
Stand Comedy Club, The ◆ ... A4
Student Centre ... C4
Surgeons' Hall ... C5
Supreme Courts ... B4
Talbot Rice, The ... C4
Teviot Place ... C4
Thistle St ... A3
Tolbooth & Highland Kirk ◆ ... B3
Torphichen Place ... C1
Torphichen St ... C2
Traverse Theatre ... C2
Tron Square ... B4
Tron, The ... B4
Union St ... A4
University ... C4
University Library ... C4
Univ of Edinburgh ... C4
Upper Grove Place ... C1
Usher Hall ... C2
Vennel ... C3
Victoria St ... B4
Viewcraig Gardens ... B5
Viewcraig St ... B5
Vue ... A4
Walker St ... B1
Waterloo Place ... A5
Waverley Bridge ... B4
Wemyss Place ... A2
West Approach Rd ... C1
West Crosscauseway ... C5
West End ... B1
West Maitland St ... C1
West of Nicholson St ... C4
West Port ... C3
West Princes Street Gardens ... B3
West Richmond St ... C5
WestTollcross ... C2
White Horse Cl ◆ ... B5
William St ... B2
Windsor St ... A5
Writer's Museum, The ... B4
York Lane ... A4
York Place ... A4
Young St ... B2

Exeter 182
Alphington St ... C1
Athelstan Rd ... C3
Bampfylde St ... B2
Barnardo Rd ... C3
Barnfield Hill ... B3
Barnfield Rd ... B2/B3
Barnfield Theatre ... B2
Bartholomew St East ... B1
Bartholomew St West ... B1
Bear St ... B2
Beaufort Rd ... C1
Bedford St ... B2
Belgrave Rd ... B3
Belmont Rd ... A3
Blackall Rd ... A2
Blackboy Rd ... A3
Bonhay Rd ... A1
Bull Meadow Rd ... C2
Bus & Coach Sta ... B3
Castle St ... B2
Catacombs ◆ ... B1
Cecil Rd ... C1
Cheeke St ... A3
Church Rd ... C1
Chute St ... A3
City Wall ... B1/B2
Civic Centre ... A2
Clifton Rd ... B3
Clifton St ... B3
Clock Tower ... B1
College Rd ... C3
Colleton Crescent ... C2
Commercial Rd ... C1
Coombe St ... B2

Cowick St ... C1
Crown Courts ... B2
Custom House Visitor Centre ... C2
CygnetTheatre ... B2
Danes' Rd ... A2
Denmark Rd ... B3
Devon County Hall ... C3
Devonshire Place ... A3
Dinham Crescent ... B1
East Grove Rd ... C3
Edmund St ... B1
Elm Grove Rd ... A3
Exe St ... B1
Exeter Cathedral † ... B2
Exeter Central ... B2
Exeter City Football Ground ... A3
Exeter College ... B2
Exeter Picture House ... B1
Fire Station ... B2
Fore St ... B1
Friars Walk ... C2
Guildhall ... B2
Guildhall Shopping Centre ... B2
Haven Rd ... C2
Heavitree Rd ... B3
Hele Rd ... A1
High St ... B2
HM Prison ... A2
Holloway St ... C2
Hoopern St ... A2
Horseguards ... A2
Howell Rd ... A1
Information Ctr ... B3
Iron Bridge ... B1
Isca Rd ... C1
Jesmond Rd ... A3
King St ... B1
King William St ... A2
Larkbeare Rd ... C2
Leisure Centre ... C1
Library ... B2
Longbrook St ... A2
LongbrookTerrace ... A2
Lower North St ... B1
Lucky Lane ... C2
Lyndhurst Rd ... C3
Magdalen Rd ... C3
Magdalen St ... C2
Market ... B2
Market St ... B2
Marlborough Rd ... C3
Mary Arches St ... B1
Matford Avenue ... C3
Matford Lane ... C3
Matford Rd ... C2
May St ... A3
Mol's Coffee Ho ... B2
New Bridge St ... B1
New North Rd ... A1/A2
North St ... B1
Northernhay St ... B1
Norwood Avenue ... C3
Odeon ... B2
Okehampton St ... C1
Old Mill Close ... C2
OldTiverton Rd ... A3
Oxford Rd ... A3
Paris St ... B2
Parr St ... A3
Paul St ... B1
Pennsylvania Rd ... A2
Portland Street ... A3
Post Office ... A3/B2/C1
Powderham Cres ... A3
Preston St ... B1
Princesshay Shopping Centre ... B2
Pyramids Leisure ... B2
Quay, The ... C2
Queen St ... B2
Queen's Terrace ... A1
Queens Rd ... C1
Radford Rd ... C3
Richmond Rd ... A1
Roberts Rd ... C2
Rougemont Castle ... B2
Rougemont Ho ◆ ... B2
Royal Albert Memorial Museum ◆ ... B2
St David's Hill ... A1
St James' Pk Sta ... A3
St James' Rd ... A3
St Leonard's Rd ... C3
St Mary Steps ... B1
St Nicholas Priory ... B1
StThomas Sta ... C1
Sandford Walk ... B3
School Rd ... C1
Sidwell St ... B2
Smythen St ... B1
Southernhay East ... B2
Southernhay West ... B2
Spicer Rd ... B3
Sports Centre ... A2
Summerland St ... B3
Sydney Rd ... C1
Tan Lane ... C1
Thornton Hill ... A2
Topsham Rd ... C2
Tucker's Hall ... B1
Tudor St ... B1
Underground Passages ◆ ... B2
University of Exeter (St Luke's Campus) B3
Velwell Rd ... A1
Verney St ... A3
Victoria St ... A3
Water Lane ... C1/C2
Weirfield Rd ... C2
Well St ... A2
West Avenue ... A2
West Grove Rd ... C3
Western Way A3/B1/B2
Willeys Avenue ... C1
Wonford Rd ... B3/C3
York Rd ... A3

Glasgow 183
Admiral St ... C2
Albert Bridge ... C5
Albion St ... B5
Anderston ... B3
Anderston Quay ... B3
Argyle Arcade ◆ ... B5
Argyle St ... A1/A2/B3/B4/B5

Argyle Street ... B5
Arlington St ... A3
Arts Centre ... B3
Ashley St ... A3
Bain St ... C6
Baird St ... A6
Baliol St ... A3
Ballater St ... C5
Barras (Mkt),The ... C6
Bath St ... A4
BBC Scotland ... C2
Bell St ... B6
Bell's Bridge ... C1
Bentinck St ... B1
Berkeley St ... B2
Black St ... A6
Blackburn St ... C2
Blackfriars St ... B6
Blantyre St ... B1
Blythswood Square A4
Blythswood St ... B4
Bothwell St ... B4
Brand St ... C2
Breadalbane St ... A2
Bridge St ... C4
Bridgegate ... C5
Briggait ... C5
Broomielaw ... B4
Broomielaw Quay Gardens ... B3
Brown St ... B4
Brunswick St ... B5
Buccleuch St ... A4
Buchanan Bus Sta ... A5
Buchanan Galleries A5
Buchanan St ... B5
Buchanan St ... B5
Cadogan St ... B4
Caledonian Univ. ... A5
Calgary St ... A6
Cambridge St ... A4
Canal St ... A6
Candleriggs ... B5
Carlton Place ... C4
Carnarvon St ... A3
Carrick St ... B4
Castle St ... A6
Cathedral Square ... B6
CathedralSt ... A5
Central Mosque ... C5
Centre for Contemporary Arts ◆ ... A4
Centre St ... C4
Cessnock ... C1
Cessnock ... C1
Charing Cross ... A3
Charlotte St ... C6
Cheapside St ... B3
Cineworld ... A5
Citizens' Theatre ... C5
City Chambers ... B5
City Halls ... B5
City of Glasgow Coll (City Campus) ... B6
City of Glasgow College (Riverside Campus) ... C4
Clairmont Gardens A2
Claremont St ... A2
ClaremontTerrace ... A2
Claythorne St ... C6
Cleveland St ... A3
Clifford Lane ... C1
Clifford St ... C1
Clifton Place ... A2
Clifton St ... A2
Clutha St ... C1
Clyde Arcade ... B5
Clyde Place ... C4
Clyde Place Quay ... C4
Clyde St ... B5
Clyde Walkway ... C4
Clydeside Distillery, The ◆ ... B1
Clydeside Expressway ... B2
Coburg St ... C4
Cochrane St ... B5
College St ... B6
Collins St ... B6
Commerce St ... C4
Cook St ... C4
Cornwall St ... C1
Couper St ... A5
Cowcaddens ... A5
Cowcaddens Rd ... A4
Crimea St ... B4
Custom House Quay Gardens ... C4
Dalhousie St ... A4
Dental Hospital ... A4
Derby St ... A2
Dobbie's Loan ... A4/A5
Dobbie's Loan PI ... A5
Dorset St ... A3
Douglas St ... B4
Doulton Fountain ◆ ... C6
Dover St ... A2
Drury St ... B4
Drygate ... B6
Dunaskin St ... A1
Dunblane St ... A5
Dundas St ... B5
Dunlop St ... C5
East Campbell St ... C6
Eastvale Place ... A1
Eglinton St ... C4
Elderslie St ... A2
Elliot St ... B2
Elmbank St ... A3
Esmond St ... A1
Exhibition Ctr ... B2
Festival Park ... C1
FilmTheatre ... A3
Finnieston Quay ... B2
Finnieston St ... B2
Fire Station ... C6
Florence St ... C5
Fox St ... C5
Gallowgate ... C6
Garnet St ... A3
Garnethill St ... A4
Garscube Rd ... A5
George Square ... B5
George St ... B5
George V Bridge ... C4
Gilbert St ... A1
Glasgow Bridge ... C4
Glasgow Cath † ... B6
Glasgow Central ... B4

Glasgow City Free Church ... B4
Glasgow Green ... C6
Glasgow Necropolis ◆ ... B6
Glasgow Royal Concert Hall ... A5
Glasgow Science Centre ◆ ... C1
Glasgow Tower ◆ ... B1
Glassford St ... B5
Glebe St ... A6
Gorbals Cross ... C5
Gorbals St ... C5
Gordon St ... B4
Govan Rd ... B1/C1/C2
Grace St ... B3
Grafton Place ... A5
Grand Ole Opry ◆ ... C3
Grant St ... A3
Granville St ... A3
Gray St ... A2
Greendyke St ... C6
Grey Eagle St ... C6
Harley St ... C1
Harvie St ... C1
Haugh Rd ... A1
Havannah St ... B6
Henry Wood Hall ... A2
High Court ... C5
High St ... B6
High Street ... B6
Hill St ... A4
Holland St ... A3
Holm St ... B4
Hope St ... A5
Houldsworth St ... A2
Houston St ... C2
Houston St ... C2
Howard St ... C5
Hunter St ... C6
Hutcheson St ... B5
Hydepark St ... B3
Imax Cinema ◆ ... C1
India St ... A3
Information Ctr ... B5
Ingram St ... B5
Jamaica St ... B4
James Watt Statue ◆ ... C6
James Watt St ... B4
John Knox St ... B6
Kelvin Hall ◆ ... A1
Kelvin Statue ◆ ... A2
Kelvin Way ... A1
Kelvingrove Art Gallery & Mus ◆ ... A1
Kelvingrove Park ... A2
Kelvinhaugh St ... A1
Kennedy St ... A6
Kent Rd ... A2
Kent St ... C6
Killermont St ... A5
King's, The ... A3
Kingston Bridge ... C3
Kingston St ... C4
Kinning Park ... C2
Kyle St ... A6
Lancefield Quay ... B2
Lancefield St ... B2
Langshot St ... C1
Lendel Place ... C1
Lighthouse, The ◆ ... B4
Lister St ... A6
Little St ... B3
London Rd ... C6
Lorne St ... C1
Lower Harbour ... C1
Lumsden St ... A1
Lymburn St ... A1
Lyndoch Crescent A3
Lyndoch Place ... A3
Lynedoch St ... A3
Macellan St ... C1
Mair St ... C2
Maitland St ... A4
Mansell St ... C2
Mavisbank Gdns ... C2
Mcalpine St ... B3
Mcaslin St ... A6
McLean Square ... C2
McLellan Gallery ... A4
McPhater St ... A4
Merchants' Ho ... B5
Middlesex St ... C1
Middleton St ... C1
Midland St ... B4
Miller St ... B5
Millennium Bridge. B6
Millroad St ... C6
Milnpark St ... C2
Milton St ... A5
Minerva St ... B2
Mitchell St West ... B4
Mitchell Lby, The ◆ ... A3
Modern Art Gallery ◆ ... B5
Moir St ... C6
Molendinar St ... C6
Moncur St ... C6
Montieth Row ... C6
Montrose St ... B5
Morrison St ... C3
Nairn St ... A1
National Piping Centre, The ◆ ... A5
Nelson Mandela Sq ◆ ... B5
Nelson St ... C4
Nelson's Monument ◆ ... C6
Newton Place ... A3
Newton St ... A3
Nicholson St ... C4
Nile St ... B5
Norfolk Court ... C4
North Frederick St ... B5
North Hanover St ... B5
North Portland St ... B6
North St ... A3
North Wallace St ... A6
O2 ABC ... A4
O2 Academy ◆ ... C4
Odeon ... A3
Old Dumbarton Rd A1
Osborne St ... B5/C5
Oswald St ... B4
Overnewton St ... A1
OVO Hydro ◆ ... B2
Oxford St ... C4
Pacific Drive ... B1
Paisley Rd ... C3
Paisley Rd West ... C1
Park Circus ... A2
Park Gardens ... A2

Park South ... A2
Park Terrace ... A2
Parkgrove Terrace ... A2
Parnie St ... C5
Parson St ... A6
Partick Bridge ... A1
Passport Office ... A4
Pavilion Theatre ... A4
Pembroke St ... A2
People's Palace ... C6
Pitt St ... A4/B4
Plantation Park ... C1
Plantation Quay ... C1
Police Museum ... B5
Police Station ... A4/A6
Port Dundas Rd ... A5
Port St ... B2
Portman St ... C2
Post Office ... A4/A5/B4/B5/C4
Prince's Dock ... C1
Princes Square ... B5
Provand's Lordship ◆ ... B6
Queen St ... B5
Queen Street ... B5
Ramshorn ... B5
Renfrew St ... A3/A4
Renton St ... A5
Richmond St ... B5
Robertson St ... B4
Rose St ... A4
Rottenrow ... B5
Royal Concert Hall ... A5
Royal Conservatoire of Scotland ... A5
Royal Crescent ... A2
Royal Exchange Sq. ... B5
Royal Highland Fusiliers Mus ◆ ... A3
West Glasgow Ambulatory Care
Royal Infirmary ... B6
RoyalTerrace ... A2
Rutland Crescent ... C2
St Andrew's in the Square ◆ ... C6
St Andrew's (RC) † ... B5
St Andrew's St ... B5
St Enoch ... B5
St Enoch Shopping Centre ... B5
St George's Rd ... A3
St James Rd ... A6
St Kent St ... B6
St Mungo Ave ... A5/A6
St Mungo Museum of Religious Life and Art ◆ ... B6
St Mungo Place ... A6
StVincent Crescent A2
StVincent Place ... B5
StVincent St ... B3/B4
StVincent Terrace ... B3
Saltmarket ... C5
Sandyford Place ... A2
Sauchiehall St ... A2/A4
SEC Armadillo ◆ ... B2
School of Art ... A4
Sclater St ... B7
Scotland St ... C2
Scotland St W ... C1
Scott St ... A4
Scottish Exhibition & Conference Ctr ◆ ... B2
Seaward St ... C2
Shaftesbury St ... A3
Sheriff Court ... C5
Shields Rd ... C1
Shopmobility ... A5
Shuttle St ... B6
Somerset Place ... A2
South Portland St ... C4
Springburn Rd ... A6
Springfield Quay ... C3
Stanley St ... C2
Stevenson St ... C6
Stewart St ... A4
Stirling Rd ... B6
Stobcross Quay ... B1
Stobcross Rd ... B1
Stock Exchange ◆ ... B5
Stockwell Place ... C5
Stockwell St ... C5
Stow College ... A4
Sussex St ... C2
Synagogue ... A3
Taylor Place ... A6
Tenement House ... A4
Teviot St ... A1
Theatre Royal ... A4
Tolbooth Steeple & Mercat Cross ◆ ... C6
Tower St ... C2
Trades House ... B5
Tradeston St ... C4
Transport Mus ◆ ... A1
Tron ◆ ... C5
Trongate ... C5
Tunnel St ... B2
Turnbull St ... C5
Union St ... B4
Univ of Strathclyde Centre, The ◆ ... A5
Victoria Bridge ... C5
Virginia St ... B5
Wallace St ... C3
Walls St ... B6
Walmer Crescent ... C1
Warroch St ... B3
Washington St ... B3
Waterloo St ... B4
Watt St ... C2
Wellington St ... B4
West Campbell St ... B4
West Graham St ... A4
West Greenhill Place ... B2
West Regent St ... A4
West Regent St ... B4
West St ... C4
Whitehall St ... B3
Wilkes St ... B3
Wilson St ... B5
Woodlands Gate ... A2
Woodlands Rd ... A3
Woodlands Terrace A2
Woodside Place ... A2
Woodside Terrace ... A2
York St ... B4
Yorkhill Parade ... A1
Yorkhill St ... A1

Gloucester 182

Albion St. C1
Alexandra Rd A3
Alfred St C3
All Saints Rd C2
Alvin St C2
Arthur St C2
Barrack Square B1
Barton St C2
Blackfriars † B1
Blenheim Rd C1
Bristol Rd C1
Brunswick Rd B2
Bruton Way B2
Bus Station B2
Cineworld ■ B2
City Council Offices B1
Clarence St B2
Commercial Rd B1
Courts B1
Cromwell St B1
Deans Way A2
Denmark Rd C3
Derby Rd C3
Docks ✦ B1
Eastgate St B2
Eastgate,The B1
Edwy Parade A2
Estcourt Close A3
Estcourt Rd A3
Falkner St C2
GL1 Leisure Centre C2
Gloucester Cath † B1
Gloucester Life B1
Gloucester Quays Outlet C1
Gloucester Mus B2
Gloucester Sta ≥ B2
Gloucestershire Archive B2
Gloucestershire Royal Hospital (A&E) H A3
Goodyere St C2
Gouda Way A1
Great Western Rd B3
Guildhall B2
Heathville Rd A3
Henry Rd B3
Henry St B3
Hinton Rd A2
HM Prison Gloucester ✦ B1
India Rd C3
Information Ctr ✦ B2
Jersey Rd C3
King's C2
King's Walk Shopping Centre B2
Kingsholm (Gloucester Rugby) A2
Kingsholm Rd A3
Lansdown Rd A3
Library C1
Llanthony Rd C1
London Rd B3
Longhorn Avenue A1
Longsmith St B1
Malvern Rd A3
Market B2
Market Parade B2
Mercia Rd A2
Metz Way C3
Midland Rd C2
Millbrook St C3
Montpellier C1
Napier St C3
National Waterways Mus Gloucester ✦ C1
Nettleton Rd C1
New Inn B2
New Olympus ■ B2
North Rd A3
Northgate St A2
Oxford Rd A2
Oxford St B2
Park & Ride Gloucester A1
Park Rd C2
Park St B2
Park,The C2
Parliament St C1
Peel Centre,The C1
Pitt St B1
Police Sta ■ B1/C3
Post Office ▣ B1
Quay St B1
Quay,The B1
Recreation Gd A1/A2
Regent St C2
Robert Raikes Ho ▣ B1
Royal Oak Rd B1
Russell St B2
Ryecroft St C2
St Aldate St B2
St Ann Way C1
St Catherine St A2
St Mark St A2
St Mary de Crypt B1
St Mary de Lode ▲ B1
St Nicholas's ▲ B1
St Oswald's Priory ✦ B1
St Oswald's Retail Park A1
St Peter's B2
Seabroke Rd A3
Sebert St A2
Severn Rd C1
Sherborne Cinema ■ B2
Sherborne St B2
Shire Hall ▣ B2
Sidney St C3
Soldiers of Gloucestershire ■ B1
Southgate St. B1/C1
Spa Field C1
Spa Rd C1
Sports Ground A2/B2
Station Rd C3
Stratton Rd C3
Stroud Rd C1
Superstore A1
Swan Rd B2
Trier Way C1/C2
Union St A2
Vauxhall Rd A2
Victoria St B2
Walham Lane A1
Wellington St B2
Westgate Retail Pk. C1
Westgate St B1
Widden St C2
Worcester St B2

Grimsby 183

Abbey Drive East C2
Abbey Drive West C2
Abbey Park Rd C2
Abbey Rd C2
Abbey Walk C2
Abbeygate Shopping Centre C2
Abbotsway C2
Adam Smith St A1/A2
Ainslie St C2
Albert St A2
Alexandra Dock A2/B2
Alexandra St A2
Alexandra Retail Pk A2
Annesley St. A1
Armstrong St A2
Arthur St B1
Augusta St C1
Bargate C1
Beeson St A1
Bethlehem St C2
Bodiam Way A1
Bradley St B3
Brighowgate C1/C2
Bus Station C2
Canterbury Drive C1
Cartergate B1/C1
Catherine St B1
Chantry Lane B1
Charlton St A1
Church Lane C2
Church St A2
Cleethorpe Rd A3
Close,The C1
College St. C1
Compton Drive C1
Corporation Bridge A2
Corporation Rd A1
Court B2/B3
Crescent St C1
Deansgate C1
Doughty Rd C1
Dover St B1
Duchess St C2
Dudley St C1
Duke of York Gardens B1
Duncombe St B1
Earl Lane B1
East Marsh St B2
East St B2
Eastgate B2
Eastside Rd A3
Eaton Court C1
Eleanor St B2
Ellis Way B3
Fisherman's Chapel A3
Fisherman's Wharf B2
Fishing Heritage Centre ■ B2
Flour Square. A3
Frederick St B3
Frederick Ward Way A2
Freeman St A3/B3
Freshney Drive B1
Freshney Place. B1
Garden St C2
Garibaldi St C2
Garth Lane B2
Grime St B3
Grimsby Docks Station ≥ A3
Grimsby Town ≥ C2
Hainton Avenue C3
Har Way. B3
Hare St C2
Harrison St B1
Haven Avenue. A1
Hay Croft Avenue B1
Hay Croft St. B1
Heneage Rd B3/C3
Henry St B1
Holme St B1
Hume St C1
James St B1
Joseph St B1
Kent St A3
King Edward St. A1
Lambert Rd. C1
Library B2
Lime St A3
Lister St. A3
Littlefield Lane C1
Lockhill A3
Lord St. B1
Lower Spring St A3
Ludford St A3
Macaulay St B1
Mallard Mews C1
Manor Avenue C2
Market B1
Market Hall B2
Market St B2
Moody Lane A1
Moss Rd C2
Nelson St A3
New St. B2
Osbourne St B2
Pasture St B3
Peaks Parkway C3
Pelham Rd C1
Police Station ▣ B3
Pyewipe Rd. A1
Railway Place. A3
Railway St. A3
Recreation Ground C2
Rendel St A2
Retail Park A2/B3
Richard St. B1
Ripon St B1
Robinson St East B1
Royal St. B1
St Hilda's Avenue C1
St James C2
Sheepfold St. B3/C3
Shopmobility B2
Sixhills St C2
South Park B2
Superstore B3/B2
Tasburgh St. C3
Tennyson St C2
Thesiger St. B2
Time Trap ▣ B2
Town Hall B1
Veal St. B1
Victoria Retail Park A3
Victoria St North A2
Victoria St South C2
Victoria St West B2
Watkin St. A1
Welholme Avenue C1
Welholme Rd C1
Wellington St B3
Wellowgate C2
Werneth Rd. B3
West Coates Rd A1
Westgate C2
Westminster Drive C2
Willingham St. C3
Wintringham Rd. C1
Wood St B3
Yarborough Drive. B1
Yarborough Hotel ▣ B1
York St. B2

Harrogate 183

Albert St. C2
Alexandra Rd B2
Arthington Avenue. C3
Ashfield Rd B2
Back Cheltenham Mount B2
Beech Grove. C1
Belmont Rd. C1
Bettys Café Tea Rooms ▣ B2
Bilton Drive A3
Bower Rd A3
Bower St. A3
Bus Station B2
Cambridge Rd B2
Cambridge St B2
Cemetery A3
Chatsworth Grove A2
Chatsworth Place A2
Chatsworth Rd A2
Chelmsford Rd B3
Cheltenham Cres. B2
Cheltenham Mt B2
Cheltenham Parade B2
Christ Church ▲ B3
Christ Church Oval. B3
Chudleigh Rd A3
Clarence Drive C1
Claro Rd A3
Claro Way A3
Coach Park B2
Coach Rd. A3
Cold Bath Rd. C1
Commercial St. A2
Coppice Avenue. A1
Coppice Drive. A1
Coppice Gate A1
Cornwall Rd C1
Council Offices. B2
Crescent Gardens B2
Crescent Rd B2
Dawson Terrace A2
Devonshire Place. A3
Dixon Rd A2
Dixon Terrace A2
Dragon Avenue A3
Dragon Parade. A3
Dragon Rd. A3
Duchy Hosp,The H C1
Duchy Rd. B1
East Parade B2
East Park Rd C2
Esplanade C2
Everyman ■ B2
Fire Station A2
Franklin Mount A2
Franklin Rd. A2
Franklin Square A2
Glebe Rd C1
Grove Park Court A3
Grove Park Terrace A3
Grove Rd. A2
Hampsthwaite Rd A1
Harcourt Drive B3
Harcourt Rd B3
Harrogate ≥ B2
Harrogate Convention Ctr. B1
Harrogate Justice Ctr (Magistrates' and County Courts) A2
Harrogate Ladies College C1
Harrogate Theatre ▣ B2
Harrogate Turkish Baths ▣ B1
Heywood Rd C1
Hollins Crescent. A1
Hollins Mews A1
Hollins Rd. A1
Hydro Leisure Centre,The A1
Information Ctr ✦ B2
James St. B2
Jenny Field Drive A1
John St. B2
Kent Drive. A1
Kent Rd A1
Kings Rd A2
Kingsway B3
Kingsway Drive B3
Lancaster Rd C1
Leeds Rd C3
Lime Grove A3
Lime St A3
Mayfield Grove. B2
Mercer ▣ B2
Montpellier Hill B2
Mornington Cres A3
Mornington Terr. A3
Mowbray Square A3
North Park Rd. B3
Oakdale Avenue A1
Oatlands Drive. C3
Odeon ■ B2
Osborne Rd. A2
Otley Rd. C1
Oxford St. B2
Parade,The. B2
Park Chase B3
Park Parade B3
Park View C2
Parliament St B2
Police Station ▣ A2
Providence Terrace A2
Queen Parade C3
Queen's Rd C1
Raglan St C2
Regent Avenue A3
Regent Grove A3
Regent Parade A3
Regent St. A3
Regent Terrace. A3
Ripon Rd A1
Robert St. C2
Royal Pump Room ■ B1
St Luke's Mount A2
St Mary's Avenue C1
St Mary's Walk C1
Scargill Rd A1
Skipton Rd A3
Skipton St. A2
Slingsby Walk. C3
South Park Rd. C1
Spring Grove A1
Springfield Avenue B1
Station Avenue B2
Station Parade. B2
Stray Rein. C3
Stray,The. C2/C3
Studley Rd A2
Superstore B2/C1
Swan Rd B1
Tower St C2
Trinity Rd C2
Union St B2
Valley Drive. C1
Valley Gardens ❀ C1
Valley Mount. C1
Victoria Avenue C2
Victoria Rd C1
Victoria Shopping Centre B2
Waterloo St. B2
West Park C2
West Park St. C2
Wood View A1
Woodfield Avenue A3
Woodfield Drive. A3
Woodfield Grove A3
Woodfield Square A3
Woodside. B3
York Place. A2
York Rd. B1

Hull 184

Adelaide St. C1
Albert Dock C1
Albion St. B2
Alfred Gelder St B2
Anlaby Rd B1
Arctic Corsair ✦ B3
Beverley Rd. A1
Blanket Row C2
Bond St. B2
Bonus Arena. B1
Bridlington Avenue A2
Brook St. B1
Brunswick Avenue. A1
Bus Station B1
Camilla Close C3
Cannon St. A2
Caroline St. A2
Carr Lane. B1
Castle St C2
Central Library. B1
Charles St. A2
Citadel Way C3
Clarence St. B3
Cleveland St. A3
Clifton St. A1
Colonial St. B1
Court. B2
Deep,The ✦ C3
Dinostar ▣ C2
Dock Office Row. A2
Dock St B2
Drypool Bridge. B3
Egton St A3
English St C1
Ferens Gallery ▣ B2
Ferensway B1
Fire Station. B1
Francis St. A2
Francis St West. A2
Freehold St. A1
Freetown Way A1
Früit Theatre ▣ C2
Garrison Rd B3
George St. B2
Gibson St. A3
Great Union St. A3
Green Lane A2
Grey St. A1
Grimston St. B2
Grosvenor St. A1
Guildhall ▣ B2
Guildhall Rd B2
Hands-on History ▣ B2
Harley St. A1
Hessle Rd C1
High St B2
Hull Minster ▲ C2
Hull Paragon Interchange Sta ≥ B1
Hull & East Riding Museum ▣ B2
Hull Ice Arena C1
Hull City Hall ▣ B2
Hull College B3
Hull History Centre A1
Hull New Theatre ▣ A2
Hull Truck Theatre ▣ B1
Humber Dock Marina. C2
Humber Dock St. C2
Humber St C2
Hyperion St. A3
Information Ctr ✦ B2
Jameson St. B1
Jarratt St. B2
Jenning St A3
King Billy Statue ✦ C2
King Edward St. B2
King St C2
Kingston Retail Pk. C1
Kingston St. C1
Liddell St. A1
Lime St. A2
Lister St. C1
Lockwood St. A2
Maister House ▣ B2
Maritime Mus ▣ B2
Market B2
Market Place C2
Millennium Bridge. C2
Minerva Pier. C2
Mulgrave St. A3
Myton Swing Bridge C2
Myton St B1
NAPA (Northern Acad of Performing Arts) B1
Nelson St C2
New Cleveland St. A3
New George St A2
Norfolk St. A1
North Bridge. A3
North St. B1
Odeon ■ C2
Old Harbour B3
Osborne St. B1
Paragon St. B2
Park St B1
Percy St. A2
Police Station ▣ B1
Porter St. C1
Portland St. B1
Post Office ▣ B1/B2
Postergate B2
Prince's Quay. B2
Prospect Centre. B1
Prospect St. A1
Queen's Gardens B2
Railway Dock Marina. C2
Railway St. B2
Reel ▣ B1
Reform St A1
Retail Park B1
Riverside Quay. C2
Roper St B2
St James St. C1
St Luke's St. B1
St Mark St C1
St Mary the Virgin ▲ B3
St Stephens Shopping Centre B1
Scale La Footbridge B3
Scott St. A2
South Bridge Rd. B3
Sport's Centre C1
Spring Bank B1
Spring St. B1
Spurn Lightship ▲ C2
Spyvee St A3
Stage @The Dock ▣ C3
Sykes St. A2
Tidal Surge Barrier ✦ C3
Tower St. B3
Trinity House Acad. B2
Vane St. A1
Victoria Pier ✦ C2
Waterhouse Lane. B2
Waterloo St. A1
Waverley St. A1
Wellington St. C2
Wellington St West C2
West St. B1
Whitefriargate. B2
Wilberforce Drive B3
Wilberforce Ho ▣ B3
Wilberforce Monument ✦ B3
William St. C1
Wincolmlee A3
Witham. A3
Wright St. A1

Inverness 184

Abban St A1
Academy St. B2
Alexander Place. B2
Anderson St. A2
Annfield Rd. C3
Ardconnel St. B3
Ardconnel Terrace. B3
Ardross Place. B2
Ardross St. B2
Argyle St. B2
Argyle Terrace B3
Attadale Rd B1
Balliefeary Rd. C1
Balliefeary Rd. C1/C2
Balnain House ✦ B2
Balnain St. B2
Bank St B2
Bellfield Park C2
Bellfield Terrace. C2
Benula Rd A1
Birnie Terrace. A1
Bishop's Rd. C2
Bowling Green ✦ B2
Bridge St. B2
Brown St. A2
Bruce Avenue. B1
Bruce Gardens. C1
Bruce Park. C1
Burial Ground. A2
Burnett Rd. A3
Bus Station B3
Caledonian Rd. B1
Cameron Rd. A1
Cameron Square A1
Carse Rd A1
Carsegate Rd Sth. A1
Castle Garrison Encounter ✦ B2
Castle Rd. B2
Castle St. B2
Celt St B2
Chapel St A2
Charles St. B3
Church St. B2
Columba Rd. B1/C1
Crown Avenue B3
Crown Circus B3
Crown Drive B3
Crown Rd. B3
Crown St. B3
Culduthel Rd. C3
Dalneigh Crescent C1
Dalneigh Rd. C1
Denny St B3
Dochfour Drive B1/C1
Douglas Row B2
Duffy Drive C2
Dunabban Rd A1
Dunain Rd. B1
Duncraig St B2
Eastgate Shopping Centre B3
Eden Court ▣ C2
Fairfield Rd. B1
Falcon Square B3
Fraser St. B2
Friars' Bridge A2
Friars' Lane. B2
Friars' St. A2
George St. A2
Gilbert St. A2
Glebe St. A2
Glendoe Terrace. A1
Gordon Terrace. B3
Gordonville Rd C2
Grant St. A2
Grant Street Park (Clachnacuddin FC). A2
Greig St. B2
Harbour Rd. A3
Harrowden Rd B1
Haugh Rd C2
Heatherley Cres C3
High St. B3
Highland Council Headquarters,The C1
Hill Park C2
Hill St C3
HM Prison. A3
Huntly Place A2
Huntly St B2
India St B2
Industrial Estate. A3
Information Ctr ✦ B2
Innes St. A3
Inverness ≥ B3
Inverness High School. C1
Inverness Museum & Art Gallery ▣ B2
Jamaica St A2
Kenneth St. B2
Kilmuir Rd. A1
King St B2
Kingsmills Rd B3
Laurel Avenue B1/C1
Library A3
Lilac Grove A1
Lindsay Avenue C1
Lochalsh Rd A1/B1
Longman Rd A3
Lotland Place A3
Lower Kessock St. A1
Madras St A2
Maxwell Drive C1
Mayfield Rd C3
Millburn Rd. B3
Mitchell's Lane. C3
Montague Row. B2
Muirfield Rd C3
Muirtown St. A1
Nelson St. A2
Ness Bank C2
Ness Bridge B2
Ness Walk B2/C2
Old Edinburgh Rd. C3
Old High Church ▲ B2
Park Rd C1
Perceval Rd B1
Planefield Rd B1
Police Station ▣ A3
Porterfield Bank C3
Porterfield Rd C3
Portland Place. A2
Post Office ▣ A2/B1/B2
Queen St B2
Queensgate B2
Railway Terrace A3
Rangemore Rd B1
Reay St B3
Riverside St B2
Rose St A2
Ross Avenue B1
Rowan Rd. A1
Royal Northern Infirmary H C2
St Andrew's Cath † B2
St John's Avenue C1
St Mary's Avenue A2
Sheriff Court B3
Shore St. A3
Smith Avenue C1
Southside Place. C3
Southside Rd C3
Spectrum Centre B3
Strothers Lane. B3
Superstore A1/B2
TA Centre C2
Telford Gardens A1
Telford Rd. A1
Telford St A1
Tomnahurich Cemetery C1
Tomnahurich St. B2
Town Hall B3
Union Rd. B3
Union St B3
Victorian Market B2
Walker Rd. A3
Walker Rd. A3
War Memorial ✦ C2
Waterloo Bridge. A2
Wells St. A1
Young St. B2

Ipswich 184

Alderman Rd B1
All Saints' Rd. A1
Alpe St. A1
Ancaster Rd. C1
Ancient House ▣ B2
Anglesea Rd. A2
Ann St. A2
Arboretum A2
Austin St. C2
Avenue,The. A3
Belstead Rd C1
Berners St. B2
Bibb Way. B1
Birkfield Drive C1
Black Horse Lane. B1
Bolton Lane A3
Bond St. B3
Bowthorpe Close B1
Bramford La A1
Bramford Rd A1
Bridge St. C2
Brookfield Rd. A1
Brooks Hall Rd A1
Broomhill Park. A1
Broomhill Rd A1
Broughton Rd. A2
Bulwer Rd. B1
Burrell Rd C2
Bus Station B3
Butter Market. B2
Buttermarket Shopping Ctr,The B2
Cardinal Park Leisure Park C2
Carr St. B3
Cecil Rd. B2
Cecilia St. B2
Chancery Rd. C2
Charles St. B2
Chevallier St. A1
Christchurch Mansion & Wolsey Art Gallery A2
Christchurch Park A3
Christchurch St. A3
Cineworld ■ C2
Civic Centre B2
Civic Drive B2
Clarkson St. B1
Cobbold St B3
Commercial Rd C2
Constable Rd. A3
Constantine Rd. C1
Constitution Hill. A2
Corder Rd A3
Corn Exchange. B2
Cotswold Avenue A1
Council Offices. C2
County Hall. B3
Crown Court. C2
Crown St. B2
Cullingham Rd B1
Cumberland St. A2
Curriers Lane. B2
Dale Hall Lane A1
Dales View Rd A1
Dalton Rd A2
Dillwyn St B2
Elliot St. A3
Elm St B2
Elsmere Rd. A3
Falcon St. B2
Felaw St C3
Fire Station. C3
Flint Wharf C2
Fonnereau Rd A2
Fore St C3
Foundation St. B2
Franciscan Way C2
Friars St. B2
Gainsborough Rd. A3
Gatacre Rd. B1
Geneva Rd. A2
Gippeswyk Avenue. C1
Gippeswyk Park C1
Grafton Way C2
Graham Rd. A1
Great Whip St. C3
Grimwade St. B3
Handford Cut. B1
Handford Rd. B1
Henley Rd. A2
Hervey St A3
High St. A2
Holly Rd A2
Ipswich Haven Marina ✦ C3
Ipswich Museum & Art Gallery ▣ A2
Ipswich School. A2
Ipswich Station ≥ C2
Ipswich Town FC (Portman Road) C2
Ivry St A2
Kensington Rd. A1
Kesteven Rd. C1
Key St. C3
Kingsfield Avenue A1
Kitchener Rd A1
Library B2
Little's Crescent. C2
London Rd B1
Low Brook St C3
Lower Orwell St B3
Luther Rd C2
Magistrates Court B2
Manor Rd A3
Mornington Ave A1
Museum St. B2
Neale St A2
New Cardinal St C2
New Cut East C3
New Wolsey ▣ B2
Newson St. A2
Norwich Rd. A1/B1
Oban St. A1
Old Custom Ho ▣ C3
Old Foundry Rd B3
Old Merchant's House ▣ C3
Orford St. A1
Paget Rd. A2
Park Rd A3
Park View Rd. A3
Peter's St. C2
Philip Rd C1
Pine Avenue A1
Pine View Rd. A1
Police Station ▣ B2
Portman Rd B2
Portmans Walk. C1
Post Office ▣ A3/B3
Princes St. B2
Prospect St. A2
Queen St. B2
Ranelagh Rd C1
Recreation Ground B1
Rectory Rd A1
Regent Theatre ▣ B3
Reg Driver Visitor Centre ✦ B3
Retail Park A3
Retail Park C1
Richmond Rd. A1
Rope Walk. B3
Rose Lane C2
Russell Rd. C2
St Edmund's Rd A2
St George's St. A2
St Helen's St. B3
Sherrington Rd A1
Shopmobility B2
Silent St. C2
Sir Alf Ramsey Way C1
Sir Bobby Robson Bridge C2
Sirdar Rd. A1
Sir John Mills Theatre ▣ B1
Soane St. A3
Springfield Lane A1
Star Lane. C3
Stevenson Rd. A1
Stoke Quay. C2
Suffolk College C3
Suffolk Retail Park C2
Surrey Rd. A1
Tacket St. B3
Tavern St. B2
Tower Ramparts B2
Tower Ramparts Shopping Centre B2
Tower St B2
Town Hall ▣ B2
Tuddenham Rd. A3
University B3
Upper Brook St. B2
Upper Orwell St. B3
Valley Rd. A2
Vermont Crescent A3
Vermont Rd. A3
Vernon St. C2
Warrington Rd A2
Waterloo Rd A3
Waterworks St. C3
Wellington St B3
West End Rd B3
Westerfield Rd A3
Westgate St. B2
Westholme Rd A1
Westwood Avenue A1
Willoughby Rd A1
Withipoll St. B3
Woodbridge Rd A3
Woodstone Avenue A3
Yarmouth Rd A3

Kendal 184

Abbot Hall Art Gallery & Mus of Lakeland Life & Industry ▣ B2
Ambulance Station A2
Anchorite Fields. C2
Anchorite Rd C2
Ann St A3
Appleby Rd A3
Archers Meadow C2
Ashleigh Rd A2
Aynam Rd B3
Bankfield Rd. B3
Beast Banks B2
Beezon Fields. A3
Beezon Rd. A3
Beezon Trading Estate A3
Belmont B2
Birchwood Close B3
Blackhall Rd B2
Brewery Arts Centre ▣ B2
Bridge St. B2
Brigsteer Rd C1
Burneside Rd. A2
Bus Station B2
Buttery Well Rd C2
Canal Head North. B3
Captain French La C2
Caroline St. A2
Castle Hill. B3
Castle Howe B2
Castle Rd. A3/B3
Castle St. A3
Cedar Grove. A1
Council Offices. B2
County Council Offices. A2
Cricket Ground. A3
Cricket Ground. C2
Cross Lane. C2
Dockray Hall Industrial Estate. A3
Dowker's Lane. B2
East View. A3
Echo Barn Hill. C1
Elephant Yard B2
Fairfield Lane. A3
Finkle St. B2
Fire Station. A2
Fletcher Square. C3
Football Ground. A3
Fowling Lane. A3
Gillinggate. C2
Glebe Rd C2
Golf Course. B1
Gooseholme. B3
Gooseholme Bridge. B3
Green St. A1
Greengate. C2
Greengate Lane C1/C2
Greenside. C1
Greenwood. C1
Gulfs Rd. B2
High Tenterfell B1
Highgate. B2
Hillswood Avenue. C1
Horncop Lane. A2
Kendal ≥ A3
Kendal Business Park A3
Kendal Castle (Remains) ▲ B3
Kendal Fell. B1
Kendal Green. A1
Kendal Ski Ctr ✦ B1
Kendal Station ≥ A3
Kent Place. A3
Kirkbarrow. C2
Kirkland. C2
Library B2
Library Rd. B2
Little Aynam. B3
Little Wood. D1
Long Close C1
Longpool A3
Lound Rd. A3
Lound St. C2
Low Fellside. B2
Lowther St. B2
Magistrates Court A2
Maple Drive A1
Market Place B2
Maude St. B2
Miller Bridge. B2
Milnthorpe Rd C2
Mint St A3
Mintsfeet Rd. A3
Mintsfeet Rd North A3
New Rd. B2
Noble's Rest. B2
Parish Church ▲ B2
Park Side Rd. C3
Parkside Business Park C3
Parr St. C3
Queen's Rd A1
Riverside Walk. C2
Rydal Mount. C3
Sandes Avenue. A2
Sandgate C3
Sandylands Rd A3
Serpentine Rd. B1
Serpentine Wood. B1
Shap Rd. A3
South Rd. C2
Stainbank Rd. C1
Station Rd. A3
Stramongate B2
Stramongate Bridge B2
Stricklandgate A2/B2
Sunnyside. C2
Thorny Hills B3
Town Hall ▣ B2
Underbarrow Rd. B1

King's Lynn 185

Albert St A2
Albion St. A2
Alive St James' Swimming Pool A2
All Saints ▲ B2
All Saints St B2
Austin Fields. A2
Austin St. B2
Avenue Rd. B3
Bank Side B1
Beech Rd. C2
Birch Tree Close B3
Birchwood St A2
Blackfriars Rd B2
Blackfriars St. B2
Boal St. B1
Bridge St. B2
Broad St. B2
Broad Walk. C3
Burkitt St A2
Bus Station B2
Carmelite Terrace C2
Chapel St A2
Checker St. C2
Church St. B2
Clough Lane. A2
Coburg St C2
Coll of West Anglia. A3
Columbia Way A3
Corn Exchange ▣ B2
County Court Rd B2
Cresswell St A2
Custom House ▣ B1
East Coast Business Park. C3
Eastgate St A2
Edma St. A2
Exton's Rd. C2
Ferry Lane. B1
Ferry St. B1
Framingham's Almshouses ▣ C2
Friars St. C2
Friars Walk. C2
Gaywood Rd A3
George St. A2
Goodwin's Rd. C2
Green Quay Discovery Ctr ✦ B1
Greyfriars' Tower ✦ B2
Guanock Terrace C2
Guildhall ▣ B2
Hansa Rd. C3
Harding's Way C2
Hardwick Rd. C2
Hextable Rd. A2
High St. B2
Holcombe Avenue C3
Hospital Walk. C2
Information Ctr ✦ B1
John Kennedy Rd. A2
Kettlewell Lane. A2
King George V Ave. B3
King St. B1
King's Lynn Art Centre ▣ B1
King's Lynn Sta ≥ B2
Library B2
Littleport St A2
Loke Rd A2
London Rd C2
Lynn Museum ▣ B2
Magistrates Court B1
Majestic ■ B2
Market Lane. A2
Millfleet C2
Milton Avenue A3
Nar Valley Walk. C2
Nelson St. C2
New Conduit St B2
Norfolk St. A2
North Lynn Discovery Centre ✦ A3
North St. B2
Oldsunway A2
Ouse Avenue. C1
Page Stair Lane B1
Park Avenue B3
Police Station ▣ B2
Portland Place. B2
Portland St. B2
Purfleet B1
Queen St. B2
Raby Avenue. A3
Railway Rd. B2
Red Mount Chapel ▲ B3
Regent Way B2
River Walk. C3
Robert St. C2
Shopmobility B2
St Ann's St A2
St James St. B2
St James' St B2
St John's Walk B3
St Margaret's ▲ B1
St Nicholas St. A2
St Peter's Rd. B2
Sir Lewis St. A2
Smith Avenue. A2
South Everard St C2
South Gate ✦ C2
South Quay. B1
Southgate St. C2
Stonegate St. B2
Stories of Lynn ▣ B1
Surrey St. A2
Sydney St. C2
Tennyson Avenue. B2
Tennyson Rd. B2
The Walks Stadium (King's Lynn FC) C3
Tower St. B2
Town Hall. B1
Town Wall (Remains) ✦ B3
True's Yard Fisherfolk Museum ▣ A2
Valingers Rd. C2
Vancouver Avenue. C2
Vancouver Quarter B2
Waterloo St. B2
Wellesley St C2
Whitefriars Terrace C2
Windsor Rd. C2
Winfarthing St. C2
Wisbech Road C2
Wyatt St A2
York Rd. C3

Lancaster 185

Aberdeen Rd. C3
Aldcliffe Rd. C2
Alfred St. B3
Ambleside Rd. B3
Ambulance & Fire Station. B2
Ashfield Avenue. B1
Ashton Rd. C2
Assembly Rooms Emporium ▣ A2
Balmoral Rd. B3
Bath House ✦ A3
Bath St B3
Blades St. B1
BMI Lancaster (private) H C3
Borrowdale Rd. C3
Bowerham Rd. C3
Brewery Lane. B2
Bridge Lane B2
Brook St C1
Bulk Rd A3
Bulk St. B2
Bus Station B2
Cable St. B2
Canal Cruises & Waterbus ✦ C2
Carlisle Bridge A1
Carr House Lane. C1
Castle ▲ B1
Castle Park B1
Caton Rd A3
China St B2
City Museum ▣ B2
Clarence St. C2
Common Garden St B2
Coniston Rd C3
Cottage Museum ▣ B2
Council Offices. C2
Courts B2
Cromwell Rd. C1
Crown Court B1
Dale St. C3
Dallas Rd. B1/C1
Dalton Rd. B3
Dalton Square B2
Damside St. B2
De Vitre St. B3
De Red. A1
Denny Avenue A1
Derby Rd. A3
Dukes,The ▣ B2
Earl St A2
East Rd B3
Eastham St C3
Edward St B3
Fairfield Nature Reserve C1
Fairfield Rd. C1
Fenton St B2
Firbank Rd A3
Friend's Meeting House ▣ B2
Garnet St. B3
George St B2
Giant Axe Field B1
Grand ▣ B2
Grasmere Rd B3
Greaves Park C1
Greaves Rd C1
Green St A3
Green St A2
Gregson Ctr,The C3
Gregson Rd. C3
Greyhound Bridge A2
Greyhound Bridge Rd A2
High St B2
Hill Side B1
Hope St. C2
Hubert Place A2
Information Ctr ✦ B1
Kelsy St. B2
Kentmere Rd C3
Keswick Road. C3
King St B2
Kingsway A3
Kirkes Rd. C2
Lancaster City Football Club B1
Lancaster Royal Grammar School B1
Lancaster St B1
Langdale Rd C3
Ley Court C1
Library B2
Lincoln Rd. C1
Lindow St. C2
Lodge St B2
Long Marsh Lane B1
Lune St A2
Lune St A2
Lune Valley Ramble A3
Mainway A2
Maritime Mus ▣ A1
Marketgate B2
Market St. B2
Meadowside. C2
Meeting Ho Lane B1
Millennium Bridge. A2
Moor Lane. B2
Moorgate C3
Morecambe Rd. A1/A2
Nelson St B3
North Rd. A2
Orchard Lane. C1
Owen Rd. A2
Park Rd B3
Parliament St A3
Patterdale Rd. C3
Penny St. B2
Police Station ▣ C1
Portland St. C2
Post Office ▣ B2/B3
Primrose St. C3
Priory ▲ B1
Prospect St. C3

206 Leeds • Leicester • Lincoln • Liverpool • Llandudno • Llanelli

Quarry Rd . . . B3
Queen St . . . C2
Regent St . . . C2
Ridge Lane . . . A3
Ridge St . . . A3
Royal Lancaster Infirmary (A&E) . . . C2
Rydal Rd . . . B3
Ryelands Park . . . A1
St Georges Quay . . . A1
St John's . . . B2
St Leonard's Gate . . . B2
St Martin's Rd . . . C3
St Nicholas Arcades Shopping Centre . . . B2
St Oswald St . . . C3
St Peter's ✝ . . . B3
St Peter's Rd . . . B3
Salisbury Rd . . . B1
Scotch Quarry Urban Park . . . C3
Sibsey St . . . B1
Skerton Bridge . . . A2
South Rd . . . C2
Station Rd . . . B1
Stirling Rd . . . C3
Storey Avenue . . . B1
Storey, The . . . B2
Sunnyside Lane . . . C1
Sylvester St . . . C1
Tarnsyke Rd . . . A1
Thurnham St . . . C2
Town Hall . . . B2
Troutbeck Rd . . . B3
Ulleswater Rd . . . B3
Univ of Cumbria . . . C3
Vicarage Field . . . B1
Vue . . . B2
West Rd . . . B1
Westbourne Drive . . . C1
Westbourne Rd . . . B1
Westham St . . . C3
Wheatfield St . . . B1
White Cross Business Park . . . C2
Williamson Rd . . . B3
Willow Lane . . . B1
Windermere Rd . . . B3
Wingate-Saul Rd . . . B1
Wolseley St . . . B3
Woodville St . . . B3
Wyresdale Rd . . . C3

Leeds 185

Aire St . . . B3
Albion Place . . . B4
Albion St . . . B4
Albion Way . . . B1
Alma St . . . A6
Ambulance Station . . . B5
Arcades . . . B4
Armley Gyratory . . . C1
Armley Rd . . . B1
Armories Drive . . . C5
Back Burley Lodge Rd . . . A1
Back Hyde Terrace . . . A2
Back Row . . . C3
Bath Rd . . . C3
Beckett St . . . A6
Bedford St . . . B3
Belgrave St . . . A4
Belle Vue Rd . . . A2
Benson St . . . A5
Black Bull St . . . C5
Blenheim Walk . . . A3
Boar Lane . . . B4
Bond St . . . B4
Bow St . . . C5
Bowman Lane . . . C4
Brewery ✦ . . . C4
Brewery Wharf . . . C5
Bridge St . . . A5/B5
Briggate . . . B4
Bruce Gardens . . . C1
Burley Rd . . . A1
Burley St . . . B1
Burmantofs St . . . B6
Bus & Coach Sta . . . B5
Butterly St . . . C4
Butts Crescent . . . B4
Byron St . . . A5
Call Lane . . . B4
Calls, The . . . B5
Calverley St . . . A3/B3
Canal St . . . B1
Canal Wharf . . . C3
Carlisle Rd . . . C5
Cavendish Rd . . . A1
Cavendish St . . . A2
Chadwick St . . . C5
Cherry Place . . . A6
Cherry Row . . . A5
City Museum . . . A4
City Varieties Music Hall . . . B4
City Square . . . B3
Civic Hall . . . A3
Clarence Road . . . C5
Clarendon Rd . . . A2
Clarendon Way . . . A3
Clark Lane . . . C6
Clay Pit Lane . . . A4
Cloberry St . . . A2
Close, The . . . B6
Clyde Approach . . . C1
Clyde Gardens . . . C1
Coleman St . . . C2
Commercial St . . . B4
Concord St . . . A5
Cookridge St . . . A4
Copley Hill . . . C1
Core, The . . . B4
Corn Exchange . . . B4
Cromer Terrace . . . A2
Cromwell St . . . A5
Cross Catherine St . . . B6
Cross Green Lane . . . C6
Cross Stamford St . . . A5
Crown & County Courts . . . A3
Crown Point Bridge . . . C5
Crown Point Rd . . . C4
Crown Point Shopping Park . . . C4
David St . . . C3
Dent St . . . C6
Derwent Place . . . C3
Dial St . . . C6
Dock St . . . C4
Dolly Lane . . . A6
Domestic St . . . C2
Drive, The . . . B6
Duke St . . . B5
Duncan St . . . B4
Dyer St . . . B5
East Field St . . . B6
East Parade . . . B3
East St . . . C5
Eastgate . . . B5
Easy Rd . . . C6
Edward St . . . B4
Ellerby Lane . . . C6
Ellerby Rd . . . C6
Emmerdale Studio Experience ✦ . . . A1
Fenton St . . . A3
Fire Station . . . B2
First Direct Arena . . . A4
Fish St . . . B4
Flax Place . . . B5
Garth, The . . . B5
Gelderd Rd . . . C1
George St . . . B4
Globe Rd . . . C2
Gower St . . . A5
Grafton St . . . A4
Grand Theatre . . . B4
Granville Rd . . . A6
Great George St . . . A3
Great Wilson St . . . C4
Greek St . . . B3
Green Lane . . . C1
Hanover Avenue . . . A2
Hanover Lane . . . A2
Hanover Square . . . A2
Hanover Way . . . A2
Harewood St . . . B4
Harrison St . . . B4
Haslewood Close . . . B6
Haslewood Drive . . . B6
Headrow, The . . . B3/B4
High Court . . . B5
Holbeck Lane . . . C2
Holdforth Close . . . C1
Holdforth Gardens . . . B1
Holdforth Grove . . . C1
Holdforth Place . . . C1
Holy Trinity . . . B4
Hope Rd . . . A5
Hunslet Lane . . . C4
Hunslet Rd . . . C4
Hyde Terrace . . . A2
Infirmary St . . . B3
Information Ctr . . . B3
Ingram Row . . . C3
ITV Yorkshire . . . A1
Junction St . . . C4
Kelso Gardens . . . A2
Kelso Rd . . . A2
Kelso St . . . A2
Kendal Lane . . . A2
Kendell St . . . C4
Kidacre St . . . C4
King Edward St . . . B4
King St . . . B3
Kippax Place . . . C6
Kirkgate . . . B4
Kirkgate Market . . . B4
Kirkstall Rd . . . A1
Kitson St . . . C6
Knight's Way Bridge . . . C5
Lady Lane . . . B4
Lands Lane . . . B4
Lane, The . . . B5
Lavender Walk . . . B6
Leeds Art Gallery . . . B3
Leeds Beckett Univ . . . A3
Leeds Bridge . . . C4
Leeds Conservatoire . . . B5
Leeds Discovery Centre . . . C5
Leeds General Infirmary (A&E) . . . A3
Leeds Grand Mosque . . . A1
Leeds Minster . . . B5
Leeds Playhouse . . . B5
Leeds Station . . . B3
Library . . . B3/B4
Light, The . . . B4
Lincoln Green Rd . . . A6
Lincoln Rd . . . A6
Lindsey Gardens . . . A6
Lindsey Rd . . . A6
Lisbon St . . . B3
Little Queen St . . . B3
Long Close Lane . . . C6
Lord St . . . C2
Lovell Park . . . A4
Lovell Park Hill . . . A4
Lovell Park Rd . . . A4
Lower Brunswick St . . . A5
Mabgate . . . A5
Macauly St . . . A5
Magistrates Court . . . A3
Manor Rd . . . C3
Mark Lane . . . B4
Marlborough St . . . B2
Marsh Lane . . . B5
Marshall St . . . C3
Meadow Lane . . . C4
Meadow Rd . . . C4
Melbourne St . . . A5
Merrion Centre . . . A4
Merrion St . . . A4
Merrion Way . . . A4
Mill St . . . B5
Millennium Square . . . A3
Monk Bridge . . . C2
Mount Preston St . . . A2
Mushroom St . . . A5
Neville St . . . C4
New Briggate . . . A4/B4
New Market St . . . B4
New York Rd . . . A5
New York St . . . B5
Nile St . . . A5
Nippet Lane . . . A6
North St . . . A4
Northern Ballet . . . B5
Northern St . . . B3
Oak Rd . . . B1
Oxford Place . . . B3
Oxford Row . . . A3
Parade, The . . . B6
Park Cross St . . . B3
Park Lane . . . A2
Park Place . . . B3
Park Row . . . B4
Park Square . . . B3
Park Square East . . . B3
Park Square West . . . B3
Park St . . . B3
Police Station . . . B5
Pontefract Lane . . . B6
Portland Crescent . . . A3
Portland Way . . . A3
Post Office . . . B4/B5
Quarry House (NHS/DSS Headquarters) . . . B5
Quebec St . . . B3
Queen St . . . B3
Radio Aire . . . A1
Railway St . . . B5
Rectory St . . . A6
Regent St . . . A5
Richmond St . . . C5
Rigton Approach . . . B6
Rigton Drive . . . B6
Rillbank Lane . . . A1
Rosebank Rd . . . A1
Rose Bowl Conference Ctr . . . A3
Royal Armouries . . . C5
Russell St . . . B3
St Anne's Cathedral (RC) ✝ . . . A4
St Anne's St . . . B4
St James' Hosp . . . A6
St John's Rd . . . A2
St Johns Centre . . . B4
St Mary's St . . . B5
St Pauls St . . . B3
Saxton Lane . . . B5
Shakespeare Ave . . . A6
Shannon St . . . B6
Sheepscar St South . . . A5
Siddall St . . . C3
Skinner Lane . . . A5
South Parade . . . B3
Sovereign St . . . C4
Spence Lane . . . C2
Springfield Mount . . . A2
Springwell Court . . . C2
Springwell Rd . . . C2
Springwell St . . . C2
Stoney Rock Lane . . . A6
Studio Rd . . . A1
Sutton St . . . C2
Sweet St . . . C3
Sweet St West . . . C3
Swinegate . . . B4
Templar St . . . B5
Tetley, The . . . C4
Thoresby Place . . . A3
Torre Rd . . . A6
Town Hall . . . A3
Trinity Leeds . . . B4
Union Place . . . C3
Union St . . . B5
University of Leeds . . . A3
Upper Accommodation Rd . . . B6
Upper Basinghall St . . . B4
Vicar Lane . . . B4
Victoria Bridge . . . C4
Victoria Gate . . . B4
Victoria Quarter . . . B4
Victoria Rd . . . C4
Vue . . . B4
Wade Lane . . . A4
Washington St . . . A1
Water Lane . . . C3
Waterloo Rd . . . C4
Wellington Place . . . B2
Wellington Rd . . . B2/C1
Wellington St . . . B3
West St . . . B2
Westfield Rd . . . A1
Westgate . . . B3
Whitehall . . . C2
Whitehall Rd . . . B3/C2
Whitelock St . . . A5
Willis St . . . C6
Willow Approach . . . A1
Willow Avenue . . . A1
Willow Terrace Rd . . . A3
Wintoun St . . . A5
Woodhouse La . . . A3/A4
Woodsley Rd . . . A1
York Place . . . B3
York Rd . . . B6

Leicester 188

Abbey St . . . A2
All Saints' . . . A1
Aylestone Rd . . . C2
Bath Lane . . . A1
Bede Park . . . C1
Bedford St . . . A3
Bedford St South . . . A3
Belgrave Gate . . . A2
Belvoir St . . . B2
Braunstone Gate . . . B1
Burleys Way . . . A2
Burnmoor St . . . C2
Bus & Coach Station . . . A2
Canning St . . . A2
Carlton St . . . C2
Castle Motte ✦ . . . B1
Castle Gardens . . . B1
Cathedral ✝ . . . B2
Charles St . . . B3
Chatham St . . . B2
Christow St . . . A3
Church Gate . . . A2
City Hall . . . B3
Clank St . . . B2
Clock Tower ✦ . . . B2
Clyde St . . . A3
Colton St . . . B3
Conduit St . . . B3
Crafton St East . . . A3
Craven St . . . A1
Crown Courts . . . B3
Curve . . . B3
De Lux . . . A2
De Montfort Hall . . . C3
De Montfort St . . . C3
De Montfort Univ . . . C1
Deacon St . . . C2
Dover St . . . B3
Duns Lane . . . B1
Dunton St . . . A1
East St . . . B3
East Bond Street . . . A2
Eastern Boulevard . . . C1
Edmonton Rd . . . A3
Erskine St . . . A3
Filbert St . . . C1
Filbert St East . . . C2
Fire Station . . . C3
Fleet St . . . A3
Friar Lane . . . B2
Friday St . . . A2
Gateway St . . . C2
Gateway, The . . . C2
Glebe St . . . B3
Granby St . . . B3
Grange Lane . . . C2
Grasmere St . . . C1
Great Central St . . . A1
Great Hall . . . B2
Guildhall . . . B2
Guru Nanak Sikh Museum . . . B1
Halford St . . . B2
Havelock St . . . C2
Haymarket Shopping Centre . . . A2
High St . . . A2
Highcross Shopping Centre . . . A2
Highcross St . . . A1
HM Prison . . . C2
Horsefair St . . . B2
Humberstone Gate . . . B2
Humberstone Rd . . . A3
Infirmary St . . . C2
Information Ctr . . . B2
Jarrom St . . . C2
Jewry Wall . . . B1
Kamloops Crescent . . . A3
King Richard III Visitor Centre ✦ . . . B2
King St . . . B2
Lancaster Rd . . . C3
LCB Depot . . . B3
Lee St . . . A3
Leicester Royal Infirmary (A&E) . . . C2
Leicester Station . . . B3
Library . . . B2
London Rd . . . C3
Lower Brown St . . . B2
Magistrates' Court . . . B2
Manitoba Rd . . . A3
Mansfield St . . . A2
Market ✦ . . . B2
Market St . . . B2
Mill Lane . . . C2
Montreal Rd . . . A3
Narborough Rd North . . . B1
Nelson Mandela Pk . . . C2
New Park St . . . B1
New St . . . B2
New Walk . . . C3
New Walk Museum & Art Gallery . . . C3
Newarke Houses . . . B2
Newarke St . . . B2
Newarke, The . . . B1
Northgate St . . . A1
Orchard St . . . A2
Ottawa Rd . . . A3
Oxford St . . . C2
Phoenix Arts Ctr . . . B3
Police Station . . . A3
Post Office . . . B2
Prebend St . . . C3
Princess Rd East . . . C3
Princess Rd West . . . C3
Queen St . . . B3
Rally Community Park, The . . . A1
Regent College . . . C3
Regent Rd . . . C2/C3
Repton St . . . A1
Rutland St . . . B3
St Augustine Rd . . . B1
St Georges Retail Pk . . . B3
St George St . . . B3
St Georges Way . . . B3
St John St . . . A2
St Margaret's . . . A2
St Margaret's Way . . . A2
St Martins . . . B2
St Mary de Castro . . . B1
St Matthew's Way . . . A3
St Nicholas . . . B1
St Nicholas Circle . . . B1
Sanvey Gate . . . A2
Silver St . . . B2
Slater St . . . A1
Soar Lane . . . A1
South Albion St . . . B3
Southampton St . . . B3
Sue Townsend Theatre . . . B2
Swain St . . . B3
Swan St . . . A1
Tigers Way . . . C3
Tower St . . . C3
Town Hall . . . B2
Tudor Rd . . . B1
Univ of Leicester . . . C3
University Rd . . . C3
Upperton Rd . . . C1
Vaughan Way . . . A2
Walnut St . . . C2
Watling St . . . A2
Welford Rd . . . B2
Welford Rd (Leicester Tigers RC) . . . C2
Wellington St . . . B2
West St . . . C3
West Walk . . . C3
Western Boulevard . . . C1
Western Rd . . . C1
Wharf St North . . . A3
Wharf St South . . . A3
Y Theatre, The . . . B3
Yeoman St . . . B3
York Rd . . . B2

Lincoln 188

Alexandra Terrace . . . B1
Anchor St . . . C1
Arboretum . . . B3
Arboretum Avenue . . . B3
Avenue, The . . . B1
Baggholme Rd . . . B3
Bailgate . . . A2
Beaumont Fee . . . B1
BMI The Lincoln Hospital . . . A2
Brayford Way . . . C1
Brayford Wharf East . . . C1
Brayford Wharf North . . . B1
Bruce Rd . . . A2
Burton Rd . . . A1
Bus Station (City) . . . C2
Canwick Rd . . . C2
Cardinal's Hat ✦ . . . B2
Carline Rd . . . B1
Castle . . . B1
Castle St . . . A1
Cathedral ✝ . . . B2
Cathedral St . . . B2
Cecil St . . . A2
Chapel Lane . . . A2
Cheviot St . . . B3
Church Lane . . . A2
City Hall . . . B1
Clasketgate . . . B2
Clayton Sports Gd . . . A3
Coach Park . . . C2
Collection, The . . . B2
County Hospital (A&E) . . . B3
County Hall . . . B1
Courts . . . C1
Cross St . . . C2
Crown Courts . . . B1
Curle Avenue . . . A3
Danesgate . . . B2
Drill Hall . . . B2
Drury Lane . . . B1
East Bight . . . A2
East Gate . . . A2
Eastcliff Rd . . . B3
Eastgate . . . B2
Egerton Rd . . . A3
Ellis Windmill ✦ . . . A1
Engine Shed, The . . . C1
Exchequer Gate ✦ . . . B2
Firth Rd . . . C1
Flaxengate . . . B2
Florence St . . . B3
George St . . . C3
Good Lane . . . A2
Gray St . . . A1
Great Northern Terr . . . C3
Greetwell Rd . . . B3
Greetwellgate . . . B3
Grove, The . . . A3
Haffenden Rd . . . A2
High St . . . B2/C1
Hungate . . . B2
James St . . . A2
Jews House & Ct . . . B2
Kesteven St . . . C2
Langworthgate . . . A2
Lawn, The . . . B1
Lee Rd . . . A3
Library . . . B2
Lincoln Central Station . . . C2
Lincoln College . . . B2
Lincolnshire Life . . . A1
Lincoln Univ Technical Coll (UTC) . . . B2
Lindum Rd . . . B2
Lindum Sports Gd . . . A3
Lindum Terrace . . . B3
Liquorice Park . . . B1
Mainwaring Rd . . . A3
Manor Rd . . . A2
Market . . . C2
Massey Rd . . . A3
Medieval Bishop's Palace . . . B2
Mildmay St . . . A1
Mill Rd . . . A1
Millman Rd . . . B3
Minster Yard . . . B2
Monks Rd . . . B3
Montague St . . . B2
Mount St . . . A1
Nettleham Rd . . . A2
Newland . . . B1
Newport . . . A2
Newport Arch . . . A2
Newport Cemetery . . . A2
Northgate . . . A2
Odeon . . . C1
Orchard St . . . B1
Oxford St . . . C2
Park St . . . B1
Pelham Bridge . . . C2
Pelham St . . . C2
Portland St . . . C2
Post Office . . . A1/B2/B3
Potter Gate . . . B2
Priory Gate . . . B2
Queensway . . . A3
Rasen Lane . . . A1
Ropewalk . . . C1
Rosemary Lane . . . B2
St Anne's Rd . . . B3
St Benedict's . . . C1
St Giles Avenue . . . A3
St Mark's Shopping Centre . . . C1
St Marks St . . . C1
St Mary-le-Wigford . . . C1
St Mary's St . . . C2
St Nicholas St . . . A2
St Rumbold's St . . . B2
St Swithin's . . . B2
Saltergate . . . C1
Saxon St . . . A1
Sewell Rd . . . B3
Silver St . . . B2
Sincil St . . . C2
Spital St . . . A2
Spring Hill . . . B1
Stamp End . . . C3
Steep Hill . . . B2
Stonebow & Guildhall . . . C2
Stonefield Avenue . . . A2
Tentercroft St . . . C1
Theatre Royal . . . B2
Tritton Rd . . . C1
Tritton Retail Park . . . C1
Union Rd . . . B1
Univ of Lincoln . . . C1
Upper Lindum St . . . B3
Upper Long Leys Rd . . . A1
Usher . . . B2
Vere St . . . A2
Victoria St . . . B1
Victoria Terrace . . . B1
Vine St . . . B3
Wake St . . . A1
Waldeck St . . . A1
Waterside North . . . C2
Waterside Shopping Centre . . . C2
Waterside South . . . C2
West Parade . . . B1
Westgate . . . A2
Wigford Way . . . C1
Williamson St . . . A2
Wilson St . . . A1
Winn St . . . B3
Wragby Rd . . . A3
Yarborough Rd . . . A1

Liverpool 188

Abercromby Square . . . C5
Addison St . . . A3
Adelaide Rd . . . B6
Albany Rd . . . B6
Albert Edward Rd . . . B6
Angela St . . . C6
Anson St . . . B4
Argyle St . . . C3
Arrad St . . . C4
Ashton St . . . B5
Audley St . . . A4
Back Leeds St . . . A2
Basnett St . . . B3
Bath St . . . A1
Beacon, The ✦ . . . B3
Beatles Story, The . . . C2
Beckwith St . . . C3
Bedford Close . . . C5
Bedford St North . . . C5
Bedford St South . . . C5
Benson St . . . C4
Berry St . . . C4
Birkett St . . . A4
Bixteth St . . . B2
Blackburne Place . . . C4
Bluecoat . . . B3
Bold Place . . . C4
Bold St . . . C4
Bolton St . . . B3
Bridport St . . . B4
Bronte St . . . B4
Brook St . . . A1
Brownlow Hill . . . B4/B5
Brownlow St . . . B5
Brunswick Rd . . . A5
Brunswick St . . . B1
Bus Station . . . C2
Butler Crescent . . . A6
Byrom St . . . A3
Caledonia St . . . C4
Cambridge St . . . C5
Camden St . . . A4
Canada Boulevard . . . B1
Canning Dock . . . C2
Canterbury St . . . A4
Cardwell St . . . C6
Carver St . . . A4
Cases St . . . B3
Castle St . . . B2
Catherine St . . . C5
Cavern Club . . . B3
Central Library . . . A3
Chapel St . . . B2
Charlotte St . . . B3
Chatham Place . . . C6
Chatham St . . . C5
Cheapside . . . B2
Chavasse Park . . . C2
Chestnut St . . . C5
Christian St . . . A3
Church St . . . B3
Clarence St . . . B4
Clayton Square Shopping Centre . . . B3
Cobden St . . . A5
Cockspur St . . . A2
College St . . . C3
College St North . . . A5
College St South . . . A5
Colquitt St . . . C4
Comus St . . . A3
Concert St . . . C3
Connaught Rd . . . B6
Cook St . . . B2
Copperas Hill . . . B4
Cornwallis St . . . C3
Covent Garden . . . B2
Craven St . . . A4
Cropper St . . . B3
Crosshall St . . . B3
Crown St . . . B5/C6
Cumberland St . . . B2
Cunard Building . . . B1
Dale St . . . B2
Dansie St . . . B4
Daulby St . . . B5
Dawson St . . . B3
Dental Hospital . . . B5
Derby Square . . . B2
Drury Lane . . . B2
Duckinfield St . . . B4
Duke St . . . C3
Earle St . . . A2
East St . . . A2
Eaton St . . . A2
Edgar St . . . A3
Edge Lane . . . B6
Edinburgh Rd . . . A6
Edmund St . . . B2
Elizabeth St . . . B5
Elliot St . . . B3
Empire Theatre . . . B4
Empress Rd . . . B6
Epstein Theatre . . . B3
Epworth St . . . A5
Erskine St . . . A5
Everyman Theatre . . . C5
Exchange St East . . . B2
FACT . . . C4
Falkland St . . . A5
Falkner St . . . C5/C6
Farnworth St . . . A6
Fenwick St . . . B2
Fielding St . . . A6
Fire Station . . . A4
Fleet St . . . C3
Fraser St . . . A4
Freemasons Row . . . A2
Gardner Row . . . A3
Gascoyne St . . . A2
George St . . . B2
Gibraltar Road . . . A1
Gilbert St . . . C3
Gildart St . . . A4
Gill St . . . B4
Goree . . . B2
Gower St . . . C2
Gradwell St . . . C3
Great Crosshall St . . . A3
Great George St . . . C4
Great Howard St . . . A1
Great Newton St . . . B4
Greek St . . . B4
Green Lane . . . B4
Greenside . . . A5
Greetham St . . . C3
Gregson St . . . A5
Grenville St . . . C3
Grinfield St . . . C6
Grove St . . . C5
Guelph St . . . A6
Hackins Hey . . . B2
Haigh St . . . A4
Hall Lane . . . B6
Hanover St . . . B3
Harbord St . . . C6
Hardman St . . . C4
Harker St . . . A4
Hart St . . . B4
Hatton Garden . . . A2
Hawke St . . . B4
Helsby St . . . B6
Henry St . . . C3
Highfield St . . . A2
Highgate St . . . B6
Hilbre St . . . B4
Hope Place . . . C4
Hope St . . . B3/C4
Hope University . . . A5
Houghton St . . . B3
Hunter St . . . A3
Hutchinson St . . . A6
Information Ctr . . . B3
Institute for the Performing Arts . . . C4
International Slavery Museum . . . C2
Irvine St . . . B6
Irwell St . . . B2
Islington . . . A4
James St . . . B2
James St Station . . . B2
Jenkinson St . . . A4
John Moores Univ . . . A2/A3/A4/B4
Johnson St . . . A3
Jubilee Drive . . . B6
Kempston St . . . A4
Kensington . . . A6
Kensington Gardens . . . B6
Kensington St . . . A6
Kent St . . . C3
King Edward St . . . A1
Kinglake St . . . B6
Knight St . . . C4
Lace St . . . A3
Langsdale St . . . A4
Law Courts . . . C2
Leece St . . . C4
Leeds St . . . A2
Leopold Rd . . . B6
Lime St . . . B3
Lime St Station . . . B4
Liver St . . . C2
Liverpool Central Station . . . B3
Liverpool Cruise Terminal . . . B1
Liverpool Landing Stage . . . B1
Liverpool Institute for Performing Arts (LIPA) . . . C4
Liverpool ONE . . . C2
Liverpool Wheel, The ✦ . . . C2
Liverpool Women's Hospital . . . C6
London Rd . . . A4/B4
Lord Nelson St . . . B4
Lord St . . . B2
Lovat St . . . C6
Low Hill . . . A5
Low Wood St . . . A6
Lydia Ann St . . . C3
M&S Bank Arena ✦ . . . C2
Mansfield St . . . A4
Marmaduke St . . . B6
Marsden St . . . A6
Martensen St . . . B6
Marybone . . . A3
Maryland St . . . C4
Mason St . . . B6
Mathew St . . . B2
May St . . . B4
Melville Place . . . C6
Merseyside Maritime Museum . . . C2
Metquarter . . . B3
Metropolitan Cathedral (RC) ✝ . . . B5
Midghall St . . . A2
Molyneux Rd . . . A6
Moor Place . . . B4
Moorfields . . . B2
Moorfields Sta . . . B2
Moss St . . . A5
Mount Pleasant . . . B4/B5
Mount St . . . C4
Mount Vernon . . . B6
Mulberry St . . . C5
Municipal Buildings . . . B2
Museum of Liverpool . . . C2
Myrtle St . . . C5
Naylor St . . . A2
Nelson St . . . C4
New Islington . . . A4
New Quay . . . B1
Newington St . . . C3
North John St . . . B2
North St . . . A3
North View . . . B6
Norton St . . . A4
O2 Academy . . . B4
Oakes St . . . B5
Odeon . . . B4
Old Hall St . . . A1
Old Leeds St . . . A2
Oldham Place . . . C4
Oldham St . . . C4
Olive St . . . C6
Open Eye Gallery . . . C2
Oriel St . . . A2
Ormond St . . . B2
Orphan St . . . C6
Overbury St . . . C6
Overton St . . . B6
Oxford St . . . C5
Paisley St . . . A1
Pall Mall . . . A2
Paradise St . . . C3
Park Lane . . . C3
Parker St . . . B3
Parr St . . . C3
Peach St . . . B5
Pembroke Place . . . B4
Pembroke St . . . B5
Philharmonic Hall . . . C5
Phythian Park . . . A6
Pickop St . . . A2
Pilgrim St . . . C4
Pitt St . . . C3
Playhouse Theatre . . . B3
Pleasant St . . . B4
Police HQ . . . C2
Police Sta . . . A4/C6
Pomona St . . . B4
Port of Liverpool Building . . . B2
Post Office . . . A2/A4/A5/B3/B4
Pownall St . . . C2
Prescot St . . . A5
Princes Dock . . . A1
Princes Gardens . . . A2
Princes Jetty . . . A1
Princes Parade . . . B1
Princes St . . . B2
Pythian St . . . A6
Queen Sq Bus Sta . . . B3
Queensland St . . . C6
Queensway Tunnel (Docks exit) . . . B1
Queensway Tunnel (Entrance) . . . B3
Radio City . . . B2
Ranelagh St . . . B3
Redcross St . . . B2
Renfrew St . . . B6
Renshaw St . . . B4
Richmond Row . . . A4
Richmond St . . . B3
Rigby St . . . A2
Roberts St . . . A1
Rock St . . . B4
Rodney St . . . C4
Roe St . . . B3
Rokeby St . . . A4
Romilly St . . . A6
Roscoe Lane . . . C4
Roscoe St . . . C4
Rose Hill . . . A3
Royal Albert Dock . . . C2
Royal Court . . . B3
Royal Liver Building . . . B1
Royal Liverpool Hospital (A&E) . . . B5
Rumford Place . . . B2
Rumford St . . . B2
Russell St . . . B4
St Andrew St . . . B4
St Anne St . . . A4
St Georges Hall . . . B3
St John's Centre . . . B3
St John's Gardens . . . B3
St John's Lane . . . B3
St Joseph's Cres . . . A4
St Minishull St . . . B5
St Nicholas Place . . . B1
Salisbury St . . . A4
Salthouse Dock . . . C2
Salthouse Quay . . . C2
Sandon St . . . C5
Saxony Rd . . . B6
Schomberg St . . . A6
School Lane . . . B2
Seel St . . . C3
Seymour St . . . B4
Shaw St . . . A5
Shopmobility . . . C2
Sidney Place . . . C6
Sir Thomas St . . . B3
Skelhorne St . . . B4
Slater St . . . C3
Smithdown Lane . . . B6
Soho Square . . . A4
Soho St . . . A4
South John St . . . B2
Springfield . . . A4
Stafford St . . . A4
Standish St . . . A3
Stanley St . . . B2
Strand St . . . C2
Strand, The . . . B2
Suffolk St . . . C3
Sydney Jones Liby . . . C5
Tabley St . . . C3
Tarleton St . . . B3
Tate Liverpool Gallery . . . C2
Teck St . . . B6
Temple St . . . B2
Titanic Memorial ✦ . . . B1
Tithebarn St . . . B2
Town Hall . . . B2
Triskelion Wy . . . A1
Trowbridge St . . . B4
Trueman St . . . A3
Union St . . . B2
Unity Theatre . . . C4
University . . . C5
Univ of Liverpool . . . B5
Upper Baker St . . . A6
Upper Duke St . . . C4
Upper Frederick St . . . C3
Vauxhall Rd . . . A2
Vernon St . . . B2
Victoria Gallery & Museum . . . B5
Victoria St . . . B2
Vine St . . . C5
Wakefield St . . . A4
Walker Art Gallery . . . A3
Walker St . . . A6
Wapping . . . C2
Water St . . . B1/B2
Waterloo Rd . . . A1
Wavertree Rd . . . B6
West Derby Rd . . . A6
West Derby St . . . B5
Western Approaches War Museum . . . B2
Whitechapel . . . B3
Whitley Gardens . . . A5
William Brown St . . . B3
William Henry St . . . A4
William Jessop Way . . . A1
Williamson Square . . . B3
Williamson St . . . B3
Williamson's Tunnels Heritage Centre ✦ . . . C6
Wood St . . . B3
World Museum, Liverpool . . . A3
York St . . . C3

Llandudno 189

Abbey Place . . . B1
Abbey Rd . . . B1
Adelphi St . . . B3
Alexandra Rd . . . C2
Anglesey Rd . . . A1
Argyll Rd . . . B3
Arvon Avenue . . . A2
Atlee Close . . . C3
Augusta St . . . B3
Back Madoc St . . . B2
Bodafon St . . . B3
Bodhyfryd Rd . . . A2
Bodnant Crescent . . . C3
Bodnant Rd . . . C3
Bridge Rd . . . C2
Bryniau Rd . . . C1
Builder St . . . B3
Builder St West . . . C2
Cabin Lift Cable Car ✦ . . . A2
Camera Obscura ✦ . . . A3
Caroline Rd . . . B2
Chapel St . . . A2
Charlton St . . . B3
Church Crescent . . . C1
Church Walks . . . A2
Claremont Rd . . . B2
Clement Avenue . . . A2
Clifton Rd . . . B2
Clonmel St . . . B3
Coach Station . . . B3
Conway Rd . . . B3
Conwy Archive Service . . . B2
Council St West . . . C3
Cricket and Recreation Gd . . . B2
Cwlach Rd . . . A2
Cwlach St . . . A1
Cwm Howard Lane . . . C3
Cwm Place . . . C3
Cwm Rd . . . C3
Dale Rd . . . C1
Deganwy Avenue . . . B2
Denness Place . . . C2
Dinas Rd . . . C2
Dolydd . . . B1
Erol Place . . . B2
Ewloe Drive . . . C3
Fairways . . . C2
Ffordd Dewi . . . C3
Ffordd Dulyn . . . C2
Ffordd Dwyfor . . . C3
Ffordd Elisabeth . . . C3
Ffordd Gwynedd . . . C3
Ffordd Las . . . C3
Ffordd Morfa . . . C3
Ffordd Penrhyn . . . C3
Ffordd Tudno . . . C3
Ffordd yr Orsedd . . . C3
Ffordd Ysbyty . . . C2
Fire & Ambulance Station . . . B3
Garage St . . . B3
George St . . . A2
Gloddaeth Avenue . . . B1
Gloddaeth St . . . B2
Gogarth Rd . . . B1
Great Orme Mines ✦ . . . A1
Great Ormes Rd . . . B1
Great Orme Tramway ✦ . . . A2
Happy Valley . . . A2
Happy Valley Rd . . . A3
Haulfre Gardens . . . A1
Herkomer Crescent . . . C1
Hill Terrace . . . A2
Home Front Museum . . . B2
Hospice . . . B1
Howard Rd . . . B3
Information Ctr . . . B2
Invalids' Walk . . . B1
James St . . . B2
Jubilee St . . . B3
King's Avenue . . . C2
King's Rd . . . C2
Knowles Rd . . . C2
Lees Rd . . . C2
Library . . . B2
Llandudno . . . A2
Llandudno (A&E) . . . C2
Llandudno Sta . . . B3
Llandudno Football Ground . . . C2
Llewelyn Avenue . . . A2
Lloyd St . . . B2
Lloyd St West . . . B1
Llwynon Rd . . . A1
Llys Maelgwn . . . C1
Madoc St . . . B2
Maelgwn Rd . . . B2
Maes-y-Cwm . . . C3
Maes-y-Orsedd . . . C3
Maesdu Bridge . . . C2
Maesdu Rd . . . C2/C3
Marian Place . . . C2
Marian Rd . . . C2
Marine Drive (Toll) . . . A3
Market St . . . A2
Miniature Golf Course . . . A1
Morfa Rd . . . B1
Mostyn . . . B3
Mostyn Broadway . . . B3
Mostyn St . . . B3
Mowbray Rd . . . C2
New St . . . A2
Norman Rd . . . B3
North Parade . . . A2
North Wales Golf Links . . . C1
Old Bank, The . . . A2
Old Rd . . . A2
Oval, The . . . B1
Oxford Rd . . . B3
Parade, The . . . B3
Parc Llandudno Retail Park . . . B3
Pier ✦ . . . A3
Plas Rd . . . A2
Police Station . . . B3
Post Office . . . A2/B3
Promenade . . . A3
Pyllau Rd . . . A1
Rectory Lane . . . A2
Rhuddlan Avenue . . . C3
St Andrew's Avenue . . . B2
St Andrew's Place . . . B2
St Beuno's Rd . . . A1
St David's Place . . . B2
St David's Rd . . . B2
St George's Place . . . A3
St Mary's Rd . . . B2
St Seriol's Rd . . . B2
Salisbury Pass . . . B1
Salisbury Rd . . . B2
Somerset St . . . B3
South Parade . . . A2
Stephen St . . . B3
Tabor Hill . . . A2
Town Hall . . . B2
Trinity Avenue . . . B1
Trinity Crescent . . . C1
Trinity Square . . . B3
Tudno St . . . A2
Ty-Coch Rd . . . A2
Ty-Gwyn Rd . . . A1/A2
Ty'n-y-Coed Rd . . . A1
Vaughan St . . . B3
Victoria Shopping Centre . . . B3
Victoria . . . A2
War Memorial ✦ . . . A2
Werny Wylan . . . C3
West Parade . . . B1
Whiston Pass . . . A2
Winllan Avenue . . . C2
Wyddfyd Rd . . . A2
York Rd . . . A2

Llanelli 189

Alban Rd . . . B3
Albert St . . . B1
Als St . . . B3
Amos St . . . C1
Andrew St . . . A3
Ann St . . . C2
Annesley St . . . B2
Arfryn Avenue . . . A3
Avenue Cilfig, The . . . A2
Belvedere Rd . . . A1
Bigyn Park Terrace . . . C3
Bigyn Rd . . . C3
Bond Avenue . . . C3
Brettenham St . . . A1
Bridge St . . . B2
Bryn Place . . . C1
Bryn Rd . . . C1
Bryn Terrace . . . C1
Bryn-More Rd . . . C1
Brynhyfryd Rd . . . A2
Brynmelyn Avenue . . . A3
Brynmor Rd . . . B1
Burry St . . . C1
Bus Station . . . B2
Caersalem Terrace . . . C2
Cambrian St . . . C1
Caswell St . . . C3
Cedric St . . . B3
Cemetery . . . A2
Chapman St . . . A1
Charles Terrace . . . C2
Church St . . . B2
Clos Caer Elms . . . A1
Clos Sant Paul . . . C2
Coastal Link Rd . . . B1/C1
Coldstream St . . . B2
Coleshill Terrace . . . B1
College Hill . . . B3
College Square . . . B3
Copperworks Rd . . . C2
Coronation Rd . . . C3
Corporation Ave . . . A3
Council Offices . . . B2
Court . . . B2
Cowell St . . . B2
Cradock St . . . C2
Craig Avenue . . . C3
Cricket Ground . . . A1
Derwent St . . . A1
Dillwyn St . . . C2
Druce St . . . C1
Eastgate Leisure Complex ✦ . . . B2
Elizabeth St . . . B2
Emma St . . . C2
Erw Rd . . . B1
Felinfoel Rd . . . A2
Fire Station . . . A3
Firth Rd . . . C3
Fron Terrace . . . C3
Furnace United Rugby Football Ground . . . A1
Gelli-On . . . B2
George St . . . C2
Gilbert Crescent . . . A2
Gilbert Rd . . . A2
Glanmor Rd . . . C2
Glanmor Terrace . . . C2
Glasfryn Terrace . . . A3
Glenalla Rd . . . B3
Glevering St . . . B3
Goring Rd . . . A2
Gorsedd Circle . . . A2
Grant St . . . C3
Graveyard . . . C2
Great Western Cl . . . C2
Greenway St . . . B1
Hall St . . . B2
Harries Avenue . . . A2
Hedley Terrace . . . A2
Heol Elli . . . B3
Heol Goffa . . . A3
Heol Nant-y-Felin . . . A3
Heol Siloh . . . B2
Hick St . . . C2
High St . . . C1
Indoor Bowls Ctr . . . B1
Inkerman St . . . B2
Island Place . . . B2
James St . . . B3
John St . . . B2
King George Ave . . . B3
Lake View Close . . . A2
Lakefield Place . . . C1
Lakefield Rd . . . C1
Langland Rd . . . C3
Leisure Centre . . . B1
Library . . . B2
Llanelli House . . . B2
Llanelli Parish Church . . . B2
Llanelli Station . . . C2
Llewellyn St . . . C2
Lliedi Crescent . . . A3
Lloyd St . . . B2
Llys Alys . . . B3
Llys Fran . . . A3
Llysnewedd . . . C1
Long Row . . . A3
Maes Gors . . . C2
Maesyrhaf . . . A3
Mansel St . . . C3
Marblehall Rd . . . B3
Marborough Rd . . . A2
Margam St . . . C3
Marged St . . . C2
Marine St . . . C1
Mariners, The . . . C1
Market . . . B2
Market St . . . B2
Marsh St . . . C2
Martin Rd . . . C3
Miles St . . . A1
Mill Lane . . . A3/B2
Mincing Lane . . . B2
Murray St . . . B2
Myn y Mor . . . B1
Nathan St . . . C1
Nelson Terrace . . . C1
Nevill St . . . C2
New Dock Rd . . . C2
New Rd . . . A1
New Zealand St . . . A1
Odeon . . . B2
Old Lodge . . . C2
Old Rd . . . A2
Paddock St . . . C2
Palace Avenue . . . B3
Parc Howard . . . A2
Parc Howard Museum & Art Gallery . . . A2
Park Crescent . . . B1
Park St . . . B2
Parkview Terrace . . . B1
Pemberton St . . . C2

Pembrey Rd A1
Peoples Park B1
Police Station ▣ B2
Post Office ✉ B2/C2
Pottery Place B3
Pottery St B3
Princess St B1
Prospect Place A2
Pryce St A1
Queen Mary's Walk C3
Queen Victoria Rd C1
Raby St B1
Railway Terrace C2
Ralph St B2
Ralph Terrace C1
Regalia Terrace B3
Rhydyrafon A3
Richard St B2
Robinson St B2
Roland Avenue A1
Russell St C3
St David's Close C1
St Elli Shopping Ctr B2
St Margaret's Drive A1
Spowart Avenue A1
Station Rd B2/C2
Stepney Place B2
Stepney St B2
Stewart St A1
Stradey Park Ave A1
Sunny Hill A2
Superstore A2
Swansea Rd A3
Talbot St C3
Temple St B3
Thomas St A2
Tinopolos TV Studios ✦ B2
Toft Place A3
Town Hall B2
Traeth Ffordd C1
Trinity Rd C3
Trinity Terrace C2
Tunnel Rd B3
Tyisha Rd C3
Union Blgs A2
Upper Robinson St B2
Vauxhall Rd B2
Walter's Rd B3
Waun Lanyrafon B2
Waun Rd A3
Wern Rd B3
West End A2
Y Bwthyn C3
Zion Row B3

London 186

Abbey Orchard St E3
Abchurch Lane D6
Abingdon St E4
Achilles Way D2
Acton St B4
Addington St E4
Air St D3
Albany St B2
Albemarle St D3
Albert Embankment F4
Aldenham St A3
Aldersgate St C6
Aldford St D2
Aldgate ⊖ C7
Aldgate High St C7
Aldwych C4
Allsop Place B1
Amwell St B5
Angel ⊖ A5
Appold St C7
Argyle Square B4
Argyle St B4
Argyll St C3
Arnold Circus B7
Artillery Lane C7
Artillery Row E3
Association of Photographers Gallery 🖼 B6
Baker St ⊖ B1
Baker St B1
Baldwin's Gardens C5
Baltic St B6
Bank ⊖ C6
Bank Museum 🏛 C6
Bank of England C6
Bankside D6
Bankside Gallery 🖼 D5
Banner St B6
Barbican ⇌⊖ C6
Barbican Centre for Arts, The C6
Barbican Gallery 🖼 C6
Basil St E1
Bastwick St B6
Bateman's Row B7
Bath St B6
Bayley St C3
Baylis Rd E5
Beak St D3
Bedford Row C4
Bedford Square C3
Bedford St D4
Bedford Way B3
Beech St C6
Belgrave Place E2
Belgrave Square E2
Bell Lane C7
Belvedere Rd E4
Berkeley Square D2
Berkeley St D2
Bernard St B4
Berners Place C3
Berners St C3
Berwick St C3
Bethnal Green Rd B7
Bevenden St B6
Bevis Marks C7
BFI (British Film Institute) 🎥 D4
BFI London IMAX Cinema 🎥 D5
Bidborough St B4
Binney St C2
Birdcage Walk E3
Bishopsgate C7
Blackfriars ⇌⊖ D5
Blackfriars Bridge D5
Blackfriars Passage D5
Blackfriars Rd E5
Blandford St C1
Blomfield St C6
Bloomsbury St C3
Bloomsbury Way C4
Bolton St D2
Bond St ⊖ C2
Borough High St E6
Boswell St C4
Bow St C4
Bowling Green La B5
Brad St D5
Bressenden Place E3
Brewer St D3
Brick St D2
Bridge St E4
Britannia Walk B6
British Film Institute (BFI) 🎥 D4
British Library ⌂ B3
British Museum 🏛 C4
Britton St B5
Broad Sanctuary E3
Broadway E3
Brook Drive F5
Brook St D2
Brunswick Place B6
Brunswick Shopping Centre, The B4
Brunswick Square B4
Brushfield St C7
Bruton St D2
Bryanston St C1
BT Centre C6
Buckingham Gate E3
Buckingham Palace 🏰 E3
Buckingham Palace Rd F2
Bunhill Row B6
Byward St D7
Cabinet War Rooms & Churchill Mus 🏛 E3
Cadogan Lane E2
Cadogan Place E1
Cadogan Square F1
Caledonian Rd A4
Calshot St A4
Calthorpe St B4
Calvert Avenue B7
Cambridge Circus C3
Camomile St C7
Cannon St D6
Cannon St ⇌⊖ D6
Capel Manor Coll B2
Carey St C4
Carlisle Lane E4
Carlisle Place E3
Carlton Ho Terrace D3
Carmelite St D5
Carnaby St C3
Carter Lane C5
Carthusian St C6
Cartwright Gardens B4
Castle Baynard St D5
Cavendish Place C2
Cavendish Square C2
Caxton Hall E3
Caxton St E3
Central St B6
Chalton St B3
Chancery Lane ⊖ C5
Chapel St E2
Charing Cross ⇌⊖ D4
Charing Cross Rd C3
Charles Dickens Museum, The B4
Charles II St D3
Charles Square B6
Charles St D2
Charlotte Rd B7
Charlotte St C3
Chart St B6
Charterhouse Sq C5
Charterhouse St C5
Cheapside C6
Chenies St C3
Chesham St E2
Chester Square F2
Chesterfield Hill D2
Chiltern St C2
Chiswell St C6
City Garden Row A5
City Rd B6
City Thameslink ⇌ C5
City University, The B5
Claremont Square A5
Clarges St D2
Clerkenwell Close B5
Clerkenwell Green B5
Clerkenwell Rd B5
Cleveland St C3
Clifford St D3
Clink Prison Mus 🏛 D6
Clock Museum 🏛 C6
Club Row B7
Cockspur St D3
Coleman St C6
Columbia Rd B7
Commercial St C7
Compton St B5
Conduit St D2
Constitution Hill E2
Copperfield St E5
Coptic St C4
Cornhill C6
Cornwall Rd D5
Coronet St B7
Courtauld Gallery 🖼 D4
Covent Garden ⊖ D4
Covent Garden ✦ D4
Cowcross St C5
Cowper St B6
Cranbourn St D3
Craven St D4
Crawford St C1
Creechurch Lane C7
Cremer St A7
Cromer St B4
Cumberland Gate D1
Cumberland Terr A2
Curtain Rd B7
Curzon St D2
Cut, The E5
D'arblay St C3
Davies St C2
Dean St C3
Deluxe Gallery 🖼 B7
Denmark St C3
Dering St C2
Devonshire St C2
Diana, Princess of Wales Meml Walk E3
Dingley Rd B6
Dorset St C1
Doughty St B4
Dover St D2
Downing St E4
Druid St E7
Drummond St B3
Drury Lane C4
Drysdale St B7
Duchess St C2
Dufferin St B6
Duke of Wellington Place E2
Duke St C2
Duke St D3
Duke St Hill D6
Duke's Place C7
Duncannon St D4
East Rd B6
Eastcastle St C3
Eastcheap D7
Eastman Dental Hospital Ⓗ B4
Eaton Place E2
Eaton Square E2
Eccleston St E2
Edgware Rd C1
Eldon St C6
Embankment ⊖ D4
Endell St C4
Endsleigh Place B3
Euston ⇌⊖ B3
Euston Rd B3
Euston Square ⊖ B3
Evelina Children's Hospital E4
Eversholt St A3
Exmouth Market B5
Fann St B6
Farringdon ⇌⊖ C5
Farringdon Rd C5
Farringdon St C5
Featherstone St B6
Fenchurch St D7
Fenchurch St ⇌ D7
Fetter Lane C5
Finsbury Circus C6
Finsbury Pavement C6
Finsbury Square B6
Fitzalan St F5
Fitzmaurice Place D2
Fleet St C5
Floral St D4
Florence Nightingale Museum 🏛 E4
Folgate St C7
Foot Hospital Ⓗ B3
Fore St C6
Foster Lane C6
Foundling Museum, The 🏛 B4
Francis St F3
Frazier St E5
Freemason's Hall C4
Friday St C6
Gainsford St E7
Garden Row E5
Gee St B6
George St C1
Gerrard St D3
Giltspur St C5
Glasshouse St D3
Gloucester Place C1
Golden Hinde ⛵ D6
Golden Lane B6
Golden Square D3
Goodge St ⊖ C3
Goodge St C3
Gordon Square B3
Goswell Rd B5
Gough St B4
Goulston St C7
Gower St B3
Gracechurch St D6
Grafton Way B3
Gray's Inn Rd B4
Great College St E4
Great Cumberland Place C1
Great Eastern St B7
Great Guildford St D6
Great Marlborough St C3
Great Ormond St B4
Great Ormond St Children's Hosp Ⓗ B4
Great Percy St B4
Great Peter St E3
Great Portland St ⊖ B2
Great Portland St C2
Great Queen St C4
Great Russell St C3
Great Scotland Yard D4
Great Smith St E3
Great Suffolk St D5
Great Titchfield St C3
Great Tower St D7
Great Windmill St D3
Greek St C3
Green Park ⊖ D3
Green St D2
Greencoat Place F3
Gresham St C6
Greville St B4/C5
Greycoat Hosp Sch E3
Greycoat Place E3
Grosvenor Crescent E2
Grosvenor Gardens E2
Grosvenor Place E2
Grosvenor Square D2
Grosvenor St D2
Guards Museum and Chapel 🏛 E3
Guildhall Art Gallery 🖼 C6
Guilford St B4
Guy's Hospital Ⓗ D6
Haberdasher St B6
Hackney Rd B7
Half Moon St D2
Halkin St E2
Hall St B5
Hallam St C2
Hampstead Rd B3
Hanover Square C2
Hans Crescent E1
Hanway St C3
Hardwick St B5
Harley St C2
Harrison St B4
Hastings St B4
Hatfields D5
Hay's Galleria D7
Hay's Mews D2
Hayles St F5
Haymarket D3
Hayward Gallery 🖼 D4
Helmet Row B6
Herbrand St B4
Hercules Rd E4
Hertford St D2
High Holborn C4
Hill St D2
HMS Belfast ⛵ D7
Hobart Place E2
Holborn ⊖ C4
Holborn C5
Holborn Viaduct C5
Holland St D5
Holmes Museum 🏛 B1
Holywell Lane B7
Horse Guards' Rd D3
Houndsditch C7
Houses of Parliament ⌂ E4
Howland St C3
Hoxton Square B7
Hoxton St B7
Hunter St B4
Hunterian Mus 🏛 C4
Hyde Park D1
Hyde Park Cnr ⊖ E2
Imperial War Museum 🏛 E5
Inner Circle B2
Ironmonger Row B6
James St C2
James St D4
Jermyn St D3
Jockey's Fields C4
John Carpenter St D5
John St B4
Judd St B4
Kennington Rd E5
King Charles St E4
King St D3
King St D4
King William St C6
King's Coll London D5
King's Cross ⇌ A4
King's Cross Rd B4
King's Cross St Pancras ⊖ A4
King's Rd E2
Kingley St C3
Kingsland Rd B7
Kingsway C4
Kinnerton St E2
Knightsbridge ⊖ E1
Lamb St C7
Lamb's Conduit St C4
Lambeth Bridge F4
Lambeth High St F4
Lambeth North ⊖ E5
Lambeth Palace 🏰 E4
Lambeth Palace Rd E4
Lambeth Rd E5
Lambeth Walk F4
Lancaster Place D4
Langham Place C2
Leadenhall St C7
Leake St E4
Leather Lane C5
Leicester Sq ⊖ D3
Leicester St D3
Leonard St B6
Lever St B6
Lexington St D3
Lidlington Place A3
Lime St D7
Lincoln's Inn Fields C4
Lindsey St C5
Lisle St D3
Liverpool St C7
Liverpool St ⇌⊖ C7
Lloyd Baker St B5
Lloyd Square B5
Lombard St C6
London Aquarium 🐟 E4
London Bridge ⇌⊖ D6
London Bridge Hospital Ⓗ D6
London City Hall ⌂ D7
London Dungeon, The 🏛 E4
London Guildhall University C6
London Rd E5
London Transport Museum 🏛 D4
London Wall C6
London Eye ✦ E4
Long Acre D4
Long Lane C5
Longford St B2
Lower Belgrave St E2
Lower Grosvenor Pl E2
Lower Marsh E5
Lower Thames St D6
Lowndes St E2
Ludgate Circus C5
Ludgate Hill C5
Luxborough St C2
Lyall St E2
Macclesfield Rd B6
Madame Tussaud's ✦ B2
Maddox St D2
Malet St C3
Mall, The E3
Manchester Square C2
Manchester St C2
Mandeville Place C2
Mansell St D7
Mansion House ⌂ C6
Mansion House ⊖ D6
Maple St C3
Marble Arch ⊖ C1
Marble Arch D1
Marchmont St B4
Margaret St C3
Margery St B5
Mark Lane D7
Marlborough Rd D3
Marshall St C3
Marsham St E3
Marylebone High St C2
Marylebone Lane C2
Marylebone Rd B2
Marylebone St C2
Mecklenburgh Sq B4
Middle Temple La C5
Middlesex St (Petticoat Lane) C7
Midland Rd A3
Minories C7
Monck St E3
Monmouth St C4
Montagu Place C1
Montagu Square C1
Montagu St C4
Montague Place C3
Monument ⊖ D6
Monument St D6
Monument, The ✦ D6
Moor Lane C6
Moorfields C6
Moorfields Eye Hospital Ⓗ B6
Moorgate C6
Moorgate ⇌⊖ C6
Moreland St B5
Morley St E5
Mortimer St C3
Mount Pleasant B5
Mount St D2
Murray Grove A6
Museum of Garden History 🏛 E4
Museum St C4
Myddelton Square B5
Myddelton St B5
National Gallery 🖼 D3
National Hospital Ⓗ B4
National Portrait Gallery 🖼 D3
Neal St C4
Nelson's Column ✦ D4
New Bond St C2/D2
New Bridge St C5
New Cavendish St C2
New Change C6
New Fetter Lane C5
New Inn Yard B7
New North Rd A6
New Oxford St C3
New Scotland Yard E3
New Square C4
Newgate St C5
Newton St C4
Nile St B6
Noble St C6
Noel St C3
North Audley St D2
North Crescent C3
North Row D2
Northampton Sq B5
Northington St B4
Northumberland Avenue D4
Norton Folgate C7
Nottingham Place C2
Obstetric Hosp Ⓗ B3
Old Bailey C5
Old Broad St C6
Old Compton St C3
Old County Hall E4
Old Gloucester St C4
Old King Edward St C6
Old Nichol St B7
Old Paradise St F4
Old Spitalfields Mkt C7
Old St B6
Old St ⇌⊖ B6
Old Vic 🎭 E5
Open Air Theatre 🎭 B2
Operating Theatre Museum 🏛 D6
Orange St D3
Orchard St C2
Ossulston St A3
Outer Circle B1
Oxford Circus ⊖ C3
Oxford St C2/C3
Paddington St C2
Palace St E3
Pall Mall D3
Pall Mall East D3
Pancras Rd A4
Panton St D3
Paris Garden D5
Park Crescent B2
Park Lane D2
Park Rd B1
Park St D2
Park St D6
Parker St C4
Parliament Square E4
Parliament St E4
Paternoster Square C5
Paul St B6
Pear Tree St B5
Penton Rise B4
Penton St A5
Pentonville Rd A4/A5
Percival St B5
Petticoat Lane (Middlesex St) C7
Petty France E3
Phoenix Place B4
Phoenix Rd A3
Photo Gallery 🖼 D3
Piccadilly D2
Piccadilly Circus ⊖ D3
Pitfield St B7
Pollock's Toy Museum 🏛 C3
Polygon Rd A3
Pont St E1
Portland Place C2
Portman Mews C2
Portman Square C2
Portman St C1
Portugal St C4
Postal Mus, The 🏛 B4
Poultry C6
Primrose St C7
Princes St C6
Procter St C4
Provost St B6
Quaker St B7
Queen Anne St C2
Queen Elizabeth Hall 🎭 D4
Queen Square B4
Queen St D6
Queen Street Place D6
Queen Victoria St D5
Queens Gallery 🖼 E3
Radnor St B6
Rathbone Place C3
Rawstorne St B5
Red Lion Square C4
Red Lion St C4
Redchurch St B7
Redcross Way D6
Regency St F3
Regent Square B4
Regent St C3
Regent's Park B2
Richmond Terrace E4
Ridgmount St C3
Rivington St B7
Robert St B2
Rochester Row F3
Ropemaker St C6
Rosebery Avenue B5
Roupell St D5
Royal Academy of Arts 🖼 D3
Royal Academy of Dramatic Art (RADA) B3
Royal Acad of Music B2
Royal Artillery Memorial ✦ E2
Royal College of Nursing C2
Royal College of Surgeons C4
Royal Festival Hall 🎭 D4
Royal London Hospital for Integrated Medicine C4
Royal National Theatre 🎭 D5
Royal National Throat, Nose and Ear Hospital Ⓗ B4
Royal Opera Ho 🎭 D4
Russell Square B3
Russell Square ⊖ B4
Sackville St D3
Sadlers Wells 🎭 B5
Saffron Hill C5
St Alban's St D3
St Andrew St C5
St Bartholomew's Hospital Ⓗ C5
St Botolph St C7
St Bride St C5
St George's Circus E5
St George's Rd E5
St Giles High St C3
St James's Palace 🏰 D3
St James's Park ⊖ E3
St James's St D3
St John St B5
St Margaret St E4
St Mark's Hosp Ⓗ B5
St Martin's Lane D4
St Martin's Le Grand C6
St Mary Axe C7
St Pancras International ⇌ A4
St Paul's ⊖ C6
St Paul's Cath ✝ C6
St Paul's Churchyard C5
St Peter's Hosp Ⓗ D4
St Thomas St D6
St Thomas' Hosp Ⓗ E4
Savile Row D3
Savoy Place D4
Savoy St D4
School of Hygiene & Tropical Medicine C3
Scrutton St B7
Sekforde St B5
Serpentine Rd D1
Seven Dials C4
Seward St B5
Seymour St C1
Shad Thames D7
Shaftesbury Ave D3
Shakespeare's Globe Theatre 🎭 D6
Shepherd Market D2
Sherwood St D3
Shoe Lane C5
Shoreditch High St B7
Shoreditch High St ⊖ B7
Shorts Gardens C4
Shrek's Adventure ✦ E4
Sidmouth St B4
Silk St C6
Sir John Soane's Museum 🏛 C4
Skinner St B5
Sloane St E1
Snow Hill C5
Soho Square C3
Somerset House ⌂ D4
South Audley St D2
South Carriage Dr E1
South Molton St C2
South Place C6
South St D2
Southampton Row C4
Southampton St D4
Southwark ⊖ D5
Southwark Bridge D6
Southwark Bridge Rd D6
Southwark Cath ✝ D6
Southwark St D6
Speakers' Corner D1
Spencer St B5
Spital Square C7
Stamford St D5
Stanhope St B3
Stephenson Way B3
Stock Exchange C5
Stoney St D6
Strand C5
Stratton St D2
Sumner St D5
Sutton's Way B6
Swanfield St B7
Swinton St B4
Tabernacle St B6
Tate Modern 🖼 D6
Tavistock Place B4
Tavistock Square B3
Tea & Coffee Museum 🏛 D6
Temple ⊖ D5
Temple Avenue D5
Temple Place D4
Terminus Place E2
Thayer St C2
Theobald's Rd C4
Thorney St F4
Threadneedle St C6
Throgmorton St C6
Tonbridge St B4
Tooley St D7
Torrington Place B3
Tothill St E3
Tottenham Court Rd B3
Tottenham Ct Rd ⊖ C3
Tottenham St C3
Tower Bridge ✦ D7
Tower Bridge App D7
Tower Bridge Rd E7
Tower Hill D7
Tower Hill ⊖ D7
Tower of London, The 🏰 D7
Toynbee St C7
Trafalgar Square D3
Trinity Square D7
Trocadero Centre D3
Tudor St D5
Turnmill St C5
Ufford St E5
Union St D5
Univ Coll Hosp Ⓗ B3
University College London (UCL) B3
Univ of London C3
Univ of Westminster C2
University St B3
Upper Belgrave St E2
Upper Berkeley St C1
Upper Brook St D2
Upper Grosvenor St D2
Upper Ground D5
Upper Montague St C1
Upper St Martin's Lane D4
Upper Thames St D6
Upper Wimpole St C2
Upper Woburn Pl B3
Vere St C2
Vernon Place C4
Vestry St B6
Victoria ⇌⊖ E2
Victoria Emb D4
Victoria Place Shopping Centre F2
Victoria St E3
Villiers St D4
Vincent Square F3
Vinopolis City of Wine 🏛 D6
Virginia Rd B7
Wakley St B5
Walbrook C6
Wallace Collection 🖼 C2
Wardour St C3/D3
Warner St B5
Warren St ⊖ B3
Warren St B3
Waterloo ⇌⊖ E5
Waterloo Bridge D4
Waterloo East ⇌ D5
Waterloo Rd E5
Watling St C6
Webber St E5
Welbeck St C2
Wellington Arch ✦ E2
Wellington Mus 🏛 E2
Wells St C3
Wenlock St A6
Wentworth St C7
West Smithfield C5
West Square E5
Westminster ⊖ E4
Westminster Abbey ✝ E4
Westminster Bridge E4
Westminster Bridge Rd E5
Westminster Cathedral (RC) ✝ E3
Westminster City Hall E3
Westminster Hall ⌂ E4
Weymouth St C2
Wharf Rd A6
Wharton St B4
Whitcomb St D3
White Cube 🖼 B7
White Lion Hill D5
White Lion St A5
Whitecross St B6
Whitefriars St C5
Whitehall D4
Whitehall Place D4
Wigmore Hall C2
Wigmore St C2
William IV St D4
Wilmington Square B5
Wilson St C6
Wilton Crescent E2
Wimpole St C2
Windmill Walk D5
Woburn Place B4
Woburn Square B3
Women's Hosp Ⓗ C3
Wood St C6
Woodbridge St B5
Wootton St D5
Wormwood St C7
Worship St B6
Wren St B4
Wynyatt St B5
Young Vic 🎭 E5
York Rd E4
York St C1
York Terrace East B2
York Terrace West B2
York Way A4

Luton 189

Adelaide St B1
Albert Rd C2
Alma St B2
Alton Rd C3
Anthony Gardens C1
Arthur St C2
Ashburnham Rd B1
Ashton Rd C2
Back St A2
Bailey St C3
Baker St C2
Biscot Rd A1
Bolton Rd B3
Boyle Close A2
Brantwood Rd B1
Bretts Mead C1
Bridge St B2
Brook St A1
Brunswick St A3
Burr St A3
Bury Park Rd A1
Bute St B2
Buxton Rd B2
Cambridge St C3
Cardiff Grove B1
Cardiff Rd B1
Cardigan St A2
Castle St B2/C2
Chapel St C2
Charles St A3
Chase St C2
Cheapside B2
Chequer St C3
Chiltern Rise C1
Church St B2/B3
Cinema 🎥 A2
Cobden St A3
College A3
Collingdon St A1
Concorde Avenue A3
Corncastle Rd C1
Cowper St C2
Crawley Green Rd B3
Crawley Rd A1
Crescent Rd A3
Crescent Rise A3
Cromwell Rd A1
Cross St A2
Cross Way, The C1
Crown Court B2
Cumberland St B2
Cutenhoe Rd C3
Dallow Rd B1
Downs Rd B1
Dudley St A2
Duke St A2
Dumfries St B1
Dunstable Place B2
Dunstable Rd A1/B1
Edward St A3
Elizabeth St C2
Essex Close C3
Farley Hill C1
Flowers Way B2
Francis St A1
Frederick St A2
Galaxy L Complex A2
George St B2
George St West B2
Gordon St B2
Grove Rd B1
Guildford St A2
Haddon Rd A3
Harcourt St C2
Hart Hill Drive A3
Hart Hill Lane A3
Hartley Rd A3
Hastings St B2
Hat Factory, The 🎭 B2
Hatters Way A1
Havelock Rd A2
Hibbert St C2
High Town Rd A3
Highbury Rd A1
Hightown Community Sports & Arts Ctr A3
Hillary Crescent C1
Hillborough Rd C1
Hitchin Rd A3
Holly St C2
Holm C1
Hucklesby Way A2
Hunts Close C1
Inkerman St A2
John St B2
Jubilee St A3
Kelvin Close C2
King St B2
Kingsland Rd C3
Larches, The A2
Latimer Rd C2
Lawn Gardens C2
Lea Rd B3
Library B2
Library Rd B2
Library Theatre 🎭 B2
Liverpool Rd B1
London Rd C2
Luton Station ⇌ A2
Lyndhurst Rd B1
Magistrates Court B2
Mall, The B2
Manchester St B2
Manor Rd B3
Manor Road Park B3
May St C3
Meyrick Avenue C1
Midland Rd A2
Mill St A2
Milton Rd B1
Moor St A1
Moor, The A1
Moorland Gardens A2
Moulton Rise A3
Napier Rd B1
New Bedford Rd A1
New Town St C2
North St A3
Old Bedford Rd A2
Old Orchard C2
Osbourne Rd C3
Oxen Rd A3
Park Square B2
Park St B3/C3
Park St West B2
Park Viaduct B3
Parkland Drive C1
Police Station ▣ B1
Pomfret Avenue A3
Pondwicks Rd B3
Post Office ✉ A1/B2
Power Court B3
Princess St B1
Red Rails C1
Regent St B2
Reginald St A2
Rothesay Rd B1
Russell Rise C1
Russell St C1
Ruthin Close C1
St Ann's Rd B3
St George's Square B2
St Mary's ⛪ B3
St Marys Rd B3
St Paul's Rd C2
St Saviour's Cres C1
Salisbury Rd B1
Seymour Avenue C3
Seymour Rd C3
Silver St B2
South Rd C2
Stanley St B1
Station Rd A2
Stockwood Cres C2
Stockwood Park C1
Strathmore Avenue C2
Stuart St B2
Studley Rd A1
Surrey St C3
Sutherland Place C1
Tavistock St C2
Taylor St A3
Telford Way A1
Tennyson Rd C2
Tenzing Grove C1
Thistle Rd B3
Town Hall B2
Townsley Close C2
UK Centre for Carnival Arts ✦ B3
Union St B2
University of Bedfordshire B3
Upper George St B2
Vicarage St B3
Villa Rd A2
Waldeck Rd A1
Wardown House Mus & Gallery 🏛🖼 A2
Wellington St B1/B2
Wenlock St A2
Whitby Rd A1
Whitehill Avenue C1
William St A2
Wilsden Avenue C1
Windmill Rd B3
Windsor St C2
Winsdon Rd B1
York St A3

Macclesfield 189

108 Steps B2
Abbey Rd A1
Alton Drive A3
Armett St C1
Athey St B1
Bank St C3
Barber St C3
Barton St C1
Beech Lane A2
Beswick St B1
Black Lane A2
Black Rd C3
Blakelow Gardens C3
Blakelow Rd C3
Bond St B1/C1
Bread St C1
Bridge St B1
Brock St A2
Brocklehurst Ave A3
Brook St B3
Brookfield Lane B3
Brough St West C1
Brown St C1
Brynton Rd A2
Buckley St C2
Bus Station B2
Buxton Rd B3
Byrons St C2
Canal St B3
Carlsbrook Avenue A3
Castle St B2
Catherine St B1
Cemetery A1
Chadwick Terrace A3
Chapel St C2
Charlotte St B2
Chester Rd B1
Chestergate B1
Christ Church ⛪ B1
Churchill Way B2
Coare St A1
Commercial Rd B2
Conway Crescent A3
Copper St C3
Cottage St B1
Crematorium A1
Crew Avenue A3
Crompton Rd B1/C1
Cross St C2
Crossall St C1
Cumberland St A1/B1
Dale St B3
Duke St B2
Eastgate B3
Exchange St B2
Fence Avenue B3
Fence Ave Ind Est A3
Flint St B3
Foden St A2
Fountain St B3
Garden St A3
Gas Rd B2
Gateway Gallery ✦ B1
George St B2
Glegg St B3
Golf Course C3
Goodall St B3
Grange Rd C1
Great King St B1
Green St B3
Grosvenor Shopping Centre B2
Gunco Lane C3
Half St C2
Hallefield Rd B3
Hatton St C1
Hawthorn Way A3
Heapy St C3
Henderson St B1
Heritage Centre 🏛 B2
Hibel Rd A2
High St C2
Hobson St C2
Hollins Rd C3
Hope St West B1
Horseshoe Drive B1
Hurdsfield Rd A3
Information Ctr ℹ B2
James St C2
Jodrell St B3
John St C2
Jordangate A2
King Edward St B2
King George's Field C3
King St B2
King's School A1
Knight Pool C3
Knight St C3
Lansdowne St A3
Library B2
Lime Grove B3
Loney St B1
Longacre St B1
Lord St C2
Lowe St C2
Lowerfield Rd A3
Lyon St B1
Macclesfield Coll C1
Macclesfield Sta ⇌ B2
MADS Little Theatre 🎭 C2
Marina B3
Market B2
Market Place B2
Masons Lane A3
Mill Lane C2
Mill Rd C2
Mill St B2
Moran Rd C1
New Hall St A2
Newton St C1
Nicholson Avenue A3
Nicholson Close A3
Northgate Avenue A2
Old Mill Lane C2
Paradise Mill 🏛 C2
Paradise St B1
Park Green B2
Park Lane C1
Park Rd C1
Park St C2
Park Vale Rd C1
Parr St B1
Peel St C2
Percyvale St A3
Peter St C1
Pickford St B2
Pierce St B1
Pinfold St B1
Pitt St C2
Police Station ▣ B2
Pool St C2
Poplar Rd C2
Post Office ✉ B2
Pownall St A2
Prestbury Rd A1/B1
Queen Victoria St B2
Queen's Avenue A3
Registrar B2
Retail Park C2
Richmond Hill C3
Riseley St B1
Roan Court B3
Roe St B2
Rowan Way A3
Ryle St C2
Ryle's Park Rd C1
St George's St C2
St Michael's ⛪ B2
Samuel St B2
Saville St C3
Shaw St B1
Silk Rd, The A2/B2
Slater St C1
Snow Hill C3
South Park C1
Spring Gardens A2
Statham St C2
Station St A2
Steeple St A3
Sunderland St B2
Superstore A1/A2/C2
Swettenham St B3
Thistleton Close C2
Thorp St B2
Town Hall B2
Townley St B2
Treacle Market ✦ B2
Turnock St C3
Union Rd B3
Union St B2
Victoria Park B3
Vincent St C2
Waters Green B2
Waterside C2
West Bond St B1
West Park A1
West Park Mus 🏛 A1
Westbrook Drive A1
Westminster Rd A1
Whalley Hayes B1
Windmill St C3
Withyfold Drive A2
York St B3

Maidstone 190

Albion Place B3
All Saints ⛪ B2
Allen St A3
Amphitheatre ✦ C2
Archbishop's Palace 🏰✿ B2
Bank St B2
Barker Rd C2
Barton Rd C3
Beaconsfield Rd C1
Bedford Place B1
Bishops Way B2
Bluett St A3
BMI The Somerfield Hospital Ⓗ A1
Bower Lane C1
Bower Mount Rd B1
Bower Place C1
Bower St B1
Boxley Rd A3
Brenchley Gardens A2
Brewer St A3
Broadway B2
Broadway Shopping Centre B2
Brunswick St C3
Buckland Hill A1
Buckland Rd B1
Bus Station B3
Campbell Rd C3
Church Rd C1
Church St B3
Cinema 🎥 C2
Clifford Way C1/C2
College Avenue C2
College Rd C2
Collis Meml Gdn C3
Cornwallis Rd B1
Corpus Christi Hall B2
Council Offices B3
County Hall A2
County Rd A3
Crompton Gardens C3
Crown & County Courts B2
Curzon Rd A3
Dixon Close C2
Douglas Rd C1
Earl St B2
Eccleston Rd C2
Fairmeadow B2
Fisher St A2
Florence Rd C1
Foley St A3
Foster St C3
Freedom Leisure Centre A1/A2
Fremlin Walk Shopping Centre B2
Gabriel's Hill B3
George St C3
Grecian St A3
Hardy St A3
Hart St C2
Hastings Rd C3
Hayle Rd C3
Hazlitt 🎭 B2
Heathorn St A3
Hedley St A3
High St B2
HM Prison A3
Holland Rd A3
Hope St A2
Information Ctr ℹ B2
James St A3
James Whatman Way A2
Jeffrey St A3
Kent County Council Offices A2
Kent History & Library Centre A2
King Edward Rd C2
King St B3
Kingsley Rd C3
Knightrider St B3
Launder Way C1
Lesley Place A1
Library B2
Little Buckland Ave A1
Lockmeadow Leisure Complex C2
London Rd B1
Lower Boxley Rd A2
Lower Fant Rd C1

Magistrates Court . B3
Maidstone Barracks
  Station . . A1
Maidstone East
  Station . . A2
Maidstone Museum &
  Bentlif Art Gall ₥ . A3
Maidstone Utd FC . A2
Maidstone West
  Station . . B2
Mall,The . . B3
Market . . C2
Market Buildings . B3
Marsham St . . B3
Medway St . . B3
Melville Rd . . C3
Mill St . . B3
Millennium Bridge. C2
Mote Rd . . B3
Muir Rd . . C3
OldTovil Rd . . C3
Palace Avenue . . B3
Perryfield St . . B3
Police Station ▨ . B3
Post Office ▣ . B2/C3
Priory Rd . . C3
Prospect Place. . C1
Pudding Lane . . B2
Queen Anne Rd. . B3
Queens Rd . . A1
Randall St . . A2
Rawdon Rd . . C3
Reginald Rd . . C1
Riverstage ♨ . . A1
Rock Place . . B1
Rocky Hill . . B1
Romney Place . . B3
Rose Yard . . B2
Rowland Close . . C1
Royal Engineers' Rd A2
Royal Star Arcade . B2
St Annes Court . . B1
St Faith's St. . . B2
St Luke's Rd . . A3
St Peter St. . . B2
St Peter's Bridge . B2
St Peter's Wharf
  Retail Park . . B2
St Philip's Avenue . C3
Salisbury Rd . . A3
Sandling Rd . . A2
Scott St . . A2
Scrubs Lane . . B3
Sheal's Crescent . C3
Somerfield Rd . . B1
Somerfield Lane . B1
Staceys St . . A2
Station Rd . . A2
Superstore . A1/B2/B3
Terrace Rd . . C3
Tonbridge Rd . . C1
Tovil Rd . . C2
Town Hall . . B2
Trinity Park . . B3
Tufton St . . B2
Tyrwhitt-Drake Mus
  of Carriages ₥ . B2
Union St . . B2
Upper Fant Rd . . C1
Upper Stone St . . B3
Victoria St. . . A1
Warwick Place . . B1
WatTyler Way . . B3
Waterloo St. . . C3
Waterloo Rd. . . A3
Week St. . . B2
Well Rd . . A3
Westree Rd . . C1
Wharf Rd. . . C1
Whatman Park . . A1
Wheeler St . . A2
Whitchurch Close . B1
Woodville Rd . . B1
Wyatt St . . B3
Wyke Manor Rd . B3

Manchester 190

Adair St. . . B6
Addington St . . A5
Adelphi St . . A1
Advent Way. . . B6
Albert Square. . C3
Albion St . . C3
Ancoats Grove . . B6
Ancoats Grove
  North. . . B6
Angela St . . C2
Aquatics Centre . . A4
Ardwick Gn North. C5
Ardwick Green Park C5
Ardwick Gn South . C5
Arlington St . . A2
Artillery St . . C2
Arundel St. . . C2
Atherton St. . . B2
Atkinson St. . . B3
Aytoun St . . B4
Back Piccadilly. . B5
Baird St. . . B5
Balloon St . . A4
Bank Place . . A1
Baring St. . . B5
Barrack St . . C1
Barrow St . . A1
Bendix St. . . A5
Bengal St . . A5
Berry St . . C5
Blackfriars Rd . . A3
Blackfriars St . . A3
Blantyre St . . C1
Bloom St . . B4
Blossom St . . A5
Boad St . . B5
Bombay St . . B4
Booth St . . A3
Booth St . . B3
Bootle St. . . B3
Brazennose St . . B3
Brewer St . . A5
Bridge St. . . B3
Bridgewater Hall . B3
Bridgewater Place. A4
Bridgewater St . . B3
Brook St . . C4
Brotherton Drive . A2
Brown St . . A3
Brown St . . B4
Brunswick St . . C6
Brydon Avenue . . B6
Buddhist Centre . . A4
Bury St . . A2
Bus & Coach Sta. . B4
Bus Station . . B4
Butler St . . A6
Buxton St . . C5
Byrom St . . B3
Cable St. . . A5
Cambridge St . C3/C4
Camp St . . B3
Canal St. . . B4
Cannon St . . A1
Cardroom Rd . . A6
Carruthers St . . A6
Castle St . . C2
Castlefield Arena . A3
Cateaton St . . A3
Cathedral † . . A3
Cathedral St . . A3
Cavendish St . . C3
Chapel St . . A1/A3
Chapeltown St . . B5
Charles St . . C4
Charlotte St . . B4
Chatham St . . C4
Chepstow St . . B3
Chester Rd . . C1/C2
Chester St. . . C4
Chetham's
  Sch of Music . . A3
China Lane . . B5
Chippenham Rd . . A6
Chorlton Rd . . C2
Chorlton St . . B4
Church St . . A2
Church St . . A5
City Park . . A4
City Rd East. . . C5
Civil Justice Centre B2
Cleminson St . . A2
Clowes St . . A3
College Land . . A3
Collier St . . B2
Commercial St . . C3
Conference Centre C4
Cooper St . . B4
Copperas St . . A4
Corn Exchange,The A4
Cornbrook ♥ . . C1
Cornell St . . A5
Corporation St . . A4
Cotter St . . C6
Cotton St . . A6
Cow Lane . . A1
Cross St . . B3
Crown Court . . B4
Crown St . . C2
Dalberg St . . C6
Dale St . . A4/B5
Dancehouse,The ♨ C4
Dantzic St . . A4
Dark Lane . . C6
Dawson St . . C2
Dean St . . A5
Deansgate . A3/B3/C2
Deansgate
  Castlefield ♥ . . C3
Deansgate Sta ⇌ . B3
Dolphin St. . . C6
Downing St . . C5
Ducie St . . B5
Duke Place . . B2
Duke St . . B2
Durling St . . C6
East Ordsall La . A2/B1
Edge St . . A4
Egerton St. . . C2
Ellesmere St . . C1
Everard St . . C1
Everyman ♨ . . B4
Every St. . . B6
Exchange Square ♥ A4
Factory,The ♨ . . B3
Fairfield St . . B5
Faulkner St. . . B4
Fennel St. . . A3
Fire Station. . . A5
Ford St . . A2
Ford St . . C6
Fountain St. . . B4
Frederick St . . A2
Gartside St . . B2
Gaythorne St . . A1
George Leigh St . . A5
George St . . B4
Gore St. . . A5
Goulden St . . A5
Granby Row . . B4
Gravel Lane . . A3
Great St. . . B6
Great Ancoats St . A5
Great Bridgewater
  St . . B3
Great George St . A1
Great Jackson St . C2
Great Marlborough
  St . . C4
Great Northern
  Leisure Complex. B3
Greengate . . A3
Grosvenor St. . . C5
Gun St . . A5
Hall St . . B3
Hampson St . . A1
Hanover St . . A4
Hanworth Close . C5
Hardman St . . B3
Harkness St . . C6
Harrison St . . B6
Hart St . . B4
Helmet St . . C6
Henry St . . A5
Heyrod St . . B6
High St . . A4
Higher Ardwick . . C5
Hilton St . . A4/A5
Holland St . . A6
HOME Entertainment
  Complex . . C3
Hood St . . A5
Hope St . . B1
Hope St . . A5
Houldsworth St . . A5
Hoyle St. . . C6
Hulme Hall Rd . . C1
Hulme St. . . A3
Hulme St. . . C3
Hyde Rd. . . C6
Islington Way . . A1
Jackson Crescent . C2
Jackson's Row . . B3
James St . . A1
Jenner Close . . C2
Jersey St . . A5
John Dalton St . . B3
John Ryland's
  Library ₥ . . B3
John St . . A2
Kennedy St . . B3
Kincardine Rd . . C5
King St . . A3
King St West . . B3
Law Courts . . B3
Laystall St . . B5
Lever St . . A5
Library . . A4
Linby St . . C2
Little Lever St . . A4
Liverpool Rd . . B1
Liverpool St . . B1
Lloyd St . . B3
Lockton Close . . C5
London Rd . . B5
Long Millgate . . A3
Longacre St . . B6
Loom St . . A5
Lower Byrom St . B2
Lower Mosley St . B3
Lower Moss Lane . C2
Lower Ormond St . C3
Loxford Lane. . . C4
Luna St . . A5
Major St . . B4
Mamucium ₥ . . B2
Manchester
  Arndale . . A4
Manchester
  Art Gallery ₥ . . B4
Manchester Central
  Convention
  Complex . . B3
Manchester
  Metropolitan Univ
  (MMU) . . B4/C4
Manchester Piccadilly
  Station ⇌ . . B5
Manchester
  Technology Ctr . . C4
Mancunian Way . . C3
Manor St . . C5
Marble St . . A4
Market St . . A4
Market St . . A5
Market St ♥ . . A4
Marsden St . . A3
Marshall St . . A5
Mayan Avenue . . A2
Medlock St . . C3
Middlewood St . . B1
Miller St . . A4
Minshull St . . B4
Mosley St . . A4
Mount St . . C2
Mulberry St . . B3
Murray St . . A5
Museum of Science &
  Industry (MOSI) ₥ B2
Nathan Drive . . A3
National Football
  Museum ₥ . . A3
Naval St . . A5
New Bailey St . . B2
New Elm Rd . . B2
New Islington . . A6
New Islington Sta ⇌ B6
New Quay St . . B2
New Union St . . A6
Newton St . . A5
Nicholas St . . B4
North Western St . C6
Oak St . . A4
Odeon ♨ . . A4/B3
Old Mill St . . A6
Oldfield Rd . . A1/C1
Oldham Rd . . A5
Oldham St . . A4
Opera House ♨ . B3
Ordsall Lane . . C1
Oxford Rd . . C4
Oxford Rd ⇌ . . C4
Oxford St . . B4
Paddock St . . C6
PalaceTheatre ♨ . B4
Pall Mall . . B4
Palmerston St . . B6
Parker St. . . B4
Peak St . . B5
Penfield Close . . C5
Peoples' History
  Museum ₥ . . B2
Peru St . . A1
Peter St. . . B3
Piccadilly . . B4
Piccadilly ♥ . . B5
Piccadilly
  Gardens ♥ . . B4
Piercy St . . A6
Poland St . . A6
Police Museum ₥ . A5
Police Station ▨ B3/B5
Pollard St . . B6
Port St. . . A5
Portland St . . B4
Portugal St East . B5
Post Office ▣
  A2/A4/A5/B3/B4/C4
Potato Wharf . . B2
Princess St . . B3/C4
Quay St . . A1
Quay St . . B2
Queen St . . B3
Radium St . . A5
Redhill St . . A5
Regent Retail Park . B1
Regent Rd . . B1
Rice St . . C3
Richmond St . . B4
River St . . C3
Roby St . . B5
Rodney St . . A6
Rosamond St . . A2
Royal Exchange ♨ . A4
Sackville St . . B4
St Andrew's St . . B6
St Ann St . . B3
St Ann's ♣ . . B3
St George's Avenue C1
St James St . . B4
St John's Cathedral
  (RC) † . . B2
St Mary's † . . A3
St Mary's Gate . . A3
St Mary's
  Parsonage . . B3
St Peter's Square ♥ B4
St Stephen St . . A2
Salford Approach. . A3
Salford Central ⇌ . A2
Sheffield St . . C5
Sherratt St . . A5
Shopmobility . . A4
Shudehill . . A4
Shudehill ♥ . . A4
Sidney St . . C4
Silk St . . A5
Silver St . . B4
Skerry Close . . C5
Snell St . . B6
South King St . . B3
Sparkle St . . B5
Spear St . . A4
Spring Gardens . . B4
Stanley St . . B2
Store St . . B5
Superstore . . B1
Swan St . . A4
Tariff St . . B5
Tatton St . . C1
Temperance St . B6/C6
Thirsk St . . C6
Thomas St . . A4
Thompson St . . A5
Tib Lane . . B3
Tib St . . A4
Town Hall
  (Manchester) . . B3
Town Hall (Salford) A2
Trafford St. . . B2
Travis St. . . B5
Trinity Way . . A2
Turner St . . A4
Union St . . C6
Univ of Manchester
  (North Campus) . C5
Univ of Salford . . A1
Upper Brook St . . C5
Upper Cleminson St A1
Upper Wharf St . . A1
Urban Exchange . . A5
Vesta St . . B6
Victoria ⇌ . . A4
Victoria Station ⇌ . A4
Wadeson Rd . . C5
Water St . . B2
Watson St . . B3
West Fleet St. . . C2
West King St . . A2
West Mosley St . . B4
Weybridge Rd . . A6
Whitworth St . . B4
Whitworth St West . C3
William St . . A1
William St . . C6
Wilmott St . . C3
Windmill St . . B3
Windsor Crescent . A1
Withy Grove . . A4
Woden St . . C1
Wood St . . B3
Woodward St . . A6
Worrall St . . C1
Worsley St . . C2
York St . . B4
York St . . A4

Merthyr Tydfil / Merthyr Tudful 190

Aberdare Rd . . B2
Abermorlais Terr. . A2
Alexandra Rd . . A1
Alma St . . C3
Arfryn Place . . C3
Argyle St . . C3
Avenue De Clichy . C2
Beacons Place
  Shopping Centre . C2
Bethesda St . . B2
Bishops Grove . . A1
Brecon Rd . . A1/B2
Briarmead . . C2
Bryn St . . C3
Bryntirion Rd . . B3/C3
Bus Station . . B2
Cae Mari Dwn . . B3
Caedraw Rd . . C2
Castle Square. . . B2
Castle St . . B2
Chapel. . . B2
Chapel Bank. . . B1
Church St . . B3
Civic Centre . . B2
Clos Penderyn . . C1
Coedcae'r Court. . C3
College Boulevard . C2
County and Crown
  Courts . . B3
Court St. . . C3
Cromwell St . . B3
Cyfarthfa Castle, Mus
  and Art Gallery ₥ . A1
Cyfarthfa Ind Est. . A1
Cyfarthfa Park . . A1
Cyfarthfa Retail Pk. A2
Dane St . . A2
Dane Terrace . . A2
Danyparc . . B2
Darren View . . A2
Dixon St . . B2
Dyke St . . B2
Dynevor St . . B2
Elwyn Drive. . . B3
Fire Station. . . B2
Fothergill St . . A2
Galonuchaf Rd . . A3
Garth St. . . B3
Georgetown . . B2
Graven Terrace . . B2
Grove Park . . B2
Grove,The. . . A2
Gurnos Rd . . A2
Gwaelodygarth
  Rd . . A2/A3
Gwaunfarren Grove A3
Gwaunfarren Rd. . A3
Gwendoline St . . A2
Hampton St . . C3
Hanover St . . B2
Heol S O Davies . . B1
Heol-Gerrig . . B2
High St . A3/B2/B3/C2
HighView . . A3
Howell Close . . B1
Jackson's Bridge . B2
James St . . B3
John St . . B3
Joseph Parry's
  Cottage ₥ . . B2
Lancaster St . . A2
Library . . A2
Llewellyn St . . B3
Llwyfen St . . A2
Llwyn Berry. . . A1
Llwyn Dic Penderyn B1
Llwyn-y-Gelynen. . C1
LowerThomas St . B3
Market . . B2
Mary St . . C3
Masonic St . . A2
MerthyrTydfil Coll . B1
MerthyrTown FC . C2
MerthyrTydfil
  Leisure Centre . . C3
MerthyrTydfil Sta ⇌ C3
Meyrick Villas . . A2
Miniature
  Railway ♣ . . A1
Mount St . . A2
Nantygwenith St . B2
NormanTerrace. . B2
Oak Rd . . C3
Old Cemetery . . B3
Pandy Close . . A1
Pantycelynen . . B1
Parade,The . . B2
ParkTerrace . . A2
Penlan View . . C2
Penry St . . B2
Pentwyn Villas . . A2
Penyard Rd . . B3
Pendarren Park . . A3
Pendarren Rd . . B3
Plymouth St . . C3
Police Station ▨ . B2
Pont Marlais West . B2
Post Office ▣ . B2
Quarry Row . . B2
Queen's Rd . . C3
Rees St . . C3
Rhydycar Link. . . C1
Riverside Park . . A1
St David's ♠ . . B1
StTydfil's ♣ . . B2
StTydfil's Avenue . C3
StTydfil's Square
  Shopping Centre . C2
Saxon St . . A2
School of Nursing . A2
Seward St . . A2
Shiloh Lane. . . A1
Stone Circles ∩ . . A1
Stuart St . . A2
Summerhill Place . A3
Superstore . . B3
Swan St. . . B2
Swansea Rd . . A1
Taff GlenView . . B3
TaffVale Court . . A3
Theatre Soar ♨ . . B1
Thomastown Park . B3
Tramroad Lane . . A3
Tramroad Side . . B3
Tramroad Side
  North . . B3
Tramroad Side
  South. . . C3
Trevithick Gardens . B3
Trevithick St . . B3
Tudor Terrace . . A2
Twynyrodyn Rd. . C3
Union St . . B3
Upper Colliers Row B1
UpperThomas St . B3
Victoria St. . . B2
Vue ♨ . . B2
Vulcan Rd . . B2
Walk,The . . C2
Warlow St . . C3
Well St . . A2
Welsh Assembly
  Government
  Offices . . C2
Wern Lane. . . C2
Wern,The
  (Merthyr RFC). . C2
West Grove . . A2
William St . . B2
Yew St . . C3
Ynysfach Engine
  House ♦ . . B1
Ynysfach Rd . . C2

Middlesbrough 191

Abingdon Rd. . . C3
Acklam Rd . . C1
Acklam Rd Hosp ⊞. C1
Albert Park . . C2
Albert Rd . . B2
AlbertTerrace. . . C2
Ambulance Station C1
Aubrey St . . C3
Avenue,The . . C2
Ayresome Gardens C2
Ayresome Gn Lane . C1
Ayresome St . . C2
Barton Rd . . A1
Bilsdale Rd . . C3
Bishopton Rd . . C3
Borough Rd . . B2/B3
Bowes Rd . . A2
Breckon Hill Rd. . B3
Bridge St West . . B2
Brighouse Rd . . A1
Burlam Rd. . . C1
Bus Station . . B2
Cannon Park. . . B1
Cannon Park Way. B1
Cannon St. . . B1
Captain Cook Sq. . B2
Carlow St . . C1
Castle Way . . B1
Chipchase Rd . . C2
Cineworld ♨ . . B3
Cleveland Centre . B2
Clive Rd. . . C2
Commercial St . . A2
Corporation Rd . . B2
Costa St. . . C2
Council Offices. . . B1
Crescent Rd . . C2
Crescent,The . . C2
Cumberland Rd . . C2
Depot Rd . . A2
Derwent St . . B1
Devonshire Rd . . C2
Diamond Rd . . B2
Dock ClockTower♦ A3
Dock St . . B2
Dorman Mus ₥ . . C2
Douglas St. . . B3
Eastbourne Rd . . C2
Eden Rd. . . C3
Fire Station. . . A3
Forty Foot Rd . . A2
Gilkes St . . B2
Grange Rd . . B2
Gresham Rd . . B2
Harford St . . C2
Hartington Rd. . . B2
Haverton Hill Rd. . A1
Hey Wood St . . B1
Highfield Rd . . C3
Hillstreet Centre . B2
Holwick Rd . . B1
Hutton Rd . . C3
Information Ctr ☑ . B2
Ironmasters Way . A2
Lambton Rd . . C3
Lancaster Rd. . . C2
Lansdowne Rd . . C3
Latham Rd . . C3
Law Courts . . B2/B3
Lees Rd. . . C3
Leeway . . B3
Library . . B2/C2
Linthorpe Cemetery C1
Linthorpe Rd . . B2
Lloyd St . . B2
Longford St . . C2
Longlands Rd . . C3
Lower East St . . A3
Lower Lake . . C2
Macmillan Acad . . C1
Maldon Rd . . C1
Marsh St . . B2
Marton Rd . . B3
Middlesbrough
  By-Pass. . B2/C1
Middlesbrough Coll B3
Middlesbrough
  Dock . . B3
Middlesbrough
  Leisure Park . . B3
Middlesbrough
  Station ⇌ . . B2
Middletown Park . B3
MIMA ₥ . . B2
Mulgrave Rd . . C2
Newport Bridge . B1
Newport Bridge
  Approach Rd. . . A1
Newport Rd . . B2
North Ormesby Rd . B3
North Rd . . B2
Northern Rd . . C1
Outram St . . C2
Oxford Rd . . C2
Park Lane . . C2
Park Rd North. . . C2
Park Rd South. . . C2
ParkVale Rd . . C3
Parliament Rd . . B1
Police Station ▨ . C2
Port Clarence Rd . A3
Portman St . . C2
Priestman Rd . . B3
Princes Rd . . B2
Python . . A3
Riverside Park Rd . A1
Riverside Stadium
  (Middlesbrough
  FC). . B3
Rockliffe Rd . . C2
Romaldkirk Rd . . B1
Roman Rd . . C2
Roseberry Rd . . C3
St Barnabas' Rd . . C2
St Paul's Rd . . B2
Saltwells Rd . . B3
Seaton Carew Rd . A3
Shepherdson Way . B3
Shopmobility . . B2
Snowdon Rd . . A2
South West
  Ironmasters Park . A2
Southfield Rd . . B2
Southwell Rd . . C2
Springfield Rd . . C2
Startforth Rd . . A2
Stockton Rd . . C1
Stockton St . . A2
Suffield St . . C2
Surrey St . . C2
Sussex St . . A1/C3
Tax Offices . . B3
TeesAMP
  Manufacturing Pk . B1
Tees Viaduct . . C1
Teessaurus Park. . A2
Teesside Tertiary
  College . . B3
Temenos ♦ . . B3
Thornfield Rd . . C3
Town Hall . . B2
Transporter Bridge
  (Toll) . . A3
Union St . . B2
Univ ofTeesside . . B2
Upper Lake . . C2
Valley Rd . . C2
Ventnor Rd . . C3
Victoria Rd . . B2
Vulcan St . . B2
Warwick St . . C2
Wellesley Rd . . B3
West Lane . . C1
Westminster Rd . . C2
Wilson St. . . B2
Windward Way . . B3
Woodlands Rd . . C2
York Rd . . C3

Milton Keynes 191

Abbey Way . . A1
Arbrook Avenue . A1
Armourer Drive . A3
Arncliffe Drive . . A1
Avebury ♥ . . B2
Avebury Boulevard C2
Bankfield ♥ . . A3
Bayard Avenue . . A3
Belvedere ♥ . . B2
Bishopstone . . A1
Blundells Rd . . A3
Boundary,The. . . C3
Boycott Avenue . . C2
Bradwell Common
  Boulevard . . B1
Bradwell Rd . . C1
Bramble Avenue. . A2
Brearley Avenue . . C3
Breckland . . A2
Brill Place . . B1
Burnham Drive. . A1
Campbell Park ♥. . B3
Cantle Avenue . . A3
Central Retail Park . B2
centre:mk. . . B2
Century Avenue . . C2
Chaffron Way . . C2
Christ the
  Cornerstone ♣ . B2
Cineworld ♨ . . B3
Civic Offices . . B2
Cleavers Avenue . B2
Colesbourne Drive A3
Conniburrow Bvd. . B2
Currier Drive . . A3
Dansteed
  Way. . A2/A3/B1
Daytona
  Go-Karting ♦ . . B1
Deltic Avenue. . . B1
Downs Barn ♥ . . A2
Downs Barn Bvd . . A2
Eaglestone ♥ . . C3
Eelbrook Avenue . B1
Elder Gate . . B1
Evans Gate . . C2
Fairford Crescent . A3
Falcon Avenue . . A3
Fennel Drive . . A2
Fishermead Bvd . . C3
Fulwoods Drive . . C3
Glazier Drive . . A3
Glovers Lane . . A1
Grafton Gate . . C2
Grafton St . . A1/C2
Gurnards Avenue . A3
Harrier Drive . . C3
Ibstone Avenue . . B1
Langcliffe Drive . . A1
Leys Rd . . C1
Library . . B2
Lincslade Grove . . C1
Linford Wood . . A2
Magistrates Court . B2
Marlborough Gate . B3
Marlborough St A2/B3
Mercers Drive. . . A1
Midsummer ♥ . . B2
Midsummer Bvd. . B2
Midsummer Place . B2
Milton Keynes
  Central ⇌ . . C1
Milton Keynes
  Hospital (A&E) ⊞. . C1
MK ♣ . . B3
Monks Way . . A1
Mullen Avenue . . A3
Mullion Place . . C3
National Film &
  Sci-Fi Museum ♨ B2
Neath Hill ♥ . . A3
North Elder ♥ . . C1
North Grafton ♥. . C1
North Overgate ♥. A3
North Row. . . B2
North Saxon ♥. . B2
North Secklow ♥. . B2
North Skeldon ♥ . A3
North Witan ♥ . . C1
Oakley Gardens . . A3
Oldbrook Bvd. . . C2
Open-Air Theatre ♨ B3
Overgate. . . A3
Overstreet . . A3
Patriot Drive. . . C3
Pencarrow Place . A3
Penryn Avenue . . A3
Perran Avenue . . A3
Pitcher Lane . . C1
Place Retail Pk,The C1
Planet Ice ♦ . . C1
Police Station ▨ . B2
Portway ♥ . . B2
Post Office ▣
  . . A1/B2/B3/C3
Precedent Drive. . A1
Quinton Drive . . A1
Ramsons Avenue . B1
Retail Park . . C2
Rockingham Drive. A2
Rooksley ♥. . . A1
Saxon Gate . . B2
Saxon St. . A1/C3
Secklow Gate . . B2
Shackleton Place . A3
Silbury Boulevard . B2
Skeldon ♥ . . A3
South Enmore . . C3
South Grafton ♥ . C1
South Row . . B2
South Saxon ♥. . C2
South Secklow ♥. . C2
South Witan ♥ . . C2
Springfield ♥. . . C3
Stainton Drive . A1/B1
Stanton Wood ♥. . A1
Stantonbury ♥ . . A1
Stantonbury Leisure
  Centre ♦ . . A1
Strudwick Drive . . C2
Sunrise Parkway . . A2
Superstore . . C1/C2
Tolcarne Avenue . A3
Towan Avenue . . A3
Trueman Place . . C3
Vauxhall . . A1
Winterhill Retail Pk C2
Witan Gate . . B2
Xscape ♦ . . B3

Newcastle upon Tyne 191

Albert St. . . C3
Argyle St. . . C3
Back New Bridge St B3
BALTIC Centre for
  Contemporary Art B3
Barker St . . A3
Barrack Rd . . A1
Bath Lane . . B1
Bessie Surtees
  House ♦ . . C2
Bigg Market . . C2
Biscuit Factory ₥ . A3
Black Gate ₥ . . C2
Blackett St . . B2
Blandford Square . C1
Boating Lake . . A1
Boyd St . . B3
Brandling Park . . A2
Bus Station . . C2
Buxton St . . B3
Byron St . . A3
Camden St . . A3
Castle Keep ₥ . . C2
Central ♥ . . C1
Central Library . . B2
Central Motorway . A2
Chester St. . . A3
Cineworld ♨ . . C2
City Hall . . B2
City Rd . . B3/C3
City Walls ♦ . . C1
Civic Centre . . B2
Claremont Rd . . A1
Clarence St . . B3
Clarence Walk . . B3
Clayton St . . C1/B1
Clayton St West . . C1
Close,The . . C2
Coach Station . . C1
College St. . . B2
Collingwood St . . C2
Copland Terrace. . B3
Coppice Way. . . B3
Corporation St . . B1
Courts . . C3
Crawhall Rd . . B3
Dean St . . C2
Dental Hospital . . A1
Dinsdale Place . . A3
Dinsdale Rd . . A3
Discovery ₥ . . C1
Doncaster Rd . . A3
Durant Rd . . B2
Eldon Square . . B1
Eldon Square
  Shopping Centre . B2
Ellison Place. . . B2
Eskdale Terrace . . A3
EslingtonTerrace . A2
Exhibition Park . . A1
Falconar St . . B3
Fenkle St. . . C1
Forth Banks . . C2
Forth St. . . C1
Gallowgate . . B1
Gate,The ♦ . . B1
Gateshead
  Millennium Bridge C3
Gateshead Quays . C3
Gibson St . . B3
Goldspink Lane . . A3
Grainger Market . . B2
Grainger St . . B2/C1
Grantham Rd . . A3
Granville Rd . . A3
Great North Children's
  Hospital ⊞ . . A1
Great North
  Mus:Hancock ₥ . A2
Grey St. . . B2
Groat Market . . C2
Guildhall ♦ . . C2
Hancock St . . A2
Hanover St . . C2
Hatton Gallery ₥ . A1
Hawks Rd . . C3
Haymarket Ⓜ . . B2
Heber St . . B1
Helmsley Rd . . A3
High Bridge . . B2
High Level Bridge . C2
Hillgate . . C2
Howard St . . B3
Hutton Terrace . . A3
Jesmond Ⓜ . . A2
Jesmond Rd . . A2/A3
John Dobson St . B2
Jubilee Rd . . A3
Kelvin Grove . . A3
Kensington Terrace A2
Laing Gallery ₥ . . B2
Lambton Rd . . A3
Leazes Crescent . . B1
Leazes Lane . . B1
Leazes Park. . . B1
Leazes Park Rd . . B1
Leazes Terrace . . B1
Library . . A2
Life Science Ctr ♦ . C1
Live ♨ . . C2
Low Friar St . . C1
Manor Chare . . C2
Manors Ⓜ . . B3
Manors Station ⇌ . B3
Market St . . B2
Melbourne St . . B3
Mill Rd . . C3
Monument Ⓜ . . B2
Monument Mall
  Shopping Centre . B2
Morpeth St . . A2
Mosley St . . C2
Napier St . . A3
New Bridge St
  West. . B2/B3
Newcastle Central
  Station ⇌ . . C1
Newcastle Helix . . B1
Newcastle Univ . . A1
Newgate St. . . B1
Newington Rd . . A3
Northern Design CtrC3
Northern Stage ♨ . A2
Northumberland Rd B2
Northumberland St B2
Northumbria Univ . B2
Northwest Radial
  Rd . . B1
O2 Academy ♦ . . C1
Oakwellgate . . C3
Open University . . B2
Orchard St . . C2
Osborne Rd . . A2
OsborneTerrace . . A3
Pandon . . B3
Pandon Bank . . B3
ParkTerrace . . A1
Percy St. . . B1
Pilgrim St . . B2
Pipewellgate . . C2
Pitt St . . B1
PlummerTower ₥ . B2
Police Station ▨ . B3
Portland Rd . . A3/B3
PortlandTerrace . . A3
Post Office ▣ . A3/B2
Pottery Lane . . C1
Prudhoe Place . . B2
Prudhoe St . . B2
Quayside. . . C3
Queen Elizabeth II
  Bridge . . C3
QueenVictoria Rd . A1
Richardson Rd . . A1
Ridley Place . . B2
Rock Terrace . . B3
RosedaleTerrace . A3
Royal Victoria
  Infirmary ⊞ . . A1
Sage Gateshead ♨ . C3
St Andrew's St . . B1
St James Ⓜ . . B1
St James' Bvd. . . C1
St James' Park
  (Newcastle Utd FC)B1
St Mary's Heritage
  Centre ♦ . . C3
St Mary's (RC) † . . C1
St Nicholas † . . C2
St Nicholas St . . C2
StThomas' St. . . B2
Sandyford Rd . A2/A3
Shield St . . B3
Shieldfield . . B3
Shopmobility . . B1
Side,The . . C2
Simpson Terrace . . B3
South Shore Rd . . C3
South St . . C1
Starbeck Avenue . A3
Stepney Rd . . B3
Stoddart St . . B3
Stowell St . . B1
Strawberry Place. . B1
Swing Bridge . . C2
Temple St . . C1
Terrace Place . . A1
Theatre Royal ♨ . B2
Times Square . . C1
Tower St . . B3
Trinity House . . C2
Tyne Bridge . . C2
Tyne Bridges ♦ . . C2
TyneTheatre &
  Opera House ♨ . C1
Tyneside ♨ . . B2
Victoria Square . . A2
Warwick St . . A3
Waterloo St . . C1
Wellington St . . B1
Westgate Rd . C1/C2
WindsorTerrace . . A2
Worswick St . . C2
Wretham Place . . B3
Youth Hostel. . . B2

Newport / Casnewydd 191

Royal Gwent ⊞ . .
AlbertTerrace. . . B1
Allt-yr-Yn Avenue . A1
Alma St . . C2
Ambulance Station C3
Bailey St . . B2
Barrack Hill . . A2
Bath St . . A3
Bedford Rd . . B3
Belle Vue Lane . . C1
Belle Vue Park . . C1
Bishop St . . A3
Blewitt St . . B1
Bolt Close . . C3
Bolt St . . C3
Bond St . . A2
Bosworth Drive . . A1
Bridge St. . . B1
Bristol St . . A3
Bryngwyn Rd . . B1
Brynhyfryd Avenue C1
Brynhyfryd Rd . . C1
Bus Station . . B2
Caerau Crescent . C1
Caerau Rd . . C1
Caerleon Rd . . A3
Capel Crescent . . C3
Cardiff Rd . . C2
Caroline St . . B3
Cedar Rd . . A3
Charles St . . B2
Charlotte Drive. . C2
Chepstow Rd . . A3
Church Rd . . A3
Cineworld ♨ . . B2
Civic Centre . . B1
Clarence Place . . A2
Clifton Place . . B1
Clifton Rd . . B1
Clyffard Crescent . B1
ClythaPark Rd . . B1
Clytha Square . . C2
Coldra Rd . . C3
Collier St . . A3
Colne St . . B3
Comfrey Close . . A1
Commercial Rd . . C3
Commercial St . . B2
Corelli St . . A3
Corn St . . B2
Corporation Rd . . B3
Coulson Close . . C2
County Court . . A2
Courts . . A1/B1
Crawford St . . B3
Cyril St . . B3
Dean St . . A3
Devon Place . . B1
Dewsland Park Rd . C2
Dolman ♨ . . B3
Dolphin St. . . C3
East Dock Rd . . C3
East St . . B2
East Usk Rd . . A3
EbbwVale Wharf . A3
Emlyn St . . B2
Enterprise Way . . A3
Eton Rd . . A3
Evans St . . A2
Factory Rd . . A2
Fields Rd . . B1
Francis Drive . . C2
Frederick St . . C2
Friars Rd . . C1
Friars Walk . . C2
Gaer Lane . . C1
George St . . C2
George St Bridge . C2
Godfrey Rd . . B1
GoldTops . . B1
Gore St . . A3
Gorsedd Circle. . B1
Grafton Rd . . A3
Graham St . . B1
Granville St . . C3
Harlequin Drive . . A1
Harrow Rd . . B3
Herbert Rd . . A3
Herbert Walk . . C2
Hereford St . . A3
High St . . B2
Hill St . . B1
Hoskins St. . . A2
Information Ctr ☑ . B2
Ivor St . . B2
Jones St. . . B1
Junction Rd . . A3
Keynshaw Avenue . C2
King St . . C2
Kingsway . . B2
Kingsway Centre . B2
Ledbury Drive. . . A1
Library . . B2
Library, Museum &
  Art Gallery ₥ . . B2
Liverpool Wharf. . B3
Llanthewy Rd . . B1
Llanvair Rd . . A3
Locke St . . A2
Lower Dock St . . C2
Lucas St . . A2
Manchester St . . A3
Market . . B2
Marlborough Rd. . B3
Mellon St . . C2
Military Preparation
  College . . A1
Mill St . . A2
Morgan St . . A3
Mountjoy Rd. . . C2
Newport Bridge . A2
Newport Centre . B2
Newport Station ⇌ B2
North St . . B2
Oakfield Rd . . B1
Park Square . . C2
Police Sta ▨ . A3/C2
Post Office ▣ . . B3
Power St. . . A1
Prince St . . A3
Pugsley St. . . A2
Queen St . . C2
Queen's Close . . A1
Queen's Hill . . B1
Queen's Hill Cres . A1
Queensway. . . B2
Railway St . . B2
Riverfront Theatre &
  Arts Centre,The ♨ B2
Riverside . . A2
Rodney Par (Dragons
  RFC & Newport
  County AFC) . . A3
Rodney Rd . . B2
Royal ♨ . . A3
Rudry St . . A3
Rugby Rd . . A3
Ruperra Lane . . A3
Ruperra St . . A3
St Edmund St . . A3
St Mark's Crescent . A1
St Mary St . . B2
St Vincent Rd . . B3
St Woolos † . . C1
St Woolos General
  (no A&E) ⊞ . . C1
St Woolos Rd . . B1
School Lane . . A2
Serpentine Rd . . B1
Shaftesbury Park . . A2
Sheaf Lane . . A1
Skinner St . . B2
Sorrel Drive . . A1
South Market St . . C3
Spencer Rd . . A1
Stow Hill . B2/C1/C2
Stow Park Avenue . C1
Stow Park Drive . . C1
Talbot St . . B2
Tennis Club. . . C1
Tregare St . . A3
Trostrey St . . A3
TunnelTerrace . . B1
Turner St . . A3
Univ of Wales Newport
  City Campus . . B3
Upper Dock St . . B2
Usk St . . A3
Usk Way . . B3/C3
Exeter Crescent . . A1
War Memorial . . A2
Waterloo Rd . . C1
West St . . B1
Wharves . . B2
Wheeler St . . A2
WhitbyPlace . . . A3
WindsorTerrace . . B1
York Place. . . C1

Newquay 192

Agar Rd . . B2
Alma Place . . B2
Ambulance Station B2
Anthony Rd . . B2
Atlantic Hotel . . A1
Bank St . . A1
Barrowfields. . . B3
BayViewTerrace . . B2
Beach Rd . . B1
Beachfield Avenue . B1
Beacon Rd . . A2
Belmont Place . . A1
Berry Rd . . B2
Blue Reef
  Aquarium ♦ . . A1
Boating Lake . . A3
Bus Station . . B2
Chapel Hill . . A1
Chester Rd . . A3
Cheviot Rd . . C1/C2
Chichester Cres . . C3
Chynance Drive . . C1
Chyverton Close. . C1
Cliff Rd . . C1
Coach Park . . B2
Colvreath Rd . . B3
Cornwall College
  Newquay. . . B3
Council Offices . . B2
Crantock St . . B1
Crescent,The. . . B1
Criggar Rocks. . . A3
Dale Close. . . C2
Dale Rd . . C2
Dane Rd . . A1
East St . . A2
Edgcumbe Avenue . B2
Edgcumbe Gardens A2
Eliot Gardens . . A3
Elm Close . . C2
Ennor's Rd . . B3
Fernhill Rd . . B1
Fire Station. . . B3
Fore St . . A1
Gannel Rd . . C2
Golf Driving Range. C3
Gover Lane . . A2
Great Western
  Beach. . . A2
Grosvenor Avenue . A2
Harbour . . A1
Hawkins Rd . . A3
Headland Rd . . A1
Hilgrove Rd . . A3/B3
Holywell Rd . . B1
HopeTerrace . . B2
Huer's Hut,The ♦ . A1
Information Ctr ☑ . A1
Island Crescent . . B2
Jubilee St . . A2
Kew Close . . C2
Killacourt Cove . . A1
King Edward Cres . A2
Lanhennor Avenue . B2
Library . . B2
Lifeboat Station . . A1
Lighthouse . . A2

Northampton • Norwich • Nottingham • Oxford • Perth • Peterborough • Plymouth • Poole • Portsmouth 209

Linden Avenue C2
Listry Rd C2
Lusty Glaze Beach A3
Lusty Glaze Rd A3
Manor Rd B1
Marcus Hill B2
Mayfield Rd B2
Meadowside C3
Mellanvrane Lane C2
Michell Avenue B2
Miniature Golf Course C3
Miniature Railway B3
Mount Wise B1
Mowhay Close C3
Narrowcliff A3
Newquay B2
Newquay Hosp B2
Newquay Town Football Ground B1
Newquay Zoo B3
North Pier A1
North Quay Hill A1
Oakleigh Terrace B2
Pargolla Rd B2
Pendragon Cres C3
Penganel Close C1
Penina Avenue C3
Pirate's Quest B1
Police Station & Courts B2
Post Office B1/B2
Quarry Park Rd B3
Rawley Lane C2
Reeds Way B1
Robartes Rd B2
St Anne's Rd A3
St Aubyn Crescent B3
St George's Rd B1
St John's Rd B1
St Mary's Rd B1
St Michael's B1
St Michael's Rd B1
St Thomas' Rd B2
Seymour Avenue B2
South Pier A1
South Quay Hill A1
Superstore B2
Sweet Briar Cres C3
Sydney Rd A1
Tolcarne Beach A2
Tolcarne Point A2
Tolcarne Rd B2
Tor Rd B2
Towan Beach A1
Towan Blystra Rd B3
Tower Rd A1
Trebarwith Cres B2
Tredour Rd C2
Treforda Rd C3
Tregoss Rd B3
Tregunnel Hill B1/C1
Tregunnel Saltings C1
Trelawney Rd B2
Treloggan Lane C3
Treloggan Rd C3
Trembath Crescent C1
Trenance Avenue B2
Trenance Gardens B2
Trenance Lane C2
Trenance Leisure Pk B3
Trenance Rd B2
Trenarth Rd B2
Treninnick Hill C3
Tretherras Rd B3
Trethewey Way C1
Trevemper Rd C2
Ulalia Rd B3
Vivian Close B2
Waterworld B3
Whitegate Rd B3
Wych Hazel Way C3

Northampton 192

78 Derngate B3
Abington Square B3
Abington St B3
Alcombe St A3
All Saints' B2
Ambush St B1
Angel St B2
Army Reserve Ctr A3
Arundel St A2
Ash St A2
Auctioneers Way C2
Bailiff St A2
Barrack Rd A2
BBOB Rugby FC A1
Beaconsfield Terr A3
Becket's Park C3
Beckett Retail Park B1
Bedford Rd B3
Billing Rd B3
Brecon St A1
Brewery C2
Bridge St C2
Broad St B2
Burns St A3
Bus Station B2
Byfield Rd B1
Campbell St A2
Castle (Site of) B2
Castle St B2
Cattle Market Rd C2
Central Museum & Art Gallery B2
Charles St A3
Cheyne Walk B3
Church Lane A2
Clare St A3
Cloutsham St A3
College St B2
Colwyn Rd A3
Cotton End C2
Countess Rd A1
County Hall B2
Craven St A3
Crown & County Courts B3
Denmark Rd B3
Derngate B3
Doddridge Church B2
Drapery B2
Duke St A3
Dunster St A3
Earl St A3
Euston Rd C2
Fire Station A3
Foot Meadow B2
Gladstone Rd A1
Gold St B2
Grafton St A2
Gray St A3
Green St B1
Greenwood Rd B1
Greyfriars B2
Grosvenor Centre B2
Grove Rd A3
Guildhall B2
Hampton St A2
Harding Terrace A2
Hazelwood Rd B3
Herbert St B2
Hervey St A3
Hester St A2
Holy Sepulchre A2
Hood St A3
Horse Market B2
Hunter St A3
Information Ctr B2
Kettering Rd A3
Kingswell St B2
Lady's Lane B2
Leicester St A2
Leslie Rd A2
Library B3
Lorne Rd A2
Lorry Park A1
Louise Rd A2
Lower Harding St A2
Lower Hester St A2
Lower Mounts B3
Lower Priory St A2
Magistrates Court A2
Main Rd C1
Marefair B2
Mkt Sq (under dev) B2
Marlborough Rd B1
Marriott St A2
Millers Meadow A1
Military Rd A3
Mounts Baths Leisure Centre A3
Nene Valley Retail Park C1
New South Bridge Rd C2
Northampton General Hospital (A&E) B3
Northampton Marina C3
Northampton Sta B1
Northcote St A2
Nunn Mills Rd C3
Old Towcester Rd C2
Overstone Rd A3
Pembroke Rd A1
Penn Court C2
Police Station B3
Post Office A1/B3
Quorn Way A2
Ransome Rd C3
Regent Square A2
Ridings,The B3
Ring Way C1
Robert St A2
Royal & Derngate Theatres B3
St Andrew's Rd B1
St Andrew's St A2
St Edmund's Rd B3
St George's St A2
St Giles B3
St Giles St B3
St Giles' Terrace B3
St James Park Rd B1
St James Rd B1
St James Retail Pk C1
St James' Mill Rd B1
St James' Mill Rd East C1
St Leonard's Rd C2
St Mary's St B2
St Michael's Rd A3
St Peter's B2
St Peter's Way Shopping Precinct B2
St Peter's Way B2
Salisbury St A2
Scarletwell St B2
Semilong Rd A2
Sheep St B2
Sol Central (Leisure Centre) B2
Somerset St A3
South Bridge C2
Southfield Avenue C2
Spencer Bridge Rd A1
Spencer Rd A3
Spring Gardens B3
Spring Lane B2
Superstore C2
Swan St B3
Tintern Avenue A1
Towcester Rd C2
Univ of Northampton (Waterside Campus) C3
Upper Bath St B2
Upper Mounts A2
Victoria Park A1
Victoria Promenade B2
Victoria Rd B3
Victoria St A2
Wellingborough Rd B3
West Bridge B1
York Rd B3

Norwich 192

Albion Way C3
All Saints Green C2
Anchor St A3
Anglia Square A2
Argyle St C3
Arts Centre B1
Ashby St C2
Assembly House B1
Bank Plain B2
Barker St A1
Barn Rd A1
Barrack St A3
Ber St C2
Bethel St B1
Bishop Bridge A3
Bishopbridge Rd A3
Bishopgate A3
Blackfriars St A2
Botolph St A2
Bracondale C3
Brazen Gate C2
Bridewell Mus B2
Brunswick Rd C1
Bull Close Rd A2
Bus Station C2
Calvert St A2
Cannell Green A3
Carrow Rd C3
Castle & Mus B2
Castle Mall B2
Castle Meadow B2
Cathedral B2
Cathedral (RC) B1
Cath Retail Park A1
Cattlemarket St B2
Chantry Place C1
Chantry Rd C1
Chapelfield East B1
Chapelfield Gardens B1
Chapelfield North B1
Chapelfield Rd B1
Cinema City B2
City Hall B1
City Rd C2
City Wall C1/C3
Close,The B2/B3
Colegate A2
Coslany St B1
Cow Hill B1
Cow Tower A3
Cowgate A2
Crown & Magistrates' Courts A2
Dragon Hall Heritage Centre C3
Duke St A1
Edward St A2
Elm Hill B2
Erpingham Gate B2
Fishergate A2
Forum,The B1
Foundry Bridge B3
Fye Bridge A2
Garden St C2
Garage,The B1
Gas Hill B3
Gentlemans Walk B2
Grapes Hill B1
Great Hospital Halls,The A3
Grove Avenue C1
Grove Rd C1
Guildhall B1
Gurney Rd A3
Hall Rd C2
Heathgate A3
Heigham St A1
Hollywood A2
Horn's Lane C2
Hungate Medieval Art B2
Ipswich Rd C1
ITV Anglia C3
James Stuart Gardens B3
King St B2
King St C3
Koblenz Avenue C3
Leisure Centre A3
Library B1
London St B2
Lower Clarence Rd B3
Maddermarket B1
Magdalen St A2
Mariners Lane C2
Market B2
Market Avenue B2
Mountergate B3
Mousehold St A3
Newmarket Rd C1
Norfolk St C1
Norwich City FC C3
Norwich Gallery B2
Norwich School B2
Norwich Station B3
Oak St A1
Odeon C3
Palace St A2
Pitt St A1
Playhouse B2
Police Station B1
Post Office A2/B2/B3/C1
Pottergate B1
Prince of Wales Rd B2
Princes St B2
Pull's Ferry B3
Puppet Theatre A2
Queen St B2
Queens Rd C2
Recorder Rd B3
Riverside Entertainment Ctr C3
Riverside Leisure Centre C3
Riverside Rd B3
Riverside Retail Pk C3
Rosary Rd B3
Rose Lane B2
Rouen Rd C2
Royal Norfolk Regimental B2
St Andrews St B2
St Augustines St A1
St Benedicts St B1
St Crispins Road A1
St Ethelbert's Gate B2
St Faiths Lane B3
St Georges St A2
St Giles St B1
St James Close A3
St Julians C2
St Leonards Rd B3
St Martin's Lane A1
St Peter Mancroft B2
St Peters St B1
St Stephens Rd C1
St Stephens St C1
Shopmobility C1
Silver Rd A2
Silver St A2
Southwell Rd C2
St Andrew's & Blackfriars' Hall B2
Strangers' Hall B1
Superstore C2
Surrey St C2
Sussex St A1
Theatre Royal B1
Theatre St B1
Thorn Lane C2
Thorpe Rd B3
Tombland B2
Union St C1
Vauxhall St B1
Victoria St C1
Vue B2
Walpole St B1
Waterfront,The C3
Wensum St A2
Wessex St C1
Westwick St A1
Wherry Rd C3
Whitefriars A2
Willow Lane B1

Nottingham 192

Abbotsford Drive A3
Addison St A1
Albert Hall B1
Alfred St Central A3
Alfreton Rd B1
All Saints St A1
Annesley Grove A2
Arboretum A1
Arboretum St A1
Arthur St A1
Arts Theatre B3
Ashforth St A3
Balmoral Rd A1
Barker Gate B3
Bath St B3
BBC Nottingham C3
Beacon Hill Rise B3
Belgrave Rooms B1
Bellar Gate B3
Belward St B3
Brewhouse Yard C2
Broad Marsh Bus Station C2
Broad St B3
Brook St B3
Burns St A1
Burton St B2
Bus Station A2
Canal St C2
Carlton St B3
Carrington St C2
Castle C2
Castle Boulevard C1
Castle Gate C2
Castle Meadow Rd C1
Castle Meadow Retail Park C1
Castle Rd C2
Castle Wharf C2
Cavendish Rd East C1
Cemetery A1/B1
Chaucer St B1
Cheapside B2
Church Rd A3
City Link C3
City of Caves C2
Clarendon St B1
Cliff Rd C3
Clumber Rd East C1
Clumber St B2
College St B1
Collin St C2
Contemporary C3
Conway Close A2
Cornerhouse, The B2
Council House B2
Cranbrook St B3
Cranmer St A2
Cromwell St B1
Curzon St B3
Derby Rd B1
Dryden St A2
Exchange Ctr,The B2
Fishpond Drive C1
Fletcher Gate B3
Forest Rd East A1
Forest Rd West A1
Friar Lane C2
Gedling Grove A1
Gedling St B3
George St B3
Gill St A2
Glasshouse St B2
Goldsmith St B2
Goose Gate B3
Great Freeman St A2
Guildhall B2
Hamilton Drive C1
Hampden St A1
Heathcote St B3
High Pavement C3
High School A1
Holles Crescent C1
Hope Drive C1
Hungerhill Rd A3
Huntingdon Drive C1
Huntingdon St A2
Information Ctr B2
Instow Rise A3
International Community Ctr A2
Kent St B3
King St B2
Lace Market B3
Lace Mkt Theatre C3
Lamartine St B3
Leisure Centre C3
Lenton Rd C1
Lewis Close A3
Library C2
Lincoln St B2
London Rd C3
Long Row B2
Low Pavement C2
Lower Parliament St B3
Magistrates' Court C2
Maid Marian Way B2
Mansfield Rd A2/B2
Middle Hill C2
Milton St B2
Mount St B2
Museum & Art Gallery C1
National Ice Centre & Motorpoint Arena C3
National Justice Museum C3
Newcastle Drive B1
Newstead Grove A2
North Sherwood St A2
Nottingham Arena C3
Nottingham Cath B1
Nottingham Coll C3
Nottingham College City Hub C3
Nottingham Station C3
Nottingham Trent University A2/B2
Old Mkt Square B2
Oliver St A1
Park Drive C1
Park Row C1
Park Terrace B1
Park Valley C1
Park,The C1
Peas Hill Rd A3
Peel St A1
Pelham St B2
Peveril Drive C1
Plantagenet St A3
Playhouse B1
Plumptre St C3
Police Station B1
Poplar St C3
Portland Rd B1
Post Office B2
Queen's Rd C3
Raleigh St A1
Regent St B1
Rick St B3
Robin Hood St B3
Robin Hood Statue C2
Ropewalk,The B1
Royal Centre B2
Royal Children Inn C2
Royal Concert Hall B2
St Ann's Hill Rd A2
St Ann's Way A2
St Ann's Well Rd A3
St James' St B2
St Mark's St B3
St Mary's Rest Gdn B3
St Mary's Gate B3
St Nicholas C2
St Peter's C2
St Peter's Gate B2
Salutation Inn C2
Shakespeare St B2
Shelton St A2
Shopmobility A2
South Parade B2
South Rd C1
South Sherwood St B2
Squire Performing Arts Centre A1
Station Street C3
Stoney St B3
Talbot St B1
Tattershall Drive C1
Tennis Drive B1
Tennyson St A1
Theatre Royal B2
Trent St C3
Trent University B2
Union Rd B3
Upper Parliament St B2
Victoria Centre B2
Victoria Leisure Ctr B3
Victoria Park B3
Victoria St B2
Walter St A1
Warser Gate B3
Watkin St A2
Waverley St A1
Wheeler Gate B2
Wilford Rd C2
Wilford St C2
Wollaton St B1
Woodborough Rd A2
Woolpack Lane B3
Ye Old Trip to Jerusalem C2
York St A2

Oxford 193

Adelaide St A1
Albert St A1
All Souls (College) B2
Ashmolean Mus B2
Balliol (College) B2
Banbury Rd A2
Bate Collection of Musical Instruments C2
Beaumont St B1
Becket St B1
Blackhall Rd A2
Blue Boar St B2
Bodleian Library B2
Botanic Garden B3
Brasenose (Coll) B2
Brewer St C2
Broad St B2
Burton-Taylor Theatre B2
Bus Station B1
Canal St A1
Cardigan St A1
Carfax Tower B2
Castle B1
Castle St B1
Catte St B2
Cemetery C1
Christ Church (Coll) B2
Christ Church Cathedral C2
Christ Church Mdw C2
City of Oxford Coll C1
Clarendon Centre B2
Cornmarket St B2
Corpus Christi (College) B2
County Hall B1
Covered Market B2
Cowley Place C3
Cranham St A1
Cranham Terrace A1
Cricket Ground B1
Crown & County Courts C2
Deer Park B3
Exeter (College) B2
Fire Station B1
Folly Bridge C2
George St B1
Great Clarendon St A1
Harris Manchester (College) B2
Hart St A1
Hertford (College) B2
High St B3
Hollybush Row B1
Holywell St B2
Hythe Bridge St B1
Ice Rink C1
Jericho St A1
Jesus (College) B2
Jowett Walk B3
Juxon St A1
Keble (College) A2
Keble Rd A2
Library B2
Linacre (College) A3
Lincoln (College) B2
Little Clarendon St A1
Longwall St B3
Magdalen (College) B3
Magdalen Bridge B2
Magdalen St B2
Magistrate's Court C2
Manor Rd B3
Mansfield (College) A2
Mansfield Rd A3
Market B1
Marlborough Rd C2
Martyrs' Meml B2
Merton (College) B3
Merton Field B3
Merton St B2
Museum of Modern Art B2
Mus of Oxford B2
Museum Rd A2
New Coll (Coll) B3
New Inn Hall St B2
New Rd B1
New Theatre B2
Norfolk St C1
Nuffield (College) B1
Observatory A1
Observatory St A1
Odeon B1/B2
Old Fire Station B1
Old Greyfriars St C2
Oriel (College) B2
Oxford Castle & Prison B1
Oxford Station B1
Oxford University Research Centres A1
Oxpens Rd C1
Paradise Square C1
Paradise St B1
Park End St B1
Parks Rd A2/B2
Pembroke (Coll) C2
Phoenix A1
Picture Gallery C2
Plantation Rd A1
Playhouse B2
Police Station C2
Post Office A1/B2
Pusey St B1
Queen's (College) B3
Queen's Lane B3
Radcliffe Camera B2
Rewley Rd B1
Richmond Rd A1
Rose Lane B3
Ruskin (College) B1
Said Bsns School B1
St Aldates C2
St Anne's (College) A1
St Antony's (Coll) A1
St Bernard's Rd A1
St Catherine's (Coll) B3
St Cross Building A3
St Cross Rd A3
St Edmund Hall (College) B3
St Giles St A2
St Hilda's (College) C3
St John St B2
St John's (College) B2
St Mary the Virgin B2
St Michael at the Northgate B2
St Peter's (College) B1
St Thomas St B1
Science Area A2
Science Museum B2
Sheldonian Theatre B2
Somerville (Coll) A1
South Parks Rd A2
Speedwell St C2
Sports Ground C3
Thames St C2
Town Hall B2
Trinity (College) B2
Turl St B2
Univ Coll (Coll) B3
Univ Natural History Mus & Pitt Rivers Mus A2
University Parks A2
Wadham (College) B2
Walton Crescent A1
Walton St A1
Western Rd C2
Westgate C2
Woodstock Rd A1
Worcester (Coll) B1

Perth 193

AK Bell Library B2
Abbot Crescent C1
Abbot St C1
Albany Terrace A1
Albert Monument A3
Alexandra St B2
Atholl St A2
Balhousie Avenue A2
Balhousie Castle & Black Watch Museum A2
Balhousie St A2
Ballantine Place A1
Barossa Place A2
Barossa St A2
Barrack St A2
Bell's Sports Centre A2
Bellwood B3
Blair St B1
Burn Park C1
Bus Station B2
Caledonian Rd B2
Canal Crescent B2
Canal St B3
Cavendish Avenue C1
Charles St B2
Charlotte Place A2
Charlotte St A3
Church St A1
City Hall B3
Club House C3
Clyde Place C1
Coach Park C3
Commercial St A3
Concert Hall B3
Council Chambers B3
County Place B2
Court B3
Craigie Place C2
Crieff Rd A1
Croft Park C2
Cross St B2
Darnhall Crescent C1
Darnhall Drive C1
Dewars Centre B1
Dundee Rd B3
Dunkeld Rd A1
Earl's Dykes B1
Edinburgh Rd C3
Elibank St B1
Fair Maid's Ho A3
Fergusson B3
Feus Rd A1
Fire Station A1
Foundary Lane A2
Friar St C1
George St B3
Glamis Place C1
Glasgow Rd B1
Glenearn Rd C2
Glover St B1/C1
Golf Course A2
Gowrie St A3
Gray St B1
Graybank Rd B1
Greyfriars Burial Gd B3
Hay St A2
High St B2/B3
Inchaffray St A1
Ind/Retail Park B1
Information Ctr B2
Isla Rd A3
James St B2
Keir St A3
King Edward St B3
King James VI Golf Course C3
King St B2
Kings Place C2
Kinnoull Causeway B2
Kinnoull St B2
Knowelea Place C1
Knowelea Terrace C1
Ladeside Bsns Ctr A1
Leisure Pool B1
Leonard St B2
Lickley St B2
Lochie Brae A3
Long Causeway A1
Low St A2
Main St A3
Marshall Place C3
Melville St A2
Mill St B3
Milne St B2
Murray Crescent C1
Murray St B2
Needless Rd C1
New Rd B2
North Inch A3
North Methven St A2
Park Place C1
Perth B2
Perth Bridge A3
Perth Business Pk B1
Perth Museum & Art Gallery B3
Perth Station C2
Pickletulllum Rd B1
Pitheavlis Crescent C1
Playhouse B2
Police Station A2
Pomarium St B2
Post Office B2/C2
Princes St B3
Priory Place C2
Queen St C1
Queen's Bridge B3
Riggs Rd B1
Riverside B3
Riverside Park B3
Rodney Gardens B3
Rose Terrace A2
St Catherine's Rd A1/A2
St Catherine's Retail Park A1
St John St B3
St John's Kirk B3
St John's Shopping Centre B2
St Leonards Bridge C2
St Ninians Cath A2
Scott Monument C2
Scott St B2
Sheriff Court B3
Shore Rd C3
Skate Park C3
South Inch C2
South Inch Bsns Ctr C3
South Inch Park C2
South Inch View C2
South Methven St B2
South St B3
South William St B2
Stables,The A1
Stanners,The B3
Stormont St A2
Strathmore St A3
Stuart Avenue C1
Superstore B1/B2
Tay St B3
Union Lane A2
Victoria St B2
Watergate B3
Wellshill Cemetery A1
West Bridge St A3
West Mill St B2
Whitefriers Cres B1
Whitefriers St B1
Wilson St C1
Windsor Terrace C1
Woodside Crescent C1
York Place B2
Young St C1

Peterborough 193

Anglia Ruskin Univ B3
Athletics Arena B3
Bishop's Palace B2
Bishop's Rd B2/B3
Bittern Way C2
Boongate A3
Bourges Boulevard A1
Bourges Retail Park B1/B2
Bridge St B2
Bright St A1
Broadway A2
Broadway A2
Brook St A2
Burghley Rd A2
Bus Station B2
Cavendish St A3
Charles St A3
Church St B2
Church Walk A2
City Road B2
Cobden Avenue A1
Cobden St A1
Cowgate B2
Craig St A2
Crawthorne Rd A2
Cromwell Rd A1
Dickens St A3
Eastfield Rd A3
Eastgate B3
Fire Station A1
Fletton Avenue C2
Frank Perkins Parkway C3
Geneva St A2
George St C1
Gladstone St A1
Glebe Rd C2
Gloucester Rd C3
Granby St B3
Grove St C1
Guildhall B2
Hadrians Court C3
Hawksbill Way C2
Henry St A2
Hereward Cross (shopping) B2
Hereward Rd B3
Information Ctr B2
Jubilee St C1
Kent Rd B1
Key Theatre C2
Kirkwood Close B1
Lea Gardens B1
Library A2
Lincoln Rd A2
London Rd C2
Long Causeway B2
Lower Bridge St C2
Magistrates Court B2
Manor House St A2
Mayor's Walk A1
Midgate B2
Midland Rd A1
Monument St A2
Morris St A3
Mus & Art Gallery B2
Nene Valley Railway C1
New Rd A2
New Rd C1
Northminster A2
Old Customs Ho C2
Oundle Rd C1
Padholme Rd A3
Palmerston Rd C1
Park Rd A2
Passport Office B2
Peterborough Cathedral B2
Peterborough Nene Valley C1
Peterborough Station B1
Police Station B2
Porters Way C3
Post Office A3/B2
Priestgate B2
Queen's Walk C2
Queensgate Centre B2
Railworld Wildlife Haven C1
Recreation Ground C3
Regional Fitness & Swimming Centre B3
River Lane B1
Rivergate Shopping Centre B2
Riverside Mead C3
Russell St A1
St John's B2
St John's St A3
St Marks St A2
St Peter's Rd B2
Saxon Rd A3
South Street B3
Spital Bridge A1
Stagshaw Drive C3
Star Rd B3
Superstore B1,B2
Thorpe Lea Rd B1
Thorpe Rd B1
Thorpe's Lea Rd B1
Tower St A2
Town Hall B2
Viersen Platz B2
Vineyard Rd B3
Wake Rd B3
Wellington St A3
Wentworth St B2
Westgate B2
Weston Homes Stadium (Peterborough United FC) The C2
Whalley St A3
Wharf Rd C1
Whitsed St A3
YMCA A3

Plymouth 193

Alma Rd A1
Anstis St B1
Armada Shopping Centre B2
Armada St A3
Armada Way B2
Arts Centre B2
Athenaeum B1
Athenaeum St C1
Barbican C3
Barbican C3
Baring St A3
Bath St B1
Beaumont Park B3
Beaumont Rd B3
Black Friars Gin Distillery C2
Box,The B2
Breton Side B3
Coach Station B2
Castle St C3
Cathedral (RC) B1
Cecil St B1
Central Park A1
Central Park Ave A2
Charles Church B3
Charles Cross B3
Charles St B2
Cineworld B2
Citadel Rd C2
Citadel Rd East C2
Civic Centre B2
Cliff Rd C1
Clifton Place A3
Cobourg St A2
College of Art B2
Continental Ferry Port B1
Cornwall St B2
Crescent,The B1
Dale Rd A2
Deptford Place A3
Derry Avenue A2
Derry's Cross B1
Drake Circus B2
Drake Circus Shopping Centre B2
Drake Statue C2
Eastlake St B2
Ebrington St B3
Elizabethan Ho C3
Elliot St C1
Endsleigh Place A2
Exeter St B3
Fire Station A3
Fish Quay C3
Gibbons St A3
Glen Park Avenue A2
Grand Parade C1
Great Western Rd C1
Greenbank Rd A3
Greenbank Terrace A3
Guildhall B2
Hampton St B3
Harwell St B1
Hill Park Crescent A3
Hoe Approach B2
Hoe Rd C2
Hoe,The C2
Hoegate St C2
Houndiscombe Rd A2
Information Ctr C3
James St A2
Kensington Rd A3
King St B1
Lambhay Hill C3
Leigham St C1
Library B2
Lipson Rd A3/B3
Lockyer St C2
Lockyers Quay C3
Madeira Rd C2
Marina B3
Market B1
Market Avenue B1
Martin St B1
Mayflower St B2
Mayflower Stone & Steps C3
Mayflower C3
Merchant's Ho B2
Millbay Rd B1
National Marine Aquarium C3
Neswick St B1
New George St B2
New St C3
North Cross A2
North Hill A3
North Quay B2
North Rd East A2
North Rd West A1
North St B3
Notte St B2
Octagon,The B1
Octagon St B1
Pennycomequick A1
Pier St C1
Plymouth Naval Memorial C2
Plymouth Pavilions B1
Plymouth Sta A2
Police Station B3
Post Office B2,C1,C3
Princess St B2
Promenade,The C2
Prysten House B2
Queen Anne's Battery Watersports Ctr C3
Radford Rd C1
Regent St B3
Rope Walk C3
Royal Citadel C2
Royal Parade B2
Royal Theatre B2
Russell Place A1
St Andrew's B2
St Andrew's Cross B2
St Andrew's St B2
St Lawrence Rd A2
Saltash Rd A2
Shopmobility B2
Smeaton's Tower C2
Southern Terrace A3
Southside St C2
Stuart Rd A1
Sutherland Rd A2
Sutton Rd B3
Sydney St A1
Teats Hill Rd C3
Tothill Avenue B3
Union St B1
Univ of Plymouth A2
Vauxhall St B2/3
Victoria Park A1
Walker Terrace C1
West Hoe Rd C1
Western Approach B1
Whittington St A1
Wyndham St B1

Poole 194

Ambulance Station A3
Baiater Gardens C2
Baiter Park C3
Ballard Close C2
Ballard Rd C2
Bay Hog Lane B1
Bridge Approach C1
Bus Station B2
Castle St B2
Catalina Drive B3
Chapel Lane B2
Church St B1
Cinnamon Lane B1
Colborne Close B3
Dear Hay Lane B2
Denmark Lane A3
Denmark Rd A3
Dolphin Centre B2
East St B2
Elizabeth Rd A3
Emerson Rd B2
Ferry Rd C1
Fire Station A2
Freightliner Terminal C1
Furnell Rd B3
Garland Rd A3
Green Rd B2
Harbour Hospital, The (Private) A3
Heckford Lane A3
Heckford Rd A3
High St B2
High St North A3
Hill St B2
Holes Bay Rd A1
Hospital (A&E) A3
Information Ctr C2
Kingland Rd B3
Kingston Rd A3
Labrador Drive C3
Lagland St B2
Lander Close C3
Lighthouse, Poole Ctr for the Arts B3
Longfleet Rd A3
Maple Rd A3
Market Close B2
Market St B2
Mount Pleasant Rd B3
New Harbour Rd C1
New Harbour Rd South C1
New Harbour Rd West C1
New Orchard B1
New Quay Rd C1
New St B2
Newfoundland Dr B2
North St B2
Old Lifeboat C2
Old Orchard B2
Parish Rd A3
Park Lake Rd B3
Parkstone Rd A3
Passenger Ferry Terminal C1
Perry Gardens B2
Pitwines Close B2
Police Station A2
Poole Central Liby B2
Poole Lifting Bridge C1
Poole Park B2
Poole Station A2
Poole Museum C1
Post Office B2
Quay,The C2
RNLI College B1
St John's Rd A3
St Margaret's Rd A2
St Mary's Maternity Unit A3
St Mary's Rd A3
Seldown Bridge B3
Seldown Lane B3
Seldown Rd B3
Serpentine Rd A2
Scaplen's Court C1
Shaftesbury Rd A3
Skinner St B2
Slipway B1
Stanley Rd C2
Sterte Avenue A2
Sterte Avenue West A1
Sterte Close A2
Sterte Esplanade A2
Sterte Rd A2
Strand St C2
Studio Poole C1
Superstore B3
Swimming Pool B3
Taverner Close B3
Thames St B1
Towngate Bridge B2
Twin Sails Bridge B1
Vallis Close C3
Waldren Close B3
West Quay B1
West Quay Rd B1
West St B1
West View Rd A2
Whatleigh Close B2
Wimborne Rd A3

Portsmouth 194

Action Stations A1
Admiralty Rd A1
Alfred Rd A2
Anglesea Rd B2
Arundel St B3
Aspex B1
Bishop Crispian Way A2
Bishop St A2
Broad St C1
Buckingham Ho C2
Burnaby Rd B2
Bus Station B1
Camber Dock C1
Cambridge Rd B2
Car Ferry to Isle of Wight B1
Cascades Shopping Centre A3
Castle Rd C3
Civic Offices B3
Clarence Pier C2
College St B1
Commercial Rd A3
Cottage Grove B3
Cross St A1
Cumberland St A2
Duisburg Way C2
Durham St A3
East St B1
Elm Grove C3
Governor's Green C1
Great Southsea St C3
Green Rd B3
Greetham St B3
Grosvenor St B3
Groundlings A2
Grove Rd North C3
Grove Rd South C3
Guildhall B3
Guildhall Walk B3
Gunwharf Quays Designer Outlet B1
Gunwharf Rd B1
Hambrook St C2
Hampshire Terrace B2
Hanover St A1
Hard,The B1
High St C2
HM Naval Base A1
HMS Nelson (Royal Naval Barracks) A2
HMS Monitor M.33 A1
HMS Victory A1
HMS Warrior A1
Hovercraft Terminal C2
Hyde Park Rd B3
Information Centre A1/B3
Isambard Brunel Rd B3
Isle of Wight Car Ferry Terminal B1
Kent Rd C3
Kent St A2
King St B3
King's Rd C3
King's Terrace C2
Lake Rd A3
Law Courts B3
Library B3
Long Curtain Rd C2

Marina B1
Market Way A3
Marmion Rd C3
Mary Rose A1
Middle St B3
Millennium Prom Walk B1/C1
Museum Rd B2
National Museum of the Royal Navy A1
Naval Rec Gd C2
Nightingale Rd C3
Norfolk St B3
North St A2
Osborne Rd C3
Paradise St A3
Park Rd B2
Passenger Catamaran to Isle of Wight B1
Passenger Ferry to Gosport B1
Pelham Rd C3
Pembroke Gardens C2
Pier Rd C2
Point Battery C1
Police Station B3
Portsmouth & Southsea Sta ≋ A3
Portsmouth Harbour Station ≋ B1
Portsmouth Historic Dockyard A1
Portsmouth Museum & Art Gallery B2
Post Office A1/A3/B3
Queen St A1
Queen's Crescent C3
Ravelin Park B2
Register Office B2
Round Tower ✦ C1
Royal Garrison Church C1
St Edward's Rd C3
St George's Rd B2
St George's Square B1
St George's Way B2
St James's Rd B3
St James's St A2
St John's Cathedral (RC) ✝ A3
St Thomas's Cath ✝ C1
St Thomas's St B2
Shopmobility A3/B1
Somers Rd B3
Southsea Common C2
Southsea Terrace C2
Spinnaker Tower ✦ B1
Square Tower ✦ C1
Station St A3
Town Fortifications ✦ C1
Unicorn Rd A2
United Services Recreation Ground B2
University of Portsmouth A2/B2
Univ of Portsmouth B3
Upper Arundel St A3
Victoria Avenue C2
Victoria Park A3
Victory Gate A1
Vue B1
Warblington St B1
Western Parade C2
White Hart Rd C1
Winston Churchill Avenue B3

Preston 194

Adelphi St A2
Anchor Court B3
Aqueduct St A1
Ardee Rd C1
Arthur St B2
Ashton St A1
Avenham Lane B3
Avenham Park C3
Avenham Rd B3
Avenham St B3
Bairstow St B3
Balderstone Rd C1
Beamont Drive A1
Beech St South C2
Bird St C1
Bow Lane B2
Brieryfield Rd A1
Broadgate C1
Brook St A2
Bus Station A3
Butler St B2
Cannon St B3
Carlton St A1
Chaddock St B3
Channel Way B1
Chapel St B3
Christ Church St B2
Christian Rd B2
Cold Bath St A2
Coleman Court C1
Connaught Rd C2
Corporation St A2/B2
County Hall B2
Cricket Ground C2
Croft St A1
Cross St B3
Crown Court A3
Crown St A3
East Cliff C3
East Cliff Rd B3
Edward St A2
Elizabeth St A3
Euston St B1
Fishergate B2/B3
Fishergate Hill B2
Fishergate Shopping Centre B2
Fitzroy St B1
Fleetwood St A1
Friargate A3
Fylde Rd A1/A2
Gerrard St B2
Glover's Court B3
Good St B2
Grafton St B2
Great George St A3
Great Shaw St A3
Greenbank St A2
Guild Way B1
Guild Hall & Charter B3
Guildhall St B3
Harrington St A2
Harris Museum B3
Hartington Rd B1
Hasset Close C2
Heatley St B2
Hind St C2
Information Ctr B3
Kilruddery Rd C1
Lancashire Archives B2
Lancaster Rd A3/B3
Latham St B3
Lauderdale St C2
Lawson St A3
Leighton St A2
Leyland Rd C1
Library A3
Library B3
Liverpool Rd C1
Lodge St B2
Lune St B3
Magistrate's Court A3
Main Sprit West B3
Maresfield Rd C1
Market St West A3
Marsh Lane B1/B2
Maudland Bank A2
Maudland Rd A2
Meadow Court C2
Meath Rd C1
Miller Arcade ✦ B3
Miller Park C3
Moor Lane A3
Mount St B3
North Rd A3
North St A3
Northcote Rd B1
Old Milestones B1
Old Tram Rd C3
Pedder St A1/A2
Peel St A2
Penwortham Bridge C2
Penwortham New Bridge C1
Pitt St B2
Playhouse A3
Police Station A3
Portway B1
Post Office B3
Preston Station ≋ B2
Retail Park B2
Ribble Bank St B2
Ribble Viaduct C2
Ribblesdale Place B3
Ringway B3
River Parade C1
Riverside C2
St George's Shopping Centre B3
St Georges B3
St John's Minster B3
St Johns Shopping Centre A3
St Mark's Rd A1
St Walburges A1
Salisbury Rd B1
Sessions House B3
Snow Hill A3
South End C2
South Meadow La C2
Spa Rd B1
Sports Ground C2
Strand Rd B1
Syke St B3
Talbot Rd B1
Taylor St C1
Tithebarn St A3
Town Hall B3
Tulketh Brow A1
University of Central Lancashire A2
Valley Rd C1
Victoria St A2
Walker St A3
Walton's Parade B2
Warwick St A3
Wellfield Bsns Park A1
Wellfield Rd A1
Wellington St A1
West Cliff C2
West Strand A1
Winckley Rd C1
Winckley Square B3
Wolseley Rd C2

Reading 194

Abbey Ruins ✝ B2
Abbey Square B2
Abbey St B2
Abbot's Walk B2
Acacia Rd C2
Addington Rd C3
Addison Rd A1
Allcroft Rd C3
Alpine St C2
Baker St B1
Berkeley Avenue C1
Bridge St B2
Brigham Rd A1
Broad St B1
Broad Street Mall B1
Carey St B1
Castle Hill C1
Castle St B1
Causeway, The A3
Caversham Rd A1
Christchurch Meadows A2
Civic Offices B1
Coley Hill C1
Coley Place C1
Craven Rd C3
Crown St C2
De Montfort Rd A1
Denmark Rd C3
Duke St B2
East St B2
Edgehill St C2
Eldon Rd B3
Eldon Terrace B3
Elgar Rd C1
Erleigh Rd C3
Field Rd C1
Fire Station A1
Fobney St B1
Forbury Gardens B2
Forbury Rd B2
Forbury Retail Park B2
Francis St C1
Friar St B1
Garrard St B1
Gas Works Rd B3
George St A2
Great Knollys St B1
Greyfriars B1
Grove, The B2
Gun St B1
Henry St C1
Hexagon Theatre, The B1
Hill's Meadow A2
Howard St B1
Inner Distribution Rd B1
Katesgrove Lane C1
Kenavon Drive B2
Kendrick Rd C2
King's Mdw Rec Gd A2
King's Rd B2
Library B2
London Rd C3
London St B2
Lynmouth Rd A1
Magistrate's Court B1
Market Place B2
Mill Lane B2
Mill Rd A2
Minster St B1
Morgan Rd C3
Mount Pleasant C2
Mus of English Rural Life (MERL) C3
Napier Rd A2
Newark St C2
Newport Rd A1
Oracle Shopping Centre, The B1
Orts Rd B3
Oxford Road B1
Pell St C1
Police Station B1
Post Office A1/B1
Queen Victoria St B1
Queen's Rd A2
Queen's Rd B2
Randolph Rd A1
Reading Auction Ctr & Farmers Mkt A1
Reading Bridge A2
Reading College B3
Reading Station ≋ A1
Redlands Rd C3
Riverside Mus B3
Rose Kiln Lane C1
Royal Berkshire Medical Mus C3
Royal Berks Hospital (A&E) C3
St Giles C2
St Laurence B2
St Mary's B1
St Mary's Butts B1
St Saviour's Rd C1
Send Rd A3
Sherman Rd C2
Sidmouth St B2
Silver St C2
South St B2
South St Arts Ctr B2
Southampton St C2
Station Hill A1
Station Rd B1
Station Shopping Park, The A1
Superstore A3
Swansea Rd A1
Thames Lido A2
Tudor Road A1
Univ of Reading C3
Valpy St B2
Vastern Rd A1
Vue B2
Waldeck St C2
Watlington St B3
West St B1
Whitby Drive C3
Wolseley St C1
York Rd A1
Zinzan St B1

St Andrews 195

Abbey St B2
Abbey Walk B3
Abbotsford Cres A1
Albany Park C3
Allan Robertson Dr C2
Ambulance Station C1
Anstruther Rd C3
Argyle St B1
Auld Burn Rd B2
Bassaguard Ind Est B1
Bell St B2
Blackfriars Chapel (Ruins) B2
Boase Avenue B2
Braid Crescent C3
Brewster Place C3
Bridge St B1
British Golf Mus A1
Broomfaulds Ave C1
Bruce Embankment A1
Bruce St C2
Bus Station A1
Byre Theatre B2
Canongate C1
Cathedral and Priory (Ruins) ✝ B3
Cemetery B1
Chamberlain St C1
Church St B2
Churchill Crescent C2
City Rd A1
Claybraes C1
Cockshaugh Public Park B1
Cosmos Community Centre B3
Council Office A2
Crawford Gardens C1
Doubledykes Rd B1
Drumcarrow Rd C1
East Sands B3
East Scores A3
Fire Station C1
Forrest St C1
Fraser Avenue C1
Freddie Tait St C2
Gateway Centre A1
Glebe Rd B2
Golf Place A1
Grange Rd C3
Greenside Place B2
Greyfriars Gardens A2
Hamilton Avenue C2
Hepburn Gardens B1
Holy Trinity B2
Horseleys Park C1
Information Ctr B2
Irvine Crescent C3
James Robb Avenue C1
James St B1
John Knox Rd C1
Kennedy Gardens B1
Kilrymont Close C3
Kilrymont Place C3
Kilrymont Rd C3
Kinburn Park B1
Kinkell Terrace C3
Kinnesburn Rd B2
Ladebraes Walk B2
Lady Buchan's Cave A3
Lamberton Place C1
Lamond Drive C2
Langlands Rd B2
Largo Rd C1
Learmonth Place C1
Library B2
Links Clubhouse A1
Links, The A1
Livingstone Cres B2
Long Rocks A2
Madras College B2
Market St A2
Martyr's Monument A1
Murray Park A2
Murray Place A2
Museum of the Univ of St Andrews (MUSA) ✦ A2
Nelson St B2
New Course, The A1
New Picture Ho A2
North Castle St A3
North St A2
Old Course, The A1
Old Station Rd A1
Pends, The B3
Pilmour Links A1
Pipeland Rd B2/C2
Police Sta A2/C1
Post Office B2/B3
Preservation Trust B3
Priestden Park C3
Priestden Place C3
Priestden Rd C3
Queen's Gardens B2
Queen's Terrace B2
Roundhill Rd C2
Royal & Ancient Golf Club A1
St Andrews B1
St Andrews Aquarium A2
St Andrews Botanic Garden B1
St Andrews Castle (Ruins) & Visitor Centre A2
St Leonard's Sch B3
St Mary St B3
St Mary's College B2
St Nicholas St C3
St Rules Tower ✦ B3
St Salvator's Coll A2
Sandyhill Crescent C2
Sandyhill Rd C2
Scooniehill Rd C2
Scores, The A2
Shields Avenue C3
Shoolbraids C2
Shore, The B3
Sloan St B1
South St B2
Spottiswoode Gardens C1
Station Rd A1
Swilcen Bridge A1
Tom Morris Drive C2
Tom Stewart Lane C1
Town Hall B2
Union St A2
Univ Chapel A2
University Library A2
Univ of St Andrews A1
Viaduct Walk B1
War Memorial A3
Wardlaw Gardens B1
Warrack St C3
Watson Avenue B2
West Port B2
West Sands A1
Westview B2
Windmill Rd A1
Winram Place C1
Wishart Gardens C2
Woodburn Park B3
Woodburn Place B3
Woodburn Terrace B3
Younger Hall A2

Salisbury 195

Albany Rd A2
Arts Centre A3
Ashley Rd A1
Avon Approach A2
Ayleswade Rd C2
Bedwin St A2
Belle Vue A2
Bishop's Walk B2
Blue Boar Row B2
Bourne Avenue A3
Bourne Hill A3
Britford Lane C2
Broad Walk C2
Brown St B2
Castle St A2
Catherine St B2
Chapter House B2
Church House B2
Churchfields Rd B1
Churchill Gardens C3
Churchill Way East B3
Churchill Way North A3
Churchill Way South C2
Churchill Way West A1
City Hall B2
Close Wall B2
Coach Park A2
Coldharbour Lane A1
College St A3
Council and Registry Offices A3
Crane Bridge Rd B2
Crane St B2
Cricket Ground C1
Culver St South B3
De Vaux Place C2
Devizes Rd A1
Dews Rd B1
Elm Grove B3
Elm Grove Rd A3
Endless St A2
Estcourt Rd A3
Exeter St C2
Fairview Rd A3
Fire Station A1
Fisherton St A1
Folkestone Rd C1
Fowlers Hill B3
Fowlers Rd B3
Friary Lane B2
Friary, The B3
Gas Lane A1
Gigant St B3
Greencroft B3
Greencroft St A3
Guildhall B2
Hall of John Halle B2
Hamilton Rd A2
Harnham Mill B1
Harnham Rd C1/C2
High St B2
House of John A'Port B2
Information Ctr B2
Kelsey Rd A3
King's Rd A2
Laverstock Rd B3
Library A2
London Rd A3
Lower St C1
Maltings, The B2
Manor Rd A3
Marsh Lane A1
Medieval Hall B2
Milford Hill B3
Milford St B3
Mill Rd B1
Mill Stream App A2
Mompesson Ho B2
New Bridge Rd C2
New Canal B2
New Harnham Rd C2
New St B2
North Canonry B2
North Gate B2
North Walk B2
Old Blandford Rd C1
Old Deanery B2
Old George Hall B2
Park St A3
Parsonage Green C1
Playhouse Theatre A2
Police Station A3
Post Office A2/B2
Poultry Cross B2
Queen Elizabeth Gardens B1
Queen's Rd A3
Rampart Rd B3
Rifles, The B2
St Ann St B2
St Ann's Gate B2
St Marks Rd A3
St Martins B3
St Nicholas' Rd C2
St Paul's A1
St Paul's Rd A1
St Thomas B2
Salisbury Cath ✝ B2
Salisbury Cath School (Bishop's Palace) C2
Salisbury Museum, The B2
Salisbury Sta ≋ A1
Salt Lane A3
Saxon Rd C1
Scots Lane A2
Shady Bower B3
Shopmobility B2
South Canonry C2
South Gate C2
Southampton Rd B2
Spire View A1
Sports Ground C3
Tollgate Rd B3
Town Path B1
Wain-a-Long Rd A3
Wessex Rd A3
West Walk C2
Wilton Rd A1
Wiltshire College B3
Winchester St B3
Windsor Rd A1
Wyndham Rd A2
York Rd A1

Scarborough 195

Aberdeen Walk B2
Albert Rd A2
Albion Rd C2
Auborough St B2
Balmoral Centre B2
Belle Vue St C1
Belmont Rd C2
Blenheim Terrace A2
Brunswick Shopping Centre B2
Castle Dykes B3
Castle Hill A3
Castle Rd B2
Castle Walls A3
Castlegate B3
Cemetery C1
Central Tramway ✦ B2
Coach Park B1
Columbus Ravine A1
Court B1
Crescent, The C2
Cricket Ground A1
Cross St B2
Crown Terrace C2
Dean Rd B1
Devonshire Drive A1
Diving Belle Statue ✦ B3
East Harbour B3
East Pier B3
Eastborough B2
Elmville Avenue B1
Esplanade C2
Falconers Rd B2
Falsgrave Rd C1
Fire Station B2
Foreshore Rd B2
Friargate B2
Gladstone Rd B1
Gladstone St B1
Hollywood Plaza A1
Holms, The A3
Hoxton Rd B1
Information Ctr B2
King St B2
Library B2
Lifeboat Station ✦ B3
Londesborough Rd C1
Longwestgate B3
Marine Drive A3
Luna Park B3
Miniature Railway A1
Nelson St B1
Newborough B2
Nicolas St B2
North Marine Rd A1
North St B2
Northway B1
Old Harbour B3
Olympia Leisure ✦ B2
Peasholm Park A1
Peasholm Rd A1
Police Station B1
Post Office B2
Princess St B3
Prospect Rd B1
Queen St B2
Queen's Parade A2
Queen's Tower (Remains) A3
Ramshill Rd C2
Roman Signal Sta A3
Roscoe St C1
Rotunda Mus C2
Royal Albert Drive A2
Royal Albert Park A2
St Martin-on-the-Hill C2
St Martin's Avenue C2
St Mary's B3
St Thomas St B2
Sandside B3
Scarborough ≋ C1
Scarborough Art Gallery C2
Scarborough Bowls Centre A1
Scarborough Castle A3
Shopmobility C2
Somerset Terrace C2
South Cliff Lift ✦ C2
Spa Theatre, The C2
Spa, The ✦ C2
Stephen Joseph Theatre C1
Tennyson Avenue B1
Tollergate B2
Town Hall B2
Trafalgar Rd B1
Trafalgar Square A1
Trafalgar St West B1
Valley Bridge Par C2
Valley Rd C1
Vernon Rd C2
Victoria Park Mount A1
Victoria Rd B1
West Pier B3
Westborough C1
Westover Rd C1
Westwood C1
Woodall Avenue A1
Woodend C2
YMCA Theatre B2
York Place B2
Yorkshire Coast College (Westwood Campus) C1

Sheffield 196

Addy Drive A2
Addy St A2
Adelphi St A3
Albert Terrace Rd A3
Albion St A2
Aldred Rd A1
Allen St A4
Alma St A4
Angel St B5
Arundel Gate B5
Arundel St C4
Ashberry Rd A2
Ashdell Rd C1
Ashgate Rd C1
Athletics Centre B2
Attercliffe Rd A6
Bailey St B4
Ball St A4
Balm Green B4
Bank St B4
Barber Rd A2
Bard St B5
Barker's Pool B4
Bates St A1
Beech Hill Rd C1
Beet St B3
Bellefield St A3
Bernard Rd A6
Bernard St B6
Birkendale A2
Birkendale Rd A2
Birkendale View A1
Bishop St C4
Blackwell Place B6
Blake St A2
Blonk St A5
Bolsover St B2
Botanical Gardens C1
Bower Rd A1
Bradley St A1
Bramall Lane C4
Bramwell St A3
Bridge St A4/A5
Brighton Terrace Rd A1
Broad Lane B3
Broad St B6
Brocco St A3
Brook Hill B3
Broomfield Rd C1
Broomgrove Rd C2
Broomhall Place C3
Broomhall Rd C2
Broomhall St C3
Broomspring Lane C2
Brown St C5
Brunswick St B3
Burgess St B3
Burlington St A2
Burns Rd A2
Cadman St A6
Cambridge St B4
Campo Lane B4
Carver St B4
Castle Square B5
Castlegate A5
Cathedral B4
Cathedral (RC) ✝ B4
Cavendish St B3
Charles St C4
Charter Row C4
Children's Hosp B2
Church St B4
City Hall B4
City Hall B4
City Rd C6
Claremont Crescent B2
Claremont Place B2
Clarke St C3
Clarkegrove Rd C2
Clarkehouse Rd C1
Clarkson St B2
Clay Wood C6
Cobden View Rd A1
Collegiate Cres C2
Commercial St B5
Commonside A1
Conduit Rd B1
Cornish St A3
Corporation St A4
Cricket Inn Rd B6
Cromwell St A1
Crookes Rd B1
Crookes Valley Park B2
Crookes Valley Rd B2
Crookesmoor Rd A2
Crown Court A4
Crucible Theatre B5
Cutlers' Hall B4
Cutlers Gate A6
Daniel Hill A2
Dental Hospital B2
Derek Dooley Way A5
Devonshire Green B3
Devonshire St B3
Division St B4
Dorset St C2
Dover St A3
Duchess Rd C5
Duke St B5
Duncombe St A1
Durham Rd B2
Earl St C4
Earl Way C4
Ecclesall Rd C3
Edmund Rd C5
Edward St B3
Effingham Rd A6
Effingham St A6
Egerton St C3
Eldon St B3
Elmore Rd B1
Exchange St B5
Eyre St C4
Fargate B4
Farm Rd C5
Fawcett St A3
Filey St B3
Fir St A1
Fire Station C4
Fitzalan Square/Ponds Forge B5
Fitzwater Rd C6
Fitzwilliam Gate C4
Fitzwilliam St B3
Flat St B5
Foley St A6
Foundry Climbing Centre A4
Fulton Rd A1
Furnace Hill A4
Furnival Rd A5
Furnival Square C4
Furnival St C4
Garden St B3
Gell St B3
Gibraltar St A4
Glebe Rd B1
Glencoe Rd C6
Glossop Rd B2/B3/C1
Gloucester St C2
Government Offices C4
Granville Rd C6
Granville Rd / The Sheffield Coll C5
Graves Gallery B5
Green Lane A4
Hadfield St A1
Hanover St C3
Hanover Way C3
Harcourt Rd B1
Harmer Lane B5
Havelock St C2
Hawley St B4
Haymarket B5
Headford St C3
Heavygate Rd A1
Henry St A3
High St B4
Hodgson St C3
Holberry Gardens C2
Hollis Croft B4
Holly St B4
Hounsfield Rd B3
Howard Rd A1
Hoyle St A3
Hyde Park A6
Hyde Park Terrace B6
Infirmary Rd A3
Infirmary Rd A3
Jericho St A3
Johnson St A5
Kelham Island Industrial A4
Lawson Rd C1
Leadmill Rd C5
Leadmill St C5
Leadmill, The C5
Leamington St A1
Leavygreave Rd B3
Lee Croft B4
Leopold St B4
Leveson St A6
Library A2/B5/C1
Light, The C4
Lyceum Theatre B5
Malinda St A3
Maltravers St A5
Manor Oaks Rd B6
Mappin St B3
Marlborough Rd B1
Mary St C4
Matilda St C4
Matlock Rd A1
Meadow St A3
Melbourn Rd A1
Melbourne Avenue C1
Millennium Galleries B5
Millsands A4
Milton St C3
Mitchell St B3
Mona Avenue A1
Mona Rd A1
Montgomery Terrace Rd A3
Montgomery Theatre B4
Monument Grounds C6
Moor Oaks Rd B1
Moor, The C4
Moor Market C4
Moore St C3
Mowbray St A4
Mushroom Lane B2
National Emergency Service Mus A4
National Videogame Museum B5
Netherthorpe Rd B3
Netherthorpe Rd B3
Newbould Lane C1
Nile St C1
Norfolk Park Rd C6
Norfolk Rd C6
Norfolk St B4
North Church St B4
Northfield Rd A1
Northumberland Rd B1
Nursery St A5
O2 Academy B5
Oakholme Rd C1
Octagon B2
Odeon B5
Old St B6
Orchard Square Shopping Centre B4
Oxford St A2
Paradise St B4
Park Lane C2
Park Square B5
Parker's Rd B1
Pearson Building (University) C2
Penistone Rd A3
Pinstone St B4
Pitt St B3
Police Station B5
Pond Hill B5
Pondorosa, The A2
Pond St B5
Ponds Forge International Sports Centre B5
Portobello St B3
Post Office A2/B3/B4/B5/C1/C3/C6
Powell St A2
Queen St B4
Queen's Rd C5
Ramsey Rd B1
Red Hill B3
Redcar Rd B1
Regent St B3
Rockingham St B4
Roebuck Rd A2
Royal Hallamshire Hospital C2
Russell St A4
Rutland Park C1
St George's Close B3
St Mary's Gate C3
St Mary's Rd C4/C5
St Philip's Rd A3
Savile St A5
School Rd B1
Scotland St A4
Severn Rd B1
Shalesmoor A4
Shalesmoor A3
Sheaf St B5
Sheffield Cath ✝ B4
Sheffield Hallam University B5
Sheffield Ice Sports Ctr – Skate Central C5
Sheffield Institute of Arts B5
Sheffield Interchange B5
Sheffield Parkway A6
Sheffield Station ≋ C5
Sheffield Station/Sheffield Hallam University B5
Sheffield University B2
Shepherd St A3
Shipton St A2
Shopmobility B3
Shoreham St C4
Showroom C5
Shrewsbury Rd C5
Sidney St C4
Site Gallery C5
Sky Edge Fields B6
Slinn St A1
Smithfield A4
Snig Hill A5
Snow Lane A4
Solly St B3
South Lane C4
South Street B5
Southbourne Rd C1
Spital Hill A5
Spital St A5
Spring Hill B1
Spring Hill Rd B1
Springvale Rd A1
Stafford Rd C6
Stafford St B6
Suffolk Rd C5
Summer St B2
Sunny Bank C3
Superstore A3/C3
Surrey St B4
Sussex St A6
Sutton St B3
Sydney Rd A2
Sylvester St C4
Talbot St B5
Taptonville Rd B1
Tenter St B4
Town Hall B4
Townend St A1
Townhead St B4
Trafalgar St B4
Tree Root Walk B2
Trinity St A4
Trippet Lane B4
Turner Museum of Glass B3
Union St B4
University Drama Studio B2
Univ of Sheffield B3
Upper Allen St A3
Upper Hanover St B3
Upperthorpe Rd A2/A3
Verdon St A5
Victoria Rd C2
Victoria Station Rd A5
Victoria St B3
Waingate B5
Watery St A3
Watson Rd C1
Wellesley Rd B2
Wellington St C3
West Bar A4
West Bar Green A4
West One Plaza B3
West St B3
West St B4
Westbourne Rd C1
Western Bank B2
Western Rd A1
Weston Park B2
Weston Pk Hosp B2
Weston Park Mus B2
Weston St B2
Wharncliffe Rd C3
Whitham Rd B1
Wicker A5
Wilkinson St B2
William St C3
Winter Garden ✦ B4
Winter St B2
York St B4
Yorkshire Artspace C4
Young St C4

Shrewsbury 195

Abbey Foregate B3
Abbey Gardens B2
Abbey Lawn Bsns Pk B3
Abbots House B2
Albert St A2
Alma St B1
Ashley St A3
Ashton Rd C1
Avondale Drive A3
Bage Way C3
Barker St B1
Beacall's Lane A2
Beeches Lane C2
Beehive Lane C1
Belle Vue Gardens C2
Belle Vue Rd C2
Belmont Bank C1
Berwick Avenue A1
Berwick Rd A1
Betton St C2
Bishop St B3
Bradford St B3
Bridge St B1
Burton St A3
Bus Station B2
Butcher Row B2
Butler Rd C1
Bynner St C2
Canon St B3
Canonbury C1
Castle Bsns Pk, The A2
Castle Foregate A2
Castle Gates B2
Castle Walk B3
Castle St B2
Cathedral (RC) ✝ C1
Chester St A2
Cineworld C3
Claremont Bank B1
Claremont Hill B1
Cleveland St B3
Coleham Head B2
Coleham Pumping Station C2
College Hill B1
Corporation Lane A1
Coton Crescent A1
Coton Hill A2
Coton Mount A1
Crescent Lane C1
Crewe St A2
Cross Hill B1
Dana, The B2
Darwin Centre B2
Dingle, The B1
Dogpole B2
English Bridge B2
Fish St B2
Frankwell B1
Gateway Ctr, The A2
Gravel Hill Lane A1
Greenhous West Mid Showground A1
Greyfriars Rd C2
Hampton Rd A3
Haycock Way C3
High St B1
Hills Lane B1
Holywell St B3
Hunter St A1
Information Ctr B1
Ireland's Mansion & Bear Steps B1
John St A3
Kennedy Rd C1
King St B3
Kingsland Bridge C1
Kingsland Bridge (toll) C1
Kingsland Rd C1
Library B2
Lime St C2
Longden Coleham C2
Longden Rd C1
Longner St B1
Luciefelde Rd C1
Mardol B1
Market B1
Monkmoor Rd B3
Moreton Crescent C2
Mount St A1
New Park Close A3
New Park Rd A2
New Park St A3
North St A2
Oakley St C1
Old Coleham C2
Old Market Hall B1
Old Potts Way C3
Parade Shops, The B2
Post Office B1/B3
Pride Hill B1
Pride Hill Centre B1
Priory Rd B1
Pritchard Way C3
Quarry Swimming & Fitness Centre, The B1
Queen St A3
Raby Crescent C2
Rad Brook C1
Rea Brook C3
Rea Brook Valley Local Nature Reserve C3
Riverside B1
Roundhill Lane A1
St Alkmund's B2
St Chad's B1
St Chad's Terrace B1
St John's Hill B1
St Julians Crescent C2
St Julians Friars C2
St Mary's B2
St Mary's St B2
Salters Lane C2
Scott St C3
Severn Theatre B1
Severn Bank A2
Severn St A2
Shrewsbury ≋ B2
Shrewsbury Abbey B3
Shrewsbury High School C1
Shrewsbury Museum & Art Gallery B1
Shrewsbury Prison Tours ✦ B2
Shrewsbury School ✦ C1
Shropshire Regimental Mus B2
Shropshire Wildlife Trust ✦ B3
Smithfield Rd B1
South Hermitage C1
Square, The B1
Superstore C3
Swan Hill B1
Sydney Avenue A3
Tankerville St B3
Tilbrook Drive A3
Town Walls C1
Trinity St C2
Underdale Rd B3
Univ Ctr Shrewsbury (Guildhall) B1
Victoria Avenue B1
Victoria Quay B1
Victoria St B2
Welsh Bridge B1
Whitehall St B3
William Way C2
Wood St A2
Wyle Cop B2

Southampton 196

Above Bar St A2
Albert Rd North B3
Albert Rd South C3
Andersons Rd B3
Argyle Rd A2
Arundel Tower ✦ B1
Bargate, The ✦ B2
BBC South A1
Bedford Place A1
Belvidere Rd A3
Bernard St C2
Blechynden Terrace A1
Brinton's Rd A2
Britannia Rd A3
Briton St C2
Brunswick Place A2
Bugle St C1
Canute Rd C3
Castle Way C2
Catchcold Tower ✦ B1
Central Bridge C3
Central Rd C2
Channel Way C3
Chapel Rd B3
City Art Gallery A1
City College B3
City Cruise Terminal C1
Civic Centre A1
Civic Centre Rd A1
Coach Station B1
Commercial Rd A1
Cumberland Place A1
Cunard Rd C2
Derby Rd A3
Devonshire Rd A1
Dock Gate 4 C2
Dock Gate 8 B1
East Park (Andrew's Park) A2
East Park Terrace A2
East St B2
Endle St B3
European Way C2
Fire Station A2
Floating Bridge Rd C3
God's House Tower ✦ C2
Golden Grove A3
Graham Rd A2
Guildhall A1
Hanover Buildings B2
Harbour Lights C3
Harbour Parade B1
Hartington Rd A3
Havelock Rd A1
Henstead Rd A1
Herbert Walker Ave B1
High St B2
Hoglands Park B2
Holy Rood (Rems), Merchant Navy Memorial B2
Houndwell Park B2
Houndwell Place B2
Hythe Ferry C2
Isle of Wight Ferry Terminal C1
James St B3
Kingsway A2
Leisure World B1
Library A1
Lime St B2
London Rd A2
Marine Parade B3
Marlands Shopping Centre, The A1
Marsh Lane B2
Mayflower Meml ✦ C1
Mayflower Park C1
Mayflower Theatre, The A1
Medieval Merchant's House C1
Melbourne St B3
Morris Rd A1
National Oceanography Centre ✦ C3
Neptune Way C3
New Rd A2
Nichols Rd A3
North Front A2
Northam Rd A3
Ocean Dock C2
Ocean Village Marina C3
Ocean Way C3
Odeon B1
Ogle Rd B1
Old Northam Rd A2
Orchard Lane B2
Oxford Avenue A2
Oxford St C2
Palmerston Park A2
Palmerston Rd A2
Parsonage Rd A3
Peel St A3
Platform Rd C2
Polygon, The A1

Southend • Stirling • Stoke-on-Trent (Hanley) • Stratford-upon-Avon • Sunderland • Swansea • Swindon • Taunton 211

Portland Terrace B1
Post Office B2
Pound Tree Rd B2
Quays Swimming & Diving Complex, The B1
Queen's Park C2
Queen's Peace Fountain ✦ A2
Queen's Terrace C2
Queensway B2
Radcliffe Rd A3
Rochester St A3
Royal Pier C1
Royal South Hants Hospital A2
St Andrew's Rd A2
St Mary's B3
St Mary St A2
St Mary's Leisure Centre A2
St Mary's Place B2
St Mary's Rd A2
St Mary's Stadium (Southampton FC) A3
St Michael's C1
SeaCity Museum A1
Showcase Cinema de Lux B1
Solent Sky C3
South Front B2
Southampton Central Station A1
Southampton Solent University A2
Terminus Terrace C2
Threefield Lane B2
Titanic Engineers' Memorial ✦ A2
Town Quay C1
Town Walls B2
Tudor House C1
Vincent's Walk B2
Westgate Hall C1
West Marlands Rd A1
West Park A1
West Park Rd A1
West Quay Rd B1
West Quay Retail Pk B1
Western Esplanade B1
Westquay Shopping Centre B1
Westquay South B1
White Star Way C2
Winton St A2

Southend-on-Sea 197

Adventure Island ✦ C3
Albany Avenue A1
Albert Rd C3
Alexandra Rd C2
Alexandra St C2
Alexandra Yacht Club ✦ C2
Ashburnham Rd B2
Avenue Rd B1
Avenue Terrace B1
Balmoral Rd B1
Baltic Avenue B3
Baxter Avenue A2/B2
Beecroft Art Gallery B2
Bircham Rd A2
Boscombe Rd B3
Boston Avenue A1/B2
Bournemouth Pk Rd A3
Browning Avenue A3
Bus Station C3
Byron Avenue A3
Cambridge Rd C1/C2
Canewdon Rd B1
Carnarvon Rd A2
Central Avenue A3
Central Museum & Planetarium B2
Chelmsford Avenue A1
Chichester Rd B2
Church Rd C3
Civic Centre A2
Clarence Rd C2
Clarence St C2
Cliff Avenue B1
Cliffs Pavilion C1
Clifftown Parade C2
Clifftown Rd C2
Colchester Rd A1
Coleman St B3
College Way B2
County Court B3
Cromer Rd B3
Crowborough Rd A2
Dryden Avenue A3
East St A2
Elmer Approach B2
Elmer Avenue B2
Forum, The B2
Gainsborough Dr A1
Gayton Rd A2
Glenhurst Rd A2
Gordon Place B2
Gordon Rd B2
Grainger Rd A2
Greyhound Retail Park A3
Greyhound Way A3
Grove, The A3
Guildford Rd B3
Hamlet Court Rd B1
Hamlet Rd C1
Harcourt Avenue A1
Hartington Rd C3
Hastings Rd B3
Herbert Grove C3
Heygate Avenue C3
High St B2/C2
Information Ctr C3
Kenway A2
Kilworth Avenue B3
Lancaster Gardens B3
Library B2
London Rd B1
Lucy Rd C3
MacDonald Avenue A1
Magistrates' Court A2
Maldon Rd A2
Marine Avenue C1
Marine Parade C3
Marine Rd C1
Milton Rd B1
Milton St B2
Napier Avenue B2
North Avenue A3
North Rd A1/B1
Odeon B2
Osborne Rd B1
Park Crescent B1
Park Rd B1
Park St B1
Park Terrace B1
Pier Hill C3
Pleasant Rd C3
Police Station A2
Post Office B2/B3
Princes St B2
Queens Rd B2
Queensway B2/B3/C3
Radio Essex C2
Rayleigh Avenue A1
Redstock Rd A2
Rochford Avenue A1
Roots Hall Stadium (Southend United FC) A1
Royal Mews C2
Royal Terrace C2
Royals Shopping Centre, The C3
Ruskin Avenue A3
St Ann's Rd B3
St Helen's Rd B1
St John's Rd B1
St Leonard's Rd C3
St Lukes Rd A3
St Vincent's Rd C1
Salisbury Ave A1/B1
Scratton Rd C2
Shakespeare Drive A1
Shopmobility B2
Short St A2
South Avenue A3
Southchurch Rd B3
Southend Central B2
South Essex Coll B2
Southend Pier Railway C3
Southend Victoria B2
Stanfield Rd A2
Stanley Rd C3
Sutton Rd A3/B3
Swanage Rd B3
Sweyne Avenue A1
Sycamore Grove A3
Tennyson Avenue A3
Tickfield Avenue A2
Tudor Rd A1
Tunbridge Rd A2
Tylers Avenue B3
Tyrrel Drive B3
Univ of Essex B2/C2
Vale Avenue A2
Victoria Avenue A2
Victoria Shopping Centre, The B2
Warrior Square B3
Wesley Rd C3
West Rd A1
West St A1
Westcliff Avenue C1
Westcliff Parade C1
Western Esplanade C1
Weston Rd C2
Whitegate Rd B3
Wilson Rd C1
Wimborne Rd B3
York Rd C3

Stirling 197

Abbey Rd A3
Abbotsford Place A3
Abercromby Place C1
Albert Halls B1
Albert Place B1
Alexandra Place A3
Allan Park C2
Ambulance Station A2
AMF Ten Pin Bowling ✦ B2
AR Centre C3
Argyll Avenue A3
Argyll's Lodging ✦ B1
Back O' Hill Ind Est A1
Back O' Hill Rd A1
Baker St B2
Ballengeich Pass A1
Balmoral Place B1
Barn Rd B1
Barnton St B2
Bastion, The ✦ C2
Bow St B1
Bruce St A2
Burghmuir Retail Park C2
Burghmuir Rd A2/B2/C2
Bus Station B2
Cambuskenneth Bridge A3
Castle Court B1
Causewayhead Rd A2
Cemetery A1
Church of the Holy Rude B1
Clarendon Place C1
Club House B1
Colquhoun St C3
Corn Exchange B2
Council Offices C2
Court B2
Cowane Centre A2
Cowane St A2
Cowane's Hosp B1
Dean Crescent A3
Douglas St A2
Drip Rd A1
Drummond Lane C1
Drummond Place C1
Drummond Pl La C1
Dumbarton Rd C2
Eastern Access Rd B2
Edward Avenue A3
Edward Rd A2
Engine Shed, The ✦ B2
Forrest Rd A2
Fort A1
Forth Crescent B2
Forth St A2
Gladstone Place C1
Glebe Avenue C1
Glebe Crescent C1
Golf Course C1
Goosecroft Rd B2
Gowanhill A1
Greenwood Avenue B1
Harvey Wynd A1
Information Ctr B1
Irvine Place B2
James St A2
John St B1
Kerse Rd C3
King's Knot ✦ B1
King's Park C1
King's Park Rd C1
Laurencecroft Rd A2
Leisure Pool B2
Library B2
Linden Avenue C2
Lovers Walk A2
Lower Back Walk B1
Lower Bridge St A2
Lower Castlehill A1
Mar Place B1
Meadow Place A3
Meadowforth Rd C3
Middlemuir Rd C3
Millar Place A3
Morris Terrace B2
Mote Hill A1
Murray Place B2
Nelson Place C2
Old Town Cemetery B1
Old Town Jail ✦ B1
Park Terrace C1
Phoenix Ind Est C3
Players Rd C3
Port St C2
Post Office A3/B2
Princes St B2
Queen St B2
Queen's Rd B1
Queenshaugh Drive A3
Ramsay Place A2
Regimental Mus A1
Riverside Drive A3
Ronald Place A1
Rosebery Place A2
Royal Gardens B1
Royal Gardens B1
St Mary's Wynd B1
St Ninian's Rd C2
Scott St A2
Seaforth Place B2
Shore Rd B2
Snowdon Place C1
Snowdon Place La C1
Spittal St B2
Springkerse Ind Est C3
Springkerse Rd C3
Stirling Arcade B2
Stirling Bsns Ctr C2
Stirling Castle A1
Stirling County Rugby Football Club A3
Stirling Enterprise Park C3
Stirling Old Bridge A2
Stirling Smith Art Gallery & Mus B1
Stirling Station B2
Superstore A1/A2
Sutherland Avenue A3
Tannery Lane A2
Thistle Ind Est C3
Thistles Shopping Centre, The B2
Tolbooth ✦ B1
Town Wall B1
Union St A2
Upper Back Walk B1
Upper Bridge St A1
Upper Castlehill B1
Upper Craigs C2
Victoria Place C1
Victoria Rd B1
Victoria Square B1/C1
Vue B2
Wallace St A2
Waverley Crescent A3
Wellgreen Rd C2
Windsor Place C1
YHA B1

Stoke-on-Trent (Hanley) 196

Acton St A3
Albion St B2
Argyle St C1
Ashbourne Grove A2
Avoca St A3
Baskerville Rd B3
Bedford Rd C1
Bedford St C1
Bethesda St B2
Birches Head Rd A3
Botteslow St C3
Boundary St A2
Broad St C2
Broom St A3
Bryan St A2
Bucknall New Rd B3
Bucknall Old Rd B3
Bus Station C3
Castlefield St C1
Cavendish St B1
Central Forest Park A2
Century Retail Park B1
Charles St B3
Cheapside B2
Chell St A3
Cineworld A2
Clarke St C1
Cleveland Rd C2
Clifford St C3
Clough St B1
Clough St East B2
Clyde St C1
College Rd C2
Cooper St C2
Corbridge Rd A1
Cricket Ground A1
Cutts St C2
Davis St C1
Denbigh St A1
Derby St C3
Dilke St A3
Dudson Ctr, The A2
Dundas St A3
Dundee Rd C1
Dyke St B3
Eastwood Rd C3
Eaton St A3
Emma Bridgewater Factory ✦ C3
Etruria Industrial C1
Etruria Park B1
Etruria Rd B1
Etruria Vale Rd C1
Festing St A3
Festival Heights Retail Park A1
Festival Retail Park A1
Fire Station C2
Five Towns C3
Foundry St B2
Franklyn St C3
Garnet St B1
Garth St B3
George St A3
Gilman St B3
Glass St B3
Goodson St B3
Greyhound Way A1
Grove Place C1
Hampton St C3
Hanley Park C2
Hanley Park C2
Harding Rd C2
Hassall St B3
Havelock Place C1
Hazlehurst St C3
Hinde St C2
Hope St B2
Houghton St C2
Hulton St A3
Information Ctr B2
Jasper St C2
Jervis St A3
John Bright St A3
John St B2
Keelings Rd A3
Kimberley Rd C1
Ladysmith Rd C1
Lawrence St C2
Leek Rd C3
Library C2
Lichfield St C3
Linfield Rd B3
Lower Bedford St C1
Lower Bryan St A2
Lower Mayer St A3
Lowther St A1
Magistrates Court C2
Malham St A2
Marsh St B2
Matlock St C3
Mayer St A3
Milton St C1
Mitchell Arts Ctr B2
Moston St A3
Mount Pleasant C1
Mulgrave St A1
Mynors St B3
Nelson Place B3
New Century St B1
Octagon Retail Park B1
Ogden Rd C3
Old Hall St B3
Old Town Rd A3
Pall Mall B2
Palmerston St C3
Parkway, The C2
Pavilion Drive A1
Pelham St C3
Percy St B2
Piccadilly B2
Picton St B3
Plough St A3
Police Station C2
Portland St A1
Post Office A3/B2
Potteries Ctr, The B2
Potteries Museum & Art Gallery B2
Potteries Way B1
Powell St A1
Pretoria Rd C1
Quadrant Rd B2
Ranelagh St C2
Raymond St C2
Rectory Rd C1
Regent Rd C2
Regent Theatre B2
Richmond Terrace C2
Ridgehouse Drive A1
Robson St C2
St Ann St B3
St Luke St B3
Sampson St B2
Shaw St A1
Sheaf St C2
Shearer St C1
Shelton New Rd C1
Shirley Rd C2
Shopmobility B3
Snow Hill C2
Spur St C3
Stafford St B2
Stubbs Lane C3
Sun St C1
Supermarket A1/B2
Superstore B2
Talbot St C3
Town Hall B2
Town Rd A3
Trinity St B2
Union St A2
Upper Hillchurch St A3
Upper Huntbach St B3
Victoria Hall B3
Warner St C2
Warwick St C1
Waterloo Rd A1
Waterloo St B3
Well St B3
Wellesley St C2
Wellington Rd B3
Wellington St B3
Whitehaven Drive A2
Whitmore St C1
Windermere St A1
Woodall St A1
Yates St C2

Stratford-upon-Avon 197

Albany Rd B1
Alcester Rd B1
Ambulance Station B1
Arden St B2
Avenue Farm A1
Ave Farm Ind Est A1
Avenue Rd A3
Baker Avenue A1
Bandstand C3
Bear Pit B2
Benson Rd A3
Birmingham Rd A2
Boat Club B3
Borden Place C1
Bridge St B2
Bridgetown Rd C3
Bridgeway B3
Broad St C2
Broad Walk C2
Brookvale Rd C1
Brunel Way B1
Bull St C2
Butterfly Farm ✦ C3
Cemetery C1
Chapel Lane B2
Cherry Orchard C1
Chestnut Walk B2
Children's Playground C3
Church St C2
Clarence Rd B1
Clopton Bridge ✦ B3
Clopton Rd A2
College B1
College Lane C2
College St C2
Community Sports Centre B1
Council Offices (District) B2
Courtyard, The C2
Cox's Yard ✦ B3
Cricket Ground C3
Ely Gardens B2
Ely St B2
Everyman B2
Evesham Rd C1
Fire Station B1
Foot Ferry C3
Fordham Avenue A2
Garrick Way C1
Gower Memorial ✦ B3
Great William St B2
Greenhill St B2
Greenway, The C2
Grove Rd B2
Guild St B2
Guildhall & Sch B2
Hall's Croft C2
Harvard House B2
Henley St B2
Hertford Rd C1
High St B2
Holton St C2
Holy Trinity C2
Information Ctr B3
Jolyffe Park Rd A2
Kipling Rd C3
Library B2
Lodge Rd B1
Maidenhead Rd A3
Mansell St B2
Masons Court B2
Masons Rd A1
Maybird Shopping Park A2
Maybrook Retail Pk A2
Maybrook Rd A1
Mayfield Avenue A2
Meer St B2
Mill Lane C2
Moat House Hotel B3
Narrow Lane C2
Nash's House & New Place B2
New St C2
Old Town C2
Orchard Way C1
Other Place, The C2
Paddock Lane C1
Park Rd A1
Payton St B2
Percy St A2
Police Station B2
Post Office A2/B2
Recreation Ground C2
Regal Road A2
Rother St B2
Rowley Crescent A3
Royal Shakespeare Theatre B3
Ryland St C2
Saffron Meadow C2
St Andrew's Cres B1
St Gregory's A3
St Gregory's Rd A3
St Mary's Rd A2
Sanctus Drive C2
Sanctus St C1
Sandfield Rd C2
Scholars Lane B2
Seven Meadows Rd C2
Shakespeare Inst C2
Shakespeare St B2
Shakespeare's Birthplace ✦ B2
Sheep St B2
Shelley Rd C3
Shipston Rd C3
Shottery Rd C1
Slingates Rd A2
Southern Lane C2
Stratford Enterprise Park A1
Stratford Hosp B2
Stratford Leisure Centre B3
Stratford Play Ho ✦ B2
Stratford Sports Club B1
Stratford-upon-Avon Station B1
Swan Theatre B3
Swan's Nest Lane B3
Talbot Rd A2
Tiddington Rd B3
Timothy's Bridge Rd A1
Town Hall B2
Town Square B2
Tramway Bridge B3
Trinity Close C2
Tudor World B2
Tyler St B2
War Meml Gardens B3
Warwick Rd B3
Waterside B3
Welcombe Rd A3
West St C2
Western Rd A2
Wharf Rd A2
Willows North, The B1
Willows, The B1
Wood St B2

Sunderland 197

Albion Place C2
Alliance Place B1
Ashwood St C1
Athenaeum St B2
Azalea Terrace C2
Beach St A1
Bedford St B2
Beechwood Terr C1
Belvedere Rd C2
Blandford St B2
Borough Rd B3
Bridge Crescent B2
Bridge St B2
Bridges, The B2
Brooke St A2
Brougham St B2
Burdon Rd C2
Burn Park C1
Burn Park Rd C1
Burn Park Tech Pk C1
Carol St B1
Charles St A3
Chester Rd C1
Chester Terrace B1
Church St A3
Civic Centre C2
Cork St B3
Coronation St B3
Cowan Terrace C2
Cresswell Terrace C2
Dame Dorothy St A2
Deptford Rd B1
Deptford Terrace A1
Derby St C2
Derwent St C2
Dock St A3
Dundas St A2
Durham Rd C1
Easington St A2
Eden House Rd C1
Egerton St C3
Empire B3
Empire Theatre B2
Farringdon Row B1
Fawcett St B2
Fire Station B1
Fox St C1
Foyle St B3
Frederick St B3
Hanover Place A1
Havelock Terrace C1
Hay St A2
Headworth Square B3
Hendon Rd B3
High St East B3
High St West B2/B3
Holmeside B2
Hylton Rd B1
John St B3
Kier Hardie Way A2
Lambton St B3
Laura St C3
Lawrence St B3
Library & Arts Ctr B3
Lily St B1
Lime St B1
Livingstone Rd B2
Low Row B2
Magistrates' Court B2
Matamba Terrace B1
Millburn St B1
Millennium Way A2
Minster B2
Monkwearmouth Station Mus A2
Mowbray Park C3
Mowbray Rd C3
Murton St C3
National Glass Centre ✦ A3
New Durham Rd C1
Newcastle Rd A2
Nile St B3
Norfolk St B3
North Bridge St A2
Northern Gallery for Contemporary Art (NGCA) A3
Otto Terrace C1
Park Lane C2
Park Lane C2
Park Rd C2
Paul's Rd B3
Peel St C3
Point, The ✦ B2
Police Station B2
Priestly Crescent A1
Queen St B2
Railway Row B1
Retail Park B1
Richmond St A2
Roker Avenue A2
Royalty Theatre C1
Royalty, The C1
Ryhope Rd C2
St Mary's Way B2
St Michael's Way B2
St Peter's A3
St Peter's A2
St Peter's Way A3
St Vincent St C3
Salem Rd C3
Salem St C3
Salisbury St C3
Sans St B3
Shopmobility B2
Silkworth Row B1
Southwick Rd A2
Stadium of Light (Sunderland AFC) A2
Stadium Way A2
Stobart St A2
Stockton Rd C2
Suffolk St C3
Sunderland B2
Sunderland Aquatic Centre A2
Sunderland College C2
Sunderland Mus B3
Sunderland St B3
Sunderland Sta B2
Tatham St C3
Tavistock Place B3
Thelma St C1
Thomas St North A2
Thornholme Rd C1
Toward Rd C3
Transport Interchange C2
Trimdon St Way B1
Tunstall Rd C2
University C1
University Library C1
Univ of Sunderland (City Campus) B1
Univ of Sunderland (St Peter's Campus) A3
University of Sunderland (Sir Tom Cowie Campus) A3
Vaux Brewery Way A2
Villiers St B3
Villiers St South B3
Vine Place C2
Violet St B1
Walton Lane B3
Waterworks Rd B1
Wearmouth Bridge B2
West Sunniside B3
West Wear St B3
Westbourne Rd B1
Western Hill C1
Wharncliffe B1
Whickham St A3
White House Rd C3
Wilson St North A2
Winter Gardens C3
Wreath Quay A1

Swansea Abertawe 198

Adelaide St C3
Albert Row C3
Alexandra Rd B3
Argyle St C1
Baptist Well Place A2
Beach St C1
Belle Vue Way B3
Berw Rd A1
Berwick Terrace A2
Bond St C1
Brangwyn Concert Hall C1
Bridge St A3
Brooklands Terrace B1
Brunswick St C1
Bryn-Syfi Terrace A2
Bryn-y-Mor Rd C1
Bullins Lane B1
Burrows Rd C1
Bus Station C2
Bus/Rail link A3
Cadfan Rd A1
Cadrawd Rd A1
Caer St B3
Carig Crescent A1
Carlton Terrace B2
Carmarthen Rd A3
Castle Square B3
Castle St B3
Catherine St C1
Civic Ctr & Library C2
Clarence St C2
Colbourne Terrace A2
Constitution Hill B1
Copr Bay Bridge C3
Court B3
Creidiol Rd A2
Cromwell St B2
Crown Courts C1
Duke St B1
Dunvant Place C2
Dyfatty Park A3
Dyfatty St A3
Dyfed Avenue A1
Dylan Thomas Ctr ✦ B3
Dylan Thomas Theatre C3
Eaton Crescent C1
Eigen Crescent A1
Elfed Rd A1
Emlyn Rd A1
Evans Terrace A3
Fairfield Terrace B1
Ffynone Drive B1
Ffynone Rd B1
Fire Station B3
Firm St A2
Fleet St C1
Francis St C1
Fullers Row B2
George St B2
Glamorgan St C2
Glynn Vivian Art Gallery B3
Gower College Swansea C1
Graig Terrace A3
Grand Theatre C2
Granogwen Rd A2
Guildhall C1
Guildhall Rd South C1
Gwent Rd A1
Gwynedd Avenue A1
Hafod St A3
Hanover St B1
Harcourt St B2
Harries St A2
Heathfield B2
Henrietta St B1
Hewson St B2
High St A3/B3
High View A2
Hill St A2
Historic Ships Berth C3
HM Prison C2
Islwyn Rd A1
King Edward's Rd C1
Kingsway, The B2
LC, The C3
Long Ridge A2
Madoc St C2
Mansel St B2
Maritime Quarter C3
Market B3
Mayhill Gardens B1
Mayhill Rd A1
Milton Terrace A2
Mission Gallery C3
Montpelier Terrace B1
Morfa Rd A3
Mount Pleasant B2
National Waterfront Museum C3
New Cut Rd A3
New St A3
Nicander Parade A2
Nicander Place A2
Nicholl St B2
Norfolk St B2
North Hill Rd A2
Northampton Lane B2
Observatory ✦ C3
Odeon B3
Orchard St B3
Oxford St B2
Oystermouth Rd C1
Page St B2
Pant-y-Celyn Rd B1
Parc Tawe North B3
Parc Tawe Shopping & Leisure Centre B3
Patti Pavilion C1
Paxton St C2
Pen-y-Graig Rd A1
Penmaen Terrace B1
Phillips Parade C1
Picton Terrace B2
Plantasia B3
Plantasia B3
Police Station B2
Post Office A1/A2/C1
Powys Avenue A1
Primrose St B2
Princess Way B3
Promenade B2
Pryder Gardens A1
Quadrant Shopping Centre C2
Quay Park B3
Rhianfa Lane B1
Rhondda St B2
Richardson St C2
Rodney St C1
Rose Hill B1
Rosehill Terrace B1
Russell St B1
St Helen's Avenue C1
St Helen's Crescent C1
St Helen's Rd C1
St James Gardens B1
St James's Crescent B1
St Mary's B3
Sea View Terrace A3
Singleton St C2
Stanley Place B2
Strand B3
Swansea Arena C3
Swansea Castle B3
Swansea Metropolitan University B2
Swansea Mus C3
Swansea Station A3
Taliesyn Rd B1
Tan y Marian Rd A1
Tegid Rd A2
Teilo Crescent A1
Tenpin Bowling ✦ B3
Terrace Rd B1/B2
Tontine St A3
Townhill Rd A1
Tramshed, The C3
Trawler Rd C3
Union St B2
Upper Strand A3
Vernon St A3
Victoria Quay C3
Victoria Rd B3
Vincent St C1
Vue C3
Walter Rd B1
Watkin St A2
Waun-Wen Rd A2
Wellington St C2
Westbury St C1
Western St C1
Westway C2
William St C2
Wind St B3
Woodlands Terrace B1
YMCA B2
York St C3

Swindon 198

Albert St C3
Albion St C1
Alfred St A2
AR Centre B1
Art Gallery & Museum C3
Ashford Rd C1
Aylesbury St A2
Bath Rd C2
Bathampton St B1
Bathurst Rd B3
Beatrice St A2
Beckhampton St B3
Bowood Rd C1
Bristol St B1
Broad St A3
Brunel Shopping Centre, The B2
Brunel Statue B2
Brunswick St C2
Bus Station B2
Cambria Bridge Rd B1
Cambria Place B1
Canal Walk B2
Carfax St B2
Carr St B1
Castle Trading Est A3
Cemetery C1/C3
Chandler Close C3
Chapel C1
Chester St B1
Christ Church C3
Church Place B1
Cirencester Way A3
Clarence St B2
Clifton St C1
Cockleberry A2
Colbourne A3
Colbourne St A3
College St B2
Commercial Rd B2
Corporation St A2
Council Offices B3
County Cricket Gd A3
County Ground (Swindon Town Football Club) A3
County Rd A3
Courts B2
Cricklade Street C3
Crombey St B1/C2
Cross St C2
Curtis St B1
Deacon St C1
Designer Outlet (Great Western) B1
Dixon St C2
Dover St C2
Dowling St C2
Drove Rd C3
Dryden St C1
Durham St C3
East St B1
Eastcott Hill C2
Eastcott Rd C2
Edgeware Rd B2
Edmund St C2
Elmina Rd A3
Emlyn Square B1
English Heritage & Historic England Archive B1
Euclid St B3
Exeter St B1
Exmouth St C1
Fairview C1
Faringdon Rd B1
Farnsby St B1
Fire Station B3
Fleet St B2
Fleming Way B2/B3
Florence St A2
Gladstone St A3
Gooch St A2
Graham St A3
Great Western Way A1/A2
Groundwell Rd B3
Hawksworth Way A1
Haydon St A2
Henry St B2
Hillside Avenue C1
Holbrook Way B2
Hunt St C3
Hydro B1
Hythe Rd C2
Information Ctr B2
Joseph St C1
Kent Rd C2
King William St C2
Kingshill Rd C1
Lansdown Rd C2
Lawn, The C3
Leicester St B3
Library B2
Lincoln St B3
Little London C3
London St B1
Magic B3
Maidstone Rd C2
Manchester Rd A3
Maxwell St B1
Milford St B2
Milton Rd B1
Morse St C2
Newcastle St B3
Newcombe Drive A1
Hawsworth Ind Est A1
National Trust HQ B1
New Coll Swindon A2
Newhall St C2
North St C2
North Star A1
North Star Avenue A1
Northampton St B3
Ocotal Way A3
Okus Rd C1
Old Town C3
Oxford St B1
Parade, The B2
Park Lane B1
Park Lane B1
Park, The B1
Pembroke St C2
Plymouth St B3
Polaris Way A2
Police Station B2
Ponting St A2
Post Office B1/B2/C3
Poulton St A3
Princes St B2
Prospect Hill C2
Prospect Place C2
Queen St B2
Queen's Park C3
Radnor St C1
Read St C1
Reading St B1
Regent Circus C2
Regent St B2
Retail Park A2/A3/B3
Rosebery St A3
St Mark's B1
Salisbury St A3
Savernake St C2
Science & Technology Facilities Council Headquarters A2
Shelley St C1
Sheppard St B1
Shopmobility B2
South St C2
Southampton St B3
Spring Gardens B3
Stafford Street C2
Stanier St C2
Station Road A2
STEAM GWR B1
Swindon Rd C2
Swindon Station A2
Tennyson St B1
Theobald St B1
Town Hall B2
Transfer Bridges A3
Union St C2
Upham Rd C3
Victoria Rd C3
Walcot Rd B3
War Memorial ✦ B2
Wells St B3
Western St C2
Westmorland Rd B3
Whalebridge B2
Whitehead St C1
Whitehouse Rd A2
William St C1
Wyvern Theatre & Arts Centre B2
York Rd B3

Taunton 198

Addison Grove A1
Albemarle Rd A1
Alfred St B3
Alma St C2
Avenue, The A1
Bath Place C1
Belvedere Rd A1
Billet St B2
Billetfield C2
Birch Grove A1
Brewhouse Theatre B2
Bridge St B1
Bridgwater & Taunton Canal A2
Broadlands Rd C1
Burton Place C1
Bus Station B1
Canal Rd A2
Cann St C1
Canon St B2
Castle St B1
Cheddon Rd A2
Chip Lane A1
Clarence St B1
Cleveland St B1
Clifton Terrace A2
Coleridge Crescent C3
Compass Hill C1
Compton Close A2
Corporation St B1
Council Offices A1
County Walk Shopping Centre C2
Courtyard B2
Cranmer Rd B2
Crescent, The C1
Critchard Way B3
Cyril St A1
Deller's Wharf B1
Duke St B2
East Reach B3
East St B3
Eastbourne Rd B2
Eastleigh Rd C3
Eaton Crescent A2
Elm Grove A1
Elms Close A1
Fons George C1
Fore St B2
Fowler St A1
French Weir Recreation Grd B1
Geoffrey Farrant Walk A2
Gray's Almshouses B2
Grays Rd B3
Greenway Avenue A1
Guildford Place C1
Hammet St B2
Haydon Rd B3
Heavitree Way A2
Herbert St A1
High St C2
Holway Avenue C3
Hugo St B3
Huish's Almshouses B2
Hurdle Way C2
Information Ctr B2
Jubilee St A1
King's College C3
Kings Close C3
Laburnum St B2
Lambrook Rd B3
Lansdowne Rd A3
Leslie Avenue A1
Leycroft Rd B3
Library C2
Linden Grove A1
Magdalene St B2
Magistrates Court B1
Malvern Terrace A2
Market House B2
Mary St C2
Middle St B2
Mitre Court B3
Mount Nebo C1
Mount St C2
Mount, The C2
Mountway C2
Mus of Somerset B1
North St B2
Northfield Avenue B1
Northfield Rd B1
Northleigh Rd C3
Obridge Allotments A3
Obridge Lane A3
Obridge Rd A3
Obridge Viaduct A3
Orch Shopping Ctr C2
Osborne Way C1
Park St C1
Paul St C2
Plais St A2
Playing Field C3
Police Station A1
Portland St B1
Post Office B1/B2
Priorswood Ind Est A3
Priorswood Rd A2
Priory Avenue B2
Priory Bridge Rd B2
Priory Fields Retail Park A3
Priory Park A2
Priory Way A3
Queen St B3
Railway St A1
Recreation Grd A1
Riverside Place B2
St Augustine St B2
St George's C2
St Georges Square C2
St James B2
St James St B2
St John's C1
St John's Rd B1
St Josephs Field C2
St Mary Magdalene's B2
Samuels Court A1
Shire Hall & Law Courts C1
Somerset County Cricket Ground B2
Somerset County Hall C1
Somerset Cricket B2
South Rd C3
South St C3
Staplegrove Rd B1
Station Approach A2
Station Rd A1
Stephen St B2
Superstore C2
Swimming Pool A1
Tancred St B2
Tangier Way B1
Tauntfield Close C3
Taunton Castle B1
Taunton Deane Cricket Club C2
Taunton Station A2
Thomas St A1
Toneway A3
Tower St B1
Trenchard Way A1
Trevor Smith Place C3
Triangle, The A2
Trinity Bsns Centre C3
Trinity Rd C3
Trinity St B3
Trull Rd C1
Tudor House B2
Upper High St C1
Venture Way A3
Victoria Gate B3
Victoria Park B3
Victoria St B3
Viney St B3
Vivary Park C2
Vivary Pk Golf Club C2
Vivary Rd C1
War Memorial ✦ C1
Wellesley St A2
Wheatley Crescent A3
Whitehall A1
Wilfred Rd B3
William St A1
Wilton Church C1
Wilton Close C1
Wilton Grove C1
Wilton St C1
Winchester St B2
Winters Field B2
Wood St B1
Yarde Place B1

Telford 198

Alma Avenue ... C1
Amphitheatre ... A2
Bowling Alley ... A3
Brandsfarm Way ... A3
Brunel Rd ... B1
Bus Station ... B2
Buxton Rd ... C1
Central Park ... B2
Chelsea Gardens ✿ ... B2
Coach Central ... B2
Coachwell Close ... B1
Colliers Way ... A2
Courts ... B2
Dale Acre Way ... A3
Darliston ... C1
Deepdale ... B2
Deercote ... B2
Dinthill ... C1
Doddington ... B3
Dodmoor Grange ... C3
Downemead ... B3
Duffryn ... B3
Dunsheath ... B3
Euston Way ... A3
Eyton Mound ... C1
Eyton Rd ... B1
Forgegate ... A2
Grange Central ... B2
Hall Park Way ... B1
Hinkshay Rd ... C2
Hollinsworth Rd ... A2
Holyhead Rd ... A3
Housing Trust ... A1
Ice Rink ... B2
Ironmasters Way ... A2
Job Centre ... B1
Land Registry ... A1
Lawn Central ... B2
Lawnswood ... C1
Library ... A1
Malinsgate ... B1
Matlock Avenue ... C1
Moor Rd ... C1
Mount Rd ... C1
Odeon 📽 ... B1
Park Lane ... A1
Police Station ◆ ... B1
Post Office
PO ... A2/B2/C1
Priorslee Avenue ... A3
Queen Elizabeth
Avenue ... A3
Queen Elizabeth
Way ... A2/B3
Queensway ... A2/B2
QEII Arena ... A3
Rampart Way ... A2
Randlay Avenue ... C3
Randlay Wood ... C3
Rhodes Avenue ... C1
Royal Way ... B1
St Leonards Rd ... B1
St Quentin Gate ... B2
Shifnal Rd ... C2
Silkin Way ... C2
Sixth Avenue ... A3
Southwater Leisure
Complex 📽 ... B2
Southwater Way ... B1
Spout Lane ... C1
Spout Mound ... C1
Spout Way ... C1
Stafford Court ... A1
Stafford Park ... B3
Stirchley Avenue ... C3
Stone Row ... C2
Superstore ... B1
Telford Bridge Retail
Park ... A1
Telford Central
Station ◆ ... A3
Telford Centre, The ... B2
Telford Forge
Shopping Park ... A1
Telford Hornets RFCC2
Telford International
Centre ... C2
Telford Way ... A1
Third Avenue ... A2
Town Park ... C2
Town Pk Visitor Ctr ... B2
Wellswood Avenue ... A1
West Centre Way ... A1
Withywood Drive ... C1
Wonderland ◆ ... C2
Woodhouse
Central ... A3
Yates Way ... A1

Torquay 199

Abbey Rd ... B2
Alexandra Rd ... A2
Alpine Rd ... B2
AMF Bowling ... B2
Ash Hill Rd ... A2
Babbacombe Rd ... B3
Bampfylde Rd ... B1
Barton Rd ... A1
Beacon Quay ... C2
Belgrave Rd ... A1/B1
Belmont Rd ... A2
Berea Rd ... A2
Braddons Hill Rd
East ... B2
Brewery Park ... B3
Bronshill Rd ... A2
Carlton Rd ... A3
Castle Circus ... A2
Castle Rd ... A2
Cavern Rd ... A2
Chatsworth Rd ... A2
Chestnut Avenue ... C1
Church St ... B1
Coach Station ... A1
Corbyn Head ... C1
Croft Hill ... B1
Croft Rd ... B1
East St ... A1
Egerton Rd ... A3
Ellacombe Church
Rd ... A3
Ellacombe Rd ... A2
English Riviera
Wheel ◆ ... C2
Falkland Rd ... B1
Fleet St ... B2
Fleet Walk
Shopping Centre ... B2
Grafton Rd ... A3
Grange Rd ... A3
Haldon Pier ... C2
Hatfield Rd ... A2
Highbury Rd ... A2
Higher Warberry Rd A3
Hillsdon Rd ... A3
Hoxton Rd ... A3
Hunsdon Rd ... B3
Information Ctr 🛈 ... B2
Inner Harbour ... C2
Kenwyn Rd ... A3
King's Drive, The ... B1
Laburnum St ... A1
Law Courts ... A1
Library ... A1
Lime Avenue ... A1
Lower Warberry Rd B3
Lucius St ... B1
Lymington Rd ... A1
Magdalene Rd ... A1
Marina ... C2
Market Forum, The ... B2
Market St ... B2
Meadfoot Lane ... C3
Meadfoot Rd ... C3
Melville St ... B2
Middle Warberry Rd B3
Mill Lane ... A1
Montpellier Rd ... C3
Morgan Avenue ... A1
Museum Rd ... B3
New Central 📽 ... B2
Newton Rd ... A1
Oakhill Rd ... A1
Outer Harbour ... C2
Parkhill Rd ... C2
Pimlico ... B2
Police Station ◆ ... B1
Post Office PO ... A1/B2
Prince of Wales
Steps ... C3
Princes Rd ... A3
Princes Rd East ... A3
Princes Rd West ... A3
Princess Gardens ... C2
Princess Pier ... C2
Princess Theatre 🎭 ... C2
Rathmore Rd ... C1
Recreation Grd ... B1
Riviera International
Centre ... B1
Rock End Avenue ... C3
Rock Rd ... B2
Rock Walk ... B2
Rosehill Rd ... A3
Royal Terr Gardens ... B2
South West
Coast Path ... C3
St Efride's Rd ... B1
St John's ... B2
St Luke's Rd ... B2
St Luke's Rd North ... B2
St Luke's Rd South ... B2
St Marychurch Rd ... A2
Scarborough Rd ... B1
Shedden Hill ... B1
South Pier ... C2
South St ... A1
Spanish Barn ... C1
Stitchill Rd ... A3
Strand ... B2
Sutherland Rd ... A3
Teignmouth Rd ... A1
Temperance St ... B2
Terrace, The ... B2
Thurlow Rd ... A1
Tor Bay ... B2
Tor Church Rd ... A1
Tor Hill Rd ... A1
Torbay Rd ... B2
Torquay Museum 🏛 B3
Torquay RFC &
Cricket Club ... B1
Torquay Station ◆ ... B1
Torquay Tennis Club B1
Torre Abbey 🏛 ... B1
Torre Abbey
Meadows ... B1
Torre Abbey Sands ... B2
Torwood Gardens ... C3
Torwood St ... C3
Town Hall ... A2
Unleashed Theatre
Company ... C2
Union Square
Shopping Centre ... A2
Union St ... A2
Upton Hill ... A2
Upton Park ... A1
Upton Rd ... A1
Vanehill Rd ... C3
Vansittart Rd ... A1
Vaughan Parade ... C2
Victoria Parade ... C3
Victoria Rd ... A2
Warberry Rd West ... A2
Warren Rd ... B2
Windsor Rd ... A2/A3
Woodville Rd ... A3

Truro 199

Adelaide Ter ... A2
Agar Rd ... C2
Arch Hill ... C2
Arundell Place ... C1
Avenue, The ... A3
Avondale Rd ... A1
Back Quay ... B3
Barrack Lane ... C3
Barton Meadow ... A1
Benson Rd ... A2
Bishops Close ... A3
Bosvean Gardens ... C1
Bosvigo Gardens ✿ A2
Bosvigo Lane ... A2
Bosvigo Rd ... B2
Bowling Alley ... B2
Broad St ... B3
Burley Close ... B3
Bus Station ... B3
Calenick St ... C3
Campfield Hill ... C2
Carclew St ... C3
Carew Rd ... A2
Carey Park ... C2
Carlyon Rd ... A3
Carvoza Rd ... A3
Castle St ... B2
Cathedral View ... A3
Chainwalk Drive ... A2
Chapel Hill ... B1
Charles St ... B3
City Hall ... B3
City Rd ... B2
Coach Park ... B3
Coinage Hall ◆ ... B3
Comprigney Hill ... A1
Coosebean Lane ... A1
Copes Gardens ... C3
County Hall ... B1
Courtney Rd ... B1
Crescent Rd ... B1
Crescent Rise ... B1
Crescent, The ... B1
Daniell Court ... C2
Daniell Rd ... C2
Daniell St ... C2
Daubuz Close ... A2
Daubuz Moors
Nature Reserve ... A3
Dobbs Lane ... B1
Edward St ... B2
Eliot Rd ... A2
Elm Court ... A3
Enys Close ... A1
Enys Rd ... A1
Fairmantle St ... B3
Falmouth Rd ... C2
Ferris Town ... B2
Fire Station ... B1
Fordh Talgarrek ... C1
Frances St ... B2
George St ... B2
Green Close ... C1
Green Lane ... C1
Grenville Rd ... C2
Gwarak Tewdar ... C2
Hall For Cornwall 🏛 B3
Hendra Park ... B2
Hendra Rd ... A1
Hendra Vean ... A1
High Cross ... B3
Higher Newham La ... C3
Higher Trehaverne ... A2
Hillcrest Avenue ... B1
Hospital H ... A2
Hunkin Close ... A2
Hurland Rd ... C3
Infirmary Hill ... B2
James Place ... A3
Kenwyn Church Rd ... A1
Kenwyn Hill ... A1
Kenwyn Rd ... A2
Kenwyn St ... B2
Kerris Gardens ... A1
King St ... B3
Leats, The ... B2
Lemon Quay ... B3
Lemon St Gallery 🏛 B3
Library ... A1
Malpas Rd ... A3
Market ... B3
Merrifield Close ... B1
Mitchell Hill ... A3
Moresk Close ... A3
Moresk Rd ... B3
Morlaix Avenue ... C3
Nancemere Rd ... A3
Newham Bsns Park C3
Newham Ind Est ... C3
Newham Rd ... C3
Northfield Drive ... C3
Oak Way ... A3
Old Bakery Studios ... B3
Palace's Terrace ... A3
Park View ... C2
Pendarves Rd ... A2
Plaza Cinema 🎬 ... B2
Police Sta ◆ ... A2/B3
Post Office PO ... B3
Prince's St ... B3
Pydar St ... B3
Quay St ... B3
Redannick
Crescent ... C2
Redannick Lane ... C2
Richard Lander
Monument ◆ ... C2
Richmond Hill ... B1
River St ... B2
Rosedale Rd ... A2
Royal Cornwall
Museum 🏛 ... B2
St Aubyn Rd ... C3
St Clement St ... B3
St George's Rd ... A1
School Lane ... C2
Spires, The ... A2
Station Rd ... B1
Stokes Rd ... A2
Strangways Terrace C3
Tabernacle St ... B2
Trehaverne Lane ... A2
Tremayne Rd ... C2
Tresawpra Drive ... C2
Treseder's Gardens A3
Treworder Rd ... B1
Treyew Rd ... B1
Truro Cathedral † ... B3
Truro Harbour
Office ... B3
Truro Station ◆ ... B3
Union St ... B3
Upper School Lane ... C2
Victoria Gardens ... B2
Waterfall Gardens ... B2

Winchester 199

Abbey Gardens ... B3
Andover Rd ... A1
Andover Road Retail
Park ... A1
Archery Lane ... C2
Arthur Rd ... A2
Bar End Rd ... C3
Beaufort Rd ... C2
Beggar's Lane ... B3
Bereweeke Avenue ... A1
Bereweeke Rd ... A1
Boscobel Rd ... A2
Brassey Rd ... A2
Broadway ... B3
Brooks Shopping
Centre, The ... B3
Bus Station ... B3
Butter Cross ◆ ... B2
Canon St ... C2
Castle Wall ... C2/C3
Cathedral † ... B2
Cheriton Rd ... A1
Chesil St ... C3
Chesil Theatre ... C3
Christchurch Rd ... C1
City Mill ◆ ... B3
City Museum 🏛 ... B2
City Rd ... B2
Clifton Rd ... B1
Clifton Terrace ... B2
Close Wall ... C2/C3
Coach Park ... B1
Colebrook St ... C3
College St ... C2
College Walk ... C3
Compton Rd ... C2
Council Offices ... C3
County Council
Offices ... C2
Cranworth Rd ... A2
Cromwell Rd ... C2
Culver Rd ... C2
Discovery
Centre ◆ ... B2
Domum Rd ... C3
Durngate Place ... B3
Eastgate St ... B3
East Hill ... C3
Edgar Rd ... C2
Egbert Rd ... A2
Elm Rd ... A1
Everyman 🎬 ... C2
Fairfield Rd ... A1
Fire Station ... A1
Fordington Avenue ... B1
Fordington Rd ... B1
Friarsgate ... B3
Gordon Rd ... B3
Great Hall & Round
Table, The ... B2
Greenhill Rd ... B1
Guildhall ... B3
Hatherley Rd ... A1
High St ... B2
Hillier Way ... A3
HM Prison ... A3
Hyde Abbey
(Remains) † ... A2
Hyde Abbey Rd ... A2
Hyde Close ... A2
Hyde St ... A2
Information Ctr 🛈 ... B2
Jane Austen's Ho 🏛 C2
Jewry St ... B2
King Alfred Place ... A3
King Alfred
Statue ◆ ... B2
Kingsgate Arch ... C2
Kingsgate Park ... C2
Kingsgate Rd ... C2
Kingsgate St ... C2
Lankhills Rd ... A2
Law Courts ... B2
Library ... B2
Lower Brook St ... B3
Magdalen Hill ... B3
Market Lane ... B2
Mews Lane ... B1
Middle Brook St ... B3
Middle Rd ... B1
Military
Museums 🏛 ... C2
Milland Rd ... C3
Milverton Rd ... A1
Monks Rd ... C3
North Hill Close ... A2
North Walls ... B3
North Walls
Recreation Grd ... A3
Nuns Rd ... A3
Oram's Arbour ... B1
Owens Rd ... A1
Parchment St ... B2
Park & Ride ... C3
Park Avenue ... B3
Playing Field ... A1
Police HQ ◆ ... C2
Portal Rd ... C3
Post Office PO ... B2/C1
Ranelagh Rd ... C1
Regimental
Museum 🏛 ... C2
River Park
Leisure Centre ... B3
Romans' Rd ... C2
Romsey Rd ... B1
Royal Hampshire
County Hospital
(A&E) H ... B1
St Cross Rd ... C1
St George's St ... B2
St Giles Hill ... C3
St James Villas ... C2
St James' Lane ... C2
St James' Terrace ... C2
St John's ... B3
St John's St ... B3
St Michael's Rd ... C2
St Paul's Hill ... B1
St Peter St ... B2
St Swithun St ... C2
St Thomas St ... C2
Saxon Rd ... A2
School of Art ... B3
Sleepers Hill Rd ... C1
Southgate St ... C2
Sparkford Rd ... C1
Square, The ... B2
Staple Gardens ... B2
Station Rd ... B2
Step Terrace ... A1
Stockbridge Rd ... A1
Stuart Crescent ... A1
Sussex St ... B2
Swan Lane ... B2
Tanner St ... B3
Theatre Royal 🎭 ... B2
Tower St ... B2
Union St ... B3
Univ of Southampton
(Winchester School
of Art) ... B3
University of
Winchester (King
Alfred Campus) ... C1
Upper Brook St ... B3
Wales St ... B3
Water Lane ... B3
Weirs, The ... C3
West End Terrace ... B1
Western Rd ... B1
Westgate 🏛 ... C2
Wharf Hill ... C3
Winchester Sta ◆ ... B2
Winnall Moors
Wildlife Reserve ... A3
Wolvesey Castle 🏛 ... C3
Worthy Lane ... A2
Worthy Rd ... A2

Windsor 199

Adelaide Square ... C3
Albany Rd ... C3
Albert St ... B1
Alexandra Gardens ... B2
Alexandra Rd ... C2
Alma Rd ... B2
Arthur Rd ... B2
Bachelors Acre ... B3
Barry Avenue ... B2
Baths Island ... A3
Beaumont Rd ... C2
Bexley St ... B1
Brocas St ... A2
Brocas, The ... A2
Brook St ... C3
Bulkeley Avenue ... C1
Castle Hill ... B3
Charles St ... B2
Claremont Rd ... C2
Clarence Crescent ... B2
Clarence Rd ... B2
Clewer Court Rd ... B1
Coach Park ... B3
College Crescent ... C1
Cricket Ground ... C3
Dagmar Rd ... C2
Datchet Rd ... B3
Devereux Rd ... C2
Dorset Rd ... C2
Duke St ... B1
Elm Rd ... C1
Eton College ◆ ... A3
Eton Coll Natural
History Mus 🏛 ... A2
Eton Court ... A2
Eton Square ... A2
Eton Wick Rd ... A1
Farm Yard ... B3
Frances Rd ... C2
Frogmore Drive ... C3
Gloucester Place ... C3
Goslar Way ... C1
Goswell Hill ... B2
Goswell Rd ... B2
Green Lane ... C1
Grove Rd ... C2
Guildhall ... B3
Helena Rd ... C2
Helston Lane ... B1
High St ... A2/B3
Holy Trinity ... B2
Home Park, The ... A3/C3
Household
Cavalry 🏛 ... B3
Imperial Rd ... C2
Information Ctr 🛈 ... B2
Keats Lane ... A2
King Edward VII Ave ... B3
King Edward VII
Hospital H ... C2
King George V
Memorial ◆ ... B3
King Stable St ... A3
King's Rd ... C3
Library ... A2/B2
Long Walk, The ... C3
Maidenhead Rd ... A1
Meadow Lane ... A2
Nell Gwynne's
House ◆ ... B3
Osborne Rd ... C2
Oxford Rd ... B1
Park St ... B3
Peascod St ... B2
Police Station ◆ ... C2
Post Office PO ... A2/C1
Princess Margaret
Hosp (private) H ... C2
Old Court Art Space,
The 🏛 ... C2
Queen Elizabeth
Bridge ... A3
Queen Victoria's
Walk ... C3
Queen's Rd ... C2
River St ... B2
Romney Island ... A3
Romney Lock ... A3
Romney Lock Rd ... A3
Russell St ... B2
St George's
Chapel ... B3
St John's ... B3
St John's Chapel ... A2
St Leonards Rd ... C1
St Mark's Rd ... C2
Sheet St ... B3
Shopmobility ... B2
South Meadow ... A3
South Meadow La ... A3
Springfield Rd ... C1
Stovell Rd ... B1
Sunbury Rd ... A2
Tangier Lane ... A2
Temple Rd ... C2
Thames St ... B3
Theatre Royal 🎭 ... B3
Trinity Place ... C2
Vansittart Rd ... B1/C1
Victoria Barracks ... C2
Victoria St ... C2
Westmead ... C1
White Lilies Island ... A1
William St ... B2
Windsor & Eton
Central ≈ ... B2
Windsor & Eton
Riverside ≈ ... A3
Windsor Bridge ... A3
Windsor Castle 🏰 ... B3
Windsor Leisure Ctr B1
Windsor Relief Rd ... A1
Windsor Royal Station
Shopping Centre ... B2
Windsor Yards ... B2
York Avenue ... C1
York Rd ... C1

Wolverhampton 200

Albion St ... B3
Arena ◆ ... B3
Art Gallery 🏛 ... B2
Ashland St ... C1
Austin St ... A1
Badger Drive ... A3
Bailey St ... B3
Bath Avenue ... B1
Bath Rd ... C2
Bell St ... C2
Berry St ... B3
Bilston Rd ... B3
Bilston St ... B3
Birmingham Canal ... A2
Bone Mill Lane ... A2
Brewery Rd ... A1
Bright St ... A1
Burton Crescent ... B3
Bus Station ... B3
Cambridge St ... A3
Camp St ... B2
Cannock Rd ... A3
Castle St ... C2
Chapel Ash ... C1
Cherry St ... C1
Chester St ... A1
Church Lane ... C2
Church St ... C2
City Archives ◆ ... B2
Civic Centre ... B2
Civic Hall ... B2
Clarence Rd ... B1
Cleveland St ... C2
Clifton St ... C1
Coach Station ... B3
Compton Rd ... B1
Corn Hill ... B3
Coven St ... A2
Craddock St ... A1
Cross St North ... A2
Crown &
County Courts ... C3
Crown St ... A2
Culwell St ... B3
Dale St ... C1
Darlington St ... C1
Devon Rd ... A1
Drummond St ... B2
Dudley Rd ... C2
Dudley St ... B2
Duke St ... C3
Dunkley St ... B1
Dunstall Avenue ... A2
Dunstall Hill ... A2
Dunstall Rd ... A1/A2
Evans St ... A1
Fawdry St ... A1
Field St ... B3
Fire Station ... C2
Fiveways ◆ ... A3
Fowler Playing
Fields ... A3
Fox's Lane ... A2
Francis St ... A2
Fryer St ... B3
Gloucester St ... B1
Gordon St ... C3
Graiseley St ... C1
Grand 🎭 ... B2
Grand Station ... B2
Granville St ... B3
Great Brickkiln St ... C1
Great Hampton St ... A1
Great Western St ... A2
Grimstone St ... B3
Harrow St ... A1
Hilton St ... A3
Hive Library, The ... B2
Horseley Fields ... B3
Humber Rd ... C1
Jack Hayward Way ... A1
Jameson St ... B1
Jenner St ... C3
Kennedy Rd ... B2
Kimberley St ... C1
King St ... B2
Laburnum St ... C1
Lansdowne Rd ... B1
Leicester St ... A1
Lever St ... C3
Library ... C1
Lichfield St ... B2
Light House 📽 ... B3
Little's Lane ... B3
Lock St ... B3
Lord St ... C2
Lowe St ... A1
Maltings, The ... A2
Mander Centre ... C2
Mander St ... C1
Market ... B2
Market St ... B2
Maxwell Rd ... C3
Merridale St ... C1
Middlecross ... C3
Molineux St ... B2
Mostyn St ... A1
Newhampton
Arts Centre ... A1
New Hampton Rd
East ... A1
Nine Elms Lane ... A3
North Rd ... A2
Oaks Crescent ... C1
Oxley St ... A2
Paget St ... A1
Park Avenue ... A1
Park Road East ... A2
Park Road West ... B1
Paul St ... C2
Pelham St ... C1
Penn Rd ... C2
Piper's Row ... B3
Piper's Row 🚌 ... B3
Pitt St ... C2
Police Station ◆ ... C2
Pool St ... C2
Poole St ... C3
Post Office PO ... A1/B2/C2/C3
Powlett St ... C3
Queen St ... B2
Raby St ... C2
Railway Drive ... B3
Red Hill St ... A2
Red Lion St ... B2
Retreat St ... C1
Ring Rd ... C2
Royal, The 🚋 ... C3
Rugby St ... A1
Russell St ... C1
St Andrew's ... A1
St David's ... B3
St George's ... C2
St George's Parade ... C2
St James St ... C3
St John's ... C2
St John's Retail Pk ... C2
St John's Square ... C2
St Mark's ... C1
St Marks Rd ... C1
St Marks St ... C1

Worcester 200

Albany Terrace ... A1
Angel Place ... B2
Angel St ... B2
Ashcroft Rd ... B3
Athelstan Rd ... C3
Avenue, The ... B2
Back Lane North ... A1
Back Lane South ... A1
Barbourne Rd ... A2
Bath Rd ... C2
Battenhall Rd ... C3
Bridge St ... B2
Britannia Square ... A2
Broad St ... B2
Bromwich Lane ... C1
Bromwich Rd ... C1
Bromyard Rd ... C1
Bus Station ... B2
Butts, The ... B2
Carden St ... C3
Castle St ... A2
Cathedral † ... B2
Cathedral Square ... B2
Charles St ... B3
Chequers Lane ... A3
Chestnut St ... A2
Chestnut Walk ... A2
Citizens' Advice
Bureau ... B2
City Walls Rd ... B2
Cole Hill ... C3
College St ... C2
Commandery,
The ◆ ... C2
Cripplegate Park ... C1
Croft Rd ... B2
Cromwell St ... B3
Cross, The ... B2
Crowngate Centre ... B2
Deansway ... B2
Diglis Parade ... C2
Diglis Rd ... C2
Edgar Tower ◆ ... C2
Farrier St ... B2
Foregate St ... B2
Fort Royal Hill ... C3
Fort Royal Park ... C3
Foundry St ... B3
Friar St ... C2
George St ... C3
Grand Stand Rd ... C1
Greenhill ... C3
Greyfriars 🏛 ... B2
Guildhall 🏛 ... B2
Henwick Rd ... B1
High St ... B2
Hill St ... C3
Hive, The ... B2
Huntington Hall 🎭 ... B2
Hylton Rd ... B1
Information Ctr 🛈 ... B2
King Charles Place
Shopping Centre ... C1
King's School ... B2
King's School
Playing Field ... C2
Kleve Walk ... C2
Lansdowne Cres ... A3
Lansdowne Walk ... A3
Laslett St ... A2
Little Chestnut St ... A2
Little London ... A2
London Rd ... C3
Lowell St ... A2
Lowesmoor ... B2
Lowesmoor Terrace ... B2
Lowesmoor Wharf ... A3
Magistrates Court ... B2
Midland Rd ... C3
Mill St ... C2
Moors Severn
Terrace, The ... A1
Museum &
Art Gallery 🏛 ... B2
Museum of Royal
Worcester 🏛 ... C2
New Rd ... B1
New St ... B2
Northfield St ... A2
Odeon 📽 ... B2
Old Palace The ... C2
Padmore St ... B3
Park St ... C2
Pheasant St ... C3
Pitchcroft
Racecourse ... A1
Portland St ... C2
Post Office PO ... A2/B2
Quay St ... B2
Queen St ... B2
Rainbow Hill ... B3
Recreation Ground ... A2
Reindeer Court ... B2
Rogers Hill ... A3
Sabrina Terrace ... A1
St Dunstan's Cres ... C3
St John's ... C1
St Martin's Gate ... B3
St Martin's Quarter ... B3
St Oswald's Rd ... A2
St Paul's St ... B3
St Swithin's
Church ... B2
St Wulstans Cres ... C3
Sansome Walk ... A2
Severn St ... C2
Shambles, The ... B2
Shaw St ... B2
Shire Hall
Crown Court ... C2
Shrub Hill Rd ... B3
Shrub Hill Retail Pk ... B3
Slingpool Walk ... C1
South Parade ... C2
Southfield St ... A2
Sports Centre ... A3
Stanley Rd ... B3
Swan, The 🦢 ... A1
Swimming Pool ... A2
Tallow Hill ... B3
Tennis Walk ... A2
Tolladine Rd ... A3
Tudor House 🏛 ... B2
Tybridge St ... B1
Tything, The ... A2
Univ of Worcester ... B2
University of
Worcester Arena ... B3
Vincent Rd ... C3
Vue 📽 ... B2
Washington St ... A3
Woolhope Rd ... C3
Worcester Bridge ... B2
Worcester County
Cricket Club ... C1
Worcester Foregate
Street ≈ ... B2
Worcester
Shrub Hill ≈ ... B3
Worcester Royal
Grammar School ... A2
Wylds Lane ... C3

Wrexham 200
Wrecsam 200

Abbot St ... C2
Acton Rd ... A3
Albert St ... C3
Alexandra Rd ... C1
Aran Rd ... A3
Barnfield ... C3
Bath Rd ... C2
Beeches, The ... A3
Beechley Rd ... C3
Belgrave Rd ... C2
Bellevue Park ... C2
Bellevue Rd ... C2
Belvedere Drive ... A1
Bennion's Rd ... C3
Berse Rd ... A1
Bersham Rd ... C1
Birch St ... C2
Bodhyfryd ... B3
Border Retail Park ... B3
Bradley Rd ... C2
Bright St ... C3
Bron-y-Nant ... C1
Brook St ... C2
Bryn-y-Cabanau
Rd ... C3
Bury St ... B3
Bus Station ... B2
Butchers Market ... B3
Caia Rd ... C3
Cambrian Ind Est ... C3
Caxton Place ... B2
Cemetery ... A1
Centenary Rd ... C1
Central Retail Park ... B2
Chapel St ... C2
Charles St ... B3
Chester Rd ... A3
Chester St ... B3
Cilcen Grove ... A3
Citizens Advice
Bureau ... B2
Cobden Rd ... C2
Council Offices ... B2
County ... B3
Crescent Rd ... B3
Crispin Lane ... A2
Croesnewyth Rd ... B1
Cross St ... A2
Cunliffe St ... C2
Derby Rd ... C3
Dolydd Rd ... C1
Duke St ... B2
Eagles Meadow ... C3
Earle St ... C2
East Avenue ... A3
Edward St ... C2
Egerton St ... B2
Empress Rd ... C1
Erddig Rd ... C2
Fairy Rd ... C2
Fire Station ... C3
Foster Rd ... A3
Foxwood Drive ... A1
Garden Rd ... A2
General Market ... B3
Gerald St ... B2
Gibson St ... C1
Greenbank St ... C1
Greenfield ... A3
Grosvenor Rd ... B2
Grove Park 🎭 ... B3
Grove Park Rd ... B3
Grove Rd ... B3
Guildhall ... B2
Haig Rd ... C3
Hampden Rd ... C2
Hazel Grove ... A3
Henhas St ... B3
High St ... B3
Hightown Rd ... C3
Hill St ... B2
Holt Rd ... B3
Holt St ... B3
Hope St ... B2
Huntroyde Avenue ... C3
Information Ctr 🛈 ... B2
Island Gn Retail Pk ... B2
Jobcentre Plus ... B2
Jubilee Rd ... B3
King St ... B2
Kingsmills Rd ... C3
Lambit St ... B3
Law Courts ... B3
Lawson Close ... A3
Lawson Rd ... A3
Lea Rd ... C2
Library & Arts Ctr ... B2
Lilac Way ... C1
Llys David Lord ... B2
Lorne St ... C2
Maesgwyn Rd ... B1
Maesdre Rd ... A2
Manley Rd ... C3
Market St ... B3
Mawddy Avenue ... A2
Mayville Avenue ... A2
Memorial Hall ... B2
Mold Rd ... A1
Mount St ... C2
Mount St Retail Pk ... C2
Neville Crescent ... A3
New Rd ... B3
North Wales Regional
Tennis Centre ... A3
Oak Drive ... A3
Odeon 📽 ... B3
Park Avenue ... A3
Park St ... B2
Peel St ... C2
Pen y Bryn ... C2
Pentre Felin ... C2
Penymaes Avenue ... A3
Peoples Market ... B3
Percy St ... C2
Pines, The ... A3
Plas Coch Rd ... A1
Plas Coch
Retail Park ... A1
Poplar Rd ... C2
Post Office PO ... A2/B3/C3
Powell Rd ... C3
Poyser St ... C3
Price's Lane ... A2
Primrose Way ... C1
Princess St ... C1
Queen St ... B3
Queens Square ... B2
Regent St ... B2
Rhosddu Rd ... A2/B2
Rhosnesni Lane ... A3
Rivulet Rd ... C3
Ruabon Rd ... C2
Ruthin Rd ... C1/C2
St Giles ... C2
St Giles Way ... C2
St James Court ... A2
St Mary's † ... B2
Salisbury Rd ... C2
Salop Rd ... C2
Sontley Rd ... C2
Spring Rd ... A2
Stanley St ... C2
Stansty Rd ... A2
Station Approach ... B2
Superstore ... A1/B3/C1
Talbot Rd ... C2
Techniquest
Glyndŵr ◆ ... C1
Town Hill ... C2
Trevor St ... C2
Trinity St ... B2
Tuttle St ... C2
Vale Park ... A1
Vernon St ... C2
Vicarage Hill ... C2
Victoria Rd ... C2
Walnut St ... C3
War Memorial ◆ ... B3
Waterworld Leisure
Centre ◆ ... B3
Watery Rd ... B1/B2
Wellington Rd ... C3
Westminster Drive ... A3
William Aston
Hall ... A1
Windsor Rd ... C1
Wrecsam
Wrexham AFC ... C1
Wrexham
Central ≈ ... B2
Wrexham
General ≈ ... B2
Wrexham Glyndwr
University Plas Coch
Campus ... A1
Wrexham Maelor
Hospital (A&E) H ... B1
Wrexham
Technology Park ... B1
Wynn Avenue ... C2
Xplore! ◆ ... B2
Yale College ... A3
Yale Grove ... A3
Yorke St ... C2

York 200

Aldwark ... B2
Barbican Rd ... C3
Bar Convent Living
Heritage Ctr 🏛 ... C1
Barley Hall 🏛 ... B2
Bishopgate St ... C2
Bishophill Senior ... C2
Bishopthorpe Rd ... C2
Blossom St ... C1
Bootham ... A1
Bootham Crescent ... A1
Bootham Terrace ... A1
Bridge St ... B2
Brook St ... A2
Brownlow St ... A3
Burton Stone Lane ... A1
Castlegate ... B2
Cemetery Rd ... C3
Cherry St ... C2
City Screen 📽 ... B2
City Wall ... A2/B1/C3
Clementhorpe ... C2
Clifford St ... B2
Clifford's Tower 🏰 ... B2
Clifton ... A1
Coach park ... A1
Coney St ... B2
Coppergate Centre ... B2
Cromwell Rd ... C2
Crown Court ... B2
Deanery Gardens ... A2
Davygate ... B2
DIG ◆ ... B2
Dodsworth Avenue ... A3
Eboracum Way ... A3
Ebor Industrial Est ... C3
Eldon St ... A2
Everyman 📽 ... C1
Fairfax House 🏛 ... B2
Fire Station ... C1
Fishergate ... C2
Foss Islands Rd ... B3
Foss Islands
Retail Park ... B3
Fossbank ... A3
Garden St ... A2
George St ... C2
Gillygate ... A2
Goodramgate ... B2
Grand Opera
House 🎭 ... B2
Grosvenor Terrace ... A1
Guildhall ... B2
Hallfield Rd ... A3
Heslington Rd ... C3
Heworth Green ... A3
Holy Trinity † ... B2
Hope St ... C2
Huntington Rd ... A3
Information Ctr 🛈 ... B2
James St ... B3
Jorvik Viking Ctr 🏛 ... B2
Kent St ... C3
Lawrence St ... C3
Layerthorpe ... B3
Leeman Rd ... B1
Lendal ... B2
Lendal Bridge ... B1
Library ... A2/B1
Longfield Terrace ... A1
Lord Mayor's Walk ... A2
Lowther St ... A2
Mansion House 🏛 ... B2
Margaret St ... C3
Marygate ... A1
Melbourne St ... C3
Merchant
Adventurers'
Hall 🏛 ... B2
Merchant Taylors'
Hall 🏛 ... B2
Micklegate ... B1
Micklegate Bar 🏛 ... C1
Monkgate ... A2
Moss St ... C1
Museum
Gardens ✿ ... B1
Museum St ... B2
National Railway
Museum 🏛 ... B1
Navigation Rd ... B3
Newton Terrace ... C2
North Parade ... A1
North St ... B2
Nunnery Lane ... C1
Nunthorpe Rd ... C1
Ouse Bridge ... B2
Paragon St ... C3
Park Grove ... A3
Park St ... C1
Parliament St ... B2
Peasholme Green ... B3
Penley's Grove St ... A2
Piccadilly ... B2
Police Station ◆ ... B3
Post Office PO ... B1/B2/B2
Priory St ... C1
Queen Anne's Rd ... A1
Regimental
Museum 🏛 ... B2
Richard III Experience
at Monk Bar 🏛 ... A2
Roman Bath 🏛 ... B2
Rowntree Park ... C2
St Andrewgate ... B2
St Benedict Rd ... C1
St John St ... A2
St Olave's Rd ... A1
St Peter's Grove ... A1
St Saviourgate ... B2
Scarcroft Hill ... C1
Scarcroft Rd ... C1
Shambles, The ... B2
Shopmobility ... B2
Skeldergate ... C2
Skeldergate
Bridge ... C2
Station Rd ... B1
Stonebow, The ... B2
Stonegate ... B2
Superstore ... B3
Sycamore Terrace ... A1
Terry Avenue ... C2
Theatre Royal 🎭 ... B2
Thorpe St ... C1
Toft Green ... B1
Tower St ... C2
Townend St ... A2
Treasurer's
House 🏛 ... A2
Trinity Lane ... B1
Undercroft
Museum 🏛 ... B2
Union Terrace ... A2
Victor St ... C2
Vine St ... C2
Walmgate ... B3
War Memorial ◆ ... B1
Wellington St ... C3
York Art Gallery 🏛 ... A1
York Barbican ◆ ... C3
York Brewery 🏛 ... B1
York Dungeon,
The 🏛 ... B2
York Minster † ... A2
York St John
University ... A2
York Station ≈ ... B1

Abbreviations used in the index

Aberdeen	Aberdeen City
Aberds	Aberdeenshire
Ald	Alderney
Anglesey	Isle of Anglesey
Angus	Angus
Argyll	Argyll and Bute
Bath	Bath and North East Somerset
BCP	Bournemouth, Christchurch and Poole
Bedford	Bedford
Blackburn	Blackburn with Darwen
Blackpool	Blackpool
Bl Gwent	Blaenau Gwent
Borders	Scottish Borders
Brack	Bracknell
Bridgend	Bridgend
Brighton	City of Brighton and Hove
Bristol	City and County of Bristol
Bucks	Buckinghamshire
Caerph	Caerphilly
Cambs	Cambridgeshire
Cardiff	Cardiff
Carms	Carmarthenshire
C Beds	Central Bedfordshire
Ceredig	Ceredigion
Ches E	Cheshire East
Ches W	Cheshire West and Chester
Clack	Clackmannanshire
Conwy	Conwy
Corn	Cornwall
Cumb	Cumberland
Darl	Darlington
Denb	Denbighshire
Derby	City of Derby
Derbys	Derbyshire
Devon	Devon
Dorset	Dorset
Dumfries	Dumfries and Galloway
Dundee	Dundee City
Durham	Durham
E Ayrs	East Ayrshire
Edin	City of Edinburgh
E Dunb	East Dunbartonshire
E Loth	East Lothian
E Renf	East Renfrewshire
Essex	Essex
E Sus	East Sussex
E Yorks	East Riding of Yorkshire
Falk	Falkirk
Fife	Fife
Flint	Flintshire
Glasgow	City of Glasgow
Glos	Gloucestershire
Gtr Man	Greater Manchester
Guern	Guernsey
Gwyn	Gwynedd
Halton	Halton
Hants	Hampshire
Hereford	Herefordshire
Herts	Hertfordshire
Highld	Highland
Hrtlpl	Hartlepool
Hull	Hull
Invclyd	Inverclyde
IoM	Isle of Man
IoW	Isle of Wight
Jersey	Jersey
Kent	Kent

How to use the index

Example

Trudoxhill Som **24** E2

- grid square
- page number
- county or unitary authority

Lancs	Lancashire
Leicester	City of Leicester
Leics	Leicestershire
Lincs	Lincolnshire
London	Greater London
Luton	Luton
Mbro	Middlesbrough
Medway	Medway
Mers	Merseyside
Midloth	Midlothian
M Keynes	Milton Keynes
Mon	Monmouthshire
Moray	Moray
M Tydf	Merthyr Tydfil
N Ayrs	North Ayrshire
Neath	Neath Port Talbot
NE Lincs	North East Lincolnshire
Newport	City and County of Newport
N Lanark	North Lanarkshire
N Lincs	North Lincolnshire
N Nhants	North Northamptonshire
Norf	Norfolk
Northumb	Northumberland
Nottingham	City of Nottingham
Notts	Nottinghamshire
N Som	North Somerset
N Yorks	North Yorkshire
Orkney	Orkney
Oxon	Oxfordshire
Pboro	Peterborough
Pembs	Pembrokeshire
Perth	Perth and Kinross
Plym	Plymouth
Powys	Powys
Ptsmth	Portsmouth
Reading	Reading
Redcar	Redcar and Cleveland
Renfs	Renfrewshire
Rhondda	Rhondda Cynon Taff
Rutland	Rutland
S Ayrs	South Ayrshire
Scilly	Scilly
S Glos	South Gloucestershire
Shetland	Shetland
Shrops	Shropshire
S Lanark	South Lanarkshire
Slough	Slough
Som	Somerset
Soton	Southampton
Southend	Southend-on-Sea
Staffs	Staffordshire
Stirling	Stirling
Stockton	Stockton-on-Tees
Stoke	Stoke-on-Trent
Suff	Suffolk
Sur	Surrey
Swansea	Swansea
Swindon	Swindon
S Yorks	South Yorkshire
T&W	Tyne and Wear
Telford	Telford and Wrekin
Thurrock	Thurrock
Torbay	Torbay
Torf	Torfaen
V Glam	The Vale of Glamorgan
W&F	Westmorland and Furness
Warks	Warwickshire
Warr	Warrington
W Berks	West Berkshire
W Dunb	West Dunbartonshire
Wilts	Wiltshire
Windsor	Windsor and Maidenhead
W Isles	Western Isles
W Loth	West Lothian
W Mid	West Midlands
W Nhants	West Northamptonshire
Wokingham	Wokingham
Worcs	Worcestershire
Wrex	Wrexham
W Sus	West Sussex
W Yorks	West Yorkshire
York	City of York

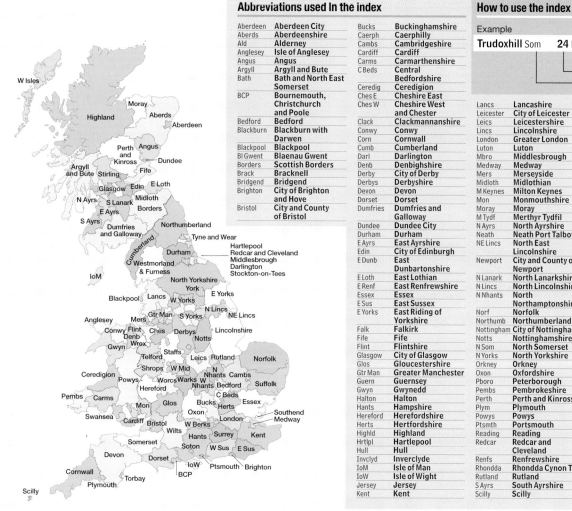

A

Abbas Combe 12 B5
Abberley 50 C2
Abberton Essex 43 C6
Worcs 50 D4
Abberwick 117 C7
Abbess Roding 42 C1
Abbey 11 C6
Abbey-cwm-hir . . . 48 B2
Abbeydale 88 F4
Abbey Dore 49 F5
Abbey Field 43 B5
Abbey Hulton 75 E6
Abbey St Bathans. 122 C3
Abbeystead 93 D5
Abbey Town 107 D8
Abbey Village. 86 B4
Abbey Wood 29 B5
Abbots Bickington. . 9 C5
Abbots Bromley . . . 62 B4
Abbotsbury 12 F3
Abbotsham 9 B6
Abbotskerswell 7 C6
Abbots Langley. . . . 40 D3
Abbots Leigh 23 B7
Abbotsley 54 D3
Abbots Morton 50 D5
Abbots Ripton 54 B3
Abbots Salford 51 D5
Abbotswood 14 B4
Abbotts Ann. 25 E8
Abcott 49 B5
Abdon 61 F5
Aber 46 E3
Aberaeron 46 C3
Aberaman 34 D4
Aberangell 58 C5
Aber-Arad 46 F2
Aberarder. 137 F7
Aberarder House . 138 B2
Aberarder Lodge . 137 F8
Aberargie 128 C3
Aberarth 46 C3
Aberavon 33 E8
Aber-banc 46 E2
Aberbeeg 35 D6
Abercanaid 34 D4
Abercarn 35 E6
Abercastle 44 B3
Abercegir 58 D5
Aberchirder 152 C6
Aber Cowarch 59 C5
Abercraf 34 C2
Abercrombie 129 D7
Abercych 45 E4
Abercynafon 34 C4
Abercynon 34 E4
Aberdalgie 128 B2
Aberdâr
=Aberdare 34 D3
Aberdare
=Aberdâr 34 D3
Aberdaron 70 E2
Aberdaugleddau
=Milford Haven . . . 44 E4
Aberdeen 141 D8
Aberdesach 82 F4
Aberdour 128 F3
Aberdovey
=Aberdyfi 58 E3
Aberdulais 34 D1
Aberdyfi
=Aberdovey 58 E3
Aberedw 48 E2
Abereiddy 44 B2
Abererch 70 D4
Aberfan 34 D4
Aberfeldy 133 E5
Aberffraw 82 E3
Aberffrwd 47 B5
Aberford 95 F7
Aberfoyle 126 D4
Abergavenny
=Y Fenni 35 C6
Abergele 72 B3
Aber-Giâr 46 E4
Abergorlech 46 F4
Abergwaun
=Fishguard 44 B4
Abergwesyn 47 D7
Abergwili 33 B5
Abergwynant 58 C3
Aber-gwynfi 34 E2
Abergwyngregyn . . 83 D6
Abergynolwyn 58 D3
Aber-Hirnant 72 F3
Aberhonddu
=Brecon 34 B4
Aberhosan 58 E5
Aberkenfig 34 F2
Aberlady 129 F6
Aberlemno 135 D5
Aberllefenni 58 D4
Abermagwr 47 B5
Abermaw
=Barmouth 58 C3
Abermeurig 46 D4
Abermule 59 E8
Abernaint 59 B8
Abernant 32 B4
Aber-nant 34 D4
Abernethy 128 C3
Abernyte 134 F2
Aberpennar
=Mountain Ash . . . 34 E4
Aberporth 45 D4
Aber-Rhiwlech 59 B6
Abersoch 70 E4
Abersychan 35 D6
Abertawe
=Swansea 33 E7
Aberteifi
=Cardigan 45 E3
Aberthin 22 B2
Abertillery
=Abertyleri 35 D6
Abertridwr Caerph. . 35 F5
Powys 59 C7
Abertyleri
=Abertillery 35 D6
Abertysswg 35 D5
Aberuthven 127 C8
Aber-Village 35 B5
Aberyscir 34 B3
Aberystwyth 58 F2
Abhainn Suidhe . . 154 G5
Abingdon-on-
Thames 38 E4
Abinger Common . 28 E2
Abinger Hammer . . 27 E8
Abington 114 B2
Abington Pigotts . . 54 E4
Ab Kettleby 64 B4
Ab Lench 50 D5
Ablington Glos 37 D8
Wilts 25 E6
Abney 75 B8
Aboyne 140 E4
Abram 86 D4
Abriachan 151 H8
Abridge 41 E7
Abronhill 119 B7
Abson 24 B2
Abthorpe 52 E4
Abune-the-Hill . . 159 F3
Aby 79 B7
Acaster Malbis 95 E8
Acaster Selby 95 E8
Accrington 87 B5
Acha 146 F4
Achabraid 145 E7
Achachork 149 D9
Achafolla 124 D3
Achagary 157 D10
Achahoish 144 F6
Achalader 133 E8
Achallader 131 E7
Acha Mor 155 E8
Achanalt 150 E5
Achanamara 144 E6
Achandunie 151 D9
Ach'an Todhair . . . 130 B4
Achany 157 J8
Achaphubuil 130 B4
Acharacle 147 E9
Acharn Highld 147 F10
Perth 132 E4
Acharole 158 E4
Achath 141 C6
Achavanich 158 F3
Achavraat 151 G12
Achddu 33 D5
Achduart 156 J3
Achentoul 157 F11
Achfary 156 F5
Achgarve 155 H13
Achiemore Highld . 156 C6
Highld 157 D11
A'Chill 148 H7
Achiltibuie 156 J3
Achina 157 C10
Achinduich 157 J8
Achinduin 124 B4
Achingills 158 D3
Achintee Highld . . . 131 B5
Highld 150 G2
Achintraid 149 E13
Achlean 138 E4
Achleck 146 G7
Achluachrach 137 F5
Achlyness 156 D5
Achmelvich 156 G3
Achmore Highld . . 149 E13
Stirling 132 F2
Achnaba Argyll 124 B5
Argyll 145 E8
Achnabat 151 H8
Achnacarnin 156 F3
Achnacarry 136 F4
Achnacloich Argyll 125 B5
Highld 149 H10
Achnaconeran . . . 137 C7
Achnacraig 146 G7
Achnacroish 130 E2
Achnadrish 146 F7
Achnafalnich 125 C8
Achnagarron 151 E9
Achnaha 146 E7
Achnahanat 151 B8
Achnahannet 139 B5
Achnairn 157 H8
Achnaluachrach . . 157 J9
Achnasaul 136 F4
Achnasheen 150 F4
Achosnich 146 E7
Achranich 147 G10
Achreamie 157 C13
Achriabhach 131 C5
Achriesgill 156 D5
Achrimsdale 157 J12
Achtoty 157 C9
Achurch 65 F7
Achuvoldrach 157 D8
Achvaich 151 B10
Achvarasdal 157 C12
Ackergill 158 E5
Acklam Mbro. 102 C2
N Yorks 96 C3
Ackleton 61 E7
Acklington 117 D8
Ackton 88 B5
Ackworth Moor
Top 88 C5
Acle 69 C7
Acock's Green 62 F5
Acol 31 C7
Acomb Northumb . . 110 C2
York 95 D8
Aconbury 49 F7
Acre 87 B5
Acrefair 73 E6
Acre Street 15 E8
Acton Ches E 74 D3
Dorset 13 G7
London 41 F5
Shrops 60 F3
Suff 56 E2
Wrex 73 D7
Acton Beauchamp . 49 D8
Acton Bridge 74 B2
Acton Burnell 60 D5
Acton Green 49 D8
Acton Pigott 60 D5
Acton Round 61 E6
Acton Scott 60 F4
Acton Trussell 62 C3
Acton Turville 37 F5
Adbaston 61 B7
Adber 12 B3
Adderley 74 E3
Adderstone 123 F7
Addiewell 120 C2
Addingham 94 E3
Addington Bucks . . . 39 B7
Kent 29 D7
London 28 C4
Addinston 121 D8
Addiscombe 28 C4
Addlestone 27 C8
Addlethorpe 79 C8
Adel 95 F5
Adeney 61 C7
Adfa 59 D7
Adforton 49 B6
Adisham 31 D6
Adlestrop 38 B2
Adlingfleet 90 B2
Adlington 86 C4
Admaston Staffs . . . 62 B4
Telford 61 C6
Admington 51 E7
Adstock 52 F5
Adstone 52 D3
Adversane 16 B4
Advie 152 E1
Adwalton 88 B3
Adwell 39 E6
Adwick le Street . . . 89 D6
Adwick upon
Dearne 89 D5
Adziel 153 C9
Ae Village 114 F2
Affleck 141 B7
Affpuddle 13 E6
Affric Lodge 136 B4
Afon-wen 72 B5
Afton 14 F4
Agglethorpe 101 F5
Agneash 84 D4
Aigburth 85 F4
Aiginis 155 D9
Aike 97 E6
Aikerness 159 C5
Aikers 159 J5
Aiketgate 108 E4
Aikton 108 D2
Ailey 48 E5
Ailstone 51 D7
Ailsworth 65 E8
Ainderby
Quernhow 102 F1
Ainderby Steeple . 101 E8
Aingers Green 43 B7
Ainsdale 85 C4
Ainsdale-on-Sea . . 85 C4
Ainstable 108 E5
Ainsworth 87 C5
Ainthorpe 103 D5
Aintree 85 E4
Aird Argyll 124 E3
Dumfries 104 C4
Highld 149 A12
W Isles 155 D10
Aird a Mhachair . . 148 D2
Aird a' Mhulaidh . . 154 F6
Aird Asaig 154 G6
Aird Dhail 155 A9
Airdens 151 B9
Aird Mhidhinis . . . 148 H2
Aird Mhighe
W Isles 154 H6
W Isles 154 J5
Aird Mhor 148 H2
Aird of Sleat 149 H10
Airdrie 119 C7
Aird Thunga 155 D9
Airdtorrisdale 157 C9
Aird Uig 154 D5
Airidh a Bhruaich . 154 F7
Airieland 106 D4
Airmyn 89 B8
Airntully 133 F7
Airor 149 H12
Airth 127 F7
Airton 94 D2
Airyhassen 105 E7
Aisby Lincs 78 F3
Lincs 90 E2
Aisgernis 148 F2
Aiskew 101 F7
Aislaby N Yorks 103 D6
N Yorks 103 F5
Stockton 102 C2
Aisthorpe 78 A2
Aith Orkney 159 G3
Shetland 160 D8
Shetland 160 H5
Aithsetter 160 K6
Aitkenhead 112 D3
Aitnoch 151 H12
Akeld 117 B5
Akeley 52 F5
Akenham 56 E5
Albaston 6 B2
Alberbury 60 C3
Albourne 17 C6
Albrighton Shrops . . 60 C4
Shrops 62 D2
Alburgh 69 F5
Albury Herts 41 B7
Sur 27 E8
Albury End 41 B7
Alby Hill 81 D7
Alcaig 151 F8
Alcaston 60 F4
Alcester 51 D5
Alciston 18 E2
Alcombe Som 21 E8
Alcombe continued
Wilts 24 C3
Alconbury 54 B2
Alconbury Weald
Cambs 54 B3
Alconbury Weston . 54 B2
Aldbar Castle 135 D5
Aldborough Norf . . . 81 D7
N Yorks 95 C7
Aldbourne 25 B7
Aldbrough 97 F8
Aldbrough St
John 101 C7
Aldbury 40 C2
Aldcliffe 92 C4
Aldclune 133 C6
Aldeburgh 57 D8
Aldeby 69 E7
Aldenham 40 E4
Alderbury 14 B2
Aldercar 76 E4
Alderford 68 C4
Alderholt 14 C2
Alderley 36 E4
Alderley Edge 74 B5
Aldermaston 26 C3
Aldermaston
Wharf 26 C4
Alderminster 51 E7
Alder's End 49 E8
Aldersey Green 73 D8
Aldershot 27 D6
Alderton Glos 50 F5
Shrops 60 B4
Suff 57 E7
Wilts 37 F5
W Nhants 52 E5
Alderwasley 76 D3
Aldfield 95 C5
Aldford 73 D8
Aldham Essex 43 B5
Suff 56 E4
Aldie 151 C10
Aldingbourne 16 D3
Aldingham 92 B2
Aldington Kent 19 B7
Worcs 51 E5
Aldington Frith 19 B7
Aldochlay 126 E2
Aldreth 54 B5
Aldridge 62 D4
Aldringham 57 C8
Aldsworth 38 C1
Aldunie 140 B2
Aldwark Derbys 76 D2
N Yorks 95 C7
Aldwick 16 E3
Aldwincle 65 F7
Aldworth 26 B3
Alexandria 118 B3
Alfardisworthy 8 C4
Alfington 11 E6
Alfold 27 F8
Alfold Bars 27 F8
Alfold Crossways . . 27 F8
Alford Aberds 140 C4
Lincs 79 B7
Som 23 F8
Alfreton 76 D4
Alfrick 50 D2
Alfrick Pound 50 D2
Alfriston 18 E2
Algaltraig 145 F9
Algarkirk 79 F5
Alhampton 23 F8
Aline Lodge 154 F6
Alisary 147 D10
Alkborough 90 B2
Alkerton 51 E8
Alkham 31 E6
Alkington 74 F2
Alkmonton 75 F8
Alladale Lodge . . . 150 C7
Allaleigh 7 D6
Allanaquoich 139 E7
Allangrange
Mains 151 F9
Allanton Borders . . 122 D4
N Lanark 119 D8
Allathasdal 148 H1
All Cannings 25 C5
Allendale Town . . . 109 D8
Allenheads 109 E8
Allensford 110 D3
Allens Green 41 C7
Allensmore 49 F6
Allenton 76 F3
Aller 12 B2
Allerby 107 F7
Allerford 21 E8
Allerston 103 F6
Allerthorpe 96 E3
Allerton Mers 86 F2
W Yorks 94 F4
Allerton Bywater . . 88 B5
Allerton
Mauleverer 95 D7
Allesley 63 F7
Allestree 76 F3
Allet 3 B6
Allexton 64 D5
Allgreave 75 C6
Allhallows 30 B2
Allhallows-on-Sea 30 B2
Alligin Shuas 149 C13
Allimore Green 62 C2
Allington Lincs 77 E8
Wilts 25 C5
Wilts 25 F7
Allithwaite 92 B3
Alloa 127 E7
Allonby 107 E7
Alloway 112 C3
All Saints South
Elmham 69 F6
All Stretton 60 E4
Allt 33 D6
Alltchaorunn 131 D5
Alltforgan 59 B6
Alltmawr 48 E2

Alltnacaillich 156 E7
Allt na h-Airbhe . . 150 B4
Allt-nan-sùgh . . . 136 B2
Alltsigh 137 C7
Alltwalis 46 F3
Alltwen 33 D8
Alltyblaca 46 E4
Allwood Green 56 B4
Almeley 48 D5
Almer 13 E7
Almholme 89 D6
Almington 74 F4
Alminstone Cross . . . 8 B5
Almondbank 128 B2
Almondbury 88 C2
Almondsbury 36 F3
Alne 95 C7
Alness 151 E9
Alnham 117 C5
Alnmouth 117 C8
Alnwick 117 C7
Alperton 40 F4
Alphamstone 56 F2
Alpheton 56 D2
Alphington 10 E4
Alport 76 C2
Alpraham 74 D2
Alresford 43 B6
Alrewas 63 C5
Alsager 74 D4
Alsagers Bank 74 E5
Alsop en le Dale . . . 75 D8
Alston Devon 11 D8
W&F 109 E7
Alstone 50 F4
Alstonefield 75 D8
Alswear 10 B2
Altandhu 156 H2
Altanduin 157 G11
Altarnun 8 F4
Altass 156 J7
Alterwall 158 D4
Altham 93 F7
Althorne 43 E5
Althorpe 90 D2
Alticry 105 D6
Altnabreac
Station 157 E13
Altnacealgach
Hotel 156 H5
Altnacraig 124 C4
Altnafeadh 131 D6
Altnaharra 157 F8
Altofts 88 B4
Alton Derbys 76 C3
Hants 26 F5
Staffs 75 E7
Alton Pancras 12 D5
Alton Priors 25 C6
Altrincham 87 F5
Altrua 136 F5
Altskeith 126 D3

Altyre House 151 F13
Alva 127 E7
Alvanley 73 B8
Alvaston 76 F3
Alvechurch 50 B5
Alvediston 13 B7
Alveley 61 F7
Alverdiscott 9 B7
Alverstoke 15 E7
Alverstone 15 F6
Alverton 77 E7
Alves 152 B1
Alvescot 38 D2
Alveston
 S Glos 36 F3
 Warks 51 D7
Alvie 138 D4
Alvingham 91 E7
Alvington 36 D3
Alwalton 65 E8
Alweston 12 C4
Alwinton 116 D5
Alwoodley 95 E5
Alyth 134 E2
Amatnatua 150 B7
Am Baile 148 G2
Ambergate 76 D3
Amber Hill 78 E5
Amberley Glos 37 D5
 W Sus 16 C4
Amble 117 D8
Amblecote 62 F2
Ambler Thorn 87 B8
Ambleside 99 D5
Ambleston 44 C5
Ambrosden 39 C6
Am Buth 124 C4
Amcotts 90 C2
Amersham 40 E2
Amesbury 25 E6
Amington 63 D6
Amisfield 114 F2
Amlwch 82 B4
Amlwch Port 82 B4
Ammanford
 = Rhydaman 33 C7
Amod 143 E8
Amotherby 96 B3
Ampfield 14 B5
Ampleforth 95 B8
Ampney Crucis 37 D7
Ampney St Mary 37 D7
Ampney St Peter ... 37 D7
Amport 25 E7
Ampthill 53 F8
Ampton 56 B2
Amroth 32 D2
Amulree 133 F5
Anagach 139 B6
Anaheilt 130 C2
Anancaun 150 E4
An Caol 149 C11
Ancaster 78 E2
Anchor 59 F8
Anchorsholme 92 E3
Ancroft 123 E5
Ancrum 116 B2
Anderby 79 B8
Anderson 13 E6
Anderton 74 B3
Andover 25 E8
Andover Down 25 E8
Andoversford 37 C7
Andreas 84 C4
Anfield 85 E4
Angarrack 2 C4
Angelbank 49 B7
Angersleigh 11 C6
Angle 44 E3
An Gleann Ur 155 D9
Angmering 16 D4
Angram N Yorks ... 100 E3
 N Yorks. 100 E3
Anie 126 C4
Ankerville 151 D11
Anlaby 90 B4
Anmer 80 E3
Annan 107 C8
Annat Argyll 125 C6
 Highld 149 C13
Anna Valley 25 E8
Annbank 112 B4
Annesley 76 D5
Annesley
 Woodhouse 76 D4
Annfield Plain ... 110 D4
Annifirth 160 J3
Annitsford 111 B5
Annscroft 60 D4
Ansdell 85 B4
Ansford 23 F8
Ansley 63 E6
Anslow 63 B6
Anslow Gate 63 B5
Anstey Herts 54 F5
 Leics. 64 D2
Anstruther
 Easter 129 D7
Anstruther
 Wester 129 D7
Ansty Hants 26 E5
 Warks 63 F7
 Wilts 13 B7
 W Sus 17 B6
Anthill Common ... 15 C7
Anthorn 107 D8
Antingham 81 D8
An t-Ob
 = Leverburgh 154 J5
Anton's Gowt 79 E5
Antonshill 127 F7
Antony 5 D8
Anwick 78 D4
Anwoth 106 D2
Aoradh 142 B3
Apes Hall 67 E5
Apethorpe 65 E7
Apeton 62 C2
Apley 78 B4
Apperknowle 76 B3
Apperley 37 B5
Apperley Bridge ... 94 F4
Appersett 100 E3
Appin 130 E3
Appin House 130 E3
Appleby 90 C3

Appleby-in-
 Westmorland ... 100 B1
Appleby Magna ... 63 D7
Appleby Parva ... 63 D7
Applecross 149 D12
Applecross
 House 149 D12
Appledore Devon ... 11 C5
 Devon. 20 F3
 Kent 19 C6
Appledore Heath ... 19 B6
Appleford 39 E5
Applegarthtown ... 114 F4
Appleshaw 25 E8
Applethwaite 98 B4
Appleton Halton ... 86 F3
 Oxon. 38 D4
Appleton-le-
 Moors 103 F5
Appleton-le-
 Street 96 B3
Appleton Roebuck .. 95 E8
Appleton Thorn ... 86 F4
Appleton Wiske ... 102 D1
Appletreehall 115 C8
Appletreewick 94 C3
Appley 11 B5
Appley Bridge 86 D3
Apse Heath 15 F6
Apsley End 54 F2
Apuldram 16 D2
Aquhythie 141 C6
Arabella 151 D11
Arbeadie 141 E5
Arberth
 = Narberth 32 C2
Arbirlot 135 E6
Arboll 151 C11
Arborfield 27 C5
Arborfield Cross .. 27 C5
Arborfield
 Garrison 27 C5
Arbourthorne 88 F4
Arbroath 135 E6
Arbuthnott 135 B7
Archiestown 152 D2
Arclid 74 C4
Ardachu 157 J9
Ardalanish 146 K6
Ardanaiseig 125 C6
Ardaneaskan ... 149 E13
Ardanstur 124 D4
Ardargie House
 Hotel 128 C2
Ardarroch 149 E13
Ardbeg Argyll ... 142 D5
 Argyll 145 E10
Ardcharnich 150 C4
Ardchiavaig 146 K6
Ardchullarie
 More 126 C4
Ardchyle 126 B4
Ard-dhubh 149 D12
Arddleen 60 C2
Ardechvie 136 E4
Ardeley 41 B6
Ardelve 149 F13
Arden 126 F2
Ardens Grafton ... 51 D6
Ardentinny 145 E10
Ardentraive 145 F9
Ardeonaig 132 F3
Ardersier 151 F10
Ardessie 150 C3
Ardfern 124 E4
Ardgartan 125 E7
Ardgay 151 B8
Ardglass 150 B4
Ardgour 130 C4
Ardheslaig 149 C12
Ardiecow 152 B5
Ardindrean 150 C4
Ardingly 17 B7
Ardington 38 F4
Ardlair 140 B4
Ardlamont House 145 G8
Ardleigh 43 B6
Ardler 134 E2
Ardley 39 B5
 Oxon. 38 F2
Ardlui 126 C2
Ardlussa 144 E5
Ardmair 150 B4
Ardmay 125 E8
Ardminish 143 D7
Ardmolich 147 D10
Ardmore Argyll .. 124 C3
 Highld 151 C10
 Highld 156 D5
Ardnacross 147 G8
Ardnadam 145 F10
Ardnagrask 151 G8
Ardnarff 149 E13
Ardnastang 130 C2
Ardnave 142 A3
Ardno 125 E7
Ardo 153 E8
Ardoch 133 F7
Ardochy House .. 136 D5
Ardo House 141 B8
Ardoyne 141 B5
Ardpatrick 144 G6
Ardpatrick House 144 H6
Ardpeaton 145 E11
Ardrishaig 145 E7
Ardross Fife 129 D7
 Highld 151 D9
Ardrossan 118 E2
Ardross Castle .. 151 D9
Ardshealach 147 E9
Ardsley 88 D4
Ardslignish 147 E8
Ardtalla 142 C5
Ardtalnaig 132 F4
Ardtoe 147 D9
Ardtrostan 127 B5
Arduaine 124 D3
Ardullie 151 E8
Ardvasar 149 H11
Ardvorlich 126 B5
Ardwell 104 E5
Ardwell Mains .. 104 E5
Ardwick 87 E6
Areley Kings 50 B3
Arford 27 F6
Argoed Caerph ... 35 E5
 Powys 47 C8
Arichamish 124 E5
Arichastlich 125 B8
Aridhglas 146 J6
Arileod 146 F4

Arinacrinachd ... 149 C12
Arinagour 146 F5
Arion 159 G3
Arisaig 147 C9
Ariundle 130 C2
Arkendale 95 C6
Arkesden 55 F5
Arkholme 93 B5
Arkle Town 101 D5
Arkley 41 E5
Arksey 89 D6
Arkwright Town ... 76 B4
Arle 37 B6
Arlecdon 98 C2
Arlesey 54 F2
Arleston 61 C6
Arley 86 F4
Arlingham 36 C4
Arlington Devon ... 20 E5
 E Sus 18 E2
 Glos 37 D8
Armadale Highld 157 C10
 W Loth 120 C2
Armadale
 Castle 149 H11
Armathwaite 108 E5
Arminghall 69 D5
Armitage 62 C4
Armley 95 F5
Armscote 51 E7
Armthorpe 89 D7
Arnabost 146 F5
Arncliffe 94 B2
Arncroach 129 D7
Arne 13 F7
Arnesby 64 E3
Arngask 128 C3
Arnisdale 149 G13
Arnish 149 D10
Arniston Engine 121 C6
Arnol 155 C8
Arnold E Yorks ... 97 E7
 Notts. 77 E5
Arnprior 126 E5
Arnside 92 B4
Aros Mains 147 G8
Arowry 73 F8
Arpafeelie 151 F9
Arrad Foot 99 F5
Arram 97 E6
Arrathorne 101 E7
Arreton 15 F6
Arrington 54 D4
Arrivain 125 B8
Arrochar 125 E8
Arrow 51 D5
Arthington 95 E5
Arthingworth 64 F4
Arthog 58 C3
Arthrath 153 E9
Arthurstone 134 E2
Artrochie 153 E10
Arundel 16 D4
Aryhoulan 130 C4
Asby 98 B2
Ascog 145 G10
Ascot 27 C7
Ascott 51 F8
Ascott-under-
 Wychwood 38 C3
Asenby 95 B6
Asfordby 64 C4
Asfordby Hill 64 C4
Asgarby Lincs 78 E4
 Lincs. 79 C6
Ash Kent 31 D6
 Kent 31 D6
 Som 12 B2
 Sur 27 D6
Ashampstead 26 B3
Ashbocking 57 D5
Ashbourne 75 E8
Ashbrittle 11 B5
Ash Bullayne 10 D2
Ashburnham
 Place 18 D3
Ashburton 7 C5
Ashbury Devon 9 E7
 Oxon. 38 F2
Ashby 90 D3
Ashby by Partney . 79 C7
Ashby cum Fenby . 91 D6
Ashby de la
 Launde 78 D3
Ashby-de-la-
 Zouch 63 C7
Ashby Folville ... 64 C4
Ashby Magna 64 E2
Ashby Parva 64 F2
Ashby Puerorum .. 79 B6
Ashby St Ledgers . 52 C3
Ashby St Mary ... 69 D6
Ashchurch 50 F4
Ashcombe 7 B7
Ashcott 23 F6
Ashdon 55 E6
Ashe 26 E3
Asheldham 43 D5
Ashen 55 E8
Ashendon 39 C7
Ashfield Carms .. 33 B7
 Stirling 127 D6
 Suff 57 C6
Ashfield Green ... 57 B6
Ashfold Crossways 17 B6
Ashford Devon ... 20 F4
 Hants 14 C2
 Kent 30 E4
 Sur 27 B8
Ashford Bowdler .. 49 B7
Ashford Carbonell 49 B7
Ashford Hill 26 C3
Ashford in the
 Water 75 C8
Ashgill 119 E7
Ash Green 63 F7
Ashill Devon 11 C5
 Norf 67 D8
 Som 11 C8
Ashingdon 42 E4
Ashington
 Northumb. 117 F8
 Som 12 B3
 W Sus 16 C5
Ashintully Castle 133 C8
Ashkirk 115 B7
Ashlett 15 D5
Ashleworth 37 B5
Ashley Cambs 55 C7
 Ches E 87 F5

Ashley continued
 Devon. 9 C8
 Dorset 14 C2
 Glos 37 E6
 Hants 14 E3
 Hants 25 F8
 N Nhants 64 E4
 Staffs 74 F4
Ashley Green 40 D2
Ashley Heath
 Dorset 14 C2
 Staffs 74 F4
Ash Magna 74 F2
Ashmanhaugh 69 B6
Ashmansworth .. 26 D2
Ashmansworthy ... 8 C5
Ash Mill 10 B2
Ashmore 13 C7
Ashorne 51 D8
Ashover 76 C3
Ashow 51 B8
Ashprington 7 D6
Ash Priors 11 B6
Ashreigney 9 C8
Ash Street 56 E4
Ashtead 28 D2
Ash Thomas 10 C5
Ashton Ches W ... 74 C2
 Corn 2 D5
 Hants 15 C6
 Hereford 49 C7
 Invclyd 118 B2
 N Nhants 65 F7
 W Nhants 53 E5
Ashton Common .. 24 D3
Ashton-in-
 Makerfield 86 E3
Ashton Keynes ... 37 E7
Ashton under Hill . 50 F4
Ashton-under-
 Lyne 87 E7
Ashton upon
 Mersey 87 E5
Ashurst Hants ... 14 C4
 Kent 18 B2
 W Sus 17 C5
Ashurstwood 28 F5
Ash Vale 27 D6
Ashwater 9 E5
Ashwell Herts ... 54 F3
 Rutland 65 C5
 Som 11 C8
Ashwellthorpe ... 68 E4
Ashwick 23 E8
Ashwicken 67 C7
Ashybank 115 C8
Askam in Furness 92 B2
Askern 89 C6
Askerswell 12 E3
Askett 39 D8
Askham Notts 77 B7
 W&F. 99 B7
Askham Bryan ... 95 E8
Askham Richard .. 95 E8
Asknish 145 D8
Askrigg 100 E4
Askwith 94 E4
Aslackby 78 F3
Aslacton 68 E4
Aslockton 77 F7
Asloun 140 C4
Aspatria 107 E8
Aspenden 41 B6
Asperton 79 F5
Aspley Guise 53 F7
Aspley Heath 53 F7
Aspull 86 D4
Asselby 89 B8
Asserby 79 B7
Assington 56 F3
Assynt House 151 E8
Astbury 74 C5
Astcote 52 D4
Asterley 60 D3
Asterton 60 E3
Asthall 38 C2
Asthall Leigh 38 C3
Astley Shrops ... 60 C5
 Warks 63 F7
 Worcs 50 C2
Astley Abbotts ... 61 E7
Astley Bridge 86 C5
Astley Cross 50 C3
Astley Green 86 E5
Aston Ches E 74 E3
 Ches W 74 B2
 Derbys 88 F2
 Hereford 49 B6
 Herts. 41 B5
 Oxon. 38 D3
 Shrops 60 B5
 Staffs 74 E4
 S Yorks 89 F5
 Telford 61 D6
 W Mid 62 F4
 Wokingham 39 F7
Aston Abbotts ... 39 B8
Aston Botterell .. 61 F6
Aston Cantlow ... 51 D6
Aston Clinton ... 40 C1
Aston Crews 36 B3
Aston Cross 50 F4
Aston End 41 B5
Aston Eyre 61 E6
Aston Fields 50 C4
Aston Flamville .. 63 E8
Aston Ingham 36 B3
Aston juxta
 Mondrum 74 D3
Aston le Walls ... 52 D2
Aston Magna 51 F6
Aston Munslow ... 60 F5
Aston on Clun ... 60 F3
Aston-on-Trent .. 63 B8
Aston Rogers 60 D3
Aston Rowant 39 E7
Aston Sandford .. 39 D7
Aston Somerville 50 F5
Aston Subedge ... 51 E6
Aston Tirrold 39 F5
Aston Upthorpe .. 39 F5
Astrop 52 F3
Astwick 54 F3
Astwood M Keynes 53 E7
Astwood Bank ... 50 C5
Aswarby 78 F3

Atcham 60 D5
Atch Lench 50 D5
Athelhampton 13 E5
Athelington 57 B6
Athelney 11 B8
Athelstaneford . 121 B8
Atherington 9 B7
Atherstone 63 E7
Atherstone on
 Stour 51 D7
Atherton 86 D4
Atley Hill 101 D7
Atlow 76 E2
Attadale 150 H2
Attadale House . 150 H2
Attenborough ... 76 F5
Atterby 90 E3
Attercliffe 88 F4
Atterton 63 E7
Attleborough Norf 68 E3
 Warks 63 E7
Attlebridge 68 C4
Atwick 97 D7
Atworth 24 C3
Aubourn 78 C2
Auchagallon 143 E9
Auchallater 139 F7
Aucharnie 153 D6
Auchattie 141 E5
Auchavan 134 C1
Auchbreck 139 B8
Auchenblae 135 B7
Auchenbrack .. 113 E7
Auchenbreck ... 145 E9
Auchencairn
 Dumfries 106 D4
 Dumfries 114 F2
 N Ayrs 143 F11
Auchencrosh ... 104 B5
Auchencrow 122 C4
Auchendinny ... 121 C5
Auchengray 120 D2
Auchenhalrig ... 152 B3
Auchenheath ... 119 E8
Auchenlochan . 145 F8
Auchenmalg ... 105 D6
Auchensoul 112 E2
Auchentiber ... 118 E3
Auchertyre ... 149 F13
Auchgourish ... 138 C5
Auchincarroch . 126 F3
Auchindrain ... 125 E6
Auchindrean ... 150 C4
Auchininna 153 D6
Auchinleck 113 B5
Auchinloch 119 B6
Auchinroath ... 152 C2
Auchintoul 140 C4
Auchiries 153 E10
Auchlee 141 E7
Auchleven 140 B5
Auchlochan ... 119 F8
Auchlossan ... 140 D4
Auchlunies 141 E7
Auchlyne 126 B4
Auchmacoy ... 153 E9
Auchmair 140 B2
Auchmantle ... 105 C5
Auchmillan ... 112 B5
Auchmithie ... 135 E6
Auchmuirbridge 128 D4
Auchmull 135 B5
Auchnacree ... 134 C4
Auchnagallin .. 151 H13
Auchnagatt ... 153 D9
Auchnaha 145 E8
Auchnashelloch 127 C6
Aucholzie 140 E2
Auchrannie ... 134 D2
Auchroisk 139 B6
Auchronie 140 F3
Auchterarder .. 127 C8
Auchteraw 137 D6
Auchterderran . 128 E4
Auchterhouse . 134 F3
Auchtermuchty . 128 C4
Auchterneed ... 150 F7
Auchtertool ... 128 E4
Auchtertyre ... 152 C1
Auchtubh 126 B4
Auckengill 158 D5
Auckley 89 D7
Audenshaw 87 E7
Audlem 74 E3
Audley 74 D4
Audley End 56 F6
Auds 153 B6
Aughton E Yorks . 96 F3
 Lancs 85 D4
 Lancs 93 C5
 S Yorks 89 F5
 Wilts 25 C7
Aughton Park ... 86 D2
Auldearn 151 F12
Aulden 49 D6
Auldgirth 114 F2
Auldhame 129 F7
Auldhouse 119 D6
Ault a'chruinn . 136 B2
Aultanrynie ... 156 F6
Aultbea 155 J13
Aultdearg 150 E5
Aultgrishan ... 155 J12
Aultguish Inn .. 150 D6
Aultibea 157 G13
Aultiphurst ... 157 C11
Aultmore 152 C4
Aultnagoire ... 137 B8
Aultnamain Inn . 151 C9
Aultnaslat 136 D4
Aulton 140 B5
Aundorach 139 C5
Aunsby 78 F3
Auquhorthies . 141 B7
Aust 36 F2
Austendike 66 B2
Austerfield 89 E7
Austrey 63 D6
Austwick 93 C7
Authorpe 91 F8
Authorpe Row ... 79 B8
Avebury 25 C6
Aveley 42 F1
Avening 37 E5
Averham 77 D7
Aveton Gifford .. 6 E4
Avielochan 138 C5
Aviemore 138 C4

Avington Hants .. 26 F3
 W Berks 25 C8
Avoch 151 F10
Avon 14 E2
Avonbridge 120 B2
Avon Dassett ... 52 E2
Avonmouth 23 B7
Avonwick 6 D5
Awbridge 14 B4
Awhirk 104 D4
Awkley 36 F2
Awliscombe 11 D6
Awre 36 D4
Awsworth 76 E4
Axbridge 23 D6
Axford Hants ... 26 E4
 Wilts 25 B7
Axminster 11 E7
Axmouth 11 E7
Axton 85 E7
Aycliff 31 E7
Aycliffe 101 B7
Aydon 110 C3
Aylburton 36 D3
Ayle 109 E7
Aylesbeare 10 E5
Aylesbury 39 C8
Aylesby 91 D6
Aylesford 29 D8
Aylesham 31 D6
Aylestone 64 D2
Aylmerton 81 D7
Aylsham 81 E7
Aylton 49 F8
Aymestrey 49 C6
Aynho 52 F3
Ayot St Lawrence 40 C4
Ayot St Peter ... 41 C5
Ayr 112 B3
Aysgarth 101 F5
Ayside 99 F5
Ayston 65 D5
Aythorpe Roding . 42 C1
Ayton 122 C5
Aywick 160 E7
Azerley 95 B5

B

Babbacombe 7 C7
Babbinswood 73 F7
Babcary 12 B3
Babel 47 F7
Babell 73 B5
Babraham 55 D6
Babworth 89 F7
Bac 155 C9
Bachau 82 C4
Back of Keppoch 147 C9
Backaland 159 E6
Backaskaill 159 C5
Backbarrow 99 F5
Backe 32 C3
Backfolds 153 C10
Backford 73 B8
 Notts. 77 D8
Backhill
 Aberds 153 E7
 Aberds 153 E10
Backhill of
 Clackriach 153 D9
Backhill of
 Fortree 153 D9
Backhill of
 Trustach 140 E5
Backies 157 J11
Backlass 158 E4
Back of Keppoch 147 C9
Back Rogerton . 113 B5
Backwell 23 C6
Backworth 111 B6
Bacon End 42 C2
Baconsthorpe ... 81 D7
Bacton Hereford . 49 F5
 Norf 81 D9
 Suff 56 C4
Bacton Green ... 56 C4
Bacup 87 B6
Badachro 149 A12
Badanloch
 Lodge 157 F10
Badavanich ... 150 F4
Badbury 38 F1
Badby 52 D3
Badcall 156 D5
Badcaul 150 B3
Baddeley Green .. 75 D6
Baddesley Clinton 51 B7
Baddesley Ensor . 63 E6
Baddidarach .. 156 G3
Baddoch 139 F7
Baddock 151 F10
Badenscoth ... 153 E7
Badenyon 140 C2
Badgall 8 F4
Badger 61 E7
Badger's Mount . 29 C5
Badgeworth 37 C6
Badgworth 23 D5
Badicaul 149 F12
Badingham 57 C7
Badlesmere 30 D4
Badlipster 158 F4
Badluarach 150 B2
Badminton 37 F5
Badnaban 156 G3
Badnagie 158 G3
Badninish 151 B10
Badrallach ... 150 B3
Badsey 51 E5
Badshot Lea 27 E6
Badsworth 89 C5
Badwell Ash 56 C3
Bae Colwyn
 = Colwyn Bay .. 83 D8
Bag Enderby 79 B6
Bagby 102 F2
Bagendon 37 D7
Bagh a Chaisteil
 = Castlebay ... 148 J1
Baghasdal 148 G2
Bagh Mor 148 C3
Bagh
 Shiarabhagh .. 148 H2
Bagillt 73 B6
Baginton 51 B8
Baglan 34 E1
Bagley 60 B4
Bagnall 75 D6
Bagnor 26 C2
Bagshot Sur 27 C7
 Wilts 25 C8

Bagthorpe Norf .. 80 D3
 Notts 76 D4
Bagworth 63 D8
Bagwy Llydiart .. 35 B8
Baildon 94 F4
Baile 154 J4
Baile Ailein ... 155 E7
Baile a'Ruiseil . 153 D9
Bailebeag 137 C8
Baile Glas 148 C3
Baile Mhartainn 148 A2
Baile Mhic Phail 148 A3
Baile Mor Argyll 146 J5
 W Isles 148 B2
Baile nan
 Cailleach 148 C2
Baile Raghaill . 148 A2
Baileyhead 108 B5
Bailiesward ... 152 E4
Baillieston 119 C6
Bailmae 106 A3
Bail'lochdrach . 148 C3
Bail Uachdraich 148 B3
Bail'Ur
 Tholastaidh .. 155 C10
Bainbridge 100 E4
Bainsford 127 F7
Bainshole 152 E6
Bainton E Yorks . 97 D5
 Pboro 65 D7
Bairnkine 116 C2
Baker's End 41 C6
Baker Street ... 42 F2
Bakewell 76 C2
Bala = Y Bala .. 72 F3
Balachuirn ... 149 D10
Balavil 138 D3
Balbeg Highld .. 137 B7
 Highld 150 H7
Balbeggie 128 B3
Balbithan 141 C6
Balbithan House 141 C6
Balblair Highld .. 151 B8
 Highld 151 E10
Balby 89 D6
Balchladich ... 156 F3
Balchraggan
 Highld 151 G8
 Highld 151 H8
Balchrick 156 D4
Balchrystie ... 129 D6
Balcladaich .. 137 B5
Balcombe 28 F4
Balcombe Lane .. 28 F4
Balcomie 129 C8
Balcurvie 128 D5
Baldersby 95 B6
Baldersby St
 James 95 B6
Balderstone 93 F6
Balderton
 Ches W 73 C7
 Notts. 77 D8
Baldhu 3 B6
Baldinnie 129 C6
Baldock 54 F3
Baldovie 134 F4
Baldrine 84 D4
Baldslow 18 D4
Baldwin 84 D3
Baldwinholme . 108 D3
Baldwin's Gate .. 74 E4
Bale 81 D6
Balearn 153 C10
Balemartine ... 146 G2
Balephuil 146 G2
Balerno 120 C4
Balevullin 146 G2
Balfield 135 C5
Balfour 159 G5
Balfron 126 F4
Balfron Station . 126 F4
Balgaveny 153 D6
Balgavies 135 D5
Balgonar 128 E2
Balgove 153 E8
Balgowan 138 E2
Balgown 149 B8
Balgrochan ... 119 B6
Balgy 149 C13
Balhaldie 127 D7
Balhalgardy ... 141 B6
Balham 28 B3
Balhary 134 E2
Baliasta 160 C8
Baligill 157 C11
Balintore Angus 134 D2
 Highld 151 D11
Balintraid 151 D10
Balk 102 F2
Balkeerie 134 E3
Balkemback 134 F3
Balkholme 89 B8
Balkissock 104 A5
Ball 60 B3
Ballabeg 84 E2
Ballacannel 84 D4
Ballachulish .. 130 D4
Ballajora 84 C4
Ballaleigh 84 D3
Ballamodha 84 E2
Ballantrae 104 A4
Ballaquine 84 D4
Ballards Gore .. 43 E5
Ballasalla IoM .. 84 C3
 IoM 84 E2
Ballater 140 E2
Ballaugh 84 C3
Ballaveare 84 E3
Ballcorach 139 B7
Ballechin 133 D6
Balleigh 151 C10
Ballencrieff ... 121 B7
Ballentoul 133 C5
Ball Haye Green . 75 D6
Ball Hill 26 C2
Ballidon 76 D2
Balliemore Argyll 124 C4
 Argyll 145 E9
Ballikinrain .. 126 F4
Ballimeanoch .. 125 D6
Ballimore Argyll 145 E8
 Stirling 126 C4
Ballinaby 142 B3
Ballindean 128 B4
Ballingdon 56 E2
Ballinger Common 40 D2

Ballingham 49 F7
Ballingry 128 E3
Ballinlick 133 E6
Ballinluig 133 D6
Ballintuim 133 D8
Balloch Angus . 134 D3
 Highld 151 G10
 N Lanark 119 B7
 W Dunb 126 F2
Ballochan 140 E4
Ballochford ... 152 E3
Ballochmorrie . 112 F2
Ballochmyle ... 113 B5
Balls Cross 16 B3
Balls Green 43 B6
Ballygown 146 G7
Ballygrant 142 B4
Ballyhaugh 146 F4
Balmacara 149 F13
Balmacara
 Square 149 F13
Balmaclellan . 106 B3
Balmacneil ... 133 D6
Balmacqueen .. 149 A9
Balmae 106 E3
Balmaha 126 E3
Balmalcolm ... 128 D5
Balmeanach .. 149 D10
Balmedie 141 C8
Balmer Heath .. 73 F8
Balmerino 129 B5
Balmerlawn 14 D4
Balmichael .. 143 E10
Balmirmer ... 135 F5
Balmore Highld . 149 D7
 Highld 151 G11
 Highld 151 H6
 Perth 133 D6
Balmule 128 F4
Balmullo 129 B6
Balmungie ... 151 F10
Balnaboth 134 C3
Balnabruaich 151 E10
Balnacoil 157 H11
Balnacra 150 G2
Balnafoich ... 151 H9
Balnagall 151 C11
Balnaguard ... 133 D6
Balnahard Argyll 144 D3
 Argyll 146 H7
Balnain 150 H7
Balnakeil 156 C6
Balnaknock ... 149 B9
Balnapaling . 151 E10
Balne 89 C6
Balochroy 143 D8
Balone 129 C6
Balornock 119 C6
Balquharn 133 F7
Balquhidder ... 126 B4
Balsall 51 B7
Balsall Common . 51 B7
Balsall Heath .. 62 F4
Balscott 51 E8
Balsham 55 D6
Baltasound 160 C8
Balterley 74 D4
Baltersan 105 C8
Balthangie 153 C8
Baltonsborough . 23 F7
Balvaird 151 F8
Balvicar 124 D3
Balvraid Highld . 149 G13
 Highld 151 H11
Bamber Bridge .. 86 B3
Bambers Green .. 42 B1
Bamburgh 123 F7
Bamff 134 D2
Bamford
 Derbys 88 F3
 Gtr Man 87 C6
Bampton Devon .. 10 B4
 Oxon. 38 D3
 W&F. 99 C7
Banavie 131 B5
Banbury 52 E2
Bancffosfelen .. 33 C5
Banchory 141 E5
Banchory-
 Devenick 141 D8
Bancycapel 33 C5
Bancyfelin 32 C4
Bancyffordd ... 46 F3
Bandirran 134 F2
Banff 153 B6
Bangor 83 D5
Bangor-is-y-coed
 = Bangor-on-Dee . 73 E7
Bangor-on-Dee
 = Bangor-is-y-coed 73 E7
Banham 68 F3
Bank 14 D3
Bankend 107 C7
Bankfoot 133 F7
Bankglen 113 C6
Bankhead
 Aberdeen 141 C7
 Aberds 141 D6
Banks
 Cumb. 109 C5
 Lancs 85 B4
Bankshill 114 F4
Banningham 81 E8
Banniskirk House 158 E3
Bannister Green . 42 B2
Bannockburn .. 127 E7
Banstead 28 D3
Bantham 6 E4
Banton 119 B7
Banwell 23 D5
Banyard's Green . 57 B6
Bapchild 30 C3

Barabhas 155 C8
Barabhas Iarach 155 C8
Barabhas Uarach 155 B8
Barachandroman 124 C2
Barassie 118 F3
Baravullin 124 E4
Barbaraville . 151 D10
Barber Booth ... 88 F2
Barbieston 112 C4
Barbon 99 F8
Barbridge 74 D3
Barbrook 21 E6
Barby 52 B3
Barcaldine 130 E3
Barcheston 51 F7
Barcombe 17 C8
Barcombe Cross . 17 C8
Barden 101 E6
Barden Scale ... 94 D3
Bardfield Saling . 42 B2
Bardister 160 F5
Bardney 78 C4
Bardon 63 C8
Bardon Mill ... 109 C7
Bardowie 119 B5
Bardrainney .. 118 B3
Bardsea 92 B3
Bardsey 95 C6
Bardwell 56 B3
Bare 92 C4
Barford Norf ... 68 D4
 Warks 51 C7
Barford St John . 52 F2
Barford St Martin 25 F5
Barford St Michael 52 F2
Barfrestone 31 D6
Bargod = Bargoed . 35 E5
Bargoed = Bargod . 35 E5
Bargrennan ... 105 B7
Barham Cambs ... 54 B2
 Kent 31 D6
 Suff 56 D5
Barharrow 106 D3
Barhill 106 C5
Bar Hill 54 C4
Barholm 65 C7
Barkby 64 D3
Barkestone-le-
 Vale 77 F7
Barkham 27 C5
Barking London . 41 F7
 Suff 56 D4
Barkingside 41 F7
Barking Tye 56 D4
Barkisland 87 C8
Barkston Lincs .. 78 E2
 N Yorks 95 F7
Barkway 54 F4
Barlaston 75 F5
Barlavington .. 16 C3
Barlborough 76 B4
Barlby 96 F2
Barlestone 63 D8
Barley Herts ... 54 F4
 Lancs 93 E8
Barley Mow ... 111 D5
Barleythorpe ... 64 D5
Barling 43 F5
Barlow Derbys .. 76 B3
 N Yorks 89 B7
 T&W. 110 C4
Barmby Moor ... 96 E3
Barmby on the
 Marsh 89 B7
Barmer 80 D4
Barmoor Castle 123 F5
Barmoor Lane
 End 123 F6
Barmouth
 = Abermaw 58 C3
Barmpton 101 C8
Barmston 97 D7
Barnack 65 D7
Barnacle 63 F7
Barnard Castle 101 C5
Barnard Gate .. 38 C4
Barnardiston ... 55 E8
Barnbarroch .. 106 D5
Barnburgh 89 D5
Barnby 69 F7
Barnby Dun 89 D7
Barnby in the
 Willows 77 D8
Barnby Moor ... 89 F7
Barnes Street .. 29 E7
Barnet 41 E5
Barnetby le Wold 90 D4
Barney 81 D5
Barnham Suff .. 56 B2
 W Sus 16 D3
Barnham Broom . 68 D3
Barnhead 135 D6
Barnhill Ches W . 73 D8
 Dundee 134 F4
 Moray 152 C1
Barnhills 104 B3
Barningham
 Durham 101 C5
 Suff 56 B3
Barnoldby le Beck 91 D6
Barnoldswick ... 93 E8
Barns Green 16 B5
Barnsley Glos ... 37 D7
 S Yorks 88 D4
Barnstaple 20 F4
Barnston Essex . 42 C2
 Mers 85 F3
Barnstone 77 F7
Barnt Green 50 B5
Barnton Ches W . 74 B3
 Edin 120 B4
Barnwell All Saints 65 F7
Barnwell St
 Andrew 65 F7
Barnwood 37 C5
Barochreal 124 C4
Barons Cross .. 49 D6
Barr 112 E2
Barra Castle .. 141 B6
Barrachan 105 E7
Barrack 153 D8
Barraglom 154 D6
Barrahormid .. 144 E6
Barran 124 C4
Barrapol 146 G2
Barras Aberds 141 F7
 W&F. 100 C3
Barrasford 110 B2
Barravullin ... 124 E4
Barregarrow ... 84 D3
Barrhead 118 D4
Barrhill 112 F2
Barrington Cambs 54 E4
 Som 11 C8
Barripper 2 C5
Barrmill 118 D3
Barrock 158 C4
Barrock House . 158 D4
Barrow Lancs ... 93 F7
 Rutland 65 C5

Barrow *continued*
Suff 55 C8
Barroway Drove 67 D5
Barrowburn 116 C4
Barrowby 77 F8
Barrowcliff 103 F8
Barrowden 65 D6
Barrowford 93 F8
Barrow Green 30 C3
Barrow Gurney 23 C7
Barrow Haven 90 B4
Barrow-in-Furness 92 C2
Barrow Island 92 C1
Barrow Nook 86 D2
Barrows Green
Ches E 74 D3
W&F 99 F7
Barrow's Green 86 F3
Barrow Street 24 F3
Barrow upon Humber 90 B4
Barrow upon Soar 64 C2
Barrow upon Trent 63 B7
Barry 135 F5
Barry = *Y Barri* 22 C3
Barry Island 22 C3
Barsby 64 C3
Barsham 69 F6
Barston 51 B7
Bartestree 49 E7
Barthol Chapel 153 E8
Barthomley 74 D4
Bartley 14 C4
Bartley Green 62 F4
Bartlow 55 E6
Barton Cambs 54 D5
Ches W 73 D8
Glos 37 B8
Lancs 85 D4
Lancs 92 F5
N Yorks 101 D7
Oxon 39 D5
Torbay 7 C7
Warks 51 D6
Barton Bendish 67 D7
Barton Hartshorn 52 F4
Barton in Fabis 76 F5
Barton in the Beans 63 D7
Barton-le-Clay 53 F8
Barton-le-Street 96 B3
Barton-le-Willows 96 C3
Barton Mills 55 B8
Barton on Sea 14 E3
Barton on the Heath 51 F7
Barton St David 23 F7
Barton Seagrave 53 B6
Barton Stacey 26 E2
Barton Turf 69 B6
Barton-under-Needwood 63 C5
Barton-upon-Humber 90 B4
Barton Waterside 90 B4
Barugh 88 D4
Barway 55 B6
Barwell 63 E8
Barwick Herts 41 C6
Som 12 C3
Barwick in Elmet 95 F6
Baschurch 60 B4
Bascote 52 C2
Basford Green 75 D6
Bashall Eaves 93 E6
Bashley 14 E3
Basildon 42 F3
Basingstoke 26 D4
Baslow 76 B2
Bason Bridge 22 E5
Bassaleg 35 F6
Bassenthwaite 108 F2
Bassett 14 C5
Bassingbourn 54 E4
Bassingfield 77 F6
Bassingham 78 C2
Bassingthorpe 65 B6
Basta 160 D7
Baston 65 C8
Bastwick 69 C7
Baswick Steer 97 E6
Batchworth Heath 40 E3
Batcombe Dorset 12 D4
Som 23 F8
Bate Heath 74 B3
Batford 40 C4
Bath 24 C2
Bathampton 24 C2
Bathealton 11 B5
Batheaston 24 C2
Bathford 24 C2
Bathgate 120 C2
Bathley 77 D7
Bathpool Corn 5 B7
Som 11 B7
Bathville 120 C2
Batley 88 B3
Batsford 51 F6
Battersby 102 D3
Battersea 28 B3
Battisborough Cross 6 E3
Battisford 56 D4
Battisford Tye 56 D4
Battle E Sus 18 D4
Powys 48 F2
Battledown 37 B6
Battlefield 60 C5
Battlesbridge 42 E3
Battlesden 40 B2
Battlesea Green 57 B6
Battleton 10 B4
Battram 63 D8
Battramsley 14 E4
Baughton 50 E3
Baughurst 26 D3
Baulking 38 E3
Baumber 78 B5
Baunton 37 D7
Baverstock 24 F5
Bawburgh 68 D4
Bawdeswell 81 E6
Bawdrip 22 F5
Bawdsey 57 E7
Bawtry 89 E7
Baxenden 87 B5
Baxterley 63 E6
Baybridge 15 B6
Baycliff 92 B2
Baydon 25 B7
Bayford Herts 41 D6
Som 12 B5
Bayles 109 E7
Baylham 56 D5
Baynard's Green 39 B5
Bayston Hill 60 D4
Baythorn End 55 E8
Bayton 49 B8
Beach 130 D1
Beachampton 53 F5
Beachamwell 67 D7
Beachans 151 G13
Beacharr 143 D7
Beachborough 19 B8
Beachley 36 E2
Beacon 11 D6
Beacon End 43 B5
Beacon Hill 27 F6
Beacon's Bottom 39 E7
Beaconsfield 40 F2
Beacrabhaic 154 H6
Beadlam 102 F4
Beadlow 54 F2
Beadnell 117 B8
Beaford 9 C7
Beal Northumb 123 E6
N Yorks 89 B6
Beamhurst 75 F7
Beaminster 12 D2
Beamish 110 D5
Beamsley 94 D3
Bean 29 B6
Beanacre 24 C4
Beanley 117 C6
Beaquoy 159 F4
Bear Cross 13 E8
Beardwood 86 B4
Beare Green 28 E2
Bearley 51 C6
Bearnus 146 G6
Bearpark 110 E5
Bearsbridge 109 D7
Bearsden 118 B5
Bearsted 29 D8
Bearstone 74 F4
Bearwood BCP 13 E8
Hereford 49 D5
W Mid 62 F4
Beattock 114 D3
Beauchamp Roding 42 C1
Beauchief 88 F4
Beaufort 35 C5
Beaufort Castle 151 G8
Beaulieu 14 D4
Beauly 151 G8
Beaumaris = *Biwmares* 83 D6
Beaumont Cumb 108 D3
Essex 43 B7
Beaumont Hill 101 C7
Beausale 51 B7
Beauworth 15 B6
Beaworthy 9 E6
Beazley End 42 B3
Bebington 85 F4
Bebside 117 F8
Beccles 69 E7
Becconsall 86 B2
Beckbury 61 D7
Beckenham 28 C4
Beckermet 98 D2
Beckfoot Cumb 98 D3
Cumb 107 E7
Beck Foot 99 E8
Beckford 50 F4
Beckhampton 25 C5
Beck Hole 103 D6
Beckingham Lincs 77 D8
Notts 89 F8
Beckington 24 D3
Beckley E Sus 19 C5
Hants 14 E3
Oxon 39 C5
Beck Row 55 B7
Beck Side 98 F4
Beckton 41 F7
Beckwithshaw 95 D5
Becontree 41 F7
Bedale 101 F7
Bedburn 110 F4
Bedchester 13 C6
Beddau 34 F4
Beddgelert 71 C6
Beddingham 17 D8
Beddington 28 C4
Bedfield 57 C6
Bedford 53 D8
Bedham 16 B4
Bedhampton 15 D8
Bedingfield 57 C5
Bedlam 95 C5
Bedlington 117 F8
Bedlington Station 117 F8
Bedlinog 34 D4
Bedminster 23 B7
Bedmond 40 D3
Bednall 62 C3
Bedrule 116 C2
Bedstone 49 B5
Bedwas 35 F5
Bedworth 63 F7
Bedworth Heath 63 F7
Bed-y-coedwr 71 E8
Beeby 64 D3
Beech Hants 26 F4
Staffs 75 F5
Beech Hill Gtr Man 86 D3
W Berks 26 C4
Beechingstoke 25 D5
Beedon 26 B2
Beeford 97 D7
Beeley 76 C2
Beelsby 91 D6
Beenham 26 C3
Beeny 8 E3
Beer 11 F7
Beercrocombe 11 B8
Beer Hackett 12 C3
Beesands 7 E6
Beesby 91 F8
Beeson 7 E6
Beeston C Beds 54 E2
Ches W 74 D2
Norf 68 C2
Notts 76 F5
Beeston *continued*
W Yorks 95 F5
Beeston Regis 81 C7
Beeswing 107 C5
Beetham 92 B4
Beetley 68 C2
Begbroke 38 C4
Begelly 32 D2
Beggar's Bush 48 C4
Beguildy 48 B3
Beighton Norf 69 D6
S Yorks 88 F5
Beighton Hill 76 D2
Beith 118 D3
Bekesbourne 31 D5
Belaugh 69 C5
Belbroughton 50 B4
Belchamp Otten 56 E2
Belchamp St Paul 55 E8
Belchamp Walter 56 E2
Belchford 79 B5
Belford 123 F7
Belhaven 122 B2
Belhelvie 141 C8
Belhinnie 140 B3
Bellabeg 140 C2
Bellamore 112 F2
Bellanoch 144 D6
Bellaty 134 D2
Bell Bar 41 D5
Bell Busk 94 D2
Belleau 79 B7
Bellehiglash 152 E1
Bell End 50 B4
Bellerby 101 E6
Bellever 6 B4
Belliehill 135 C5
Bellingdon 40 D2
Bellingham 116 F4
Belloch 143 E7
Bellochantuy 143 E7
Bell o'th'Hill 74 E2
Bellsbank 112 D4
Bellshill N Lanark 119 C7
Northumb 123 F7
Bellspool 120 F4
Bellsquarry 120 C3
Bells Yew Green 18 B3
Belmaduthy 151 F9
Belmesthorpe 65 C7
Belmont Blackburn 86 C4
London 28 C3
S Ayrs 112 B3
Shetland 160 C7
Belnacraig 140 C2
Belowda 4 C4
Belper 76 E3
Belper Lane End 76 E3
Belsay 110 B4
Belses 115 B8
Belsford 7 D5
Belstead 56 E5
Belston 112 B3
Belstone 9 E8
Belthorn 86 B5
Beltinge 31 C5
Beltoft 90 D2
Belton Leics 63 B8
Lincs 78 F2
N Lincs 89 D8
Norf 69 D7
Belton in Rutland 64 D5
Beltring 29 E7
Belts of Collonach 141 E5
Belvedere 29 B5
Belvoir 77 F8
Bembridge 15 F7
Bemersyde 121 F8
Bemerton 25 F6
Bempton 97 B7
Benacre 69 F8
Ben Alder Lodge 132 B2
Ben Armine Lodge 157 H10
Benbuie 113 E7
Ben Casgro 155 E9
Benderloch 124 B5
Bendronaig Lodge 150 H3
Benenden 18 B5
Benfield 105 C7
Bengate 69 B6
Bengeworth 50 E5
Benhall Green 57 C7
Benhall Street 57 C7
Benholm 135 C8
Beningbrough 95 D8
Benington Herts 41 B5
Lincs 79 E6
Benllech 82 C5
Benmore Argyll 145 E10
Stirling 126 B3
Benmore Lodge 156 H6
Bennacott 8 E4
Bennan 143 F10
Benniworth 91 F6
Benover 29 E8
Ben Rhydding 94 E4
Bensham 110 C5
Benslie 118 E3
Benson 39 E6
Bent 135 B6
Bent Gate 87 B5
Benthall Northumb 117 B8
Shrops 61 D6
Bentham 37 C6
Benthoul 141 D7
Bentlawnt 60 D3
Bentley E Yorks 97 F6
Hants 27 E5
Suff 56 F5
S Yorks 89 D6
Warks 63 E6
Worcs 50 C4
Bentley Heath 51 B6
Benton 21 F5
Bentpath 115 E6
Bents 120 C2
Bentworth 26 E4
Benvie 134 F3
Benwick 66 E3
Beoley 51 C5
Beoraidbeg 147 B9
Bepton 16 C2
Berden 41 B7
Bere Alston 6 C2
Bere Ferrers 6 C2
Berepper 3 D5
Bere Regis 13 E6
Bergh Apton 69 D6
Berinsfield 39 E5
Berkeley 36 E3
Berkhamsted 40 D2
Berkley 24 E3
Berkswell 51 B7
Bermondsey 28 B4
Bernera 149 F13
Bernice 145 D10
Bernisdale 149 C9
Berrick Salome 39 E6
Berriedale 158 H3
Berrier 99 B5
Berriew 59 D8
Berrington Northumb 123 E6
Shrops 60 D5
Berrow 22 D5
Berrow Green 50 D2
Berry Down Cross 20 E4
Berryfield 39 C7
Berry Hill Glos 36 C2
Pembs 45 E2
Berryhillock 152 B5
Berrynarbor 20 E4
Berry Pomeroy 7 C6
Bersham 73 E7
Berstane 159 G5
Berwick 18 E2
Berwick Bassett 25 B5
Berwick Hill 110 B4
Berwick St James 25 F5
Berwick St John 13 B7
Berwick St Leonard 24 F4
Berwick-upon-Tweed 123 D5
Bescar 85 C4
Besford 50 E4
Bessacarr 89 D7
Bessels Leigh 38 D4
Bessingby 97 C7
Bessingham 81 D7
Bestbeech Hill 18 B3
Besthorpe Norf 68 E3
Notts 77 C8
Bestwood 77 E5
Bestwood Village 77 E5
Beswick 97 E6
Betchworth 28 E3
Bethania Ceredig 46 C4
Gwyn 71 C8
Gwyn 83 F6
Bethel Anglesey 82 D3
Gwyn 72 F3
Gwyn 82 E5
Bethersden 30 E3
Bethesda Gwyn 83 E6
Pembs 32 C1
Bethlehem 33 B7
Bethnal Green 41 F6
Betley 74 E4
Betsham 29 B7
Betteshanger 31 D7
Bettiscombe 11 E8
Bettisfield 73 F8
Betton Shrops 60 D3
Shrops 74 F3
Bettws Bridgend 34 F3
Mon 35 C6
Newport 35 E6
Bettws Cedewain 59 E8
Bettws Gwerfil Goch 72 E4
Bettws Ifan 46 E2
Bettws Newydd 35 D7
Bettws-y-crwyn 60 F2
Bettyhill 157 C10
Betws 33 C7
Betws Bledrws 46 D4
Betws-Garmon 82 F5
Betws-y-Coed 83 F7
Betws-yn-Rhos 72 B3
Beulah Ceredig 45 E4
Powys 47 D8
Bevendean 17 D7
Bevercotes 77 B6
Beverley 97 F6
Beverston 37 E5
Bevington 36 E3
Bewaldeth 108 F2
Bewcastle 109 B5
Bewdley 50 B2
Bewerley 94 C4
Bewholme 97 D7
Bexhill 18 E4
Bexley 29 B5
Bexleyheath 29 B5
Bexwell 67 D6
Beyton 56 C3
Bhaltos 154 D5
Bhatarsaigh 148 J1
Bibury 37 D8
Bicester 39 B5
Bickenhall 11 C7
Bickenhill 63 F5
Bicker 78 F5
Bickershaw 86 D4
Bickerstaffe 86 D2
Bickerton Ches E 74 D2
N Yorks 95 D7
Bickington Devon 7 B5
Devon 20 F4
Bickleigh Devon 6 C3
Devon 10 D4
Bickleton 20 F4
Bickley 28 C5
Bickley Moss 74 E2
Bicknacre 42 D3
Bicknoller 22 F3
Bicknor 30 D2
Bickton 14 C2
Bicton Shrops 60 C4
Shrops 60 F2
Bidborough 29 E6
Biddenden 19 B5
Biddenham 53 E8
Biddestone 24 B3
Biddisham 23 D5
Biddlesden 52 E4
Biddlestone 117 D5
Biddulph 75 D5
Biddulph Moor 75 D6
Bideford 9 B6
Bidford-on-Avon 51 D6
Bidston 85 E3
Bielby 96 E3
Bieldside 141 D7
Bierley IoW 15 G6
Bierley *continued*
W Yorks 94 F4
Bierton 39 C8
Bigbury 6 E4
Bigbury on Sea 6 E4
Bigby 90 D4
Biggar S Lanark 120 F3
W&F 92 C1
Biggin Derbys 75 D8
Derbys 76 E2
N Yorks 95 F8
Biggings 160 G3
Biggin Hill 28 D5
Biggleswade 54 E2
Bighouse 157 C11
Bighton 26 F4
Bignor 16 C3
Big Sand 149 A12
Bigton 160 L5
Bilberry 4 C5
Bilborough 76 E5
Bilbrook 22 E2
Bilbrough 95 E8
Bilbster 158 E4
Bildershaw 101 B7
Bildeston 56 E3
Billericay 42 E2
Billesdon 64 D4
Billesley 51 D6
Billingborough 78 F4
Billinge 86 D3
Billingford 81 E6
Billingham 102 B2
Billinghay 78 D4
Billingley 88 D5
Billingshurst 16 B4
Billingsley 61 F7
Billington C Beds 40 B2
Lancs 93 F7
Billockby 69 C7
Billy Row 110 F4
Bilsborrow 92 F5
Bilsby 79 B7
Bilsham 16 D3
Bilsington 19 B7
Bilson Green 36 C3
Bilsthorpe 77 C6
Bilsthorpe Moor 77 D6
Bilston Midloth 121 C5
W Mid 62 E3
Bilstone 63 D7
Bilting 30 E4
Bilton E Yorks 97 F7
Northumb 117 C8
Warks 52 B2
Bilton in Ainsty 95 E7
Bimbister 159 G4
Binbrook 91 E6
Binchester Blocks 110 F5
Bincombe 12 F4
Bindal 151 C12
Binegar 23 E8
Binfield 27 B6
Binfield Heath 26 B5
Bingfield 110 B2
Bingham 77 F7
Bingley 94 F4
Bings Heath 60 C5
Binham 81 D5
Binley Hants 26 D2
W Mid 51 B8
Binley Woods 51 B8
Binniehill 119 B8
Binsoe 94 B5
Binstead 15 E6
Binsted 27 E5
Binton 51 D6
Bintree 81 E6
Binweston 60 D3
Birch Essex 43 C5
Gtr Man 87 D6
Bircham Newton 80 D3
Bircham Tofts 80 D3
Birchanger 41 B8
Birchencliffe 88 C2
Bircher 49 C6
Birch Green 43 C5
Birchgrove Cardiff 22 B3
Swansea 33 E8
Birch Heath 74 C2
Birch Hill 74 B2
Birchington 31 C6
Birchmoor 63 D6
Birchover 76 C2
Birch Vale 87 F8
Birchwood Lincs 78 C2
Warr 86 E4
Bircotes 89 E7
Birdbrook 55 E8
Birdforth 95 B7
Birdham 16 E2
Birdholme 76 C3
Birdingbury 52 C2
Birdlip 37 C6
Birdsall 96 C4
Birds Edge 88 D3
Birdsgreen 61 F7
Birdsmoor Gate 11 D8
Birdston 119 B6
Birdwell 88 D4
Birdwood 36 C4
Birgham 122 F3
Birkby 101 D8
Birkdale 85 C4
Birkenhead 85 F4
Birkenhills 153 D7
Birkenshaw N Lanark 119 C6
W Yorks 88 B3
Birkhall 140 E2
Birkhill Angus 134 F3
Borders 114 C5
Birkholme 65 B6
Birkin 89 B6
Birley 49 D6
Birling Kent 29 C7
Northumb 117 D8
Birling Gap 18 F2
Birlingham 50 E4
Birmingham 62 F4
Birnam 133 E7
Birse 140 E4
Birsemore 140 E4
Birstall Leics 64 D2
W Yorks 88 B3
Birstwith 94 D5
Birthorpe 78 F4
Birtley Hereford 49 C5
Birtley *continued*
Northumb 109 B8
T&W 111 D5
Birts Street 50 F2
Bisbrooke 65 E5
Biscathorpe 91 F6
Biscot 40 B3
Bisham 39 F8
Bishampton 50 D4
Bish Mill 10 B2
Bishop Auckland 101 B7
Bishopbridge 90 E4
Bishopbriggs 119 C6
Bishop Burton 97 F5
Bishop Middleham 111 F6
Bishopmill 152 B2
Bishop Monkton 95 C6
Bishop Norton 90 E3
Bishopsbourne 31 D5
Bishops Cannings 24 C5
Bishop's Castle 60 F3
Bishop's Caundle 12 C4
Bishop's Cleeve 37 B6
Bishops Frome 49 E8
Bishop's Green 42 C2
Bishop's Hull 11 B7
Bishop's Itchington 51 D8
Bishops Lydeard 11 B6
Bishops Nympton 10 B2
Bishop's Offley 61 B7
Bishop's Stortford 41 B7
Bishop's Sutton 26 F4
Bishop's Tachbrook 51 C8
Bishops Tawton 20 F4
Bishopsteignton 7 B7
Bishopstoke 15 C5
Bishopston 33 F6
Bishopstone Bucks 39 C8
E Sus 17 D8
Hereford 49 E6
Swindon 38 F2
Wilts 13 B8
Bishopstrow 24 E3
Bishop Sutton 23 D7
Bishop's Waltham 15 C6
Bishopswood 11 C7
Bishop's Wood 62 D2
Bishopsworth 23 C7
Bishop Thornton 95 C5
Bishopthorpe 95 E8
Bishopton Darl 102 B1
Dumfries 105 E8
N Yorks 95 B6
Renfs 118 B4
Warks 51 D6
Bishop Wilton 96 D3
Bishton 35 F7
Bisley Glos 37 D6
Sur 27 D7
Bispham 92 E3
Bispham Green 86 C2
Bissoe 3 B6
Bisterne Close 14 D3
Bitchfield 65 B6
Bittadon 20 E4
Bittaford 6 D4
Bittering 68 C2
Bitterley 49 B7
Bitterne 15 C5
Bitteswell 64 F2
Bitton 23 C8
Biwmares = *Beaumaris* 83 D6
Bix 39 F7
Bixter 160 H5
Blaby 64 E2
Blackacre 114 E3
Blackadder West 122 D4
Blackawton 7 D6
Blackborough 11 D5
Blackborough End 67 C6
Black Bourton 38 D2
Blackboys 18 C2
Blackbrook Derbys 76 E3
Mers 86 E3
Staffs 74 F4
Blackburn Aberds 141 C7
Aberds 152 E5
Blackburn 86 B4
W Loth 120 C2
Black Callerton 110 C4
Black Clauchrie 112 F2
Black Corries Lodge 131 D6
Blackcraig 113 F7
Black Crofts 124 B5
Blackden Heath 74 B4
Blackdog 141 C8
Black Dog 10 D3
Blackfell 111 D5
Blackfield 14 D5
Blackford Cumb 108 C3
Perth 127 D7
Som 12 B4
Som 23 E6
Blackfordby 63 C7
Blackgang 15 G5
Blackhall Colliery 111 F7
Blackhall Mill 110 D4
Blackhall Rocks 111 F7
Blackham 29 F5
Blackhaugh 121 F7
Blackheath Essex 43 B6
Suff 57 B8
Sur 27 E8
W Mid 62 F3
Black Heddon 110 B3
Blackhill Aberds 153 C10
Aberds 153 D10
Highld 149 C8
Blackhills Highld 151 F12
Moray 152 C2
Blackhorse 23 B8
Blackland 24 C5
Black Lane 87 D5
Blacklaw 153 C6
Blackley 87 D6
Blacklunans 134 C1
Black Marsh 60 E3
Blackmill 34 F3
Blackmoor 27 F5
Blackmoor Gate 21 E5
Blackmore 42 D2
Blackmore End Essex 55 F8
Herts 40 C4
Black Mount 131 E6
Blackness 120 B3
Blacknest 27 E5
Black Notley 42 B3
Blacko 93 E8
Black Pill 33 E7
Blackpool Blackpool 92 F3
Devon 7 E6
Pembs 32 C1
Blackpool Gate 108 B5
Blackridge 119 C8
Blackrock Argyll 142 B4
Mon 35 C6
Blackrod 86 C4
Blackshaw 107 C7
Blackshaw Head 87 B7
Blacksmith's Green 56 C5
Blackstone 17 C6
Black Tar 44 E4
Blackthorn 39 C6
Blackthorpe 56 C3
Blacktoft 90 B2
Blacktop 141 D7
Black Torrington 9 D6
Blacktown 35 F6
Blackwall Tunnel 41 F6
Blackwater Corn 3 B6
Hants 27 D6
IoW 15 F6
Blackwaterfoot 143 F9
Blackwell Darl 101 C7
Derbys 75 B8
Derbys 76 D4
Warks 51 E7
Worcs 50 B4
W Sus 28 F4
Blackwood 119 E7
Blackwood = *Coed Duon* 35 E5
Blackwood Hill 75 D6
Blacon 73 C7
Bladnoch 105 D8
Bladon 38 C4
Blaenannerch 45 E4
Blaenau Ffestiniog 71 C8
Blaenavon 35 D6
Blaencelyn 46 D2
Blaendyryn 47 F8
Blaenffos 45 F3
Blaengarw 34 E3
Blaengwrach 34 D2
Blaen-gwynfi 34 E2
Blaenpennal 46 C5
Blaenplwyf 46 B4
Blaenporth 45 E4
Blaenrhondda 34 D3
Blaen-waun 32 B3
Blaen-y-coed 32 B4
Blaenycwm 47 B7
Blaen-y-Cwm Denb 72 F4
Gwyn 71 E8
Powys 59 B7
Blagdon N Som 23 D7
Torbay 7 C6
Blagdon Hill 11 C7
Blagill 109 E7
Blaguegate 86 D2
Blaich 130 B4
Blain 147 E9
Blaina 35 D6
Blair Atholl 133 C5
Blairbeg 143 E11
Blairdaff 141 C5
Blair Drummond 127 E6
Blairglas 126 F2
Blairgowrie 134 E1
Blairhall 128 F2
Blairingone 127 E8
Blairland 118 E3
Blairlogie 127 E7
Blairlomond 125 F7
Blairmore 145 E10
Blairnamarrow 139 C8
Blairquhosh 126 F4
Blair's Ferry 145 G8
Blairskaith 119 B5
Blaisdon 36 C4
Blakebrook 50 B3
Blakedown 50 B3
Blakelaw 122 F3
Blakeley 62 E2
Blakeley Lane 75 E6
Blakemere 49 E5
Blakeney Glos 36 D3
Norf 81 C6
Blakenhall Ches E 74 E4
W Mid 62 E3
Blakeshall 62 F2
Blakesley 52 D4
Blanchland 110 D2
Blandford Forum 13 D6
Blandford St Mary 13 D6
Bland Hill 94 D5
Blanefield 119 B5
Blankney 78 C3
Blantyre 119 D6
Blar a'Chaorainn 131 C5
Blaran 124 D4
Blarghour 125 D5
Blarmachfoldach 130 C4
Blarnalearoch 150 B4
Blashford 14 D2
Blaston 64 E5
Blatherwycke 65 E6
Blawith 98 F4
Blaxhall 57 D7
Blaxton 89 D7
Blaydon 110 C4
Bleadon 22 D5
Bleak Hey Nook 87 D8
Blean 30 C5
Bleasby Lincs 90 F5
Notts 77 E7
Bleasdale 93 E5
Bleatarn 100 C2
Blebocraigs 129 C6
Bleddfa 48 C4
Bledington 38 B2
Bledlow 39 D7
Bledlow Ridge 39 E7
Blegbie 121 C7
Blencarn 109 F6
Blencogo 107 E8
Blendworth 15 C8
Blenheim Park 80 D4
Blennerhasset 107 E8
Blervie Castle 151 F13
Bletchingdon 39 C5
Bletchingley 28 D4
Bletchley M Keynes 53 F6
Shrops 74 F3
Bletherston 32 B1
Bletsoe 53 D8
Blewbury 39 F5
Blickling 81 E7
Blidworth 77 D5
Blindburn 116 C4
Blindcrake 107 F8
Blindley Heath 28 E4
Blisland 5 B6
Blissford 14 C2
Bliss Gate 50 B2
Blisworth 52 D5
Blithbury 62 B4
Blitterlees 107 D8
Blockley 51 F6
Blofield 69 D6
Blofield Heath 69 C6
Blo' Norton 56 B4
Bloomfield 115 B8
Blore 75 E8
Blount's Green 75 F7
Blowick 85 C4
Bloxham 52 F2
Bloxholm 78 D3
Bloxwich 62 D3
Bloxworth 13 E6
Blubberhouses 94 D4
Blue Anchor Som 22 E2
Swansea 33 E6
Blue Row 43 C6
Blundeston 69 E8
Blunham 54 D2
Blunsdon St Andrew 37 F8
Bluntington 50 B3
Bluntisham 54 B4
Blunts 5 C8
Blyborough 90 E3
Blyford 57 B8
Blymhill 62 C2
Blyth Northumb 117 F9
Notts 89 F7
Blyth Bridge 120 E4
Blythburgh 57 B8
Blythe 121 E8
Blythe Bridge 75 E6
Blyton 90 E2
Boarhills 129 C7
Boarhunt 15 D7
Boarshead 18 B2
Boars Head 86 D3
Boars Hill 38 D4
Boarstall 39 C6
Boasley Cross 9 E6
Boath 151 D8
Boat of Garten 138 C5
Bobbing 30 C2
Bobbington 62 E2
Bobbingworth 41 D8
Bocaddon 5 D6
Bochastle 126 D5
Bocking 42 B3
Bocking Churchstreet 42 B3
Boddam Aberds 153 D11
Shetland 160 M5
Boddington 37 B5
Bodedern 82 C3
Bodelwyddan 72 B4
Bodenham Hereford 49 D7
Wilts 14 B2
Bodenham Moor 49 D7
Bodermid 70 E2
Bodewryd 82 B3
Bodfari 72 B4
Bodffordd 82 D4
Bodham 81 C7
Bodiam 18 C4
Bodicote 52 F2
Bodieve 4 B4
Bodinnick 5 D6
Bodle Street Green 18 D3
Bodmin 5 C5
Bodney 67 E8
Bodorgan 82 E3
Bodsham 30 E5
Boduan 70 D4
Bodymoor Heath 63 E5
Bogallan 151 F9
Bogbrae 153 E10
Bogend Borders 122 E3
S Ayrs 118 F3
Boghall 120 C2
Boghead 119 E7
Bogmoor 152 B3
Bogniebrae 152 D5
Bognor Regis 16 E3
Bograxie 141 C6
Bogside 119 D8
Bogton 153 C6
Bogue 113 F6
Bohenie 137 F5
Bohortha 3 C7
Bohuntine 137 F5
Boirseam 154 J5
Bojewyan 2 C2
Bolam Durham 101 B6
Northumb 117 F6
Bolberry 6 F4
Bold Heath 86 F3
Boldon 111 C6
Boldon Colliery 111 C6
Boldre 14 E4
Boldron 101 C5
Bole 89 F8
Bolehill 76 D2
Boleside 121 F7
Bolham 10 C4
Bolham Water 11 C6
Bolingey 4 D2
Bollington 75 B6
Bollington Cross 75 B6
Bolney 17 B6
Bolnhurst 53 D8
Bolshan 135 D6
Bolsover 76 B4
Bolsterstone 88 E3
Bolstone 49 F7
Boltby 102 F2
Bolter End 39 E7
Bolton E Loth 121 B8
E Yorks 96 D3
Gtr Man 86 D5
Northumb 117 C7
Bolton *continued*
W&F 99 B8
Bolton Abbey 94 D3
Bolton Bridge 94 D3
Bolton-by-Bowland 93 E7
Boltonfellend 108 C4
Boltongate 108 E2
Bolton-le-Sands 92 C4
Bolton Low Houses 108 E2
Bolton-on-Swale 101 E7
Bolton Percy 95 E8
Bolton Town End 92 C4
Bolton upon Dearne 89 D5
Bolventor 5 B6
Bomere Heath 60 C4
Bonar Bridge 151 B9
Bonawe 125 B6
Bonby 90 C4
Boncath 45 F4
Bonchester Bridge 115 C8
Bonchurch 15 G6
Bondleigh 9 D8
Bonehill Devon 6 B5
Staffs 63 D5
Bo'ness 127 F8
Bonhill 118 B3
Boningale 62 D2
Bonjedward 116 B2
Bonkle 119 D8
Bonnavoulin 147 F8
Bonnington Edin 120 C4
Kent 19 B7
Bonnybank 129 D5
Bonnybridge 127 F7
Bonnykelly 153 C8
Bonnyrigg and Lasswade 121 C6
Bonnyton Aberds 153 E6
Angus 134 F3
Angus 135 D6
Bonsall 76 D2
Bonskeid House 133 C5
Bont 35 C7
Bontddu 58 C3
Bont-Dolgadfan 59 D5
Bont-goch 58 F3
Bonthorpe 79 B7
Bontnewydd Ceredig 46 C5
Gwyn 82 F4
Bont-newydd 72 B4
Bont Newydd Gwyn 71 C8
Gwyn 71 E8
Bontuchel 72 D4
Bonvilston 22 B2
Bon-y-maen 33 E7
Booker 39 E8
Boon 121 E8
Boosbeck 102 C4
Boot 98 D3
Booth 87 B8
Boothby Graffoe 78 D2
Boothby Pagnell 78 F2
Boothen 75 E5
Boothferry 89 B8
Boothville 53 C5
Booth Wood 87 C8
Bootle Cumb 98 F3
Mers 85 E4
Booton 81 E7
Boot Street 57 E6
Boquhan 126 F4
Boraston 49 B8
Borden Kent 30 C2
W Sus 16 B2
Bordley 94 C2
Bordon 27 F6
Bordon Camp 27 F5
Boreham Essex 42 D3
Wilts 24 E3
Boreham Street 18 D3
Borehamwood 40 E4
Boreland Dumfries 114 E4
Stirling 132 F2
Borgh W Isles 148 H1
W Isles 154 J4
Borghastan 154 C7
Borgie 157 D9
Borgue Dumfries 106 E3
Highld 158 H3
Borley 56 E2
Bornais 148 F2
Bornesketaig 149 A8
Borness 106 E3
Boroughbridge 95 C6
Borough Green 29 D7
Borras Head 73 D7
Borreraig 148 C6
Borrobol Lodge 157 G11
Borrowash 76 F4
Borrowby 102 F2
Borrowdale 98 C4
Borrowfield 141 E7
Borth 58 E3
Borthwickbrae 115 C7
Borthwickshiels 115 C7
Borth-y-Gest 71 D6
Borve 149 D9
Borve Lodge 154 H5
Borwick 92 B5
Bosavern 2 C2
Bosbury 49 E8
Boscastle 8 E3
Boscombe BCP 14 E2
Wilts 25 F7
Boscoppa 4 D5
Bosham 16 D2
Bosherston 44 F4
Boskenna 2 D3
Bosley 75 C6
Bossall 96 C3
Bossiney 8 F2
Bossingham 31 E5
Bossington 21 E7
Bostock Green 74 C3
Boston 79 E6
Boston Long Hedges 79 E6
Boston Spa 95 E7
Boston West 79 E5
Boswinger 3 B8
Botallack 2 C2

Botany Bay 41 E5
Botcherby 108 D4
Botcheston 63 D8
Botesdale 56 B4
Bothal 117 F8
Bothamsall 77 B6
Bothel 107 F8
Bothenhampton 12 E2
Bothwell 119 D7
Botley Bucks 40 D2
　Hants 15 C6
　Oxon 38 D4
Botolph Claydon . . . 39 B7
Botolphs 17 D5
Bottacks 150 E7
Bottesford Leics 77 F8
　N Lincs 90 D2
Bottisham 55 C6
Bottlesford 25 D6
Bottom Boat 88 B4
Bottomcraig 129 B5
Bottom House 75 D7
Bottom of Hutton . . 86 B2
Bottom o'th'Moor . . 86 C2
Botusfleming 6 C2
Botwnnog 70 D3
Bough Beech 29 E5
Boughrood 48 F3
Boughspring 36 E2
Boughton Norf 67 D6
　Notts 77 C6
　W Nhants 53 C5
Boughton Aluph 30 E4
Boughton Lees 30 E4
Boughton
　Malherbe 30 E2
Boughton
　Monchelsea 29 D8
Boughton Street 30 D4
Boulby 103 C5
Boulden 60 F5
Boulmer 117 C8
Boulston 44 D4
Boultenstone 140 C3
Boultham 78 C2
Bourn 54 D4
Bourne 65 B7
Bourne End Bucks . . 40 F1
　C Beds 53 E7
　Herts 40 D3
Bournemouth 13 E8
Bournes Green
　Glos 37 D6
　Southend 43 F5
Bournheath 50 B4
Bournmoor 111 D6
Bournville 62 F4
Bourton Dorset 24 F2
　N Som 23 C5
　Oxon 38 F2
　Shrops 61 E5
Bourton on
　Dunsmore 52 B2
Bourton on the
　Hill 51 F6
Bourton-on-the-
　Water 38 B1
Bousd 146 E5
Boustead Hill 108 D2
Bouth 99 F5
Bouthwaite 94 B4
Boveney 27 B7
Boverton 21 C8
Bovey Tracey 7 B6
Bovingdon 40 D3
Bovingdon Green
　Bucks 39 F8
　Herts 40 D3
Bovinger 41 D8
Bovington Camp . . . 13 F6
Bow Borders 121 E7
　Devon 10 D2
　Orkney 159 J4
Bowbank 100 B4
Bow Brickhill 53 F7
Bowburn 111 F6
Bowcombe 15 F5
Bowd 11 E6
Bowden Borders . . . 121 F8
　Devon 7 E6
Bowden Hill 24 C4
Bowderdale 100 D1
Bowdon 87 F5
Bower 116 F3
Bowerchalke 13 B8
Bowerhill 24 C4
Bower Hinton 12 C2
Bowermadden 158 D4
Bowers Gifford 42 F3
Bowershall 128 E2
Bowertower 158 D4
Bowes 100 C4
Bowgreave 92 E4
Bowgreen 87 F5
Bowhill 115 B7
Bowhouse 107 C7
Bowland Bridge 99 F6
Bowley 49 D7
Bowlhead Green 27 F7
Bowling W Dunb . . . 118 B4
　W Yorks 94 F4
Bowling Bank 73 E7
Bowling Green 50 D3
Bowmanstead 99 E5
Bowmore 142 C4
Bowness-on-
　Solway 108 C2
Bowness-on-
　Windermere 99 E6
Bow of Fife 128 C5
Bowsden 123 E5
Bowside Lodge 157 C11
Bowston 99 E6
Bow Street 58 F3
Bowthorpe 68 D4
Box Glos 37 D5
　Wilts 24 C3
Boxbush 36 C4
Box End 53 E8
Boxford Suff 56 E3
　W Berks 26 B2
Boxgrove 16 D3
Boxley 29 D8
Boxmoor 40 D3
Boxted Essex 56 F4
　Suff 56 D2

Boxted Cross 56 F4
Boxted Heath 56 F4
Boxworth 54 C4
Boxworth End 54 C4
Boyden Gate 31 C6
Boylestone 75 F8
Boyndie 153 B6
Boynton 97 C7
Boysack 135 E6
Boyton Corn 8 E4
　Suff 57 E7
　Wilts 24 F4
Boyton Cross 42 D2
Boyton End 55 E8
Bozeat 53 D7
Braaid 84 E3
Braal Castle 158 D3
Brabling Green 57 C6
Brabourne 30 E4
Brabourne Lees 30 E4
Brabster 158 D5
Bracadale 149 E8
Bracara 147 B10
Braceborough 65 C7
Bracebridge 78 C2
Bracebridge Heath 78 C2
Bracebridge Low
　Fields 78 C2
Braceby 78 F3
Bracewell 93 E8
Brackenfield 76 D3
Brackenthwaite
　Cumb 108 E2
　N Yorks 95 D5
Bracklesham 16 E2
Brackletter 136 F4
Brackley Argyll 143 D8
　W Nhants 52 F3
Brackloch 156 G4
Bracknell 27 C6
Braco 127 D7
Bracobrae 152 C5
Bracon Ash 68 E4
Bracorina 147 B10
Bradbourne 76 D2
Bradbury 101 B8
Bradda 84 F1
Bradden 52 E4
Braddock 5 C6
Bradeley 75 D5
Bradenham Bucks . . 39 E8
　Norf 68 D2
Bradenstoke 24 B5
Bradfield Essex 56 F5
　Norf 81 D8
　W Berks 26 B4
Bradfield Combust 56 D2
Bradfield Green 74 D3
Bradfield Heath 43 B7
Bradfield St Clare . 56 D3
Bradfield St
　George 56 C3
Bradford Corn 5 B6
　Derbys 76 C2
　Devon 9 D6
　Northumb 123 F7
　W Yorks 94 F4
Bradford Abbas 12 C3
Bradford Leigh 24 C3
Bradford-on-Avon 24 C3
Bradford-on-Tone 11 B6
Bradford Peverell . . 12 E4
Brading 15 F7
Bradley Derbys 76 E2
　Hants 26 E4
　NE Lincs 91 D6
　Staffs 62 C2
　W Mid 62 E3
　W Yorks 88 B2
Bradley Green 50 C4
Bradley in the
　Moors 75 E7
Bradley Stoke 36 F3
Bradlow 50 F2
Bradmore Notts 77 F5
　W Mid 62 E2
Bradninch 10 D5
Bradnop 75 D7
Bradpole 12 E2
Bradshaw Gtr Man . . 86 C5
　W Yorks 87 C8
Bradstone 9 F5
Bradwall Green 74 C4
Bradway 88 F4
Bradwell Derbys . . . 88 F2
　Essex 42 B4
　M Keynes 53 F6
　Norf 69 D8
　Staffs 74 E5
Bradwell Grove 38 D2
Bradwell on Sea . . . 43 D6
Bradwell
　Waterside 43 D5
Bradworthy 8 C5
Bradworthy Cross . . 8 C5
Brae Dumfries 107 B6
　Highld 155 J13
　Highld 156 J7
　Shetland 160 G5
Braeantra 151 D8
Braedownie 134 B2
Braefield 150 H7
Braegrum 128 B2
Braehead
　Dumfries 105 D8
　Orkney 159 D5
　Orkney 159 H6
　S Lanark 119 F8
　S Lanark 120 D2
Braehead of
　Lunan 135 D6
Braehoulland 160 F4
Braehungie 158 G3
Braelangwell
　Lodge 151 B8
Braemar 139 E7
Braemore Highld . . 150 D4
　Highld 158 G2
Brae of
　Achnahaird 156 H3
Brae Roy Lodge . . . 137 E6
Braeside 118 B2
Braes of Enzie 152 C3
Braeswick 159 E7
Braewick 160 H5
Brafferton Darl . . . 101 B7
　N Yorks 95 B7
Brafield-on-the-
　Green 53 D6

Bragar 155 C7
Bragbury End 41 B5
Bragleenmore 124 C5
Braichmelyn 83 E6
Braid 120 C5
Braides 92 D4
Braidley 101 F5
Braidwood 119 E8
Braigo 142 B3
Brailsford 76 E2
Brainshaugh 117 D8
Braintree 42 B3
Braiseworth 56 B5
Braishfield 14 B4
Braithwaite Cumb . . 98 B4
　S Yorks 89 C7
　W Yorks 94 E3
Braithwell 89 E6
Bramber 17 C5
Bramcote Notts 76 F5
　Warks 63 F8
Bramdean 15 B7
Bramerton 69 D5
Bramfield Herts 41 C5
　Suff 57 B7
Bramford 56 E5
Bramhall 87 F6
Bramham 95 E7
Bramhope 95 E5
Bramley Hants 26 D4
　Sur 27 E8
　S Yorks 89 E5
　W Yorks 94 F5
Bramling 31 D6
Brampford Speke . . 10 E4
Brampton Cambs . . 54 B3
　Cumb 108 C5
　Derbys 76 B3
　Hereford 49 F6
　Lincs 77 B8
　Norf 81 E8
　Suff 69 F7
　S Yorks 88 D5
　W&F 100 B1
Brampton Abbotts 36 B3
Brampton Ash 64 F4
Brampton Bryan . . . 49 B5
Brampton en le
　Morthen 89 F5
Bramshall 75 F7
Bramshaw 14 C3
Bramshill 26 C5
Bramshott 27 F6
Branault 147 E8
Brancaster 80 C3
Brancaster Staithe 80 C3
Brancepeth 110 F5
Branch End 110 C3
Branchill 151 F13
Branderburgh 152 A2
Brandesburton 97 E7
Brandeston 57 C6
Brand Green 36 B4
Brandhill 49 B6
Brandis Corner 9 D6
Brandiston 81 E7
Brandon Durham . . 110 F5
　Lincs 78 E2
　Northumb 117 C6
　Suff 67 F7
　Warks 52 B2
Brandon Bank 67 F6
Brandon Creek 67 E6
Brandon Parva 68 D3
Brandsby 95 B8
Brandy Wharf 90 E4
Brane 2 D3
Bran End 42 B2
Branksome 13 E8
Branksome Park . . . 13 E8
Bransby 77 B8
Branscombe 11 F6
Bransford 50 D2
Bransgore 14 E2
Branshill 127 E7
Bransholme 97 F7
Branson's Cross . . . 51 B5
Branston Leics 64 B5
　Lincs 78 C3
　Staffs 63 B6
Branston Booths . . . 78 C3
Branstone 15 F6
Bransty 98 C1
Brant Broughton . . 78 D2
Brantham 56 F5
Branthwaite Cumb . 108 F2
　Cumb 108 F2
Brantingham 90 B3
Branton Northumb . 117 C6
　S Yorks 89 D7
Branxholme 115 C7
Branxholm Park . . . 115 C7
Branxton 122 F4
Brassey Green 74 C2
Brassington 76 D2
Brasted 29 D5
Brasted Chart 29 D5
Brathens 141 E5
Bratoft 79 C7
Brattleby 90 F3
Bratton Telford 61 C6
　Wilts 24 D4
Bratton Clovelly 9 E6
Bratton Fleming . . . 20 F5
Bratton Seymour . . 12 B4
Braughing 41 B6
Braunston 52 C3
Braunstone Town . . 64 D2
Braunston-in-
　Rutland 64 D5
Braunton 20 F3
Brawby 96 B3
Brawl 157 C11
Brawlbin 158 E2
Bray 27 B7
Braybrooke 64 F4
Braye 16 I1
Brayford 21 F5
Bray Shop 5 B8
Braystones 98 D2
Braythorn 94 E5
Braytown 13 F6
Brazacott 8 E4
Breach 30 C2
Breachacha
　Castle 146 F4
Breachwood
　Green 40 B4

Breacleit 154 D6
Breaden Heath 73 F8
Breadsall 76 F3
Breadstone 36 D4
Breage 2 D5
Breakachy 150 G7
Bream 36 D3
Breamore 14 C2
Brean 22 D4
Breanais 154 E4
Brearton 95 C6
Breascleit 154 D7
Breaston 76 F4
Brechfa 46 F4
Brechin 135 C5
Breckan 159 H3
Breck of Cruan 159 G4
Breckrey 149 B10
Brecon
　= Aberhonddu . . 34 B4
Bredbury 87 E7
Brede 18 D5
Bredenbury 49 D8
Bredfield 57 D6
Bredgar 30 C2
Bredhurst 29 C8
Bredicot 50 D4
Bredon 50 F4
Bredon's Norton . . 50 F4
Bredwardine 48 E5
Breedon on the
　Hill 63 B8
Breibhig W Isles . . 148 J1
　W Isles 155 D9
Breich 120 C2
Breightmet 86 D5
Breighton 96 F3
Breinton 49 F6
Breinton Common 49 E6
Breiwick 160 J6
Bremhill 24 B4
Bremirehoull 160 L6
Brenachoile 67 F7
Brenchley 29 E7
Brendon 21 E6
Brenkley 110 B5
Brent Eleigh 56 E3
Brentford 28 B2
Brentingby 64 C4
Brent Knoll 22 D5
Brent Pelham 54 F5
Brentwood 42 E1
Brenzett 19 C7
Brereton 62 C4
Brereton Green . . . 74 C4
Brereton Heath . . . 74 C5
Bressingham 68 F3
Bretby 63 B6
Bretford 52 B2
Bretforton 51 E5
Bretherdale Head . 99 D7
Bretherton 86 B2
Brettabister 160 H6
Brettenham Norf . . 68 F2
　Suff 56 D3
Bretton Derbys 76 B2
　Flint 73 C7
Brewer Street 28 D4
Brewlands
　Bridge 134 C1
Brewood 62 D2
Briach 151 F13
Briants Puddle 13 E6
Brick End 42 B1
Brickendon 41 D6
Bricket Wood 40 D4
Bricklehampton . . . 50 E4
Bride 84 B4
Bridekirk 107 F8
Bridell 45 E3
Bridestowe 9 F7
Brideswell 152 E5
Bridford 10 F3
Bridfordmills 10 F3
Bridge 31 D5
Bridge End Angus . 134 F3
　Cumb 98 B2
Bridge End 55 F5
Bridgehampton . . . 12 B3
Bridge Hewick 95 B6
Bridgehill 110 D3
Bridgemary 15 D6
Bridgemont 87 F8
Bridgend Aberds . . 140 C4
　Aberds 152 E5
　Angus 135 C5
　Argyll 142 B4
　Argyll 143 E8
　Argyll 145 D7
　Fife 129 C5
　Moray 152 E3
　N Lanark 119 B6
　Pembs 45 E3
　W&F 99 C5
　W Loth 120 B3
Bridgend = Pen-y-
　Bont Ar Ogwr . . . 21 B8
Bridgend of
　Lintrathen 134 D2
Bridge of Alford . . 140 C4
Bridge of Allan . . . 127 E6
Bridge of Avon . . . 152 E1
Bridge of Awe 125 C6
Bridge of Balgie . . 132 E2
Bridge of Cally . . . 133 D8
Bridge of Canny . . 141 E5
Bridge of
　Craigisla 134 D2
Bridge of Dee 106 D4
Bridge of Don 141 C8
Bridge of Dun 135 D6
Bridge of Dye 141 F5
Bridge of Earn 128 C3
Bridge of Ericht . . 132 D2
Bridge of Feugh . . 141 E6
Bridge of Forss . . . 157 C13
Bridge of Gairn . . . 140 E2
Bridge of Gaur . . . 132 D2
Bridge of
　Muchalls 141 E7
Bridge of Oich 137 D6
Bridge of Orchy . . 125 B8
Bridge of Waith . . . 159 G3
Bridge of Walls . . . 160 H4
Bridge of Weir 118 C3
Bridgerule 8 D4
Bridges 60 E3
Bridge Sollers 49 E6
Bridge Street 56 E2

Bridgeton 119 C6
Bridgetown Corn . . . 8 F5
　Som 21 F8
Bridge Trafford . . . 73 B8
Bridge Yate 23 B8
Bridgham 68 F2
Bridgnorth 61 E7
Bridgtown 62 D3
Bridgwater 22 F5
Bridlington 97 C7
Bridport 12 E2
Bridstow 36 B2
Brierfield 93 F8
Brierley Glos 36 C3
　Hereford 49 D6
　S Yorks 88 C5
Brierley Hill 62 F3
Briery Hill 35 D5
Brigg 90 D4
Briggswath 103 D6
Brigham Cumb 107 F7
　E Yorks 97 D6
Brighouse 88 B2
Brighstone 14 F5
Brightgate 76 D2
Brighthampton 38 D3
Brightling 18 C3
Brightlingsea 43 C6
Brighton Brighton . . 17 D7
　Corn 4 D4
Brighton Hill 26 E4
Brightons 120 B2
Brightwalton 26 B2
Brightwell 57 E6
Brightwell
　Baldwin 39 E6
Brightwell cum
　Sotwell 39 E5
Brignall 101 C5
Brig o'Turk 126 D4
Brigsley 91 D6
Brigsteer 99 F6
Brigstock 65 F6
Brill 39 C6
Brilley 48 E4
Brimaston 44 C4
Brimfield 49 C7
Brimington 76 B4
Brimley 7 B5
Brimpsfield 37 C6
Brimpton 26 C3
Brims 159 K3
Brimscombe 37 D5
Brimstage 85 F4
Brinacory 147 B10
Brind 96 F3
Brindister
　Shetland 160 H4
　Shetland 160 K6
Brindle 86 B4
Brindley Ford 75 D5
Brineton 62 C2
Bringhurst 64 E5
Brington 53 B8
Brinian 159 F5
Briningham 81 D6
Brinkhill 79 B6
Brinkley 55 D7
Brinklow 52 B2
Brinkworth 37 F7
Brinmore 138 B2
Brinscall 86 B4
Brinsea 23 C6
Brinsley 76 E4
Brinsop 49 E6
Brinsworth 88 F5
Brinton 81 D6
Brisco 108 D4
Brisley 81 E5
Brislington 23 B8
Bristol 23 B7
Briston 81 D6
Britannia 87 B6
Britford 14 B2
Brithdir 58 C4
British Legion
　Village 29 D8
Briton Ferry 33 E8
Britwell Salome . . . 39 E6
Brixham Devon 7 D7
Brixton Devon 6 D3
　London 28 B4
Brixton Deverill . . . 24 F3
Brixworth 52 B5
Brize Norton 38 D3
Broad Blunsdon . . 38 E1
Broadbottom 87 E7
Broadbridge 16 D2
Broadbridge Heath 28 F2
Broad Campden . . . 51 F6
Broad Chalke 13 B8
Broadclyst 10 E4
Broadfield Gtr Man . 87 C6
　Lancs 86 B3
　Pembs 32 D2
　W Sus 28 F3
Broadford 149 F11
Broadford Bridge . . 16 B4
Broad Green
　C Beds 53 E7
　Essex 42 B4
　Worcs 50 D2
Broadhaugh 115 D7
Broadhaven 158 E5
Broad Haven 44 D3
Broadheath 87 F5
Broad Heath 49 C8
Broadhembury . . . 11 D6
Broadhempston . . . 7 C6
Broad Hill 55 B6
Broad Hinton 25 B6
Broadholme Derbys 76 E3
　Lincs 77 B8
Broadland Row . . . 18 D5
Broadlay 32 D4
Broad Laying 26 C2
Broadley Lancs 87 C6
　Moray 152 B3
Broadley Common 41 D7
Broad Marston 51 E6
Broadmayne 12 F5
Broadmeadows . . . 121 F7
Broadmere 26 E4
Broadmoor 32 D1
Broadoak 31 C5
Broad Oak Carms . . 33 B6
　Cumb 98 E3
　Dorset 12 E2
　Dorset 13 C5

Broad Oak continued
　E Sus 18 C3
　E Sus 18 D5
　Hereford 36 B1
　Mers 86 E3
Broadrashes 152 C4
Broadsea 153 B9
Broadstairs 31 C7
Broadstone BCP . . . 13 E8
　Shrops 60 F5
Broad Street 30 D2
Broad Street
　Green 42 D4
Broad Town 25 B5
Broadtown Lane . . . 25 B5
Broadwas 50 D2
Broadwater Herts . . 41 B5
　W Sus 17 D5
Broadway Carms . . . 32 D3
　Pembs 44 D3
　Som 11 C8
　Suff 57 B7
　Worcs 51 F5
Broadwell Glos 36 C2
　Glos 38 B2
　Oxon 38 D2
　Warks 52 C2
Broadwell House . . 110 D2
Broadwey 12 F4
Broadwindsor 12 D2
Broadwoodkelly . . 9 D8
Broadwoodwidger 9 F6
Brobury 48 E5
Brochel 149 D10
Brochloch 113 E5
Brochroy 125 B6
Brockamin 50 D2
Brockbridge 15 C7
Brockdam 117 B7
Brockdish 57 B6
Brockenhurst 14 D4
Brocketsbrae 119 F8
Brockford Street . . . 56 C5
Brockhall 52 C4
Brockhampton 28 E2
Brockhampton
　Glos 37 D7
　Hereford 49 F7
Brockholes 88 C2
Brockhurst Derbys . 76 C3
　Hants 15 D7
Brocklebank 108 E3
Brocklesby 90 C5
Brockley 23 C6
Brockley Green 56 D2
Brockleymoor 108 F4
Brockton Shrops . . . 60 D3
　Shrops 60 F3
　Shrops 61 D7
　Shrops 61 E5
　Telford 61 C7
Brockweir 36 D2
Brockwood 15 B7
Brockworth 37 C5
Brocton 62 C3
Brodick 143 E11
Brodsworth 89 D6
Brogaig 149 B9
Brogborough 53 F7
Brokenborough . . . 37 F6
Broken Cross
　Ches E 75 B5
　Ches W 74 B3
Bromborough 85 F4
Brome 56 B5
Brome Street 57 B5
Bromeswell 57 D7
Bromfield Cumb . . . 107 E8
　Shrops 49 B6
Bromham Bedford . 53 D8
　Wilts 24 C4
Bromley London . . . 28 C5
　W Mid 62 F3
Bromley Common . 28 C5
Bromley Green 19 B6
Brompton Medway . 29 C8
　N Yorks 102 E1
　N Yorks 103 F7
Brompton-on-
　Swale 101 D7
Brompton Ralph . . . 22 F2
Brompton Regis . . . 21 F8
Bromsash 36 B3
Bromsberrow
　Heath 50 F2
Bromsgrove 50 B4
Bromyard 49 D8
Bromyard Downs . . 49 D8
Bronaber 71 D8
Brongest 46 E2
Bronington 73 F8
Bronllys 48 F3
Bronnant 46 C5
Bronwydd Arms . . . 33 B5
Bronydd 48 E4
Brongarth 72 B3
Brook Carms 32 D3
　Hants 14 C3
　Hants 14 C4
　IoW 14 F4
　Kent 30 E4
　Sur 27 E8
Brooke Norf 69 E5
　Rutland 64 D5
Brookenby 91 E6
Brook End 53 C8
Brookfield 118 C4
Brook Hill 14 C3
Brookhouse 92 C5
Brookhouse Green 74 C5
Brookland 19 C6
Brooklands
　Dumfries 106 B5
　Gtr Man 87 E5
　Shrops 74 E2
Brookmans Park . . 41 D5
Brooks 59 E8
Brooks Green 16 B5
Brook Street Kent . . 19 B6
　Kent 29 E6
　W Sus 17 B7
Brookthorpe 37 C5
Brookville 67 E7
Brookwood 27 D7
Broom C Beds 54 E2
　S Yorks 88 E5
　Warks 51 D5

Broom continued
　Worcs 50 B4
Broome Norf 69 E6
　Shrops 60 F4
Broomedge 86 F5
Broome Park 117 C7
Broomer's Corner . 16 B5
Broomfield Aberds 153 E9
　Essex 42 C3
　Kent 30 D2
　Kent 31 C5
　Som 22 F4
Broomfleet 90 B2
Broomhall Ches E . . 74 E3
　Windsor 27 C7
Broomhaugh 110 C3
Broomhill Norf 67 D6
　Northumb 117 D8
　S Yorks 88 D5
Broom Hill 13 D8
Broomholm 81 D9
Broomley 110 C3
Broompark 110 E5
Broom's Green 50 F2
Broomy Lodge 14 C3
Brora 157 J12
Brotherhouse Bar . 66 C2
Brotherstone 122 F2
Brothertoft 79 E5
Brotherton 89 B5
Brotton 102 C4
Broubster 157 C13
Brough Derbys 88 F2
　E Yorks 90 B3
　Highld 158 C4
　Notts 77 D8
　Orkney 159 G4
　Shetland 160 F6
　Shetland 160 F7
　Shetland 160 G7
　Shetland 160 H6
　Shetland 160 J7
　W&F 100 C2
Broughall 74 E2
Brough Lodge 160 D7
Brough Sowerby . . 100 C2
Broughton
　Borders 120 F4
　Cambs 54 B3
　Flint 73 C7
　Hants 25 F8
　Lancs 92 F5
　M Keynes 53 E6
　N Lincs 90 D3
　N Nhants 53 B6
　N Yorks 94 D2
　N Yorks 96 B3
　Orkney 159 D5
　Oxon 52 F2
　V Glam 21 B8
Broughton Astley . . 64 E2
Broughton Beck . . . 98 F4
Broughton
　Common 24 C3
Broughton Gifford . 24 C3
Broughton
　Hackett 50 D4
Broughton in
　Furness 98 F4
Broughton Mills . . . 98 E4
Broughton Moor . . 107 F7
Broughton Park . . . 87 D6
Broughton Poggs . 38 D2
Broughtown 159 D7
Broughty Ferry . . . 134 F4
Browhouses 108 C2
Browland 160 H4
Brown Candover . . 26 F3
Brown Edge Lancs . 85 C4
　Staffs 75 D6
Brown Heath 73 C8
Brownhill Aberds . 153 D6
　Aberds 153 D8
　Blackburn 93 F6
　Shrops 60 B4
Brownhills Fife 129 C7
　W Mid 62 D4
Brownlow 74 C5
Brownlow Heath . . 74 C5
Brownmuir 135 B7
Brown's End 50 F2
Brownshill 37 D5
Brownston 6 D4
Brownyside 117 B7
Broxa 103 E7
Broxbourne 41 D6
Broxburn E Loth . . 122 B2
　W Loth 120 B3
Broxholme 78 B2
Broxted 42 B1
Broxton 73 D8
Broxwood 49 D5
Broyle Side 17 C8
Brù 155 C8
Bruairnis 148 H2
Bruan 158 G5
Bruar Lodge 133 B5
Brucehill 118 B3
Bruera 73 C8
Bruichladdich 142 B3
Bruisyard 57 C7
Brumby 90 D2
Brund 75 C8
Brundall 69 D6
Brundish 57 C6
Brundish Street . . . 57 B6
Brunery 147 D10
Brunshaw 93 F8
Brunswick
　Village 110 B5
Bruntcliffe 88 B3
Bruntingthorpe . . . 64 E3
Brunton Fife 128 B5
　Northumb 117 B8
　Wilts 25 D7
Brushford Devon . . 9 D8
　Som 10 B4
Bruton 23 F8
Bryanston 13 D6
Brydekirk 107 B8
Bryher 2 E3
Brymbo 73 D6
Brympton 12 C3
Bryn Carms 33 D6
　Gtr Man 86 D3
　Neath 34 E2

Bryn continued
　Shrops 60 F2
Brynamman 33 C8
Brynberian 45 F3
Brynbryddan 34 E1
Brynbuga = Usk . . . 35 D7
Bryncae 34 F3
Bryncethin 34 F3
Bryncir 71 C5
Bryn-coch 33 E8
Bryncroes 70 D3
Bryncrug 58 D3
Bryn Du 82 D3
Bryneglwys 72 E5
Brynford 73 B5
Bryn Gates 86 D3
Bryn-glas 83 E8
Bryn Golau 34 F3
Bryngwran 82 D3
Bryngwyn Ceredig . 46 E2
　Mon 35 D7
　Powys 48 E3
Brynhenllan 45 F3
Brynhoffnant 46 D2
Brynithel 35 D6
Bryn-Iwan 46 F2
Brynmawr 35 C5
Bryn-mawr 70 D3
Brynmenyn 34 F3
Brynmill 33 E7
Bryn-nantllech 72 C3
Brynna 34 F3
Bryn-nantllech-oryr . 72 C3
Brynrefail Anglesey . 82 C4
Gwyn 83 E5
Brynsadler 34 F4
Bryn Saith
　Marchog 72 D4
Brynsiencyn 82 E4
Bryn Sion 59 C5
Brynteg Anglesey . . 82 C4
Ceredig 46 E3
Bryn-y-gwenin 35 C7
Bryn-y-maen 83 D8
Bryn-yr-eryr 70 C4
Buaile nam
　Bodach 148 H2
Bualintur 149 F9
Buarthmeini 72 F2
Bubbenhall 51 B8
Bubwith 96 F3
Buccleuch 115 C6
Buchanhaven 153 D11
Buchanty 127 B8
Buchlyvie 126 E4
Buckabank 108 E3
Buckden Cambs . . . 54 C2
　N Yorks 94 B2
Buckenham 69 D6
Buckerell 11 D6
Buckfast 6 C5
Buckfastleigh 6 C5
Buckhaven 129 E5
Buckholm 121 F7
Buckholt 36 C2
Buckhorn Weston . 13 B5
Buckhurst Hill 41 E7
Buckie 152 B4
Buckies 158 D3
Buckingham 52 F4
Buckland Bucks . . . 40 C1
　Devon 6 E4
　Glos 51 F5
　Hants 14 E4
　Herts 54 F4
　Kent 31 E7
　Oxon 38 E3
　Sur 28 D3
Buckland Brewer . . 9 B6
Buckland
　Common 40 D2
Buckland Dinham . 24 D2
Buckland Filleigh . . 9 D6
Buckland in the
　Moor 6 B5
Buckland
　Monachorum . . . 6 C2
Buckland Newton . 12 D4
Buckland St Mary . 11 C7
Bucklebury 26 B3
Bucklegate 79 F6
Bucklerheads 134 F4
Bucklers Hard 14 E5
Bucklesham 57 E6
Buckley = Bwcle . . . 73 C6
Bucklow Hill 86 F5
Buckminster 65 B5
Bucknall Lincs 78 C4
　Stoke 75 E6
Bucknell Oxon 39 B5
　Shrops 49 B5
Buckpool 152 B4
Buck's Cross 8 B5
Bucksburn 141 D7
Buck's Green 27 F8
Buckshaw Village . . 86 B3
Bucks Horn Oak . . . 27 E6
Buckskin 26 D4
Buck's Mills 9 B5
Buckton Ches E 74 D3
　E Yorks 97 B7
　Hereford 49 B5
　Northumb 123 F6
Buckworth 54 B2
Budbrooke 51 C7
Budby 77 C6
Budd's Titson 8 D4
Bude 8 D4
Budlake 10 E4
Budle 123 F7
Budleigh Salterton 11 F5
Budock Water 3 C6
Buerton 74 E3
Buffler's Holt 52 F4
Bugbrooke 52 D4
Buglawton 75 C5
Bugle 4 D5
Bugley 24 E3
Bugthorpe 96 D3
Buildwas 61 D6
Builth Road 48 D2
Builth Wells = Llanfair-
　ym-Muallt 48 D2
Buirgh 154 H5
Bulby 65 B7
Bulcote 77 E6
Buldoo 157 C12
Bulford 25 E6

Bulford Camp 25 E6
Bulkeley 74 D2
Bulkington Warks . . 63 F7
　Wilts 24 D4
Bulkworthy 9 C5
Bullamoor 102 E1
Bullbridge 76 D3
Bullbrook 27 C6
Bulley 36 C4
Bullgill 107 F7
Bull Hill 14 E4
Bullington Hants . . 26 E2
　Lincs 78 B3
Bull's Green 41 C5
Bullwood 145 F10
Bulmer Essex 56 E2
　N Yorks 96 C3
Bulmer Tye 56 F2
Bulphan 42 F2
Bulverhythe 18 E4
Bulwark 153 D9
Bulwell 76 E5
Bulwick 65 E6
Bumble's Green . . . 41 D7
Bun Abhainn
　Eadarra 154 G6
Bunacaimb 147 C9
Bun a'Mhuilinn . . . 148 G2
Bunarkaig 136 F4
Bunbury 74 D2
Bunbury Heath . . . 74 D2
Bunchrew 151 G9
Bundalloch 149 F13
Buness 160 C8
Bunessan 146 J6
Bungay 69 F6
Bunkers Hill 38 C4
Bunker's Hill Lincs . 78 B2
　Lincs 79 D5
Bunloit 137 B8
Bun Loyne 136 D5
Bunnahabhain . . . 142 A5
Bunny 64 B2
Buntait 150 H6
Buntingford 41 B6
Bunwell 68 E4
Burbage Derbys . . . 75 B7
　Leics 63 E8
　Wilts 25 C7
Burchett's Green . . 39 F8
Burcombe 25 F5
Burcot 39 E5
Burcott 40 B1
Burdon 111 D6
Bures 56 F3
Bures Green 56 F3
Burford Ches E 74 D3
　Oxon 38 C2
　Shrops 49 C7
Burg 146 G6
Burgar 159 F4
Burgate Hants 14 C2
　Suff 56 B4
Burgess Hill 17 C7
Burgh 57 D6
Burgh by Sands . . . 108 D3
Burgh Castle 69 D7
Burghclere 26 C2
Burghead 151 E14
Burghfield 26 C4
Burghfield
　Common 26 C4
Burghfield Hill 26 C4
Burgh Heath 28 D3
Burghill 49 E6
Burgh le Marsh . . . 79 C8
Burgh Muir 141 B6
Burgh next
　Aylsham 81 E8
Burgh on Bain 91 F6
Burgh St Margaret 69 C7
Burgh St Peter . . . 69 E7
Burghwallis 89 C6
Burham 29 C8
Buriton 15 B8
Burland 74 D3
Burlawn 4 B4
Burleigh 27 C6
Burlescombe 11 C5
Burleston 13 E5
Burley Hants 14 D3
　Rutland 65 C5
　W Yorks 95 F5
Burleydam 74 E3
Burley Gate 49 E7
Burley in
　Wharfedale 94 E4
Burley Lodge 14 D3
Burley Street 14 D3
Burlingjobb 48 D4
Burlow 18 D2
Burlton 60 B4
Burmarsh 19 B7
Burmington 51 F7
Burn 89 B6
Burnaston 76 F2
Burnbank 119 D7
Burnby 96 E4
Burncross 88 E4
Burneside 99 E7
Burness 159 D7
Burneston 101 F8
Burnett 23 C8
Burnfoot Borders . . 115 C7
　E Ayrs 112 D4
　Perth 127 D8
Burnham Bucks . . . 40 F2
　N Lincs 90 C4
Burnham
　Deepdale 80 C4
Burnham Green . . . 41 C5
Burnham Market . . 80 C4
Burnham Norton . . 80 C4
Burnham-on-
　Crouch 43 E5
Burnham-on-Sea . 22 E5
Burnham Overy
　Staithe 80 C4
Burnham Overy
　Town 80 C4
Burnham Thorpe . 80 C4
Burnhead
　Dumfries 113 E8
　S Ayrs 112 D2
Burnhervie 141 C6
Burnhill Green 61 D7
Burnhope 110 E4
Burnhouse 118 D3

Burniston.........103 F8
Burnlee...........88 D2
Burnley............93 F8
Burnley Lane......93 F8
Burnmouth........123 C5
Burn of Cambus....127 D6
Burnopfield......110 D4
Burnsall...........94 C3
Burnside Angus...135 D5
  E Ayrs...........113 C5
  Fife.............128 D3
  Shetland........160 F4
  S Lanark........119 C6
  W Loth..........120 B3
Burnside of
  Duntrune.......134 F4
Burnswark.......107 B8
Burntcommon.....27 D8
Burnt Heath......76 B2
Burnthouse........3 C6
Burnt Houses....101 B6
Burntisland......128 F4
Burnton.........112 D4
Burntwood........62 D4
Burnt Yates......95 C5
Burnwynd........120 C4
Burpham Sur......27 D8
  W Sus...........16 D4
Burradon
  Northumb.......117 D5
  T&W............111 B5
Burrafirth.......160 B8
Burraland Shetland 160 F5
  Shetland........160 J4
Burras............3 C5
Burravoe Shetland 160 F7
  Shetland........160 G5
Burray Village...159 J5
Burrells..........100 C1
Burrelton.......134 F2
Burridge Devon....20 F4
  Hants...........15 C6
Burrill..........101 F7
Burringham........90 D2
Burrington Devon...9 C8
  Hereford........49 B6
  N Som...........23 D6
Burrough Green...55 D7
Burrough on the
  Hill............64 C4
Burrow-bridge....11 B8
Burrowhill.......27 C7
Burry.............33 E5
Burry Green......33 E5
Burry Port
  = Porth Tywyn...33 D5
Burscough........86 C2
Burscough Bridge..86 C2
Bursea............96 F4
Burshill..........97 E6
Bursledon........15 D5
Burslem...........75 E5
Burstall..........56 E4
Burstock.........12 D2
Burston Norf.....68 F4
  Staffs..........75 F6
Burstow..........28 E4
Burstwick........91 B6
Burtersett......100 F3
Burtle...........23 E5
Burton BCP.......14 E2
  Ches W..........73 B7
  Ches W..........74 C2
  Lincs...........78 B2
  Northumb.......123 F7
  Pembs...........44 E4
  Som.............22 E3
  Wilts...........24 B3
Burton Agnes.....97 C7
Burton Bradstock.12 F2
Burton Dassett...51 D8
Burton Fleming...97 B6
Burton Green
  W Mid...........51 B7
  Wrex............73 D7
Burton Hastings..63 E8
Burton-in-Kendal.99 F7
Burton in Lonsdale.93 B6
Burton Joyce......77 E6
Burton Latimer...53 B7
Burton Lazars....64 C4
Burton-le-Coggles.65 B6
Burton Leonard...95 C6
Burton on the
  Wolds...........64 B2
Burton Overy.....64 E3
Burton
  Pedwardine.....78 E4
Burton Pidsea....97 F8
Burton Salmon....89 B5
Burton Stather...90 C2
Burton upon
  Stather.........90 C2
Burton upon Trent.63 B6
Burtonwood.......86 E3
Burwardsley......74 D2
Burwarton........61 F6
Burwash..........18 C3
Burwash Common...18 C3
Burwash Weald....18 C3
Burwell Cambs....55 C6
  Lincs...........79 B6
Burwen...........82 B4
Burwick.........159 K5
Bury Cambs.......66 F2
  Gtr Man.........87 C6
  Som.............10 B4
  W Sus...........16 C4
Bury Green.......41 B7
Bury St Edmunds...56 C2
Burythorpe.......96 C3
Busby...........119 D5
Buscot...........38 E2
Bush Bank........49 D6
Bushbury.........62 D3
Bushby...........64 D3
Bush Crathie....139 E8
Bushey...........40 E4
Bushey Heath.....40 E4
Bush Green.......68 F5
Bushley..........50 F3
Bushton..........25 B5
Buslingthorpe....90 F4
Busta...........160 G5
Butcher's Cross..18 C2
Butcombe.........23 C7
Butetown.........22 B3
Butleigh.........23 F7
Butleigh Wootton.23 F7

Butler's Cross...39 D8
Butler's End.....63 F6
Butlers Marston..51 E8
Butley............57 D7
Butley High
  Corner..........57 E7
Butterburn......109 B6
Buttercrambe.....96 D3
Butterknowle....101 B6
Butterleigh......10 D4
Buttermere Cumb..98 C3
  Wilts...........25 C8
Buttershaw.......88 B2
Butterstone.....133 E7
Butterton.........75 D7
Butterwick
  Durham.........102 B1
  Lincs...........79 E6
  N Yorks.........96 B3
  N Yorks.........97 B5
Butt Green.......74 D3
Buttington.......60 D2
Buttonoak........50 B2
Buttsash.........14 D5
Butt's Green.....14 B4
Buxhall..........56 D4
Buxhall Fen Street.56 D4
Buxley..........122 D4
Buxted...........18 B8
Buxton Derbys....75 B7
  Norf............81 E8
Buxworth.........87 F8
Bwcle = Buckley...73 C6
  Oxon............38 C4
  Rutland.........65 E5
Bwlch............35 B5
Bwlchgwyn........73 D6
Bwlch-Llan.......46 D4
Bwlchnewydd......32 B4
Bwlchtocyn.......70 E4
Bwlch-y-cibau....59 C8
Bwlch-y-fadfa....46 E3
Bwlch-y-ffridd...59 E7
Bwlchgroes.......45 F4
Bwlch-y-sarnau...48 B2
Byermoor........110 D4
Byers Green.....110 F5
Byfield..........52 D3
Byfleet..........27 C8
Byford...........49 E5
Bygrave..........54 F3
Byker...........111 C5
Bylchau..........72 C3
Byley............74 C4
Bynea............33 E6
Byrness.........116 D3
Bythorn..........53 B8
Byton............49 C5
Byworth..........16 B3

C

Cabharstadh.....155 E8
Cablea..........133 F6
Cabourne.........90 D5
Cabrach Argyll...144 G3
  Moray..........140 B2
Cabrich.........151 G8
Cabus............92 E4
Cackle Street....17 B8
Cadbury..........10 D4
Cadbury Barton....9 C8
Cadder..........119 B6
Caddington.......40 C3
Caddonfoot......121 F7
Cadeby Leics.....63 D8
  S Yorks.........89 D6
Cadeleigh........10 D4
Cade Street......18 C3
Cadgwith..........3 E6
Cadham..........128 D4
Cadishead........86 E5
Cadle............33 E7
Cadley Lancs.....92 F5
  Wilts...........25 C7
  Wilts...........25 D7
Cadmore End......39 E7
Cadnam...........14 C3
Cadney...........90 D4
Cadole...........73 C6
Cadoxton........22 C3
Cadoxton-Juxta-
  Neath..........34 E1
Cadshaw..........86 C5
Cadzow.........119 D7
Caeathro.........82 E4
Caehopkin........34 C2
Caenby...........90 F4
Caenby Corner....90 F3
Caerau Bridgend...34 E2
  Cardiff.........22 B3
Caér-bryn........33 C6
Caerdeon.........58 C3
Caerdydd = Cardiff.22 B3
Caerfarchell.....44 C2
Caerffili
  = Caerphilly....35 F5
Caerfyrddin
  = Carmarthen...33 B5
Caergeiliog......82 D3
Caergwrle........73 D7
Caergybi
  = Holyhead.....82 C2
Caerleon.........35 E7
  = Caerllion.....35 E7
Caer Llan........36 D1
Caerllion
  = Caerleon......35 E7
Caernarfon.......82 E4
Caerphilly
  = Caerffili.....35 F5
Caersws..........59 E7
Caerwedros.......46 E2
Caerwent.........36 E1
Caerwych.........71 D7
Caerwys..........72 B5
Caethle..........58 E3
Caim.............83 C6
Caio.............47 F5
Cairinis........148 B3
Cairisiadar.....154 D5
Cairminis.......154 J5
Cairnbaan.......145 D7
Cairnbanno
  House..........153 D8
Cairnborrow.....152 D4
Cairnbrogie.....141 B7
Cairnbulg Castle 153 B10
Cairncross Angus.134 B4

Cairncross continued
  Borders.........122 C4
Cairndow........125 D7
Cairness........153 B10
Cairneyhill.....128 F2
Cairnfield House.152 B4
Cairngaan.......104 F5
Cairngarroch....104 E4
Cairnhill.......153 E6
Cairnie Aberds..141 D7
  Aberds.........152 D1
Cairnorrie......153 D8
Cairnpark.......141 C7
Cairnryan.......104 C4
Cairnton........159 H4
Caister-on-Sea...69 C8
Caistor..........90 D5
Caistor St Edmund 68 D5
Caistron........117 D5
Caitha Bowland..121 E7
Calais Street....56 F3
Calanais........154 D7
Calbost.........155 F9
Calbourne........14 F5
Calceby..........79 B6
Calcot Row.......26 B4
Calcott..........31 C5
Caldback........160 C8
Caldbeck........108 F3
Caldbergh.......101 F5
Caldecote Cambs..54 D4
  Cambs...........65 F8
  Herts...........54 F3
  W Nhants........52 D4
Caldecott N Nhants 53 C7
  Oxon............38 C4
  Rutland.........65 E5
Calder bank.....119 C7
Calder Bridge....98 D2
Calderbrook......87 C7
Caldercruix.....119 C8
Calder Hall......98 D2
Calder Mains....158 E2
Caldermill......119 E6
Calder Vale......92 E5
Calderwood.....119 D6
Caldhame........134 E4
Caldicot.........36 F1
Caldwell Derbys..63 C6
  N Yorks........101 C6
Caldy............85 F3
Caledrhydiau....46 D3
Calfsound......159 E6
Calgary.........146 F6
Califer.........151 F13
California Falk..120 B2
  Norf............69 C8
Calke............63 B7
Callakille.....149 C11
Callaly.........117 D6
Callander.......126 D5
Callaughton......61 E6
Callestick........4 D2
Calligarry.....149 H11
Callington........5 C8
Callow...........49 F6
Callow End.......50 E3
Callow Hill Wilts.37 F7
  Worcs...........50 B2
Callows Grave....49 C7
Calmore.........14 C4
Calmsden.........37 D7
Calne............24 B5
Calow............76 B4
Calshot..........15 D5
Calstock..........6 C2
Calstone
  Wellington.....24 C5
Calthorpe........81 D7
Calthwaite......108 E4
Calton N Yorks...94 D2
  Staffs..........75 D8
Calveley.........74 D2
Calver...........76 B2
Calverhall.......74 F3
Calver Hill......49 E5
Calverleigh......10 C4
Calverley........94 F5
Calvert..........39 B6
Calverton M Keynes 53 F5
  Notts...........77 E6
Calvine.........133 C5
Calvo...........107 D8
Cam..............36 E4
Camas-luinie....136 B2
Camasnacroise...130 D2
Camastianavaig.149 E10
Camasunary.....149 G10
Camault Muir....151 G8
Camb............160 D7
Camber...........19 D6
Camberley........27 C6
Camberwell.......28 B4
Camblesforth.....89 B7
Cambo...........117 F6
Cambois.........117 F9
Camborne..........3 C5
Cambridge Cambs..55 D5
  Glos............36 D4
Cambridge Town...43 F5
Cambus..........127 E7
Cambusavie
  Farm...........151 B10
Cambusbarron....127 E6
Cambuskenneth...127 E7
Cambuslang.....119 C6
Cambusmore
  Lodge..........151 B10
Camden...........41 F5
Camelford........9 E7
Camelsdale.......27 F6
Camerory.......151 H13
Camer's Green....50 F2
Camerton Bath....24 D2
  Cumb...........107 F7
  E Yorks.........91 B6
Camghouran.....132 D2
Cammachmore....141 E8
Cammeringham....90 F3
Camore.........151 B10
Campbeltown....143 F8
Camperdown.....111 B5
Camp Hill........63 E7
Campmuir.......134 F2
Campsall.........89 C6
Campsey Ash.....57 D7
Campton..........54 F2
Camptown.......116 C2

Camrose..........44 C4
Camserney......133 E5
Camster.........158 F4
Camuschoirk....130 C1
Camuscross.....149 G11
Camusnagaul
  Highld.........130 B4
  Highld.........150 C3
Camusrory......147 B11
Camusteel......149 D12
Camusterrach...149 D12
Camusvrachan...132 E3
Canada...........14 C3
Canadia..........18 D4
Canal Side.......89 C7
Candacraig
  House..........140 C2
Candlesby........79 C7
Candy Mill......120 E3
Cane End.........26 B4
Canewdon.........42 E4
Canford Bottom...13 D8
Canford Cliffs...13 F8
Canford Magna....13 E8
Canham's Green...56 C4
Canholes.........75 B7
Canisbay.......158 C5
Cann.............13 B6
Cannard's Grave..23 E8
Cann Common.....13 B6
Cannich.........150 H6
Cannington.......22 F4
Cannock..........62 D3
Cannock Wood....62 C4
Canonbie........108 B3
Canon Bridge....49 E6
Canon Frome.....49 E8
Canon Pyon......49 E6
Canons Ashby....52 D3
Canonstown.......2 C4
Canterbury.......30 D5
Cantley Norf.....69 D6
  S Yorks.........89 D7
Cantlop..........60 D5
Canton...........22 B3
Cantraybruich..151 G10
Cantraydoune...151 G10
Cantraywood....151 G10
Cantsfield.......93 B6
Canvey Island....42 F3
Canwick..........78 C2
Canworthy Water...8 E4
Caol............131 B5
Caolas..........154 D5
Caolas Scalpaigh 154 H7
Caolas Stocinis.154 H6
Caol Ila........142 A5
Capel............28 E2
Capel Bangor.....58 F3
Capel Betws
  Lleucu..........46 D5
Capel Carmel.....70 E2
Capel Coch.......82 C4
Capel Curig......83 F7
Capel Cynon......46 E2
Capel Dewi Carms..33 B5
  Ceredig.........46 E3
  Ceredig.........58 F3
Capel Garmon....83 F8
Capel-gwyn......82 D3
Capel Gwyn.......33 B5
Capel Gwynfe....33 B8
Capel Hendre....33 C6
Capel Hermon....71 E8
Capel Isaac......33 B6
Capel Iwan.......45 F4
Capel le Ferne...31 F6
Capel Llanilltern.34 F4
Capel Mawr......82 D4
Capel St Andrew..57 E7
Capel St Mary....56 F4
Capel Seion......46 B5
Capel Tygwydd....45 E4
Capel Uchaf......70 C5
Capelulo.........83 D7
Capel-y-graig....82 E5
Capenhurst......73 B7
Capernwray.......92 B5
Capheaton......117 F6
Cappercleuch...115 B5
Capplegill......114 C4
Capton...........7 D6
Caputh.........133 F7
Carbis Bay........2 C4
Carbost Highld..149 D9
  Highld.........149 E8
Carbrook.........88 F4
Carbrooke........68 D2
Carburton........77 B6
Carcant.........121 D6
Carcary........135 D6
Carclaze..........4 D5
Car Colston......77 E7
Carcroft.........89 C6
Cardenden......128 E4
Cardeston........60 C3
Cardiff = Cardydd.22 B3
Cardigan
  = Aberteifi.....45 E3
Cardington Bedford.53 E8
  Shrops..........60 E5
Cardinham.........5 C6
Cardonald......118 C5
Cardow.........152 D1
Cardrona.......121 F6
Cardross.......118 B3
Cardurnock.....107 D8
Careby...........65 C7
Careston Castle.135 D5
Carew............32 D1
Carew Cheriton...32 D1
Carew Newton....32 D1
Carey............49 F7
Carfrae.........121 C8
Cargenbridge...107 B6
Cargill.........134 F1
Cargo...........108 D3
Cargreen..........6 C2
Carham.........122 F4
Carhampton.......22 E2
Carharrack........3 B6
Carie Perth.....132 D3
  Perth..........132 F3
Carines...........4 D2
Carisbrooke......15 F5
Cark.............92 B3
Carlabhagh.....154 C7
Carland Cross.....4 D3
Carlby...........65 C7

Carlecotes.......88 D2
Carlesmoor.......94 B4
Carleton Cumb...108 D4
  Lancs...........92 F3
  N Yorks.........94 E2
  W&F.............99 B7
Carleton Forehoe.68 D3
Carleton Rode....68 E4
Carlingcott......23 D8
Carlin How......103 C5
Carlisle........108 D4
  Cambs...........55 D7
  Leics...........63 D7
  Notts...........77 E6
  N Yorks.........89 B7
  N Yorks........101 C6
  N Yorks........101 F5
  N Yorks........102 F1
  Stockton.......102 B1
  Suff............57 C7
  S Yorks.........88 C4
  W Yorks.........88 B4
Carlton Colville.69 F8
Carlton Curlieu..64 E3
Carlton
  Husthwaite.....95 B7
Carlton in
  Cleveland.....102 D3
Carlton in Lindrick 89 F6
Carlton le
  Moorland.......78 D2
Carlton Miniott.102 F1
Carlton on Trent.77 C7
Carlton Scroop...78 E2
Carluke.........119 D8
Carmarthen
  = Caerfyrddin...33 B5
Carmel Anglesey..82 C3
  Carms...........33 C6
  Flint...........73 B5
  Guern...........16 I2
  Gwyn............82 F4
Carmont........141 F7
Carmunnock.....119 D6
Carmyle.........119 C6
Carmyllie......135 E5
Carnaby..........97 C7
Carnach Highld..136 B3
  Highld.........150 B3
  W Isles........154 H7
Carnachy.......157 D10
Càrnais........154 D5
Carnbee........129 D7
Carnbo.........128 D2
Carnbrea..........3 B5
Carnduff.......119 E6
Carnduncan.....142 B3
Carne............3 C8
Carnforth........92 B4
Carn-gorm......136 B2
Carnhedryn......44 C3
Carnhell Green....2 C5
Carnkie Corn......3 C6
  Corn............3 C6
Carno............59 E6
Carnoch Highld..150 F5
  Highld.........150 H6
Carnock........128 F2
Carnon Downs.....3 B6
Carnousie......153 C6
Carnoustie.....135 F5
Carnwath.......120 E2
Carnyorth........2 C2
Carperby.......101 F5
Carpley Green...100 F4
Carr.............89 E6
Carradale.......143 E9
Carragraich.....154 H6
Carrbridge.....138 B5
Carrefour Selous.17 I3
Carreglefn......82 C3
Carreg-wen.......45 E4
Carr Hill.......111 C5
Carrick Argyll..145 E8
  Fife...........129 B6
Carrick Castle..145 D10
Carrick House...159 E6
Carriden.......128 F2
Carrington Gtr Man.86 E5
  Lincs...........79 D6
  Midloth........121 C6
Carrog Conwy.....71 C8
  Denb............72 E5
Carron Falk.....127 F7
  Moray..........152 D2
Carronbridge....113 E8
Carron Bridge...127 F6
Carronshore.....127 F7
Carrshield......109 E8
Carrutherstown.107 B8
Carrville......111 E6
Carsaig Argyll..144 E6
  Argyll.........147 J8
Carscreugh.....105 D6
Carsegowan.....105 D8
Carse Gray.....134 D4
Carse House.....144 G6
Carseriggan....105 C7
Carsethorn.....107 D6
Carshalton......28 C3
Carsington......76 D2
Carskiey.......143 H7
Carsluith......105 D8
Carsphairn.....113 E5
Carstairs......120 E2
Carstairs
  Junction......120 E2
Carswell Marsh...38 E3
Carter's Clay....14 B4
Carterton.......38 D2
Carterway Heads.110 D3
Carthew...........4 D5
Carthorpe.......101 F8
Cartington.....117 D6
Cartland.......119 E8
Cartmel..........92 B3
Cartmel Fell.....99 F6
Carway...........33 D5
Cary Fitzpaine...12 B3
Cascob...........48 C4
Cas-gwent
  = Chepstow.....36 E2
Cashlie........132 E1
Cashmoor........13 C7
Casnewydd
  = Newport.......35 F7
Cassey Compton...37 C7
Cassington......38 C4

Cassop..........111 F6
Castell..........72 C5
Castellau........34 F4
Castell Howell...46 E3
Castell Newydd Emlyn
  = Newcastle Emlyn 46 E2
Castell-y-bwch...35 E6
Castellau........34 F4
Castle Acre......67 C8
Castle Ashby.....53 D6
Castlebay
  = Bagh a Chaisteil 148 J1
Castle Bolton...101 E5
Castle Bromwich..62 F5
Castle Bytham....65 C6
Castle Caereinion.59 D8
Castle Carrock..108 D5
Castlecary.....119 B7
Castle Combe.....24 B3
Castlecraig....151 E11
Castle Donington.63 B8
Castle Douglas..106 C4
Castle Eaton.....37 E8
Castle Eden....111 F7
Castlefairn....113 F7
Castle Forbes...140 C5
Castleford.......88 B5
Castle Frome.....49 E8
Castle Green.....27 C7
Castle Gresley...63 C6
Castle Heaton..122 E5
Castle Hedingham 55 F8
Castlehill Borders 120 F5
  Highld.........158 D3
  W Dunb.........118 B3
Castle Hill......29 E7
Castle Huntly...128 B5
Castle Kennedy..104 D5
Castlemaddy....113 F5
Castlemartin.....44 F4
Castlemilk
  Dumfries.......107 B8
  Glasgow........119 D6
Castlemorris.....44 B4
Castlemorton....50 F2
Castle O'er.....115 E5
Castle
  Pulverbatch....60 D4
Castle Rising....67 B6
Castleside.....110 E3
Castle Stuart..151 G10
Castlethorpe....53 E6
Castleton Angus..134 E3
  Argyll.........145 E7
  Derbys..........88 F2
  Gtr Man.........87 C6
  Newport.........35 F6
  N Yorks........102 D4
Castletown
  Ches W..........73 D8
  Highld.........151 G10
  Highld.........158 D3
  IoM.............84 F2
  T&W............111 D6
Castleweary....115 D7
Castley..........95 E5
Caston...........68 E2
Castor...........65 E8
Catacol.........143 D10
Catbrain.........36 F2
Catbrook.........36 D2
Catchall..........2 D3
Catchems Corner..51 B7
Catchgate......110 D4
Catcleugh......116 D3
Catcliffe........88 F5
Catcott..........23 F5
Caterham.........28 D4
Catfield.........69 B6
Catfirth........160 H6
Catford..........28 B4
Catforth.........92 F4
Cathays..........22 B3
Cathcart.......119 C5
Cathedine.......35 B5
Catherington.....15 C7
Catherton........49 B8
Catlodge........138 E2
Catlowdy........108 B4
Catmore..........26 E2
Caton............92 C5
Caton Green......92 C5
Catrine........113 B5
Cat's Ash........35 E7
Catsfield........18 D4
Catshill.........50 B4
Cattal...........95 D7
Cattawade........56 F5
Catterall........92 E4
Catterick......101 E7
Catterick Bridge.101 E7
Catterick
  Garrison......101 E6
Catterlen......108 F4
Catterline.....135 B8
Catterton........95 E8
Catthorpe........52 B3
Cattistock.......12 E3
Catton Northumb.109 D8
  N Yorks.........95 B6
Catwick..........97 E7
Catworth.........53 B8
Caudlesprings...68 D2
Caulcott.........39 B5
Cauldcots......135 E6
Cauldhame......126 E5
Cauldmill......115 C8
Cauldon..........75 E7
Caulkerbush....107 D6
Caulside.......115 F7
Caunsall.........62 F2
Caunton..........77 D7
Causeway
  Causewayend...120 F3
  Causeway End...105 C8
  Causeway Foot...94 F3
  Causewayhead
    Cumb.........107 D8
    Stirling.....127 E6
  Causeway Park
    Bridge.......117 E7
Causey Park.....117 E7
Cautley........100 E1
Cavendish........56 E2

Cavendish Bridge..63 B8
Cavenham........55 C8
Caversfield......39 B5
Caversham........26 B5
Caverswall.......75 E6
Cavil............96 F3
Cawdor.........151 F11
Cawkwell.........79 B5
Cawood...........95 F8
Cawsand..........6 D2
Cawston..........81 E7
Cawthorne........88 D3
Cawthorpe........65 B7
Cawton...........96 B2
Caxton...........54 D4
Caynham.........49 B7
Caythorpe Lincs..78 E2
  Notts...........77 E6
Cayton.........103 F8
Ceann a Bhaigh..148 B2
Ceannacroc
  Lodge..........136 C5
Ceann a Deas Loch
  Baghasdail.....148 G2
Ceann Shiphoirt..155 F7
Ceann
  Tarabhaigh....154 F7
Cearsiadair.....155 E8
Cefn Berain......72 C3
Cefn-brith.......72 D3
Cefn Canol.......73 F6
Cefn-coch........83 E8
Cefn Coch........59 B8
Cefn-coed-y-
  cymmer.........34 D4
Cefn Cribbwr....34 F2
Cefn Cross......34 F2
Cefn-ddwysarn....72 F3
Cefn Einion......60 F2
Cefneithin.......33 C6
Cefn-gorwydd....47 E8
Cefn-mawr.......73 E6
Cefn-y-bedd.....73 D7
Cefn-y-pant.....32 B2
Cei-bach.........46 D3
Ceinewydd
  = New Quay......46 D2
Ceint............82 D4
Cellan...........46 E5
Cellarhead.......75 E6
Cemaes...........82 B3
Cemmaes.........58 D5
Cemmaes Road....58 D5
Cenarth..........45 E4
Cenin............71 C5
Central.........118 B2
Ceos...........155 E8
Ceres..........129 C6
Cerne Abbas......12 D4
Cerney Wick......37 E7
Cerrigceinwen...82 D4
Cerrigydrudion...72 E3
Cessford.......116 B3
Ceunant..........82 E5
Chaceley.........50 F3
Chacewater.......3 B6
Chackmore.......52 F4
Chacombe........52 E2
Chadderton......87 D6
Chadderton Fold..87 D6
Chaddesden.......76 F3
Chaddesley
  Corbett........50 B3
Chaddleworth....26 B2
Chadlington.....38 B3
Chadshunt.......51 D8
Chad Valley......62 F4
Chadwell........64 B4
Chadwell St Mary..29 B7
Chadwick End....51 B7
Chadwick Green...86 E3
Chaffcombe......11 C8
Chagford.........10 F2
Chailey..........17 C7
Chainbridge.....66 D4
Chain Bridge....79 E6
Chainhurst......29 E8
Chalbury.........13 D8
Chalbury Common.13 D8
Chaldon..........28 D4
Chaldon Herring..13 F5
Chale............15 G5
Chale Green......15 G5
Chalfont Common..40 E3
Chalfont St Giles.40 E2
Chalfont St Peter.40 E3
Chalford.........37 D5
Chalgrove.......39 E6
Chalk............29 B7
Challacombe......21 E5
Challoch........105 C7
Challock.........30 D4
Chalton C Beds...40 B3
  Hants...........15 C8
Chalvington......18 E2
Chancery.........46 B4
Chandler's Ford..14 B5
Channel Tunnel...19 B8
Channerwick....160 L6
Chantry Som......24 E2
  Suff............56 E5
Chapel..........128 E4
Chapel Allerton
  Som............23 D6
  W Yorks.........95 F6
Chapel Amble......4 B4
Chapel Brampton..52 C5
Chapel Chorlton..74 F5
Chapel End.......63 E7
Chapel-en-
  le-Frith.......87 F8
Chapelgate.......66 B4
Chapel Green
  Warks..........52 C2
  Warks..........51 B8
Chapel Haddlesey.89 B6
Chapelhall.....119 C7
Chapel Head.....66 F3
Chapelhill
  Dumfries.......114 E3
  Highld.........151 D11
  N Ayrs.........118 E2
  Perth..........128 B3
  Perth..........133 F7
Chapel Hill
  Aberds.........153 E10
  Lincs...........78 D5
  Mon.............36 E2
  N Yorks.........95 E6

Chapelknowe....108 B3
Chapel Lawn.....48 B5
Chapel-le-Dale..93 B7
Chapel Milton....87 F8
Chapel of
  Garioch.......141 B6
Chapel Row......26 C3
Chapel St
  Leonards.......79 B8
Chapel Stile.....99 D5
Chapelton Angus.135 E6
  Devon...........9 B7
  Highld.........138 C5
  S Lanark.......119 E6
Chapeltown
  Blackburn......86 C5
  Moray..........139 B8
  S Yorks.........88 E4
Chapmanslade....24 E3
Chapmans Well....9 E5
Chapmore End....41 C6
Chappel..........42 B4
Chard............11 D8
Chardstock......11 D8
Charfield........36 E4
Charford.........50 C4
Charing..........30 E3
Charing Cross....14 C2
Charing Heath....30 E3
Charingworth.....51 F7
Charlbury........38 C3
Charlcombe......24 C2
Charlecote.......51 D7
Charles..........21 F5
Charlesfield...107 C8
Charleston Angus.134 E3
  Renfs..........118 C4
Charlestown
  Aberdeen......141 D8
  Corn............4 D5
  Derbys..........87 E8
  Dorset.........12 G4
  Fife...........128 F2
  Gtr Man.........87 D6
  Highld.........149 A13
  Highld.........151 G9
  W Yorks.........87 B7
Charlestown of
  Aberlour......152 D2
Charles Tye......56 D4
Charlesworth.....87 E8
Charlton Hants...25 E8
  Herts...........40 B4
  London..........28 B5
  Northumb.......116 F4
  Som............23 D8
  Telford.........61 C5
  Wilts...........13 B7
  Wilts...........25 D6
  Wilts...........37 F6
  W Nhants........52 F3
  W Sus...........16 C2
  Worcs...........50 E5
  W Sus...........16 C2
Charlton Abbots..37 B7
Charlton Adam...12 B3
Charlton-All-
  Saints.........14 B2
Charlton Down....12 E4
Charlton
  Horethorne....12 B5
Charlton Kings...37 B6
Charlton
  Mackerell......12 B3
Charlton Marshall 13 D6
Charlton
  Musgrove......12 B5
Charlton on
  Otmoor.........39 C5
Charltons......102 C4
Charlwood.......28 E3
Charlynch.......22 F4
Charminster.....12 E4
Charmouth.......11 E8
Charndon........39 B6
Charney Bassett..38 E3
Charnock Richard.86 C3
Charsfield.......57 D6
Chart Corner....29 D8
Charter Alley....26 D3
Charterhouse....23 D6
Charterville
  Allotments.....38 C3
Chartham........30 D5
Chartham Hatch...30 D5
Chartridge......40 D2
Chart Sutton....30 E2
Charvil..........27 B5
Charwelton......52 D3
Chasetown.......62 D4
Chastleton......38 B2
Chasty...........8 D5
Chatburn.........93 E7
Chatcull.........74 F4
Chatham..........29 C8
Chathill.......117 B7
Chattenden......28 B8
Chatteris........66 F3
Chattisham......56 E4
Chatto..........116 C3
Chatton........117 B6
Chawleigh.......10 C2
Chawley.........38 D4
Chawston........54 D2
Chawton.........26 F5
Cheadle Gtr Man..87 F6
  Staffs..........75 E7
Cheadle Heath....87 F6
Cheadle Hulme....87 F6
Cheam...........28 C3
Cheapside.......27 C8
Chearsley.......39 C7
Chebsey.........62 B2
Checkendon......39 F6
Checkley Ches E..74 E4
  Hereford........49 F7
  Staffs..........75 F7
Chedburgh.......55 D8
Cheddar..........23 D6
Cheddington.....40 C2
Cheddleton......75 D6
Cheddon Fitzpaine 11 B7
Chedglow........37 E6
Chedgrave.......69 E6
Chedington......12 D2
Chediston........57 B7
Chedworth.......37 C7
Chedzoy..........22 F5
Cheeklaw.......122 D3

Cheeseman's
  Green..........19 B7
Cheglinch.......20 E4
Cheldon.........10 C2
Chelford........74 B5
Chellaston......76 F3
Chell Heath......75 D5
Chellington.....53 D7
Chelmarsh.......61 F7
Chelmer Village..42 D3
Chelmondiston...57 F6
Chelmorton......75 C8
Chelmsford......42 D3
Chelsea.........28 B3
Chelsfield......29 C5
Chelsworth......56 E3
Cheltenham......37 B6
Chelveston......53 C7
Chelvey..........23 C6
Chelwood........23 C8
Chelwood
  Common........17 B8
Chelwood Gate...17 B8
Chelworth.......37 E6
Chelworth Green..37 E7
Chemistry.......74 E2
Chenies.........40 E3
Cheny Longville..60 F4
Chepstow
  = Cas-gwent....36 E2
Chequerfield....89 B5
Cherhill........24 B5
Cherington Glos..37 E6
  Warks..........51 F7
Cheriton Devon...21 E6
  Hants..........15 B6
  Kent...........19 B8
  Swansea.........33 E5
Cheriton Bishop..10 E2
Cheriton Fitzpaine 10 D3
Cheriton or Stackpole
  Elidor.........44 F4
Cherrington.....61 B6
Cherrybank.....128 B3
Cherry Burton...97 E5
Cherry Hinton...55 D5
Cherry Orchard...50 D3
Cherry Willingham 78 B3
Chertsey........27 C8
Cheselbourne....13 E5
Chesham.........40 E2
Chesham Bois....40 E2
Cheshunt........41 D6
Cheslyn Hay.....62 D3
Chessington.....28 C2
Chester.........73 C8
Chesterblade....23 E8
Chesterfield....76 B3
Chester-le-
  Street........111 D5
Chester Moor...111 E5
Chesters Borders.116 B2
  Borders........116 C2
Chesterton Cambs.55 C5
  Cambs...........65 E8
  Glos............37 D7
  Oxon............39 B5
  Shrops..........61 E7
  Staffs..........74 E5
  Warks...........51 D8
Chesterwood....109 C8
Chestfield.......30 C5
Cheston.........6 D4
Cheswardine.....61 B7
Cheswick.......123 E6
Chetnole........12 D4
Chettiscombe....10 C4
Chettisham......66 F5
Chettle.........13 C7
Chetton.........61 E6
Chetwode........39 B6
Chetwynd Aston..61 C7
Cheveley........55 C7
Chevening.......29 D5
Chevington......55 D8
Chevithorne.....10 C4
Chew Magna......23 C7
Chew Stoke......23 C7
Chewton
  Keynsham......23 C8
Chewton Mendip..23 D7
Chichcley.......53 E7
Chichester......16 D2
Chickerell......12 F4
Chicklade.......24 F4
Chicksgrove.....24 F4
Chidden.........15 C7
Chiddingfold....27 F7
Chiddingly......18 D2
Chiddingstone...29 E5
Chiddingstone
  Causeway.......29 E6
Chiddingstone
  Hoath..........29 E5
Chideock........12 E2
Chidham.........15 D8
Chidswell.......88 B3
Chieveley.......26 B2
Chignall St James.42 D2
Chignall Smealy..42 C2
Chigwell........41 E7
Chigwell Row....41 E7
Chilbolton......25 F8
Chilcomb........15 B6
Chilcombe.......12 E3
Chilcompton.....23 D8
Chilcote........63 C6
Childer Thornton.73 B7
Child Okeford....13 C6
Childrey........38 F3
Child's Ercall...61 B6
Childswickham...51 F5
Childwall........86 F2
Childwick Green..40 C4
Chilfrome.......12 E3
Chilgrove.......16 C2
Chilham.........30 D4
Chilhampton.....25 F5
Chilla...........9 D6
Chillaton........9 F6
Chillenden......31 D6
Chillerton......15 F5
Chillesford......57 D7
Chillingham....117 B6
Chillington Devon.7 E5
  Som............11 C8

Chilmark...24 F4
Chilson...38 C3
Chilsworthy Corn...6 B2
  Devon...8 C5
Chilthorne Domer.12 C3
Chiltington...17 C7
Chilton Bucks...39 C6
  Durham...101 B7
  Oxon...38 F4
Chilton Cantelo...12 B3
Chilton Foliat...25 B8
Chilton Lane...111 F6
Chilton Polden...23 F5
Chilton Street...55 E8
Chilton Trinity...22 F4
Chilvers Coton...63 E7
Chilwell...76 F5
Chilworth Hants...14 C5
  Sur...27 E8
Chimney...38 D3
Chineham...26 D4
Chingford...41 E6
Chinley...87 F8
Chinley Head...87 F8
Chinnor...39 D7
Chipnall...74 F4
Chippenhall Green 57 B6
Chippenham Cambs 55 C7
  Wilts...24 B4
Chipperfield...40 D3
Chipping Herts...54 F4
  Lancs...93 E6
Chipping
  Campden...51 F6
Chipping Hill...42 C4
Chipping Norton...38 B3
Chipping Ongar...42 D1
Chipping Sodbury...36 F4
Chipping Warden...52 E2
Chipstable...10 B5
Chipstead Kent...29 D5
  Sur...28 D3
Chirbury...60 E2
Chirk = Y Waun...73 F6
Chirk Bank...73 F6
Chirmorrie...105 B6
Chirnside...122 D4
Chirnsidebridge.122 D4
Chirton...25 D5
Chisbury...25 C7
Chiselborough...12 C2
Chiseldon...25 B6
Chiserley...87 B8
Chislehampton...39 E5
Chislehurst...28 B5
Chislet...31 C6
Chiswell Green...40 D4
Chiswick...28 B3
Chiswick End...54 E4
Chisworth...87 E7
Chithurst...16 B2
Chittering...55 B5
Chitterne...24 E4
Chittlehamholt...9 B8
Chittlehampton...9 B8
Chittoe...24 C4
Chivenor...20 F4
Chobham...27 C7
Choicelee...122 D3
Cholderton...25 E7
Cholesbury...40 D2
Chollerford...110 B2
Chollerton...110 B2
Cholmondeston...74 C3
Cholsey...39 F5
Cholstrey...49 D6
Chop Gate...102 E3
Choppington...117 F8
Chopwell...110 D4
Chorley Ches E...74 D2
  Lancs...86 C3
  Shrops...61 F6
  Staffs...62 C4
Chorleywood...40 E3
Chorlton cum
  Hardy...87 E6
Chorlton Lane...73 E8
Choulton...60 F3
Chowdene...111 D5
Chowley...73 D8
Chrishall...54 F5
Christchurch BCP..14 E2
  Cambs...66 E4
  Glos...36 C2
  Newport...35 F7
Christian Malford..24 B4
Christleton...73 C8
Christmas
  Common...39 E7
Christon...23 D5
Christon Bank...117 B8
Christow...10 F3
Chryston...119 B6
Chudleigh...7 B6
Chudleigh Knighton..7 B6
Chulmleigh...9 C8
Chunal...87 E8
Church...86 B5
Churcham...36 C4
Church Aston...61 C7
Churchbank...48 B4
Church Brampton.52 C5
Churchbridge...62 D3
Church Broughton 76 F2
Church Crookham.27 D6
Churchdown...37 C5
Church Eaton...62 C2
Churchend Essex...42 E2
  Essex...43 E6
  S Glos...36 E4
Church End Cambs..66 D3
  Cambs...66 F2
  C Beds...40 B2
  C Beds...54 F2
  Essex...55 E6
  E Yorks...97 C6
  Hants...26 D4
  Lincs...78 F5
  Warks...63 E6
  Wilts...24 B5
Church Enstone...38 B3
Church Fenton...95 F8
Churchfield...62 E4
Churchgate Street.41 C7

Church Green
  Devon...11 E6
  Norf...68 E3
Church Gresley...63 C6
Church
  Hanborough...38 C4
Church Hill...74 C3
Church Houses...102 E4
Churchill Devon...11 D8
  Devon...20 E4
  N Som...23 D6
  Oxon...38 C3
  Worcs...50 B3
  Worcs...50 D4
Churchinford...11 C7
Church Knowle...13 F7
Church Laneham...77 B8
Church Langton...64 E4
Church Lawford...52 B2
Church Lawton...74 D5
Church Leigh...75 F7
Church Lench...50 D5
Church Mayfield...75 E8
Church Minshull...74 C3
Church Norton...16 E2
Churchover...64 F2
Church Preen...60 E5
Church
  Pulverbatch...60 D4
Churchstanton...11 C6
Church Stoke...60 E2
Churchstow...6 E5
Church Stowe...52 D4
Church Street...29 B8
Church Stretton...60 E4
Churchtown Derbys 76 C2
  IoM...84 C4
  Lancs...92 E4
  Mers...85 C4
Church Town
  N Lincs...89 D8
  Sur...28 D4
Church Village...34 F4
Church Warsop...77 C5
Churston Ferrers...7 D7
Churt...27 F6
Churton...73 D8
Churwell...88 B3
Chute Standen...25 D8
Chwilog...70 D5
Chyandour...2 C3
Cilan Uchaf...70 E3
Cilcain...73 C5
Cilcennin...46 C4
Cilfor...71 D6
Cilfrew...34 D1
Cilfynydd...34 E4
Cilgerran...45 E3
Cilgwyn Carms...33 B8
  Gwyn...82 F4
  Pembs...45 F2
Ciliau Aeron...46 D3
Cill Donnain...148 F2
Cille Bhrighde...148 G2
Cille Pheadair...148 G2
Cilmeri = Cilmery..48 D2
Cilmery = Cilmeri..48 D2
Cilsan...33 B6
Ciltalgarth...72 E2
Cilwendeg...45 F4
Cilybebyll...33 D8
Cilycwm...47 F6
Cimla...34 E1
Cinderford...36 C3
Cippyn...45 E3
Circebost...154 D6
Cirencester...37 D7
Ciribhig...154 C6
City London...41 F6
  Powys...60 F2
City Dulas...82 C4
Clachaig...145 E10
Clachan Argyll...124 D3
  Argyll...125 D7
  Argyll...130 E2
  Argyll...144 H6
  Highld...149 E10
  W Isles...148 D2
Clachaneasy...105 B7
Clachanmore...104 E4
Clachan na Luib..148 B3
Clachan of
  Campsie...119 B6
Clachan of
  Glendaruel...145 E8
Clachan-Seil...124 D3
Clachan Strachur.125 E6
Clachbreck...144 F6
Clachnabrain...134 C3
Clachtoll...156 G3
Clackmannan...127 E8
Clacton-on-Sea...43 C7
Cladach
  Chireboist...148 B2
Cladach-
  knockline...148 B2
Claddach...125 C6
Claggan Highld...131 B5
  Highld...147 G9
Claigan...148 C7
Claines...50 D3
Clandown...23 D8
Clanfield Hants...15 C7
  Oxon...38 D2
Clanville...25 E8
Claonaig...145 H7
Claonel...157 J8
Clapgate Dorset...13 D8
  Herts...41 B7
Clapham Bedford..53 D8
  London...28 B3
  N Yorks...93 C7
  W Sus...16 D4
Clap Hill...19 B7
Clappers...122 D5
Clappersgate...99 D5
Clapton...12 D2
Clapton-in-
  Gordano...23 B6
Clapworthy...9 B8
Clarach...58 F3
Clara Vale...110 C4
Clarbeston...32 B1
Clarbeston Road...32 B1
Clarborough...89 F8
Clardon...158 D3

Clare...55 E8
Clarebrand...106 C4
Clarencefield...107 C7
Clarilaw...115 C8
Clark's Green...28 F2
Clarkston...119 D5
Clashandorran...151 G8
Clashcoig...151 B9
Clashindarroch..152 E4
Clashmore
  Highld...151 C10
  Highld...156 F3
Clashnessie...156 F3
Clashnoir...139 B8
Clate...160 G7
Clathy...127 C8
Clatt...140 B4
Clatter...59 E6
Clatterford...15 F5
Clatterin Bridge..135 B6
Clatworthy...22 F2
Claughton Lancs...93 C5
  Lancs...93 B5
  Mers...85 E4
Claverdon...51 C6
Claverham...23 C6
Clavering...55 F5
Claverley...61 E7
Claverton...24 C2
Clawdd-newydd..72 D4
Clawthorpe...92 B5
Clawton...9 E5
Claxby Lincs...79 B7
  Lincs...90 E5
Claxton Norf...69 D6
  N Yorks...96 C2
Claybokie...139 E6
Claybrooke Magna 63 F8
Claybrooke Parva..63 F8
Clay Common...69 F7
Clay Coton...52 B3
Clay Cross...76 C3
Claydon Oxon...52 D2
  Suff...56 D5
Claygate Dumfries 108 B3
  Kent...29 E8
  Sur...28 C2
Claygate Cross...29 D7
Clayhanger Devon..10 B5
  W Mid...62 D4
Clayhidon...11 C6
Clayhill E Sus...18 C5
  Hants...14 D4
Clay Hill...26 B3
Clay Lake...66 B2
Clayock...158 E3
Claypole...77 E8
Clayton Staffs...75 E5
  S Yorks...89 D5
  W Sus...17 C6
  W Yorks...94 F4
Clayton Green...86 B3
Clayton-le-Moors.93 F7
Clayton-le-Woods 86 B3
Clayton West...88 C3
Clayworth...89 F8
Cleadale...146 C7
Cleadon...111 C6
Clearbrook...6 C3
Clearwell...36 D2
Cleasby...101 C7
Cleat...159 K5
Cleatlam...101 C6
Cleator...98 C2
Cleator Moor...98 C2
Clebrig...157 F8
Cleckheaton...88 B2
Cleedownton...61 F5
Cleehill...49 B7
Clee St Margaret..61 F5
Cleethorpes...91 D7
Cleeton St Mary..49 B8
Cleeve...23 C6
Cleeve Hill...37 B6
Cleeve Prior...51 E5
Clegyrnant...59 D6
Clehonger...49 F6
Cleish...128 E2
Cleland...119 D8
Clench Common..25 C6
Clenchwarton...67 B5
Clent...50 B4
Cleobury
  Mortimer...49 B8
Cleobury North...61 F6
Cleongart...143 E7
Clephanton...151 F11
Clerklands...115 B8
Clestrain...159 H4
Cleuch Head...115 C8
Cleughbrae...107 B7
Clevancy...25 B5
Clevedon...23 B6
Cleveley...38 B3
Cleveleys...92 E3
Cleverton...37 F6
Clevis...21 B7
Clewer...23 D6
Cley next the Sea..81 C6
Cliaid...148 H1
Cliasmol...154 G5
Cliburn...99 B7
Click Mill...159 F4
Cliddesden...26 E4
Cliffburn...135 E6
Cliffe Medway...29 B8
  N Yorks...96 F2
Cliff End...19 D5
Cliffe Woods...29 B8
Clifford Hereford..48 E4
  W Yorks...95 E7
Clifford Chambers.51 D6
Clifford's Mesne...36 C4
Cliffsend...31 C7
Clifton Bristol...23 B7
  C Beds...54 F2
  Derbys...75 E8
  Lancs...92 F4
  Nottingham...77 F5
  N Yorks...94 E4
  Oxon...52 F2
  Stirling...131 F7
  S Yorks...89 E6
  W&F...99 B7
  Worcs...50 E3
  York...95 D8
Clifton Campville..63 C6
Cliftoncote...116 B4

Clifton Green...87 D5
Clifton Hampden...39 E5
Clifton Reynes...53 D7
Clifton upon
  Dunsmore...52 B3
Clifton upon Teme.50 C2
Cliftonville...31 B7
Climaen gwyn...33 D8
Climping...16 D3
Climpy...120 D2
Clink...24 E2
Clint...95 D5
Clint Green...68 C3
Clintmains...122 F2
Cliobh...154 D5
Clippesby...69 C7
Clipsham...65 C6
Clipston...64 F4
Clipstone...77 C5
Clitheroe...93 E7
Cliuthar...154 H6
Clive...60 B5
Clivocast...160 C8
Clixby...90 D5
Clocaenog...72 D4
Clochan...152 B4
Clock Face...86 E3
Clockmill...122 D3
Cloddiau...60 D2
Clodock...35 B7
Clola...153 D10
Clophill...53 F8
Clopton N Nhants..65 F7
  Suff...57 D6
Clopton Corner...57 D6
Clopton Green...55 D8
Closeburn...113 E8
Close Clark...84 E2
Closworth...12 C3
Clothall...54 F3
Clotton...74 C2
Clough Foot...87 B7
Cloughton...103 E8
Cloughton
  Newlands...103 E8
Clousta...160 H5
Clouston...159 G3
Clova Aberds...140 B3
  Angus...134 B3
Clovelly...8 B5
Clove Lodge...100 C4
Clovenfords...121 F7
Clovenstone...141 C6
Clovullin...130 C4
Clow Bridge...87 B6
Clowne...76 B4
Clows Top...50 B2
Cloy...73 E7
Cluanie Inn...136 C3
Cluanie Lodge...136 C3
Clun...60 F3
Clunbury...60 F3
Clunderwen...32 C2
Clune...138 B3
Clunes...136 F5
Clungunford...49 B5
Clunie Aberds...153 C6
  Perth...133 E8
Clunton...60 F3
Cluny...128 E4
Cluny Castle...138 E2
Clutton Bath...23 D8
  Ches W...73 D8
Clwt-grugoer...72 C3
Clwt-y-bont...83 E5
Clydach Mon...35 C6
  Swansea...33 D7
Clydach Vale...34 E3
Clydebank...118 B4
Clydey...45 F4
Clyffe Pypard...25 B5
Clynder...145 E11
Clyne...34 D2
Clynelish...157 J11
Clynnog-fawr...82 F4
Clyro...48 E4
Clyst Honiton...10 E4
Clyst Hydon...10 D5
Clyst St George...10 F4
Clyst St Lawrence.10 D5
Clyst St Mary...10 E4
Cnoc Amhlaigh.155 D10
Cnwch-coch...47 B5
Coachford...152 D4
Coad's Green...5 B7
Coal Aston...76 B3
Coalbrookdale...61 D6
Coalbrookvale...35 D5
Coalburn...119 F8
Coalburns...110 C4
Coalcleugh...109 E8
Coaley...36 D4
Coalhall...112 C4
Coalhill...42 E3
Coalpit Heath...36 F3
Coalport...61 D6
Coalsnaughton...127 E8
Coaltown of
  Balgonie...128 E4
Coaltown of
  Wemyss...128 E5
Coalville...63 C8
Coalway...36 C2
Coat...12 B2
Coatbridge...119 C7
Coatdyke...119 C7
Coate Swindon...38 F1
  Wilts...24 C5
Coates Cambs...66 E3
  Glos...37 D6
  Lancs...93 E8
  Notts...90 F2
  W Sus...16 C3
Coatham...102 B3
Coatham
  Mundeville...101 B7
Coatsgate...114 D3
Cobbaton...9 B8
Cobbler's Green...69 E5
Coberley...37 C6
Cobham Kent...29 C7
  Sur...28 C2
Cobholm Island...69 D8
Cobleland...126 E4
Cobnash...49 C6
Coburty...153 B9
Cockayne...102 E4
Cockayne Hatley...54 E3
Cock Bank...73 E7

Cock Bridge...139 D8
Cockburnspath...122 B3
Cock Clarks...42 D4
Cockenzie and Port
  Seton...121 B7
Cockerham...92 D4
Cockermouth...107 F8
Cockernhoe Green 40 B4
Cockfield Durham.101 B6
  Suff...56 D3
Cockfosters...41 E5
Cocking...16 C2
Cockington...7 C6
Cocklake...23 D6
Cockley Beck...98 D4
Cockley Cley...67 D7
Cockshutt...60 B4
Cockthorpe...81 C5
Cockwood...10 F4
Cockyard...49 F6
Codda...5 B6
Coddenham...56 D5
Coddington
  Ches W...73 D8
  Hereford...50 E2
  Notts...77 D8
Codford St Mary..24 F4
Codford St Peter..24 F4
Codicote...41 C5
Codmore Hill...16 B4
Codnor...76 E4
Codrington...24 B2
Codsall...62 D2
Codsall Wood...62 D2
Coed Duon
  = Blackwood...35 E5
Coedely...34 F4
Coedkernew...35 F6
Coed Mawr...83 D5
Coed Morgan...35 C7
Coedpoeth...73 D6
Coed-Talon...73 D6
Coedway...60 C3
Coed-y-bryn...46 E2
Coed-y-paen...35 E7
Coed-yr-ynys...35 B5
Coed Ystumgwern.71 E6
Coelbren...34 C2
Coffinswell...7 C6
Cofton Hackett...50 B5
Cogan...22 B3
Cogenhoe...53 C6
Cogges...38 D3
Coggeshall...42 B4
Coggeshall Hamlet 42 B4
Coggins Mill...18 C2
Coignafearn
  Lodge...138 C2
Coig
  Peighinnean..155 A10
Coig Peighinnean
  Bhuirgh...155 B9
Coilacriech...140 E2
Coilantogle...126 D4
Coilleag...148 G2
Coillore...149 E8
Coity...34 F3
Col...155 C9
Colaboll...157 H8
Colan...4 C3
Colaton Raleigh...11 F5
Colbost...148 D7
Colburn...101 E6
Colby IoM...84 E2
  Norf...81 D8
  W&F...100 B1
Colchester...43 B6
Colcot...22 C3
Cold Ash...26 C3
Cold Ashby...52 B4
Cold Ashton...24 B2
Cold Aston...37 C8
Coldbackie...157 D9
Coldbeck...100 D2
Cold Blow...32 C2
Cold Brayfield...53 D7
Coldean...17 D7
Coldeast...7 B6
Colden...87 B7
Colden Common...15 B5
Coldfair Green...57 C8
Coldham...66 D4
Cold Hanworth...90 F4
Coldharbour Glos..36 D2
  Kent...29 D6
  Sur...28 E2
Cold Harbour...78 F2
Cold Hatton...61 B6
Cold Hesledon...111 E7
Cold Higham...52 D4
Coldingham...122 C5
Cold Kirby...102 F3
Cold Newton...64 D4
Cold Northcott...8 F4
Cold Norton...42 D4
Cold Overton...64 C5
Coldrain...128 D2
Coldred...31 E6
Coldridge...9 D8
Coldstream Angus.134 F3
  Borders...122 F4
Coldwaltham...16 C4
Coldwells...153 D11
Coldwells Croft...140 B4
Coldyeld...60 E3
Cole...23 F8
Colebatch...60 F3
Colebrook...10 D5
Colebrooke...10 E2
Coleby Lincs...78 C2
  N Lincs...90 C2
Coleford Devon...10 D2
  Glos...36 C2
  Som...23 E8
Cole Green...41 C5
Cole Henley...26 D2
Colehill...13 D8
Coleman's Hatch..29 F5
Colemere...73 F8
Colemore...26 F5
Coleorton...63 C8
Colerne...24 B3
Cole's Green...57 C6
Coleshill Bucks...40 E2
  Oxon...38 E2

Coleshill continued
  Warks...63 F6
Colestocks...11 D5
Colgate...28 F3
Colgrain...126 F2
Colinsburgh...129 D6
Colinton...120 C5
Colintraive...145 F9
Colkirk...80 E5
Collace...134 F2
Collafirth...160 G6
Collaton St Mary..7 D6
College Milton...119 D6
Collessie...128 C4
Collier Row...41 E8
Collier's End...41 B6
Collier's Green...18 B4
Collier Street...29 E8
Colliery Row...111 E6
Collieston...141 B9
Collin...107 B7
Collingbourne
  Ducis...25 D7
Collingbourne
  Kingston...25 D7
Collingham Notts..77 C8
  W Yorks...95 E6
Collington...49 C8
Collingtree...53 D5
Collins Green...86 E3
Colliston...135 E6
Collycroft...63 F7
Collynie...153 E8
Collyweston...65 D6
Colmonell...104 A5
Colmworth...54 D2
Colnabaichin...139 D8
Colnbrook...27 B8
Colne Cambs...54 B4
  Lancs...93 E8
Colne Engaine...56 F2
Colney...68 D4
Colney Heath...41 D5
Colney Street...40 D4
Coln Rogers...37 D7
Coln St Aldwyn's..37 D8
Coln St Dennis...37 C7
Colpy...153 E6
Colquhar...121 E6
Colsterdale...101 F6
Colsterworth...65 B6
Colston Bassett...77 F6
Coltfield...151 E14
Colthouse...99 E5
Coltishall...69 C5
Coltness...119 D8
Colton Norf...68 D4
  N Yorks...95 E8
  Staffs...62 B4
  W&F...99 F5
  W Yorks...95 F6
Col Uarach...155 D9
Colva...48 D4
Colvend...107 D5
Colvister...160 D7
Colwall Green...50 E2
Colwall Stone...50 E2
Colwell...110 B2
Colwich...62 B4
Colwick...77 E6
Colwinston...21 B8
Colworth...16 D3
Colwyn Bay
  = Bae Colwyn...83 D8
Colyford...11 E7
Colyton...11 E7
Combe Hereford...48 C5
  Oxon...38 C4
  W Berks...25 C8
Combe Common...27 F7
Combe Down...24 C2
Combe Florey...22 F3
Combe Hay...24 D2
Combe Martin...20 E4
Combe Moor...49 C5
Combe Raleigh...11 D6
Comberbach...74 B3
Comberton Cambs..54 D4
  Hereford...49 C6
Combe St
  Nicholas...11 C8
Combpyne...11 E7
Combridge...75 F7
Combrook...51 D8
Combs Derbys...75 B7
  Suff...56 D4
Combs Ford...56 D4
Combwich...22 E4
Comers...141 D5
Comins Coch...58 F3
Commins Coch...59 D5
Commercial End...55 C6
Commins Capel
  Betws...46 D5
Commondale...102 C4
Common Edge...92 F3
Commonmoor...5 C7
Commonside...74 E2
Common Side...76 B3
Compstall...87 E7
Compton Devon...7 C6
  Hants...15 B5
  Sur...27 E6
  Sur...27 E7
  W Berks...26 B3
  Wilts...25 D6
  W Sus...15 C8
Compton Abbas...13 C6
Compton Abdale...37 C7
Compton Bassett..24 B5
Compton
  Beauchamp...38 F2
Compton Bishop...23 D5
Compton
  Chamberlayne...13 B8
Compton Dando...23 C8
Compton Dundon..23 F6
Compton Martin...23 D7
Compton
  Pauncefoot...12 B4
Compton Valence..12 E3
Comrie Fife...128 F2
  Perth...127 B6
Conaglen House..130 C4
Conchra...145 E9
Concraigie...133 E8
Conder Green...92 D4

Conderton...50 F4
Condicote...38 B1
Condorrat...119 B7
Condover...60 D4
Coneyhurst...16 B5
Coneysthorpe...96 B3
Coney Weston...56 B3
Conford...27 F6
Congash...139 B6
Congdon's Shop...5 B7
Congerstone...63 D7
Congham...80 E3
Congl-y-wal...71 C8
Congresbury...23 C6
Congreve...62 C3
Conicavel...151 F12
Coningsby...78 D5
Conington Cambs..54 C4
  Cambs...65 F8
Conisbrough...89 E6
Conisby...142 B3
Conisholme...91 E8
Coniston E Yorks...97 F7
  W&F...99 E5
Coniston Cold...94 D2
Conistone...94 C2
Connah's Quay...73 C6
Connel...124 B5
Connel Park...113 C6
Connor Downs...2 C4
Conon Bridge...151 F8
Conon House...151 F8
Cononley...94 E2
Conordan...149 E10
Consall...75 E6
Consett...110 D4
Constable Burton 101 E6
Constantine...3 D6
Constantine Bay...4 B3
Contin...150 F7
Contlaw...141 D7
Conwy...83 D7
Conyer...30 C3
Conyers Green...56 C2
Cooden...18 E4
Cooil...84 E3
Cookbury...9 D6
Cookham...40 F1
Cookham Dean...40 F1
Cookham Rise...40 F1
Cookhill...51 D5
Cookley Suff...57 B7
  Worcs...62 F2
Cookley Green...39 E6
Cookney...141 E7
Cooksbridge...17 C8
Cooksmill Green...42 D2
Coolham...16 B5
Cooling...29 B8
Coombe Corn...4 D4
  Corn...8 C4
  Hants...15 B7
  Wilts...25 D6
Coombe Bissett...14 B2
Coombe Hill...37 B5
Coombe Keynes...13 F6
Coombes...17 D5
Coopersale
  Common...41 D7
Cootham...16 C4
Copdock...56 E5
Copford Green...43 B5
Copgrove...95 C6
Copister...160 F6
Cople...54 E2
Copley...101 B5
Coplow Dale...75 B8
Copmanthorpe...95 E8
Coppathorne...8 D4
Coppenhall...62 C3
Coppenhall Moss..74 D4
Copperhouse...2 C4
Coppingford...65 F8
Copplestone...10 D2
Coppull...86 C3
Coppull Moor...86 C3
Copsale...17 B5
Copster Green...93 F6
Copston Magna...63 F8
Copt Heath...51 B6
Copt Hewick...95 B6
Copthorne Shrops..60 C4
  Sur...28 F4
Copt Oak...63 C8
Copy's Green...80 D5
Copythorne...14 C4
Corbets Tey...42 F1
Corbridge...110 C2
Corby...65 F5
Corby Glen...65 B6
Cordon...143 E11
Coreley...49 B8
Cores End...40 F2
Corfe...11 C7
Corfe Castle...13 F7
Corfe Mullen...13 E7
Corfton...60 F4
Corgarff...139 D8
Corhampton...15 B7
Corlae...113 E6
Corley...63 F7
Corley Ash...63 F6
Corley Moor...63 F6
Cornaa...84 D4
Cornabus...142 D4
Cornel...83 E7
Corner Row...92 F4
Corney...98 E3
Cornforth...111 F6
Cornhill...152 C5
Cornhill-on-
  Tweed...122 F4
Cornholme...87 B7
Cornish Hall End...55 F7
Cornquoy...159 J6
Cornsay...110 E4
Cornsay Colliery..110 E4
Corntown Highld..151 F8
  V Glam...21 B8
Cornwell...38 B2
Cornwood...6 D4
Cornworthy...7 D6
Corpach...130 B4
Corpusty...81 D7
Corran Highld...130 C4
  Highld...149 H13

Corranbuie...145 G7
Corrany...84 D4
Corrie...143 D11
Corrie Common...114 F5
Corriecravie...143 F10
Corriemoillie...150 E6
Corriemulzie
  Lodge...150 B6
Corrievarkie
  Lodge...132 B2
Corrievorrie...138 B3
Corrimony...150 H6
Corringham Lincs..90 E2
  Thurrock...42 F3
Corris...58 D4
Corris Uchaf...58 D4
Corrour Shooting
  Lodge...131 C8
Corrow...125 E7
Corry...149 F11
Corry of
  Ardnagrask...151 G8
Corsback...158 C4
Corscombe...12 D3
Corse Aberds...152 D6
  Glos...36 B4
Corse Lawn...50 F3
Corse of Kinnoir..152 D5
Corsewall...104 C4
Corsham...24 B3
Corsindae...141 D5
Corsley...24 E3
Corsley Heath...24 E3
Corsock...106 B4
Corston Bath...23 C8
  Wilts...37 F6
Corstorphine...120 B4
Cors-y-Gedol...71 E6
Cortachy...134 D3
Corton Suff...69 E8
  Wilts...24 E4
Corton Denham...12 B4
Coruanan Lodge..130 C4
Corunna...148 B3
Corwen...72 E4
Coryton Devon...9 F6
  Thurrock...42 F3
Cosby...64 E2
Coseley...62 E3
Cosgrove...53 E5
Cosham...15 D7
Cosheston...32 D1
Coskills...90 D4
Cosmeston...22 C3
Cossall...76 E4
Cossington Leics..64 C3
  Som...23 E5
Costa...159 F4
Costessey...68 C4
Costock...64 B2
Coston...64 C5
Cote...38 D3
Cotebrook...74 C2
Cotehill...108 D4
Cotes Leics...64 B2
  Staffs...74 F5
  W&F...99 F6
Cotesbach...64 F2
Cotgrave...77 F6
Cotham...77 E7
Cothelstone...22 F3
Cotherstone...101 C5
Cothill...38 E4
Cotleigh...11 D7
Cotmanhay...76 E4
Cotmaton...11 F6
Coton Cambs...54 D5
  Staffs...62 B2
  Staffs...75 F6
  W Nhants...52 B4
Coton Clanford...62 B2
Coton Hill Shrops..60 C4
  Staffs...75 F6
Coton in the Elms..63 C6
Cott...7 C5
Cottam E Yorks...97 C5
  Lancs...92 F5
  Notts...77 B8
Cottartown...151 H13
Cottenham...54 C5
Cotterdale...100 E3
Cottered...41 B6
Cotteridge...50 B5
Cotterstock...65 E7
Cottesbrooke...52 B5
Cottesmore...65 C6
Cotteylands...10 C4
Cottingham
  E Yorks...97 F6
  N Nhants...64 E5
Cottingley...94 F4
Cottisford...52 F3
Cotton Staffs...75 E7
  Suff...56 C4
Cotton End...53 E8
Cottown Aberds...140 B4
  Aberds...141 C6
  Aberds...153 D8
Cotwalton...75 F6
Couch's Mill...5 D6
Coughton Hereford..36 B2
  Warks...51 C5
Coulaghailtro...144 G6
Coulags...150 G2
Coulby Newham...102 C3
Coulderton...98 D1
Couldoran...150 F3
Coulin...150 F3
Coull Aberds...140 D4
  Argyll...142 B3
Coulport...145 E11
Coulsdon...28 D3
Coulston...24 D4
Coulter...120 F3
Coulton...96 B3
Cound...61 D5
Coundon Durham..101 B7
  W Mid...63 F7
Coundon Grange..101 B7
Countersett...100 F4
Countess...25 E6
Countess Wear...10 F4
Countesthorpe...64 E2
Countisbury...21 E6
County Oak...28 F3
Coup Angus...134 E2
Coup Green...86 B3
Coupland...122 F5

Cour...143 D9
Courance...114 E3
Court-at-Street...19 B7
Courteenhall...53 D5
Court Henry...33 B6
Courtsend...43 E6
Courtway...22 F4
Cousland...121 C6
Cousley Wood...18 B3
Cove Argyll...145 E11
  Borders...122 B3
  Devon...10 C4
  Hants...27 D6
  Highld...155 H13
Cove Bay...141 D8
Cove Bottom...57 B8
Covehithe...69 F8
Coven...62 D3
Coveney...66 F4
Covenham St
  Bartholomew...91 E7
Covenham St Mary 91 E7
Coventry...51 B8
Coverack...3 E6
Coverham...101 F6
Covesea...152 A1
Covington Cambs..53 B8
  S Lanark...120 F2
Cowan Bridge...93 B6
Cow Ark...93 E6
Cowbeech...18 D3
Cowbit...66 C2
Cowbridge Lincs...79 E6
  Som...21 E8
Cowbridge
  = Y Bont-Faen...21 B8
Cowdale...75 B7
Cowden...29 E5
Cowdenbeath...128 E3
Cowdenburn...120 D5
Cowers Lane...76 E3
Cowes...15 E5
Cowesby...102 F2
Cowfold...17 B6
Cowgill...100 F2
Cowie Aberds...141 F7
  Stirling...127 F7
Cowley Devon...10 E4
  Glos...37 C6
  London...40 F3
  Oxon...39 D5
Cowleymoor...10 C4
Cowling Lancs...86 C3
  N Yorks...94 E2
  N Yorks...101 F7
Cowlinge...55 D8
Cowpe...87 B6
Cowpen...117 F8
Cowpen Bewley...102 B2
Cowplain...15 C7
Cowshill...109 E8
Cowslip Green...23 C6
Cowstrandburn...128 E2
Cowthorpe...95 D7
Coxbank...74 E3
Coxbench...76 E3
Cox Common...69 F6
Coxford Norf...80 E4
  Soton...14 C4
Cox Green...29 E8
Coxheath...29 D8
Coxhill...31 E6
Coxhoe...111 F6
Coxley...23 E7
Cox Moor...76 D5
Coxwold...95 B8
Coychurch...21 B8
Coylton...112 B4
Coylumbridge...138 C5
Coynach...140 D3
Coynachie...152 E4
Coytrahen...34 F2
Crabadon...7 D5
Crabbs Cross...50 C5
Crabtree...17 B6
Crackenthorpe...100 B1
Crackington Haven..8 E3
Crackley...51 B7
Cracklybank...61 C7
Crackpot...100 E4
Cracoe...94 C2
Craddock...11 C5
Cradhlastadh...154 D5
Cradley...50 E2
Cradley Heath...62 F3
Crafthole...5 D8
Craggan...139 B6
Craggie Highld...151 H10
  Highld...157 H11
Cragg Vale...87 B8
Craghead...110 D5
Crai...34 B2
Craibstone...152 C4
Craichie...135 E5
Craig Dumfries...106 B3
  Dumfries...106 C3
  Highld...150 G3
Craiganour Lodge.132 D3
Craig Castle...140 B3
Craig-cefn-parc...33 D7
Craigdam...153 E8
Craigdarroch
  Dumfries...113 E7
  Highld...150 F7
Craigdhu...150 G7
Craigearn...141 C6
Craigellachie...152 D2
Craigencross...104 C4
Craigend Perth...128 B3
  Stirling...127 F6
Craigendoran...145 E11
Craigends...118 C4
Craigens Argyll...142 B3
  E Ayrs...113 C5
Craighat...126 F3
Craighead...129 D8
Craighlaw Mains..105 C7
Craighouse...144 G4
Craigie Aberds...141 C8
  Dundee...134 F4
  Perth...128 B3
  Perth...133 E8
  S Ayrs...118 F4
Craigielaw...121 B7
Craiglockhart...120 B5
Craigmalloch...112 E4
Craigmaud...153 C8

Craigmillar 121 B5
Craigmore 145 G10
Craignant 73 F6
Craigneuk
N Lanark 119 C7
N Lanark 119 D7
Craignure 124 B3
Craigo 135 C6
Craigow 128 D2
Craig Penllyn 21 B8
Craigrothie 129 C5
Craigroy 151 F14
Craigruie 126 B3
Craigston Castle 153 C7
Craigton Aberdeen 141 D7
Angus 134 D3
Angus 135 F5
Highld 151 B9
Craigtown 157 D11
Craig-y-don 83 C7
Craig-y-nos 34 C2
Craik 115 D6
Crail 129 D8
Crailing 116 B2
Crailinghall 116 B2
Craiselound 89 E8
Crakehill 95 B7
Crakemarsh 75 F7
Crambe 96 C3
Cramlington 111 B5
Cramond 120 B4
Cramond Bridge 120 B4
Cranage 74 C4
Cranberry 74 F5
Cranborne 13 C8
Cranbourne 27 B7
Cranbrook Devon 10 E5
Kent 18 B4
Cranbrook
Common 18 B4
Crane Moor 88 D4
Crane's Corner 68 C2
Cranfield 53 E7
Cranford 28 B2
Cranford St
Andrew 53 B7
Cranford St John 53 B7
Cranham Glos 37 C5
London 42 F1
Crank 86 E3
Crank Wood 86 D4
Cranleigh 27 F8
Cranley 57 B5
Cranmer Green 56 B4
Cranmore 14 F4
Cranna 153 C6
Crannich 147 G8
Crannoch 152 C4
Cranoe 64 E4
Cransford 57 C7
Cranshaws 122 C2
Cranstal 84 B4
Crantock 4 C2
Cranwell 78 E3
Cranwich 67 E7
Cranworth 68 D2
Craobh Haven 124 E3
Crapstone 6 C3
Crarae 125 F5
Crask Inn 157 G8
Craskins 140 D4
Crask of Aigas 150 G7
Craster 117 C8
Craswall 48 F4
Cratfield 57 B7
Crathes 141 E6
Crathie Aberds 139 E8
Highld 137 E8
Crathorne 102 D2
Craven Arms 60 F4
Crawcrook 110 C4
Crawford Lancs 86 D2
S Lanark 114 B2
Crawfordjohn 113 B8
Crawick 113 C7
Crawley Hants 26 F2
Oxon 38 C3
W Sus 28 F3
Crawley Down 28 F4
Crawleyside 110 E2
Crawshawbooth 87 B6
Crawton 135 B8
Cray N Yorks 94 B2
Perth 133 C8
Crayford 29 B6
Crayke 95 B8
Crays Hill 42 E3
Cray's Pond 39 F6
Creacombe 10 C3
Creagan 130 E3
Creag Ghoraidh 148 D2
Creaguaineach
Lodge 131 C7
Creaksea 43 E5
Creaton 52 B5
Creca 108 B2
Credenhill 49 E6
Crediton 10 D3
Creebridge 105 C8
Creech Heathfield 11 B7
Creech St Michael 11 B7
Creed 3 B8
Creekmouth 41 F7
Creeting Bottoms 56 D5
Creeting St Mary 56 D4
Creeton 65 B7
Creetown 105 D8
Creggans 125 E6
Cregneash 84 F1
Creg-ny-Baa 84 D3
Cregrina 48 D3
Creich 128 B5
Creigiau 34 F4
Cremyll 6 D2
Creslow 39 B8
Cressage 61 D5
Cressbrook 75 B8
Cresselly 32 D1
Cressing 42 B3
Cresswell
Northumb 117 E8
Staffs 75 F6
Cresswell Quay 32 D1
Creswell 76 B5
Cretingham 57 C6
Cretshengan 144 G6
Crewe Ches E 74 D4
Ches W 73 D8
Crewgreen 60 C3
Crewkerne 12 D2
Crianlarich 126 B2
Cribyn 46 D4
Criccieth 71 D5
Crich 76 D3
Crichie 153 D9
Crichton 121 C6
Crick Mon 36 E1
W Nhants 52 B3
Crickadarn 48 E2
Cricket Malherbie 11 C8
Cricket St Thomas 11 D8
Crickheath 60 B2
Crickhowell 35 C6
Cricklade 37 E8
Cricklewood 41 F5
Cridling Stubbs 89 B6
Crieff 127 B7
Criggion 60 C2
Crigglestone 88 C4
Crimond 153 C10
Crimonmogate 153 C10
Crimplesham 67 D6
Crinan 144 D6
Cringleford 68 D4
Cringles 94 E3
Crinow 32 C2
Cripplesease 2 C4
Cripplestyle 13 C8
Cripp's Corner 18 C4
Croasdale 98 C2
Crockenhill 29 C6
Crockernwell 10 E2
Crockerton 24 E3
Crocketford or
Ninemile Bar 106 B5
Crockey Hill 96 E2
Crockham Hill 28 D5
Crockleford Heath 43 B6
Crockness 159 J4
Crock Street 11 C8
Croeserw 34 E2
Croes-goch 44 B3
Croes-lan 46 E2
Croesor 71 C7
Croesyceiliog
Carms 33 C5
Torf 35 E7
Croes-y-mwyalch 35 E7
Croesywaun 82 F5
Croft Leics 64 E2
Lincs 79 C8
Pembs 45 E3
Warr 86 E4
Croftamie 126 F3
Croftmalloch 120 C2
Crofton Wilts 25 C7
W Yorks 88 C4
Croft-on-Tees 101 D7
Crofts of
Benachielt 158 G3
Crofts of Haddo 153 E8
Crofts of
Inverthernie 153 D7
Crofts of Meikle
Ardo 153 D8
Crofty 33 E6
Croggan 124 C3
Croglin 109 E5
Croich 150 B7
Crois Dughaill 148 F2
Cromarty 151 E10
Cromblet 153 E7
Cromdale 139 B6
Cromer Herts 41 B5
Norf 81 C8
Cromford 76 D2
Cromhall 36 E3
Cromhall Common 36 F3
Cromor 155 E9
Cromra 137 E8
Cromwell 77 C7
Cronberry 113 B6
Crondall 27 E5
Cronk-y-Voddy 84 D3
Cronton 86 F2
Crook Durham 110 F4
W&F 99 E6
Crookedholm 118 F4
Crookes 88 F4
Crookham
Northumb 122 F5
W Berks 26 C3
Crookham Village 27 D5
Crookhaugh 114 B4
Crookhouse 116 B3
Crooklands 99 F7
Crook of Devon 128 D2
Cropredy 52 E2
Cropston 64 C2
Cropthorne 50 E4
Cropton 103 F5
Cropwell Bishop 77 F6
Cropwell Butler 77 F6
Cros 155 A10
Crosbost 155 E8
Crosby Cumb 107 F7
IoM 84 E3
N Lincs 90 C2
Crosby Garrett 100 D2
Crosby
Ravensworth 99 C8
Crosby Villa 107 F7
Croscombe 23 E7
Cross 23 D6
Crossaig 143 C9
Crossal 149 E9
Crossapol 146 G2
Cross Ash 35 C8
Cross-at-Hand 29 E8
Crossburn 119 B8
Crossbush 16 D4
Crosscanonby 107 F7
Crossdale Street 81 D8
Crossens 85 C4
Crossflatts 94 E4
Crossford Fife 128 F2
S Lanark 119 E8
Crossgate 66 B2
Crossgatehall 121 C6
Crossgates Fife 128 F3
Powys 48 C2
Crossgill 93 C5
Cross Green Devon 9 F5
Suff 56 D2
Suff 56 D3
Warks 51 D8
Cross-hands 32 B2
Cross Hands Carms 33 C6
Cross Hands *continued*
Pembs 32 C1
Crosshill E Ayrs 112 B4
Fife 128 E3
S Ayrs 112 D3
Cross Hill 76 E4
Crosshouse 118 F3
Cross Houses 60 D5
Crossings 108 B5
Cross in Hand
E Sus 18 C2
Leics 64 F2
Cross Inn Ceredig 46 C4
Ceredig 46 D2
Rhondda 34 F4
Crosskeys 35 E6
Cross Keys 29 D6
Crosskirk 157 B13
Cross Lane Head 61 E7
Crosslanes 60 C3
Cross Lanes Corn 3 D5
N Yorks 95 C8
Wrex 73 E7
Crossle 118 C4
Crosslee 115 C6
Crossmichael 106 C4
Crossmoor 92 F4
Cross Oak 35 B5
Cross of
Jackston 153 E7
Cross o'th'hands 76 E2
Crossroads Aberds 141 E6
E Ayrs 118 F4
Cross Street 57 B5
Crossway Hereford 49 F8
Mon 35 C8
Powys 48 D2
Crossway Green 50 C3
Crossways 13 F5
Crosswell 45 F3
Crosswood 47 B5
Crosthwaite 99 E6
Croston 86 C2
Crostwick 69 C5
Crostwight 69 B6
Crothair 154 D6
Crouch 29 D7
Croucheston 13 B8
Crouch Hill 12 C5
Crouch House
Green 28 E5
Croughton 52 F3
Crovie 153 B8
Crowan 2 C5
Crowborough 18 B2
Crowcombe 22 F3
Crowdecote 75 C8
Crowden 87 E8
Crow Edge 88 D2
Crowell 39 E7
Crowfield Suff 56 D5
W Nhants 52 E4
Crow Hill 36 B3
Crowhurst E Sus 18 D4
Sur 28 E4
Crowhurst Lane
End 28 E4
Crowland 66 C2
Crowlas 2 C4
Crowle N Lincs 89 C8
Worcs 50 D4
Crowmarsh
Gifford 39 F6
Crown Corner 57 B6
Crownhill 6 D2
Crownland 56 C4
Crownthorpe 68 D3
Crowntown 2 C5
Crows-an-wra 2 D2
Crowshill 68 D2
Crowsnest 60 D3
Crowthorne 27 C6
Crowton 74 B2
Croxall 63 C5
Croxby 91 E5
Croxdale 111 F5
Croxden 75 F7
Croxley Green 40 E3
Croxton Cambs 54 C3
N Lincs 90 C4
Norf 67 F8
Staffs 74 F4
Croxtonbank 74 F4
Croxton Kerrial 64 B5
Croy Highld 151 G10
N Lanark 119 B7
Croyde 20 F3
Croydon Cambs 54 E4
London 28 C4
Crubenmore
Lodge 138 E2
Cruckmeole 60 D4
Cruckton 60 C4
Cruden Bay 153 E10
Crudgington 61 C6
Crudwell 37 E6
Crug 48 B3
Crugmeer 4 B4
Crugybar 47 F5
Crulabhig 154 D6
Crumlin = Crymlyn 35 E6
Crumpsall 87 D6
Crundale Kent 30 E4
Pembs 44 D4
Crwys Morchard 10 C3
Crux Easton 26 D2
Crwbin 33 C5
Crya 159 H4
Cryers Hill 40 E1
Crymlyn 83 D6
Crymlyn = Crumlin 35 E6
Crymych 45 F3
Crynant 34 D1
Crynfryn 46 C4
Cuaig 149 C12
Cuan 124 D3
Cubbington 51 C8
Cubeck 100 F4
Cubert 4 D2
Cubley 88 D3
Cubley Common 75 F8
Cublington Bucks 39 B8
Hereford 49 F6
Cuckfield 17 B7
Cucklington 13 B5
Cuckney 77 B5
Cuckoo Hill 89 E8
Cuddesdon 39 D6
Cuddington Bucks 39 C7
Cuddington *continued*
Ches W 74 B3
Cuddington Heath 73 E8
Cuddy Hill 92 F4
Cudham 28 D5
Cudliptown 6 B3
Cudworth Som 11 C8
S Yorks 88 D4
Cuffley 41 D6
Cuiashader 155 B10
Cuidhir 148 H1
Cuidhtinis 154 J5
Culbo 151 E9
Culbokie 151 F9
Culburnie 150 G7
Culcabock 151 G9
Culcairn 151 E9
Culcharry 151 F11
Culcheth 86 E4
Culdrain 152 E5
Culduie 149 D12
Culford 56 B2
Culgaith 99 B8
Culham 39 E5
Culkein 156 F3
Culkein Drumbeg 156 F4
Culkerton 37 E6
Cullachie 139 B5
Cullen 152 B5
Cullercoats 111 B6
Cullicudden 151 E9
Cullingworth 94 F3
Cullipool 124 D3
Cullivoe 160 C7
Culloch 127 C6
Culloden 151 G10
Cullompton 10 D5
Culmaily 151 B11
Culmazie 105 D7
Culmington 60 F4
Culmstock 11 C6
Culnacraig 156 J3
Culnaknock 149 B10
Culpho 57 E6
Culrain 151 B8
Culross 127 F8
Culroy 112 C3
Culsh Aberds 140 E2
Aberds 153 D8
Culshabbin 105 D7
Culswick 160 J4
Cultercullen 141 B8
Cults Aberdeen 141 D7
Aberds 152 E5
Dumfries 105 E8
Culverstone Green 29 C7
Culverthorpe 78 E3
Culworth 52 E3
Culzie Lodge 151 D8
Cumbernauld 119 B7
Cumbernauld
Village 119 B7
Cumberworth 79 B8
Cuminestown 153 C8
Cumlewick 160 L6
Cummersdale 108 D3
Cummertrees 107 C8
Cummingston 152 B1
Cumnock 113 B5
Cumnor 38 D4
Cumrew 108 D5
Cumwhinton 108 D4
Cumwhitton 108 D5
Cundall 95 B7
Cunninghamhead 118 E3
Cunnister 160 D7
Cupar 129 C5
Cupar Muir 129 C5
Cupernham 14 B4
Curbar 76 B2
Curbridge Hants 15 C6
Oxon 38 D3
Curdridge 15 C6
Curdworth 63 E5
Curland 11 C7
Curlew Green 57 C7
Currarie 112 E1
Curridge 26 B2
Currie 120 C4
Curry Mallet 11 B8
Curry Rivel 11 B8
Curtisden Green 29 E8
Curtisknowle 6 D5
Cury 3 D5
Cushnie 153 B7
Cushuish 22 F3
Cusop 48 E4
Cutcloy 105 F8
Cutcombe 21 F8
Cutgate 87 C6
Cutiau 58 C3
Cutlers Green 55 F6
Cutnall Green 50 C3
Cutsdean 51 F5
Cutthorpe 76 B3
Cutts 160 K6
Cuxham 39 E6
Cuxton 29 C8
Cuxwold 91 D5
Cwm Bl Gwent 35 D5
Denb 72 B4
Swansea 33 E7
Cwmafan 34 E1
Cwmaman 34 E4
Cwmann 46 E4
Cwmavon 35 D6
Cwmbach Carms 32 B3
Carms 33 D5
Powys 48 D2
Powys 48 F3
Cwmbâch 34 D4
Cwmbelan 59 F6
Cwmbran
= Cwmbrân 35 E6
Cwmbrwyno 58 F4
Cwm-byr 46 F5
Cwmcarn 35 E6
Cwmcarvan 36 D1
Cwm-Cewydd 59 C5
Cwm-cou 45 E4
Cwmcych 45 F4
Cwmdare 34 D3
Cwmderwen 59 D6
Cwmdu Carms 46 F5
Powys 35 B5
Swansea 33 E7
Cwmduad 46 F2
Cwm-Dulais 33 D7
Cwmdwr 47 F6
Cwmfelin Bridgend 34 F2
M Tydf 34 D4
Cwmfelin Boeth 32 C2
Cwm-felin-fach 35 E5
Cwmfelin Mynach 32 B3
Cwmffrwd 33 C5
Cwm Ffrwd-oer 35 D6
Cwmgiedd 34 C1
Cwmgors 33 C8
Cwmgwili 33 C6
Cwmgwrach 34 D2
Cwm-hesgen 71 E8
Cwmhiraeth 46 F2
Cwm-hwnt 34 D3
Cwmifor 33 B7
Cwm Irfon 47 E7
Cwmisfael 33 C5
Cwm-Llinau 58 D5
Cwmllynfell 33 C8
Cwm-mawr 33 C6
Cwmorgan 45 F4
Cwm-parc 34 E3
Cwmpengraig 46 F2
Cwm Penmachno 71 C8
Cwmrhos 35 B5
Cwmsychpant 46 E3
Cwmtillery 35 D6
Cwm-twrch Isaf 34 C1
Cwm-twrch Uchaf 34 C1
Cwmwysg 34 B2
Cwm-y-glo Carms 33 C6
Gwyn 82 E5
Cwmyoy 35 B6
Cwmystwyth 47 B6
Cwrt 58 D3
Cwrt-newydd 46 E3
Cwrt-y-cadno 47 E5
Cwrt-y-gollen 35 C6
Cydweli
= Kidwelly 33 D5
Cyffordd Llandudno
= Llandudno
Junction 83 D7
Cyffylliog 72 D4
Cyfronydd 59 D8
Cymer 34 E2
Cyncoed 35 F6
Cynghordy 47 E7
Cynheidre 33 D5
Cynwyd 72 E4
Cynwyl Elfed 32 B4
Cywarch 59 C5

D

Dacre N Yorks 94 C4
W&F 99 B6
Dacre Banks 94 C4
Daddry Shield 109 F8
Dadford 52 F4
Dadlington 63 E8
Dafarn Faig 71 C5
Dafen 33 D6
Daffy Green 68 D2
Dagenham 41 F7
Daglingworth 37 D6
Dagnall 40 C2
Dail Beag 154 C7
Dail bho Dheas 155 A9
Dail bho Thuath 155 A9
Daill 142 B4
Dailly 112 D2
Dail Mor 154 C7
Dairsie or
Osnaburgh 129 C6
Daisy Hill 86 D4
Dalabrog 148 F2
Dalavich 125 D5
Dalbeattie 106 C5
Dalblair 113 C6
Dalbog 135 B5
Dalbury 76 F2
Dalby IoM 84 E2
N Yorks 96 B2
Dalchalloch 132 C4
Dalchalm 157 J12
Dalchenna 125 E6
Dalchirach 152 E1
Dalchork 157 H8
Dalchreichart 137 C5
Dalchruin 127 C6
Dalderby 78 C5
Dale 44 E3
Dale Abbey 76 F4
Dale Head 99 C6
Dalelia 147 E10
Dale of Walls 160 H3
Daless 151 H11
Dalfaber 138 C5
Dalgarven 118 E2
Dalgety Bay 128 F3
Dalginross 127 B6
Dalguise 133 E6
Dalhalvaig 157 D11
Dalham 55 C8
Dalinlongart 145 E10
Dalkeith 121 C6
Dallam 86 E3
Dallas 151 F14
Dalleagles 113 C5
Dallinghoo 57 D6
Dallington E Sus 18 D3
W Nhants 52 C5
Dallow 94 B4
Dalmadilly 141 C6
Dalmally 125 C7
Dalmarnock 119 C6
Dalmary 126 E4
Dalmellington 112 D4
Dalmeny 120 B4
Dalmigavie 138 C3
Dalmigavie
Lodge 138 B3
Dalmore 151 E9
Dalmuir 118 B4
Dalnabreck 147 E9
Dalnacardoch
Lodge 132 B4
Dalnacroich 150 F6
Dalnaglar Castle 133 C8
Dalnahaitnach 138 B4
Dalnaspidal
Lodge 132 B3
Dalnavaid 133 C7
Dalnavie 151 D9
Dalnawillan
Lodge 157 E13
Dalness 131 D5
Dalnessie 157 H9
Dalqueich 128 D2
Dalreavoch 157 J10
Dalry 118 E2
Dalrymple 112 C3
Dalserf 119 D8
Dalston 108 D3
Dalswinton 114 F2
Dalton Dumfries 107 B8
Lancs 86 D2
Northumb 110 B4
Northumb 110 D2
N Yorks 95 B7
N Yorks 101 D6
S Yorks 89 E5
Dalton-in-Furness 92 B2
Dalton-le-Dale 111 E7
Dalton-on-Tees 101 D7
Dalton Piercy 111 F7
Dalveich 126 B5
Dalvina Lodge 157 E9
Dalwhinnie 138 F2
Dalwood 11 D7
Dalwyne 112 E3
Damerham 14 C2
Damgate 69 D7
Dam Green 68 F3
Damnaglaur 104 F5
Damside 120 E4
Dam Side 92 E4
Danbury 42 D3
Danby 103 D5
Danby Wiske 101 E8
Dandaleith 152 D2
Danderhall 121 C6
Danebridge 75 C6
Dane End 41 B6
Danehill 17 B8
Danemoor Green 68 D3
Danesford 61 E7
Daneshill 26 D4
Dangerous Corner 86 C3
Danskine 121 C8
Darcy Lever 86 D5
Darenth 29 B6
Daresbury 86 F3
Darfield 88 D5
Darfoulds 77 B5
Dargate 30 C4
Dargavel Renfs 118 B3
Darite 5 C7
Darlaston 62 E3
Darley 94 D5
Darley Bridge 76 C2
Darley Head 94 D4
Darlingscott 51 E7
Darlington 101 C7
Darliston 74 F2
Darlton 77 B7
Darnall 88 F4
Darnick 121 F8
Darowen 58 D5
Darra 153 D7
Darracott 20 F3
Darras Hall 110 B4
Darrington 89 B5
Darsham 57 C8
Dartford 29 B6
Dartford Crossing 29 B6
Dartington 7 C5
Dartmeet 6 B4
Dartmouth 7 D6
Darton 88 D4
Darvel 119 F5
Darwell Hole 18 D3
Darwen 86 B4
Datchet 27 B7
Datchworth 41 C5
Datchworth Green 41 C5
Daubhill 86 D5
Daugh of
Kinermony 152 D2
Dauntsey 37 F6
Dava 151 H13
Davenham 74 B3
Davenport Green 74 B5
Daventry 52 C3
Davidson's Mains 120 B5
Davidstow 8 F3
David's Well 48 B2
Davington 115 D5
Daviot Aberds 141 B6
Highld 151 H10
Davoch of
Grange 152 C4
Davyhulme 87 E5
Dawley 61 D6
Dawlish 7 B7
Dawlish Warren 7 B7
Dawn 83 D8
Daws Heath 42 F4
Daw's House 8 F5
Dawsmere 79 F7
Dayhills 75 F6
Daylesford 38 B2
Ddôl-Cownwy 59 C7
Ddrydwy 82 D3
Deadwater 116 E2
Deaf Hill 111 F6
Deal 31 D7
Deal Hall 43 E6
Dean Cumb 98 B2
Devon 6 C5
Devon 20 E4
Dorset 13 C7
Hants 15 C6
Som 23 E8
Deanburnhaugh 115 C6
Deane Gtr Man 86 D4
Hants 26 D3
Deanich Lodge 150 C6
Deanland 13 C7
Dean Prior 6 C5
Dean Row 87 F6
Deans 120 C3
Deanscales 98 B2
Deanshanger 53 F5
Deanston 127 D6
Dearham 107 F7
Debach 57 D6
Debden Essex 41 E7
Essex 55 F6
Debden Cross 55 F6
Debenham 57 C5
Dechmont 120 B3
Deddington 52 F2
Dedham 56 F4
Dedham Heath 56 F4
Deebank 141 E5
Deene 65 E6
Deenethorpe 65 E6
Deepcar 88 E3
Deepcut 27 D7
Deepdale 100 F2
Deeping Gate 65 D8
Deeping St James 65 D8
Deeping St
Nicholas 66 C2
Deerhill 152 C4
Deerhurst 37 B5
Deerness 159 H6
Defford 50 E4
Defynnog 34 B3
Deganwy 83 D7
Deighton N Yorks 102 D1
W Yorks 88 C2
York 96 E2
Deiniolen 83 E5
Delabole 8 F2
Delamere 74 C2
Delfrigs 141 B8
Delliefure 151 H13
Dell Lodge 139 C6
Delnabo 139 C7
Delnadamph 139 D8
Delph 87 D7
Delves 110 E4
Delvine 133 E8
Dembleby 78 F3
Denaby Main 89 E5
Denbigh
= Dinbych 72 C4
Denbury 7 C6
Denby 76 E3
Denby Dale 88 D3
Denchworth 38 E3
Dendron 92 B2
Denel End 53 F8
Denend 152 E6
Denford 53 B7
Dengie 43 D5
Denham Bucks 40 F3
Suff 55 C8
Suff 57 B5
Denham Street 57 B5
Denhead Aberds 153 C9
Fife 129 C6
Denhead of
Arbilot 135 E5
Denhead of Gray 134 F3
Denholm 115 C8
Denholme 94 F3
Denholme Clough 94 F3
Denio 70 D4
Denmead 15 C7
Denmore 141 C8
Denmoss 153 D6
Dennington 57 C6
Denny 127 F7
Dennyloanhead 127 F7
Denny Lodge 14 D4
Denshaw 87 C7
Denside 141 E7
Densole 31 E6
Denston 55 D8
Denstone 75 E8
Dent 100 F2
Denton Cambs 65 F8
Darl 101 C7
E Sus 17 D8
Gtr Man 87 E7
Kent 31 E6
Lincs 77 F8
Norf 69 F5
N Yorks 94 E4
Oxon 39 D5
W Nhants 53 D6
Denton's Green 86 E2
Denver 67 D6
Denwick 117 C8
Deopham 68 D3
Deopham Green 68 E3
Depden 55 D8
Depden Green 55 D8
Deptford London 28 B4
Wilts 24 F5
Derby 76 F3
Derbyhaven 84 F2
Dereham 68 C2
Deri 35 D5
Derril 8 D5
Derringstone 31 E6
Derrington 62 B2
Derriton 8 D5
Derryguaig 146 H7
Derry Hill 24 B4
Derrythorpe 90 D2
Dersingham 80 D2
Dervaig 146 F7
Derwen 72 D4
Derwenlas 58 E4
Desborough 64 F5
Desford 63 D8
Detchant 123 F6
Detling 29 D8
Deuddwr 60 C2
Devauden 36 E1
Devil's Bridge 47 B6
Devizes 24 C5
Devol 118 B3
Devonport 6 D2
Devonside 127 E8
Devoran 3 C6
Dewar 121 E6
Dewlish 13 E5
Dewsbury 88 B3
Dewsbury Moor 88 B3
Dewshall Court 49 F6
Dhoon 84 D4
Dhoor 84 C4
Dhowin 84 B4
Dial Post 17 C5
Dibden 14 D5
Dibden Purlieu 14 D5
Dickleburgh 68 F4
Didbrook 51 F5
Didcot 39 F5
Diddington 54 C2
Diddlebury 60 F5
Didley 49 F6
Didling 16 C2
Didmarton 37 F5
Didsbury 87 E6
Didworthy 6 C4
Digby 78 D3
Digg 149 B9
Diggle 87 D8
Digmoor 86 D2
Digswell Park 41 C5
Dihewyd 46 D3
Dilham 69 B6
Dilhorne 75 E6
Dillarburn 119 E8
Dillington 54 C2
Dilston 110 C2
Dilton Marsh 24 E3
Dilwyn 49 D6
Dinas Carms 45 F4
Gwyn 70 D3
Dinas Cross 45 F2
Dinas Dinlle 82 F4
Dinas-Mawddwy 59 C5
Dinas Powys 22 B3
Dinbych
= Denbigh 72 C4
Dinbych-y-Pysgod
= Tenby 32 D2
Dinder 23 E7
Dinedor 49 F7
Dingestow 36 C1
Dingle 85 F4
Dingleden 18 B5
Dingley 64 F4
Dingwall 151 F8
Dinlabyre 115 E8
Dinmael 72 E4
Dinnet 140 E3
Dinnington Som 12 C2
S Yorks 89 F6
T&W 110 B5
Dinorwic 83 E5
Dinton Bucks 39 C7
Wilts 24 F5
Dinwoodie Mains 114 E4
Dinworthy 8 C5
Dippen 143 F11
Dippenhall 27 E6
Dipple Moray 152 C3
S Ayrs 112 D2
Diptford 6 D5
Dipton 110 D4
Dirdhu 139 B6
Dirleton 129 F7
Dirt Pot 109 E8
Discoed 48 C4
Diseworth 63 B8
Dishes 159 F7
Dishforth 95 B6
Disley 87 F7
Diss 56 B5
Disserth 48 D2
Distington 98 B2
Ditchampton 25 F5
Ditcheat 23 F8
Ditchingham 69 E6
Ditchling 17 C7
Ditherington 60 C5
Dittisham 7 D6
Ditton Halton 86 F2
Kent 29 D8
Ditton Green 55 D7
Ditton Priors 61 F6
Divach 137 B7
Divlyn 47 F6
Dixton Glos 50 F4
Mon 36 C2
Dobcross 87 D7
Dobwalls 5 C7
Doccombe 10 F2
Dochfour House 151 H9
Dochgarroch 151 G9
Docking 80 D3
Docklow 49 D7
Dockray 99 B5
Dockroyd 94 F3
Doc Penfro
= Pembroke Dock 44 E4
Dodburn 115 D7
Doddinghurst 42 E1
Doddington Cambs 66 E3
Kent 30 D3
Lincs 78 B2
Northumb 123 F5
Shrops 49 B8
Doddiscombsleigh 10 F3
Dodford
W Nhants 52 C4
Worcs 50 B4
Dodington 24 A2
Dodleston 73 C7
Dods Leigh 75 F7
Dodworth 88 D4
Doe Green 86 F3
Doe Lea 76 C4
Dogdyke 78 D5
Dogmersfield 27 D5
Dogridge 37 F7
Dogsthorpe 65 D8
Dog Village 10 E4
Dolanog 59 C7
Dolau Powys 48 C3
Rhondda 34 F3
Dolbenmaen 71 C6
Dolfach 59 D6
Dolfor 59 F8
Dol-fôr 58 D5
Dolgarrog 83 E7
Dolgellau 58 C4
Dolgran 46 F3
Dolhendre 72 F2
Doll 157 J11
Dollar 127 E8
Dolley Green 48 C4
Dollwen 58 F3
Dolphin 73 B5
Dolphinholme 92 D5
Dolphinton 120 E4
Dolton 9 C7
Dolwen Conwy 83 D8
Powys 59 D6
Dolwyd 83 D8
Dolwyddelan 83 F7
Dôl-y-Bont 58 F3
Dol-y-cannau 48 E4
Dolyhir 48 D4
Doncaster 89 D6
Dones Green 74 B3
Donhead St
Andrew 13 B7
Donhead St Mary 13 B7
Donibristle 128 F3
Donington 78 F5
Donington on Bain 91 F6
Donington South
Ing 78 F5
Donisthorpe 63 C7
Donkey Town 27 C7
Donnington Glos 38 B1
Hereford 50 F2
Shrops 61 D5
Telford 61 C7
W Berks 26 C3
W Sus 16 D2
Donnington Wood 61 C7
Donyatt 11 C8
Doonfoot 112 C3
Dorback Lodge 139 C6
Dorchester Dorset 12 E4
Oxon 39 E5
Dordon 63 D6
Dore 88 F4
Dores 151 H8
Dorking 28 E2
Dormansland 28 E5
Dormanstown 102 B3
Dormington 49 E7
Dormston 50 D4
Dornal 105 B6
Dorney 27 B7
Dornie 149 F13
Dornoch 151 C10
Dornock 108 C2
Dorrery 158 E2
Dorridge 51 B6
Dorrington Lincs 78 D3
Shrops 60 D4
Dorsington 51 E6
Dorstone 48 E5
Dorton 39 C6
Dorusduain 136 B2
Dosthill 63 E6
Dottery 12 E2
Doublebois 5 C6
Dougarie 143 E9
Doughton 37 E5
Douglas IoM 84 E3
S Lanark 119 F8
Douglas & Angus 134 F4
Douglastown 134 E4
Douglas Water 119 F8
Douglas West 119 F8
Doulting 23 E8
Dounby 159 F3
Doune Highld 156 J7
Stirling 127 D6
Doune Park 153 B7
Douneside 140 D3
Dounie 151 B8
Dounreay 157 C12
Dousland 6 C3
Dovaston 60 B3
Dove Holes 75 B7
Dovenby 107 F7
Dover 31 E7
Dovercourt 57 F6
Doverdale 50 C3
Doveridge 75 F8
Doversgreen 28 E3
Dowally 133 E7
Dowbridge 92 F4
Dowdeswell 37 C6
Dowlais 34 D4
Dowland 9 C7
Dowlish Wake 11 C8
Down Ampney 37 E8
Downcraig
Ferry 145 H10
Downderry 5 D8
Downe 28 C5
Downend IoW 15 F6
S Glos 23 B8
W Berks 26 B2
Downfield 134 F3
Downgate 5 B8
Downham Essex 42 E3
Lancs 93 E7
Northumb 122 F4
Downham Market 67 D6
Down Hatherley 37 B5
Downhead 23 E8
Downhill Perth 133 F7
T&W 111 D6
Downholland
Cross 85 D4
Downholme 101 E6
Downies 141 E8
Downley 39 E8
Down St Mary 10 D2
Downside Som 23 E8
Sur 28 D2
Down Thomas 6 D3
Downton Hants 14 E3
Wilts 14 B2
Downton on the
Rock 49 B6
Dowsby 65 B8
Dowsdale 66 C2
Dowthwaitehead 99 B5
Doxey 62 B3
Doxford 117 B7
Doxford Park 111 D6
Doynton 24 B2
Draffan 119 E7
Dragonby 90 C3
Drakeland Corner 6 D3
Drakemyre 118 D2
Drake's Broughton 50 E4
Drakes Cross 51 B5
Drakewalls 6 B2
Draughton N Yorks 94 D3
W Nhants 53 B5
Drax 89 B7
Draycote 52 B2
Draycott Derbys 76 F4
Glos 51 F6
Som 23 D6
Draycott in the
Clay 63 B5
Draycott in the
Moors 75 E6
Drayford 10 C2
Drayton Leics 64 E5
Lincs 78 F5
Norf 68 C4
Oxon 38 E4
Oxon 52 E2
Ptsmth 15 D7
Som 12 B2
Worcs 50 B4
Drayton Bassett 63 D5
Drayton
Beauchamp 40 C2
Drayton Parslow 39 B8

Drayton St
  Leonard 39 E5
Drebley 94 D3
Dreemskerry 84 C4
Dreenhill 44 D4
Drefach Carms 33 C6
  Carms 46 F2
Dre-fach Carms 33 C7
  Ceredig 46 E4
Drefelin 46 F2
Dreghorn 118 F3
Drellingore 31 E6
Drem 121 B8
Dresden 75 E6
Dreumasdal 148 E2
Drewsteignton 10 E2
Driby 79 B6
Driffield E Yorks 97 D6
  Glos 37 E7
Drigg 98 E2
Drighlington 88 B3
Drimnin 147 F8
Drimpton 12 D2
Drimsynie 125 E7
Drinisiadar 154 H6
Drinkstone 56 C3
Drinkstone Green 56 C3
Drishaig 125 D7
Drissaig 124 D5
Drochil 120 E4
Droitwich 50 C3
Droitwich Spa 50 C3
Droman 156 D4
Dron 128 C3
Dronfield 76 B3
Dronfield
  Woodhouse 76 B3
Drongan 112 C4
Dronley 134 F3
Droxford 15 C7
Droylsden 87 E7
Druid 72 E4
Druidston 44 D3
Druimarbin 130 B4
Druimavuic 130 E4
Druimdrishaig 144 F6
Druimindarroch 147 C9
Druimyeon More . 143 C7
Drum Argyll 145 F8
  Perth 128 D2
Drumbeg 156 F4
Drumblade 152 D5
Drumblair 153 D6
Drumbuie
  Dumfries 113 F5
  Highld 149 E12
Drumburgh 108 D2
Drumburn 107 C6
Drumchapel 118 B5
Drumchardine 151 G8
Drumchork 155 J13
Drumclog 119 F6
Drumderfit 151 F9
Drumeldrie 129 D6
Drumelzier 120 F4
Drumfearn 149 G11
Drumgask 138 E2
Drumgley 134 D4
Drumguish 138 E3
Drumin 152 E1
Drumlasie 140 D5
Drumlemble 143 G7
Drumligair 141 C8
Drumlithie 141 F6
Drummoddie 105 E7
Drummond 151 E9
Drummore 104 F5
Drummuir 152 D3
Drummuir Castle . 152 D3
Drumnadrochit . 137 B8
Drumnagorrach . 152 C5
Drumoak 141 E6
Drumpark 107 A5
Drumphail 105 C6
Drumrash 106 B3
Drumrunie 156 J4
Drums 141 B8
Drumsallie 130 B3
Drumstinchall 107 C5
Drumsturdy 134 F4
Drumtochty
  Castle 135 B6
Drumtroddan 105 E7
Drumuie 149 D9
Drumuillie 138 B5
Drumvaich 127 C5
Drumwhindle 153 E6
Drunkendub 135 E6
Drury 73 C6
Drury Square 68 C2
Drybeck 100 C1
Drybridge Moray . 152 B4
  N Ayrs 118 F3
Drybrook 36 C3
Dryburgh 121 F8
Dry Doddington . . 77 E8
Dry Drayton 54 C4
Dryhope 115 B5
Drylaw 120 B5
Drym 2 C5
Drymen 126 F3
Drymuir 153 D9
Drynoch 149 E9
Dryslwyn 33 B6
Dryton 61 D5
Dubford 153 B8
Dubton 135 D5
Duchally 156 H6
Duck Corner 57 E7
Duckington 73 D8
Ducklington 38 D3
Duckmanton 76 B4
Duck's Cross 54 D2
Duddenhoe End 55 F5
Duddingston 121 B5
Duddington 65 D6
Duddleswell 17 B8
Duddon 74 C2
Duddon Bridge 98 F4
Dudleston 73 F7
Dudleston Heath . . . 73 F7
Dudley T&W 111 B5
  W Mid 62 E3
Dudley Port 62 E3

Duffield 76 E3
Duffryn Neath 34 E2
  Newport 35 F6
Dufftown 152 E3
Duffus 152 B1
Dufton 100 B1
Duggleby 96 C4
Duirinish 149 E12
Duisdalemore . 149 G12
Duisky 130 B4
Dukestown 35 C5
Dukinfield 87 E7
Dulas 82 C4
Dulcote 23 E7
Dulford 11 D5
Dull 133 E5
Dullatur 119 B7
Dullingham 55 D7
Dulnain Bridge . 139 B5
Duloe Bedford 54 C2
  Corn 5 D7
Dulsie 151 G12
Dulverton 10 B4
Dulwich 28 B4
Dumbarton 118 B3
Dumbleton 50 F5
Dumcrieff 114 D4
Dumfries 107 B6
Dumgoyne 126 F4
Dummer 26 E3
Dumpford 16 B2
Dumpton 31 C7
Dun 135 D6
Dunain House 151 G9
Dunalastair 132 D4
Dunan Argyll 145 F10
  Highld 149 F10
Dunball 22 E5
Dunbar 122 B2
Dunbeath 158 H3
Dunbeg 124 B4
Dunblane 127 D6
Dunbog 128 C4
Duncanston 151 F8
Duncanstone 140 B4
Dun
  Charlabhaigh . . . 154 C6
Dunchurch 52 B2
Duncote 52 D4
Duncow 114 F2
Duncraggan 126 D4
Duncrievie 128 D3
Duncton 16 C3
Dundas House 159 K5
Dundee 134 F4
Dundeugh 113 F5
Dundon 23 F6
Dundonald 118 F3
Dundonnell 150 C3
Dundonnell Hotel 150 C3
Dundonnell
  House 150 C4
Dundraw 108 E2
Dundreggan 137 C6
Dundreggan
  Lodge 137 C6
Dundrennan 106 E4
Dundry 23 C7
Dunecht 141 D6
Dunfermline 128 F2
Dunfield 37 E8
Dunford Bridge 88 D2
Dungworth 88 F3
Dunham 77 B8
Dunham-on-the-
  Hill 73 B8
Dunhampton 50 C3
Dunham Town 86 F5
Dunholme 78 B3
Dunino 129 C7
Dunipace 127 F7
Dunira 127 B6
Dunkeld 133 E7
Dunkerton 24 D2
Dunkeswell 11 D6
Dunkeswick 95 E6
Dunkirk Kent 30 D4
  Norf 81 E8
Dunk's Green 29 D7
Dunlappie 135 C5
Dunley Hants 26 D2
  Worcs 50 C2
Dunlichity Lodge . 151 H9
Dunlop 118 E4
Dunmaglass
  Lodge 137 B8
Dunmore Argyll . 144 G6
  Falk 127 F7
Dunnet 158 C4
Dunnichen 135 E5
Dunninald 135 D7
Dunning 128 C2
Dunnington
  E Yorks 97 D7
  Warks 51 D5
  York 96 D2
Dunnockshaw 87 B6
Dunollie 124 B4
Dunoon 145 F10
Dunragit 105 D5
Dunrostan 144 E6
Duns 122 D3
Dunsby 65 B8
Dunscore 113 F8
Dunscroft 89 D7
Dunsdale 102 C4
Dunsden Green 26 B5
Dunsfold 27 F8
Dunsford 10 F3
Dunshalt 128 C4
Dunshillock 153 D9
Dunsley 103 C6
Dunsmore 40 D1
Dunsop Bridge 93 D6
Dunstable 40 B3
Dunstall 63 B5
Dunstall Common . 50 E3
Dunstall Green 55 C8
Dunstan 117 C8
Dunstan Steads . . 117 B8
Dunster 21 E8
Duns Tew 38 B4
Dunston Lincs 78 C3
  Norf 68 D5
  Staffs 62 C3
  T&W 110 C5
Dunsville 89 D7
Dunswell 97 F6

Dunsyre 120 E3
Dunterton 5 B8
Duntisbourne
  Abbots 37 D6
Duntisbourne Leer 37 D6
Duntisbourne
  Rouse 37 D6
Duntish 12 D4
Duntocher 118 B4
Dunton Bucks 39 B8
  C Beds 54 E3
  Norf 80 D4
Dunton Bassett . . 64 E2
Dunton Green 29 D6
Dunton Wayletts . . 42 E2
Duntulm 149 A9
Dunure 112 C2
Dunvant 33 E6
Dunvegan 148 D7
Dunwich 57 B8
Dunwood 75 D6
Dupplin Castle 128 C2
Durdar 108 D4
Durgates 18 B3
Durham 111 E5
Durisdeer 113 D8
Durisdeermill 113 D8
Durkar 88 C4
Durleigh 22 F4
Durley Hants 15 C6
  Wilts 25 C7
Durlow Hill 42 B2
Durnamuck 150 B3
Durness 156 C7
Durno 141 B6
Duror 130 D3
Durran Argyll 125 E5
  Highld 158 C3
Durrington Wilts . . . 25 E6
  W Sus 16 D5
Dursley 36 E4
Durston 11 B7
Durweston 13 D6
Dury 160 G6
Duston 52 C5
Duthil 138 B5
Dutlas 48 B4
Duton Hill 42 B2
Dutson 8 F5
Dutton 74 B2
Duxford Cambs 55 E5
  Oxon 38 E3
Dwygyfylchi 83 D7
Dwyran 82 E4
Dyce 141 C7
Dye House 110 D2
Dyffryn Bridgend . . . 34 E2
  Carms 32 B4
  Pembs 44 B4
Dyffryn Ardudwy . . 71 E6
Dyffryn Castell 58 F4
Dyffryn Ceidrych . . 33 B8
Dyffryn Cellwen . . . 34 D2
Dyke Lincs 65 B8
  Moray 151 F13
Dykehead Angus . . 134 C3
  N Lanark 119 D8
  Stirling 126 E4
Dykelands 135 C7
Dykends 134 D2
Dykeside 153 D7
Dykesmains 118 E2
Dylife 59 E5
Dymchurch 19 C7
Dymock 50 F2
Dyrham 24 B2
Dysart 128 E5
Dyserth 72 B4

E

Eadar Dha
  Fhadhail 154 D5
Eagland Hill 92 E4
Eagle 77 C8
Eagle Barnsdale . . 77 C8
Eagle Moor 77 C8
Eaglescliffe 102 C2
Eaglesfield Cumb . . 98 B2
  Dumfries 108 B2
Eaglesham 119 D5
Eaglethorpe 65 E7
Eairy 84 E2
Eakley Lanes 53 D6
Eakring 77 C6
Ealand 89 C8
Ealing 40 F4
Eals 109 D6
Eamont Bridge 99 B7
Earby 94 E2
Earcroft 86 B4
Eardington 61 E7
Eardisland 49 D6
Eardisley 48 E5
Eardiston Shrops . . 60 B3
  Worcs 49 C8
Earith 54 B4
Earl Sterndale 75 C7
Earle 117 B5
Earley 27 B5
Earlham 68 D5
Earlish 149 B8
Earls Barton 53 C6
Earls Colne 42 B4
Earl's Croome 50 E3
Earlsdon 51 B8
Earlsferry 129 E6
Earlsfield 78 F2
Earlsford 153 E8
Earl's Green 56 C4
Earlsheaton 88 B3
Earl Shilton 63 E8
Earlsmill 151 F12
Earl Soham 57 C6
Earl Sterndale 75 C7
Earlston Borders . . 121 F8
  E Ayrs 118 F4
Earl Stonham 56 D5
Earlswood Mon . . . 36 E1
  Sur 28 E3
  Warks 51 B6
Earnley 16 E2
Earsairidh 148 J2
Earsdon 111 B6
Earsham 69 F6
Earswick 96 D2
Eartham 16 D3
Easby N Yorks 101 D6
  N Yorks 102 D3
Easdale 124 D3

Easebourne 16 B2
Easenhall 52 B2
Eashing 27 E7
Easington Bucks . . 39 C6
  Durham 111 E7
  E Yorks 91 C7
  Northumb 123 F7
  Oxon 39 E6
  Oxon 52 F2
  Redcar 103 C5
Easington
  Colliery 111 E7
Easington Lane 111 E6
Easingwold 95 C8
Easole Street 31 D6
Eassie 134 E3
East Aberthaw 22 C2
East Adderbury 52 F2
East Allington 7 E5
East Anstey 10 B3
East Appleton 101 E7
East Ardsley 88 B4
East Ashling 16 D2
East Auchronie . . . 141 D7
East Ayton 103 F7
East Bank 35 D6
East Barkwith 91 F5
East Barming 29 D8
East Barnby 103 C6
East Barnet 41 E5
East Barns 122 B3
East Barsham 80 D5
East Beckham 81 D7
East Bedfont 27 B8
East Bergholt 56 F4
East Bilney 68 C2
East Blatchington . 22 C6
East Boldre 14 D4
Eastbourne 18 F3
East Brent 22 D5
Eastbridge 57 C8
East Bridgford 77 E6
East Buckland 21 F5
East Budleigh 11 F5
Eastburn 94 E3
East Burrafirth . . . 160 H5
East Burton 13 F6
Eastbury London . . 40 E3
  W Berks 25 B8
East Butsfield 110 E4
East Butterwick . . . 90 D2
Eastby 94 D3
East Cairnbeg 135 B7
East Calder 120 C3
East Carleton 68 D4
East Carlton
  N Nhants 64 F5
  W Yorks 94 E5
East Chaldon 13 F5
East Challow 38 F3
East Chiltington . . 17 C7
East Chinnock 12 C2
East Chisenbury . . 25 D6
Eastchurch 30 B3
East Clandon 27 D8
East Claydon 39 B7
East Clyne 157 J12
East Coker 12 C3
East Combe 22 F3
East Common 96 F2
East Compton 23 E8
Eastcote London . . 40 F4
  W Mid 51 B6
  W Nhants 52 D4
Eastcott Corn 8 C4
  Wilts 25 D5
East Cottingwith . . 96 E3
Eastcourt Wilts 25 C7
  Wilts 37 E6
East Cowes 15 E6
East Cowick 89 B7
East Cowton 101 D8
East Cramlington . 111 B5
East Cranmore 23 E8
East Creech 13 F7
East Croachy 138 B2
East Croftmore . . . 139 C5
East Curthwaite . . . 108 E3
East Dean E Sus . . . 18 F2
  Hants 14 B3
  W Sus 16 C3
East Down 20 E5
East Drayton 77 B7
East Ella 90 B4
East End Dorset . . . 13 E7
  E Yorks 91 B6
  Hants 14 E4
  Hants 26 C2
  Herts 41 B7
  Kent 18 B5
  N Som 23 B6
  Oxon 38 C3
Easter Ardross . . . 151 D9
Easter Balmoral . . 139 E8
Easter Boleskine . . 137 B8
Easter Compton . . . 36 A2
Easter Cringate . . . 127 F6
Easter Davoch 140 D3
Easter Earshaig . . 114 D3
Easter Fearn 151 C9
Easter
  Galcantray . . . 151 G11
Eastergate 16 D3
Easterhouse 119 C6
Easter Howgate . . . 120 C5
Easter Howlaws . . 122 E3
Easter Kinkell 151 F8
Easter Lednathie . 134 C3
Easter Moniack . . 151 G8
Eastern Green 63 F6
Easter Ord 141 D7
Easter Quarff 160 K6
Easter Rhynd 128 C3
Easter Row 127 D6
Easter Silverford . 153 B7
Easter Skeld 160 J5
Easterton 24 D5
Eastertown 22 D5
Eastertown of
  Auchleuchries . 153 E10
Easter Whyntie . . 152 B6
East Farleigh 29 D8
East Farndon 64 F4
East Ferry 90 E2
Eastfield N Lanark . 119 C8
  N Yorks 103 F8

Eastfield Hall 117 D8
East Fortune 121 B8
East Garston 25 B8
Eastgate Durham . 110 F2
  Norf 81 E7
East Ginge 38 F4
East Goscote 64 C3
East Grafton 25 C7
East Grimstead 14 B3
East Grinstead 28 F4
East Guldeford 19 C6
East Haddon 52 C4
East Hagbourne . . . 39 F5
East Halton 90 C5
East Ham 41 F7
Eastham 85 F4
Eastham Ferry 85 F4
Easthampstead 27 C6
East Hanney 38 E4
East Hanningfield . . 42 D3
East Hardwick 89 C5
East Harling 68 F2
East Harlsey 102 E2
East Harnham 14 B2
East Harptree 23 D7
East Hartford 111 B5
East Harting 15 C8
East Hatley 54 D3
East Hauxwell 101 E6
East Haven 135 F5
East Heckington . . 78 E4
East Hedleyhope . . 110 E4
East Hendred 38 F4
East Herrington . . 111 D6
East Heslerton 96 B5
East Hoathly 18 D2
Easthope 61 E5
Easthorpe Essex . . 43 B5
  Leics 77 F8
  Notts 77 D7
East Horrington . . 23 E7
East Horsley 27 D8
East Horton 123 F6
Easthouses 121 C6
East Huntspill 22 E5
East Hyde 40 C4
East Ilkerton 21 E6
East Ilsley 38 F4
East Keal 79 C6
East Kennett 25 C6
East Keswick 95 E6
East Kilbride 119 D6
East Kirkby 79 C6
East Knapton 96 B4
East Knighton 13 F6
East Knoyle 24 F3
East Kyloe 123 F6
East Lambrook 12 C2
East Lamington . . 151 D10
East Langdon 31 E7
East Langton 64 E4
East Langwell 157 J10
East Lavant 16 D2
East Lavington 16 C3
East Layton 101 D6
Eastleach Martin . . 38 D2
Eastleach Turville . 38 D1
East Leake 64 B2
East Learmouth . . 122 F4
Eastleigh Devon . . . 9 B6
  Hants 14 C5
East Leigh 9 D8
East Lexham 67 C8
East Lilburn 117 B6
Eastling 30 D3
East Linton 121 B8
East Liss 15 B8
East Looe 5 D7
East Lound 89 E8
East Lulworth 13 F6
East Lutton 96 C5
East Lydford 23 F7
East Mains 141 E5
East Malling 29 D8
East March 134 F4
East Marden 16 C2
East Markham 77 B7
East Marton 94 D2
East Meon 15 B7
East Mere 10 C4
East Mersea 43 C6
East Mey 158 C5
East Molesey 28 C2
Eastmoor Derbys . . 76 B3
  Norf 67 D7
East Morden 13 E7
East Morton 94 E3
East Ness 96 B2
East Newton 97 F8
Eastney 15 E7
Eastnor 50 F2
East Norton 64 D4
East Nynehead 11 B6
East Oakley 26 D3
Eastoft 90 C2
East Ogwell 7 B6
Eastoke 15 E8
Easton Cambs 54 B2
  Cumb 108 B4
  Cumb 108 C2
  Devon 10 F2
  Dorset 12 G4
  Hants 26 F3
  Lincs 65 B6
  Norf 68 C4
  Som 23 E7
  Suff 57 D6
  Wilts 24 B3
Easton Grey 37 F5
Easton-in-
  Gordano 23 B7
Eastongate 126 E2
Easton Maudit 53 D6
Easton on the Hill . . 65 D7
Easton Royal 25 C7
East Orchard 13 C6
East Ord 123 D5
East Panson 9 E5
Eastpark 107 C7
East Peckham 29 E7
East Pennard 23 F7
East Perry 54 C2
East Portlemouth . . 6 F5
East Prawle 7 F5
East Preston 16 D4
East Putford 9 C5

East Quantoxhead . . 22 E3
East Rainton 111 E6
East Ravendale 91 E6
East Raynham 80 E4
East Rhidorroch
  Lodge 150 B5
East Rigton 95 E6
East Rounton 102 D2
East Row 103 C6
East Rudham 80 E4
East Runton 81 C7
East Ruston 69 B6
Eastry 31 D7
East Saltoun 121 C7
East Sleekburn . . 117 F8
East Somerton 69 C7
East Stockwith 89 E8
East Stoke Dorset . 13 F6
  Notts 77 E7
East Stour 13 B6
East Stourmouth . . 31 C6
East Stowford 9 B8
East Stratton 26 F3
East Studdal 31 E7
East Suisnish 149 E10
East Taphouse 5 C6
East-the-Water 9 B6
East Thirston 117 E7
East Tilbury 29 B7
East Tisted 26 F5
East Torrington . . 90 F5
East Tuddenham . . 68 C3
East Tytherley 14 B3
East Tytherton 24 B4
East Village 10 D3
East Wall 60 E5
East Walton 67 C7
East Wellow 14 B4
East Wemyss 128 E5
East Whitburn 120 C2
Eastwick Herts 41 C7
  Shetland 160 F5
East Williamston . . 32 D1
East Winch 67 C6
East Winterslow . . 25 F7
East Wittering 15 E8
East Witton 101 F6
Eastwood Notts . . . 76 E4
  Southend 42 F4
  W Yorks 87 B7
East Woodburn . . 116 F5
East Woodhay 26 C2
East Worldham 26 F5
East Worlington . . 10 C2
East Worthing 17 D5
Easthorpe 51 C8
Eaton Ches E 75 C5
  Ches W 74 C2
  Leics 64 B4
  Norf 68 D5
  Notts 77 B7
  Oxon 38 D4
  Shrops 60 F3
  Shrops 60 F5
Eaton Bishop 49 F6
Eaton Bray 40 B2
Eaton Constantine . 61 D5
Eaton Green 40 B2
Eaton Hastings 38 E2
Eaton on Tern 61 B6
Eaton Socon 54 D2
Eavestone 94 C5
Ebberston 103 F6
Ebbesbourne
  Wake 13 B7
Ebbw Vale
  =Glyn Ebwy . . . 35 D5
Ebchester 110 D4
Ebford 10 F4
Ebley 37 D5
Ebnal 73 E8
Ebrington 51 E6
Ecchinswell 26 D2
Ecclaw 122 C3
Ecclefechan 107 B8
Eccles Borders . . 122 E3
  Gtr Man 87 E5
  Kent 29 C8
Ecclesall 88 F4
Ecclesfield 88 E4
Ecclesgreig 135 C7
Eccleshall 62 B2
Eccleshill 94 F4
Ecclesmachan . . . 120 B3
Eccles on Sea 69 B7
Eccles Road 68 E3
Eccleston Ches W . 73 C8
  Lancs 86 C3
  Mers 86 E2
Eccleston Park 86 E2
Eccup 95 E5
Echt 141 D6
Eckford 116 B3
Eckington Derbys . . 76 B4
  Worcs 50 E4
Ecton 53 C6
Edale 88 F2
Edburton 17 C6
Edderside 107 E7
Edderton 151 C10
Eddistone 8 B4
Eddleston 120 E5
Edenbridge 28 E5
Edenfield 87 C5
Edenhall 109 F5
Edenham 65 B7
Eden Park 28 C4
Edensor 76 C2
Edentaggart 126 E2
Edenthorpe 89 D7
Edentown 108 D3
Ederline 124 E4
Edern 70 D3
Edgarley 23 F7
Edgbaston 62 F4
Edgcote 52 E2
Edgcott Bucks 39 B6
  Som 21 F7
Edge 60 D3
Edgebolton 61 B5
Edge End 36 C2
Edgefield 81 D6
Edgefield Street . . 81 D6
Edge Green 73 D8

Edge Hill 85 F4
Edgeside 87 B6
Edgeworth 37 D6
Edgmond 61 C7
Edgmond Marsh 61 B7
Edgton 60 F3
Edgware 40 E4
Edgworth 86 C5
Edinample 126 B4
Edinbane 149 C8
Edinburgh 121 B5
Edingale 63 C6
Edingight House . . 152 C5
Edingley 77 D6
Edingthorpe 69 A6
Edingthorpe
  Green 69 A6
Edington Som 23 F5
  Wilts 24 D4
Edintore 152 D4
Edithmead 22 E5
Edith Weston 65 D6
Edlesborough 40 C2
Edlingham 117 D7
Edlington 78 B5
Edmondsham 13 C8
Edmondsley 110 E5
Edmondthorpe 65 C5
Edmonstone 159 F6
Edmonton 41 E6
Edmundbyers 110 D3
Ednam 122 F3
Ednaston 76 E2
Edradynate 133 D5
Edrom 122 D4
Edstaston 74 F2
Edstone 51 C6
Edvin Loach 49 D8
Edwalton 77 F5
Edwardstone 56 E3
Edwinsford 46 F5
Edwinstowe 77 C6
Edworth 54 E3
Edwyn Ralph 49 D8
Edzell 135 C5
Efail Isaf 34 F4
Efailnewydd 70 D4
Efailwen 32 B2
Efenechtyd 72 D5
Effingham 28 D2
Effirth 160 H5
Efford 10 D3
Egdon 50 D4
Egerton Gtr Man . . 86 C5
  Kent 30 E3
Egerton Forstal . . . 30 E2
Eggborough 89 B6
Eggbuckland 6 D3
Eggington 40 B2
Egginton 63 B6
Egglescliffe 102 C2
Eggleston 100 B4
Egham 27 B8
Egleton 65 D5
Eglingham 117 C7
Egloshayle 4 B5
Egloskerry 8 F4
Eglwysbach 83 D8
Eglwys-Brewis 22 C2
Eglwys Cross 73 E8
Eglwys Fach 58 E3
Eglwyswen 45 F3
Eglwyswrw 45 F3
Egmanton 77 C7
Egremont Cumb . . . 98 C2
  Mers 85 E4
Egton 103 D6
Egton Bridge 103 D6
Eight Ash Green . . 43 B5
Eignaig 130 E1
Eil 138 C4
Eilanreach 149 G13
Eileanach Lodge . . 151 E8
Eilean Darach 150 C4
Einacleite 154 E6
Eisgean 155 F8
Eisingrug 71 D7
Elan Village 47 C8
Elberton 36 F3
Elburton 6 D3
Elcho 128 B3
Elcombe 37 F8
Eldernell 66 E3
Eldersfield 50 F3
Eldersli 118 C4
Eldon 101 B7
Eldroth 93 C7
Eldwick 94 E4
Elfhowe 99 E6
Elford Northumb . . 123 F7
  Staffs 63 C5
Elgin 152 B2
Elgol 149 G10
Elham 31 E5
Elie 129 D6
Elim 82 C3
Eling 14 C4
Elishader 149 B10
Elishaw 116 E4
Elkesley 77 B6
Elkstone 37 C6
Ellan 138 B4
Elland 88 B2
Ellary 144 F6
Ellastone 75 E8
Ellemford 122 C3
Ellenbrook 84 E2
Ellenhall 62 B2
Ellen's Green 27 F8
Ellerbeck 102 E2
Ellerburn 103 F6
Ellerby 103 C5
Ellerdine Heath . . . 61 B6
Ellerhayes 10 D4
Elleric 130 E4
Ellerker 90 B3
Ellerton E Yorks . . . 96 F3
  Shrops 61 B7

Ellisfield 26 E4
Ellistown 63 C8
Ellon 153 E9
Ellonby 108 F4
Ellough 69 F7
Elloughton 90 B3
Ellwood 36 D2
Elm 66 D4
Elmbridge 50 C4
Elmdon Essex 55 F5
  W Mid 63 F5
Elmdon Heath 63 F5
Elmers End 28 C4
Elmesthorpe 63 E8
Elmfield 15 E7
Elm Hill 13 B6
Elmhurst 62 C5
Elmley Castle 50 E4
Elmley Lovett 50 C3
Elmore 36 C4
Elmore Back 36 C4
Elm Park 41 F8
Elmscott 8 B4
Elmsett 56 E4
Elmstead Market . . 43 B6
Elmsted 30 E5
Elmstone 31 C6
Elmstone
  Hardwicke . . . 37 B6
Elmswell E Yorks . . 97 D5
  Suff 56 C3
Elmton 76 B5
Elphin 156 H5
Elphinstone 121 B6
Elrick 141 D7
Elrig 105 E7
Elsdon 117 E5
Elsecar 88 E4
Elsenham 41 B8
Elsfield 39 C5
Elsham 90 C4
Elsing 68 C3
Elslack 94 E2
Elson 73 F7
Elsrickle 120 E3
Elstead 27 E7
Elsted 16 C2
Elsthorpe 65 B7
Elston Notts 77 E7
  Wilts 25 E5
Elstone 9 C8
Elstow 53 E8
Elstree 40 E4
Elstronwick 97 F8
Elswick 92 F4
Elsworth 54 C4
Elterwater 99 D5
Eltham 28 B5
Eltisley 54 D3
Elton Cambs 65 E7
  Ches W 73 B8
  Derbys 76 C2
  Glos 36 C4
  Hereford 49 B6
  Notts 77 F7
  Stockton 102 C2
Elton Green 73 B8
Elvanfoot 114 C2
Elvaston 76 F4
Elveden 56 B2
Elvingston 121 B7
Elvington Kent 31 D6
  York 96 E2
Elwick Hrtlpl 111 F7
  Northumb 123 F7
Elworth 74 C4
Elworthy 22 F2
Ely Cambs 66 F5
  Cardiff 22 B3
Emberton 53 E6
Embleton Cumb . . 107 F8
  Northumb 117 B8
Embo 151 B11
Emborough 23 D8
Embo Street 151 B11
Embsay 94 D3
Emersons Green . . 23 B8
Emery Down 14 D3
Emley 88 C3
Emmbrook 27 C5
Emmer Green 26 B5
Emmington 39 D7
Emneth 66 D4
Emneth Hungate . . 66 D5
Empingham 65 D6
Empshott 27 F5
Emstrey 60 D5
Emsworth 15 D8
Enborne 26 C2
Enchmarsh 60 E5
Enderby 64 E2
Endmoor 99 F7
Endon 75 D6
Endon Bank 75 D6
Enfield 41 E6
Enfield Wash 41 E6
Enford 25 D6
Engamoor 160 H4
Engine Common . . . 36 F3
Englefield 26 B4
Englefield Green . . 27 B7
Englesea-brook . . . 74 D4
English Bicknor . . . 36 C2
Englishcombe 24 C2
English Frankton . . 60 B4
Enham Alamein . . . 25 E8
Enmore 22 F4
Ennerdale Bridge . . 98 C2
Enoch 113 D8
Enochdhu 133 C7
Ensay 146 G6
Ensbury 13 E8
Ensdon 60 C4
Ensis 9 B7
Enstone 38 B3
Enterkinfoot 113 D8
Enterpen 102 D2
Eolaigearraidh . . 148 H2
Eorabus 146 J6
Eòropaidh 155 A10
Epperstone 77 E6
Epping 41 D7
Epping Green
  Essex 41 D7
  Herts 41 D5
Epping Upland . . . 41 D7
Eppleby 101 C6

Epplesworth 97 F6
Epsom 28 C3
Epwell 51 E8
Epworth 89 D8
Epworth Turbary . . 89 D8
Erbistock 73 E7
Erbusaig 149 F12
Erchless Castle . . 150 G7
Erddig 73 E7
Erdington 62 E5
Eredine 125 E5
Eriboll 156 D7
Ericstane 114 C3
Eridge Green 18 B2
Erines 145 F7
Eriswell 55 B8
Erith 29 B6
Erlestoke 24 D4
Ermine 78 B2
Ermington 6 D4
Erpingham 81 D7
Errogie 137 B8
Errol 128 B4
Erskine 118 B4
Erskine Bridge . . . 118 B4
Ervie 104 C4
Erwarton 57 F6
Erwood 48 E2
Eryholme 101 D8
Eryrys 73 D6
Escomb 101 B6
Escrick 96 E2
Esgairdawe 46 E4
Esgairgeiliog 58 D4
Esh 110 E4
Esher 28 C2
Esholt 94 E4
Eshott 117 E8
Eshton 94 D2
Esh Winning 110 E4
Eskadale 150 H7
Eskbank 121 C6
Eskdale Green 98 D3
Eskdalemuir 115 E5
Eske 97 E6
Eskham 91 E7
Esprick 92 F4
Essendine 65 C7
Essendon 41 D5
Essich 151 H9
Essington 62 D3
Eston 102 C3
Eswick 160 H6
Etal 122 F5
Etchilhampton . . . 24 C5
Etchingham 18 C4
Etchinghill Kent . . . 19 B8
  Staffs 62 C4
Ethie Castle 135 E6
Ethie Mains 135 E6
Etling Green 68 C3
Eton 27 B7
Eton Wick 27 B7
Etteridge 138 E2
Ettersgill 100 B3
Ettingshall 62 E3
Ettington 51 E7
Etton E Yorks 97 E5
  Pboro 65 D8
Ettrick 115 C5
Ettrickbridge 115 B6
Ettrickhill 115 C5
Etwall 76 F2
Euston 56 B2
Euximoor Drove . . 66 E4
Euxton 86 C3
Evanstan 151 E9
Evanton 151 E9
Evedon 78 E3
Evelix 151 B10
Evenjobb 48 C4
Evenley 52 F3
Evenlode 38 B2
Evenwood 101 B6
Evenwood Gate . . 101 B6
Everbay 159 F7
Evercreech 23 F8
Everdon 52 D3
Everingham 96 E4
Everleigh 25 D7
Everley 103 F7
Eversholt 53 F7
Evershot 12 D3
Eversley 27 C5
Eversley Cross . . . 27 C5
Everthorpe 96 F5
Everton C Beds . . . 54 D3
  Hants 14 E3
  Mers 85 E4
  Notts 89 E7
Evertown 108 B3
Evesbatch 49 E8
Evesham 50 E5
Evington 64 D3
Ewden Village 88 E3
Ewell 28 C3
Ewell Minnis 31 E6
Ewelme 39 E6
Ewen 37 E7
Ewenny 21 B8
Ewerby 78 E4
Ewerby Thorpe . . . 78 E4
Ewes 115 E6
Ewesley 117 E7
Ewhurst 27 E8
Ewhurst Green
  E Sus 18 C4
  Sur 27 F8
Ewloe 73 C7
Ewloe Green 73 C6
Ewood 86 B4
Eworthy 9 E6
Ewshot 27 E6
Ewyas Harold 35 B7
Exbourne 9 D8
Exbury 14 E5
Exebridge 10 B4
Exelby 101 F7
Exeter 10 E4
Exford 21 F7
Exhall 51 D6
Exley Head 94 F3
Exminster 10 F4
Exmouth 10 F5
Exnaboe 160 M5
Exning 55 C7
Exton Devon 10 F4
  Hants 15 B7

Exton *continued*
Rutland 65 C6
Som 21 F8
Exwick. 10 E4
Eyam. 76 B2
Eydon. 52 D3
Eye *Hereford* . . .49 C6
Pboro. 66 D2
Suff. 56 B5
Eye Green. 66 D2
Eyemouth. 122 C5
Eyeworth. 54 E3
Eyhorne Street . . .30 D2
Eyke. 57 D7
Eynesbury. 54 D2
Eynort 149 F8
Eynsford 29 C6
Eynsham. 38 D4
Eype. 12 E2
Eyre *Highld*. 149 C9
Highld. 149 E10
Eythorne. 31 E6
Eyton *Hereford* . . .49 C6
Shrops. 60 F3
Wrex 73 E7
Eyton upon the Weald
Moors 61 C6

F

Faceby. 102 D2
Facit. 87 C6
Faddiley. 74 D2
Fadmoor. 102 F4
Faerdre. 33 D7
Failand. 23 B7
Failford. 112 B4
Failsworth. 87 D6
Fain. 150 D4
Fairbourne. 58 C3
Fairburn. 89 B5
Fairfield *Derbys* . .75 B7
Stockton. 102 C2
Worcs. 50 B4
Worcs. 50 E5
Fairford. 38 D1
Fair Green. 67 C6
Fairhaven. 85 B4
Fair Hill. 108 F5
Fairlie. 118 D2
Fairlight. 19 D5
Fairlight Cove. 19 D5
Fairmile. 11 E5
Fairmilehead. 120 C5
Fairoak. 74 F4
Fair Oak. 15 C5
Fair Oak Green. . . .26 C4
Fairseat. 29 C7
Fairstead *Essex* . . .42 C3
Norf. 67 C6
Fairwarp. 17 B8
Fairy Cottage 84 D4
Fairy Cross 9 B6
Fakenham. 80 E5
Fakenham Magna. .56 B3
Fala. 121 C7
Fala Dam. 121 C7
Falahill. 121 D6
Falcon. 49 F2
Faldingworth. 90 F4
Falfield. 36 E3
Falkenham. 57 F6
Falkirk. 119 B8
Falkland. 128 D4
Falla. 116 C3
Fallgate. 76 C3
Fallin. 127 E7
Fallowfield. 87 E2
Fallsidehill. 122 E2
Falmer. 17 D7
Falmouth. 3 C7
Falsgrave. 103 F8
Falstone. 116 F3
Fanagmore. 156 E4
Fangdale Beck. . .102 E3
Fangfoss. 96 D3
Fankerton. 127 F6
Fanmore. 150 E5
Fannich Lodge. . .150 E5
Fans. 122 E2
Far Bank. 89 C7
Far Bletchley. 53 F6
Farcet. 66 E2
Far Cotton. 53 D5
Farden. 49 B7
Fareham. 15 D6
Farewell. 62 C4
Far Forest. 50 B2
Farforth. 79 B6
Faringdon. 38 E2
Farington. 86 B3
Farlam. 109 D5
Farlary. 157 J10
Far Laund. 76 E3
Farleigh *N Som* . . .23 C6
Sur. 28 C4
Farleigh
Hungerford. . . .24 D3
Farleigh Wallop. .26 E4
Farlesthorpe. 79 B7
Farleton *Lancs* . . .93 C5
W&F. 99 F7
Farley *Shrops* 60 D3
Staffs. 75 E7
Wilts. 14 B3
Farley Green. 27 E8
Farley Hill *Luton* . .40 B3
Wokingham. 26 C5
Farleys End. 36 C4
Farlington. 96 C2
Farlow. 61 F6
Farmborough. 23 C8
Farmcote *Glos* . . .37 B7
Shrops. 61 E7
Farmington. 37 C8
Farmoor. 38 D4
Farmtown. 152 C6
Farnborough *Hants* 27 D6
London. 28 C5
Warks. 52 E2
W Berks. 38 F4
Farnborough
Green. 27 D6
Farncombe. 27 E7
Farndish. 53 C7
Farndon *Ches W* . .73 D8
Notts. 77 D7
Farnell. 135 D6

Farnham *Dorset* . .13 C7
Essex. 41 B7
N Yorks. 95 C6
Suff. 57 C7
Sur. 27 E7
Farnham Common 40 F2
Farnham Green. . .41 B7
Farnham Royal. . .40 F2
Farnhill. 94 E3
Farningham. 29 C6
Farnley *N Yorks* . .94 E5
W Yorks. 95 F5
Farnley Tyas. 88 C2
Farnsfield. 77 D6
Farnworth *Gtr Man* .86 D5
Halton. 86 F3
Farr *Highld*. 138 D4
Highld. 151 H9
Highld. 157 C10
Farr House. 151 H9
Farrington. 10 E5
Farrington Gurney. 23 D8
Far Sawrey. 99 E5
Farsley. 94 F5
Farthinghoe. 52 F3
Farthingloe. 31 E6
Farthingstone. . . .52 D4
Fartown. 88 C2
Farway. 11 E6
Fasag. 149 C13
Fascadale. 147 D8
Faslane Port 145 E11
Fasnacloich. 130 E4
Fasnakyle Ho. . . .137 B6
Fassfern. 130 B4
Fatfield. 111 D6
Fattahead. 153 C6
Faugh. 108 D5
Fauldhouse. 120 C2
Faulkbourne. 42 C3
Faulkland. 24 D2
Fauls. 74 F2
Faversham. 30 C4
Favillar. 152 E2
Fawdington. 95 B7
Fawfieldhead. 75 C7
Fawkham Green. . .29 C6
Fawler. 38 C3
Fawley *Bucks* 39 F7
Hants. 15 D5
W Berks. 38 F3
Fawley Chapel 36 B2
Fawley Waterside .15 D5
Faxfleet. 90 B2
Faygate. 28 F3
Fazakerley. 85 E4
Fazeley. 63 D6
Fearby. 101 F6
Fearn. 151 D11
Fearnan. 132 E4
Fearnbeg. 149 C12
Fearnhead. 86 E4
Fearn Lodge 151 C9
Fearnmore. 149 B12
Fearn Station. . . .151 D11
Featherstone *Staffs* .88 B5
W Yorks. 88 B5
Featherwood. 116 D4
Feckenham. 50 C5
Feering. 42 B4
Feetham. 100 E4
Feizor. 93 C7
Felbridge. 28 F4
Felbrigg. 81 D8
Felcourt. 28 E4
Felden. 40 D3
Felin-Crai. 34 B2
Felindre *Carms* . . .33 B6
Carms. 33 B8
Carms. 46 F2
Carms. 47 F5
Ceredig. 46 D4
Powys. 59 F8
Swansea. 33 D7
Felindre Farchog .45 F3
Felinfach *Ceredig*. .46 D4
Powys. 48 F2
Felinfoel. 33 D6
Felingwmisaf. 33 B6
Felingwmuchaf. . .33 B6
Felinwynt. 45 D4
Felixkirk. 102 F2
Felixstowe. 57 F6
Felixstowe Ferry. .57 F7
Felkington. 122 F5
Felkirk. 88 C4
Felling. 111 C5
Fell Side. 108 F3
Felmersham. 53 D7
Felmingham. 81 E8
Felpham. 16 E3
Felsham. 56 D3
Felsted. 42 B2
Feltham. 28 B2
Felthorpe. 68 C4
Felton *Hereford* . . .49 E7
Northumb. 117 D7
N Som. 23 C7
Felton Butler. . . .60 C3
Feltwell. 67 E7
Fenay Bridge. 88 C2
Fence. 93 F8
Fence Houses. . . .111 D6
Fen Ditton. 55 C5
Fen Drayton. 54 C4
Fen End. 51 B7
Fengate *Norf* 81 E7
Pboro. 66 E2
Fenham. 123 E6
Fenhouses. 79 E5
Feniscliffe. 86 B4
Feniscowles. 86 B4
Feniton. 11 E6
Fenlake. 53 E8
Fenny Bentley. . . .75 D8
Fenny Bridges. . . .11 E6
Fenny Compton. . .52 D2
Fenny Drayton. . . .63 E7
Fenny Stratford. .53 F6
Fenrother. 117 E7
Fen Side. 79 D6
Fenstanton. 54 C4
Fenton *Cambs* . . .54 B4
Lincs. 77 B8
Lincs. 77 D8
Stoke. 75 E5
Fenton Barns. . . .129 F7
Fenton Town. . . .123 F5
Fenwick *E Ayrs* . .118 E4

Fenwick *continued*
Northumb. 110 B3
Northumb. 123 E6
S Yorks. 89 C6
Feochaig. 143 G8
Feock. 3 C7
Feolin Ferry. . . .144 G3
Ferindonald. . . .149 H11
Feriniquarrie. . .148 C6
Ferlochan. 130 E3
Fern. 134 C4
Ferndale. 34 E4
Ferndown. 13 D8
Ferness. 151 G12
Ferney Green. 99 E6
Fernham. 38 E2
Fernhill Heath. . . .50 D3
Fernhurst. 16 B2
Fernie. 128 C5
Ferniegair. 119 D7
Fernilea. 149 E8
Fernilee. 75 B7
Ferrensby. 95 C6
Ferring. 16 D4
Ferrybridge. 89 B5
Ferryden. 135 D7
Ferryhill *Aberdeen* 141 D8
Durham. 111 F5
Ferry Hill. 66 F3
Ferryhill Station. 111 F6
Ferry Point. 151 C10
Ferryside. 32 C4
Fersfield. 68 F3
Fersit. 131 B7
Ferwig. 45 E3
Feshiebridge. . . .138 D4
Fetcham. 28 D2
Fetterangus. 153 C9
Fettercairn. 135 B6
Fettes. 151 F11
Fewcott. 39 B5
Fewston. 94 D4
F Faccombe. 25 D8
Ffairfach. 33 B7
Ffair-Rhos. 47 C6
Ffaldybrenin. 46 E5
Ffarmers. 47 E5
Ffawyddog. 35 C6
Fforest. 33 D6
Fforest-fâch. 33 E7
Ffostrasol. 46 E2
Ffos-y-ffin. 46 C3
Ffridd-Uchaf. 83 F5
Ffrith. 73 D6
Ffrwd. 82 F4
Ffynnon ddrain. . .33 B5
Ffynnongroyw. . . .85 F2
Ffynnon-oer. 46 D4
Fidden. 146 J6
Fiddes. 141 F7
Fiddington *Glos* . .50 F4
Som. 22 E4
Fiddleford. 13 C6
Fiddlers Hamlet. .41 D7
Field. 75 F7
Field Broughton. .99 F5
Field Dalling. 81 D6
Field Head. 63 D8
Fifehead
Magdalen. 13 B5
Fifehead Neville. .13 C5
Fifield *Oxon*. 38 C2
Wilts. 25 D6
Windsor. 27 B7
Fifield Bavant. . . .13 B8
Figheldean. 25 E6
Filands. 37 F6
Filby. 69 C7
Filey. 97 A7
Filgrave. 53 E6
Filkins. 38 D2
Filleigh *Devon* 9 B8
Devon. 10 C2
Fillingham. 90 F3
Fillongley. 63 F6
Filton. 23 B8
Fimber. 96 C4
Finavon. 134 D4
Finchairn. 124 E5
Fincham. 67 D6
Finchampstead. . .27 C5
Finchdean. 15 C8
Finchingfield. 55 F7
Finchley. 41 E5
Findern. 76 F3
Findhorn. 151 E13
Findhorn Bridge. .138 B4
Findochty. 152 B4
Findo Gask. 128 B2
Findon *Aberds* . . .141 E8
W Sus. 16 D5
Findon Mains. . . .151 E9
Findrack House. .140 D5
Finedon. 53 B7
Fingal Street. 57 C6
Fingask. 141 B6
Fingerpost. 50 B2
Fingest. 39 E7
Finghall. 101 F6
Fingland *Cumb* . .108 D2
Dumfries. 113 C7
Finglesham. 31 D7
Fingringhoe. 43 B6
Finlarig. 132 F2
Finmere. 52 F4
Finnart. 132 D2
Finningham. 56 C4
Finningley. 89 E7
Finnygaud. 152 C5
Finsbury. 41 F6
Finstall. 50 C4
Finsthwaite. 99 F5
Finstock. 38 C3
Finstown. 159 G4
Fintry *Aberds* . . .153 C7
Dundee. 134 F4
Stirling. 126 F5
Finzean. 140 E5
Fionnphort. 146 J6
Fionnsbhagh. . . .154 J5
Firbeck. 89 F6
Firby *N Yorks* 96 C3
N Yorks. 101 F7
Firgrove. 87 C7
Firsby. 79 C7
Firsdown. 25 F7
First Coast. 150 B2
Fir Tree. 110 F4
Fishbourne *IoW* . . .15 E6

Fishbourne *continued*
W Sus. 16 D2
Fishburn. 111 F6
Fishcross. 127 E7
Fisherford. 153 E6
Fisher Place. 99 C5
Fisher's Pond. . . .15 B5
Fisherstreet. 27 F7
Fisherton *Highld*. .151 F10
S Ayrs. 112 C2
Fishguard
= *Abergwaun* 44 B4
Fishlake. 89 C7
Fishleigh Barton . .9 B7
Fishpond. 36 B3
Fishponds. 23 B8
Fishpool. 36 B3
Fishtoft. 79 E6
Fishtoft Drove. . . .79 E6
Fishtown of Usan. 135 D7
Fishwick. 122 D5
Fiskavaig. 149 E8
Fiskerton *Lincs* . . .78 B3
Notts. 77 D7
Fitling. 97 F8
Fittleton. 25 E6
Fittleworth. 16 C4
Fitton End. 66 C4
Fitz. 60 C4
Fitzhead. 11 B6
Fitzwilliam. 88 C5
Fiunary. 147 G9
Five Acres. 36 C2
Five Ashes. 18 C2
Fivecrosses. 74 B2
Fivehead. 11 B8
Five Oak Green. . .29 E7
Five Oaks *Jersey* . .17 I3
W Sus. 16 B4
Five Roads. 33 D5
Flack's Green. 42 C3
Flackwell Heath. .40 F1
Fladbury. 50 E4
Fladdabister. 160 K6
Flagg. 75 C8
Flamborough. 97 B8
Flamstead. 40 C3
Flamstead End. . .41 D6
Flansham. 16 D3
Flanshaw. 88 B4
Flasby. 94 D2
Flash. 75 C7
Flashader. 149 C8
Flask Inn. 103 D7
Flaunden. 40 D3
Flawborough. 77 E7
Flawith. 95 C7
Flax Bourton. 23 C7
Flaxby. 95 D6
Flaxholme. 76 E3
Flaxley. 36 C3
Flaxpool. 22 F3
Flaxton. 96 C2
Fleckney. 64 E3
Flecknoe. 52 C3
Fledborough. 77 B8
Fleet *Hants* 15 D8
Hants. 27 D6
Lincs. 66 B3
Fleetham. 117 B7
Fleet Hargate. . . .66 B3
Fleetlands. 15 D6
Fleetville. 40 D4
Fleetwood. 92 E3
Flemingston. 22 B2
Flemington. 119 D6
Flempton. 56 C2
Fleoideabhagh. . .154 J5
Fletchertown. . . .108 E2
Fletching. 17 B8
Fleur-de-lis. 35 E5
Flexbury. 8 D4
Flexford. 27 E7
Flimby. 107 F7
Flimwell. 18 B4
Flint = *Y Fflint*. .73 B6
Flintham. 77 E7
Flint Mountain. . .73 B6
Flinton. 97 F8
Flintsham. 48 D5
Flitcham. 80 E3
Flitton. 53 F8
Flitwick. 53 F8
Flixborough. 90 C2
Flixborough
Stather. 90 C2
Flixton *Gtr Man* . .86 E5
N Yorks. 97 B6
Suff. 69 F6
Flockton. 88 C3
Flodaigh. 148 C3
Flodden. 122 F5
Flodigarry. 149 A9
Flood's Ferry. 66 E3
Flookburgh. 92 B3
Florden. 68 E4
Flore. 52 C4
Flotterton. 117 D5
Flowton. 56 E4
Flush House. 88 D2
Flushing *Aberds* . .153 D10
Corn. 3 C7
Flyford Flavell. . . .50 D4
Foals Green. 57 B6
Fobbing. 42 F3
Fochabers. 152 C3
Fochriw. 35 D5
Fockerby. 90 C2
Fodderletter. 139 B7
Fodderty. 151 F8
Foel. 59 C6
Foel-gastell. 33 C6
Foffarty. 134 E4
Foggathorpe. 96 F3
Fogo. 122 E3
Fogorig. 122 E3
Foindle. 156 E4
Folda. 134 C1
Fole. 75 F7
Foleshill. 63 F7
Folke. 12 C4
Folkestone. 31 F6
Folkingham. 78 F3
Folkington. 18 E2
Folksworth. 65 F8
Folkton. 97 B6
Folla Rule. 153 E7
Follifoot. 95 D6
Folly Gate. 9 E7
Fonthill Bishop. . .24 F4
Fonthill Gifford. .24 F4

Fontmell Magna. . .13 C6
Fontwell. 16 D3
Foolow. 75 B8
Foots Cray. 29 B5
Forbestown. 140 C2
Force Mills. 99 E5
Forcett. 101 C6
Ford *Argyll*. 124 E4
Bucks. 39 D7
Devon. 9 B6
Glos. 37 B7
Northumb. 122 F5
Shrops. 60 C4
Staffs. 75 D7
Wilts. 24 B3
W Sus. 16 D3
Fordcombe. 29 E6
Fordell. 128 F3
Forden. 60 D2
Ford End. 42 C2
Forder Green. 7 C5
Fordham *Cambs* . .55 B7
Essex. 43 B5
Norf. 67 E6
Fordhouses. 62 D3
Fordingbridge. . . .14 C2
Fordon. 97 B6
Fordoun. 135 B7
Ford's Green. 56 C4
Fordstreet. 43 B5
Ford Street. 11 C6
Fordwells. 38 C3
Fordwich. 31 D5
Fordyce. 152 B5
Forebridge. 62 B3
Forest. 109 F8
Forest Becks. 93 D7
Forestburn Gate. .117 E6
Foresterseat. 152 C1
Forest Gate. 41 F7
Forest Green. 28 E2
Forest Hall. 99 D7
Forest Head. 39 D5
Forest Lane Head. .95 D6
Forest Lodge
Argyll. 131 K6
Highld. 139 C6
Perth. 133 B6
Forest Mill. 127 E8
Forest Row. 28 F5
Forestside. 15 C8
Forest Town. 77 C5
Forfar. 134 D4
Forgandenny. . . .128 C2
Forge. 58 E4
Forge Side. 35 D6
Forgewood. 119 D7
Forgie. 152 C3
Forglen House. . .153 C6
Formby. 85 D4
Forncett End. 68 E4
Forncett St Mary. .68 E4
Forncett St Peter. 68 E4
Forneth. 133 E7
Fornham All
Saints. 56 C2
Fornham St
Martin. 56 C2
Forres. 151 F13
Forrestfield. 119 C8
Forrest Lodge. . .113 F5
Forsbrook. 75 E6
Forse. 158 G4
Forse House. 158 G4
Forsinain. 157 E12
Forsinard. 157 E11
Forsinard
Station. 157 E11
Forston. 12 E4
Fort Augustus. . .137 D6
Forteviot. 128 C2
Fortevrin. 128 C2
Fort George *Guern* .16 I2
Highld. 151 F10
Forth. 120 D2
Forthampton. 50 F3
Forth Road
Bridge. 120 B4
Fortingall. 132 E4
Forton *Hants* 26 E2
Lancs. 92 D4
Shrops. 60 C4
Som. 11 B8
Staffs. 61 B7
Forton Heath. . . .60 C4
Fortrie. 153 D6
Fortrose. 151 F10
Fortuneswell. 12 G4
Fort William. . . .131 B5
Forty Green. 40 E2
Forty Hill. 41 E6
Forward Green. . .56 D4
Fosbury. 25 D8
Fosdyke. 79 F6
Foss. 132 D4
Foss Cross. 37 C7
Fossebridge. 37 C7
Fosterhouses. 89 C7
Foster Street. 41 D7
Foston *Derbys* . . .75 F8
Lincs. 77 E8
N Yorks. 96 C2
Foston on the
Wolds. 97 D7
Fotherby. 91 E7
Fotheringhay. 65 E7
Foubister. 159 H6
Foulby. 88 C4
Foulden *Borders* . .122 D5
Norf. 67 E7
Foulis Castle. . . .151 E8
Foul Mile. 18 D3
Foulridge. 93 E8
Foulsham. 81 E6
Fountainhall. . . .121 E7
Four Ashes *Staffs* .62 F2
Suff. 56 B4
Four Crosses
Powys. 59 D7
Powys. 60 C2
Wrex. 73 D6
Four Elms. 29 E5
Four Forks. 22 F4
Four Gotes. 66 C4
Fourlane Ends. . . .76 D3
Four Lane Ends. . .74 C2
Four Lanes. 3 C5
Fourlanes End. . . .74 D5
Four Marks. 26 F4

Four Mile Bridge. .82 D2
Four Oaks *E Sus* . .19 C5
W Mid. 62 E5
W Mid. 63 F6
Fourpenny. 151 B11
Four Roads *Carms* .33 D5
IoM. 84 F2
Fourstones. 109 C8
Four Throws. 18 C4
Fovant. 13 B8
Foveran. 141 B8
Fowey. 5 D6
Fowley Common. .86 E4
Fowlis. 134 F3
Fowlis Wester. . .127 B8
Fowlmere. 54 E5
Fownhope. 49 F7
Foxbar. 118 C4
Foxcombe Hill. . . .38 D4
Fox Corner. 27 D7
Foxdale. 84 E2
Foxearth. 56 E2
Foxfield. 98 F4
Foxham. 24 B4
Foxhole *Corn*. 4 D4
Swansea. 33 E7
Foxholes. 97 B6
Foxhunt Green. . .18 D2
Fox Lane. 27 D6
Foxley *Norf*. 81 E6
Wilts. 37 F5
Fox Street. 43 B6
Foxt. 75 E7
Foxton *Cambs* . . .54 E5
Durham. 102 B1
Leics. 64 F4
Foxup. 93 B8
Foxwist Green. . . .74 C3
Foxwood. 49 B8
Foy. 36 B2
Foyers. 137 B7
Fraddam. 2 C4
Fraddon. 4 D4
Fradley. 63 C5
Fradswell. 75 F6
Fraisthorpe. 97 C7
Framfield. 17 B8
Framingham Earl. .69 D5
Framingham Pigot. 69 D5
Framlingham. 57 C6
Frampton *Dorset* . .12 E4
Lincs. 79 F6
Frampton
Cotterell. 36 F3
Frampton Mansell. 37 D6
Frampton on
Severn. 36 D4
Frampton West
End. 79 E6
Framsden. 57 D5
Framwellgate
Moor. 111 E5
Franche. 50 B3
Frankby. 85 F3
Frankley. 62 F3
Frank's Bridge. . . .48 D3
Frankton. 52 B2
Frant. 18 B2
Fraserburgh. 153 B9
Frating Green. . . .43 B6
Fratton. 15 E7
Freathy. 5 D8
Freckenham. 55 B7
Freckleton. 86 B2
Freeby. 64 B5
Freehay. 75 E7
Freeland. 38 C4
Freester. 160 H6
Freethorpe. 69 D7
Freiston. 79 E6
Fremington *Devon*. 20 F4
N Yorks. 101 E5
Frenchay. 23 B8
Frenchbeer. 9 F8
Frenich. 126 D3
Frensham. 27 E6
Fresgoe. 157 C12
Freshfield. 85 D3
Freshford. 24 C2
Freshwater. 14 F4
Freshwater Bay. . .14 F4
Freshwater East. .32 E1
Fressingfield. 57 B6
Freston. 57 F5
Freswick. 158 D5
Fretherne. 36 D4
Frettenham. 68 C5
Freuchie. 128 D4
Freuchies. 134 C2
Freystrop. 44 D4
Friar's Gate. 29 F5
Friarton. 128 B3
Friday Bridge. 66 D4
Friday Street. 18 E3
Fridaythorpe. 96 D4
Friern Barnet. . . .41 E5
Friesland. 146 F4
Friesthorpe. 90 F4
Frieston. 78 E2
Frieth. 39 E7
Frilford. 38 E4
Frilsham. 26 B3
Frimley. 27 D6
Frimley Green. . . .27 D6
Frindsbury. 29 B8
Fring. 80 D3
Fringford. 39 B6
Frinsted. 30 D2
Frinton-on-Sea. . .43 B8
Friockheim. 135 E5
Friog. 58 C3
Frisby on the
Wreake. 64 C3
Friskney. 79 D7
Friskney Eaudike. 79 D7
Friskney Tofts. . . .79 D7
Friston *E Sus* 18 F2
Suff. 57 C8
Fritchley. 76 D3
Fritham. 14 C3
Frith Bank. 79 E6
Frith Common. . . .49 C8
Frithelstock. 9 C6
Frithelstock Stone. 9 C6
Frithville. 79 D6
Frittenden. 30 E2
Frittiscombe. 7 E6
Fritton *Norf*. 68 E5
Norf. 69 D7

Fritwell. 39 B5
Frizinghall. 94 F4
Frizington. 98 C2
Frocester. 36 D4
Frodesley. 60 D5
Frodingham. 90 C2
Frodsham. 74 B2
Frogatt. 76 B2
Froghall. 75 E7
Frogham *Devon*. . . .7 E5
Hants. 27 D6
Frognall. 65 C8
Frogshail. 81 D8
Frolesworth. 64 E2
Frome. 24 E2
Frome St Quintin. 12 D3
Fromes Hill. 49 E8
Fron *Denb*. 72 C4
Gwyn. 70 D4
Gwyn. 82 F5
Powys. 48 C2
Powys. 59 E8
Powys. 60 D2
Froncysyllte. 73 E6
Frongoch. 72 F3
Frostenden. 69 F7
Frosterley. 110 F3
Frotoft. 159 F5
Froxfield. 25 C7
Froxfield Green. . .15 B8
Froyle. 27 E5
Fryerning. 42 D2
Fryton. 96 B2
Fulbeck. 78 D2
Fulbourn. 55 D6
Fulbrook. 38 C2
Fulford *Som*. 11 B7
Staffs. 75 F6
York. 96 E2
Fulham. 28 B3
Fulking. 17 C6
Fullarton *Glasgow*. 119 C6
N Ayrs. 118 F3
Fuller's Moor. 73 D8
Fuller Street. 42 C3
Fullerton. 25 F8
Fulletby. 79 B5
Full Sutton. 96 D3
Fullwood. 118 D4
Fulmer. 40 F2
Fulmodeston. 81 D5
Fulnetby. 78 B3
Fulstow. 91 E7
Fulwell. 111 D6
Fulwood *Lancs*. . .92 F5
S Yorks. 88 F4
Fundenhall. 68 E4
Fundenhall Street. 68 E4
Funtington. 15 D8
Funtley. 15 D6
Funtullich. 127 B6
Funzie. 160 D8
Furley. 11 D7
Furnace *Argyll*. . .125 E6
Carms. 33 D6
Furnace End. 63 E6
Furneaux Pelham. 41 B7
Furness Vale. 87 F8
Furzehill. 21 E6
Furze Platt. 40 F1
Fyfett. 11 C7
Fyfield *Essex* 42 D1
Glos. 38 D2
Hants. 25 E7
Oxon. 38 E4
Wilts. 25 C7
Fylingthorpe. . . .103 D7
Fyvie. 153 E7

G

Gabhsann bho
Dheas. 155 B9
Gabhsann bho
Thuath. 155 B9
Gablon. 151 B10
Gabroc Hill. 118 D4
Gaddesby. 64 C3
Gadebridge. 40 D3
Gaer. 35 B5
Gaerllwyd. 35 E8
Gaerwen. 82 D4
Gagingwell. 38 B4
Gaick Lodge. 138 F3
Gailey. 62 C3
Gainford. 101 C6
Gainsborough *Lincs* 90 E2
Suff. 57 E5
Gainsford End. . . .55 F8
Gairloch. 149 A13
Gairlochy. 136 F4
Gairney Bank. . . .128 E3
Gairnshiel Lodge. 139 D8
Gaisgill. 99 D8
Gaitsgill. 108 E3
Galashiels. 121 F7
Galgate. 92 D4
Galhampton. 12 B4
Gallaberry. 114 F2
Gallachoille. 144 E6
Gallanach *Argyll*. 124 C4
Argyll. 146 E5
Gallantry Bank. . .74 D2
Gallatown. 128 E4
Galley Common. . .63 E7
Galley Hill. 54 C4
Galleyend. 42 D3
Galleywood. 42 D3
Gallin. 132 E2
Gallowfauld. 134 E4
Gallows Green. . . .75 E7
Galltair. 149 F13
Galmisdale. 146 C7
Galmpton *Devon*. . .6 E4
Torbay. 7 D6
Galphay. 95 B5
Galston. 118 F5
Galtrigill. 148 C6
Gamblesby. 109 F6
Gamesley. 87 E8
Gamlingay. 54 D3
Gammersgill. 101 F5
Gamston. 77 B7
Ganarew. 36 C2
Ganavan. 124 B4
Gang. 5 C8
Ganllwyd. 71 E8

Ext–Gla 221

Gannochy *Angus*. .135 C5
Perth. 128 B3
Gansclet. 158 F5
Ganstead. 97 F7
Ganthorpe. 96 B2
Ganton. 97 B5
Garbat. 150 E7
Garbhallt. 125 F5
Garboldisham. . . .68 F3
Garden City. 73 C7
Gardenstown. . . .153 B7
Garden Village
Wrex. 73 D7
W Yorks. 95 F7
Garderhouse. 160 J5
Gardham. 97 E5
Gardin. 160 G6
Gare Hill. 24 E2
Garelochhead. . . .145 D11
Garford. 38 E4
Garforth. 95 F7
Gargrave. 94 D2
Gargunnock. 127 E6
Garlic Street. 68 F5
Garlieston. 105 E8
Garlinge Green. . .30 D5
Garlogie. 141 D6
Garmond. 153 C8
Garmony. 147 G9
Garmouth. 152 B3
Garn. 33 C7
Garndiffaith. 35 D6
Garndolbenmaen .71 C5
Garnedd. 83 F7
Garnett Bridge. . . .99 E7
Garnfadryn. 70 D3
Garnkirk. 119 C6
Garnlydan. 35 C5
Garnswllt. 33 D7
Garn-yr-erw. 35 C6
Garrabost. 155 D10
Garraron. 124 E4
Garras. 3 D6
Garreg. 71 C7
Garrick. 127 C7
Garrigill. 109 E7
Garriston. 101 E6
Garroch. 113 F5
Garrogie Lodge. .137 C8
Garros. 149 B9
Garrow. 133 E5
Garryhorn. 113 E5
Garsdale. 100 F2
Garsdale Head. . .100 E2
Garsdon. 37 F6
Garshall Green. . .75 F6
Garsington. 39 D5
Garstang. 92 E4
Garston. 86 F2
Garswood. 86 E3
Gartcosh. 119 C6
Garth *Bridgend* . .34 E2
Gwyn. 83 D5
Powys. 47 E8
Shetland. 160 H4
Wrex. 73 E6
Garthamlock. . . .119 C6
Garthbrengy. 48 F2
Garthdee. 141 D8
Gartheli. 46 D4
Garthmyl. 59 E8
Garthorpe *Leics* . .64 B5
N Lincs. 90 C2
Gartly. 152 E5
Gartmore. 126 E4
Gartnagrenach. . .144 H6
Gartness *N Lanark*. 119 C7
Stirling. 126 F4
Gartocharn. 126 F3
Garton. 97 F8
Garton-on-the-
Wolds. 97 D5
Gartsherrie. 119 C7
Gartymore. 157 H13
Garvald. 121 B8
Garvamore. 137 E8
Garvard. 146 D2
Garvault Hotel . .157 F10
Garve. 150 E6
Garvestone. 68 D3
Garvock *Aberds*. .135 B7
Inverclyd. 118 B2
Garway. 36 B1
Garway Hill. 35 B8
Gaskan. 130 B1
Gastard. 24 C3
Gasthorpe. 68 F2
Gatcombe. 15 F5
Gateacre. 86 F2
Gatebeck. 99 F7
Gate Burton. 90 F2
Gateford. 89 F6
Gateforth. 89 B6
Gatehead. 118 F3
Gate Helmsley. . . .96 D2
Gatehouse. 116 F3
Gatehouse of
Fleet. 106 D3
Gatelawbridge. . .114 E2
Gateley. 81 E5
Gatenby. 101 F8
Gateshead. 111 C5
Gatesheath. 73 C8
Gateside *Aberds*. .140 C5
Angus. 134 E4
E Renf. 118 D4
Fife. 128 D3
N Ayrs. 118 D3
Gateslack. 114 D2
Gathurst. 86 D3
Gatley. 87 F6
Gattonside. 121 F8
Gaufron. 47 C8
Gaulby. 64 D3
Gauldry. 129 B5
Gaunt's Common. .13 D8
Gautby. 78 B4
Gavinton. 122 D3
Gawber. 88 D4
Gawcott. 52 F4
Gawsworth. 75 C5
Gawthorpe. 88 B3
Gawthrop. 100 F1
Gawthwaite. 98 F4
Gaydon. 51 D8
Gayfield. 159 C5
Gayhurst. 53 E6
Gayle. 100 F3

Gayles. 101 D6
Gay Street. 16 B4
Gayton *Mers*. 85 F3
Norf. 67 C7
Staffs. 62 B3
W Nhants. 52 D5
Gayton le Marsh. .91 F8
Gayton le Wold. . .91 F6
Gayton Thorpe. . .67 C7
Gaywood. 67 B6
Gazeley. 55 C8
Geanies House . .151 D11
Gearraidh
Bhailteas. 148 F2
Gearraidh Bhaird. 155 E8
Gearraidh na h-
Aibhne. 154 D7
Gearraidh na
Monadh. 148 G2
Geary. 148 B7
Geddes House . .151 F11
Gedding. 56 D3
Geddington. 65 F5
Gedintailor. 149 E10
Gedling. 77 E6
Gedney. 66 B4
Gedney Broadgate. 66 B4
Gedney Drove End. 66 B4
Gedney Dyke. 66 B4
Gedney Hill. 66 C3
Gee Cross. 87 E7
Geilston. 118 B3
Geirinis. 148 D2
Geise. 158 D3
Geisiadar. 154 D6
Geldeston. 69 E6
Gell. 83 E8
Gelli *Pembs*. 32 C1
Rhondda. 34 E3
Gellideg. 34 D4
Gellifor. 72 C5
Gelligaer. 35 E5
Gellilydan. 71 D7
Gellinudd. 33 D8
Gellyburn. 133 F7
Gellywen. 32 B3
Gelston *Dumfries*. 106 D4
Lincs. 78 E2
Gembling. 97 D7
Gentleshaw. 62 C4
Geocrab. 154 H6
Georgefield. 115 E5
George Green. 40 F3
George Nympton. .10 B2
Georgetown. 35 D5
Gerlan. 83 E6
Germansweek. 9 E6
Germoe. 2 D4
Gerrans. 3 C7
Gerrards Cross. . .40 F3
Gestingthorpe. . . .56 F2
Geuffordt. 60 C2
Gibbet Hill. 64 F2
Gibbshill. 106 B4
Gib Hill. 74 B3
Gidea Park. 41 F8
Gidleigh. 9 F8
Giffnock. 119 D5
Gifford. 121 C8
Giffordland. 118 E2
Giffordtown. 128 C4
Giggleswick. 93 C8
Gilberdyke. 90 B2
Gilchriston. 121 C7
Gilcrux. 107 F8
Gildersome. 88 B3
Gildingwells. 89 F6
Gileston. 22 C2
Gilfach. 35 E5
Gilfach Goch. 34 F3
Gilfachrheda. 46 D3
Gilamoor. 102 F4
Gillar's Green. . . .86 E2
Gillen. 148 C7
Gilling East. 96 B2
Gillingham *Dorset*. 13 B6
Medway. 29 C8
Norf. 69 E7
Gilling West. 101 D6
Gillock. 158 E4
Gillow Heath. 75 D5
Gills. 158 C5
Gill's Green. 18 B4
Gilmanscleuch. . .115 B6
Gilmerton *Edin*. .121 C5
Perth. 127 B7
Gilmonby. 100 C4
Gilmorton. 64 F2
Gilmourton. 119 E6
Gilsland. 109 C6
Gilsland Spa. . . .109 C6
Gilston *Borders*. .121 D7
Herts. 41 C7
Gilwern. 35 C6
Gimingham. 81 D8
Giosla. 154 E6
Gipping. 56 C4
Gipsey Bridge. . . .79 E5
Girdle Toll. 118 E3
Girlsta. 160 H6
Girsby. 102 D1
Girthon. 54 D2
Girton *Cambs*. . . .54 C5
Notts. 77 C8
Girvan. 112 E1
Gisburn. 93 E8
Gisleham. 69 F8
Gislingham. 56 B4
Gissing. 68 F4
Gittisham. 11 E6
Gladestry. 48 D4
Gladsmuir. 121 B7
Glais. 33 D8
Glaisdale. 103 D5
Glame. 149 D10
Glamis. 134 E3
Glan Adda. 83 D5
Glanaman. 33 C7
Glan Conwy *Conwy*. 83 D8
Conwy. 83 F8
Glandford. 81 C6
Glan-Duar. 46 E4
Glandwr. 32 B2
Glan-Dwyfach. . . .71 C5

Glandy Cross....32 B2
Glandyfi....58 E3
Glan Gors....82 D4
Glangrwyney....35 C6
Glanmule....59 E8
Glanrafon....58 F3
Glanrhyd Gwyn....70 D3
  Pembs....45 E3
Glan-rhyd....82 F4
Glanton....117 C6
Glanton Pike....117 C6
Glan-traeth....82 D2
Glanvilles
  Wootton....12 D4
Glan-y-don....73 B5
Glan-y-nant....59 F6
Glan-yr-afon
  Anglesey....83 C6
  Gwyn....72 E3
  Gwyn....72 E4
Glan-y-wern....71 D7
Glapthorn....65 E7
Glapwell....76 C4
Glas-allt Shiel....139 F8
Glasbury....48 F3
Glaschoil....151 H13
Glascoed Denb....72 B3
  Mon....35 D7
  Powys....59 C8
Glascorrie....140 E2
Glascote....63 D6
Glascwm....48 D3
Glasdrum....130 E4
Glasfryn....72 D3
Glasgow....119 C5
Glashvin....149 B9
Glasinfryn....83 E5
Glasnacardoch....147 B9
Glasnakille....149 G10
Glasphein....148 D6
Glaspwll....58 E4
Glassburn....150 H6
Glasserton....105 F8
Glassford....119 E7
Glasshouse Hill....36 B4
Glasshouses....94 C4
Glasslie....128 D4
Glasson Cumb....108 C2
  Lancs....92 D4
Glassonby....109 F5
Glasterlaw....135 D5
Glaston....65 D5
Glastonbury....23 F7
Glatton....65 F8
Glazebrook....86 E4
Glazebury....86 E4
Glazeley....61 F7
Gleadless....88 F4
Gleadsmoss....74 C5
Gleann
  Tholàstaidh....155 C10
Gleaston....92 B2
Gleiniant....59 E6
Glemsford....56 E2
Glen Dumfries....106 B5
  Dumfries....106 D2
Glenamachrie....124 C5
Glen Auldyn....84 C4
Glenbarr....143 E7
Glenbeg Highld....138 B6
  Highld....147 E8
Glen Bernisdale....149 D8
Glenbervie....141 F6
Glenboig....119 C7
Glenborrodale....147 E9
Glenbranter....125 F7
Glenbreck....114 B3
Glenbrein Lodge....137 C7
Glenbrittle House 149 F9
Glenbuchat
  Lodge....140 C2
Glenbuck....113 B7
Glenburn....118 C4
Glencalvie Lodge.150 C2
Glencanisp
  Lodge....156 G4
Glencaple....107 C6
Glencarron
  Lodge....150 F3
Glencarse....128 B3
Glencassley
  Castle....156 J7
Glenceitlein....131 E5
Glencoe....130 D4
Glencraig....128 E3
Glencripesdale....147 F9
Glencrosh....113 F7
Glendavan House 140 D3
Glendevon....127 D8
Glendoebeg....137 D7
Glendoe Lodge....137 D7
Glendoick....128 B4
Glendoll Lodge....134 B2
Glendoune....112 E1
Glenduckie....128 C4
Glendye Lodge....140 F5
Gleneagles
  House....127 D8
Glenegedale....142 C4
Glenelg....149 G13
Glenernie....151 G13
Glenfarg....128 C3
Glenfarquhar
  Lodge....141 F6
Glenferness
  House....151 G12
Glenfeshie Lodge 138 E4
Glenfield....64 D2
Glenfinnan....147 C11
Glenfoot....128 C3
Glenfyne Lodge..125 D8
Glengap....106 D3
Glengarnock....118 D3
Glengorm Castle.146 F7
Glengrasco....149 D9
Glenhead Farm..134 C2
Glen Ho....121 F5
Glenhoul....113 F6
Glenhurich....130 C2
Glenkerry....115 C5
Glenkiln....106 B5
Glenkindie....140 C3
Glenlatterach....152 C1
Glenlee....113 F6
Glenlichorn....127 C6

Glenlivet....139 B7
Glenlochsie....133 B7
Glenloig....143 E10
Glenluce....105 D6
Glenmallan....125 F8
Glenmarksie....150 F6
Glenmavis....160 G5
Glenmaye....84 E2
Glenmidge....113 F8
Glen Mona....84 D4
Glenmore Argyll....124 C3
  Highld....149 D9
Glenmore Lodge .139 D5
Glenmoy....134 C4
Glen Nevis House. 131 B5
Glenogil....134 C4
Glenprosen
  Village....134 C3
Glenprosen
  Mains....145 H7
Glenree....143 F10
Glenridding....99 C5
Glenrossal....156 J7
Glenrothes....128 D4
Glensanda....130 E2
Glensaugh....135 B6
Glenshero Lodge 137 E8
Glen Sluain....125 F6
Glenstockadale....104 C4
Glenstriven....145 F9
Glentaggart....113 B8
Glen Tanar
  House....140 E3
Glentham....90 E4
Glentirranmuir....127 E5
Glenton....140 B5
Glentress....121 F5
Glentromie
  Lodge....138 E3
Glen Trool Lodge. 112 F4
Glentrool Village. 105 B7
Glentruan....84 B4
Glentruim House 138 E2
Glentworth....90 F3
Glenuig....147 D9
Glenurquhart....151 E10
Glen Village....119 B8
Glen Vine....84 E3
Glespin....113 B8
Gletness....160 H6
Glewstone....36 B2
Glinton....65 D8
Glooston....64 E4
Glororum....123 F7
Glossop....87 E8
Gloster Hill....117 D8
Gloucester....37 C5
Gloup....160 C7
Glusburn....94 E3
Glutt Lodge....157 F12
Glutton Bridge....75 C7
Glympton....38 B4
Glynarthen....46 E2
Glynbrochan....59 F6
Glyn-Ceiriog....73 F6
Glyncoch....34 E4
Glyncorrwg....34 E2
Glyn-cywarch....71 D7
Glynde....17 D8
Glyndebourne....17 C8
Glyndyfrdwy....72 E5
Glyn Ebwy
  = Ebbw Vale....35 D5
Glynedd
  = Glynneath....34 D2
Glyn-neath
  = Glynedd....34 D2
Glynogwr....34 F3
Glyntaff....34 F4
Glyntawe....34 C2
Gnosall....62 B2
Gnosall Heath....62 B2
Goadby....64 E4
Goadby Marwood . 64 B4
Goatacre....24 B5
Goathill....12 C4
Goathland....103 D6
Goathurst....22 F4
Goat Lees....30 E4
Gobernuisgach
  Lodge....156 E7
Gobhaig....154 G5
Gobowen....73 F7
Godalming....27 E7
Godley....87 E7
Godmanchester....54 B3
Godmanstone....12 E4
Godmersham....30 D4
Godney....23 E6
Godolphin Cross....2 C5
Godre'r-graig....34 D1
Godshill Hants....14 C2
  IoW....15 F6
Godstone....28 D4
Godwinscroft....14 E2
Goetre....35 D7
Goferydd....82 C2
Goff's Oak....41 D6
Gogar....120 B4
Goginan....58 F3
Golan....71 C6
Golant....5 D6
Golberdon....5 B8
Golborne....86 E4
Golcar....88 C2
Goldcliff....35 F7
Golden Cross....18 D2
Golden Green....29 E7
  Denb....72 B4
Golden Grove....33 C6
Goldenhill....75 D5
Golden Hill....14 E3
Golden Pot....26 E5
Golden Valley....37 B6
Golders Green....41 F5
Goldhanger....43 D5
Gold Hill....66 E5
Golding....60 D5
Goldington....53 D8
Goldsborough
  N Yorks....95 D6
  N Yorks....103 C6
Goldsithney....2 C4
Goldsworthy....9 B5
Goldthorpe....89 D5

Gollanfield....151 F11
Golspie....157 J11
Golval....157 C11
Gomeldon....25 F6
Gomersal....88 B3
Gomshall....27 E8
Gonalston....77 E6
Gonfirth....160 G5
Good Easter....42 C2
Gooderstone....67 D7
Goodleigh....20 F5
Goodmanham....96 E4
Goodnestone Kent .30 C4
  Kent....31 D6
Goodrich....36 C2
Goodrington....7 D6
Goodshaw....87 B6
Goodwick = Wdig.. 44 B4
Goodworth
  Clatford....25 E8
Goole....89 B8
Goonbell....3 B6
Goonhavern....4 D2
Goose Eye....94 E3
Goose Green
  Gtr Man....86 D3
  Norf....68 F4
  W Sus....16 C5
Gooseham....38 E3
Goosey....38 E3
Goosnargh....93 F5
Goostrey....74 B4
Gorcott Hill....51 C5
Gord....160 L6
Gordon....122 E2
Gordonbush....157 J11
Gordonsburgh....152 B1
Gordonstoun....152 B1
Gordonstown
  Aberds....152 C5
  Aberds....153 E7
Gore....31 D7
Gorebridge....121 C6
Gore Cross....24 D5
Gorefield....66 C4
Gore Pit....42 C4
Gorey....17 I3
Gorgie....120 B5
Goring....39 F6
Goring-by-Sea....16 D4
Goring Heath....26 B4
Gorleston-on-Sea 69 D8
Gornalwood....62 E3
Gorrachie....153 C7
Gorran Churchtown .3 B8
Gorran Haven....3 B9
Gorrenberry....115 C7
Gors....46 B5
Gorsedd....73 B5
Gorse Hill....38 F1
Gorseinon....33 E6
Gorseness....159 G5
Gorsgoch....46 D3
Gorslas....33 C6
Gorsley....36 B3
Gorstan....150 F6
Gorstanvorran....130 B2
Gorsteyhill....74 D4
Gorsty Hill....62 B5
Gortantaoid....142 A4
Gorton....87 E6
Gosbeck....57 D5
Gosberton....78 F5
Gosberton Clough . 65 B8
Gosfield....42 B3
Gosford....49 C7
Gosforth Cumb....98 D2
  T&W....110 C5
Gosmore....40 B4
Gosport....15 E7
Gossabrough....160 E7
Gossington....36 D4
Goswick....123 E6
Gotham....76 F5
Gotherington....37 B6
Gott....160 J6
Goudhurst....18 B4
Goulceby....79 B5
Gourdas....153 D7
Gourdon....135 B8
Gourock....118 B2
Govan....119 C5
Govanhill....119 C5
Goveton....7 E5
Govilon....35 C6
Gowanhill....153 B10
Gowdall....89 B7
Gowerton....33 E6
Gowkhall....128 F2
Gowthorpe....96 D3
Goxhill E Yorks....97 F7
  N Lincs....90 B5
Goxhill Haven....90 B5
Goytre....34 F1
Grabhair....155 F8
Graby....65 B7
Grade....3 E6
Graffham....16 C3
Grafham Cambs....54 C2
  Sur....27 E8
Grafton Hereford....49 F6
  N Yorks....95 C7
  Oxon....38 D2
  Shrops....60 C4
  Worcs....49 C7
Grafton Flyford....50 D4
Grafton Regis....53 E5
Grafton
  Underwood....65 F6
Grafty Green....30 E2
Graianrhyd....73 D6
Graig Conwy....83 D8
  Denb....72 B4
Graig-fechan....72 D5
Grain....30 B2
Grainsby....91 E6
Grainthorpe....91 E7
Grampound....3 B8
Grampound Road .. 4 D4
Gramsdal....148 C3
Granborough....39 B7
Granby....77 F7
Grandborough....52 C2
Grandtully....133 D6
Grange Cumb....98 C4
  E Yorks....118 F4
  Medway....29 C8
  Mers....85 F3
  Perth....128 B4

Grange
  Crossroads....152 C4
Grange Hall....151 E13
Grange Hill....41 E7
Grangemill....76 D2
Grange Moor....88 C3
Grangemouth....127 F8
Grange of
  Lindores....128 C4
Grange-over-
  Sands....92 B4
Grangepans....128 F2
Grange Villa....110 D5
Granish....138 C5
Granston....44 B3
Grantchester....54 D5
Grantham....78 F2
Grantley....94 C5
Grantlodge....141 C6
Granton Dumfries.114 D3
  Edin....120 B5
Grantown-on-
  Spey....139 B6
Grantshouse....122 C4
Grappenhall....86 F4
Grasby....90 D4
Grasmere....99 D5
Grasscroft....87 D7
Grassendale....85 F4
Grassholme....100 B4
Grassington....94 C3
Grassmoor....76 C4
Grassthorpe....77 C7
Grateley....25 E7
Gratwich....75 F7
Graveley Cambs....54 C3
  Herts....41 B5
Gravelly Hill....62 E5
Gravels....60 D3
Graven....160 F6
Graveney....30 C4
Gravesend Herts....41 B7
  Kent....29 B7
Grayingham....90 E3
Grayrigg....99 E7
Grays....29 B7
Grayshott....27 F6
Grayswood....27 F7
Graythorp....102 B3
Grazeley....26 C4
Greasbrough....88 E5
Greasby....85 F3
Great Abington....55 E6
Great Addington....53 B7
Great Alne....51 D6
Great Altcar....85 D4
Great Amwell....41 C6
Great Asby....100 C1
Great Ashfield....56 C3
Great Ayton....102 C3
Great Baddow....42 D3
Great Bardfield....55 F7
Great Barford....54 D2
Great Barr....62 E4
Great Barrington....38 C2
Great Barrow....73 C8
Great Barton....56 C2
Great Barugh....96 B3
Great Bavington....117 F5
Great Bealings....57 E6
Great Bedwyn....25 C7
Great Bentley....43 B7
Great Billing....53 C6
Great Bircham....80 D3
Great Blakenham....56 D5
Great Blencow....108 F4
Great Bolas....61 B6
Great Bookham....28 D2
Great Bourton....52 E2
Great Bowden....64 F4
Great Bradley....55 D7
Great Braxted....42 C4
Great Bricett....56 D4
Great Brickhill....53 F7
Great Bridge....62 E3
Great Bridgeford....62 B2
Great Brington....52 C4
Great Bromley....43 B6
Great Broughton
  Cumb....107 F7
  N Yorks....102 D3
Great Budworth....74 B3
Great Burdon....101 C8
Great Burgh....28 D3
Great Burstead....42 E2
Great Busby....102 D3
Great Canfield....42 C1
Great Carlton....91 F8
Great Casterton....65 D7
Great Chart....30 E3
Great Chatwell....61 C7
Great Chesterford..55 E6
Great Cheverell....24 D4
Great Chishill....54 F5
Great Clacton....43 C7
Great Cliff....88 C4
Great Clifton....98 B2
Great Coates....91 D6
Great Comberton....50 E4
Great Corby....108 D4
Great Cornard....56 E2
Great Cowden....97 E8
Great Coxwell....38 E2
Great Crakehall....101 E7
Great Cransley....53 B6
Great
  Cressingham....67 D8
Great Crosby....85 E4
Great Cubley....75 F8
Great Dalby....64 C4
Great Denham....53 E8
Great Doddington...53 C6
Great Dunham....67 C8
Great Dunmow....42 C2
Great Durnford....25 F6
Great Easton Essex. 42 B2
  Leics....64 E5
Great Eccleston....92 E4
Great Edstone....103 F5
Great Ellingham....68 E3
Great Elm....24 E2
Greater Doward....36 C2
Great Eversden....54 D4
Great Fencote....101 E7
Great Finborough....56 D4
Greatford....65 C7

Great Fransham....67 C8
Great Yeldham....55 F8
Greatgate....75 E7
Great Gidding....65 F8
Great Givendale....96 D4
Great Glen....64 E3
Great Gonerby....77 F8
Great Gransden....54 D3
Great Green Norf....56 D3
  Suff....56 D3
Great Habton....96 B3
Great Hale....78 E4
Great Hallingbury. 41 C8
Greatham Hants....27 F5
  Hrtlpl....102 B2
  W Sus....16 C4
Great Hampden....39 D8
Great Harrowden....53 B6
Great Harwood....93 F7
Great Haseley....39 D6
Great Hatfield....97 E7
Great Haywood....62 B4
Great Heath....63 F7
Great Heck....89 B6
Great Henny....56 F2
Great Hinton....24 D4
Great Hockham....68 E2
Great Holland....43 C8
Great Horkesley....56 F3
Great Hormead....41 B6
Great Horton....94 F4
Great Horwood....53 F5
Great Houghton
  S Yorks....88 D5
  W Nhants....53 D5
Great Hucklow....75 B8
Great Kelk....97 D7
Great Kimble....39 D8
Great Kingshill....40 E1
Great Langton....101 E7
Great Leighs....42 C3
Great Lever....86 D5
Great Limber....90 D5
Great Linford....53 E6
Great Livermere....56 B2
Great Longstone....76 B2
Great Lumley....111 E5
Great Lyth....60 D4
Great Malvern....50 E2
Great Maplestead....56 F2
Great Marton....92 F3
Great Massingham 80 E3
Great Melton....68 D4
Great Milton....39 D6
Great Missenden....40 D1
Great Mitton....93 F7
Great Mongeham....31 D7
Great Moulton....68 E4
Great Munden....41 B6
Great Musgrave....100 C2
Great Ness....60 C3
Great Notley....42 B3
Great Oakley Essex .43 B7
  N Nhants....65 F5
Great Offley....40 B4
Great Ormside....100 C2
Great Orton....108 D3
Great Ouseburn....95 C7
Great Oxendon....64 F4
Great Oxney
  Green....42 D2
Great Palgrave....67 C8
Great Parndon....41 D7
Great Paxton....54 C3
Great Plumpton....92 F3
Great Plumstead....69 C6
Great Ponton....78 F2
Great Preston....88 B5
Great Raveley....66 F2
Great Rissington....38 C1
Great Rollright....51 F8
Great Ryburgh....81 E5
Great Ryle....117 C6
Great Ryton....60 D4
Great Saling....42 B3
Great Salkeld....109 F5
Great Sampford....55 F7
Great Sankey....86 F3
Great Saxham....55 C8
Great Shefford....25 B8
Great Shelford....55 D5
Great Smeaton....101 D8
Great Snoring....80 D5
Great Somerford....37 F6
Great Stainton....101 B8
Great Stambridge .42 E4
Great Staughton....54 C2
Great Steeping....79 C7
Great Stonar....31 D7
Great Strickland....99 B7
Great Stukeley....54 B3
Great Sturton....78 B5
Great Sutton
  Ches W....73 B7
  Shrops....60 F5
Great Swinburne. 110 B2
Great Tew....38 B3
Great Tey....42 B4
Great Thurkleby....95 B7
Great Thurlow....55 D7
Great Torrington....9 C6
Great Totham....42 C4
Great Tows....91 E6
Great Urswick....92 B2
Great Wakering....43 E5
Great Waldingfield 56 E3
Great Walsingham. 80 D5
Great Waltham....42 C3
Great Warley....42 E1
Great Washbourne. 50 F4
Great Weldon....65 F6
Great Welnetham...56 D2
Great Wenham....56 F4
Great
  Whittington....110 B3
Great Wigborough. 43 C5
Great Wilbraham....55 D6
Great Wishford....25 F5
Great Witcombe....37 C5
Great Witley....50 C2
Great Wolford....51 F7
Great Wratting....55 E7
Great Wymondley. 41 B5
Great Wyrley....62 D3
Great Wytheford....61 C5

Great Yarmouth....69 D8
Greave....87 B6
Greeba....84 D3
Green....72 C4
Greenbank....160 C7
Greenburn....120 C2
Greendikes....117 B6
Green End....54 D2
Greenfield C Beds....53 F8
  Flint....73 B5
  Gtr Man....87 D7
  Highld....136 D5
  Oxon....39 E7
Greenford....40 F4
Greengairs....119 B7
Greenham....26 C2
Green
  Hammerton....95 D7
Greenhaugh....116 F3
Greenhead....109 C6
Greenhill Falk....119 B8
  Kent....31 C5
  Leics....63 C8
  London....40 F4
Greenhills....118 D3
Greenhithe....29 B6
Greenholm....118 F5
Greenholme....99 D7
Greenhouse....115 B8
Greenhow Hill....94 C4
Greenigoe....159 H5
Greenland....158 D4
Greenlands....39 F7
Green Lane....59 E8
Greenlaw Aberds..153 C6
  Borders....122 C3
Greenlea....107 B7
Greenloaning....127 D7
Greenmount....87 C5
Greenmow....160 L6
Greenock....118 B2
Greenock West....118 B2
Greenodd....99 F5
Green Ore....23 D7
Greenrow....107 D8
Green St Green....29 C5
Greenside....110 C4
Greensidehill....117 C5
Greens Norton....52 E4
Greenstead
  Green....42 B4
Greensted....41 D8
Green Street....40 E4
Greenway....34 F2
Greenwich....28 B4
Greet....50 F5
Greete....49 B7
Greetham Lincs....79 B6
  Rutland....65 C6
Greetland....87 B8
Gregg Hall....99 E6
Gregson Lane....86 B3
Greinetobht....148 A3
Greinton....23 F6
Gremista....160 J6
Grenaby....84 E3
Grendon N Nhants .53 C6
  Warks....63 D6
Grendon Common. 63 E6
Grendon Green....49 D7
Grendon
  Underwood....39 B6
Grenofen....6 B2
Grenoside....88 E4
Greosabhagh....154 H6
Gresford....73 D7
Gresham....81 D7
Greshornish....149 C8
Gressenhall....68 C2
Gressingham....93 C5
Gresty Green....74 D4
Greta Bridge....101 C5
Gretna....108 C3
Gretna Green....108 C3
Gretton Glos....50 F5
  N Nhants....65 E5
  Shrops....60 E5
Grewelthorpe....94 B5
Greygarth....94 B4
Grey Green....89 D8
Greynor....33 D6
Greyrigg....107 B8
Greysouthen....98 B2
Greystoke....108 F4
Greystone Angus. 135 E5
  Dumfries....107 B6
Greywell....26 D5
Griais....155 C9
Grianan....155 D9
Gribthorpe....96 F3
Gribun....146 H7
Gridley Corner....9 E5
Griff....63 F7
Griffithstown....35 E6
Grimbister....159 G4
Grimblethorpe....91 F6
Grimeford Village.. 86 C4
Grimethorpe....88 D5
Griminis....148 C2
Grimister....160 D6
Grimley....50 C3
Grimness....159 J5
Grimoldby....91 F7
Grimpo....60 B3
Grimsargh....93 F5
Grimsbury....52 E2
Grimsby....91 C6
Grimscote....52 D4
Grimscott....8 D4
Grimshader....155 E9
Grimsthorpe....65 B7
Grimston E Yorks...97 F8
  Leics....64 B3
  Norf....80 E3
  York....96 D2
Grimstone....12 E4
Grinacombe Moor. 9 E6
Grindale....97 B7
Grindigar....159 H6
Grindiscol....160 K6
Grindle....61 D7
Grindleford....76 B2
Grindleton....93 E7
Grindley....62 B4
Grindley Brook....74 E2
Grindlow....75 B8
Grindon Northumb. 122 E5
  Staffs....75 D7
Grindonmoor
  Gate....75 D7
Gringley on
  the Hill....89 E8

Grinsdale....108 D3
Grinshill....60 B5
Grinton....101 E5
Griomsidar....155 E8
Grishipoll....146 F4
Grisling Common....17 B8
Gristhorpe....103 F8
Griston....68 E2
Gritley....159 H6
Grittenham....37 F7
Grittleton....37 F5
Grizebeck....98 F4
Grizedale....99 E5
Grobister....159 F7
Groby....64 D2
Groes Conwy....72 C4
  Neath....34 F1
Groes-faen....34 F4
Groesffordd Marli . 72 B4
Groeslon Gwyn....82 E5
  Gwyn....82 F4
Groes-lwyd....60 C2
Grogport....143 D9
Gromford....57 D7
Gronant....72 A4
Groombridge....18 B2
Grosmont Mon....35 B8
  N Yorks....103 D6
Groton....56 E3
Grougfoot....120 B3
Grouville....17 I3
Grove Dorset....12 G5
  Kent....31 C6
  Notts....77 B7
  Oxon....38 E4
Grove Park....28 B5
Grovesend....33 D6
Grove Vale....62 E4
Grudie....150 E6
Gruids....157 J8
Gruinard House . 150 B2
Grula....149 F8
Gruline....147 G8
Grunasound....160 K5
Grundisburgh....57 D6
Grunsagill....93 D7
Grutness....160 N6
Gualachulain....131 E5
Gualin House....156 D6
Guardbridge....129 C6
Guarlford....50 E3
Guay....133 E7
Guestling
  Green....19 D5
Guestling Thorn....19 D5
Guestwick....81 E6
Guestwick Green... 81 E6
Guide....86 B5
Guide Post....117 F8
Guilden Morden....54 E3
Guilden Sutton....73 C8
Guildford....27 E7
Guildtown....133 F8
Guilsborough....52 B4
Guilsfield....60 C2
Guilton....31 D6
Guineaford....20 F4
Guisborough....102 C4
Guiseley....94 E4
Guist....81 E5
Guith....159 E6
Guiting Power....37 B7
Gulberwick....160 K6
Gullane....129 F6
Gulval....2 C3
Gulworthy....6 B2
Gumfreston....32 D2
Gumley....64 E3
Gummow's Shop.... 4 D3
Gunby E Yorks....96 F3
  Lincs....65 B6
Gundleton....26 F4
Gun Hill....18 D2
Gunn....20 F5
Gunnerside....100 E4
Gunnerton....110 B2
Gunness....90 C2
Gunnislake....6 B2
Gunnista....160 J6
Gunthorpe Norf....81 D6
  Notts....77 E6
  Pboro....65 D8
Gunville....15 F5
Gunwalloe....3 D5
Gurnard....15 E5
Gurnett....75 B6
Gurney Slade....23 E8
Gurnos....34 D1
Gussage
  All Saints....13 C8
Gussage
  St Michael....13 C7
Guston....31 E7
Gutcher....160 D7
Guthrie....135 D5
Guyhirn....66 D3
Guyhirn Gull....66 D3
Guy's Head....66 B4
Guy's Marsh....13 B6
Guyzance....117 D8
Gwaenysgor....72 A4
Gwalchmai....82 D3
Gwaun-Cae-
  Gurwen....33 C8
Gwaun-Leision....33 C8
Gwbert....45 E3
Gweek....3 C6
Gwehelog....35 D7
Gwenddwr....48 E2
Gwennap....3 C6
Gwenter....3 E6
Gwernaffield....73 C6
Gwernesney....35 D8
Gwernogle....46 F4
Gwernymynydd....73 C6
Gwersyllt....73 D7
Gwespyr....85 F2
Gwithian....2 B4
Gwredog....82 C4
Gwyddelwern....72 E4
Gwyddgrug....46 F3
Gwydyr Uchaf....83 E7
Gwynfryn....73 D7
Gwystre....48 C2
Gwytherin....83 E8
Gyfelia....73 E7
Gyffin....83 D7
Gyre....159 H4
Gyrn-goch....70 C5

H
Habberley....60 D3
Habergham....93 F8
Habrough....90 C5
Haceby....78 F3
Hacheston....57 D7
Hackbridge....28 C3
Hackenthorpe....88 F5
Hackford....68 D3
Hackforth....101 E7
Hackland....159 F4
Hackleton....53 D6
Hackness N Yorks..103 E7
  Orkney....159 J4
Hackney....41 F6
Hackthorn....90 F3
Hackthorpe....99 B7
Haconby....65 B8
Hacton....41 F8
Hadden....122 F3
Haddenham Bucks . 39 D7
  Cambs....55 B5
Haddington
  E Loth....121 B8
  Lincs....78 C2
Haddiscoe....69 E7
Haddon Cambs....65 E8
  Ches E....75 C6
Hade Edge....88 D2
Hademore....63 D5
Hadfield....87 E8
Hadham Cross....41 C7
Hadham Ford....41 B7
Hadleigh Essex....42 F4
  Suff....56 E4
Hadley....61 C6
Hadley End....62 B5
Hadlow....29 E7
Hadlow Down....18 C2
Hadnall....60 C5
Hadstock....55 E6
Hady....76 B3
Hadzor....50 C4
Haffenden Quarter 30 E2
Hafod-Dinbych....83 F8
Hafod-lom....83 D8
Haggate....93 F8
Haggbeck....108 B4
Haggerston....123 E6
Haggrister....160 F5
Hagley Hereford....49 E7
  Worcs....62 F3
Hagworthingham. 79 C6
Haigh Gtr Man....86 D4
  S Yorks....88 C3
Haigh Moor....88 B3
Haighton Green....93 F5
Haile....98 D2
Hailes....50 F5
Hailey Herts....41 C6
  Oxon....38 C3
Hailsham....18 E2
Hail Weston....54 C2
Hainault....41 E7
Hainford....68 C5
Hainton....91 F5
Hairmyres....119 D6
Haisthorpe....97 C7
Hakin....44 E3
Halam....77 D6
Halbeath....128 F3
Halberton....10 C5
Halcro....158 D4
Hale Gtr Man....87 F5
  Halton....86 F2
  Hants....14 C2
Hale Bank....86 F2
Halebarns....87 F5
Hales Norf....69 E6
  Staffs....74 F4
Halesfield....61 D7
Halesgate....66 B3
Halesowen....62 F3
Hales Place....30 D5
Halesworth....57 B7
Halewood....86 F2
Halford Shrops....60 F4
  Warks....51 E7
Halfpenny Furze....32 C3
Halfpenny Green....62 E2
Halfway Carms....46 F5
  Carms....47 F7
  W Berks....26 C2
Halfway House....60 C3
Halfway Houses....30 B3
Halifax....87 B8
Halket....118 D4
Halkirk....158 E3
Halkyn....73 B6
Halland....18 D2
Hallaton....64 E4
Hallatrow....23 D8
Hallbankgate....109 D5
Hall Dunnerdale....98 E4
Hallen....36 F2
Hall Green W Mid...62 F5
  W Yorks....88 C4
Halliburton....122 E2
Hallin....148 C7
Halling....29 C8
Hallington Lincs....91 F7
  Northumb....110 B2
Halliwell....86 C5
Hall of
  Tankerness....159 H6
Hall of the Forest . 60 F2
Halloughton....77 D6
Hallow....50 D3
Hallrule....115 C8
Halls....122 B2
Hallsands....7 F6
Hall's Green....41 B5
Hallthwaites....98 F3
Hallworthy....8 F3
Hallyburton
  House....134 F2
Hallyne....120 E4
Halmer End....74 E4
Halmore....36 D3
Halmyre Mains....120 E4
Halnaker....16 D3
Halsall....85 C4
Halse Som....11 B6

Halse continued
  W Nhants....52 E3
Halsetown....2 C4
Halsham....91 B6
Halsinger....20 F4
Halstead Essex....56 F2
  Kent....29 C5
  Leics....64 D4
Halstock....12 D3
Haltham....78 C5
Haltoft End....79 E6
Halton Bucks....40 C1
  Halton....86 F3
  Lancs....92 C5
  Northumb....110 C2
  W Yorks....95 F6
  Wrex....73 F7
Halton East....94 D3
Halton Gill....93 B8
Halton Holegate....79 C7
Halton Lea Gate.. 109 D6
Halton West....93 D8
Haltwhistle....109 C7
Halvergate....69 D7
Halwell....7 D5
Halwill....9 E6
Halwill Junction....9 D6
Ham Devon....11 D7
  Glos....36 E3
  Highld....158 C4
  Kent....31 D7
  London....28 B2
  Shetland....160 K1
  Wilts....25 C8
Hambleden....39 F7
Hambledon Hants . 15 C7
  Sur....27 F7
Hamble-le-Rice....15 D5
Hambleton Lancs.. 92 E3
  N Yorks....95 F8
Hambridge....11 B8
Hambrook S Glos...23 B8
  W Sus....15 D8
Ham Common....13 B6
Hameringham....79 C6
Hamerton....54 B2
Hametoun....160 K1
Ham Green
  Hereford....50 E2
  Kent....19 C5
  Kent....30 C2
  N Som....23 B7
  Worcs....50 C5
Hamilton....119 D7
Hammer....27 F6
Hammerpot....16 D4
Hammersmith....28 B3
Hammerwich....62 D4
Hammerwood....28 F5
Hammond Street.. 41 D6
Hammoon....13 C6
Hamnavoe
  Shetland....160 E4
  Shetland....160 F6
  Shetland....160 E6
  Shetland....160 K5
Hampden Park....18 E3
Hamperden End....55 F6
Hampnett....37 C7
Hampole....89 C6
Hampreston....13 E8
Hampstead....41 F5
Hampstead
  Norreys....26 B3
Hampsthwaite....95 D5
Hampton Pboro....65 E8
  London....28 C2
  Shrops....61 F7
  Worcs....50 E5
Hampton Bishop....49 F7
Hampton Heath....73 E8
Hampton in Arden. 63 F6
Hampton Loade....61 F7
Hampton Lovett....50 C3
Hampton Lucy....51 D7
Hampton on the
  Hill....51 C7
Hampton Poyle....39 C5
Hamrow....80 E5
Hamsey....17 C8
Hamsey Green....28 D4
Hamstall Ridware. 62 C5
Hamstead IoW....14 E5
  W Mid....62 E4
Hamstead
  Marshall....26 C2
Hamsterley
  Durham....110 D4
  Durham....110 F4
Hamstreet....19 B7
Ham Street....23 F7
Hamworthy....13 E7
Hanbury Staffs....63 B5
  Worcs....50 C4
Hanbury Woodend 63 B5
Hanby....78 F3
Hanchurch....74 E5
Handbridge....73 C8
Handcross....17 B6
Handforth....87 F6
Handley....73 D8
Handsacre....62 C4
Handsworth
  S Yorks....88 F5
  W Mid....62 E4
Handy Cross....9 B6
Hanford....75 E5
Hanging Langford. 24 F5
Hangleton....16 D4
Hanham....23 B8
Hankelow....74 E3
Hankerton....37 E6
Hankham....18 E3
Hanley....75 E5
Hanley Castle....50 E3
Hanley Child....49 C8
Hanley Swan....50 E3
Hanley William....49 C8
Hanmer....73 F8
Hannah....79 B8
Hannington Hants . 26 D3
  Swindon....38 E1
  W Nhants....53 B6
Hannington Wick...38 E1
Hansel Village....118 F3
Hanslope....53 E6
Hanthorpe....65 B7
Hanwell London....40 F4

Hanwell continued
Oxon............52 E2
Hanwood............60 D4
Hanworth London...28 B2
Norf............81 D7
Happendon............119 F8
Happisburgh............69 A6
Happisburgh
Common............69 B6
Hapsford............73 B8
Hapton Lancs............93 F7
Norf............68 E4
Harberton............7 D5
Harbertonford............7 D5
Harbledown............30 D5
Harborne............62 F4
Harborough
Magna............52 B2
Harbottle............117 D5
Harbury............51 D8
Harby Leics............77 F7
Notts............77 B8
Harcombe............11 E6
Harden W Mid............62 D4
W Yorks............94 F3
Hardgate............141 D6
Hardham............16 C4
Hardingham............68 D3
Hardingstone............53 D5
Hardington............24 D2
Hardington
Mandeville............12 C3
Hardington Marsh.12 D3
Hardley............14 D5
Hardley Street............69 D6
Hardmead............53 E7
Hardrow............100 E3
Hardstoft............76 C4
Hardway Hants............15 D7
Som............24 F2
Hardwick Bucks............39 C8
Cambs............54 D4
N Nhants............53 C6
Norf............67 C6
Norf............68 F5
Notts............77 B6
Oxon............38 D3
Oxon............39 B5
W Mid............62 E4
Hardwicke Glos............36 C4
Glos............37 B6
Hereford............48 E4
Hardy's Green............43 B5
Hareby............79 C6
Hareden............93 D6
Harefield............40 E3
Hare Green............43 B6
Hare Hatch............27 B6
Harehills............95 F6
Harehope............117 B6
Haresceugh............109 E6
Harescombe............37 C5
Haresfield............37 C5
Hareshaw............119 C8
Hareshaw Head.116 F4
Hare Street............41 B6
Harewood............95 E6
Harewood End............36 B2
Harford Carms............46 E5
Devon............6 D4
Hargate............68 E4
Hargatewall............75 B8
Hargrave Ches W..73 C8
N Nhants............53 B8
Suff............55 C8
Harker............108 C3
Harkland............160 E6
Harkstead............57 F5
Harlaston............63 C6
Harlaw House..141 B6
Harlaxton............77 F8
Harlech............71 D6
Harlequin............77 F6
Harlescott............60 C5
Harlesden............41 F5
Harleston Devon............7 E5
Norf............68 F4
Suff............56 D4
Harlestone............52 C5
Harle Syke............93 F8
Harley Shrops............61 D5
S Yorks............88 E4
Harleyholm............120 F2
Harlington C Beds..53 F10
London............40 F4
S Yorks............89 D5
Harlosh............149 D7
Harlow............41 C7
Harlow Hill
Northumb............110 C3
N Yorks............95 D5
Harlthorpe............96 F3
Harlton............54 D4
Harman's Cross..13 F7
Harmby............101 F6
Harmer Green..41 C5
Harmer Hill............60 B4
Harmondsworth..27 B8
Harmston............78 C2
Harnham............110 B3
Harnhill............37 D7
Harold Hill............41 E8
Haroldston West..44 D3
Haroldswick............160 B8
Harold Wood............41 E8
Harome............102 F4
Harpenden............40 C4
Harpford............11 E5
Harpham............97 C6
Worcs............49 C8
Harpole............52 C4
Harpsdale............158 E3
Harpsden............39 F7
Harpswell............90 F3
Harpurhey............87 D6
Harpur Hill............75 B7
Harraby............108 D4
Harrapool..149 F11
Harrier............160 J1
Harrietfield............127 B8
Harrietsham............30 D2
Harrington Cumb..98 B1
Lincs............79 B6
N Nhants............64 F4
Harringworth............65 E6
Harris............146 B6
Harrogate............95 D6

Harrold............53 D7
Harrow............40 F4
Harrowbarrow............5 C8
Harrowden............53 E8
Harrowgate Hill..101 C7
Harrow on the Hill..40 F4
Harrow Street............56 F3
Harrow Weald............40 E4
Harston Cambs............54 D5
Leics............77 F8
Harswell............96 E4
Hart............111 F7
Hartburn
Northumb............117 F6
Stockton............102 C2
Hart Common............86 D4
Hartest............56 D2
Hartfield............29 F5
Hartford Cambs............54 B3
Ches W............74 B3
Hartfordbridge............27 D5
Hartford End............42 C2
Harthill Ches W..74 D2
N Lanark............120 C2
S Yorks............89 F5
Hart Hill............40 B4
Hartington............75 C8
Hartland............8 B4
Hartlebury............50 B3
Hartlepool............111 F8
Hartley Kent............18 B4
Kent............29 C7
Northumb............111 B6
W&F............100 D2
Hartley Westpall..26 D4
Hartley Wintney..27 D5
Hartlip............30 C2
Hartoft End............103 E5
Harton N Yorks............96 C3
Shrops............60 F4
T&W............111 C6
Hartpury............36 B4
Hartshead............88 B2
Hartshill............63 E7
Hartshorne............63 B7
Hartsop............99 C6
Hart Station............111 F7
Hartwell............53 D5
Hartwood............119 D8
Harvieston............126 F4
Harvington............51 E5
Harvington Cross..51 E5
Harwell............38 F4
Harwich............57 F6
Harwood Durham..109 F8
Gtr Man............86 C5
Harwood Dale..103 E7
Harworth............89 E7
Hasbury............62 F3
Hascombe............27 E7
Haselbech............52 B5
Haselbury
Plucknett............12 C2
Haseley............51 C7
Haselor............51 D6
Hasfield............37 B5
Hasguard............44 E3
Haskayne............85 D4
Hasketon............57 D6
Hasland............76 C3
Haslemere............27 F7
Haslingden............87 B5
Haslingfield............54 D5
Haslington............74 D4
Hassall............74 D4
Hassall Green............74 D4
Hassall Street............30 E4
Hassendean............115 B8
Hassingham............69 D6
Hassocks............17 C6
Hassop............76 B2
Hastigrow............158 D4
Hastingleigh............30 E4
Hastings............18 E5
Hastingwood............41 D7
Hastoe............40 D2
Haswell............111 E6
Haswell Plough..111 E6
Hatch C Beds............54 E2
Hants............26 D4
Wilts............13 B7
Hatch Beauchamp.11 B8
Hatch End............40 E4
Hatchet Gate............14 D4
Hatch Green............11 C8
Hatching Green..40 C4
Hatchmere............74 B2
Hatcliffe............91 D6
Hatfield Hereford..49 D7
Herts............41 D5
S Yorks............89 D7
Worcs............50 D3
Hatfield Broad
Oak............41 C8
Hatfield Garden
Village............41 D5
Hatfield Heath..41 C8
Hatfield Hyde..41 C5
Hatfield Peverel..42 C3
Hatfield
Woodhouse............89 D7
Hatford............38 E3
Hatherden............25 D8
Hatherleigh............9 D7
Hathern............63 B8
Hatherop............38 D1
Hathersage............88 F3
Hathershaw............87 D7
Hatherton Ches E..74 E3
Staffs............62 E3
Hatley St George..54 D3
Hatt............5 C8
Hattingley............26 F4
Hatton Aberds..153 E10
Derbys............63 B6
Lincs............78 B4
Shrops............60 E4
Warks............51 C7
Warr............86 F3
Hatton Castle..153 D7
Hattoncrook..141 B7
Hatton Heath..73 C8
Hatton of Fintray.141 C7
Haugh E Ayrs............112 B4
Gtr Man............87 C7
Lincs............79 B7
Haugham............91 F7
Haugh Head............117 B6

Haughley............56 C4
Haughley Green..56 C4
Haugh of Glass..152 E4
Haugh of Urr..106 C5
Haughs of
Clinterty............141 C7
Haughton Notts............77 B6
Shrops............60 B3
Shrops............61 C5
Shrops............61 D7
Shrops............61 E6
Staffs............62 B2
Haughton Castle .110 B2
Haughton Green..87 E7
Haughton Moss..74 D2
Haultwick............41 B6
Haunn Argyll..146 G6
W Isles............148 G2
Haunton............63 C6
Hauxley............117 D8
Hauxton............54 D5
Havannah............75 C5
Havant............15 D8
Haven............49 D6
Haven Bank............78 D5
Haven Side............91 B5
Havenstreet............15 E6
Havercroft............88 C4
Haverfordwest
= Hwlffordd............44 D4
Haverhill............55 E7
Haverigg............92 B1
Havering-atte-
Bower............41 E8
Haveringland............81 E7
Haversham............53 E6
Haverthwaite............99 F5
Haverton Hill............102 B2
Hawarden
= Penarlâg............73 C7
Hawcoat............92 B2
Hawen............46 E2
Hawes............100 F3
Hawes' Green............68 E5
Hawes Side............92 F3
Hawford............50 C3
Hawick............115 C8
Hawkchurch............11 D8
Hawkedon............55 D8
Hawkenbury Kent..18 B2
Kent............30 E2
Hawkeridge............24 D3
Hawkerland............11 F5
Hawkesbury S Glos..36 F4
Warks............52 B2
Hawkesbury Upton 36 F4
Hawkes End............63 F7
Hawk Green............87 F7
Hawkhill............117 C8
Hawkhurst............18 B4
Hawkinge............31 F6
Hawkley............15 B8
Hawkridge............21 F7
Hawkshead............99 E5
Hawkshead Hill..99 E5
Hawksland............119 F8
Hawkswick............94 B2
Hawksworth Notts..77 E7
W Yorks............94 E4
W Yorks............95 F5
Hawkwell............42 E4
Hawley Hants............27 D6
Kent............29 B6
Hawling............37 B7
Hawnby............102 F3
Haworth............94 F3
Hawstead............56 D2
Hawthorn Durham..111 E7
Rhondda............35 F5
Wilts............24 C3
Hawthorn Hill
Brack............27 B6
Lincs............78 D5
Hawthorpe............65 B7
Hawton............77 D7
Haxby............96 D2
Haxey............89 D8
Haydock............86 E3
Haydon............12 C4
Haydon Bridge..109 C8
Haydon Wick............37 F8
Haye............5 C8
Hayes London............28 C5
London............40 F4
Hayfield Derbys............87 F8
Fife............128 F4
Hay Green............66 C5
Hayhill............112 C4
Hayhillock............135 E5
Hayle............2 C4
Haynes............53 E8
Haynes Church
End............53 E8
Hay-on-Wye
= Y Gelli Gandryll..48 E4
Hayscastle............44 C3
Hayscastle Cross..44 C4
Hayshead............135 E6
Hay Street............41 B6
Hayton Aberdeen..141 D8
Cumb............107 E8
Cumb............108 D5
E Yorks............96 E4
Notts............89 F8
Hayton's Bent............60 F5
Haytor Vale............7 B5
Haywards Heath..17 B7
Haywood............89 C6
Haywood Oaks..77 D6
Hazelbank............119 E8
Hazelbury Bryan..12 D5
Hazeley............26 D5
Hazel Grove............87 F7
Hazelhurst............87 D7
Hazelslade............62 C4
Hazel Street............18 B3
Hazelton............37 C7
Hazelton Walls..128 B5
Hazelwood............76 E3
Hazlemere............40 E1
Hazlerigg............110 B5
Hazlewood............94 D3
Hazon............117 D7
Heacham............80 D2
Headbourne
Worthy............26 F2
Headbrook............48 D5
Headcorn............30 E2
Headingley............95 F5
Headington............39 D5

Headlam............101 C6
Headless Cross..50 C5
Headley Hants............26 C3
Hants............27 F6
Sur............28 D3
Head of Muir..127 F7
Headon............77 B7
Heads............119 E7
Heads Nook............108 D4
Heage............76 D3
Healaugh N Yorks..95 E7
N Yorks............101 E5
Heald Green............87 F6
Heale Devon............20 E5
Som............23 E8
Healey Gtr Man..87 C6
Northumb............110 D3
N Yorks............101 F6
Healing............91 C6
Heamoor............2 C3
Heanish............146 G3
Heanor............76 E4
Heanton
Punchardon............20 F4
Heapham............90 F2
Hearthstane............114 B4
Heasley Mill............21 F6
Heast............149 G11
Heath Cardiff............22 B3
Derbys............76 C4
Heath and Reach..40 B2
Heathcote............75 C8
Heath End Hants..26 C3
Sur............27 E6
Warks............51 C7
Heather............63 C7
Heatherfield..149 D9
Heathfield Devon..7 B6
E Sus............18 C2
Som............11 B6
Heathhall............107 B6
Heath Hayes............62 C4
Heath Hill............61 C7
Heath House............23 E6
Heathrow Airport..27 B8
Heathstock............11 D7
Heathton............62 E2
Heath Town............62 E3
Heatley............86 F5
Heaton Lancs............92 C4
Staffs............75 C6
T&W............111 C5
W Yorks............94 F4
Heaton Moor............87 E6
Heaverham............29 D6
Heaviley............87 F7
Heavitree............10 E4
Hebburn............111 C6
Hebden............94 C3
Hebden Bridge..87 B7
Hebron Anglesey..82 C4
Carms............32 B2
Northumb............117 F7
Heck............114 F3
Heckfield............26 C5
Heckfield Green..57 B5
Heckfordbridge..43 B5
Heckington............78 E4
Heckmondwike..88 B3
Heddington............24 C4
Heddle............159 G4
Heddon-on-the-
Wall............110 C4
Hedenham............69 E6
Hedge End............15 C5
Hedgerley............40 F2
Hedging............11 B8
Hedley on the
Hill............110 D3
Hednesford............62 C4
Hedon............91 B5
Hedsor............40 F2
Hedworth............111 C6
Hegdon Hill............49 D7
Heggerscales..100 C3
Heglibister..160 H5
Heighington Darl 101 B7
Lincs............78 C3
Heights of Brae..151 E8
Heights of
Kinlochewe..150 E3
Heilam............156 C7
Heiton............122 F3
Hele Devon............10 D4
Devon............20 E4
Helensburgh..145 E11
Helford............3 D6
Helford Passage..3 D6
Helhoughton............80 E4
Helions
Bumpstead............55 E7
Hellaby............89 E6
Helland............5 B5
Hellesdon............68 C5
Hellidon............52 D3
Hellifield............93 D8
Hellingly............18 D2
Hellington............69 D6
Hellister............160 J5
Helmdon............52 E3
Helmingham............57 D5
Helmington Row..110 F4
Helmsdale............157 H13
Helmshore............87 B5
Helmsley............102 F4
Helperby............95 C7
Helperthorpe............97 B5
Helpringham............78 E4
Helpston............65 D8
Helsby............73 B8
Helsey............79 B8
Helston............3 D5
Helstone............8 F2
Helton............99 B7
Helwith Bridge..93 C8
Hemblington............69 C6
Hemel Hempstead. 40 D3
Hemingbrough..96 F2
Hemingby............78 B5
Hemingford
Abbots............54 B3
Hemingford Grey..54 B3
Hemingstone............57 D5
Hemington Leics..63 B8
N Nhants............65 F7
Som............24 D2
Hemley............57 E6
Hemlington............102 C3

Hemp Green............57 C7
Hempholme............97 D6
Hempnall............68 E5
Hempnall Green..68 E5
Hempriggs
House............158 F5
Hempstead Essex..55 F7
Essex............42 C3
Medway............29 C8
Norf............69 B7
Norf............81 D7
Hempsted............37 C5
Hempton Norf............80 E5
Oxon............52 F2
Hemsby............69 C7
Hemswell............90 E3
Hemswell Cliff..90 F3
Hemsworth............88 C5
Hemyock............11 C6
Henbury Bristol..23 B7
Ches E............75 B5
Hendon London..41 F5
T&W............111 D7
Hendre............73 C5
Hendre-ddu............83 E8
Hendreforgan............34 F3
Hendy............33 D6
Heneglwys............82 D4
Hen-feddau fawr..45 F4
Henfield............17 C6
Henford............9 E5
Henghurst............19 B6
Hengoed Caerph..35 E5
Powys............48 D4
Shrops............73 F6
Hengrave............56 C2
Henham............41 B8
Heniarth............59 D8
Henlade............11 B7
Henley Shrops............49 B7
Som............23 F6
Suff............57 D5
W Sus............16 B2
Henley-in-Arden..51 C6
Henley-on-
Thames............39 F7
Henley's Down..18 D4
Henllan Ceredig..46 E2
Denb............72 C4
Henllan Amgoed..32 B2
Henllys............35 E6
Henlow............54 F2
Hennock............10 F3
Henny Street............56 F2
Henryd............83 D7
Henry's Moat............32 B1
Hensall............89 B6
Henshaw............109 C7
Hensingham............98 C1
Henstead............69 F7
Henstridge............12 C5
Henstridge Ash..12 B5
Henstridge Marsh..12 B5
Henton Oxon............39 D7
Som............23 E6
Henwood............5 B7
Heogan............160 J6
Heol-las............33 E7
Heol-y-Cyw............34 F3
Hepburn............117 B6
Hepple............117 D5
Hepscott............117 F8
Heptonstall............87 B7
Hepworth Suff............56 B3
W Yorks............88 D2
Herbrandston............44 E3
Hereford............49 E7
Heriot............121 D6
Hermiston............120 B4
Hermitage
Borders............115 E8
Dorset............12 D4
W Berks............26 B3
W Sus............15 D8
Hermon Anglesey..82 E3
Carms............33 B7
Carms............46 F2
Pembs............45 F4
Herne............31 C5
Herne Bay............31 C5
Herner............9 B7
Hernhill............30 C4
Herodsfoot............5 C7
Herongate............42 E2
Heronsford..104 A5
Herriard............26 E4
Herringfleet............69 E7
Herringswell............55 B8
Hersden............31 C6
Hersham Corn............8 D4
Sur............28 C2
Herstmonceux............18 D3
Herston............159 J5
Hertford............41 C6
Hertford Heath..41 C6
Hertingfordbury..41 C6
Hesket Bank............86 B2
Hesketh Lane............93 E6
Hesket
Newmarket..108 F3
Heskin Green............86 C3
Hesleden............111 F7
Hesleyside............116 F4
Heslington............96 D2
Hessay............95 D8
Hessenford............5 D8
Hessett............56 C3
Hessle............90 B4
Hest Bank............92 C4
Heston............28 B2
Hestwall............159 G3
Heswall............85 F3
Hethe............39 B5
Hethersett............68 D4
Hethersgill............108 C4
Hethpool............116 B4
Hett............111 F5
Hetton............94 D2
Hetton-le-Hole..111 E6
Hetton Steads..123 F6
Heugh............110 B3
Heugh-head............140 C2
Heveningham............57 B7
Hever............29 E5
Heversham............99 F6
Hevingham............81 E7
Hewas Water............3 B8
Hewelsfield............36 D2
Hewish N Som............23 C6

Howich continued
Som............12 D2
Heworth............96 D2
Hexham............110 C2
Hextable............29 B6
Hexton............54 F2
Hexworthy............6 B4
Hey............93 E8
Heybridge Essex..42 D3
Essex............42 E2
Heybridge Basin..42 D3
Heybrook Bay............4 F5
Heydon Cambs............54 E5
Norf............81 E7
Heydour............78 F3
Heyford Park Oxon..39 B5
Heylipol............146 G2
Heylor............160 E4
Heysham............92 C4
Heyshott............16 C2
Heyside............87 D7
Heytesbury............24 E4
Heythrop............38 B3
Heywood Gtr Man..87 C6
Wilts............24 D3
Hibaldstow............90 D3
Hickleton............89 D5
Hickling Norf............69 B7
Notts............64 B3
Hickling Green..69 B7
Hickling Heath..69 B7
Hickstead............17 B6
Hidcote Boyce..51 E6
High Ackworth..88 C5
Higham Derbys..76 D3
Kent............29 B8
Lancs............93 F8
Suff............55 C8
Suff............56 F4
Higham Dykes..110 B4
Higham Ferrers..53 C7
Higham Gobion..54 F2
Higham on the Hill 63 E7
Highampton............9 D6
Higham Wood..29 E6
High Angerton..117 F6
High Bankhill..109 E5
High Barnes..111 D6
High Beach............41 E7
High Bentham..93 C6
High Bickington..9 B8
High Birkwith..93 B7
High Blantyre..119 D6
High
Bonnybridge..119 B8
High Bradfield..88 E3
High Bray............21 F5
Highbridge Highld..136 F4
Som............22 E5
Highbrook............28 F4
High Brooms..29 E6
High Bullen............9 B7
Highburton............88 C2
Highbury............23 E8
High Buston..117 D8
High Callerton..110 B4
High Catton..96 D3
Highclere............26 C2
Highcliffe............14 E3
High Cogges............38 D3
High Coniscliffe..101 C7
High Cross Hants..15 B8
Herts............41 C6
High Easter............42 C2
High Eggborough..89 B6
High Ellington..101 F6
Higher Ansty............13 D5
Higher Ashton............10 F3
Higher Ballam..92 F3
Higher Bartle..92 F5
Higher Boscaswell..2 C2
Higher
Burwardsley..74 D2
High Ercall............61 C5
Higher Clovelly..8 B5
Higher End............86 D3
Higher Kinnerton..73 C7
Higher
Penwortham..86 B3
Higher Town............2 E4
Higher Walreddon..6 B2
Higher Walton
Lancs............86 B3
Warr............86 F3
Higher Wheelton..86 B4
Higher Whitley..86 F4
Higher Wincham..74 B3
Higher Wych............73 E8
High Etherley..101 B6
Highfield E Yorks..96 F3
Gtr Man............86 D5
N Ayrs............118 D3
Oxon............39 B5
S Yorks............88 F4
T&W............110 D4
Highfields Cambs..54 D4
Northumb............123 D5
High Garrett............42 B3
Highgate............41 F5
High Grange............110 F4
High Green Norf..68 D4
S Yorks............88 E4
Worcs............50 E3
High Halden............19 B5
High Halstow............29 B8
High Ham............23 F6
High Harrington..98 B2
High Hatton............61 B6
High Hawsker..103 D7
High Hesket............108 E4
High Hesleden..111 F7
High Hoyland..88 C3
High Hunsley..97 F5
High Hurstwood..17 B8
High Hutton............96 C3
High Ireby............108 F2
High Kelling............81 C7
High Kilburn..95 B8
Highlane Ches E..75 C5
Derbys............88 F5
High Lane Gtr Man..87 F7
Worcs............49 C8
High Laver............41 D8
Highlaws............107 E8
Highleadon............36 B4
High Legh............86 F5
Highleigh............16 E2
High Leven............102 C2

Highley............61 F7
High Littleton..23 D8
High Lorton............98 B3
High Marishes..96 B4
High Marnham..77 B8
High Melton............89 D6
High Mickley..110 C3
High Mindork..105 D7
Highmoor Cross..39 F7
Highmoor Hill..36 F1
Highnam............36 C4
Highnam Green..36 B4
High Newton..99 F6
High Newton-by-the-
Sea............117 B8
High Nibthwaite..98 F4
High Offley............61 B7
High Ongar............42 D1
High Onn............62 C2
High Roding............42 C2
High Row............108 F3
High Salvington..16 D5
High Sellafield..98 D2
High Shaw............100 E3
High Spen............110 D4
Highsted............30 C3
High Stoop............110 E4
High Street Corn..4 D4
Kent............18 B4
Suff............56 E2
Suff............57 B8
Suff............57 D8
Highstreet Green..56 F3
High Street Green 56 D4
Hightae............107 B7
High Throston..111 F7
Hightown Ches E..75 C5
Mers............85 D3
Hightown Green..56 D3
High Toynton..79 C5
High Trewhitt..117 D6
High Valleyfield..128 F2
Highway............24 B5
Highweek............7 B6
High Westwood..110 D4
Highworth............38 E2
High Wray............99 E5
High Wych............41 C7
High Wycombe..40 E1
Hilborough............67 D8
Hilcote............76 D4
Hilcott............25 D6
Hildenborough..29 E6
Hilden Park............29 E6
Hildersham............55 E6
Hilderstone............75 F6
Hilderthorpe............97 C7
Hilfield............12 D4
Hilgay............67 E6
Hill S Glos............36 E3
W Mid............62 E5
Hillam............89 B6
Hillbeck............100 C2
Hillborough............31 C6
Hillbrae Aberds..141 B6
Aberds............152 D6
Hill Brow............15 B8
Hillbutts............13 D7
Hillclifflane............76 E2
Hillcommon............11 B6
Hill Dale............86 C2
Hill Dyke............79 E6
Hillend............128 F3
Hill End Durham..110 F3
Fife............128 E2
N Yorks............94 D3
Hillerton............10 E2
Hillesden............39 B6
Hillesley............36 F4
Hillfarance............11 B6
Hillhead Aberds..152 E5
Devon............7 D7
S Ayrs............112 C4
Hill Head Hants..15 D6
Hillhead of
Auchentumb..153 C9
Hillhouse............121 D8
Hilliclay............158 D3
Hillingdon............40 F3
Hillington Glasgow 118 C5
Norf............80 E3
Hillmorton............52 B3
Hill Mountain..44 E4
Hillockhead
Aberds............140 C3
Aberds............140 D2
Hill of Beath..128 E3
Hill of Fearn..151 D11
Hill of
Mountblairy..153 C6
Hill Ridware..62 C4
Angus............135 C7
Mers............85 C4
Orkney............159 J5
Shetland............160 G6
Hillside Aberds..141 E8
Angus............135 C7
Mers............85 C4
Orkney............159 J5
Shetland............160 G6
Hillswick............160 F4
Hill Top Durham..100 B4
Hants............14 D5
W Mid............62 E3
W Yorks............88 C4
Hillview............13 E7
Hillway............15 F7
Hillwell............160 M5
Hilmarton............24 B5
Hilperton............24 D3
Hilsea............15 D7
Hilston............97 F8
Hilton Aberds..153 E9
Cambs............54 C3
Derbys............76 F2
Dorset............13 D5
Durham..101 B6
Highld............151 C10
Shrops............61 E7
Stockton............102 C2
W&F............100 B2

Hinderwell............103 C5
Hindford............73 F7
Hindhead............27 F6
Hindley............86 D4
Hindley Green..86 D4
Hindlip............50 D3
Hindolveston..81 E6
Hindon............24 F4
Hindringham..81 D5
Hingham............68 D3
Hinstock............61 B6
Hintlesham............56 E4
Hinton Hants............14 E3
Hereford............48 F5
S Glos............24 B2
Shrops............60 D4
W Nhants............52 D3
Hinton Ampner..15 B6
Hinton Blewett..23 D7
Hinton
Charterhouse..24 D2
Hinton-in-the-
Hedges............52 F3
Hinton Martell..13 D8
Hinton on the
Green............50 E5
Hinton Parva..38 F2
Hinton St George..12 C2
Hinton St Mary..13 C5
Hinton Waldrist..38 E3
Hints Shrops............49 B8
Staffs............63 D5
Hinwick............53 C7
Hinxhill............30 E4
Hinxton............55 E5
Hinxworth............54 E3
Hipperholme..88 B2
Hipswell............101 E6
Hirael............83 D5
Hiraeth............32 B2
Hirn............141 D6
Hirnant............59 B7
Hirst N Lanark..119 C8
Northumb............117 F8
Hirst Courtney..89 B7
Hirwaen............72 C5
Hirwaun............34 D3
Hiscott............9 B7
Histon............54 C5
Hitcham............56 D3
Hitchin............40 B4
Hither Green..28 B4
Hittisleigh............10 E2
Hive............96 F4
Hixon............62 B4
Hoaden............31 D6
Hoaldalbert............35 B7
Hoar Cross............62 B5
Hoarwithy............36 B2
Hoath............31 C6
Hobarris............48 B5
Hobbister..159 H4
Hobkirk............115 C8
Hobson............110 D4
Hoby............64 C3
Hockering............68 C3
Hockerton............77 D7
Hockley............42 E4
Hockley Heath..51 B6
Hockliffe............40 B2
Hockwold cum
Wilton............67 F7
Hockworthy............10 C5
Hoddesdon............41 D6
Hoddlesden............86 B5
Hoddomcross..107 B8
Hoddom Mains..107 B8
Hodgeston............32 E1
Hodley............59 E8
Hodnet............61 B6
Hodthorpe............76 B5
Hoe Hants............15 C6
Norf............68 C2
Hoe Gate............15 C7
Hoff............100 C1
Hoggard's Green..56 D2
Hoggeston............39 B8
Hogha Gearraidh.148 A2
Hoghton............86 B4
Hognaston............76 D2
Hog Patch............27 E6
Hogsthorpe............79 B8
Holbeach............66 B3
Holbeach Bank..66 B3
Holbeach Clough..66 B3
Holbeach Drove..66 C3
Holbeach Hurn..66 B3
Holbeach St Johns 66 C3
Holbeach St Marks 79 F6
Holbeach St
Matthew............79 F7
Holbeck Notts............76 B5
W Yorks............95 F5
Holbeck
Woodhouse..76 B5
Holberrow Green..50 D5
Holbeton............6 D4
Holborn............41 F6
Holbrook Derbys..76 E3
S Yorks............88 F5
Suff............57 F5
Holburn............123 F6
Holbury............14 D5
Holcombe Devon..7 B7
Som............23 E8
Holcombe Rogus..11 C5
Holcot............53 C5
Holden............93 E7
Holdenby............52 C4
Holdenhurst............14 E2
Holdgate............61 F5
Holdingham............78 E3
Holditch............11 D8
Hole-in-the-Wall..36 B3
Holemoor............9 D6
Holestane............113 E8
Holford............22 E3
Holgate............95 D8
Holker............92 B3
Holkham............80 C4
Hollacombe............9 D5
Holland Arley..159 C5
Orkney............159 F7
Holland Fen............78 E5
Holland-on-Sea..43 C8
Hollandstoun..159 C8
Hollee............108 C2

Hollesley............57 E7
Hollicombe............7 C6
Hollingbourne..30 D2
Hollington Derbys..76 F2
E Sus............18 D4
Staffs............75 F7
Hollington Grove..76 F2
Hollingworth............87 E8
Hollins............87 D6
Hollinsclough..75 C7
Hollins Green..86 E4
Hollins Lane..92 D4
Hollinwood
Gtr Man............87 D7
Shrops............74 F2
Hollocombe............9 C8
Holloway............76 D3
Hollowell............52 B4
Hollow Meadows..88 F3
Hollybush Caerph..35 D5
E Ayrs............112 C3
Worcs............50 F2
Holly End............66 D4
Holly Green............50 E3
Hollym............91 B7
Hollywood............51 B5
Holmbridge............88 D2
Holmbury St Mary.28 E2
Holmbush............4 D5
Holmcroft............62 B3
Holme Cambs............65 F8
Notts............77 D8
N Yorks............102 F1
W&F............92 B5
W Yorks............88 D2
Holme Chapel..87 B6
Holme Green..95 E8
Holme Hale..67 D8
Holme Lacy..49 F7
Holme Marsh..48 D5
Holme next the
Sea............80 C3
Holme-on-Spalding-
Moor............96 F4
Holme on the
Wolds............97 E5
Holme Pierrepont..77 F6
Holmer............49 E7
Holmer Green..40 E2
Holme St
Cuthbert............107 E8
Holmes Chapel..74 C4
Holmesfield............76 B3
Holmeswood............86 C2
Holmewood............76 C4
Holme Wood..94 F4
Holmfirth............88 D2
Holmhead
Dumfries............113 F7
E Ayrs............113 B5
Holmisdale............148 D6
Holmpton............91 B7
Holmrook............98 E2
Holmsgarth..160 J6
Holmwrangle..108 E5
Holne............6 C5
Holnest............12 D4
Holsworthy............8 D5
Holsworthy Beacon..9 D5
Holt Dorset............13 D8
Norf............81 D7
Wilts............24 C3
Worcs............50 C3
Wrex............73 D8
Holtby............96 D2
Holt End Hants..26 F4
Worcs............50 C5
Holt Fleet............50 C3
Holt Heath............50 C3
Holton Oxon............39 D6
Som............12 B4
Suff............57 B7
Holton cum
Beckering............90 F5
Holton Heath..13 E7
Holton le Clay..91 D6
Holton le Moor..90 E4
Holton St Mary..56 F4
Holt Park............95 E5
Holwell Dorset..12 C5
Herts............54 F2
Leics............64 B4
Oxon............38 D2
Holwick............100 B4
Holworth............13 F5
Holybourne............26 E5
Holy Cross............50 B4
Holyhead
= Caergybi............82 C2
Holy Island............123 E7
Holymoorside..76 C3
Holyport............27 B6
Holystone............117 D5
Holytown............119 C7
Holywell Cambs..54 B4
Corn............4 D2
Dorset............12 D3
E Sus............18 F2
Northumb............111 B6
Holywell
= Treffynnon............73 B5
Holywell Green..87 C8
Holywell Lake..11 B6
Holywell Row..55 B8
Holywood............114 F2
Homer............61 D6
Homersfield............69 F5
Hom Green............36 B2
Homington............14 B2
Honeyborough..44 E4
Honeybourne..51 E6
Honeychurch............9 D8
Honey Hill............30 C5
Honey Street..25 C6
Honey Tye............56 F3
Honiley............51 B7
Honing............69 B6
Honingham............68 C4
Honington Lincs..78 E2
Suff............56 B3
Warks............51 E7
Honiton............11 D6
Honley............88 C2
Hood Green............88 D4
Hooe E Sus............18 E3
Plym............6 D3

Hooe Common 18 D3
Hoo Green 86 F5
Hook E Yorks 89 B8
Hants 26 D5
London 28 C2
Pembs 44 D4
Wilts 37 F7
Hooke 12 E3
Hookgate 74 F4
Hook Green Kent . . . 18 B3
Kent 29 C7
Hook Norton 51 F8
Hookway 10 E3
Hookwood 28 E3
Hoole 73 C8
Hooley 28 D3
Hoop 36 D2
Hoo St Werburgh . . 29 B8
Hooton 73 B7
Hooton Levitt 89 E6
Hooton Pagnell 89 D5
Hooton Roberts . . . 89 E5
Hope Derbys 88 F2
Devon 6 F4
Highld 156 B7
Powys 60 D2
Shrops 60 D3
Staffs 75 D8
Hope = Yr Hôb 73 D7
Hope Bagot 49 B7
Hope Bowdler 60 E4
Hope End Green . . . 42 B1
Hope Green 87 F7
Hopeman 152 B1
Hope Mansell 36 C3
Hopesay 60 F3
Hope's Green 42 F3
Hope under Dinmore 49 D7
Hopley's Green 48 D5
Hopperton 95 D7
Hop Pole 65 C8
Hopstone 61 E7
Hopton Shrops 60 B3
Shrops 61 B5
Staffs 62 B3
Suff 56 B3
Hopton Cangeford . 60 F5
Hopton Castle 49 B5
Hoptonheath 49 B5
Hopton on Sea 69 D8
Hopton Wafers 49 B8
Hopwas 63 D5
Hopwood Gtr Man . . 87 D6
Worcs 50 B5
Horam 18 D2
Horbling 78 F4
Horbury 88 C3
Horcott 38 D1
Horden 111 E7
Horderley 60 F4
Hordle 14 E3
Hordley 73 F7
Horeb Carms 33 B6
Carms 33 D5
Ceredig 46 E2
Horfield 23 B8
Horham 57 B6
Horkesley Heath . . . 43 B5
Horkstow 90 C3
Horley Oxon 52 E2
Sur 28 E3
Hornblotton Green 23 F7
Hornby Lancs 93 C5
N Yorks 101 E7
N Yorks 102 D1
Horncastle 79 C5
Hornchurch 41 F8
Horncliffe 122 E5
Horndean Borders . 122 E4
Hants 15 C8
Horndon 6 B3
Horndon on the Hill 42 F2
Horne 28 E4
Horniehaugh 134 C4
Horning 69 C6
Horninghold 64 E5
Horninglow 63 B6
Horningsea 55 C5
Horningsham 24 E3
Horningtoft 80 E5
Hornsby 108 D5
Horns Corner 18 C4
Horns Cross Devon . . . 9 B5
E Sus 18 C5
Hornsea 97 E8
Hornsea Bridge 97 E8
Hornsey 41 F6
Hornton 51 E8
Horrabridge 6 C3
Horringer 56 C2
Horringford 15 F6
Horsebridge Devon . . 6 B2
Hants 25 F8
Horse Bridge 75 D6
Horsebrook 62 C2
Horsehay 61 D6
Horseheath 55 E7
Horsehouse 101 F5
Horsell 27 D7
Horseman's Green 73 E8
Horseway 66 F4
Horsey 69 B7
Horsford 68 C4
Horsforth 94 F5
Horsham Worcs 50 D2
W Sus 28 F2
Horsham St Faith . . 68 C5
Horsington Lincs 78 C4
Som 12 B5
Horsley Derbys 76 E3
Glos 37 E5
Northumb 110 C3
Northumb 116 E4
Horsley Cross 43 B7
Horsleycross Street 43 B7
Horsleyhill 115 C8
Horsleyhope 110 E3
Horsley Woodhouse 76 E3
Horsmonden 29 E7
Horspath 39 D5
Horstead 69 C5
Horsted Keynes . . . 17 B7
Horton Bucks 40 C2
Dorset 13 D8
Lancs 93 D8
S Glos 36 F4
Shrops 60 B4
Som 11 C8
Staffs 75 D6
Swansea 33 F5
Wilts 25 C5
Windsor 27 B8
W Nhants 53 D6
Horton-cum-Studley 39 C5
Horton Green 73 E8
Horton Heath 15 C5
Horton in Ribblesdale 93 B8
Horton Kirby 29 C6
Hortonlane 60 C4
Horwich 86 C4
Horwich End 87 F8
Horwood 9 B7
Hose 64 B4
Hoselaw 122 F4
Hoses 98 E4
Hosh 127 B7
Hosta 148 A2
Hoswick 160 L6
Hotham 96 F4
Hothfield 30 E3
Hoton 64 B2
Houbie 160 D8
Houdston 112 E1
Hough Ches E 74 D4
Ches E 75 B5
Hougham 77 E8
Hough Green 86 F2
Hough-on-the-Hill 78 E2
Houghton Cambs 54 B3
Cumb 108 D4
Hants 25 F8
Pembs 44 E4
W Sus 16 C4
Houghton Conquest 53 E8
Houghton Green E Sus 19 C6
Warr 86 E4
Houghton-le-Side 101 B7
Houghton-le-Spring 111 E6
Houghton on the Hill 64 D3
Houghton Regis . . . 40 B3
Houghton St Giles . 80 D5
Houlland Shetland . 160 F7
Shetland 160 H5
Houlsyke 103 D5
Houlton Warks 52 B3
Hound 15 D5
Hound Green 26 D5
Houndslow 122 E2
Houndwood 122 C4
Hounslow 28 B2
Hounslow Green . . 42 C2
Housay 160 F8
House of Daviot . 151 G10
House of Glenmuick 140 E2
Housetter 160 E5
Houss 160 K5
Houston 118 C4
Houstry 158 G3
Houton 159 H4
Hove 17 D6
Hoveringham 77 E6
Hoveton 69 C6
Hovingham 96 B2
How 108 D5
Howbrook 88 E4
How Caple 49 F8
Howden Borders . . . 116 B2
E Yorks 89 B8
Howden-le-Wear 110 F4
Howe Highld 158 D5
Norf 69 D5
N Yorks 101 F8
Howe Bridge 86 D4
Howe Green 42 D3
Howell 78 E4
How End 53 E8
Howe of Teuchar . 153 D7
Howe Street Essex . 42 C2
Essex 55 F7
Howey 48 D2
Howgate 120 D5
How Green 29 E5
Howick 117 C8
Howle Durham 101 B5
Telford 61 B6
Howlett End 55 F6
Howley 11 D7
Hownam 116 C3
Hownam Mains . . . 116 B3
Howpasley 115 D6
Howsham N Lincs . . . 90 D4
N Yorks 96 C3
Howslack 114 D3
Howtel 122 F4
Howton 35 B8
Howtown 99 C6
Howwood 118 C3
Hoxne 57 B5
Hoy 159 H3
Hoylake 85 F3
Hoyland 88 D4
Hoylandswaine 88 D3
Hubberholme 94 B2
Hubbert's Bridge . . 79 E5
Huby N Yorks 95 C8
N Yorks 95 E5
Hucclecote 37 C5
Hucking 30 D2
Hucknall 76 E5
Huddersfield 88 C2
Huddington 50 D4
Hudswell 101 D6
Huggate 96 D4
Hugglescote 63 C8
Hughenden Valley . 40 E1
Hughley 61 E5
Hugh Town 2 E4
Huish Devon 9 C7
Wilts 25 C6
Huish Champflower . . . 11 B5
Huish Episcopi 12 B2
Huisinis 154 F4
Hulcott 40 C1
Hulland 76 E2
Hulland Ward 76 E2
Hullavington 37 F5
Hullbridge 42 E4
Hulme 87 E6
Hulme End 75 D8
Hulme Walfield 74 C5
Hulverstone 14 F4
Hulver Street 69 F7
Humber 49 D7
Humber Bridge 90 B4
Humberston 91 D7
Humbie 121 C7
Humbleton E Yorks . . 97 F8
Northumb 117 B5
Humby 78 F3
Hume 122 E3
Humshaugh 110 B2
Huna 158 C5
Huncoat 93 F7
Huncote 64 E2
Hundalee 116 C2
Hunderthwaite . . . 100 B4
Hundleby 79 C6
Hundle Houses 79 D5
Hundleton 44 E4
Hundon 55 E8
Hundred Acres 15 C6
Hundred End 86 B2
Hundred House 48 D3
Hungarton 64 D3
Hungerford Hants . . 14 C2
W Berks 25 C8
Hungerford Newtown 25 B8
Hungerton 65 B5
Hungladder 149 A8
Hunmanby 97 B6
Hunmanby Moor . . . 97 B7
Hunningham 51 C8
Hunny Hill 15 F5
Hunsdon 41 C7
Hunsingore 95 D7
Hunslet 95 F6
Hunsonby 109 F5
Hunspow 158 C4
Hunstanton 80 C2
Hunstanworth 110 E2
Hunsterson 74 E3
Hunston Suff 56 C3
W Sus 16 D2
Hunstrete 23 C8
Hunt End 50 C5
Hunter's Quay . . . 145 F10
Hunthill Lodge . . . 134 B4
Huntingdon 54 B3
Huntingfield 57 B7
Huntingford 24 F3
Huntington E Loth . 121 B7
Hereford 48 D4
Staffs 62 C3
York 96 D2
Huntingtower 128 B2
Huntley 36 C4
Huntly 152 E5
Huntlywood 122 E2
Hunton Kent 29 E8
N Yorks 101 E6
Hunt's Corner 68 F3
Hunt's Cross 86 F2
Huntsham 10 B5
Huntspill 22 E5
Huntworth 22 F5
Hunwick 110 F4
Hunworth 81 D6
Hurdsfield 75 B6
Hurley Warks 63 E6
Windsor 39 F8
Hurlford 118 F4
Hurliness 159 K3
Hurn 14 E2
Hurn's End 79 E7
Hursley 14 B5
Hurst N Yorks 101 D5
Som 12 C2
Wokingham 27 B5
Hurstbourne Priors 26 E2
Hurstbourne Tarrant 25 D8
Hurst Green E Sus . . 18 C4
Lancs 93 F6
Hurstpierpoint 17 C6
Hurst Wickham 17 C6
Hurstwood 93 F8
Hurtmore 27 E7
Hurworth Place . . . 101 D7
Hury 100 C4
Husabost 148 C7
Husbands Bosworth 64 F3
Husborne Crawley . 53 F7
Husthwaite 95 B8
Hutchwns 21 B7
Huthwaite 76 D4
Huttoft 79 B8
Hutton Borders 122 D5
Essex 42 E2
E Yorks 97 D6
Lancs 86 B2
N Som 22 D5
W&F 99 B6
Hutton Buscel 103 F7
Hutton Conyers . . . 95 B6
Hutton Cranswick . 97 D6
Hutton End 108 F4
Hutton Gate 102 C3
Hutton Henry 111 F7
Hutton-le-Hole . . 103 E5
Hutton Magna 101 C6
Hutton Roof W&F . . 93 B5
W&F 108 F3
Hutton Rudby 102 D2
Hutton Sessay 95 B7
Hutton Village 102 C3
Hutton Wandesley . 95 D8
Huxley 74 C2
Huxter Shetland . . . 160 G7
Shetland 160 H5
Huxton 122 C4
Huyton 86 E2
Hwlffordd = Haverfordwest . . 44 D4
Hycemoor 98 F2
Hyde Glos 37 D5
Gtr Man 87 E7
Hants 14 C2
Hyde Heath 40 D2
Hyde Park 89 D6
Hydestile 27 E7
Hylton Castle 111 D6
Hyndford Bridge . 120 E2
Hynish 146 H2
Hyssington 60 E3
Hythe Hants 14 D5
Kent 19 B8
Hythe End 27 B8
Hythie 153 C10

I

Ibberton 13 D5
Ible 76 D2
Ibsley 14 D2
Ibstock 63 C8
Ibstone 39 E7
Ibthorpe 25 D8
Ibworth 26 D3
Ichrachan 125 B6
Ickburgh 67 E8
Ickenham 40 F3
Ickford 39 D6
Ickham 31 D6
Ickleford 54 F2
Icklesham 19 D5
Ickleton 55 E5
Icklingham 55 B8
Ickwell Green 54 E2
Icomb 38 B2
Idbury 38 C2
Iddesleigh 9 D7
Ide 10 E3
Ideford 7 B6
Ide Hill 29 D5
Iden 19 C6
Iden Green Kent 18 B4
Kent 18 B5
Idle 94 F4
Idlicote 51 E7
Idmiston 25 F6
Idole 33 C5
Idridgehay 76 E2
Idrigill 149 B8
Idstone 38 F2
Idvies 135 E5
Iffley 39 D5
Ifield 28 F3
Ifold 27 F8
Iford 17 D8
Ifton Heath 73 F7
Ightfield 74 F2
Ightham 29 D6
Iken 57 D8
Ilam 75 D8
Ilchester 12 B3
Ilderton 117 B6
Ilford 41 F7
Ilfracombe 20 E4
Ilkeston 76 E4
Ilketshall St Andrew 69 F6
Ilketshall St Lawrence 69 F6
Ilketshall St Margaret 69 F6
Ilkley 94 E4
Illey 62 F3
Illingworth 87 B8
Illogan 3 B5
Illston on the Hill . . 64 E4
Ilmer 39 D7
Ilmington 51 E7
Ilminster 11 C8
Ilsington 7 B5
Ilston 33 E6
Ilton N Yorks 94 B4
Som 11 C8
Imachar 143 D9
Imeraval 142 D4
Immingham 91 C5
Impington 54 C5
Ince 73 B8
Ince Blundell 85 D4
Ince in Makerfield . 86 D3
Inchbare 135 C6
Inchberry 152 C3
Inchbraoch 135 D7
Incheril 150 E3
Inchgrundle 134 B4
Inchina 150 B2
Inchinnan 118 C4
Inchkinloch 157 E8
Inchlaggan 136 D4
Inchlumpie 151 D8
Inchmore 150 G6
Inchnacardoch Hotel 137 C6
Inchnadamph 156 G5
Inch of Arnhall . . . 135 B6
Inchree 130 C4
Inchture 128 B4
Inchyra 128 B3
Indian Queens 4 D4
Inerval 142 D4
Ingatestone 42 E2
Ingbirchworth 88 D3
Ingestre 62 B3
Ingham Lincs 90 F3
Norf 69 B6
Suff 56 B2
Ingham Corner 69 B6
Ingleborough 66 C4
Ingleby Derbys 63 B7
Lincs 77 B8
Ingleby Arncliffe . 102 D2
Ingleby Barwick . . 102 C2
Ingleby Greenhow 102 D3
Inglemire 97 F6
Inglesbatch 24 C2
Inglesham 38 E2
Ingleton Durham . . 101 B6
N Yorks 93 B6
Inglewhite 92 E5
Ingliston 120 B4
Ingoe 110 B3
Ingol 92 F5
Ingoldisthorpe 80 D2
Ingoldmells 79 C8
Ingoldsby 78 F3
Ingon 51 D7
Ingram 117 C6
Ingrow 94 F3
Ings 99 E6
Ingst 36 F2
Ingworth 81 E7
Inham's End 66 E2
Inkberrow 50 D5
Inkpen 25 C8
Inkstack 158 C4
Inn 99 D6
Innellan 145 F10
Innerleithen 121 F6
Innerleven 129 D5
Innermessan 104 C4
Innerwick E Loth . . 122 B3
Perth 132 E2
Innis Chonain 125 C7
Insch 140 B5
Insh 138 D4
Inshore 156 C6
Inskip 92 F4
Instoneville 89 C6
Instow 20 F3
Intake 89 D6
Inver Aberds 139 E8
Highld 151 C11
Perth 133 E7
Inverailort 147 C10
Inveraldie 134 F4
Inveralligin 149 C13
Inverallochy 153 B10
Inveran 151 B8
Inveraray 125 E6
Inverarish 149 E10
Inverarity 134 E4
Inverarnan 126 C2
Inverasdale 155 J13
Inverbeg 126 E2
Inverbervie 135 B8
Inverboyndie 153 B6
Inverbroom 150 C4
Invercassley 156 J7
Invercauld House . 139 E7
Inverchaolain 145 F9
Invercharnan 131 E5
Inverchoran 150 F5
Invercreran 130 E4
Inverdruie 138 C5
Inverebrie 153 E9
Invereck 145 E10
Inverernan House 140 C2
Invereshie House . 138 D4
Inveresk 121 B6
Inverey 139 F6
Inverfarigaig 137 B8
Invergarry 137 D6
Invergelder 139 E8
Invergeldie 127 B6
Invergordon 151 E10
Invergowrie 134 F3
Inverguseran 149 H12
Inverhadden 132 D3
Inverharroch 152 E3
Inverherive 126 B2
Inverie 147 B10
Inverinan 125 D5
Inverinate 136 B2
Inverkeilor 135 E6
Inverkeithing 128 F3
Inverkeithny 153 D6
Inverkip 118 B2
Inverkirkaig 156 H3
Inverlael 150 C4
Inverlochlarig 126 C3
Inverlochy Argyll . . 125 C7
Highld 131 B5
Inverlussa 144 E5
Inver Mallie 136 F4
Invermark Lodge . 140 F3
Invermoidart 147 D9
Invermoriston 137 C7
Invernaver 157 C10
Inverneill 145 E7
Inverness 151 G9
Invernettie 153 D11
Invernoaden 125 F7
Inveroran Hotel . . . 131 E6
Inverpolly Lodge . 156 H3
Inverquharity 134 D4
Inverquhomery . . 153 D10
Inverroy 137 F5
Inversanda 130 D3
Invershiel 136 C2
Invershin 151 B8
Inversnaid Hotel . . 126 D2
Inverugie 153 D11
Inveruglas 126 D2
Inveruglass 138 D4
Inverurie 141 B6
Invervar 132 E3
Inverythan 153 D7
Inwardleigh 9 E7
Inworth 42 C4
Iochdar 148 D2
Iping 16 B2
Ipplepen 7 C6
Ipsden 39 F6
Ipsley 51 C5
Ipstones 75 D7
Ipswich 57 E5
Irby 85 F3
Irby in the Marsh . . 79 C7
Irby upon Humber . 91 D5
Irchester 53 C7
Ireby Cumb 108 F2
Lancs 93 B6
Ireland Orkney 159 H4
Shetland 160 L5
Ireland's Cross 74 E4
Ireleth 92 B2
Ireshopeburn 109 F8
Irlam 86 E5
Irnham 65 B7
Iron Acton 36 F3
Ironbridge 61 D6
Iron Cross 51 D5
Irongray 107 B6
Ironmacannie 106 B3
Ironside 153 C8
Ironville 76 D4
Irstead 69 B6
Irthington 108 C4
Irthlingborough . . . 53 B7
Irton 103 F8
Irvine 118 F3
Isauld 157 C12
Isbister Orkney . . . 159 F3
Orkney 159 G4
Shetland 160 D5
Shetland 160 G7
Isfield 17 C8
Isham 53 B6
Isle Abbotts 11 B8
Isle Brewers 11 B8
Isleham 55 B7
Isle of Whithorn . . 105 F8
Isleornsay 149 G12
Islesburgh 160 G5
Islesteps 107 B6
Isleworth 28 B2
Isley Walton 63 B8
Islibhig 154 E4
Islington 41 F6
Islip N Nhants 53 B7
Oxon 39 C5
Istead Rise 29 C7
Isycoed 73 D8
Itchen 14 C5
Itchen Abbas 26 F3
Itchen Stoke 26 F3
Itchingfield 16 B5
Itchington 36 F3
Itteringham 81 D7
Itton 9 E8
Itton Common 36 E1
Ivegill 108 E4
Iver 40 F3
Iver Heath 40 F3
Iveston 110 D4
Ivinghoe 40 C2
Ivinghoe Aston 40 C2
Ivington 49 D6
Ivington Green 49 D6
Ivybridge 6 D4
Ivy Chimneys 41 D7
Ivychurch 19 C7
Ivy Cross 13 B6
Ivy Hatch 29 D6
Iwade 30 C3
Iwerne Courtney or Shroton 13 C6
Iwerne Minster 13 C6
Ixworth 56 B3
Ixworth Thorpe 56 B3

J

Jack Hill 94 D5
Jack in the Green . . 10 E5
Jacksdale 76 D4
Jackstown 153 E7
Jacobstow 8 E3
Jacobstowe 9 D7
Jameston 32 E1
Jamestown Dumfries 115 E6
Highld 150 F7
W Dunb 126 F2
Jarrow 111 C6
Jarvis Brook 18 C2
Jasper's Green 42 B3
Java 124 B3
Jawcraig 119 B8
Jaywick 43 C7
Jealott's Hill 27 B6
Jedburgh 116 B2
Jeffreyston 32 D1
Jellyhill 119 B6
Jemimaville 151 E10
Jersey Farm 40 D4
Jesmond 111 C5
Jevington 18 E2
Jockey End 40 C3
Johnby 108 F4
John o'Groats 158 C5
John's Cross 18 C4
Johnshaven 135 C7
Johnston E Renfs . . 118 C4
Pembs 44 D4
Johnstonebridge . 114 E3
Johnstown Carms . . 33 C5
Wrex 73 E7
Joppa Edin 121 B6
S Ayrs 112 C4
Jordans 40 E2
Jordanthorpe 88 F4
Jump 88 D4
Jumpers Green 14 E2
Juniper Green 120 C4
Jurby East 84 C3
Jurby West 84 C3

K

Kaber 100 C2
Kaimend 120 E2
Kaimes 121 C5
Kalemouth 116 B3
Kames Argyll 124 D4
Argyll 145 F8
E Ayrs 113 B6
Kea 3 B7
Keadby 90 C2
Keal Cotes 79 C6
Kearsley 87 D5
Kearstwick 99 F8
Kearton 100 E4
Kearvaig 156 B5
Keasden 93 C7
Keckwick 86 F3
Keddington 91 F7
Kedington 55 E8
Kedleston 76 E3
Keelby 91 C5
Keele 74 E5
Keeley Green 53 E8
Keeston 44 D4
Keevil 24 D4
Kegworth 63 B8
Kehelland 2 B5
Keig 140 C5
Keighley 94 E3
Keil 130 D3
Keilarsbrae 127 E7
Keilhill 153 C7
Keillmore 144 E5
Keillor 134 E2
Keillour 127 B8
Keills 142 B5
Keils 144 G4
Keinton Mandeville 23 F7
Keir Mill 113 E8
Keisby 65 B7
Keiss 158 D5
Keith 152 C4
Keith Inch 153 D11
Keithock 135 C6
Kelbrook 94 E2
Kelby 78 E3
Keld N Yorks 100 D3
W&F 99 C7
Keldholme 103 F5
Kelfield N Lincs 90 D2
N Yorks 95 F8
Kelham 77 D7
Kellan 147 G8
Kellas Angus 134 F4
Moray 152 C1
Kellaton 7 F6
Kelleth 100 D1
Kelleythorpe 97 D5
Kelling 81 C6
Kellingley 89 B6
Kellington 89 B6
Kelloe 111 F6
Kelloholm 113 C7
Kelly 9 F5
Kelly Bray 5 B8
Kelmarsh 52 B5
Kelmscot 38 E2
Kelsale 57 C7
Kelsall 74 C2
Kelsall Hill 74 C2
Kelshall 54 F4
Kelsick 107 D8
Kelso 122 F3
Kelstedge 76 C3
Kelstern 91 E6
Kelston 24 C2
Keltneyburn 132 E4
Kelton 107 B6
Kelty 128 E3
Kelvedon 42 C4
Kelvedon Hatch . . . 42 E1
Kelvin 119 D6
Kelvinside 119 C5
Kelynack 2 C2
Kemback 129 C6
Kemberton 61 D7
Kemble 37 E6
Kemerton 50 F4
Kemeys Commander 35 D7
Kemnay 141 C6
Kempley 36 B3
Kempsey 50 E3
Kempsford 38 E1
Kemps Green 51 B6
Kempshott 26 D4
Kempston 53 E8
Kempston Hardwick 53 E8
Kempton 60 F3
Kemp Town 17 D7
Kemsing 29 D6
Kemsley 30 C3
Kenardington 19 B6
Kenchester 49 E6
Kencot 38 D2
Kendal 99 E7
Kendoon 113 F6
Kendray 88 D4
Kenfig 34 F2
Kenfig Hill 34 F2
Kenilworth 51 B7
Kenknock 132 F1
Kenley London 28 D4
Shrops 61 D5
Kenmore Highld . . 149 C12
Perth 132 E4
Kenn Devon 10 F4
N Som 23 C6
Kennacley 154 H6
Kennacraig 145 G7
Kennerleigh 10 D3
Kennet 127 E8
Kennethmont 140 B4
Kennett 55 C7
Kennford 10 F4
Kenninghall 68 F3
Kenninghall Heath 68 F3
Kennington Kent 30 E4
Oxon 39 D5
Kennoway 129 D5
Kenny Hill 55 B7
Kennythorpe 96 C3
Kenovay 146 G2
Kensaleyre 149 C9
Kensington 28 B3
Kensworth 40 C3
Kensworth Common 40 C3
Kentallen 130 D4
Kentchurch 35 B8
Kentford 55 C8
Kentisbeare 11 D5
Kentisbury 20 E5
Kentisbury Ford . . . 20 E5
Kentmere 99 D6
Kenton Devon 10 F4
Suff 57 C5
T&W 110 C5
Kenton Bankfoot . 110 C5
Kentra 147 E9
Kents Bank 92 B3
Kent's Green 36 B4
Kent's Oak 14 B4
Kent Street E Sus . . . 18 D4
Kent 29 D7
W Sus 17 B6
Kenwick 73 F8
Kenwyn 3 B7
Keoldale 156 C6
Keppanach 130 C4
Keppoch 136 B2
Keprigan 143 G7
Kepwick 102 E2
Kerchesters 122 F3
Keresley 63 F7
Kernborough 7 E5
Kerne Bridge 36 C2
Kerris 2 D3
Kerry 59 F8
Kerrycroy 145 G10
Kerrysdale 149 A13
Kerry's Gate 49 F5
Kersall 77 C7
Kersey 56 E4
Kershopefoot 115 F7
Kersoe 50 E4
Kerswell 11 D5
Kerswell Green 50 E3
Kesgrave 57 E6
Kessingland 69 F8
Kessingland Beach 69 F8
Kessington 119 B5
Kestle 3 B8
Kestle Mill 4 D3
Keston 28 C5
Keswick Cumb 98 B4
Norf 68 D5
Norf 81 D9
Ketley 61 C6
Ketley Bank 61 C6
Ketsby 79 B6
Kettering 53 B6
Ketteringham 68 D4
Kettins 134 F2
Kettlebaston 56 D3
Kettlebridge 128 D5
Kettleburgh 57 C6
Kettlehill 128 D5
Kettleholm 107 B8
Kettleness 103 C6
Kettleshume 75 B6
Kettlesing Bottom . 94 D5
Kettlesing Head . . . 94 D5
Kettlestone 81 D5
Kettlethorpe 77 B8
Kettletoft 159 E7
Kettlewell 94 B2
Ketton 65 D6
Kew 28 B2
Kew Bridge 28 B2
Kewstoke 22 C5
Kexbrough 88 D4
Kexby Lincs 90 F2
York 96 D3
Key Green 75 C5
Keyham 64 D3
Keyhaven 14 E4
Keyingham 91 B6
Keymer 17 C7
Keynsham 23 C8
Keysoe 53 C8
Keysoe Row 53 C8
Keyston 53 B8
Keyworth 77 F6
Kibblesworth 110 D5
Kibworth Beauchamp 64 E3
Kibworth Harcourt 64 E3
Kidbrooke 28 B5
Kiddemore Green . 62 D2
Kidderminster 50 B3
Kiddington 38 B4
Kidlington 38 C4
Kidmore End 26 B4
Kidsgrove 74 D5
Kidstones 100 F4
Kidwelly = Cydweli 33 D5
Kiel Crofts 124 B5
Kielder 116 E2
Kierfiold Ho 159 G3
Kilbagie 127 F8
Kilbarchan 118 C4
Kilbeg 149 H11
Kilberry 144 G6
Kilbirnie 118 D3
Kilbride Argyll 124 C4
Argyll 124 C5
Highld 149 F10
Kilburn Angus 134 C3
Derbys 76 E3
London 41 F5
N Yorks 95 B8
Kilby 64 E3
Kilchamaig 145 G7
Kilchattan 144 D2
Kilchattan Bay . . . 145 H10
Kilchenzie 143 F7
Kilcheran 124 B4
Kilchiaran 142 B3
Kilchoan Argyll 124 D3
Highld 146 E7
Kilchoman 142 B3
Kilchrenan 125 C6
Kilconquhar 129 D6
Kilcot 36 B3
Kilcoy 151 F8
Kilcreggan 145 E11
Kildale 102 D4
Kildalloig 143 G8
Kildary 151 D10
Kildermorie Lodge 151 D8
Kildonan 143 F11
Kildonan Lodge . 157 G12
Kildonnan 146 C7
Kildrummy 140 C3
Kildwick 94 E3
Kilfinan 145 F8
Kilfinnan 137 E5
Kilgetty 32 D2
Kilgwrrwg Common 36 E1
Kilham E Yorks 97 C6
Northumb 122 F4
Kilkenneth 146 G2
Kilkerran 143 G8
Kilkhampton 9 E6
Killamarsh 89 F5
Killay 33 E7
Killbeg 147 G9
Killean 143 D7
Killearn 126 F4
Killen 151 F9
Killerby 101 C6
Killichonan 132 D2
Killiechonate 136 F5
Killiechronan 147 G8
Killiecrankie 133 C6
Killiemor 146 H7
Killiemore House . 146 J7
Killilan 150 H2
Killimster 158 E5
Killin 132 F2
Killinallan 142 A4
Killinghall 95 D5
Killington 99 F8
Killingworth 111 B5
Killin Lodge 137 D8
Killmahumaig 144 D6
Killochyett 121 E7
Killocraw 143 E7
Killundine 147 G8
Kilmacolm 118 C3
Kilmaha 124 E5
Kilmahog 126 D5
Kilmalieu 130 D2
Kilmaluag 149 A9
Kilmany 129 B5
Kilmarie 149 G10
Kilmarnock 118 F4
Kilmaron Castle . . 129 C5
Kilmartin 124 F4
Kilmaurs 118 E4
Kilmelford 124 D4
Kilmeny 142 B4
Kilmersdon 23 D8
Kilmeston 15 B6
Kilmichael 143 F7
Kilmichael Glassary 145 D7
Kilmichael of Inverlussa 144 E6
Kilmington Devon . . . 11 E7
Wilts 24 F2
Kilmonivaig 136 F4
Kilmorack 150 G7
Kilmore Argyll 124 C4
Highld 149 H11
Kilmory Argyll 144 F6
Highld 147 D8
Highld 149 H8
N Ayrs 143 F10
Kilmuir Highld 148 D7
Highld 149 A8
Highld 151 D10
Highld 151 G9
Kilmun Argyll 124 D5
Argyll 145 E10
Kilncadzow 119 E8
Kilndown 18 B4
Kilnhurst 89 E5
Kilninian 146 G6
Kilninver 124 C4
Kiln Pit Hill 110 D3
Kilnsea 91 C8
Kilnsey 94 C2
Kilnwick 97 E5
Kilnwick Percy 96 D4
Kiloran 144 D2
Kilpatrick 143 F10
Kilpeck 49 F6
Kilphedir 157 H12
Kilpin 89 B8
Kilpin Pike 89 B8
Kilrenny 129 D7
Kilsby 52 B3
Kilspindie 128 B4
Kilsyth 119 B7
Kiltarlity 151 G8
Kilton Notts 77 B5
Som 22 E3
Kilton Thorpe 102 C4
Kilvaxter 149 B8
Kilve 22 E3
Kilvington 77 E7
Kilwinning 118 E3
Kimberley Norf 68 D3
Notts 76 E5
Kimberworth 88 E5
Kimblesworth 111 E5
Kimble Wick 39 D8
Kimbolton Cambs . . . 53 C8
Hereford 49 C7
Kimcote 64 F2
Kimmeridge 13 G7
Kimmerston 123 F5
Kimpton Hants 25 E7
Herts 40 C4
Kinbrace 157 F11
Kinbuck 127 D6
Kincaple 129 C6
Kincardine Fife 127 F8
Highld 151 C9
Kincardine Bridge 127 F8
Kincardine O'Neil 140 E4
Kinclaven 134 F1
Kincorth 141 D8
Kincorth House . 151 E13
Kincraig 138 D4
Kincraigie 133 E6
Kindallachan 133 E6
Kineton Glos 37 B7
Warks 51 D8
Kinfauns 128 B3
Kingairloch 130 D2
Kingarth 145 H9
Kingcoed 35 D8
King Edward 153 C7
Kingerby 90 E4
Kingham 38 B2
Kingholm Quay . . . 107 B6
Kinghorn 128 F4
Kingie 136 D4
Kinglassie 128 E4
Kingoodie 128 B5
King's Acre 49 E6
Kingsand 6 D2
Kingsbarns 129 C7
Kingsbridge Devon . . 6 E5
Som 21 F8
King's Bromley 62 C5
Kingsburgh 149 C8
Kingsbury London . . 41 F5
Warks 63 E6
Kingsbury Episcopi 12 B2
King's Caple 36 B2
Kingsclere 26 D3
King's Cliffe 65 E7
Kingscote 37 E5
Kingscott 9 C7
King's Coughton . . 51 D5
Kingscross 143 F11
Kingsdon 12 B3
Kingsdown 31 E7
Kingseat 128 E3
Kingsey 39 D7
Kingsfold 28 F2
Kingsford E Ayrs . . . 118 E4
Worcs 62 F2
Kingsforth 90 C4
Kingsgate 31 B7
Kingsheanton 20 F4
King's Heath 62 F4
Kings Hedges 55 C5
King's Hill 29 D7
Kingshouse Hotel 131 D6
Kingside Hill 107 D8
Kingskerswell 7 C6
Kingskettle 128 D5
Kingsland Anglesey . 82 C2
Hereford 49 C6
Kings Langley 40 D3
Kingsley Ches W 74 B2
Hants 27 F5
Staffs 75 E7
Kingsley Green 27 F6
Kingsley Holt 75 E7

Kin–Lit 225

Kingsley Park 53 C5
King's Lynn 67 B6
King's Meaburn 99 B8
King's Mills 73 E7
Kingsmuir Angus 134 E4
Fife 129 D7
Kings Muir 121 F5
King's Newnham 52 B2
King's Newton 63 B7
Kingsnorth 19 B7
King's Norton Leics 64 D3
W Mid 51 B5
King's Nympton 9 C8
King's Pyon 49 D6
King's Ripton 54 B3
King's Somborne 25 F8
King's Stag 12 C5
King's Stanley 37 D5
King's Sutton 52 F2
Kingstanding 62 E4
Kingsteignton 7 B6
King Sterndale 75 B7
King's Thorn 49 F7
Kingsthorpe 53 C5
Kingston Cambs 54 D4
Devon 6 E4
Dorset 13 D5
Dorset 13 G7
E Loth 129 F7
Hants 14 D2
IoW 15 F5
Kent 31 D5
Moray 152 B3
Kingston Bagpuize 38 E4
Kingston Blount 39 E7
Kingston by Sea 17 D6
Kingston Deverill 24 F3
Kingstone Hereford 49 F6
Som 11 C8
Staffs 62 B4
Kingston Gorse 16 D4
Kingston Lisle 38 F3
Kingston Maurward 12 E5
Kingston near Lewes 17 D7
Kingston on Soar 64 B2
Kingston Russell 12 E3
Kingston St Mary 11 B7
Kingston Seymour 23 C6
Kingston upon Hull 90 B4
Kingston upon Thames 28 C2
Kingston Vale 28 B3
Kingstown 108 D3
King's Walden 40 B4
Kingswear 7 D6
Kingswells 141 D7
Kingswinford 62 F2
Kingswood Bucks 39 C6
Glos 36 E4
Hereford 48 D4
Kent 30 D2
Powys 60 D2
S Glos 23 B8
Sur 28 D3
Warks 51 B6
Kings Worthy 26 F2
Kingthorpe 78 B4
Kington Hereford 48 D4
Worcs 50 D4
Kington Langley 24 B4
Kington Magna 13 B5
Kington St Michael 24 B4
Kingussie 138 D3
Kingweston 23 F7
Kininvie House 152 D3
Kinkell Bridge 127 C8
Kinknockie 153 D10
Kinlet 61 F7
Kinloch Fife 128 C4
Highld 146 B6
Highld 149 G11
Highld 156 F6
Perth 133 E8
Perth 134 E2
Kinlochan 130 C2
Kinlochard 126 D3
Kinlochbeoraid 147 C11
Kinlochbervie 156 D5
Kinlocheil 130 B3
Kinlochewe 150 E3
Kinloch Hourn 136 D2
Kinloch Laggan 137 F8
Kinlochleven 131 C5
Kinloch Lodge 157 D8
Kinlochmoidart 147 D10
Kinlochmorar 147 B11
Kinlochmore 131 C5
Kinloch Rannoch 132 D3
Kinlochspelve 124 C2
Kinloid 147 C9
Kinloss 151 E13
Kinmel Bay 72 A3
Kinmuck 141 C7
Kinmundy 141 C7
Kinnadie 153 D9
Kinnaird 128 B4
Kinnaird Castle 135 D6
Kinneff 135 B8
Kinnelhead 114 D3
Kinnell 135 D6
Kinnerley 60 B3
Kinnersley Hereford 48 E5
Worcs 50 E3
Kinnerton 48 C4
Kinnesswood 128 D3
Kinninvie 101 B5
Kinnordy 134 D3
Kinoulton 77 F6
Kinross 128 D3
Kinrossie 134 F1
Kinsbourne Green 40 C4
Kinsey Heath 74 E3
Kinsham Hereford 49 C5
Worcs 50 F4
Kinsley 88 C5
Kinson 13 E8
Kintbury 25 C8
Kintessack 151 E12
Kintillo 128 C3
Kintocher 140 D4
Kinton Hereford 49 B6
Shrops 60 C3
Kintore 141 C6
Kintour 142 C5
Kintra Argyll 142 D4
Kintra *continued*
Argyll 146 J6
Kintraw 124 E4
Kinuachdrachd 124 F3
Kinveachy 138 C5
Kinver 62 F2
Kippax 95 F7
Kippen 127 E5
Kippford or Scaur 106 D5
Kirbister Orkney 159 F7
Orkney 159 H4
Kirbuster 159 F3
Kirby Bedon 69 D5
Kirby Bellars 64 C4
Kirby Cane 69 E6
Kirby Cross 43 B8
Kirby Grindalythe 96 C5
Kirby Hill N Yorks 95 C6
N Yorks 101 D6
Kirby Knowle 102 F2
Kirby-le-Soken 43 B8
Kirby Misperton 96 B3
Kirby Muxloe 64 D2
Kirby Row 69 E6
Kirby Sigston 102 E2
Kirby Underdale 96 D4
Kirby Wiske 102 F1
Kirdford 16 B4
Kirk 158 E4
Kirkabister 160 K6
Kirkandrews 106 E3
Kirkandrews upon Eden 108 D3
Kirkbampton 108 D3
Kirkbean 107 D6
Kirk Bramwith 89 C7
Kirkbride 108 D2
Kirkbuddo 135 E5
Kirkburn Borders 121 F5
E Yorks 97 D5
Kirkburton 88 C2
Kirkby Lincs 90 E4
Mers 86 E2
N Yorks 102 D3
Kirkby Fleetham 101 E7
Kirkby Green 78 D3
Kirkby-in-Ashfield 76 D5
Kirkby-in-Furness 98 F4
Kirkby la Thorpe 78 E3
Kirkby Lonsdale 93 B6
Kirkby Malham 93 C8
Kirkby Mallory 63 D8
Kirkby Malzeard 94 B5
Kirkby Mills 103 F5
Kirkbymoorside 102 F4
Kirkby on Bain 78 C5
Kirkby Overflow 95 E6
Kirkby Stephen 100 D2
Kirkby Thore 99 B8
Kirkby Underwood 65 B7
Kirkby Wharfe 95 E8
Kirkcaldy 128 E4
Kirkcambeck 108 C5
Kirkcarswell 106 E4
Kirkcolm 104 C4
Kirkconnel 113 C7
Kirkconnell 107 C6
Kirkcowan 105 C7
Kirkcudbright 106 D3
Kirkdale 85 E4
Kirk Deighton 95 D6
Kirk Ella 90 B4
Kirkfieldbank 119 E8
Kirkgunzeon 107 C5
Kirk Hallam 76 E4
Kirkham Lancs 92 F4
N Yorks 96 C3
Kirkhamgate 88 B3
Kirk Hammerton 95 D7
Kirkharle 117 F6
Kirkheaton Northumb 110 B3
W Yorks 88 C2
Kirkhill Angus 135 C6
Highld 151 G8
Midloth 120 C5
Moray 152 E2
Kirkhope 115 B6
Kirkhouse 121 F6
Kirkiboll 157 D8
Kirkibost 149 G10
Kirkinch 134 E3
Kirkinner 105 D8
Kirkintilloch 119 B6
Kirk Ireton 76 D2
Kirkland Cumb 98 C2
Dumfries 113 C7
Dumfries 113 E8
W&F 109 F6
Kirk Langley 76 F2
Kirkleatham 102 B3
Kirklevington 102 D2
Kirkley 69 E8
Kirklington Notts 77 D6
N Yorks 101 F8
Kirklinton 108 C4
Kirkliston 120 B4
Kirkmaiden 104 F5
Kirk Merrington 111 F5
Kirkmichael Perth 133 D7
S Ayrs 112 D3
Kirk Michael 84 C3
Kirkmuirhill 119 E7
Kirknewton Northumb 122 F5
W Loth 120 C4
Kirkney 152 E5
Kirk of Shotts 119 C8
Kirkoswald S Ayrs 112 D2
W&F 109 E5
Kirkpatrick Durham 106 B4
Kirkpatrick-Fleming 108 B2
Kirk Sandall 89 D7
Kirksanton 98 F3
Kirk Smeaton 89 C6
Kirkstall 95 F5
Kirkstead 78 C4
Kirkstile 152 E5
Kirkstyle 158 C5
Kirkton Aberds 140 B5
Aberds 153 D6
Angus 134 E4
Angus 134 F4
Borders 115 C8
Dumfries 114 F2
Kirkton *continued*
Fife 129 B5
Highld 149 F13
Highld 150 G2
Highld 151 B10
Highld 151 F10
Perth 127 C8
S Lanark 114 B2
Stirling 126 D4
Kirktonhill 121 D7
Kirkton Manor 120 F5
Kirkton of Airlie 134 D3
Kirkton of Auchterhouse 134 F3
Kirkton of Auchterless 153 D7
Kirkton of Barevan 151 G11
Kirkton of Bourtie 141 B7
Kirkton of Collace 134 F1
Kirkton of Craig 135 D7
Kirkton of Culsalmond 153 E6
Kirkton of Durris 141 E6
Kirkton of Glenbuchat 140 C2
Kirkton of Glenisla 134 C2
Kirkton of Kingoldrum 134 D3
Kirkton of Largo 129 D6
Kirkton of Lethendy 133 E8
Kirkton of Logie Buchan 141 B8
Kirkton of Maryculter 141 E7
Kirkton of Menmuir 135 C5
Kirkton of Monikie 135 F5
Kirkton of Oyne 141 B5
Kirkton of Rayne 153 F6
Kirkton of Skene 141 D7
Kirkton of Tough 140 C5
Kirktown 153 C10
Kirktown of Alvah 153 B6
Kirktown of Deskford 152 B5
Kirktown of Fetteresso 141 F7
Kirktown of Mortlach 152 E3
Kirktown of Slains 141 B9
Kirkurd 120 E4
Kirkwall 159 G5
Kirkwhelpington 117 F5
Kirk Yetholm 116 B4
Kirmington 90 C5
Kirmond le Mire 91 E5
Kirn 145 F10
Kirriemuir 134 D3
Kirstead Green 69 E5
Kirtlebridge 108 B2
Kirtleton 115 F5
Kirtling 55 D7
Kirtling Green 55 D7
Kirtlington 38 C4
Kirtomy 157 C10
Kirton Lincs 79 F6
Notts 77 C6
Suff 57 F6
Kirton End 79 E5
Kirton Holme 79 E5
Kirton in Lindsey 90 E3
Kislingbury 52 D4
Kites Hardwick 52 C2
Kittisford 11 B5
Kittle 33 F6
Kitt's Green 63 F5
Kitt's Moss 87 F6
Kittybrewster 141 D8
Kitwood 26 F4
Kivernoll 49 F6
Kiveton Park 89 F5
Knaith 90 F2
Knaith Park 90 F2
Knap Corner 13 B6
Knaphill 27 D7
Knapp Perth 134 F2
Som 11 B8
Knapthorpe 77 D7
Knapton Norf 81 D9
York 95 D8
Knapton Green 49 D6
Knapwell 54 C4
Knaresborough 95 D6
Knarsdale 109 D6
Knauchland 152 C5
Knaven 153 D8
Knayton 102 F2
Knebworth 41 B5
Knedlington 89 B8
Kneesall 77 C7
Kneesworth 54 E4
Kneeton 77 E7
Knelston 33 F5
Knenhall 75 F6
Knettishall 68 F2
Knightacott 21 F5
Knightcote 51 D8
Knightley Dale 62 B2
Knighton Devon 6 E3
Leicester 64 D2
Staffs 61 B7
Staffs 74 E4
Knighton = Tref-y-Clawdd 48 B4
Knightswood 118 C5
Knightwick 50 D2
Knill 48 C4
Knipton 77 F8
Knitsley 110 E4
Kniveton 76 D2
Knock Argyll 147 H8
Moray 152 C5
W&F 100 B1
Knockally 158 H3
Knockan 156 H5
Knockandhu 139 B8
Knockando 152 D1
Knockando House 152 D2
Knockbain 151 F9
Knockbreck 148 B7
Knockbrex 106 E2
Knockdee 158 D3
Knockdolian 104 A5
Knockenkelly 143 F11
Knockentiber 118 F3
Knockespock House 140 B4
Knockfarrel 151 F8
Knockglass 104 D4
Knockholt 29 D5
Knockholt Pound 29 D5
Knockie Lodge 137 C7
Knockin 60 B3
Knockinlaw 118 F4
Knocklearn 106 B4
Knocknaha 143 G7
Knocknain 104 C3
Knockrome 144 F4
Knocksharry 84 D2
Knodishall 57 C8
Knolls Green 74 B5
Knolton 73 F7
Knolton Bryn 73 F7
Knook 24 E4
Knossington 64 D5
Knott End-on-Sea 92 E3
Knotting 53 C8
Knotting Green 53 C8
Knottingley 89 B6
Knotts Lancs 93 D7
W&F 99 B6
Knotty Ash 86 E2
Knotty Green 40 E2
Knowbury 49 B7
Knowe 105 B7
Knowehead 113 E6
Knowesgate 117 F5
Knowes of Elrick 152 C6
Knoweton 119 D7
Knowhead 153 C9
Knowle Bristol 23 B8
Devon 10 D2
Devon 11 F5
Devon 20 F3
Shrops 49 B7
W Mid 51 B6
Knowle Green 93 F6
Knowle Park 94 E3
Knowl Hill 27 B6
Knowlton Dorset 13 C8
Kent 31 D6
Knowsley 86 E2
Knowstone 10 B3
Knox Bridge 29 E8
Knucklas 48 B4
Knuston 53 C7
Knutsford 74 B4
Knutton 74 E5
Knypersley 75 D5
Kuggar 3 E6
Kyleakin 149 F12
Kyle of Lochalsh 149 F12
Kylerhea 149 F12
Kylesknoydart 147 B11
Kylesku 156 F5
Kylesmorar 147 B11
Kylestrome 156 F5
Kyllachy House 138 B3
Kynaston 60 B3
Kynnersley 61 C6
Kyre Magna 49 C8

L

Labost 155 C7
Lacasaidh 155 E8
Lacasdal 155 D9
Laceby 91 D6
Lacey Green 39 E8
Lach Dennis 74 B4
Lackford 55 B8
Lacock 24 C4
Ladbroke 52 D2
Laddingford 29 E7
Lade Bank 79 D6
Ladock 4 D3
Lady 159 D7
Ladybank 128 C5
Ladykirk 122 E4
Ladysford 153 B9
La Fontenelle 16 I2
Laga 147 E9
Lagalochan 124 D4
Lagavulin 142 D5
Lagg Argyll 144 F4
N Ayrs 143 F10
Laggan Argyll 142 C3
Highld 137 E5
Highld 138 E2
Highld 147 D10
S Ayrs 112 F2
Lagganulva 146 G7
Laide 155 H13
Laigh Fenwick 118 E4
Laigh Glengall 112 C3
Laighmuir 118 E4
Laindon 42 F2
Lair 150 G3
Lairg 157 J8
Lairg Lodge 157 J8
Lairgmore 151 H8
Lairg Muir 157 J8
Laisterdyke 94 F4
Laithes 108 F4
Lake IoW 15 F6
Wilts 25 F6
Lakenham 68 D5
Lakenheath 67 F7
Lakesend 66 E5
Lakeside 99 F5
Laleham 27 C8
Laleston 21 B7
Lamarsh 56 F2
Lamas 81 E8
Lambden 122 E3
Lamberhurst 18 B3
Lamberhurst Quarter 18 B3
Lamberton 123 D5
Lambeth 28 B4
Lambhill 119 C5
Lambley Northumb 109 D6
Notts 77 E6
Lamborough Hill 38 D4
Lambourn 25 B8
Lambourne End 41 E7
Lambs Green 28 F3
Lambston 44 D4
Lambton 111 D5
Lamerton 6 B2
Lamesley 111 D5
Laminess 159 E7
Lamington Highld 151 D10
S Lanark 120 F2
Lamlash 143 E11
Lamloch 112 E5
Lamonby 108 F4
Lamorna 2 D3
Lamorran 3 B7
Lampardbrook 57 C6
Lampeter = Llanbedr Pont Steffan 46 E4
Lampeter Velfrey 32 C2
Lamphey 32 D1
Lamplugh 98 B2
Lamport 53 B5
Lamyatt 23 F8
Lana 8 E5
Lanark 119 E8
Lancaster 92 C4
Lanchester 110 E4
Lancing 17 D5
Landbeach 55 C5
Landcross 9 B6
Landerberry 141 D6
Landford 14 C3
Landford Manor 14 B3
Landimore 33 E5
Landkey 20 F4
Landore 33 E7
Landrake 5 C8
Landscove 7 C5
Landshipping 32 C1
Landshipping Quay 32 C1
Landulph 6 C2
Landwade 55 C7
Lane 4 C3
Laneast 8 F4
Lane End Bucks 39 E8
Cumb 98 E3
Dorset 13 E6
Hants 15 B6
IoW 15 F7
Lancs 93 E8
Lane Ends Lancs 93 D7
Lancs 93 F7
N Yorks 94 E2
Laneham 77 B8
Lanehead Durham 109 E8
Northumb 116 F3
Lane Head Derbys 75 B8
Durham 101 C6
Gtr Man 86 E4
W Yorks 88 D2
Lanercost 109 C5
Laneshaw Bridge 94 E2
Lane Side 87 B5
Lanfach 35 E6
Langar 77 F7
Langbank 118 B3
Langbar 94 D3
Langburnshiels 115 D8
Langcliffe 93 C8
Langdale 157 E9
Langdale End 103 E7
Langdon 8 F5
Langdon Beck 109 F8
Langdon Hills 42 F2
Langdyke 128 D5
Langenhoe 43 C6
Langford C Beds 54 E2
Devon 10 D5
Essex 42 D4
Notts 77 D8
Oxon 38 D2
Langford Budville 11 B6
Langham Essex 56 F4
Norf 81 C6
Rutland 64 C5
Suff 56 C3
Langhaugh 120 F5
Langho 93 F7
Langholm 115 F6
Langleeford 117 B5
Langley Ches E 75 B6
Hants 14 D5
Herts 41 B5
Kent 30 D2
Northumb 109 C8
Slough 27 B8
Warks 51 C6
W Sus 16 B2
Langley Burrell 24 B4
Langley Common 76 F2
Langley Heath 30 D2
Langley Lower Green 54 F5
Langley Marsh 11 B5
Langley Park 110 E5
Langley Street 69 D6
Langley Upper Green 54 F5
Langney 18 E3
Langold 89 F6
Langore 8 F5
Langport 12 B2
Langrick 79 E5
Langridge 24 C2
Langridge Ford 9 B7
Langrigg 107 E8
Langrish 15 B8
Langsett 88 D3
Langshaw 121 F8
Langside 127 C6
Langskaill 159 D5
Langstone Hants 15 D8
Newport 35 E7
Langthorne 101 E7
Langthorpe 95 C6
Langthwaite 101 D5
Langtoft E Yorks 97 C6
Lincs 65 C8
Langton Durham 101 C6
Lincs 78 C5
Lincs 79 B6
N Yorks 96 C3
Langton by Wragby 78 B4
Langton Green Kent 18 B2
Suff 56 B5
Langton Herring 12 F4
Langton Matravers 13 G8
Langtree 9 C6
Langwathby 109 F5
Langwell House 158 H3
Langwell Lodge 156 J4
Langwith 76 C5
Langwith Junction 76 C5
Langworth 78 B3
Lanivet 4 C5
Lanlivery 5 D5
Lanner 3 C6
Lanreath 5 D6
Lansallos 5 D6
Lansdown 37 B6
Lanteglos Highway 5 D6
Lanton Borders 116 B2
Northumb 122 F5
Lapford 10 D2
Laphroaig 142 D4
La Planque 16 I2
Lapley 62 C2
Lapworth 51 B6
Larachbeg 147 G9
Larbert 127 F7
Larden Green 74 D2
Largie 152 E6
Largiemore 145 E8
Largoward 129 D6
Largs 118 D2
Largybeg 143 F11
Largymore 143 F11
Larkfield 118 B2
Larkhall 119 D7
Larkhill 25 E6
Larling 68 F2
Larriston 115 E8
Lartington 101 C5
Lary 140 D2
Lasham 26 E4
Lashenden 30 E2
Lassington 36 B4
Lassodie 128 E3
Lastingham 103 E5
Latcham 23 E6
Latchford Herts 41 B6
Warr 86 F4
Latchingdon 42 D4
Latchley 6 B2
Lately Common 86 E4
Lathbury 53 E6
Latheron 158 G3
Latheronwheel 158 G3
Latheronwheel House 158 G3
Lathones 129 D6
Latimer 40 E3
Latteridge 36 F3
Lattiford 12 B4
Latton 37 E7
Latton Bush 41 D7
Lauchintilly 141 C6
Lauder 121 E8
Laugharne 32 C4
Laughterton 77 B8
Laughton E Sus 18 D2
Leics 64 F3
Lincs 78 F3
Lincs 90 E2
Laughton Common 89 F6
Laughton en le Morthen 89 F6
Launcells 8 D4
Launceston 8 F5
Launton 39 B6
Laurencekirk 135 B7
Laurieston Dumfries 106 C3
Falk 120 B2
Lavendon 53 D7
Lavenham 56 E3
Laverhay 114 E4
Laversdale 108 C4
Laverstock 25 F6
Laverstoke 26 E2
Laverton Glos 51 F5
N Yorks 94 B5
Som 24 D2
Lavister 73 D7
Law 119 D8
Lawers Perth 127 B6
Perth 132 F3
Lawford 56 F4
Lawhitton 9 F5
Lawkland 93 C7
Lawley 61 D6
Lawnhead 62 B2
Lawrenny 32 D1
Lawshall 56 D2
Lawton 49 D6
Laxey 84 D4
Laxfield 57 B6
Laxfirth Shetland 160 H6
Shetland 160 J6
Laxford Bridge 156 E5
Laxo 160 G6
Laxobigging 160 F6
Laxton E Yorks 89 B8
N Nhants 65 E6
Notts 77 C7
Laycock 94 E3
Layer Breton 43 C5
Layer de la Haye 43 C5
Layer Marney 43 C5
Layham 56 E4
Laylands Green 25 C8
Laytham 96 F3
Layton 92 F3
Lazenby 102 B3
Lazonby 108 F5
Lea Derbys 76 D3
Hereford 36 B3
Lincs 90 F2
Shrops 60 D4
Shrops 60 F3
Wilts 37 F6
Leabrooks 76 D4
Leac a Li 154 H6
Leachkin 151 G9
Leadburn 120 D5
Leadenham 78 D2
Leaden Roding 42 C1
Leadgate Durham 110 D4
T&W 110 D4
W&F 109 E7
Leadhills 113 C8
Leafield 38 C3
Leagrave 40 B3
Leake 102 E2
Leake Commonside 79 D6
Lealholm 103 D5
Lealt Argyll 144 D5
Highld 149 B10
Lea Marston 63 E6
Leamington Hastings 52 C2
Leamonsley 62 D5
Leamside 111 E6
Leanaig 151 F8
Leargybreck 144 F4
Leasgill 99 F6
Leasingham 78 E3
Leasingthorne 101 B7
Leasowe 85 E3
Leatherhead 28 D2
Leatherhead Common 28 D2
Leathley 94 E5
Leaton 60 C4
Lea Town 92 F4
Leaveland 30 D4
Leavening 96 C3
Leaves Green 28 C5
Leazes 110 D4
Lebberston 103 F8
Lechlade-on-Thames 38 E2
Leck 93 B6
Leckford 25 F8
Leckfurin 157 D10
Leckgruinart 142 B3
Leckhampstead Bucks 52 F5
W Berks 26 B2
Leckhampstead Thicket 26 B2
Leckhampton 37 C6
Leckie 150 E3
Leckmelm 150 B4
Leckwith 22 B3
Leconfield 97 E6
Ledaig 124 B5
Ledburn 40 B2
Ledbury 50 F2
Ledcharrie 126 B4
Ledgemoor 49 D6
Ledicot 49 C6
Ledmore 156 H5
Lednagullin 157 C10
Ledsham Ches W 73 B7
W Yorks 89 B5
Ledston 88 B5
Ledston Luck 95 F7
Ledwell 38 B4
Lee Argyll 146 J7
Devon 20 E3
Hants 14 C4
Lancs 93 D5
Shrops 73 F8
Leeans 160 J5
Leebotten 160 L6
Leebotwood 60 E4
Lee Brockhurst 60 B5
Leece 92 C2
Leechpool 44 D4
Lee Clump 40 D2
Leeds Kent 30 D2
W Yorks 95 F5
Leedstown 2 C5
Leek 75 D6
Leekbrook 75 D6
Leek Wootton 51 C7
Lee Mill 6 D4
Leeming 101 F7
Leeming Bar 101 E7
Lee Moor 6 C3
Lee-on-the-Solent 15 D6
Lees Derbys 76 F2
Gtr Man 87 D7
W Yorks 94 F3
Leeswood 73 C6
Legbourne 91 F7
Legerwood 121 E8
Legsby 90 F5
Leicester 64 D2
Leicester Forest East 64 D2
Leigh Dorset 12 D4
Glos 37 B5
Gtr Man 86 D4
Kent 29 E6
Shrops 60 D3
Sur 28 E3
Wilts 37 E7
Worcs 50 D2
Leigh Beck 42 F4
Leigh Common 12 B5
Leigh Delamere 24 B3
Leigh Green 19 B6
Leigh on Sea 42 F4
Leigh Park 15 D8
Leigh Sinton 50 D2
Leighswood 62 D4
Leighterton 37 E5
Leighton N Yorks 94 B4
Powys 60 D2
Shrops 61 D6
Som 24 E2
Leighton Bromswold 54 B2
Leighton Buzzard 40 B2
Leigh upon Mendip 23 E8
Leigh Woods 23 B7
Leinthall Earls 49 C6
Leinthall Starkes 49 C6
Leintwardine 49 B6
Leire 64 E2
Leirinmore 156 C7
Leiston 57 C8
Leitfie 134 E2
Leith 121 B5
Leitholm 122 E3
Lelant 2 C4
Lelley 97 F8
Lem Hill 50 B2
Lemmington Hall 117 C7
Lempitlaw 122 F3
Lenchwick 50 E5
Lendalfoot 112 F1
Lendrick Lodge 126 D4
Lenham 30 D2
Lenham Heath 30 E3
Lennel 122 E4
Lennoxtown 119 B6
Lenton Lincs 78 F3
Nottingham 77 F5
Lentran 151 G8
Lenwade 68 C3
Leny House 126 D5
Lenzie 119 B6
Leoch 134 F3
Leochel-Cushnie 140 C4
Leominster 49 D6
Leonard Stanley 37 D5
Leorin 142 D4
Lepe 15 E5
Lephin 148 D6
Lephinchapel 145 D8
Lephinmore 145 D8
Le Planel 16 I2
Leppington 96 C3
Lepton 88 C3
Lerryn 5 D6
Lerwick 160 J6
Lesbury 117 C8
Le Skerne Haughton 101 C8
Leslie Aberds 140 B4
Fife 128 D4
Lesmahagow 119 F8
Lesnewth 8 E3
Lessendrum 152 D5
Lessingham 69 B6
Lessonhall 108 D2
Leswalt 104 C4
Letchmore Heath 40 E4
Letchworth Garden City 54 F3
Letcombe Bassett 38 F3
Letcombe Regis 38 F3
Letham Angus 135 E5
Falk 127 F7
Fife 128 C5
Perth 128 B2
Letham Grange 135 E6
Lethenty 153 D8
Letheringham 57 D6
Letheringsett 81 D6
Lettaford 10 F2
Lettan 159 D8
Letterewe 150 D2
Letterfearn 149 F13
Letterfinlay 137 E5
Lettermorar 147 C10
Lettermore 146 G7
Letters 150 C4
Letterston 44 C4
Lettoch Highld 139 C6
Highld 151 H13
Letton Hereford 48 E5
Hereford 49 B5
Letton Green 68 D2
Letty Green 41 C5
Letwell 89 F6
Leuchars 129 B6
Leuchars House 152 B2
Leumrabhagh 155 F8
Levan 118 B2
Levaneap 160 G6
Levedale 62 C2
Leven E Yorks 97 E7
Fife 129 D5
Levencorroch 143 F11
Levens 99 F6
Levens Green 41 B6
Levenshulme 87 E6
Levenwick 160 L6
Leverburgh = An t-Ob 154 J5
Leverington 66 C4
Leverton 79 E7
Leverton Highgate 79 E7
Leverton Lucasgate 79 E7
Leverton Outgate 79 E7
Le Villocq 16 I2
Levington 57 F6
Levisham 103 E6
Levishie 137 C7
Lew 38 D3
Lewannick 8 F4
Lewdown 9 F6
Lewes 17 C8
Leweston 44 C4
Lewisham 28 B4
Lewiston 137 B8
Lewistown 34 F3
Lewknor 39 E7
Leworthy Devon 8 D5
Devon 21 F5
Lewtrenchard 9 F6
Lexden 43 B5
Ley Aberds 140 C4
Corn 5 C6
Leybourne 29 D7
Leyburn 101 E6
Leyfields 63 D6
Leyhill 40 D2
Leyland 86 B3
Leylodge 141 C6
Leymoor 88 C2
Leys Aberds 153 C10
Perth 134 F2
Leys Castle 151 G9
Leysdown-on-Sea 30 B4
Leysmill 135 E6
Leys of Cossans 134 E3
Leysters Pole 49 C7
Leyton 41 F6
Leytonstone 41 F6
Lezant 5 B8
Leziate 67 C6
Lhanbryde 152 B2
Liatrie 150 H5
Libanus 34 B3
Libberton 120 E2
Liberton 121 C5
Liceasto 154 H6
Lichfield 62 D5
Lickey 50 B4
Lickey End 50 B4
Lickfold 16 B3
Liddel 159 K5
Liddesdale 130 D1
Liddington 38 F2
Lidgate 55 D8
Lidget 89 D7
Lidget Green 94 F4
Lidgett 77 C6
Lidlington 53 F7
Lidstone 38 B3
Lieurary 158 D2
Liff 134 F3
Lifton 9 F5
Liftondown 9 F5
Lighthorne 51 D8
Lightwater 27 C7
Lightwood 75 E6
Lightwood Green Ches E 74 E3
Wrex 73 E7
Lilbourne 52 B3
Lilburn Tower 117 B6
Lilleshall 61 C7
Lilley Herts 40 B4
W Berks 26 B2
Lilliesleaf 115 B8
Lillingstone Dayrell 52 F5
Lillingstone Lovell 52 E5
Lillington Dorset 12 C4
Warks 51 C8
Lilliput 13 E8
Lilstock 22 E3
Lilyhurst 61 C7
Limbury 40 B3
Limebrook 49 C5
Limefield 87 C6
Limekilnburn 119 D7
Limekilns 128 F2
Limerigg 119 B8
Limerstone 14 F5
Limington 12 B3
Limpenhoe 69 D6
Limpley Stoke 24 C2
Limpsfield 28 D5
Limpsfield Chart 28 D5
Linby 76 D5
Linchmere 27 F6
Lincluden 107 B6
Lincoln 78 B2
Lincomb 50 C3
Lincombe 6 D5
Lindale 99 F6
Lindal in Furness 92 B2
Lindean 121 F7
Lindfield 17 B7
Lindford 27 F6
Lindifferon 128 C5
Lindley 88 C2
Lindley Green 94 E5
Lindores 128 C4
Lindridge 49 C8
Lindsell 42 B2
Lindsey 56 E3
Linford Hants 14 D2
Thurrock 29 B7
Lingague 84 E2
Lingards Wood 87 C8
Lingbob 94 F3
Lingdale 102 C4
Lingen 49 C5
Lingfield 28 E4
Lingreabhagh 154 J5
Lingwood 69 D6
Linicro 149 B8
Linkenholt 25 D8
Linkhill 18 C5
Linkinhorne 5 B8
Linklater 159 K5
Linksness 159 H3
Linktown 128 E4
Linley 60 E3
Linley Green 49 D8
Linlithgow 120 B3
Linlithgow Bridge 120 B2
Linshiels 116 D4
Linsiadar 154 D7
Linsidemore 151 B8
Linslade 40 B2
Linstead Parva 57 B7
Linstock 108 D4
Linthwaite 88 C2
Lintlaw 122 D4
Lintmill 152 B5
Linton Borders 116 B3
Cambs 55 E6
Derbys 63 C6
Hereford 36 B3
Kent 29 E8
Northumb 117 E8
N Yorks 94 C2
W Yorks 95 E6
Linton-on-Ouse 95 C7
Linwood Hants 14 D2
Lincs 90 F5
Renfs 118 C4
Lionacleit 148 D2
Lional 155 A10
Liphook 27 F6
Liscard 85 E4
Liscombe 21 F7
Liskeard 5 C7
L'Islet 16 I2
Liss 15 B8
Lissett 97 D7
Liss Forest 15 B8
Lissington 90 F5
Lisvane 35 F5
Liswerry 35 F7
Litcham 67 C8
Litchborough 52 D4
Litchfield 26 D2
Litherland 85 E4
Litlington Cambs 54 E4
E Sus 18 E2
Little Abington 55 E6
Little Addington 53 B7
Little Alne 51 C6
Little Altcar 85 D4
Little Asby 100 D1
Little Assynt 156 G4
Little Aston 62 D4
Little Atherfield 15 F5
Little Ayre 159 J4
Little-ayre 160 G5
Little Ayton 102 C3
Little Baddow 42 D3
Little Badminton 37 F5
Little Ballinluig 133 D6
Little Bampton 108 D2
Little Bardfield 55 F7
Little Barford 54 D2
Little Barningham 81 D7
Little Barrington 38 C2
Little Barrow 73 B8
Little Barugh 96 B3
Little Bavington 110 B2
Little Bealings 57 E6
Littlebeck 103 D6
Little Bedwyn 25 C7
Little Bentley 43 B7

Little
Berkhamsted 41 D5
Little Billing 53 C6
Little Birch 49 F7
Little Blakenham 56 E5
Little Blencow 108 F4
Little Bollington 86 F5
Little Bookham 28 D2
Littleborough
Gtr Man 87 C7
Notts 90 F2
Littlebourne 31 D6
Little Bowden 64 F4
Little Bradley 55 D7
Little Brampton 60 F3
Little Brechin 135 C5
Littlebredy 12 F3
Little Brickhill 53 F7
Little Brington 52 C4
Little Bromley 43 B6
Little Broughton 107 F7
Little Budworth 74 C2
Little Burstead 42 E2
Littlebury 55 F6
Littlebury Green 55 F5
Little Bytham 65 C7
Little Carlton Lincs 91 F7
Notts 77 D7
Little Casterton 65 D7
Little Cawthorpe 91 F7
Little Chalfont 40 E2
Little Chart 30 E3
Little Chesterford 55 E6
Little Cheverell 24 D4
Little Chishill 54 F5
Little Clacton 43 C7
Little Clifton 98 B2
Little Colp 153 D7
Little Comberton 50 E4
Little Common 18 E4
Little Compton 51 F7
Little Cornard 56 F2
Little Cowarne 49 D8
Little Coxwell 38 E2
Little Crakehall 101 E7
Little Cressingham 67 D8
Little Crosby 85 D4
Little Dalby 64 C4
Little Dawley 61 D6
Littledean 36 C3
Little Dens 153 D10
Little Dewchurch 49 F7
Little Downham 66 F5
Little Driffield 97 D6
Little Dunham 67 C8
Little Dunkeld 133 E7
Little Dunmow 42 B2
Little Easton 42 B2
Little Eaton 76 E3
Little Eccleston 92 E4
Little Ellingham 68 E3
Little End 41 D8
Little Eversden 54 D4
Little Faringdon 38 D2
Little Fencote 101 E7
Little Fenton 95 F8
Littleferry 151 B11
Little Finborough 56 D4
Little Fransham 68 C2
Little Gaddesden 40 C2
Little Gidding 65 F8
Little Glemham 57 D7
Little Glenshee 133 F6
Little Gransden 54 D3
Little Green 24 E2
Little Grimsby 91 E7
Little Gruinard 150 C2
Little Habton 96 B3
Little Hadham 41 B7
Little Hale 78 E4
Little Hallingbury 41 C7
Littleham Devon 9 B6
Devon 10 F5
Little Hampden 40 D1
Littlehampton 16 D4
Little Harrowden 53 B6
Little Haseley 39 D6
Little Hatfield 97 E7
Little Hautbois 81 E8
Little Haven 44 D3
Little Hay 62 D5
Little Hayfield 87 F8
Little Haywood 62 B4
Little Heath 63 F7
Littlehempston 7 C6
Little Hereford 49 C7
Little Horkesley 56 F3
Little Horsted 17 C8
Little Horton 94 F4
Little Horwood 53 F5
Littlehoughton 117 C8
Little Houghton
S Yorks 88 D5
W Nhants 53 D6
Little Hucklow 75 B8
Little Hulton 86 D5
Little Humber 91 B5
Little Hungerford 26 B3
Little Irchester 53 C7
Little Kimble 39 D8
Little Kineton 51 D8
Little Kingshill 40 E1
Little Langdale 99 D5
Little Langford 25 F5
Little Laver 41 D8
Little Leigh 74 B3
Little Leighs 42 C3
Little Lever 87 D5
Little London Bucks 39 C6
E Sus 18 D2
Hants 25 E8
Hants 26 D4
Lincs 66 B2
Lincs 66 B4
Norf 81 E7
Powys 59 F7
Little Longstone 75 B8
Little Lynturk 140 C4
Little Malvern 50 E2
Little Maplestead 56 F2
Little Marcle 49 F8
Little Marlow 40 F1
Little Marsden 93 F8
Little Massingham 80 E3
Little Melton 68 D4
Littlemill Aberds 140 E2
Littlemill continued
E Ayrs 112 C4
Highld 151 F12
Northumb 117 C8
Little Mill 35 D7
Little Milton 39 D6
Little Missenden 40 E2
Littlemoor 12 F4
Littlemore 39 D5
Little Musgrave 100 C2
Little Ness 60 C4
Little Neston 73 B6
Little Newcastle 44 C4
Little Newsham 101 C6
Little Oakley Essex 43 B8
N Nhants 65 F5
Little Orton 108 D3
Little Ouseburn 95 C7
Littleover 76 F3
Little Paxton 54 C2
Little Petherick 4 B4
Little Pitlurg 152 D4
Little Plumpton 92 F3
Little Plumstead 69 C6
Little Ponton 78 F2
Littleport 67 F5
Little Raveley 54 B3
Little Reedness 90 B2
Little Ribston 95 D6
Little Rissington 38 C1
Little Ryburgh 81 E5
Little Ryle 117 C6
Little Salkeld 109 F5
Little Sampford 55 F7
Little Sandhurst 27 C6
Little Saxham 55 C8
Little Scatwell 150 F6
Little Sessay 95 B7
Little Shelford 54 D5
Little Singleton 92 F3
Little
Skillymarno 153 C9
Little Smeaton 89 C6
Little Snoring 81 D5
Little Sodbury 36 F4
Little Somborne 25 F8
Little Somerford 37 F6
Little Stainforth 93 C8
Little Stainton 101 B8
Little Stanney 73 B8
Little Staughton 54 C2
Little Steeping 79 C7
Little Stoke 75 F6
Littlestone on Sea 19 C7
Little Stonham 56 C5
Little Stretton Leics 64 D3
Shrops 60 E4
Little Strickland 99 C7
Little Stukeley 54 B3
Little Sutton 73 B7
Little Tew 38 B3
Little Thetford 55 B6
Little Thirkleby 95 B7
Littlethorpe Leics 64 E2
N Yorks 95 C6
Little Thurlow 55 D7
Little Thurrock 29 B7
Littleton Ches W 73 C8
Hants 26 F2
Perth 134 F2
Som 23 F6
Sur 27 C8
Sur 27 E7
Littleton Drew 37 F5
Littleton-on-
Severn 36 F2
Littleton Pannell 24 D5
Little Torboll 151 B10
Little Torrington 9 C6
Little Totham 42 C4
Little Toux 152 C5
Littletown 111 E6
Little Town Cumb 98 C4
Lancs 93 F6
Little Urswick 92 B2
Little Wakering 43 F5
Little Walden 55 E6
Little Waldingfield 56 E3
Little Walsingham 80 D5
Little Waltham 42 C3
Little Warley 42 E2
Little Weighton 97 F5
Little Weldon 65 F6
Little Welnetham 56 C2
Little Wenlock 61 D6
Little Whittingham
Green 57 B6
Littlewick Green 27 B6
Little Wilbraham 55 D6
Little Wishford 25 F5
Little Witley 50 C2
Little Wittenham 39 E5
Little Wolford 51 F7
Littleworth Bedford 53 E8
Glos 37 D5
Oxon 38 E3
Staffs 62 C4
Worcs 50 D3
Little Wratting 55 E7
Little Wymington 53 C7
Little Wymondley 41 B5
Little Wyrley 62 D4
Little Yeldham 55 F8
Litton Derbys 75 B8
N Yorks 94 B2
Som 23 D7
Litton Cheney 12 E3
Liurbost 155 E8
Liverpool 85 E4
Liverpool Airport 86 F2
Liversedge 88 B3
Liverton Devon 7 B6
Redcar 103 C5
Livingston 120 C3
Livingston
Village 120 C3
Lixwm 73 B5
Lizard 3 E6
Llaingoch 82 C2
Llaithddu 59 F7
Llan 59 D5
Llanaber 58 C3
Llanaelhaearn 70 C4
Llanafan 47 B5
Llanafan-fawr 47 D8
Llanallgo 82 C4
Llanandras
= Presteigne 48 C5
Llanarmon 70 D5
Llanarmon Dyffryn
Ceiriog 73 F5
Llanarmon-yn-Ial 73 D5
Llanarth Ceredig 46 D3
Mon 35 C7
Llanarthne 33 B6
Llanasa 85 F2
Llanbabo 82 C3
Llanbadarn Fawr 58 F3
Llanbadarn Fynydd 48 B3
Llanbadarn-y-
Garreg 48 E3
Llanbadoc 35 E7
Llanbadrig 82 B3
Llanbeder 35 E7
Llanbedr Gwyn 71 E6
Powys 35 B6
Powys 48 E3
Llanbedr-Dyffryn-
Clwyd 72 D5
Llanbedrgoch 82 C5
Llanbedrog 70 D4
Llanbedr Pont Steffan
= Lampeter 46 E4
Llanbedr-
y-cennin 83 E7
Llanberis 83 E5
Llanbethêry 22 C2
Llanbister 48 B3
Llanblethian 21 B8
Llanboidy 32 B3
Llanbradach 35 E5
Llanbrynmair 59 D5
Llancarfan 22 B2
Llancayo 35 D7
Llancloudy 36 B1
Llancynfelyn 58 E3
Llandaff 22 B3
Llandanwg 71 E6
Llandarcy 33 E8
Llandawke 32 C3
Llanddaniel Fab 82 D4
Llanddarog 33 C6
Llanddeiniol 46 B4
Llanddeiniolen 82 E5
Llandderfel 72 F3
Llanddeusant
Anglesey 82 C3
Carms 34 B1
Llanddew 48 F2
Llanddewi 33 F5
Llanddewi-Brefi 47 D5
Llanddewi'r Cwm 48 E2
Llanddewi
Rhydderch 35 C7
Llanddewi Velfrey 32 C2
Llanddoged 83 E8
Llanddona 83 D5
Llanddowror 32 C3
Llanddulas 72 B3
Llanddwywe 71 E6
Llanddyfynan 82 D5
Llandefaelog Fach 48 F2
Llandefaelog-
tre'rgraig 35 B5
Llandefalle 48 F3
Llandegai 83 D5
Llandegfan 83 D5
Llandegla 73 D5
Llandegley 48 C3
Llandegveth 35 E7
Llandegwning 70 D3
Llandeilo 33 B7
Llandeilo Graban 48 E2
Llandeilo'r Fan 47 F7
Llandeloy 44 C3
Llandenny 35 D8
Llandevenny 35 F8
Llandewednock 3 E6
Llandewi
Ystradenny 48 C3
Llandinabo 36 B2
Llandinam 59 F7
Llandissilio 32 B2
Llandogo 36 D2
Llandough V Glam 21 B8
V Glam 22 B3
Llandovery
= Llanymddyfri 47 F6
Llandow 21 B8
Llandre Carms 47 E5
Ceredig 58 F3
Llandrillo 72 F4
Llandrillo-yn-
Rhos 83 C8
Llandrindod =
Llandrindod Wells 48 C2
Llandrindod Wells
= Llandrindod 48 C2
Llandrinio 60 C2
Llandudno 83 C7
Llandudno Junction
= Cyffordd
Llandudno 83 D7
Llandwrog 82 F4
Llandybie 33 C7
Llandyfaelog 33 C5
Llandyfan 33 C7
Llandyfriog 46 E2
Llandyfrydog 82 C4
Llandygwydd 45 E4
Llandynan 73 E5
Llandyrnog 72 C5
Llandysilio 60 C2
Llandyssil 59 E8
Llandysul 46 E3
Llanedeyrn 35 F6
Llanedi 33 D6
Llaneglwys 48 F2
Llanegryn 58 D2
Llanegwad 33 B6
Llaneilian 82 B4
Llanelian-
yn-Rhos 83 D8
Llanelidan 72 D5
Llanelieu 48 F3
Llanellen 35 C7
Llanelli 33 E6
Llanelltyd 58 C4
Llanelly 35 C6
Llanelly Hill 35 C6
Llanelwedd 48 D2
Llanelwy = St Asaph 72 B4
Llanenddwyn 71 E6
Llanengan 70 E3
Llanerchymedd 82 C4
Llanerfyl 59 D7
Llanfachraeth 82 C3
Llanfachreth 71 E8
Llanfaelog 82 D3
Llanfaelrhys 70 E3
Llanfaenor 35 C8
Llanfaes Anglesey 83 D6
Powys 34 B4
Llanfaethlu 82 C3
Llanfaglan 82 E4
Llanfair 71 E6
Llanfair-ar-y-bryn 47 F7
Llanfair
Caereinion 59 D8
Llanfair Clydogau 46 D5
Llanfair-Dyffryn-
Clwyd 72 D5
Llanfairfechan 83 D6
Llanfair
Kilgheddin 35 D7
Llanfair-Nant-
Gwyn 45 F3
Llanfairpwllgwyngyll
82 D5
Llanfair Talhaiarn 72 B3
Llanfair Waterdine 48 B4
Llanfair-ym-Muallt
= Builth Wells 48 D2
Llanfairyneubwll 82 D3
Llanfairynghornwy 82 B3
Llanfallteg 32 C2
Llanfaredd 48 D2
Llanfarian 46 B4
Llanfechain 59 B8
Llanfechan 47 D8
Llanfechell 82 B3
Llanfendigaid 58 D2
Llanferres 73 C5
Llan Ffestiniog 71 C8
Llanfflewyn 82 C3
Llanfihangel-
ararth 46 F3
Llanfihangel-
Crucorney 35 B7
Llanfihangel Glyn
Myfyr 72 E3
Llanfihangel Nant
Bran 47 F8
Llanfihangel-nant-
Melan 48 D3
Llanfihangel
Rhydithon 48 C3
Llanfihangel
Rogiet 35 F8
Llanfihangel Tal-y-
llyn 35 B5
Llanfihangel-uwch-
Gwili 33 B5
Llanfihangel-y-
Creuddyn 47 B5
Llanfihangel-yn-
Ngwynfa 59 C7
Llanfihangel yn
Nhowyn 82 D3
Llanfihangel-y-
pennant
Gwyn 58 D3
Gwyn 71 C6
Llanfihangel-y-
traethau 71 D6
Llanfilo 48 F3
Llanfoist 35 C6
Llanfor 72 F3
Llanfrechfa 35 E7
Llanfrothen 71 C7
Llanfrynach 34 B4
Llanfwrog Anglesey 82 C3
Denb 72 D5
Llanfyllin 59 C8
Llanfynydd Carms 33 B6
Flint 73 D6
Llanfyrnach 45 F4
Llangadfan 59 C7
Llangadog 33 B8
Llangadwaladr
Anglesey 82 E3
Powys 73 F5
Llangaffo 82 E4
Llangain 32 C4
Llangammarch
Wells 47 E8
Llangan 21 B8
Llangarron 36 B2
Llangasty Talyllyn 35 B5
Llangathen 33 B6
Llangattock 35 C6
Llangattock
Lingoed 35 B7
Llangattock nigh
Usk 35 D7
Llangattock-Vibon-
Avel 36 C1
Llangedwyn 59 B8
Llangefni 82 D4
Llangeinor 34 F3
Llangeitho 46 D5
Llangeler 46 F2
Llangelynin 58 D2
Llangendeirne 33 C5
Llangennech 33 D6
Llangennith 33 E5
Llangenny 35 C6
Llangernyw 83 E8
Llangian 70 E3
Llanglydwen 32 B2
Llangoed 83 D6
Llangoedmor 45 E3
Llangollen 73 E6
Llangolman 32 B2
Llangors 35 B5
Llangovan 36 D1
Llangower 72 F3
Llangrannog 46 D2
Llangristiolus 82 D4
Llangrove 36 C2
Llangua 35 B7
Llangunllo 48 B4
Llangunnor 33 C5
Llangurig 47 B8
Llangwm Conwy 72 E3
Mon 35 D8
Pembs 44 E4
Llangwnnadl 70 D3
Llangwyfan 72 C5
Llangwyfan-isaf 82 E3
Llangwyllog 82 D4
Llangwyryfon 46 B4
Llangybi Ceredig 46 D5
Gwyn 70 C5
Mon 35 E7
Llangyfelach 33 E7
Llangynhafal 72 C5
Llangynidr 35 C5
Llangynin 32 C3
Llangynog Carms 32 C4
Powys 59 B7
Llangynwyd 34 F2
Llanhamlach 34 B4
Llanharan 34 F4
Llanharry 34 F4
Llanhennock 35 E7
Llanhiledd
= Llanhilleth 35 D6
Llanhilleth
= Llanhiledd 35 D6
Llanidloes 59 F6
Llaniestyn 70 D3
Llanifyny 59 F5
Llanigon 48 F4
Llanilar 46 B5
Llanilid 34 F3
Llanilltud Fawr
= Llantwit Major 21 C8
Llanishen Cardiff 35 F5
Mon 36 D1
Llanllawddog 33 B5
Llanllechid 83 E6
Llanllowell 35 E7
Llanllugan 59 D7
Llanllwch 32 C4
Llanllwchaiarn 59 E8
Llanllwni 46 F3
Llanllyfni 82 F4
Llanmadoc 33 E5
Llanmaes 21 C8
Llanmartin 35 F7
Llanmihangel 21 B8
Llanmorlais 33 E6
Llannefydd 72 B3
Llannon 33 D6
Llannor 70 D4
Llanon 46 C4
Llanover 35 D7
Llanpumsaint 33 B5
Llanreithan 44 C3
Llanrhaeadr 72 C4
Llanrhaeadr-ym-
Mochnant 59 B8
Llanrhian 44 B3
Llanrhidian 33 E5
Llanrhos 83 C7
Llanrhyddlad 82 C3
Llanrhystud 46 C4
Llanrosser 48 F4
Llanrothal 36 C1
Llanrug 82 E5
Llanrumney 35 F6
Llanrwst 83 E8
Llansadurnen 32 C3
Llansadwrn
Anglesey 83 D5
Carms 47 F5
Llansaint 32 D4
Llansamlet 33 E7
Llansanffraid-ym-
Mechain 60 B2
Llansannan 72 C3
Llansannor 21 B8
Llansantffraed
Ceredig 46 C4
Powys 35 B5
Llansantffraed
Cwmdeuddwr 47 C8
Llansantffraed-in-
Elvel 48 D2
Llansawel 46 F5
Llansilin 60 B2
Llansoy 35 D8
Llanspyddid 34 B4
Llanstadwell 44 E4
Llansteffan 32 C4
Llanstephan 48 E3
Llantarnam 35 E7
Llanteg 32 C2
Llanthony 35 B6
Llantilio
Crossenny 35 C7
Llantilio Pertholey 35 C7
Llantood 45 E3
Llantrisant
Anglesey 82 C3
Mon 35 E7
Rhondda 34 F4
Llantrithyd 22 B2
Llantwit Fardre 34 F4
Llantwit Major
= Llanilltud Fawr 21 C8
Llanuwchllyn 72 F2
Llanvaches 35 E8
Llanvair Discoed 35 E8
Llanvapley 35 C7
Llanvetherine 35 C7
Llanveynoe 48 F5
Llanvihangel
Gobion 35 D7
Llanvihangel-Ystern-
Llewern 35 C8
Llanwarne 36 B2
Llanwddyn 59 C7
Llanwenog 46 E3
Llanwern 35 F7
Llanwinio 32 B3
Llanwnda Gwyn 82 F4
Pembs 44 B4
Llanwnnen 46 E4
Llanwnog 59 E7
Llanwrda 47 F6
Llanwrin 58 D4
Llanwrthwl 47 C8
Llanwrtud
= Llanwrtyd Wells 47 E7
Llanwrtyd 47 E7
Llanwrtyd Wells
= Llanwrtud 47 E7
Llanwyddelan 59 D7
Llanyblodwel 60 B2
Llanybri 32 C4
Llanybydder 46 E4
Llanycefn 32 B1
Llanychaer 44 B4
Llanycil 72 F3
Llanycrwys 46 E5
Llanymawddwy 59 C6
Llanymddyfri
= Llandovery 47 F6
Llanymynech 60 B2
Llanynghenedl 82 C3
Llanynys 72 C5
Llan-y-pwll 73 D7
Llanyre 48 C2
Llanystumdwy 71 D5
Llanywern 35 B5
Llawhaden 32 C1
Llawnt 73 F6
Llawr Dref 70 E3
Llawryglyn 59 E6
Llay 73 D7
Llechcynfarwy 82 C3
Llecheiddior 71 C5
Llechfaen 34 B4
Llechryd Caerph 35 D5
Ceredig 45 E4
Llechrydau 73 F6
Lledrod 46 B5
Llenmerewig 59 E8
Llethrid 33 E6
Llidiad Nenog 46 F4
Llidiardau 72 F2
Llidiart-y-parc 72 E5
Llithfaen 70 C4
Llong 73 C6
Llowes 48 E3
Llundain-fach 46 D4
Llwydcoed 34 D3
Llwyn 60 F2
Llwyncelyn 46 D3
Llwyndafydd 46 D2
Llwynderw 60 D2
Llwyn-du 35 C6
Llwyndyrys 70 C4
Llwyngwril 58 D2
Llwyn-hendy 33 E6
Llwynmawr 73 F6
Llwyn-têg 33 D6
Llwyn-y-brain 32 C2
Llwyn-y-groes 46 D4
Llwynypia 34 E3
Llynclys 60 B2
Llynfaes 82 D4
Llysfaen 83 D8
Llyswen 48 F3
Llysworney 21 B8
Llys-y-frân 32 B1
Llywel 47 F7
Loan 120 B2
Loanend 122 D5
Loanhead 121 C5
Loans 118 F3
Loans of Tullich 151 D11
Lobb 20 F3
Loch a Charnain 148 D3
Loch a'
Ghainmhich 155 E7
Lochailort 147 C10
Lochaline 147 G9
Lochanhully 138 B5
Lochans 104 D4
Locharbriggs 114 F2
Lochassynt
Lodge 156 G4
Lochavich House 124 D5
Lochawe 125 C7
Loch Baghasdail
= Lochboisdale 148 G2
Lochboisdale =
Loch Baghasdail 148 G2
Lochbuie 124 C2
Lochcarron 149 E13
Loch Choire
Lodge 157 F9
Lochdhu 157 E13
Lochdochart
House 126 B3
Lochdon 124 B3
Lochdrum 150 D5
Lochead 144 F6
Lochearnhead 126 B4
Lochee 134 F3
Lochend Highld 151 H8
Highld 158 D4
Locherben 114 E2
Loch Euphoirt 148 B3
Lochfoot 107 B5
Lochgair 145 D8
Lochgarthside 137 C8
Lochgelly 128 E3
Lochgilphead 145 E7
Lochgoilhead 125 E8
Loch Head 105 E7
Lochhill 152 B2
Lochindorb
Lodge 151 H12
Lochinver 156 G3
Lochlane 127 B7
Loch Loyal Lodge 157 E9
Lochluichart 150 E6
Lochmaben 114 F3
Lochmaddy =
Loch nam Madadh 148 B4
Lochmore
Cottage 158 F2
Lochmore Lodge 156 F5
Loch nam Madadh
= Lochmaddy 148 B4
Lochore 128 E3
Lochportain 148 A4
Lochranza 143 C10
Lochs Crofts 152 B3
Loch Sgioport 148 E3
Lochside Aberds 135 C7
Highld 151 F11
Highld 156 D7
Highld 157 F11
Lochslin 151 C11
Lochstack Lodge 156 E5
Lochton 141 E6
Lochty Angus 135 C5
Fife 129 D7
Perth 128 B2
Lochuisge 130 D1
Lochurr 113 F7
Lochwinnoch 118 D3
Lochwood 114 E3
Lochyside 131 B5
Lockengate 4 C5
Lockerbie 114 F4
Lockeridge 25 C6
Lockerley 14 B3
Locking 23 D5
Lockinge 38 F4
Lockington E Yorks 97 E5
Leics 63 B8
Lockleywood 61 B6
Locks Heath 15 D6
Lockton 103 E6
Lockwood 88 C2
Loddington Leics 64 D4
N Nhants 53 B6
Loddiswell 6 E5
Loddon 69 E6
Lode 55 C6
Loders 12 E2
Lodsworth 16 B3
Lofthouse N Yorks 94 B4
W Yorks 88 B4
Loftus 103 C5
Logan 113 B5
Loganlea 120 C2
Logan Mains 104 E4
Loggerheads 74 F4
Logie Angus 135 C6
Fife 129 B6
Moray 151 F13
Logiealmond
Lodge 133 F6
Logie Coldstone 140 D3
Logie Hill 151 D10
Logie Newton 153 E6
Logie Pert 135 C6
Logierait 133 D6
Login 32 B2
Lolworth 54 C4
Lonbain 149 C11
Londesborough 96 E4
London Colney 40 D4
Londonderry 101 F8
Londonthorpe 78 F2
Londubh 155 J13
Lonemore 151 C10
Long Ashton 23 B7
Longbar 118 D3
Long Bennington 77 E8
Longbenton 111 C5
Longborough 38 B1
Long Bredy 12 E3
Longbridge Warks 51 C7
W Mid 50 B5
Longbridge
Deverill 24 E3
Long Buckby 52 C4
Longburton 12 C4
Long Clawson 64 B4
Longcliffe 76 D2
Long Common 15 C6
Long Compton
Staffs 62 B2
Warks 51 F7
Longcot 38 E2
Long Crendon 39 D6
Long Crichel 13 C7
Longcroft 119 B7
Longden 60 D4
Long Ditton 28 C2
Longdon Staffs 62 C4
Worcs 50 F3
Longdon Green 62 C4
Longdon on Tern 61 C6
Longdown 10 E3
Longdowns 3 C6
Long Drax 89 B7
Long Duckmanton 76 B4
Long Eaton 76 F4
Longfield Kent 29 C7
Shetland 160 M5
Longford Derbys 76 F2
Glos 37 B5
London 27 B8
Shrops 74 F3
Telford 61 C7
W Mid 63 F7
Longfordlane 76 F2
Longforgan 128 B5
Longformacus 122 D2
Longframlington 117 D7
Long Green 50 F3
Longham Dorset 13 E8
Norf 68 C2
Long Hanborough 38 C4
Longhaven 153 E11
Longhill 153 C9
Longhirst 117 F8
Longhope Glos 36 C3
Orkney 159 J4
Longhorsley 117 E7
Longhoughton 117 C8
Long Itchington 52 C2
Longlane Derbys 76 F2
W Berks 26 B2
Long Lawford 52 B2
Longlevens 37 B5
Longley 88 D2
Longley Green 50 D2
Long Load 12 B2
Longmanhill 153 B7
Long Marston
Herts 40 C1
N Yorks 95 D8
Warks 51 E6
Long Marton 100 B1
Long Melford 56 E2
Longmoor Camp 27 F5
Longmorn 152 C2
Long Newnton 37 E6
Longnewton
Borders 115 B8
Stockton 102 C1
Long Newton 121 C8
Longney 36 C4
Longniddry 121 B7
Longnor Shrops 60 D4
Staffs 75 C7
Longparish 26 E2
Longport 75 E5
Long Preston 93 D8
Longridge Lancs 93 F6
Staffs 62 C3
W Loth 120 C2
Longriggend 119 B8
Long Riston 97 E7
Longrock 2 C4
Longsdon 75 D6
Longshaw 86 D3
Longside 153 D10
Long Sight 87 D7
Longstanton 54 C4
Longstock 25 F8
Longstone 32 D2
Longstowe 54 D4
Long Stratton 68 E4
Long Street 53 E5
Long Sutton Hants 26 E5
Lincs 66 B4
Som 12 B2
Longthorpe 65 E8
Long Thurlow 56 C4
Longthwaite 99 B6
Longton Lancs 86 B2
Stoke 75 E6
Longtown Cumb 108 C3
Hereford 35 B7
Longview 86 E2
Longville in the
Dale 60 E5
Long Whatton 63 B8
Longwick 39 D7
Long Wittenham 39 E5
Longwitton 117 F6
Longwood 61 D6
Longworth 38 E3
Longyester 121 C8
Lonmay 153 C10
Lonmore 148 D7
Looe 5 D7
Loose 29 D8
Loosley Row 39 D8
Lopcombe Corner 25 F7
Lopen 12 C2
Loppington 60 B4
Lopwell 6 C2
Lorbottle 117 D6
Lorbottle Hall 117 D6
Lornty 134 E1
Loscoe 76 E4
Losgaintir 154 H5
Lossiemouth 152 A2
Lossit 142 C2
Lostford 74 F3
Lostock Gralam 74 B3
Lostock Green 74 B3
Lostock Hall 86 B3
Lostock Junction 86 D4
Lostwithiel 5 D6
Loth 159 E7
Lothbeg 157 H12
Lothersdale 94 E2
Lothmore 157 H12
Loudwater 40 E2
Loughborough 64 C2
Loughor 33 E6
Loughton Essex 41 E7
M Keynes 53 F6
Shrops 61 F6
Lound Lincs 65 C7
Notts 89 F7
Suff 69 E8
Lount 63 C7
Louth 91 F7
Love Clough 87 B6
Lovedean 15 C7
Lover 14 B3
Loversall 89 E6
Loves Green 42 D2
Lovesome Hill 102 E1
Loveston 32 D1
Lovington 23 F7
Low Ackworth 89 C5
Low Barlings 78 B3
Low Bentham 93 C6
Low Bradfield 88 E3
Low Bradley 94 E3
Low Braithwaite 108 E4
Lowbridge House 99 D7
Low Brunton 110 B2
Low Burnham 89 D8
Low Burton 101 F7
Low Buston 117 D8
Lowca 98 B1
Low Catton 96 D3
Low Clanyard 104 F5
Low Coniscliffe 101 C7
Low Crosby 108 D4
Low Dalby 103 F6
Lowdham 77 E6
Low Dinsdale 101 C8
Lowe 74 F2
Lowe Hill 75 D6
Low Ellington 101 F7
Lower Aisholt 22 F4
Lower Arncott 39 C6
Lower Ashton 10 F3
Lower Assendon 39 F7
Lower Badcall 156 E4
Lower Bartle 92 F4
Lower Basildon 26 B4
Lower Beeding 17 B6
Lower Benefield 65 F6
Lower Boddington 52 D2
Lower Brailes 51 F8
Lower Breakish 149 F11
Lower Broadheath 50 D3
Lower Bullingham 49 F7
Lower Cam 36 D4
Lower Chapel 48 F2
Lower Chute 25 D8
Lower Cragabus 142 D4
Lower Crossings 87 F8
Lower
Cumberworth 88 D3
Lower Darwen 86 B4
Lower Dean 53 C8
Lower Diabaig 149 B12
Lower Dicker 18 D2
Lower Dinchope 60 F4
Lower Down 60 F3
Lower Drift 2 D3
Lower Dunsforth 95 C7
Lower Egleton 49 E8
Lower Elkstone 75 D7
Lower End 40 B2
Lower Everleigh 25 D6
Lower Farringdon 26 F5
Lower Foxdale 84 E2
Lower Frankton 73 F7
Lower Froyle 27 E5
Lower Gledfield 151 B8
Lower Green 81 D5
Lower Hacheston 57 D7
Lower Halistra 148 C7
Lower Halstow 30 C2
Lower Hardres 31 D5
Lower Hawthwaite 98 F4
Lower Heath 75 C5
Lower
Hempriggs 151 E14
Lower Hergest 48 D4
Lower Heyford 38 B4
Lower Higham 29 B8
Lower Holbrook 57 F5
Lower Hordley 60 B3
Lower
Horsebridge 18 D2
Lower Killeyan 142 D3
Lower Kingswood 28 D3
Lower Kinnerton 73 C7
Lower Langford 23 C6
Lower Largo 129 D6
Lower Leigh 75 F7
Lower Lemington 51 F7
Lower Lenie 137 B8
Lower Lydbrook 36 C2
Lower Lye 49 C6
Lower Machen 35 F6
Lower Maes-coed 48 F5
Lower Mayland 43 D5
Lower Midway 63 B7
Lower Milovaig 148 C6
Lower Moor 50 E4
Lower Nazeing 41 D6
Lower Netchwood 61 E6
Lower Ollach 149 E10
Lower Penarth 22 B3
Lower Penn 62 E2
Lower Pennington 14 E4
Lower Peover 74 B4
Lower Pexhill 75 B5
Lower Place 87 C7
Lower Quinton 51 E6
Lower Rochford 49 C8
Lower Seagry 37 F6
Lower Shelton 53 E7
Lower Shiplake 27 B5
Lower
Shuckburgh 52 C2
Lower Slaughter 38 B1
Lower Stanton St
Quintin 37 F6
Lower Stoke 30 B2
Lower Stondon 54 F2
Lower Stow Bedon 68 E2
Lower Street Norf 69 C6
Norf 81 D8
Lower Strensham 50 E4
Lower Stretton 86 F4
Lower Sundon 40 B3
Lower Swanwick 15 D5
Lower Swell 38 B1
Lower Tean 75 F7
Lower Thurlton 69 E7
Lower Tote 149 B10
Lower Town 44 B4
Lower Tysoe 51 E8
Lower Upham 15 C6
Lower Vexford 22 F3
Lower Weare 23 D6
Lower Welson 48 D4
Lower Whitley 74 B3
Lower Wield 26 E4
Lower
Winchendon 39 C7
Lower Withington 74 C5
Lower Woodend 39 F8
Lower Woodford 25 F6
Lower Wyche 50 E2
Lowesby 64 D4
Lowestoft 69 E8
Loweswater 98 B3
Low Etherley 101 B6
Low Fell 111 D5
Lowford 15 C5
Low Fulney 66 B2
Low Garth 103 D5
Low Gate 110 C2
Lowgill Lancs 93 C6
W&F 99 E8
Low Grantley 94 B5
Low Habberley 50 B3
Low Ham 12 B2
Low Hesket 108 E4
Low Hesleyhurst 117 E6
Low Hutton 96 C3
Lowick N Nhants 65 F6
Northumb 123 F6
Lowick Bridge 98 F4
Lowick Green 98 F4
Low Laithe 94 C4
Lowlands 35 E6
Low Leighton 87 F8
Low Lorton 98 B3
Low Marishes 96 B4
Low Marnham 77 C8
Low Mill 102 E4
Low Moor Lancs 93 E7
W Yorks 88 B2
Lowmoor Row 99 B8
Low Moorsley 111 E6
Low Newton 99 F6
Low Newton-by-the-
Sea 117 B8
Lownie Moor 134 E4
Low Row Cumb 108 F3
Cumb 109 C5
N Yorks 100 E4
Low Salchrie 104 C4
Low Smerby 143 F8
Lowsonford 51 C6
Lowther 99 B7
Lowthorpe 97 C6
Lowton 86 E4
Lowton Common 86 E4
Low Torry 128 F2
Low Worsall 102 D1
Low Wray 99 D5
Loxbeare 10 C4
Loxhill 27 F8
Loxhore 20 F5
Loxley 51 D7
Loxton 23 D5
Loxwood 27 F8
Lubcroy 156 J6
Lubenham 64 F4
Luccombe 21 E8
Luccombe Village 15 G6
Lucker 123 F7
Luckett 5 B8
Luckington 37 F5
Lucklawhill 129 B6
Luckwell Bridge 21 F8
Lucton 49 C6
Ludag 148 G2
Ludborough 91 E6
Ludchurch 32 C2
Luddenden 87 B8
Luddenden Foot 87 B8
Luddesdown 29 C7
Luddington N Lincs 90 C2
Warks 51 D6
Luddington in the
Brook 65 F8
Lude House 133 C5
Ludford Lincs 91 F6
Shrops 49 B7
Ludgershall Bucks 39 C6
Wilts 25 D7
Ludgvan 2 C4
Ludham 69 C6
Ludlow 49 B7
Ludwell 13 B7
Ludworth 111 E6

Luffincott 8 E5
Lugar 113 F5
Luggate Burn 122 B2
Lugg Green 49 C6
Luggiebank 119 B7
Lugton 118 D4
Lugwardine 49 E7
Luib 149 F10
Lulham 49 E6
Lullenden 28 E5
Lullington Derbys 63 C6
Som 24 D2
Lulsgate Bottom 23 C7
Lulsley 50 D2
Lumb 87 B8
Lumby 95 F7
Lumloch 119 C6
Lumphanan 140 D4
Lumphinnans 128 E3
Lumsdaine 122 C4
Lumsden 140 B3
Lunan 135 D6
Lunanhead 134 D4
Luncarty 128 B2
Lund E Yorks 97 E5
N Yorks 96 F2
Shetland 160 C7
Lunderton 153 D11
Lundie Angus 134 F2
Highld 136 C4
Lundin Links 129 D6
Lunga 124 E3
Lunna 160 G6
Lunning 160 G7
Lunnon 33 F6
Lunsford's Cross 18 D4
Lunt 85 D4
Luntley 49 D5
Luppitt 11 D6
Lupset 88 C4
Lupton 99 F7
Lurgashall 16 B3
Lusby 79 C6
Luson 6 E4
Luss 126 E2
Lussagiven 144 E5
Lusta 149 C7
Lustleigh 10 F2
Luston 49 C6
Luthermuir 135 C6
Luthrie 128 C5
Luton Devon 7 B7
Luton 40 B3
Medway 29 C8
Lutterworth 64 F2
Lutton Devon 6 D3
Lincs 66 B4
N Nhants 65 F8
Lutworthy 10 C2
Luxborough 21 F8
Luxulyan 5 D5
Lybster 158 G4
Lydbury North 60 F3
Lydcott 21 F5
Lydd 19 C7
Lydden 31 E6
Lyddington 65 E5
Lydd on Sea 19 C7
Lydeard St Lawrence 22 F3
Lyde Green 26 D5
Lydford 9 F7
Lydford-on-Fosse 23 F7
Lydgate 87 B7
Lydham 60 E3
Lydiard Green 37 F7
Lydiard Millicent 37 F7
Lydiate 85 D4
Lydlinch 12 C5
Lydney 36 D3
Lydstep 32 E1
Lye 62 F3
Lye Green Bucks 40 D2
E Sus 18 B2
Lyford 38 E3
Lymbridge Green 30 E5
Lyme Regis 11 E8
Lyminge 31 E5
Lymington 14 E4
Lyminster 16 D4
Lymm 86 F4
Lymore 14 E3
Lympne 19 B8
Lympsham 22 D5
Lympstone 10 F4
Lynchat 138 D3
Lyndale House 149 C8
Lyndhurst 14 D4
Lyndon 65 D6
Lyne 27 C8
Lyneal 73 F8
Lyne Down 49 F8
Lyneham Oxon 38 B2
Wilts 24 B5
Lynemore 139 B6
Lynemouth 117 E8
Lyne of Gorthleck 137 B8
Lyne of Skene 141 C6
Lyness 159 J4
Lyng Norf 68 C3
Som 11 B8
Lynmouth 21 E6
Lynsted 30 C3
Lynton 21 E6
Lyon's Gate 12 D4
Lyonshall 48 D5
Lytchett Matravers 13 E7
Lytchett Minster 13 E7
Lyth 158 D4
Lytham 85 B4
Lytham St Anne's 85 B4
Lythe 103 C6
Lythes 159 K5

M

Mabe Burnthouse 3 C6
Mabie 107 B6
Mablethorpe 91 F9
Macclesfield 75 B6
Macclesfield Forest 75 B6
Macduff 153 B7
Mace Green 56 E5
Macharioch 143 H8
Machen 35 F6
Machrihanish 143 F7
Machynlleth 58 D4
Machynys 33 E6
Mackerel's Common 16 B4
Mackworth 76 F3
Macmerry 121 B7
Madderty 127 B8
Maddiston 120 B2
Madehurst 16 C3
Madeley Staffs 74 E4
Telford 61 D6
Madeley Heath 74 E4
Madeley Park 74 E4
Madingley 54 C4
Madley 49 F6
Madresfield 50 E3
Madron 2 C3
Maenaddwyn 82 C4
Maenclochog 32 B1
Maendy 22 B2
Maentwrog 71 C7
Maen-y-groes 46 D2
Maer 74 F4
Maerdy Conwy 72 E4
Rhondda 34 E3
Maesbrook 60 B2
Maesbury 60 B3
Maesbury Marsh 60 B3
Maesgwyn-Isaf 59 C8
Maesgwynne 32 B3
Maeshafn 73 C6
Maesllyn 46 E2
Maesmynis 48 E2
Maesteg 34 E2
Maestir 46 E4
Maes-Treylow 48 C4
Maesybont 33 C6
Maesycrugiau 46 E3
Maesy cwmmer 35 E5
Maesymeillion 46 E3
Magdalen Laver 41 D8
Maggieknockater 152 D3
Magham Down 18 D3
Maghull 85 D4
Magor 35 F8
Magpie Green 56 B4
Maiden Bradley 24 F3
Maidencombe 7 C7
Maidenhall 57 E5
Maidenhead 40 F1
Maiden Law 110 E4
Maiden Newton 12 E3
Maidens 112 D2
Maidensgrave 57 E6
Maiden's Green 27 B6
Maidenwell Corn 5 B6
Lincs 79 B6
Maiden Wells 44 F4
Maidford 52 D4
Maids Moreton 52 F5
Maidstone 29 D8
Maidwell 52 B5
Mail 160 L6
Main 59 C8
Maindee 35 F7
Mainsforth 111 F6
Mains of Airies 104 C3
Mains of Allardice 135 B8
Mains of Annochie 153 D9
Mains of Ardestie 135 F5
Mains of Balhall 135 C5
Mains of Ballindarg 134 D4
Mains of Balnakettle 135 B6
Mains of Birness 153 E9
Mains of Burgie 151 F13
Mains of Clunas 151 G11
Mains of Crichie 153 D9
Mains of Dalvey 151 H14
Mains of Dellavaird 141 F6
Mains of Drum 141 E7
Mains of Edingight 152 C5
Mains of Fedderate 153 D8
Mains of Inkhorn 153 E9
Mains of Mayen 152 D5
Mains of Melgund 135 D5
Mains of Thornton 135 B6
Mains of Watten 158 E4
Mainsriddle 107 D6
Mainstone 60 F2
Maisemore 37 B5
Malacleit 148 A2
Malborough 6 F5
Malcoff 87 F8
Maldon 42 D4
Malham 94 C2
Maligar 149 B9
Mallaig 147 B9
Malleny Mills 120 C4
Malling 126 D4
Malltraeth 82 E4
Mallwyd 59 C5
Malmesbury 37 F6
Malmsmead 21 E6
Malpas Ches W 73 E8
Corn 3 B7
Newport 35 E7
Malswick 36 B4
Maltby Stockton 102 C2
S Yorks 89 E6
Maltby le Marsh 91 F8
Malting Green 43 B5
Maltman's Hill 30 E3
Malton 96 B3
Malvern Link 50 E2
Malvern Wells 50 E2
Mamble 49 B8
Manaccan 3 D6
Manafon 59 D8
Manais 154 J6
Manar House 141 B6
Manaton 10 F2
Manby 91 F7
Mancetter 63 E7
Manchester 87 E6
Manchester Airport 87 F6
Mancot 73 C7
Mandally 137 D5
Manea 66 F4
Manfield 101 C7
Mangaster 160 F5
Mangotsfield 23 B8
Mangurstadh 154 D5
Mankinholes 87 B7
Manley 74 B2
Manmoel 35 D5
Mannal 146 G2
Mannerston 120 B3
Manningford Bohune 25 D6
Manningford Bruce 25 D6
Manningham 94 F4
Mannings Heath 17 B6
Mannington 13 D8
Manningtree 56 F4
Mannofield 141 D8
Manor 41 F7
Manorbier 32 E1
Manordeilo 33 B7
Manor Estate 88 F4
Manorhill 122 F2
Manorowen 44 B4
Manselfield 33 F6
Mansel Lacy 49 E6
Mansell Gamage 49 E5
Mansergh 99 F8
Mansfield E Ayrs 113 C6
Notts 76 C5
Mansfield Woodhouse 76 C5
Mansriggs 98 F4
Manston Dorset 13 C6
Kent 31 C7
W Yorks 95 F6
Manswood 13 D7
Manthorpe Lincs 65 C7
Lincs 78 F2
Manton N Lincs 90 D3
Notts 77 B5
Rutland 65 D5
Wilts 25 C6
Manuden 41 B7
Maperton 12 B4
Maplebeck 77 C7
Maple Cross 40 E3
Mapledurham 26 B4
Mapledurwell 26 D4
Maplehurst 17 B5
Maplescombe 29 C6
Mapleton 75 E8
Mapperley 76 E4
Mapperley Park 77 E5
Mapperton 12 E3
Mappleborough Green 51 C5
Mappleton 97 E8
Mappowder 12 D5
Maraig 154 G6
Marazanvose 4 D3
Marazion 2 C4
Marbhig 155 F9
Marbury 74 E2
March Cambs 66 E4
S Lanark 114 C2
Marcham 38 E4
Marchamley 61 B5
Marchington 75 F8
Marchington Woodlands 62 B5
Marchroes 70 E4
Marchwiel 73 E7
Marchwood 14 C4
Marcross 21 C8
Marden Hereford 49 E7
Kent 29 E8
T&W 111 B6
Wilts 25 D5
Marden Beech 29 E8
Marden Thorn 29 E8
Mardy 35 C7
Marefield 64 D4
Mareham le Fen 79 C5
Mareham on the Hill 79 C5
Marehay 76 E3
Marehill 16 C4
Maresfield 17 B8
Marfleet 90 B5
Marford 73 D7
Margam 34 F1
Margaret Marsh 13 C6
Margaret Roding 42 C1
Margaretting 42 D2
Margate 31 B7
Margnaheglish 143 E11
Margrove Park 102 C4
Marham 67 C7
Marhamchurch 8 D4
Marholm 65 D8
Mariandyrys 83 C6
Marianglas 82 C5
Mariansleigh 10 B2
Marionburgh 141 D6
Marishader 149 B9
Marjoriebanks 114 F3
Mark Dumfries 104 D5
S Ayrs 104 B4
Som 23 E5
Markbeech 29 E5
Markby 79 B7
Mark Causeway 23 E5
Mark Cross E Sus 17 C8
E Sus 18 B2
Market Bosworth 63 D8
Market Deeping 65 D8
Market Drayton 74 F3
Market Harborough 64 F4
Markethill 134 F2
Market Lavington 24 D5
Market Overton 65 C5
Market Rasen 90 F5
Market Stainton 78 B5
Market Warsop 77 C5
Market Weighton 96 E4
Market Weston 56 B3
Markfield 63 C8
Markham 35 D5
Markham Moor 77 B7
Markinch 128 D4
Markington 95 C5
Marksbury 23 C8
Marks Tey 43 B5
Markyate 40 C3
Marland 87 C6
Marlborough 25 C6
Marlbrook Hereford 49 D7
Worcs 50 B4
Marlcliff 51 D5
Marldon 7 C6
Marlesford 57 D7
Marley Green 74 E2
Marley Hill 110 D5
Marley Mount 14 E3
Marlingford 68 D4
Mar Lodge 139 E6
Marloes 44 E2
Marlow Bucks 39 F8
Hereford 49 B6
Marlow Bottom 40 F1
Marlpit Hill 28 E5
Marlpool 76 E4
Marnhull 13 C5
Marnoch 152 C5
Marnock 119 C7
Marple 87 F7
Marple Bridge 87 F7
Marr 89 D6
Marrel 157 H13
Marrick 101 E5
Marrister 160 G7
Marros 32 D3
Marsden T&W 111 C6
W Yorks 87 C8
Marsett 100 F4
Marsh Devon 11 C7
W Yorks 94 F3
Marshall's Heath 40 C4
Marshalsea 11 D8
Marshalswick 40 D4
Marsham 81 E7
Marshaw 93 D5
Marsh Baldon 39 E5
Marshborough 31 D7
Marshbrook 60 F4
Marshchapel 91 E7
Marshfield Newport 35 F6
S Glos 24 B2
Marshgate 8 E3
Marsh Gibbon 39 B6
Marsh Green Devon 10 E5
Kent 28 E5
Staffs 75 D5
Marshland St James 66 D5
Marsh Lane 76 B4
Marshside 85 C4
Marsh Street 21 E8
Marshwood 11 E8
Marske 101 D6
Marske-by-the-Sea 102 B4
Marston Ches W 74 B3
Hereford 49 D5
Lincs 77 E8
Oxon 39 D5
Staffs 62 B3
Staffs 62 C2
Warks 63 E6
Wilts 24 D4
Marston Doles 52 D2
Marston Green 63 F5
Marston Magna 12 B3
Marston Meysey 37 E8
Marston Montgomery 75 F8
Marston Moretaine 53 E7
Marston on Dove 63 B6
Marston St Lawrence 52 E3
Marston Stannett 49 D7
Marston Trussell 64 F3
Marstow 36 C2
Marsworth 40 C2
Marten 25 D7
Marthall 74 B5
Martham 69 C7
Martin Hants 13 C8
Kent 31 E7
Lincs 78 C5
Lincs 78 D4
Martin Dales 78 C4
Martin Drove End 13 B8
Martinhoe 21 E5
Martinhoe Cross 21 E5
Martin Hussingtree 50 C3
Martin Mill 31 E7
Martinscroft 86 F4
Martinstown 12 F4
Martlesham 57 E6
Martlesham Heath 57 E6
Martletwy 32 C1
Martley 50 D2
Martock 12 C2
Marton Ches E 75 C5
E Yorks 97 F7
Lincs 90 F2
Mbro 102 C3
N Yorks 95 C7
N Yorks 103 F5
Shrops 60 B4
Shrops 60 D2
Warks 52 C2
Marton-le-Moor 95 B6
Martyr's Green 27 D8
Martyr Worthy 26 F3
Marwick 159 F3
Marwood 20 F4
Marybank 150 F7
Maryburgh 151 F8
Maryhill 119 C5
Marykirk 135 C6
Marylebone 86 D3
Marypark 152 E1
Maryport Cumb 107 F7
Dumfries 104 F5
Mary Tavy 6 B3
Maryton 135 D6
Marywell Aberds 140 E4
Aberds 141 E8
Angus 135 E6
Masham 101 F7
Mashbury 42 C2
Masongill 93 B6
Masonhill 112 B3
Mastin Moor 76 B4
Mastrick 141 D7
Matching 41 C8
Matching Green 41 C8
Matching Tye 41 C8
Matfen 110 B3
Matfield 29 E7
Mathern 36 E2
Mathon 50 E2
Mathry 44 B3
Matlaske 81 D7
Matlock 76 C2
Matlock Bath 76 D2
Matson 37 C5
Matterdale End 99 B5
Mattersey 89 F7
Mattersey Thorpe 89 F7
Mattingley 26 D5
Mattishall 68 C3
Mattishall Burgh 68 C3
Mauchline 112 B4
Maud 153 D9
Maugersbury 38 B2
Maughold 84 C4
Mauld 150 H7
Maulden 53 F8
Maulds Meaburn 99 C8
Maunby 102 F1
Maund Bryan 49 D7
Maundown 11 B5
Mautby 69 C7
Mavis Enderby 79 C6
Mawbray 107 E7
Mawdesley 86 C2
Mawdlam 34 F2
Mawgan 3 D6
Mawgan Porth 4 C3
Maw Green 74 D4
Mawla 3 B6
Mawnan 3 D6
Mawnan Smith 3 D6
Mawsley 53 B6
Maxey 65 D8
Maxstoke 63 F6
Maxton Borders 122 F2
Kent 31 E7
Maxwellheugh 122 F3
Maxwelltown 107 B6
Maxworthy 8 E4
Mayals 33 E7
May Bank 75 E5
Maybole 112 D3
Mayfield E Sus 18 C2
Midloth 121 C6
Staffs 75 E8
W Loth 120 C2
Mayford 27 D7
Mayland 43 D5
Maynard's Green 18 D2
Maypole Mon 36 C1
Scilly 2 E4
Maypole Green Essex 43 B5
Norf 69 E7
Suff 57 C6
Maywick 160 L5
Meadle 39 D8
Meadowtown 60 D3
Meaford 75 F5
Mealabost 155 D9
Mealabost Bhuirgh 155 B9
Meal Bank 99 E7
Mealsgate 108 E2
Meanwood 95 F5
Mearbeck 93 C8
Meare 23 E6
Meare Green 11 B8
Mears Ashby 53 C6
Measham 63 C7
Meath Green 28 E3
Meathop 99 F6
Meaux 97 F6
Meavy 6 C3
Medbourne 64 E4
Medburn 110 B4
Meddon 8 C4
Meden Vale 77 C5
Medlam 79 D6
Medmenham 39 F8
Medomsley 110 D4
Medstead 26 F4
Meerbrook 75 C6
Meer End 51 B7
Meers Bridge 91 F8
Meesden 54 F5
Meeth 9 D7
Meggethead 114 B4
Meidrim 32 B3
Meifod Denb 72 D4
Powys 59 C8
Meigle N Ayrs 118 C1
Perth 134 E2
Meikle Earnock 119 D7
Meikle Ferry 151 C10
Meikle Forter 134 C1
Meikle Gluich 151 C9
Meikleour 134 F1
Meikle Pinkerton 122 B3
Meikle Strath 135 B6
Meikle Tarty 141 B8
Meikle Wartle 153 E7
Meinciau 33 C5
Meir 75 E6
Meir Heath 75 E6
Melbourn 54 E4
Melbourne Derbys 63 B7
E Yorks 96 E3
S Lanark 120 E3
Melbury Abbas 13 B6
Melbury Bubb 12 D3
Melbury Osmond 12 D3
Melbury Sampford 12 D3
Melby 160 H3
Melchbourne 53 C8
Melcombe Bingham 13 D5
Melcombe Regis 12 F4
Meldon Devon 9 E7
Northumb 117 F7
Meldreth 54 E4
Meldrum House 141 B7
Melfort 124 D4
Melgarve 137 E7
Meliden 72 A4
Melinbyrhedyn 58 E5
Melincourt 34 D2
Melin-y-coed 83 E8
Melin-y-ddôl 59 D7
Melin-y-grug 59 D7
Melin-y-Wig 72 E4
Melkinthorpe 99 B7
Melkridge 109 C7
Melksham 24 C4
Melldalloch 145 F8
Melling Lancs 93 B5
Mers 85 D4
Melling Mount 86 D2
Mellis 56 B5
Mellon Charles 155 H13
Mellon Udrigle 155 H13
Mellor Gtr Man 87 F7
Lancs 93 F6
Mellor Brook 93 F6
Mells 24 E2
Melmerby N Yorks 95 B6
N Yorks 101 F5
W&F 109 F6
Melplash 12 E2
Melrose 121 F8
Melsetter 159 K3
Melsonby 101 D6
Meltham 88 C2
Melton 57 D6
Meltonby 96 D3
Melton Constable 81 D6
Melton Mowbray 64 C4
Melton Ross 90 C4
Melvaig 155 J12
Melverley 60 C3
Melverley Green 60 C3
Melvich 157 C11
Membury 11 D7
Memsie 153 B9
Memus 134 D4
Menabilly 5 D5
Menai Bridge = Porthaethwy 83 D5
Mendham 69 F5
Mendlesham 56 C5
Mendlesham Green 56 C4
Menheniot 5 C7
Mennock 113 D8
Menston 94 E4
Menstrie 127 E7
Menthorpe 96 F2
Mentmore 40 C2
Meoble 147 C10
Meole Brace 60 C4
Meols 85 E3
Meonstoke 15 C7
Meopham 29 C7
Meopham Station 29 C7
Mepal 66 F4
Meppershall 54 F2
Merbach 48 E5
Mere Ches E 86 F5
Wilts 24 F3
Mere Brow 86 C2
Mereclough 93 F8
Mere Green 62 E5
Mereside 92 F3
Mereworth 29 D7
Mergie 141 F6
Meriden 63 F6
Merkadale 149 E8
Merkland Dumfries 106 B4
S Ayrs 112 E2
Merkland Lodge 156 G7
Merley 13 E8
Merlin's Bridge 44 D4
Merrington 60 B4
Merrion 44 F4
Merriott 12 C2
Merrivale 6 B3
Merrow 27 D8
Merrymeet 5 C7
Mersham 19 B7
Merstham 28 D3
Merston 16 D2
Merstone 15 F6
Merther 3 B7
Merthyr 32 B4
Merthyr Cynog 47 F8
Merthyr-Dyfan 22 C3
Merthyr Mawr 21 B7
Merthyr Tudful = Merthyr Tydfil 34 D4
Merthyr Tydfil = Merthyr Tudful 34 D4
Merthyr Vale 34 E4
Merton Devon 9 C7
London 28 B3
Norf 68 E2
Oxon 39 C5
Mervinslaw 116 C2
Meshaw 10 C2
Messing 42 C4
Messingham 90 D2
Metfield 69 F5
Metheringham 78 C3
Methil 129 E5
Methlem 70 D2
Methley 88 B4
Methlick 153 E8
Methven 128 B2
Methwold 67 E7
Methwold Hythe 67 E7
Mettingham 69 F6
Mevagissey 3 B9
Mewith Head 93 C7
Mexborough 89 D5
Mey 158 C4
Meysey Hampton 37 E8
Miabhag W Isles 154 G5
W Isles 154 H6
Miabhig 154 D5
Michaelchurch 36 B2
Michaelchurch Escley 48 F5
Michaelchurch on Arrow 48 D4
Michaelston-le-Pit 22 B3
Michaelston-y-Fedw 35 F6
Michaelstow 5 B5
Michealston-super-Ely 22 B3
Micheldever 26 F3
Michelmersh 14 B4
Mickfield 56 C5
Micklebring 89 E6
Mickleby 103 C6
Mickleham 28 D2
Mickleover 76 F3
Micklethwaite 94 E4
Mickleton Durham 100 B4
Glos 51 E6
Mickletown 88 B4
Mickle Trafford 73 C8
Mickley 95 B5
Mickley Square 110 C3
Mid Ardlaw 153 B9
Mid Auchinlech 118 B3
Midbea 159 D5
Mid Beltie 140 D5
Mid Calder 120 C3
Mid Cloch Forbie 153 C7
Mid Clyth 158 G4
Middle Assendon 39 F7
Middle Aston 38 B4
Middle Barton 38 B4
Middlebie 108 B2
Middle Cairncake 153 D8
Middle Claydon 39 B7
Middle Drums 135 D5
Middleforth Green 86 B3
Middleham 101 F6
Middle Handley 76 B4
Middlehope 60 F4
Middle Littleton 51 E5
Middle Maes-coed 48 F5
Middlemarsh 12 D4
Middle Mill 44 C3
Middlemuir 141 B8
Middle Rasen 90 F4
Middle Rigg 128 D2
Middlesbrough 102 B2
Middleshaw Dumfries 107 B8
W&F 99 F7
Middlesmoor 94 B3
Middlestone 111 F5
Middlestone Moor 110 F5
Middlestown 88 C3
Middlethird 122 E2
Middleton Aberds 141 C7
Argyll 146 G2
Derbys 75 C8
Derbys 76 D2
Essex 56 F2
Gtr Man 87 D6
Hants 26 E2
Hereford 49 C7
Lancs 92 D4
Midloth 121 D6
N Nhants 64 F5
Norf 67 C6
Northumb 117 F6
Northumb 123 F7
N Yorks 94 E4
N Yorks 103 F5
Perth 128 D3
Perth 133 E8
Shrops 49 B7
Shrops 60 B3
Shrops 60 E2
Suff 57 C8
Swansea 33 F5
Warks 63 E5
W&F 99 F8
W Yorks 88 B3
Middleton Cheney 52 E2
Middleton Green 75 F6
Middleton Hall 117 B5
Middleton-in-Teesdale 100 B4
Middleton Moor 57 C8
Middleton One Row 102 C1
Middleton-on-Leven 102 D2
Middleton-on-Sea 16 D3
Middleton on the Hill 49 C7
Middleton-on-the-Wolds 96 E5
Middleton Priors 61 E6
Middleton Quernham 95 B6
Middleton St George 101 C8
Middleton Scriven 61 F6
Middleton Stoney 39 B5
Middleton Tyas 101 D7
Middletown Cumb 98 D1
Powys 60 C3
Middle Tysoe 51 E8
Middle Wallop 25 F7
Middlewich 74 C3
Middle Winterslow 25 F7
Middle Woodford 25 F6
Middlewood Green 56 C4
Middlezoy 23 F5
Middridge 101 B7
Midfield 157 C8
Midge Hall 86 B3
Midgeholme 109 D6
Midgham 26 C3
Midgley W Yorks 87 B8
W Yorks 88 C3
Midhopestones 88 E3
Midhurst 16 B2
Mid Lavant 16 D2
Midlem 115 B8
Mid Main 150 H7
Midmar 141 D5
Midsomer Norton 23 D8
Midton 118 B2
Midtown Highld 155 J13
Highld 157 C8
Midtown of Buchromb 152 D3
Mid Urchany 151 G11
Midville 79 D6
Mid Walls 160 H4
Midway 87 F7
Mid Yell 160 D7
Migdale 151 B9
Migvie 140 D3
Milarrochy 126 E3
Milborne Port 12 C4
Milborne St Andrew 13 E6
Milborne Wick 12 B4
Milbourne 110 B4
Milburn 100 B1
Milbury Heath 36 E3
Milcombe 52 F2
Milden 56 E3
Mildenhall Suff 55 B8
Wilts 25 C7
Milebrook 48 B5
Milebush 29 E8
Mile Cross 68 C5
Mile Elm 24 C4
Mile End Essex 43 B5
Glos 36 C2
Mileham 68 C2
Mile Oak 17 D6
Milesmark 128 F2
Milfield 122 F5
Milford Derbys 76 E3
Devon 8 B4
Powys 59 E7
Staffs 62 B3
Sur 27 E7
Wilts 14 B2
Milford Haven = Aberdaugleddau 44 E4
Milford on Sea 14 E3
Milkwall 36 D2
Milkwell 13 B7
Milland 16 B2
Millarston 118 C4
Millbank Aberds 153 D11
Highld 158 D3
Mill Bank 87 B8
Millbeck 98 B4
Millbounds 159 E6
Millbreck 153 D10
Millbridge 27 E6
Millbrook C Beds 53 F8
Corn 6 D2
Soton 14 C4
Millburn 112 B4
Millcombe 7 E6
Mill Common 69 F7
Millcorner 18 C5
Milldale 75 D8
Millden Lodge 135 B5
Milldens 135 D5
Mill End Bucks 39 F7
Herts 54 F4
Millerhill 121 C6
Miller's Dale 75 B8
Miller's Green 76 D2
Millgreen 61 B6
Mill Green Essex 42 D2
Norf 68 F4
Suff 56 E3
Millhalf 48 E4
Millhayes 11 D7
Millhead 92 B4
Millheugh 119 D7
Mill Hill 41 E5
Millholme 99 E7
Millhouse Argyll 145 F8
W&F 108 F3
Millhousebridge 114 F4
Millhouse Green 88 D3
Millhouses 88 F4
Millikenpark 118 C4
Millin Cross 44 D4
Millington 96 D4
Mill Lane 27 D5
Millmeece 74 F5
Mill of Kingoodie 141 B7
Mill of Muiresk 153 D6
Mill of Sterin 140 E2
Mill of Uras 141 F7
Millom 98 F3
Millook 8 E3
Mill Place 90 D3
Millpool 5 B6
Millport 145 H10
Millquarter 113 F6
Mill Side 99 F6
Mill Street 68 C3
Millthorpe 78 F4
Millthrop 100 E1
Milltimber 141 D7
Milltown Corn 5 D6
Derbys 76 C3
Devon 20 F4
Dumfries 108 B3
Milltown of Aberdalgie 128 B2
Milltown of Auchindoun 152 D3
Milltown of Craigston 153 C7
Milltown of Edinvillie 152 D2
Milltown of Kildrummy 140 C3
Milltown of Rothiemay 152 D5
Milltown of Towie 140 C3
Milnathort 128 D3
Milner's Heath 73 C8
Milngavie 119 B5
Milnrow 87 C7
Milnshaw 87 B5
Milnthorpe 99 F6
Milo 33 C6
Milson 49 B8
Milstead 30 D3
Milston 25 E6
Milton Angus 134 E3
Cambs 55 C5
Cumb 109 C5
Derbys 63 B7
Dumfries 105 D6
Dumfries 106 B5
Dumfries 113 F8
Highld 150 F6
Highld 150 H7
Highld 151 D10
Highld 151 G8
Highld 158 E5
Moray 152 B5
Notts 77 B7
N Som 22 C5
Oxon 38 E4
Oxon 52 F2
Pembs 32 D1
Perth 127 C8
Ptsmth 15 E7
Stirling 126 D4
Stoke 75 D6
W Dunb 118 B4
Milton Abbas 13 D6
Milton Abbot 6 B2
Milton Bridge 120 C5
Milton Bryan 53 F7
Milton Clevedon 23 F8
Milton Coldwells 153 E9
Milton Combe 6 C2
Milton Damerel 9 C5
Miltonduff 152 B1
Milton End 37 D8
Milton Ernest 53 D8
Milton Green 73 D8
Miltonhill 151 E13
Milton Hill 38 E4
Miltonise 105 B5
Milton Keynes 53 F6
Milton Keynes Village 53 F6
Milton Lilbourne 25 C6
Milton Malsor 52 D5
Milton Morenish 132 F3
Milton of Auchinhove 140 D4
Milton of Balgonie 128 D5
Milton of Buchanan 126 E3
Milton of Campfield 140 D5
Milton of Campsie 119 B6
Milton of Corsindae 141 D5
Milton of Cushnie 140 C4
Milton of Dalcapon 133 D6
Milton of Edradour 133 D6
Milton of Gollanfield 151 F10
Milton of Lesmore 140 B3
Milton of Logie 140 D3
Milton of Murtle 141 D7
Milton of Noth 140 B4
Milton of Tullich 140 E2
Milton on Stour 13 B5
Milton Regis 30 C3
Milton under Wychwood 38 C2
Milverton Som 11 B6
Warks 51 C8
Milwich 75 F6
Minard 125 F5
Minchinhampton 37 D5
Mindrum 122 F4
Minehead 21 E8
Minera 73 D6
Minety 37 E7
Minffordd Gwyn 58 C4
Gwyn 71 D6
Gwyn 83 D5
Miningsby 79 C6
Minions 5 B7
Minishant 112 C3
Minllyn 59 C5
Minnes 141 B8
Minngearraidh 148 F2
Minnigaff 105 C8
Minnonie 153 B7
Minskip 95 C6
Minstead 14 C3
Minsted 16 B2
Minster Kent 30 B3
Kent 31 C7
Minsterley 60 D3
Minster Lovell 38 C3
Minsterworth 36 C4
Minterne Magna 12 D4
Minting 78 B4
Mintlaw 153 D9
Minto 115 B8
Minton 60 E4
Minwear 32 C1
Minworth 63 E5
Mirbister 159 F4
Mirehouse 98 C1
Mireland 158 D5
Mirfield 88 C3
Miserden 37 D6
Miskin 34 F4
Misson 89 E7
Misterton Leics 64 F2
Notts 89 E8
Som 12 D2
Mistley 56 F5
Mitcham 28 C3
Mitcheldean 36 C3
Mitchell 4 D3
Mitchel Troy 36 C1
Mitcheltroy Common 36 D1
Mitford 117 F7
Mithian 4 D2
Mitton 62 C2
Mixbury 52 F4
Moat 108 B4
Moats Tye 56 D4
Mobberley Ches E 74 B4
Staffs 75 E7
Moccas 49 E5
Mochdre Conwy 83 D8
Powys 59 F7
Mochrum 105 E7
Mockbeggar 14 D2
Mockerkin 98 B2
Modbury 6 D4
Moddershall 75 F6
Moelfre Anglesey 82 C5
Powys 59 B8
Moffat 114 D3
Moggerhanger 54 E2
Moira 63 C7
Molash 30 D4
Mol-chlach 149 G9
Mold = Yr Wyddgrug 73 C6
Moldgreen 88 C2
Molehill Green 42 B1
Molescroft 97 E6
Molesden 117 F7
Molesworth 53 B8
Moll 149 E10
Molland 10 B3
Mollington Ches W 73 B7
Oxon 52 E2
Mollinsburn 119 B7
Monachty 46 C4
Monachylemore 126 C3
Monar Lodge 150 G5
Monaughty 48 C4
Monboddo House 135 B7
Mondynes 135 B7
Monevechadan 125 E7
Monewden 57 D6
Moneydie 128 B2
Moniaive 113 E7
Monifieth 134 F4
Monikie 135 F4
Monimail 128 C4
Monington 45 E3

Monk Bretton.......88 D4
Monken Hadley....41 E5
Monk Fryston.....89 B6
Monkhopton......61 E6
Monkland........49 D6
Monkleigh.........9 B6
Monknash........21 B8
Monkokehampton. 9 D7
Monkseaton.....111 B6
Monks Eleigh.....56 E3
Monk's Gate......17 B6
Monks Heath.....74 B5
Monk Sherborne. .26 D4
Monkshill.......153 D7
Monksilver........22 F2
Monks Kirby......63 F8
Monk Soham......57 C6
Monkspath.......51 B6
Monks Risborough 39 D8
Monk Street......42 B2
Monkswood......35 D7
Monkton Devon ...11 D6
  Kent..........31 C6
  Pembs........44 E4
  S Ayrs.......112 B3
Monkton Combe . .24 C2
Monkton Deverill . 24 F3
Monkton Farleigh . 24 C3
Monkton
  Heathfield......11 B7
Monkton Up
  Wimborne......13 C8
Monkwearmouth.111 D6
Monkwood.......26 F4
Monmouth
  =Trefynwy......36 C2
Monmouth Cap. ..35 B7
Monnington on
  Wye...........49 E5
Monreith.......105 E7
Monreith Mains .105 E7
Montacute.......12 C2
Montcoffer
  House........153 B6
Montford Argyll .145 G10
  Shrops.......60 C4
Montford Bridge . .60 C4
Montgarrie.....140 C4
Montgomery
  =Trefaldwyn....60 E2
Montrave.......129 D5
Montrose.......135 D7
Mont Saint.......16 I2
Montsale........43 E6
Monxton.........25 E8
Monyash.........75 C8
Monymusk......141 C5
Monzie.........127 B7
Monzie Castle...127 B7
Moodiesburn....119 B6
Moonzie........128 C5
Moor Allerton....95 F5
Moorby..........79 C5
Moor Crichel.....13 D7
Moordown.......13 E8
Moore...........86 F3
Moor End E Yorks..96 F4
  York..........96 D2
Moorends........89 C7
Moorgate........88 E5
Moorgreen......76 E4
Moorhall.........76 B3
Moorhampton....49 E5
Moorhead........94 F4
Moorhouse Cumb .108 D3
  Notts.........77 C7
Moorlinch........23 F5
Moor Monkton....95 D8
Moor of Granary. 151 F12
Moor of
  Ravenstone....105 E7
Moor Row........98 C2
Moorsholm.....102 C4
Moorside.........87 D7
Moor Street......30 C2
Moorthorpe......89 C5
Moortown Hants .14 D2
  IoW...........14 F5
  Lincs.........90 E4
Morangie.......151 C10
Morar..........147 B9
Morborne........65 E8
Morchard Bishop. .10 D2
Morcombelake. ...12 E2
Morcott.........65 D6
Morda...........60 B2
Morden Dorset....13 E7
  London........28 C3
Mordiford.......49 F7
Mordon.........101 B8
More............60 E3
Morebath........10 B4
Morebattle.....116 B3
Morecambe......92 C4
Morefield......150 B4
Moreleigh........7 D5
Morenish.......132 F2
Moresby.........98 B1
Moresby Parks. ...98 B1
Morestead........15 B6
Moreton Dorset....13 F6
  Essex.........41 D8
  Mers..........85 E3
  Oxon..........39 D6
  Staffs........61 C7
Moreton Corbet . .61 B5
Moretonhampstead
............10 F2
Moreton-in-Marsh 51 F7
Moreton Jeffries . .49 E8
Moreton Morrell . 51 D8
Moreton on Lugg . 49 E7
Moreton Pinkney. .52 E3
Moreton Say......74 F3
Moreton Valence . 36 D4
Morfa Carms......33 C6
  Carms.........33 E6
Morfa Bach........32 C4
Morfa Bychan.....71 D6
Morfa Dinlle......82 F4
Morfa Glas........34 D2
Morfa Nefyn......70 C3
Morfydd.........72 E5
Morgan's Vale. ...14 B2
Moriah..........46 B5

Morland.........99 B7
Morley Derbys....76 E3
  Durham.......101 B6
  W Yorks.......88 B3
Morley Green.....87 F6
Morley St Botolph. 68 E3
Morningside Edin .120 B5
  N Lanark......119 D8
Morningthorpe....68 E5
Morpeth........117 F8
Morphie.......135 C7
Morrey..........62 C5
Morris Green.....55 F8
Morriston........33 E7
Morston.........81 C6
Mortehoe........20 E3
Mortimer........26 C4
Mortimer's Cross . .49 C6
Mortimer West
  End...........26 C4
Mortlake........28 B3
Morton Cumb.....108 D3
  Derbys........76 C4
  Lincs.........65 B7
  Lincs.........77 C8
  Lincs.........90 E2
  Norf..........68 C4
  Notts.........77 D7
  S Glos........36 E3
  Shrops........60 B2
Morton Bagot 51 C6
Morton-on-
  Swale........101 E8
Morvah...........2 C3
Morval...........5 D7
Morvich Highld....136 B2
  Highld.......157 J10
Morville........61 E6
Morville Heath....61 E6
Morwenstow......8 C4
Mosborough......88 F5
Moscow.........118 E4
Mosedale.......108 F3
Moseley W Mid. ...62 E3
  W Mid.........62 F4
  Worcs.........50 D3
Moss Argyll.....146 G2
  Highld.......147 E9
  S Yorks.......89 C6
  Wrex.........73 D7
Mossat.........140 C3
Mossbank.......160 F6
Mossbay.........98 B1
Mossblown......112 B4
Mossbrow........86 F5
Mossburnford....116 C2
Mossdale.......106 B3
Moss Edge.......92 E4
Mossend........119 C7
Moss End........27 B6
Mosser..........98 B3
Mossfield......151 D9
Mossgiel.......112 B4
Mosside........134 D4
Mossley Ches E....75 C5
  Gtr Man.......87 D7
Mossley Hill.....85 F4
Moss of
  Barmuckity....152 B2
Moss Pit.........62 B3
Moss-side.....151 F11
  N Yorks.......92 F3
Mosstodloch....152 B3
Mosston........135 E5
Mossy Lea.......86 C3
Mosterton.......12 D2
Moston Gtr Man....87 D6
  Shrops........61 B5
Mostyn..........85 F2
Mostyn Quay.....85 F2
Motcombe........13 B6
Motherby........99 B6
Motherwell.....119 D7
Mottingham......28 B5
Mottisfont......14 B4
Mottistone......14 F5
Mottram in
  Longdendale....87 E7
Mottram St
  Andrew........75 B5
Mouilpied........16 I2
Mouldsworth.....74 B2
Moulin.........133 D6
Moulsecoomb.....17 D7
Moulsford........39 F5
Moulsoe.........53 E7
Moulton Ches W....74 C3
  Lincs.........66 B3
  N Yorks.......101 D7
  Suff..........55 C7
  V Glam........22 B2
  W Nhants......53 C5
Moulton Chapel . .66 C2
Moulton Eaugate . 66 C3
Moulton St Mary . 69 D6
Moulton Seas End . 66 B3
Mounie Castle...141 B6
Mount Corn.......4 D2
  Corn...........5 C6
  Highld.......151 G12
Mountain........94 F3
Mountain Ash
  =Aberpennar....34 E4
Mountain Cross .120 E4
Mountain Water . .44 C4
Mountbenger....115 B6
Mountfield......18 C4
Mountgerald....151 E8
Mount Hawke......3 E6
Mountjoy.........4 C3
Mountnessing....42 E2
Mounton.........36 E2
Mount Pleasant
  Ches E........74 D5
  Derbys........63 C6
  Derbys........76 E3
  Flint.........73 C6
  Hants.........14 E3
  W Yorks.......88 B3
Mountsorrel.....64 C2
Mount Sorrel.....13 C6
Mount Tabor.....87 B8
Mousehole........2 D3
Mousen.........123 F7

Mouswald.......107 B7
Mow Cop.........75 D5
Mowhaugh.......116 B4
Mowsley.........64 F3
Moxley..........62 E3
Moy Highld......137 F7
Moy Hall........151 H9
Moy House......151 E13
Moyles Court.....14 D2
Moylgrove........45 E3
Moy Lodge......137 F7
Muasdale.......143 D7
Muchalls.......141 E8
Much Birch.......49 F7
Much Cowarne....49 E8
Much Dewchurch . 49 F6
Muchelney.......12 B2
Much Hadham....41 C7
Much Hoole......86 B2
Muchlarnick.......5 D7
Much Marcle......49 F8
Muchrachd.......150 H5
Much Wenlock....61 D6
Muckernich.....151 F8
Mucking.........42 F2
Muckleford......12 E4
Mucklestone.....74 F4
Muckleton.......61 B5
Muckletown....140 B4
Muckley Corner . .62 D4
Muckton.........91 F7
Mudale.........157 F8
Muddiford.......20 F4
Mudeford........14 E2
Mudford.........12 C3
Mudgley.........23 E6
Mugdock.......119 B5
Mugeary........149 E9
Mugginton......76 E2
Muggleswick....110 E3
Muie...........157 J9
Muir..........139 F6
Muirden.......153 C7
Muirdrum.......135 F5
Muirhead Angus...134 F3
  Fife.........128 D4
  N Lanark......119 C6
  S Ayrs.......118 F3
Muirhouselaw....116 B2
Muirhouses.....128 F2
Muirkirk.......113 B6
Muirmill.......127 F6
Muir of Fairburn . 150 F7
Muir of Fowlis....140 C4
Muir of Ord.....151 F8
Muir of Pert....134 F4
Muirshearlich...136 F4
Muirskie.......141 E7
Muirtack.......153 D10
Muirton Highld....151 E10
  Perth........127 C8
  Perth........128 B3
Muirton Mains....150 F7
Muirton of
  Ardblair.....134 E1
Muirton of
  Ballochy.....135 C6
Muiryfold......153 C7
Muker.........100 E4
Mulbarton......68 D4
Mulben.........152 C3
Mulindry.......142 C4
Mullardoch
  House........150 H5
Mullion..........3 E5
Mullion Cove......3 E5
Mumby..........79 B8
Munderfield
  Stocks........49 D8
Munderfield Row . 49 D8
Mundesley......81 D9
Mundford.......67 E8
Mundham.......69 E6
Mundon.........42 D4
Munerigie......137 D5
Muness.........160 C8
Mungasdale.....150 B2
Mungrisdale....108 F3
Munlochy.......151 F9
Munsley.........49 E8
Munslow.........60 F5
Murchington......9 F8
Murcott.........39 C5
Murkle.........158 C3
Murlaggan Highld .136 E3
  Highld.......137 F6
Murra.........159 H3
Murrayfield....120 B5
Murrow.........66 D3
Mursley.........39 B8
Murthill.......134 D4
Murthly.......133 F8
Murton Durham...111 E6
  Northumb......123 E5
  W&F..........100 B2
  York..........96 D2
Musbury........11 E7
Muscoates......102 F4
Musdale........124 C5
Musselburgh....121 B6
Mustard Hyrn....69 C7
Muston Leics....77 F8
  N Yorks.......97 B6
Mustow Green....50 B3
Mutehill.......106 E3
Mutford.........69 F7
Muthill.........127 C7
Mutterton.......10 D5
Muxton.........61 C7
Mybster........158 E3
Myddfai.........34 B1
Myddle..........60 B4
Mydroilyn.......46 D3
Myerscough......92 F4
Mylor Bridge......3 C7
Mynachlog-ddu...45 F3
Myndtown.......60 F3
Mynydd Bach.....47 B6
Mynydd-bach.....36 E1
Mynydd Bodafon . 82 C4
Mynydd Isa......73 C6
Mynyddygarreg ...33 D5
Mynytho.........70 D4
Myrebird.......141 E6
Myrelandhorn...158 E4
Myreside.......128 B4
Myrtle Hill......47 F6
Mytchett........27 D6

Mytholm.........87 B7
Mytholmroyd.....87 B8
Myton-on-Swale...95 C7
Mytton..........60 C4

N

Naast.........155 J13
Naburn.........95 E8
Nackington......31 D5
Nacton.........57 E6
Nafferton.......97 D6
Na Gearrannan...154 C6
Nailbridge......36 C3
Nailsbourne.....11 B7
Nailsea.........23 B6
Nailstone.......63 D8
Nailsworth......37 E5
Nairn.........151 F11
Nalderswood....28 E3
Nancegollan......2 C5
Nancledra........2 C3
Nanhoron........70 D3
Nannau..........71 E8
Nannerch........73 C5
Nanpantan......64 C2
Nanpean..........4 D4
Nansledan........4 C3
Nanstallon.......4 C5
Nant-ddu........34 C4
Nanternis........46 D2
Nantgaredig......33 B5
Nantgarw........35 F5
Nant-glas........47 C8
Nantglyn.........72 C4
Nantgwyn........47 B8
Nantlle..........82 F5
Nantmawr........60 B2
Nantmel.........48 C2
Nantmor.........71 C7
Nant Peris.......83 F6
Nant Uchaf......72 D4
Nantwich.........74 D3
Nantycaws.......33 C5
Nant-y-derry....35 D7
Nant-y-ffin......46 F4
Nantyffyllon....34 E2
Nantyglo.........35 C5
Nant-y-moel.....34 E3
Nant-y-pandy....83 D6
Naphill.........39 E8
Nappa...........93 D8
Napton on the Hill . 52 C2
Narberth
  =Arberth......32 C2
Narborough Leics . 64 E2
  Norf..........67 C7
Nasareth........82 F4
Naseby..........52 B4
Nash Bucks......53 F5
  Hereford......48 C5
  Newport.......35 F7
  Shrops........49 B8
Nash Lee........39 D8
Nassington......65 E7
Nasty...........41 B6
Nateby Lancs....92 E4
  W&F..........100 D2
Natland.........99 F7
Naughton........56 E4
Naunton Glos....37 B8
  Worcs.........50 F3
Naunton
  Beauchamp....50 D4
Navenby.........78 D2
Navestock Heath . .41 E8
Navestock Side....42 E1
Navidale.......157 H13
Nawton.........102 F4
Nayland.........56 F3
Nazeing.........41 D7
Neacroft........14 E2
Neal's Green.....63 F7
Neap..........160 H7
Near Sawrey......99 E5
Neasham........101 C8
Neath
  =Castell-Nedd....33 E8
Neath Abbey.....33 E8
Neatishead......69 B6
Nebo Anglesey....82 B4
  Ceredig.......46 C4
  Conwy.........83 F8
  Gwyn..........82 F4
Necton..........67 D8
Nedd..........156 F4
Nedderton.......117 F8
Nedging Tye.....56 E4
Needham.........68 F5
Needham Market . 56 D4
Needingworth....54 B4
Needwood........63 B5
Neen Savage.....49 B8
Neen Sollars....49 B8
Neenton.........61 F6
Nefyn...........70 C4
Neilston.......118 D4
Neinthirion.....59 D6
Neithrop........52 E2
Nelly Andrews
  Green.........60 D2
Nelson Caerph....35 E5
  Lancs.........93 F8
Nelson Village...111 B5
Nemphlar.......119 E8
Nempnett
  Thrubwell....23 C7
Nene Terrace.....66 D2
Nenthall.......109 E7
Nenthead.......109 E7
Nenthorn.......122 F2
Nerabus........142 C3
Nercwys.........73 C6
Nerston........119 D6
Nesbit.........123 F5
Ness...........89 F7
Nesscliffe......60 C3
Neston Ches W....73 B6
  Wilts.........24 C3
Nether Alderley . .74 B5
Netheravon......25 E6
Nether Blainslie . .121 E8
Nether Booth....88 F2
Netherbrae.....153 C7
Netherbrough...159 G4
Nether Broughton . 64 B3

Netherburn.....119 E8
Netherbury......12 E2
Netherby Cumb...108 B3
  N Yorks.......95 E6
Nether Cerne....12 E4
Nether Compton . .12 C3
Nethercote......52 C3
Nethercott......20 F3
Nether Crimond . .141 B7
Nether Dalgliesh .115 C6
Nether Dallachy . .152 B3
Nether Exe......10 D4
Netherend.......36 D2
Netherfield......18 D4
Nether Glasslaw . .153 C8
Netherhampton . .14 B2
Nether Handwick .134 E3
Nether Haugh....88 E5
Nether Heage....76 D3
Nether Heyford . .52 D4
Nether Hindhope .116 C3
Nether
  Howcleuch....114 C3
Nether Kellet....92 C5
Nether
  Kinmundy....153 D10
Nether Langwith . 76 B5
Netherlaw.......106 E4
Nether Leask....153 E10
Netherley Aberds .141 E7
  Mers..........86 F2
Nethermill.......114 F3
Nether Monynut . .122 C3
Nethermuir......153 D9
Nether Padley....76 B3
Nether Park....153 C10
Netherplace.....118 D5
Nether Poppleton . 95 D8
Netherseal......63 C6
Nether Silton...102 E2
Nether Stowey....22 F3
Netherthird.....113 C5
Netherthong.....88 D2
Netherthorpe....89 F6
Netherton Angus .135 D5
  Devon..........7 B6
  Hants.........25 D8
  Mers..........85 D4
  Northumb......117 D5
  Oxon..........38 E4
  Perth........133 D8
  Stirling......119 B5
  W Mid.........62 F3
  W Yorks.......88 C2
  W Yorks.......88 C3
Nethertown Cumb . 98 D1
  Highld.......158 C5
Nether Urquhart .128 D3
Nether Wallop....25 F8
Nether Wasdale . .98 D3
Nether Whitacre . 63 E6
Netherwitton....117 E7
Netherwood.....113 B6
Nether Worton....52 F2
Nethy Bridge....139 B6
Netley..........15 D5
Netley Marsh....14 C4
Nettacott.......11 C7
Nettlebed.......39 F7
Nettlebridge....23 E8
Nettlecombe.....12 E3
Nettleden.......40 C3
Nettleham.......78 B3
Nettlestead.....29 D7
Nettlestead Green . 29 D7
Nettlestone.....15 E7
Nettlesworth....111 E5
Nettleton Lincs....90 D5
  Wilts.........24 B3
Neuadd.........33 B7
Nevendon.......42 E3
Nevern..........45 E2
Neuadd.........33 B7
New Abbey......107 C6
New Aberdour...153 B8
New Addington . .28 C4
New Alresford. ...26 F3
New Alyth......134 E2
Newark Orkney...159 D8
Newark-on-Trent . 77 D7
New Arley.......63 F6
Newarthill.....119 D7
New Ash Green....29 C7
New Barn........29 C7
New Barnetby....90 C4
Newbarns........92 B2
New Barton......53 C6
Newbattle......121 C6
New Bewick.....117 B6
Newbiggin Cumb . 98 E2
  Durham.......100 B4
  N Yorks.......100 E4
  N Yorks.......100 F4
  W&F...........92 C2
  W&F...........99 B8
  W&F...........99 B8
Newbiggin-by-the-
  Sea..........117 F9
Newbigging Angus 134 E2
  Angus........134 F4
  S Lanark......120 E3
New Bilton......52 B2
Newbold Derbys...76 B3
Newbold on Avon . 52 B2
Newbold on Stour . 51 E7
Newbold Pacey....51 D7
Newbold Verdon . .63 D8
New Bolingbroke . 79 D6
Newborough
  Anglesey......82 E4
  Pboro.........66 D2
  Staffs........62 B5
Newbottle T&W....111 D6
New Boultham....78 B2
New Bradwell....53 E6
New Brancepeth . .110 E5
Newbridge Caerph . 35 E6
  Ceredig.......46 D4
  Corn...........2 C3

Newbridge continued
  Corn...........5 C8
  Dumfries.....107 B6
  Edin.........120 B4
  Hants.........14 C3
  IoW...........14 F5
  Pembs.........44 B4
New Bridge......73 E6
Newbridge Green . 50 F3
Newbridge-on-
  Usk...........35 E7
Newbridge on
  Wye...........48 D2
New Brighton Flint . 73 C6
  Mers..........85 E4
New Brinsley....76 D4
Newbrough.....109 C8
New Broughton . .73 D7
New Buckenham . .68 E3
Newbuildings....10 D2
Newburgh Aberds .141 B8
  Aberds.......153 C9
  Borders......115 C6
  Fife.........128 C4
  Lancs.........86 C2
Newburn.......110 C4
Newbury........26 C2
Newbury Park....41 F7
Newby Lancs....93 E8
  N Yorks.......93 B7
  N Yorks.......102 C3
  N Yorks.......103 E8
  W&F...........99 B7
Newby Bridge....99 F5
New Byth.......153 C8
Newby West.....108 D4
Newby Wiske....102 F1
Newcastle Mon....35 C8
  Shrops........60 F2
Newcastle Emlyn
  =Castell Newydd
  Emlyn.........46 E2
Newcastleton or
  Copshaw Holm .115 F7
Newcastle-under-
  Lyme..........74 E5
Newcastle upon
  Tyne.........110 C5
New Catton......68 C5
Newchapel Pembs . 45 F4
  Powys.........59 F6
  Staffs........75 D5
  Sur...........28 E4
New Cheriton....15 B6
Newchurch Carms . 32 B4
  IoW...........15 F6
  Kent..........19 B7
  Lancs.........93 F8
  Mon...........36 E1
  Powys.........48 D4
  Staffs........62 B5
Newcott.........11 D7
New Costessey....68 C4
New Cowper.....107 E8
Newcraighall....121 B6
New Cross Ceredig . 46 B5
  London........28 B4
New Cumnock....113 C6
New Deer.......153 D8
New Delaval....111 B5
New Duston......52 C5
New Earswick....96 D2
New Edlington....89 E6
New Elgin......152 B2
New Ellerby......97 F7
Newell Green....27 B6
New Eltham......28 B5
New End........51 D5
Newenden.......18 C5
Newent.........36 B4
Newerne........36 D3
New Farnley.....94 F5
New Ferry......85 F4
Newfield Durham .110 F5
  Highld.......151 D10
Newford.........2 E4
Newfound........26 D3
New Fryston.....89 B5
Newgale.........44 C3
New Galloway...106 B3
Newgate.........81 C6
Newgate Street....41 D6
New Gilston....129 D6
New Grimsby......2 E3
New Hainford....68 C5
Newhall Ches E...74 E3
  Derbys........63 B6
Newhall House...151 E9
Newhall Point...151 E10
Newham........117 B7
Newham Hall....117 B7
New Hartley....111 B6
Newhaven E Sus...18 E2
  Edin.........121 B5
  E Sus.........17 D8
New Haw........27 C8
New Hedges.....32 D2
New Herrington . .111 D6
Newhey.........87 C7
New Hinksey....39 D5
New Holkham....80 D4
New Holland.....90 B4
Newholm.......103 C6
New Houghton
  Derbys........76 C5
  Norf..........80 E3
Newhouse......119 C7
New Houses.....93 B8
New Humberstone 64 D3
New Hutton......99 E7
New Hythe......29 D8
Newick..........17 B8
Newingreen......19 B8
Newington Kent...19 B8
  Kent..........30 C2
  Kent..........31 C7
  Notts.........89 E7
  Oxon..........39 E6
  Shrops........60 F4
  Shrops........73 D7
New Inn Carms....46 F3
  Mon...........36 D1
  Pembs.........45 F2
  Torf..........35 E7
New Invention
  Shrops........48 B4
  W Mid.........62 D3
New Kelso......150 G2

New Kingston....64 B2
New Lanark.....119 E8
Newland Glos....36 D2
  Hull..........97 F6
  N Yorks.......89 B7
  Notts.........77 E6
  Worcs.........50 E2
Newlandrig.....121 C6
Newlands Borders .115 E8
  Highld.......151 G10
  Moray........152 C3
  Northumb......110 D3
Newland's Corner . 27 E8
Newlandsmuir...119 D6
Newlands of
  Geise........158 D2
Newlands of
  Tynet........152 B3
Newlands Park....82 C2
New Lane........86 C2
New Lane End....86 E4
New Leake.......79 D7
New Leeds......153 C9
New Longton.....86 B3
Newlot.........159 G6
New Luce.......105 C5
Newlyn...........2 D3
Newmachar.....141 C7
Newmains......119 D8
New Malden......28 C3
Newmarket Suff....55 C7
  W Isles.......155 D9
New Marske.....102 B4
New Marton......73 F7
New Mickelfield . .95 F7
Newmill Borders...115 C7
  Corn...........2 C3
  Moray........152 C4
New Mill Aberds..141 F6
  Herts.........40 C2
  Wilts.........25 C6
  W Yorks.......88 D2
Newmill of
  Inshewan.....134 C4
New Mills Ches E...87 F5
  Corn...........4 D3
  Derbys........87 F7
  Powys.........59 D7
Newmills of
  Boyne........152 C5
Newmiln.......133 F8
Newmilns......118 F5
New Mistley....56 F5
New Moat.......32 B1
Newnham Cambs . .54 D5
  Glos..........36 C3
  Hants.........26 D5
  Herts.........54 F3
  Kent..........30 D3
  W Nhants......52 D3
Newnham Bridge . 49 C8
New Ollerton....77 C6
New Oscott......62 E4
Newpark.......129 C6
New Park........95 D5
New Pitsligo...153 C8
New Polzeath......4 B4
Newport Devon....20 F4
  Essex.........55 F6
  E Yorks.......96 F4
  Highld.......158 H3
  IoW...........15 F6
  Norf..........69 C8
  Telford.......61 C7
Newport
  =Casnewydd....35 F7
Newport
  =Trefdraeth....45 F2
Newport-on-Tay . 129 B6
Newport Pagnell . 53 E6
Newpound
  Common.......16 B4
Newquay.........4 C3
New Quay
  =Ceinewydd....46 D2
New Rackheath . .69 C6
New Radnor......48 C4
New Rent.......108 F4
New Ridley.....110 D3
New Road Side....94 E2
New Romney.....19 C7
New Rossington . .89 E7
New Row Ceredig . .46 B5
  Lancs.........93 F6
  N Yorks.......102 C4
New Sarum......25 F6
Newsbank........74 C5
Newseat Aberds . .153 D10
  Aberds.......153 E7
Newsham Northumb 111 B6
  N Yorks.......101 C6
  N Yorks.......102 F1
Newsholme E Yorks 89 B8
  Lancs.........93 D8
New Silksworth . .111 D6
Newsome........88 C2
Newstead Borders .121 F8
  Northumb......117 B7
  Notts.........76 D5
New Stevenston . .119 D7
New Street......75 D7
New Street Lane . .74 F3
New Swanage....13 F8
Newthorpe......95 F7
Newton Argyll...125 F6
  Borders......116 B2
  Bridgend......21 B7
  Cambs.........54 E5
  Cambs.........66 C4
  Cardiff.......22 B4
  Ches W........73 C8
  Ches W........74 B2
  Ches W........74 D2
  Cumb.........92 B2
  Derbys........76 D4
  Dorset........13 C6
  Dumfries.....108 B2
  Dumfries.....114 E4
  Gtr Man.......87 E7
  Hereford......48 F5
  Hereford......49 D7
  Highld.......151 E10
  Highld.......151 G10
  Highld.......156 F5
  Highld.......158 H4
  IoM...........84 E3
  Lancs.........86 F4
  Lancs.........92 E3
  Lancs.........93 B5
  Lancs.........93 B7
  Lincs.........78 F3

Newton continued
  Moray........152 B1
  N Nhants......65 F5
  Norf..........67 C8
  Northumb......110 C3
  Notts.........77 E6
  Perth........133 F5
  S Lanark......119 C6
  S Lanark......120 F2
  Staffs........62 B4
  Suff..........56 E3
  Swansea.......33 F7
  S Yorks.......89 D6
  Warks.........52 B3
  W&F...........98 F4
  Wilts.........14 B3
  W Loth.......120 B3
Newton Abbot......7 B6
Newtonairds....113 F8
Newton Arlosh...107 D8
Newton Aycliffe . .101 B7
Newton Bewley . .102 B2
Newton
  Blossomville....53 D7
Newton
  Bromswold....53 C7
Newton
  Burgoland....63 D7
Newton by Toft . .90 F4
Newton Ferrers....6 E3
Newton Flotman . .68 E5
Newtongrange...121 C6
Newton Hall....110 C3
Newton Harcourt . 64 E3
Newton Heath....87 E6
Newton House....141 B5
Newton Kyme....95 E7
Newton-le-Willows
  Mers..........86 E3
  N Yorks.......101 F7
Newton Longville . 53 F6
Newton Mearns . .118 D5
Newtonmill.....135 C6
Newtonmore....138 E3
Newton Morrell . .101 D7
Newton
  Mulgrave.....103 C5
Newton of
  Ardtoe.......147 D9
Newton of
  Balcanquhal...128 C3
Newton of
  Falkland.....128 D4
Newton on Ayr...112 B3
Newton on Ouse . .95 D8
Newton-on-
  Rawcliffe.....103 E6
Newton-on-the-
  Moor.........117 D7
Newton on Trent . 77 B8
Newton Park....145 G10
Newton
  Poppleford....11 F5
Newton Purcell . .52 F4
Newton Regis....63 D6
Newton Reigny . .108 F4
Newton St Cyres . .10 E3
Newton St Faith . .68 C5
Newton St Loe....24 C2
Newton St Petrock . 9 C6
Newton Solney....63 B6
Newton Stacey....26 E2
Newton Stewart .105 C8
Newton Tony....25 E7
Newton Tracey......9 B7
Newton under
  Roseberry....102 C3
Newton upon
  Derwent.......96 E3
Newton Valence . .26 F5
New Totley......76 B3
Newtown Argyll...125 E6
  BCP...........13 E8
  Ches W........74 B2
  Corn...........3 D6
  Cumb.........107 D7
  Cumb.........108 C5
  Derbys........87 F7
  Devon.........10 B2
  Glos..........36 D3
  Glos..........50 F4
  Hants.........14 B4
  Hants.........14 C3
  Hants.........15 C5
  Hants.........15 C6
  Hereford......49 E8
  Highld.......137 D6
  IoM...........84 E3
  IoW...........14 E5
  Northumb......117 B6
  Northumb......117 D6
  Northumb......123 F5
  Shrops........73 F8
  Staffs........75 C6
  Staffs........75 C7
  Wilts.........13 B7
Newtown
  =Y Drenewydd....59 E8
Newtown Linford . 64 D2
Newtown St
  Boswells.....121 F8
Newtown Unthank. 63 D8
New Tredegar =
  Tredegar Newydd. 35 D5
New Trows......119 F8
Newtyle.......134 E2
New Ulva.......144 E6
New Walsoken....66 D4
New Waltham....91 D6
New Whittington . .76 B3
New Wimpole....54 E4
New Winton.....121 B7
New Yatt........38 C3
New York Lincs....78 D5
  N Yorks.......94 C4
Neyland.........44 E4
Niarbyl.........84 E2
Nibley..........36 E3
Nibley Green....36 E4
Nibon.........160 F5
Nicholashayne . .11 C6
Nicholaston.....33 F6
Nidd...........95 C6
Nigg Aberdeen...141 D8

Nigg continued
  Highld.......151 D10
Nigg Ferry.....151 E10
Nightcott.......10 B3
Nilig...........72 D4
Nine Ashes......42 D1
Ninebanks......109 D7
Nine Mile Burn . .120 D4
Nine Wells......44 C2
Ninfield........18 D4
Ningwood........14 F4
Nisbet.........116 B2
Nisthouse Orkney .159 G4
  Shetland......160 H6
Niton...........15 G6
Nitshill.......118 C5
Noak Hill.......41 E8
Noblethorpe.....88 D3
Nobottle........52 C4
Nocton..........78 C3
Noke............39 C5
Nolton..........44 D3
Nolton Haven....44 D3
No Man's Heath
  Ches W........74 E2
  Warks.........63 D6
Nomansland Devon . 10 C3
  Wilts.........14 C3
Noneley........60 B4
Nonikiln.......151 D9
Nonington......31 D6
Noonsbrough....160 H4
Norbreck........92 E3
Norbridge.......50 E2
Norbury Ches E....74 E2
  Derbys........75 E8
  Shrops........60 E3
  Staffs........61 B7
Nordelph........66 D5
Norden..........87 C6
Norden Heath....13 F7
Nordley.........61 E6
Norham........122 E5
Norley..........74 B2
Norleywood......14 E4
Normanby N Lincs . 90 C2
  N Yorks.......103 F5
  Redcar.......102 C3
Normanby-by-
  Spital........90 F4
Normanby by Stow 90 F2
Normanby le Wold . 90 E5
Norman Cross....65 E8
Normandy........27 D7
Norman's Bay....18 E3
Norman's Green. .11 D5
Normanstone.....69 E8
Normanton Derby . 76 F3
  Leics.........77 E8
  Lincs.........78 E2
  Notts.........77 D7
  Rutland.......65 D6
  W Yorks.......88 B4
Normanton le
  Heath.........63 C7
Normanton on
  Soar..........64 B2
Normanton-on-the-
  Wolds.........77 F6
Normanton on
  Trent.........77 C7
Normoss........92 F3
Norney..........27 E7
Norrington
  Common.......24 C3
Norris Green....85 E4
Norris Hill.....63 C7
Northacre.......68 E2
Northallerton...102 E1
Northam Devon......9 B6
  Soton.........14 C5
Northampton....53 C5
North Anston....89 F6
North Aston....38 B4
Northaw.........41 D5
North Baddesley . 14 C4
North
  Ballachulish....130 C4
North Barrow....12 B4
North Barsham. ...80 D5
Northbeck.......78 E3
North Benfleet....42 F3
North Bersted....16 D3
North Berwick....129 F7
North Boarhunt . .15 C7
Northborough....65 D8
Northbourne.....31 D7
North Bovey.....10 F2
North Bradley....24 D3
North Brentor......9 F6
North Brewham . .24 F2
Northbridge
  Street........18 C4
North Buckland . .20 E3
North Burlingham . 69 C6
North Cadbury....12 B4
North Cairn....104 B3
North Carlton....78 B2
North Carrine...143 H7
North Cave......96 F4
North Cerney....37 D7
Northchapel.....16 B3
North Charford . .14 C2
North Charlton...117 B7
North Cheriton. ...12 B4
Northchurch.....40 D2
North Cliff......97 E8
North Cliffe.....96 F4
North Clifton....77 B8
North
  Cockerington. .91 E7
North Coker.....12 C3
North Collafirth . .160 E5
North Common. .17 B7
North Connel....124 B5
North Cotes.....91 D7
Northcott........8 E5
North Cove......69 F7
North Cowton...101 D7
North Crawley....53 E7
North Cray......29 B5
North Creake....80 D4
North Curry......11 B8
North Dalton....96 D5
North Dawn....159 H5
Northdown......31 B7
North Duffield....96 F2

Northduke ... 159 F3
North Elkington ... 91 F6
North Elmham ... 81 E5
North Ellistaiin ... 89 C7
Northend Bath ... 24 C2
  Bucks ... 39 E7
  Warks ... 51 D8
North End Bucks ... 39 B8
  Essex ... 42 C2
  E Yorks ... 97 F8
  Hants ... 26 C2
  Lincs ... 78 E5
  N Som ... 23 C6
  Ptsmth ... 15 D7
  Som ... 11 B7
  W Sus ... 16 D5
Northenden ... 87 E6
North Erradale ... 155 J12
North Fambridge ... 42 E4
North Fearns ... 149 E10
North Featherstone ... 88 B5
North Ferriby ... 90 B3
Northfield
  Aberdeen ... 141 D8
  Borders ... 122 C5
  E Yorks ... 90 B4
  W Mid ... 50 B5
Northfields ... 65 D7
Northfleet ... 29 B7
North Frodingham ... 97 D7
Northgate ... 65 B8
North Gluss ... 160 F5
North Gorley ... 14 C2
North Green Norf ... 69 F6
  Suff ... 57 C7
North Greetwell ... 78 B3
North Grimston ... 96 C4
North Halley ... 159 H6
North Halling ... 29 C8
North Hayling ... 15 D8
North Hazelrigg ... 123 F6
North Heasley ... 21 F6
North Heath ... 16 B4
North Hill Cambs ... 55 B5
  Corn ... 5 B7
North Hinksey ... 38 D4
North Holmwood ... 28 E2
Northhouse ... 115 D7
North Howden ... 96 F3
North Hykeham ... 78 C2
Northiam ... 18 C5
Northill ... 54 E2
Northington ... 26 F3
North Johnston ... 44 D4
North Kelsey ... 90 D4
North Kelsey Moor ... 90 D4
North Kessock ... 151 G9
North Killingholme ... 90 C5
North Kilvington ... 102 F2
North Kilworth ... 64 F3
North Kirkton ... 153 C11
North Kiscadale ... 143 F11
North Kyme ... 78 D4
North Lancing ... 17 D5
Northlands ... 79 D6
Northlea ... 111 D7
Northleach ... 37 C8
North Lee ... 39 D8
Northleigh ... 11 E6
North Leigh ... 38 C3
North Leverton with
  Habblesthorpe ... 89 F8
Northlew ... 9 E7
North Littleton ... 51 E5
North Lopham ... 68 F3
North Luffenham ... 65 D6
North Marden ... 16 C2
North Marston ... 39 B7
North Middleton
  Midloth ... 121 D6
  Northumb ... 117 B6
North Molton ... 10 B2
Northmoor ... 38 D4
Northmoor Green or
  Moorland ... 22 F5
North Moreton ... 39 F5
Northmuir ... 134 D3
North Mundham ... 16 D2
North Muskham ... 77 D7
North Newbald ... 96 F5
North Newington ... 52 F2
North Newnton ... 25 D6
North Newton ... 22 F4
Northney ... 15 D8
North Nibley ... 36 E4
North Oakley ... 26 D3
North Ockendon ... 42 F1
Northolt ... 40 F4
Northop ... 73 C6
Northop Hall ... 73 C6
North Ormesby ... 102 B3
North Ormsby ... 91 E6
Northorpe Lincs ... 65 C7
  Lincs ... 78 F5
  Lincs ... 90 E2
North Otterington ... 102 F1
Northover Som ... 12 B3
  Som ... 23 F6
North Owersby ... 90 E4
Northowram ... 88 B2
North Perrott ... 12 D2
North Petherton ... 22 F4
North Petherwin ... 8 F4
North Pickenham ... 67 D8
North Piddle ... 50 D4
North Poorton ... 12 E3
Northport ... 13 F7
North Port ... 125 C6
Northpunds ... 160 L6
North Queensferry ... 128 F3
North Radworthy ... 21 F6
North Rauceby ... 78 E3
Northrepps ... 81 D8
North Reston ... 91 F7
North Rigton ... 95 E5
North Rode ... 75 C5
North Roe ... 160 E5
North Runcton ... 67 C6
North Sandwick ... 160 D7
North Scale ... 92 C1
North Scarle ... 77 C8
North Seaton ... 117 F8
North Shian ... 130 E3
North Shields ... 111 C6

North Shoebury ... 43 F5
North Shore ... 92 F3
North Side Cumb ... 98 B2
  Pboro ... 66 E2
North Skelton ... 102 C4
North Somercotes ... 91 E8
North Stainley ... 95 B5
North Stainmore ... 100 C3
North Stifford ... 42 F2
North Stoke Bath ... 24 C2
  Oxon ... 39 F6
  W Sus ... 16 C4
Northstowe ... 54 C5
North Street Hants ... 26 F4
  Kent ... 30 D4
  Medway ... 30 B2
  W Berks ... 26 B4
North Sunderland ... 123 F8
North Tamerton ... 8 E5
North Tawton ... 9 D8
North Thoresby ... 91 E6
North Tidworth ... 25 E7
North Togston ... 117 D8
Northtown ... 159 J5
North Tuddenham ... 68 C3
North Walbottle ... 110 C4
North Walsham ... 81 D8
North Waltham ... 26 E3
North Warnborough ... 26 D5
North Water Bridge ... 135 C6
North Watten ... 158 E4
Northway ... 50 F4
North Weald Bassett ... 41 D7
North Wheatley ... 89 F8
North Whilborough ... 7 C6
Northwich ... 74 B3
Northwick ... 36 F2
North Wick ... 23 C7
North Willingham ... 91 F5
North Wingfield ... 76 C4
North Witham ... 65 B6
Northwold ... 67 E7
Northwood Derbys ... 76 C2
  IoW ... 15 E5
  Kent ... 31 C7
  London ... 40 E3
  Shrops ... 73 F8
Northwood Green ... 36 C4
North Woolwich ... 28 B5
North Wootton Dorset ... 12 C4
  Norf ... 67 B6
  Som ... 23 E7
North Wraxall ... 24 B3
North Wroughton ... 38 F1
Norton E Sus ... 17 D8
  Glos ... 37 B5
  Halton ... 86 F3
  Herts ... 54 F3
  IoW ... 14 F4
  Mon ... 35 C8
  Notts ... 77 B5
  Powys ... 48 C5
  Shrops ... 60 F4
  Shrops ... 61 D5
  Shrops ... 61 D7
  Stockton ... 102 B2
  Suff ... 56 C3
  S Yorks ... 89 C6
  Wilts ... 37 F5
  W Nhants ... 52 C4
  Worcs ... 50 D3
  Worcs ... 50 E5
  W Sus ... 16 D3
  W Sus ... 16 E2
Norton Bavant ... 24 E4
Norton Bridge ... 75 F5
Norton Canes ... 62 D4
Norton Canon ... 49 E5
Norton Corner ... 81 E6
Norton Disney ... 77 D8
Norton East ... 62 D4
Norton Ferris ... 24 F2
Norton Fitzwarren ... 11 B6
Norton Green ... 14 F4
Norton Hawkfield ... 23 C7
Norton Heath ... 42 D2
Norton in Hales ... 74 F4
Norton-in-the-Moors ... 75 D5
Norton-Juxta-Twycross ... 63 D7
Norton-le-Clay ... 95 B7
Norton Lindsey ... 51 C7
Norton Malreward ... 23 C8
Norton Mandeville ... 42 D1
Norton-on-Derwent ... 96 B3
Norton St Philip ... 24 D2
Norton sub Hamdon ... 12 C2
Norton Woodseats ... 88 F4
Norwell ... 77 C7
Norwell Woodhouse ... 77 C7
Norwich ... 68 D5
Norwick ... 160 B8
Norwood ... 89 F5
Norwood Hill ... 28 E3
Norwoodside ... 66 E4
Noseley ... 64 E4
Noss ... 160 M5
Noss Mayo ... 6 E3
Nosterfield ... 101 F7
Nostie ... 149 F13
Notgrove ... 37 B8
Nottage ... 34 D2
Nottingham ... 77 F5
Nottington ... 12 F4
Notton Wilts ... 24 C4
  W Yorks ... 88 C4
Nounsley ... 42 C3
Noutard's Green ... 50 C2
Novar House ... 151 E9
Nox ... 60 C4
Nuffield ... 39 F6
Nunburnholme ... 96 E4
Nuncargate ... 76 D5
Nuneaton ... 63 E7
Nuneham Courtenay ... 39 E5
Nun Hills ... 87 B6
Nun Monkton ... 95 D8
Nunney ... 24 E2
Nunnington ... 96 B2

Nunnykirk ... 117 F6
Nunsthorpe ... 91 D6
Nunthorpe Mbro ... 102 C3
  York ... 96 D1
Nunton ... 14 B2
Nunwick ... 95 B6
Nupend ... 36 D4
Nursling ... 14 C4
Nursted ... 15 B8
Nutbourne W Sus ... 15 D8
  W Sus ... 16 C4
Nutfield ... 28 D4
Nuthall ... 76 E5
Nuthampstead ... 54 F5
Nuthurst ... 17 B5
Nutley E Sus ... 17 B8
  Hants ... 26 E4
Nutwell ... 89 D7
Nybster ... 158 D5
Nyetimber ... 16 E2
Nyewood ... 16 B2
Nymet Rowland ... 10 D2
Nymet Tracey ... 10 D2
Nympsfield ... 37 D5
Nynehead ... 11 B6
Nyton ... 16 D3

O

Oadby ... 64 D3
Oad Street ... 30 C2
Oakamoor ... 75 E7
Oakbank ... 120 C3
Oak Cross ... 9 E7
Oakdale ... 35 E5
Oake ... 11 B6
Oaken ... 62 D2
Oakenclough ... 92 E5
Oakengates ... 61 C7
Oakenholt ... 73 B6
Oakenshaw Durham ... 110 F5
  W Yorks ... 88 B2
Oakerthorpe ... 76 D3
Oakes ... 88 C2
Oakfield ... 35 E7
Oakford Ceredig ... 46 D3
  Devon ... 10 B4
Oakfordbridge ... 10 B4
Oakgrove ... 75 C6
Oakham ... 65 D5
Oakhanger ... 27 F5
Oakhill ... 23 E8
Oakhurst ... 29 D6
Oakington ... 54 C5
Oaklands Herts ... 41 C5
  Powys ... 48 D2
Oakle Street ... 36 C4
Oakley BCP ... 13 E8
  Bedford ... 53 D8
  Bucks ... 39 C6
  Fife ... 128 F2
  Hants ... 26 D3
  Oxon ... 39 D7
  Suff ... 57 B5
Oakley Green ... 27 B7
Oakley Park ... 59 F6
Oakmere ... 74 C2
Oakridge Glos ... 37 D6
  Hants ... 26 D4
Oaks ... 60 D4
Oaksey ... 37 E6
Oaks Green ... 75 F8
Oakthorpe ... 63 C7
Oakwoodhill ... 28 F2
Oakworth ... 94 F3
Oape ... 156 J7
Oare Kent ... 30 C4
  Som ... 21 E7
  W Berks ... 26 B3
  Wilts ... 25 C6
Oasby ... 78 F3
Oathlaw ... 134 D4
Oatlands ... 95 D6
Oban Argyll ... 124 C4
  Highld ... 147 C11
Oborne ... 12 C4
Obthorpe ... 65 C7
Occlestone Green ... 74 C3
Occold ... 57 B5
Ochiltree ... 112 B5
Ochtermuthill ... 127 C7
Ochtertyre ... 127 B7
Ockbrook ... 76 F4
Ockham ... 27 D8
Ockle ... 147 D8
Ockley ... 28 F2
Ocle Pychard ... 49 E7
Octon ... 97 C6
Octon Cross Roads ... 97 C6
Odcombe ... 12 C3
Odd Down ... 24 C2
Oddendale ... 99 C7
Odder ... 78 B2
Oddingley ... 50 D4
Oddington Glos ... 38 B2
  Oxon ... 39 C5
Odell ... 53 D7
Odie ... 159 F7
Odiham ... 26 D5
Odstock ... 14 B2
Odstone ... 63 D7
Offchurch ... 51 C8
Offenham ... 51 E5
Offham E Sus ... 17 C7
  Kent ... 29 D7
  W Sus ... 16 D4
Offord Cluny ... 54 C3
Offord Darcy ... 54 C3
Offton ... 56 E4
Offwell ... 11 E6
Ogbourne Maizey ... 25 B6
Ogbourne St Andrew ... 25 B6
Ogbourne St George ... 25 B7
Ogil ... 134 C4
Ogle ... 110 B4
Ogmore ... 21 B7
Ogmore-by-Sea ... 21 B7
Ogmore Vale ... 34 E3
Okeford Fitzpaine ... 13 C6
Okehampton ... 9 E7
Okehampton Camp ... 9 E7
Okraquoy ... 160 K6
Old ... 53 B5
Old Aberdeen ... 141 D8

Old Alresford ... 26 F3
Oldany ... 156 F4
Old Arley ... 63 E6
Old Basford ... 76 E5
Old Basing ... 26 D4
Oldberrow ... 51 C6
Old Bewick ... 117 B6
Old Bolingbroke ... 79 C6
Oldborough ... 10 D2
Old Brampton ... 76 B3
Old Bridge of Tilt ... 133 C5
Old Bridge of Urr ... 106 C4
Old Buckenham ... 68 E3
Old Burghclere ... 26 D2
Oldbury Shrops ... 61 E7
  Warks ... 63 E7
  W Mid ... 62 F3
Oldbury-on-Severn ... 36 E3
Oldbury on the Hill ... 37 F5
Old Byland ... 102 F3
Old Cassop ... 111 F6
Oldcastle Bridgend ... 21 B8
  Mon ... 35 B7
Old Castleton ... 115 E8
Old Catton ... 68 C5
Old Clee ... 91 D6
Old Cleeve ... 22 E2
Old Clipstone ... 77 C6
Old Colwyn ... 83 D8
Oldcotes ... 89 F6
Old Coulsdon ... 28 D4
Old Crombie ... 152 C5
Old Dailly ... 112 E2
Old Dalby ... 64 B3
Old Deer ... 153 D9
Old Denaby ... 89 E5
Old Edlington ... 89 E6
Old Eldon ... 101 B7
Old Ellerby ... 97 F7
Oldfallow ... 62 C3
Old Felixstowe ... 57 F7
Oldfield ... 50 C3
Old Fletton ... 65 E8
Oldford ... 24 D2
Old Glossop ... 87 E8
Old Goole ... 89 B8
Old Hall ... 59 F6
Oldham ... 87 D7
Oldhamstocks ... 122 B3
Old Heath ... 43 B6
Old Heathfield ... 18 C2
Old Hill ... 62 F3
Old Hunstanton ... 80 C2
Old Hurst ... 54 B3
Old Hutton ... 99 F7
Old Kea ... 3 B7
Old Kilpatrick ... 118 B4
Old Kinnernie ... 141 D6
Old Knebworth ... 41 B5
Old Langho ... 93 F7
Old Laxey ... 84 D4
Old Leake ... 79 D7
Old Malton ... 96 B3
Oldmeldrum ... 141 B7
Old Micklefield ... 95 F7
Old Milton ... 14 E3
Old Milverton ... 51 C7
Old Monkland ... 119 C7
Old Netley ... 15 D5
Old Philpstoun ... 120 B3
Old Quarrington ... 111 F6
Old Radnor ... 48 D4
Old Rattray ... 153 C10
Old Rayne ... 141 B5
Old Romney ... 19 C7
Oldshore Beg ... 156 D4
Oldshoremore ... 156 D5
Old Sodbury ... 36 F4
Old Somerby ... 78 F2
Oldstead ... 102 F3
Old Stratford ... 53 E5
Old Thirsk ... 102 F2
Oldtown ... 140 B4
Old Town Northumb ... 116 E4
  Scilly ... 2 C3
  W&F ... 99 F7
  W&F ... 108 E4
Oldtown of Ord ... 152 C6
Old Trafford ... 87 E6
Old Tupton ... 76 C3
Old Warden ... 54 E2
Oldway ... 33 F6
Oldways End ... 10 B3
Oldwhat ... 153 C8
Old Weston ... 53 B8
Old Whittington ... 76 B3
Old Wick ... 158 E5
Old Windsor ... 27 B7
Old Wives Lees ... 30 D4
Old Woking ... 27 D8
Old Woodhall ... 78 C5
Oliver's Battery ... 15 B5
Ollaberry ... 160 E5
Ollerton Ches E ... 74 B4
  Notts ... 77 C6
  Shrops ... 61 B6
Olmarch ... 46 D5
Olney ... 53 D6
Olrig House ... 158 D3
Olton ... 62 F5
Olveston ... 36 F3
Olwen ... 46 E4
Ombersley ... 50 C3
Ompton ... 77 C6
Onchan ... 84 E3
Onecote ... 75 D7
Onen ... 35 C8
Ongar Hill ... 67 B5
Ongar Street ... 49 C5
Onibury ... 49 B6
Onich ... 130 C4
Onllwyn ... 34 C2
Onneley ... 74 E4
Onslow Village ... 27 E7
Onthank ... 118 E4
Openwoodgate ... 76 E3
Opinan Highld ... 149 A12
  Highld ... 155 H13
Orange Lane ... 122 E3
Orange Row ... 66 B5
Orasaigh ... 155 F8
Orbliston ... 152 C3
Orbost ... 148 D7
Orby ... 79 C7

Orchard Hill ... 9 B6
Orchard Portman ... 11 B7
Orcheston ... 25 E5
Orcop ... 36 B1
Orcop Hill ... 36 B1
Ord ... 149 G11
Ordhead ... 141 C5
Ordie ... 140 D3
Ordiequish ... 152 C3
Ordsall ... 89 F7
Ore ... 18 D5
Oreton ... 61 F6
Orford Suff ... 57 E8
  Warr ... 86 E4
Orgreave ... 63 C5
Orlestone ... 19 B6
Orleton Hereford ... 49 C6
  Worcs ... 49 C8
Orlingbury ... 53 B6
Ormesby ... 102 C3
Ormesby St Margaret ... 69 C7
Ormesby St Michael ... 69 C7
Ormiclate Castle ... 148 E2
Ormiscaig ... 155 H13
Ormiston ... 121 C7
Ormsaigbeg ... 146 E7
Ormsaigmore ... 146 E7
Ormsary ... 144 F6
Ormsgill ... 92 B1
Ormskirk ... 86 D2
Orpington ... 29 C5
Orrell Gtr Man ... 86 D3
  Mers ... 85 E4
Orrisdale ... 84 C3
Orroland ... 106 E4
Orsett ... 42 F2
Orslow ... 62 C2
Orston ... 77 E7
Orthwaite ... 108 F2
Ortner ... 92 D5
Orton N Nhants ... 53 B6
Orton W&F ... 99 C8
Orton Longueville ... 65 E8
Orton-on-the-Hill ... 63 D7
Orton Waterville ... 65 E8
Orwell ... 54 D4
Osbaldeston ... 93 F6
Osbaldwick ... 96 D2
Osbaston ... 60 B3
Osbournby ... 78 F3
Oscroft ... 74 C2
Ose ... 149 D8
Osgathorpe ... 63 C8
Osgodby Lincs ... 90 E4
  N Yorks ... 96 F2
  N Yorks ... 103 F8
Oskaig ... 149 E10
Oskamull ... 146 G7
Osmaston Derby ... 76 F3
  Derbys ... 76 E2
Osmington ... 12 F5
Osmington Mills ... 12 F5
Osmotherley ... 102 E2
Ospisdale ... 151 C10
Ospringe ... 30 C4
Ossett ... 88 B3
Ossington ... 77 C7
Ostend ... 43 E5
Oswaldkirk ... 96 B2
Oswaldtwistle ... 86 B5
Oswestry ... 60 B2
Otford ... 29 D6
Otham ... 29 D8
Othery ... 23 F5
Otley Suff ... 57 D6
  W Yorks ... 94 E5
Otterbourne ... 15 B5
Otterburn Northumb ... 116 E4
  N Yorks ... 93 D8
Otterburn Camp ... 116 E4
Otter Ferry ... 145 E8
Otterham ... 8 E3
Otterhampton ... 22 E4
Ottershaw ... 27 C8
Otterswick ... 160 E7
Otterton ... 11 F5
Ottery St Mary ... 11 E6
Ottinge ... 31 E5
Ottringham ... 91 B6
Oughterby ... 108 D2
Oughtershaw ... 100 F3
Oughterside ... 107 E8
Oughtibridge ... 88 E4
Oughtrington ... 86 F4
Oulston ... 95 B8
Oulton Cumb ... 108 D2
  Norf ... 81 E7
  Staffs ... 75 F6
  Suff ... 69 E8
  W Yorks ... 88 B4
Oulton Broad ... 69 E8
Oulton Street ... 81 E7
Oundle ... 65 F7
Ousby ... 109 F6
Ousdale ... 158 H2
Ousefleet ... 90 B2
Ouston Durham ... 111 D5
  Northumb ... 110 B3
Outertown ... 159 G3
Outgate ... 99 E5
Outhgill ... 100 D2
Outlane ... 87 C8
Out Newton ... 91 B7
Out Rawcliffe ... 92 E4
Outwell ... 66 D5
Outwick ... 14 C2
Outwood Sur ... 28 E4
  W Yorks ... 88 B4
Outwoods ... 61 C7
Ovenden ... 87 B8
Ovenscloss ... 121 F7
Over Cambs ... 54 B4
  Ches W ... 74 C3
  S Glos ... 36 F2
Overbister ... 159 D7
Overbury ... 50 F4
Overcombe ... 12 F4
Over Compton ... 12 C3
Overgreen ... 76 B3
Over Green ... 63 E5
Over Haddon ... 76 C2
Over Hulton ... 86 D4
Over Kellet ... 92 B5
Over Kiddington ... 38 B4
Over Knutsford ... 74 B4

Overleigh ... 23 F6
Overley Green ... 51 D5
Over Monnow ... 36 C2
Over Norton ... 38 B3
Over Peover ... 74 B4
Overpool ... 73 B7
Overscaig Hotel ... 156 G7
Overseal ... 63 C6
Over Silton ... 102 E2
Oversland ... 30 D4
Overstone ... 53 C6
Over Stowey ... 22 F3
Overstrand ... 81 C8
Over Stratton ... 12 C2
Over Tabley ... 86 F5
Overthorpe ... 52 E2
Overton Aberdeen ... 141 C7
  Ches W ... 74 B2
  Dumfries ... 107 C6
  Hants ... 26 E3
  Lancs ... 92 D4
  N Yorks ... 95 D8
  Shrops ... 49 B7
  Swansea ... 33 F5
  W Yorks ... 88 C3
Overton = Owrtyn ... 73 E7
Overton Bridge ... 73 E7
Overtown ... 119 D8
Over Wallop ... 25 F7
Over Whitacre ... 63 E6
Over Worton ... 38 B4
Oving Bucks ... 39 B7
  W Sus ... 16 D3
Ovingdean ... 17 D7
Ovingham ... 110 C3
Ovington Durham ... 101 C6
  Essex ... 55 E8
  Hants ... 26 F3
  Norf ... 68 D2
  Northumb ... 110 C3
Ower ... 14 C4
Owermoigne ... 13 F5
Owlbury ... 60 E3
Owler Bar ... 76 B2
Owlerton ... 88 F4
Owl's Green ... 57 C6
Owlswick ... 39 D7
Owmby ... 90 D4
Owmby-by-Spital ... 90 F4
Owrtyn = Overton ... 73 E7
Owslebury ... 15 B6
Owston Leics ... 64 D4
  S Yorks ... 89 C6
Owston Ferry ... 90 E2
Owstwick ... 97 F8
Owthorne ... 91 B7
Owthorpe ... 77 F6
Oxborough ... 67 D7
Oxcombe ... 79 B6
Oxenholme ... 99 F7
Oxenhope ... 94 F3
Oxen Park ... 99 F5
Oxenton ... 50 F4
Oxenwood ... 25 D8
Oxford ... 39 D5
Oxhey ... 40 E4
Oxhill ... 51 E8
Oxley ... 62 D3
Oxley Green ... 43 C5
Oxley's Green ... 18 C3
Oxnam ... 116 C2
Oxshott ... 28 C2
Oxspring ... 88 D3
Oxted ... 28 D4
Oxton Borders ... 121 D7
  Notts ... 77 D6
Oxwich ... 33 F5
Oxwick ... 80 E5
Oykel Bridge ... 156 J6
Oyne ... 141 B5

P

Pabail Iarach ... 155 D10
Pabail Uarach ... 155 D10
Pace Gate ... 94 D4
Packington ... 63 C7
Padanaram ... 134 D4
Padbury ... 52 F5
Paddington ... 41 F5
Paddlesworth ... 19 B8
Paddockhaugh ... 152 C2
Paddockhole ... 115 F5
Paddock Wood ... 29 E7
Padfield ... 87 E8
Padiham ... 93 F7
Padog ... 83 F8
Padside ... 94 D4
Padstow ... 4 B4
Padworth ... 26 C4
Page Bank ... 110 F5
Pagham ... 16 E2
Paglesham Churchend ... 43 E5
Paglesham Eastend ... 43 E5
Paibeil ... 148 B2
Paible ... 154 H5
Paignton ... 7 C6
Pailton ... 63 F8
Painscastle ... 48 E3
Painshawfield ... 110 C3
Painsthorpe ... 96 D4
Painswick ... 37 D5
Pairc Shiaboist ... 154 C7
Paisley ... 118 C4
Pakefield ... 69 E8
Pakenham ... 56 C3
Pale ... 72 F3
Palestine ... 25 E7
Paley Street ... 27 B6
Palfrey ... 62 E4
Palgowan ... 112 F3
Palgrave ... 56 B5
Pallion ... 111 D6
Palmarsh ... 19 B8
Palnackie ... 106 D5
Palnure ... 105 C8
Palterton ... 76 C4
Pamber End ... 26 D4
Pamber Green ... 26 D4
Pamber Heath ... 26 C4
Pamphill ... 13 D7
Pampisford ... 55 E5
Pan ... 159 J4
Panbride ... 135 F5
Pancrasweek ... 8 D4
Pandy Gwyn ... 58 D3

Pandy continued
  Mon ... 35 B7
  Powys ... 59 D6
  Wrex ... 73 F5
Pandy Tudur ... 83 E8
Panfield ... 42 B3
Pangbourne ... 26 B4
Pannal ... 95 D6
Panshanger ... 41 C5
Pant ... 60 B2
Pant-glas Carms ... 33 B6
  Gwyn ... 71 C5
Pant-glâs ... 58 E4
Pant-glas ... 71 C5
Pantgwyn Carms ... 33 B6
  Ceredig ... 45 E4
Pant-lasau ... 33 E7
Pant Mawr ... 59 F5
Panton ... 78 B4
Pantperthog ... 58 D4
Pant-teg ... 33 B5
Pant-y-Caws ... 32 B2
Pant-y-dwr ... 47 B8
Pant-y-ffridd ... 59 D8
Pantyffynnon ... 33 C7
Pantymwyn ... 73 C5
Pant-yr-awel ... 34 F3
Pant-y-Wacco ... 72 B5
Panxworth ... 69 C6
Papcastle ... 107 F8
Papigoe ... 158 E5
Papil ... 160 K5
Papley ... 159 J5
Papple ... 121 B8
Papplewick ... 76 D5
Papworth Everard ... 54 C3
Papworth St Agnes ... 54 C3
Par ... 5 D5
Parbold ... 86 C2
Parbrook Som ... 23 F7
  W Sus ... 16 B4
Parc ... 72 F2
Parcllyn ... 45 D4
Parc-Seymour ... 35 E8
Parc-y-rhôs ... 46 E4
Pardshaw ... 98 B2
Parham ... 57 C7
Park ... 114 E2
Park Corner Oxon ... 39 F6
  Windsor ... 40 F1
Parkend ... 36 D3
Park End Mbro ... 102 C3
  Northumb ... 109 B8
Parkeston ... 57 F6
Parkgate Ches W ... 73 B6
  Dumfries ... 114 F3
  Kent ... 19 B5
  Sur ... 28 E3
Park Gate ... 15 D6
Parkham ... 9 B5
Parkham Ash ... 9 B5
Park Hill Notts ... 77 D6
  N Yorks ... 95 C6
Parkhill House ... 141 C7
Parkhouse ... 36 D1
Parkhouse Green ... 76 C4
Parkhurst ... 15 E5
Parkmill ... 33 F6
Parkneuk ... 135 B7
Parkstone ... 13 E8
Park Street ... 28 F2
Parley Cross ... 13 E8
Parracombe ... 21 E5
Parrog ... 45 F2
Parsley Hay ... 75 C8
Parsonage Green ... 42 D3
Parsonby ... 107 F8
Parson Cross ... 88 E4
Parson Drove ... 66 D3
Parson's Heath ... 43 B6
Partick ... 119 C5
Partington ... 86 E5
Partney ... 79 C7
Parton Cumb ... 98 B1
  Dumfries ... 106 B3
  Glos ... 37 B5
Partridge Green ... 17 C5
Parwich ... 75 D8
Passenham ... 53 F5
Paston ... 81 D9
Patchacott ... 9 E6
Patcham ... 17 D7
Patching ... 16 D4
Patchole ... 20 E5
Pateley Bridge ... 94 C4
Paternoster Heath ... 43 C5
Pathe ... 23 F5
Pathhead Aberds ... 135 C7
  E Ayrs ... 113 C6
  Fife ... 128 E4
  Midloth ... 121 C6
Path of Condie ... 128 C2
Pathstruie ... 128 C2
Patna ... 112 C4
Patney ... 25 D5
Patrick ... 84 D2
Patrick Brompton ... 101 E7
Patrington ... 91 B7
Patrixbourne ... 31 D5
Patterdale ... 99 C5
Pattingham ... 62 E2
Pattishall ... 52 D4
Pattiswick Green ... 42 B4
Patton Bridge ... 99 E7
Paul ... 2 D3
Paulerspury ... 52 E5
Paull ... 91 B5
Paulton ... 23 D8
Pavenham ... 53 D7
Pawlett ... 22 E5
Pawston ... 122 F4
Paxford ... 51 F6
Paxton ... 122 D5
Payhembury ... 11 D5
Paythorne ... 93 D8
Peacehaven ... 17 D8
Peak Dale ... 75 B7
Peak Forest ... 75 B8
Peakirk ... 65 D8
Pearsie ... 134 D3
Peasedown St John ... 24 D2
Peasehill ... 76 E3
Peasemore ... 26 B2
Peasenhall ... 57 C7
Pease Pottage ... 28 F3
Peaslake ... 27 E8
Peasley Cross ... 86 E3

Peasmarsh ... 19 C5
Peaston ... 121 C7
Peastonbank ... 121 C7
Peat Inn ... 129 D6
Peatling Magna ... 64 E2
Peatling Parva ... 64 F2
Peaton ... 60 F5
Peats Corner ... 57 C5
Pebmarsh ... 56 F2
Pebworth ... 51 E6
Pecket Well ... 87 B7
Peckforton ... 74 D2
Peckham ... 28 B4
Peckleton ... 63 D8
Pedlinge ... 19 B8
Pedmore ... 62 F3
Pedwell ... 23 F6
Peebles ... 121 E5
Peel ... 84 D2
Peel Common ... 15 D6
Peel Park ... 119 D6
Peening Quarter ... 19 C5
Pegsdon ... 54 F2
Pegswood ... 117 F8
Pegwell ... 31 C7
Peinchorran ... 149 E10
Peinlich ... 149 C9
Pelaw ... 111 C5
Pelcomb Bridge ... 44 D4
Pelcomb Cross ... 44 D4
Peldon ... 43 C5
Pellon ... 87 B8
Pelsall ... 62 D4
Pelton ... 111 D5
Pelutho ... 107 E8
Pelynt ... 5 D7
Pemberton ... 86 D3
Pembrey ... 33 D5
Pembridge ... 49 D5
Pembroke = Penfro ... 44 E4
Pembroke Dock = Doc Penfro ... 44 E4
Pembury ... 29 E7
Penallt ... 36 C2
Penally ... 32 E2
Penalt ... 36 B2
Penare ... 3 B8
Penarlâg = Hawarden ... 73 C7
Penarth ... 22 B3
Pen-bont Rhydybeddau ... 58 F3
Penbryn ... 45 D4
Pencader ... 46 F3
Pencaenewydd ... 70 C5
Pencaitland ... 121 C7
Pencarnisiog ... 82 D3
Pencarreg ... 46 E4
Pencelli ... 34 B4
Pen-clawdd ... 33 E6
Pencoed ... 34 F3
Pencombe ... 49 D7
Pencoyd ... 36 B2
Pencraig Hereford ... 36 B2
  Powys ... 59 B7
Pendeen ... 2 C2
Penderyn ... 34 D3
Pendine ... 32 D3
Pendlebury ... 87 D5
Pendleton ... 93 F7
Pendock ... 50 F2
Pendoggett ... 4 B5
Pendomer ... 12 C3
Pendoylan ... 22 B2
Pendre ... 34 F3
Penegoes ... 58 D4
Pen-ffordd ... 32 B1
Penfro = Pembroke ... 44 E4
Pengam ... 35 E5
Penge ... 28 B4
Pengenffordd ... 48 F3
Pengorffwysfa ... 82 B4
Pengover Green ... 5 C7
Pen-groes-oped ... 35 D7
Penhale Corn ... 3 E5
  Corn ... 4 D4
Penhalvaen ... 3 C6
Penhill ... 38 F1
Penhow ... 35 E8
Penhurst ... 18 D3
Peniarth ... 58 D3
Penicuik ... 120 C5
Peniel Carms ... 33 B5
  Denb ... 72 C4
Penifiler ... 149 D9
Peninver ... 143 F8
Penisarwaun ... 83 E5
Penistone ... 88 D3
Penjerrick ... 3 C6
Penketh ... 86 F3
Penkill ... 112 E2
Penkridge ... 62 C3
Penley ... 73 F8
Penllergaer ... 33 E7
Penllyn ... 21 B8
Pen-llyn ... 82 C3
Pen-lon ... 82 E4
Penmachno ... 83 F7
Penmaen ... 33 F6
Penmaenan ... 83 D7
Penmaenmawr ... 83 D7
Penmaenpool ... 58 C3
Penmark ... 22 C2
Penmarth ... 3 C6
Penmon ... 83 C6
Penmore Mill ... 146 F7
Penmorfa Ceredig ... 46 D2
  Gwyn ... 71 C6
Penmynydd ... 82 D5
Penn Bucks ... 40 E2
  W Mid ... 62 E2
Pennal ... 58 D4
Pennan ... 153 B8
Pennant Ceredig ... 46 C4
  Denb ... 72 F4
  Powys ... 59 E5
Pennant Melangell ... 59 B7
Pennard ... 33 F6
Pennerley ... 60 E3
Pennington
  Gtr Man ... 86 E4
  Hants ... 14 E4
  W&F ... 92 B2
Penny Bridge ... 99 F5
Pennycross ... 147 J8
Pennygate ... 69 B6
Pennygown ... 147 G8
Pennymoor ... 10 C3
Pennywell ... 111 D6
Penparc Ceredig ... 45 E4
  Pembs ... 44 B3
Penparcau ... 58 F2
Penperlleni ... 35 D7
Penpillick ... 5 D5
Penpol ... 3 C7
Penpoll ... 5 D6
Penpont Dumfries ... 113 E8
  Powys ... 34 B3
Penrherber ... 45 F4
Penrhiw-fawr ... 34 E4
Penrhiw goch ... 33 C6
Penrhiw-llan ... 46 E2
Penrhiw-pâl ... 46 E2
Penrhos ... 70 D4
Penrhôs ... 35 C8
Penrhos ... 34 C1
Penrhosfeilw ... 82 C2
Penrhyn Bay ... 83 C8
Penrhyn-coch ... 58 F3
Penrhyndeudraeth ... 71 D7
Penrhynside ... 83 C8
Penrice ... 33 F5
Penrith ... 108 F5
Penrose ... 4 B3
Penruddock ... 99 B6
Penryn ... 3 C6
Pensarn Carms ... 33 C5
  Conwy ... 72 B3
Pen-sarn Gwyn ... 70 C5
  Gwyn ... 71 E6
Pensax ... 50 C2
Pensby ... 85 F3
Penselwood ... 24 F2
Pensford ... 23 C8
Penshaw ... 111 D6
Penshurst ... 29 E6
Pensilva ... 5 C7
Penston ... 121 B7
Pentewan ... 3 B9
Pentir ... 83 E5
Pentire ... 4 C2
Pentlow ... 56 E2
Pentney ... 67 C7
Penton Mewsey ... 25 E8
Pentraeth ... 82 D5
Pentre Carms ... 33 C6
  Powys ... 59 F7
  Powys ... 60 C3
  Rhondda ... 34 E3
  Shrops ... 60 C3
  Wrex ... 72 F5
  Wrex ... 73 E6
Pentrebach M Tydf ... 34 D4
  Swansea ... 33 D7
Pentre-bâch ... 46 E4
Pentre-bach ... 47 F8
Pentrebeirdd ... 59 C8
Pentre Berw ... 82 D4
Pentre-bont ... 83 F7
Pentrecagal ... 46 E2
Pentre-celyn Denb ... 72 D5
  Powys ... 59 D5
Pentre-chwyth ... 33 E7
Pentre-cwrt ... 46 F2
Pentre Dolau-Honddu ... 47 E8
Pentredwr ... 73 E5
Pentre-dwr ... 33 E7
Pentrefelin Carms ... 33 B6
  Ceredig ... 46 E5
  Conwy ... 83 D8
  Gwyn ... 71 D6
Pentrefoelas ... 83 F8
Pentre-galar ... 45 F3
Pentregat ... 46 D2
Pentre-Gwenlais ... 33 C7
Pentre Gwynfryn ... 71 E6
Pentre Halkyn ... 73 B5
Pentreheyling ... 60 E2
Pentre-Isaf ... 83 E8
Pentre Llanrhaeadr ... 72 C4
Pentre-llwyn-ll yd ... 47 E8
Pentre-llyn ... 46 B5
Pentre-llyn cymmer ... 72 D3
Pentre Meyrick ... 21 B8
Pentre-piod ... 35 F6
Pentre'r Felin ... 83 E8
Pentre'r-felin ... 47 D5
Pentre-tafarn-yfedw ... 83 E8
Pentre-ty-gwyn ... 47 F7
Pentrich ... 76 D3
Pentridge ... 13 C8
Pen-twyn ... 36 D2
Pentyrch ... 35 F5
Penuchadre ... 21 B7
Penuwch ... 46 C4
Penwithick ... 4 D5
Penwyllt ... 34 C2
Penybanc ... 33 C7
Pen-y-banc ... 33 B7
Pen-y-bont Carms ... 32 B4
  Gwyn ... 58 D4
  Gwyn ... 71 E7
  Powys ... 60 B2
Pen-y-Bont Ar Ogwr = Bridgend ... 21 B8
Penybontfawr ... 59 B7
Pen-y-bryn Gwyn ... 58 D2
  Pembs ... 45 E3
Penycae ... 73 E6
Pen-y-cae ... 34 C2
Pen-y-cae-mawr ... 35 E8
Pen-y-cefn ... 72 B5
Pen-y-clawdd ... 36 D1
Pen-y-coedcae ... 34 F4
Penycwm ... 44 C3
Pen-y-fai ... 34 F2
Penyffordd ... 73 C7
Penyffridd ... 82 F5
Pen-y-garn Carms ... 46 F4
  Ceredig ... 58 F3
Pen-y-garnedd ... 59 B8
Pen-y-garnedd ... 82 D5

Pen-y-gop 72 E3
Penygraig 34 E3
Pen-y-graig 70 D2
Penygroes Gwyn . . 82 F4
. . . . Pembs 45 F3
Pen-y-groes 33 C6
Pen-y-groeslon . . . 70 D3
Pen-y-Gwryd
  Hotel 83 F6
Penyrheol 35 F5
Pen-yr-heol 35 C8
Pen-yr-
  Heolgerrig 34 D4
Penysarn 82 B4
Pen-y-stryt 73 D5
Penywaun 34 D3
Penzance 2 C3
Peopleton 50 D4
Peover Heath 74 B4
Peper Harow 27 E7
Perceton 118 E3
Percie 140 E4
Percyhorner 153 B9
Periton 21 E8
Perivale 40 F4
Perkinsville 111 D5
Perlethorpe 77 B6
Perranarworthal . . 3 C6
Perranporth 4 D2
Perranuthnoe 2 D4
Perranzabuloe 4 D2
Perry Barr 62 E4
Perryfoot 88 F2
Perry Green Herts . 41 C7
. . . . Wilts 37 F6
Perry Street 29 B7
Pershall 74 F5
Pershore 50 E4
Pert 135 C6
Pertenhall 53 C8
Perth 128 B3
Perthy 73 F7
Perton 62 E2
Pertwood 24 F3
Peterborough 65 E8
Peterburn 155 J12
Peterchurch 48 F5
Peterculter 141 D7
Peterhead 153 D11
Peterlee 111 E7
Petersfield 15 B8
Peter's Green 40 C4
Peters Marland . . . 9 C6
Peterstone
  Wentlooge 35 F6
Peterston-super-
  Ely 22 B2
Peterstow 36 B2
Peter Tavy 6 B3
Petertown 159 H4
Petham 30 D5
Petrockstow 9 D7
Pett 19 D5
Pettaugh 57 D5
Petteridge 29 E7
Pettinain 120 E2
Pettistree 57 D6
Petton Devon 10 B5
. . . . Shrops . . . 60 B4
Petts Wood 28 C5
Petty 153 E7
Pettycur 128 F4
Pettymuick 141 B8
Petworth 16 B3
Pevensey 18 E3
Pevensey Bay 18 E3
Pewsey 25 C6
Philham 8 B4
Philiphaugh 115 B7
Phillack 2 C4
Philleigh 3 C7
Philpstoun 120 B3
Phocle Green 36 B3
Phoenix Green . . . 27 D5
Pica 98 B2
Piccotts End 40 D3
Pickering 103 F5
Picket Piece 25 E8
Picket Post 14 D2
Pickhill 101 F8
Picklescott 60 E4
Pickletillem 129 B6
Pickmere 74 B3
Pickney 11 B6
Pickstock 61 B7
Pickwell Devon . . . 20 E3
. . . . Leics 64 C4
Pickworth Lincs . . 78 F3
. . . . Rutland . . 65 D6
Picton Ches W 73 B8
. . . . Flint 85 F2
. . . . N Yorks . 102 D3
Piddinghoe 17 D8
Piddington Oxon . 39 C6
. . . . W Nhants . 53 D6
Piddlehinton 12 E5
Piddletrenthide . . 12 E5
Pidley 54 B4
Piercebridge 101 C7
Pierowall 159 D5
Pigdon 117 F7
Pikehall 75 D8
Pilgrims Hatch . . . 42 E1
Pilham 90 E2
Pill 23 B7
Pillaton 5 C8
Pillerton Hersey . . 51 E8
Pillerton Priors . . . 51 E8
Pilleth 48 C4
Pilley Hants 14 E4
. . . . S Yorks . . 88 D4
Pilling 92 E4
Pilling Lane 92 E3
Pillowell 36 D3
Pillwell 13 C5
Pilning 36 F2
Pilsbury 75 C8
Pilsdon 12 E2
Pilsgate 65 D7
Pilsley Derbys . . . 76 B3
. . . . Derbys . . . 76 C4
Pilton Devon 20 F4
. . . . N Nhants . 65 F7
. . . . Rutland . . 65 D6
. . . . Som 23 E7
Pilton Green 33 F5

Pimperne 13 D7
Pinchbeck 66 B2
Pinchbeck Bars . . . 65 B8
Pinchbeck West . . 66 B2
Pincheon Green . . 89 C7
Pinehurst 38 F1
Pinfold 85 C4
Pinged 33 D5
Pinhoe 10 E4
Pinkneys Green . . 40 F1
Pinley 51 B8
Pin Mill 57 F6
Pinminnoch 112 E1
Pinmore 112 E2
Pinmore Mains . . 112 E2
Pinner 40 F4
Pinvin 50 E4
Pinwherry 112 F1
Pinxton 76 D4
Pipe and Lyde . . . 49 E7
Pipe Gate 74 E4
Piperhill 151 F11
Piper's Pool 8 F4
Pippacott 20 F4
Pipton 48 F3
Pirbright 27 D7
Pirnmill 143 D9
. . . . Worcs 50 E3
Pisgah Ceredig . . . 47 B5
. . . . Stirling . 127 D6
Pishill 39 F7
Pistyll 70 C4
Pitagowan 133 C5
Pitblae 153 B9
Pitcairngreen . . . 128 B2
Pitcalnie 151 D11
Pitcaple 141 B6
Pitchcombe 37 D5
Pitchcott 39 B7
Pitchford 60 D5
Pitch Green 39 D7
Pitch Place 27 D7
Pitcombe 23 F8
Pitcorthie 129 D7
Pitcox 122 B2
Pitcur 134 F2
Pitfichie 141 C5
Pitforthie 135 B8
Pitgrudy 151 B10
Pitkennedy 135 D5
Pitkevy 128 D4
Pitkierie 129 D7
Pitlessie 128 D5
Pitlochry 133 D6
Pitmachie 141 B5
Pitmain 138 D3
Pitmedden 141 B7
Pitminster 11 C7
Pitmuies 135 E5
Pitmunie 141 C5
Pitney 12 B2
Pitscottie 129 C6
Pitsea 42 F3
Pitsford 53 C5
Pitsmoor 88 F4
Pitstone 40 C2
Pitstone Green . . 40 C2
Pittendreich 152 B1
Pittentrail 157 J10
Pittenweem 129 D7
Pittington 111 E6
Pittodrie 141 B5
Pitton 25 F7
Pittswood 29 E7
Pittulie 153 B9
Pityme 4 B4
Pity Me 111 E5
Pityoulish 138 C5
Pixey Green 57 B6
Pixham 28 D2
Pixley 49 F8
Place Newton . . . 96 B4
Plaidy 153 C7
Plains 119 C7
Plaish 60 E5
Plaistow 27 F8
Plaitford 14 C3
Plank Lane 86 E4
Plas Gogerddan . . 58 F3
Plas Llwyngwern . 58 D4
Plas Nantyr 73 F5
Plastow Green . . . 26 C3
Plas-yn-Cefn 72 B4
Platt 29 D7
Platt Bridge 86 D4
Platts Common . . 88 D4
Plawsworth 111 E5
Plaxtol 29 D7
Playden 19 C6
Playford 57 E6
Play Hatch 26 B5
Playing Place 3 B7
Playley Green 50 F2
Plealey 60 D4
Plean 127 F7
Pleasington 86 B4
Pleasley 76 C5
Pleckgate 93 F6
Plenmeller 109 C7
Pleshey 42 C2
Plockton 149 E13
Plocrapol 154 H6
Ploughfield 49 E5
Plowden 60 F3
Ploxgreen 60 D3
Pluckley 30 E3
Pluckley Thorne . 30 E3
Plumbland 107 F8
Plumley 74 B4
Plumpton E Sus . . 17 C7
. . . . W&F 108 F4
Plumpton Green . 17 C7
Plumpton Head . . 108 F5
Plumstead London . 29 B5
. . . . Norf 81 D7
Plumtree 77 F6
Plungar 77 F7
Plush 12 D5
Plwmp 46 D2
Plymouth 6 D2
Plympton 6 D3
Plymstock 6 D3
Plymtree 11 D5
Pockley 102 F4
Pocklington 96 E4
Pode Hole 66 B2

Podimore 12 B3
Podington 53 C7
Podmore 74 F4
Point Clear 43 C6
Pointon 78 F4
Pokesdown 14 E2
Pol a Charra 148 G2
Polbae 105 B6
Polbain 156 H2
Polbathic 5 D8
Polbeth 120 C3
Polchar 138 D4
Polebrook 65 F7
Pole Elm 50 E3
Polegate 18 E2
Poles 151 B10
Polesworth 63 D6
Polgigga 2 D2
Polglass 156 J3
Polgooth 4 D4
Poling 16 D4
Polkerris 5 D5
Polla 156 D6
Pollington 89 C7
Polloch 130 C1
Pollok 118 C5
Pollokshields . . . 119 C5
Polmassick 3 B8
Polmont 120 B2
Polnessan 112 C4
Polnish 147 C10
Polperro 5 D7
Polruan 5 D6
Polsham 23 E7
Polstead 56 F3
Poltalloch 124 F4
Poltimore 10 E4
Polton 121 C5
Polwarth 122 D3
Polyphant 8 F4
Polzeath 4 B4
Pondersbridge . . . 66 E2
Ponders End 41 E6
Pondtail 27 D6
Ponsanooth 3 C6
Ponsworthy 6 B5
Pont Aber 33 B8
Pont Aber-Geirw . . 71 E8
Pontamman 33 C7
Pontantwn 33 C5
Pontardawe 33 D8
Pontarddulais . . . 33 D6
Pont-ar-gothi 33 B6
Pont ar Hydfer . . . 34 B2
Pont-ar-llechau . . 33 B8
Pontarsais 33 B5
Pontblyddyn 73 C6
Pontbren Araeth . 33 B7
Pontbren Llwyd . . 34 D3
Pont Cwm Pydew . 72 F4
Pont Cyfyng 83 F7
Pont Cysyllte 73 E6
Pont Dolydd
  Prysor 71 D8
Pontefract 89 B5
Ponteland 110 B4
Ponterwyd 58 F4
Pontesbury 60 D3
Pontfadog 73 F6
Pontfaen 45 F2
Pont-faen 47 F8
Pont Fronwydd . . 58 B5
Pont-gareg 45 E3
Pontgarreg 46 D2
Pont-Henri 33 D5
Ponthir 35 E7
Ponthirwaun 45 E4
Pontllanfraith . . . 35 E5
Pontlliw 33 D7
Pont-Llogel 59 C7
Pontlottyn 35 D5
Pontneddfechan . 34 D3
Pontnewydd 35 E6
Pont Pen-y-
  benglog 83 E6
Pontrhydfendigaid 47 C6
Pont Rhyd-goch . . 83 E6
Pont-Rhyd-sarn . . 59 B5
Pont Rhyd-y-cyff. . 34 F2
Pontrhydyfen . . . 34 E1
Pont-rhyd-y-
  groes 47 B6
Pontrilas 35 B7
Pontrobert 59 C8
Pont-rug 82 E5
Pont Senni
  = Sennybridge . . 34 B3
Ponts Green 18 D3
Pontshill 36 B3
Pont-siân 46 E3
Pontsticill 34 C4
Pontwgan 83 D7
Pontyates 33 D5
Pontyberem 33 C6
Pontyclun 34 F4
Pontycymer 34 E3
Pontyglasier 45 F3
Pont-y-gwaith . . . 34 E4
Pont-y-pant 83 F7
Pont y Pennant . . 59 B6
Pontypool
  = Pont-y-pŵl . . . 35 D6
Pontypridd 34 F4
Pont-y-pŵl
  = Pontypool 35 D6
Pont yr Afon-Gam . 71 C8
Pont-yr-hafod . . . 44 C4
Pontywaun 35 E6
Pooksgreen 14 C4
Pool Corn 3 B5
. . . . W Yorks . . 94 F5
Poole 13 E8
Poole Keynes 37 E6
Poolend 75 D6
Pooley Bridge . . . 99 B6
Poolfold 75 D5
Poolhill 36 B4
Pool o'Muckhart . 128 D2
Pool Quay 60 C2
Poolsbrook 76 B4
Pootings 29 E5
Popham 26 E3
Popeswood 27 C6
Poplar 41 F6
Popley 26 D4
Porchester 77 E5

Porchfield 14 E5
Porin 150 F6
Poringland 69 D5
Porkellis 3 C5
Porlock 21 E7
Porlock Weir 21 E7
Portachoillan . . . 144 H6
Port Ann 145 E8
Port Appin 130 E3
Port Arthur 160 K5
Port Askaig 142 B5
Portavadie 145 G8
Port Bannatyne . 145 G9
Portbury 23 B7
Port Carlisle 108 C2
Port Charlotte . . 142 C3
Portchester 15 D7
Portclair 137 C7
Port Clarence . . . 102 B2
Port Driseach . . . 145 F8
Port Ellen 142 D4
Port Elphinstone . 141 C6
Portencalzie 104 B4
Portencross 118 E1
Port Erin 84 F1
Portesham 12 F4
Portessie 152 B4
Port e Vullen 84 C4
Port-Eynon 33 F5
Portfield Gate . . . 44 D4
Portgate 9 F6
Port Gaverne 8 F2
Port Glasgow . . . 118 B3
Portgordon 152 B3
Portgower 157 H13
Porth Corn 4 C3
. . . . Rhondda . 34 E4
Porthaethwy
  = Menai Bridge . . 83 D5
Porthallow Corn . . 3 D6
. . . . Corn 5 D7
Porthcawl 21 B7
Porthcothan 4 B3
Porthcurno 2 D2
Port Henderson . 149 A12
Porthgain 44 B3
Porthill 60 C4
Porthkerry 22 C2
Porthleven 2 D5
Porthllechog 82 B4
Porthmadog 71 D6
Porthmeor 2 C3
Porth Navas 3 D6
Portholland 3 B8
Porthoustock 3 D7
Porthpean 4 D5
Porthtowan 3 B5
Porth Tywyn
  = Burry Port 33 D5
Porthyrhyd Carms . 33 C6
. . . . Carms . . . 47 F6
Porth-y-waen . . . 60 B2
Portincaple 145 D11
Portington 96 F3
Portinnisherrich . 125 D5
Portinscale 98 B4
Port Isaac 4 A4
Portishead 23 B6
Portkil 145 E11
Portknockie 152 B4
Port Lamont 145 F9
Portlethen 141 E8
Portling 107 D5
Port Lion 44 E4
Portloe 3 C8
Port Logan 104 E4
Portmahomack . . 151 C12
Portmeirion 71 D6
Portmellon 3 B9
Port Mholair 155 D10
Port Mor 146 D7
Portmore 14 E4
Port Mulgrave . . 103 C5
Portnacroish . . . 130 E3
Portnahaven 142 C2
Portnalong 149 E8
Portnaluchaig . . . 147 C9
Portnancon 156 C7
Port Nan
  Giùran 155 D10
Port nan Long . . . 148 A3
Portnellan 126 B3
Port Nis 155 A10
Portobello 121 B6
Port of Menteith . 126 D5
Porton 25 F6
Portpatrick 104 D4
Port Quin 4 A4
Port Ramsay 130 E2
Portreath 3 B5
Portree 149 D9
Port St Mary 84 F2
Portscatho 3 C7
Portsea 15 D7
Portskerra 157 C11
Portskewett 36 F2
Portslade 17 D6
Portslade-by-Sea . 17 D6
Portsmouth Ptsmth . 15 D7
. . . . W Yorks . . 87 B7
Portsonachan . . . 125 C6
Portsoy 152 B5
Port Sunlight 85 F4
Portswood 14 C5
Port Talbot 34 E1
Porttanachy 152 B3
PortTennant 33 E7
Portuairk 146 E7
Portway Hereford . 49 F6
. . . . Worcs . . . 51 B5
Port Wemyss 142 C2
Port William 105 E7
Portwrinkle 5 D8
Poslingford 55 E8
Postbridge 6 B4
Postcombe 39 E7
Posting 19 B8
Postwick 69 D5
Potholm 115 F6
Potsgrove 40 B2
Potten End 40 D3
Potter Brompton . 97 B5
Potterhanworth . . 78 C3
Potterhanworth
  Booths 78 C3
Potter Heigham . . 69 C7
Potterne 24 D4
Potterne Wick . . . 24 D5

Potternewton . . . 95 F6
Potters Bar 41 D5
Potter's Cross . . . 62 F2
Pottery 53 E5
Potter Street 41 D7
Potterton Aberds . 141 C8
. . . . W Yorks . . 95 F7
Potto 102 D2
Potton 54 E3
Pott Row 80 E3
Pott Shrigley 75 B6
Poughill Corn 8 D4
. . . . Devon 10 D3
Poulshot 24 D4
Poulton Glos 37 D8
. . . . Mers 85 E4
Poulton-le-Fylde . 92 F3
Pound Bank 50 B2
Poundbury 12 E4
Poundfield 18 B2
Pound Green
  E Sus 18 C2
  IoW 14 F4
. . . . Worcs 50 B2
Poundland 112 F1
Poundon 39 B6
Poundsgate 6 B5
Poundstock 8 E4
Powburn 117 C6
Powderham 10 F4
Powerstock 12 E3
Powfoot 107 C8
Powick 50 D3
Powmill 128 E2
Poxwell 12 F5
Poyle 27 B8
Poynings 17 C6
Poyntington 12 C4
Poynton 87 F7
Poynton Green . . 61 C5
Poystreet Green . 56 D3
Praa Sands 2 D4
Pratt's Bottom . . 29 C5
Praze 2 C5
Praze-an-Beeble . 2 C5
Predannack Wollas . 3 E5
Prees 74 F2
Preesall 92 E3
Prees Green 74 F2
Preesgweene 73 F6
Prees Heath 74 F2
Prees Higher
  Heath 74 F2
Prees Lower Heath 74 F2
Prendergast 122 D5
Prendwick 117 C6
Prengwyn 46 E3
Prenteg 71 C6
Prenton 85 F4
Prescot 86 E2
Prescott 60 B4
Pressen 122 F4
Prestatyn 72 A4
Prestbury Ches E . 75 B6
. . . . Glos 37 B6
Presteigne
  = Llanandras . . . 48 C5
Presthope 61 E5
Prestleigh 23 E8
Preston Borders . 122 D3
. . . . Brighton . 17 D7
. . . . Devon 7 B6
. . . . Dorset . . . 12 F5
. . . . E Loth . . . 121 B8
. . . . E Yorks . . . 97 F7
. . . . Glos 37 D7
. . . . Glos 49 F8
. . . . Herts 40 B4
. . . . Kent 30 C4
. . . . Kent 31 C6
. . . . Lancs 86 B3
. . . . Northumb . 117 B7
. . . . Rutland . . 65 D5
. . . . Shrops . . . 60 C5
. . . . Wilts 24 B5
. . . . Wilts 25 B7
Preston Bagot . . . 51 C6
Preston Bissett . . 39 B6
Preston Bowyer . 11 B6
Preston
  Brockhurst 60 B5
Preston Brook . . . 86 F3
Preston Candover . 26 E4
Preston Capes . . . 52 D3
Preston
  Crowmarsh 39 E6
Preston Gubbals . 60 C4
Prestonmill 107 D6
Preston on Stour . 51 E7
Preston on the Hill 86 F3
Preston on Wye . . 49 E5
Prestonpans 121 B6
Preston Plucknett . 12 C3
Preston St Mary . 56 D3
Preston-under-
  Scar 101 E5
Preston upon the
  Weald Moors . . . 61 C6
Preston Wynne . . 49 E7
Prestwich 87 D6
. . . . Flint 73 C7
Prestwick
  Crossing 110 B4
. . . . S Ayrs . . 112 B3
Prestwood 40 D1
Price Town 34 E3
Prickwillow 67 F5
Priddy 23 D7
Priesthaugh 115 D7
Priest Hutton 92 B5
Priest Weston . . . 60 E2
Priesthorpe 94 F5
Primethorpe 64 E2
Primrose Green . . 68 C3
Primrosehill 40 D3
Primrose Valley . . 97 B7
Princes Gate 32 C2
Princes
  Risborough . . . 39 D8
Princethorpe 52 B2
Princetown Caerph . 35 C5
. . . . Devon 6 B3
Prion 72 C4
Prior Muir 129 C7
Prior Park 123 D5
Priors Frome 49 F7
Priors Hardwick . 52 D2
Priorslee 61 C7
Priors Marston . . 52 D2
Priory Wood 48 E4

Priston 23 C8
Pristow Green . . . 68 F4
Prittlewell 42 F4
Privett 15 B7
Prixford 20 F4
Probus 3 B7
Proncy 151 B10
Prospect 107 E8
Prudhoe 110 C3
Ptarmigan Lodge . 126 D2
Pubil 132 E1
Puckeridge 41 B6
Puckington 11 C8
Pucklechurch . . . 23 B8
Pucknall 14 B4
Puckrup 50 F3
Puddinglake 74 C4
Puddington
  Ches W 73 B7
. . . . Devon . . . 10 C3
Puddledock 68 E3
Puddletown 12 E5
Pudleston 49 D7
Pudsey 94 F5
Pulborough 16 C4
Puleston 61 B7
Pulford 73 D7
Pulham 12 D5
Pulham Market . . 68 F4
Pulham St Mary . 68 F5
Pulloxhill 53 F8
Pumpherston . . . 120 C3
Pumsaint 47 E5
Puncheston 32 B1
Puncknowle 12 F3
Punnett's Town . . 18 C3
Purbrook 15 D7
Purewell 14 E2
Purfleet 29 B6
Puriton 22 E5
Purleigh 42 D4
Purley London . . . 28 C4
. . . . W Berks . . 26 B4
Purlogue 48 B4
Purls Bridge 66 F4
Purse Caundle . . . 12 C4
Purslow 60 F3
Purston Jaglin . . . 88 C5
Purton Glos 36 D3
. . . . Wilts 37 F7
Purton Stoke 37 E7
Pury End 52 E5
Pusey 38 E3
Putley 49 F8
Putney 28 B3
Putsborough 20 E3
Puttenham Herts . 40 C1
. . . . Sur 27 E7
Puxton 23 C6
Pwll 33 D5
Pwllcrochan 44 E4
Pwll-glas 72 D5
Pwllgloyw 48 F2
Pwllheli 70 D4
Pwllmeyric 36 E2
Pwll-trap 32 C3
Pwll-y-glaw 34 E1
Pyecombe 17 C6
Pye Corner 35 F7
Pye Green 62 C3
Pyewipe 91 C6
Pyle 34 F2
Pyle = Y Pîl 34 F2
Pylle 23 F8
Pymoor 66 F4
Pyrford 27 D8
Pyrton 39 E6
Pytchley 53 B6
Pyworthy 8 D5

Q

Quabbs 60 F2
Quadring 78 F5
Quainton 39 C7
Quarley 25 E7
Quarndon 76 E3
Quarrier's
  Homes 118 C3
Quarrington 78 E3
Quarrington Hill . 111 F6
Quarry Bank 62 F3
Quarryford 121 C8
Quarryhill 151 C10
Quarrywood 152 B1
Quarter 119 D7
Quatford 61 E7
Quatt 61 F7
Quebec 110 E4
Quedgeley 37 C5
Queen Adelaide . . 67 F5
Queen Camel 12 B3
Queen Charlton . . 23 C8
Queen Dart 10 C3
Queenhill 50 F3
Queen Oak 24 F2
Queensbury 94 F4
Queensferry Edin . 120 B4
. . . . Flint 73 C7
Queensferry
  Crossing 110 B4
Queen's Head . . . 60 B3
Queen's Park
. . . . Bedford . . 53 E8
. . . . W Nhants . 52 C5
Queenstown 92 F3
Queen Street Kent . 29 E7
. . . . Wilts 37 F7
Queenzieburn . . . 119 B6
Quemerford 24 C5
Quendale 160 M5
Quendon 55 F6
Queniborough . . . 64 C3
Quenington 37 D8
Quernmore 92 D5
Quethiock 5 C8
Quholm 159 G3
Quicks Green 26 B3
Quidenham 68 F3
Quidhampton
. . . . Hants . . . 26 D3
. . . . Wilts 25 F6
Quilquox 153 E9
Quina Brook 74 F2
Quindry 159 J5
Quinton W Mid . . 62 F3
. . . . W Nhants . 53 D5

Quintrell Downs . . 4 C3
Quixhill 75 E8
Quoditch 9 E6
Quoig 127 B7
Quorndon 64 C2
Quothquan 120 F2
Quoyloo 159 F3
Quoyness 159 H3
Quoys Shetland . . 160 B8
. . . . Shetland . 160 G6

R

Raasay House . . . 149 E10
Rabbit's Cross . . . 29 E8
Raby 73 B7
Rachan Mill 120 F4
Rachub 83 E6
Rackenford 10 C3
Rackham 16 C4
Rackheath 69 C5
Racks 107 B7
Rackwick Orkney . 159 D5
. . . . Orkney . . 159 J3
Radbourne 76 F2
Radcliffe Gtr Man . 87 D5
. . . . Northumb . 117 D8
Radcliffe on Trent . 77 F6
Radclive 52 F4
Radcot 38 E2
Raddery 151 F10
Radernie 129 D6
Radford Semele . . 51 C8
Radipole 12 F4
Radlett 40 E4
Radley 39 E5
Radmanthwaite . . 76 C5
Radmoor 61 B6
Radmore Green . . 74 D2
Radnage 39 E7
Radstock 23 D8
Radstone 52 E3
Radway 51 E8
Radway Green . . . 74 D4
Radwell Bedford . . 53 D8
. . . . Herts 54 F3
Radwinter 55 F7
Radyr 35 F5
Rafford 151 F13
Ragdale 64 C3
Raglan 35 D8
Ragnall 77 B8
Rahane 145 E11
Rainford 86 D2
Rainford Junction . 86 D2
Rainham London . . 41 F8
. . . . Medway . . 30 C2
Rainhill 86 E2
Rainhill Stoops . . 86 E3
Rainow 75 B6
Rainton 95 B6
Rainworth 77 D5
Raisbeck 99 D8
Raise 109 E7
Rait 128 B4
Raithby Lincs 79 C6
. . . . Lincs 91 F7
Rake 16 B2
Rakewood 87 C7
Ram 46 E4
Ramasaig 148 D6
Rame Corn 3 C6
. . . . Corn 6 E2
Ram Lane 30 E3
Ramnageo 160 C8
Rampisham 12 D3
Rampside 92 C2
Rampton Cambs . . 54 C5
. . . . Notts 77 B7
Ramsbottom 87 C5
Ramsbury 25 B7
Ramscraigs 158 H3
Ramsdean 15 B8
Ramsdell 26 D3
Ramsden 38 C3
Ramsden
  Bellhouse 42 E3
Ramsden Heath . . 42 E3
Ramsey Cambs . . . 66 F2
. . . . Essex 57 F6
. . . . IoM 84 C4
Ramseycleuch . . 115 C5
Ramsey Forty Foot 66 F3
Ramsey Heights . . 66 F2
Ramsey Island . . . 43 D8
Ramsey Mereside . 66 F2
Ramsey St Mary's . 66 F2
Ramsgate 31 C7
Ramsgill 94 B4
Ramshorn 75 E7
Ramsnest
  Common 27 F7
Ranais 155 E9
Ranby Lincs 78 B5
. . . . Notts 89 F7
Rand 78 B4
Randwick 37 D5
Ranfurly 118 C3
Rangag 158 F3
Rangemore 63 B5
Rangeworthy 36 F3
Rankinston 112 C4
Ranmoor 88 F4
Ranmore Common 28 D2
Rannerdale 98 C3
Rannoch Station . 131 D8
Ranochan 147 C11
Ranskill 89 F7
Ranton 62 B2
Ranworth 69 C6
Raploch 127 E6
Rapness 159 D6
Rascal Moor 96 F4
Rascarrel 106 E4
Rashiereive 141 B8
Raskelf 95 B7
Rassau 35 C5
Rastrick 88 B2
Ratagan 136 C2
Ratby 64 D2
Ratcliffe Culey . . . 63 E7
Ratcliffe on Soar . 63 B8
Ratcliffe on the
  Wreake 64 C3
Rathen 153 B10
Rathillet 129 B5

Rathmell 93 D8
Ratho 120 B4
Ratho Station . . . 120 B4
Rathven 152 B4
Ratley 51 E8
Ratlinghope 60 E4
Rattar 158 C4
Ratten Row 92 E4
Rattery 6 C5
Rattlesden 56 D3
Rattray 134 E1
Raughton Head . . 108 E3
Raunds 53 B7
Ravenfield 89 E5
Ravenglass 98 E2
Raveningham . . . 69 E6
Ravenscar 103 D7
Ravenscraig 118 B2
Ravensdale 84 C3
Ravensden 53 D8
Ravenseat 100 D3
Ravenshead 77 D5
Ravensmoor 74 D3
Ravensthorpe
. . . . W Nhants . 52 B4
. . . . W Yorks . . 88 B3
Ravenstone Leics . 63 C8
. . . . M Keynes . 53 D6
Ravenstonedale . 100 D2
Ravenstown 92 B3
Ravenstruther . . 120 E2
Ravensworth . . . 101 D6
Raw 103 D7
Rawcliffe E Yorks . 89 B7
. . . . York 95 D8
Rawcliffe Bridge . 89 B7
Rawdon 94 F5
Rawmarsh 88 E5
Rawreth 42 E3
Rawridge 11 D7
Rawtenstall 87 B6
Raxton 153 E8
Raydon 56 F4
Raylees 117 E5
Rayleigh 42 E4
Rayne 42 B3
Rayners Lane 40 F4
Raynes Park 28 C3
Reach 55 C6
Read 93 F7
Reading 26 B5
Reading Street . . 19 B6
Reagill 99 C8
Rearquhar 151 B10
Rearsby 64 C3
Reaster 158 D4
Reawick 160 J5
Reay 157 C12
Rechullin 149 C13
Reculver 31 C6
Redberth 32 D1
Redbourn 40 C4
Redbourne 90 E3
Redbrook Mon . . . 36 C2
. . . . Wrex 74 E2
Redburn Highld . . 151 G11
. . . . Highld . . 151 G12
. . . . Northumb . 109 C7
Redcar 102 B4
Redcastle Angus . 135 D6
. . . . Highld . . . 151 G8
Redcliff Bay 23 B6
Red Dial 108 E2
Redding 120 B2
Reddingmuirhead
. . . . 120 B2
Reddish 87 E6
Redditch 50 C5
Rede 56 D2
Redenhall 69 F5
Redesdale Camp . 116 E4
Redesmouth 116 F4
Redford Aberds . . 135 B7
. . . . Angus . . 135 E5
. . . . Durham . . 110 F3
Redfordgreen . . . 115 C6
Redgorton 128 B2
Redgrave 56 B4
Redhill Aberds . . . 141 D6
. . . . Aberds . . 153 E6
. . . . N Som . . . 23 C7
. . . . Sur 28 D3
Red Hill 50 D2
Redhouse 145 G7
Redhouses 142 B4
Red Houses . . . . . 11 —
Redisham 69 F7
Redland Bristol . . 23 B7
. . . . Orkney . . 159 F4
Redlingfield 57 B5
Red Lodge 55 B7
Redlynch Som . . . 23 F9
. . . . Wilts 14 B3
Redmarley
  D'Abitot 50 F2
Redmarshall 102 B1
Redmile 77 F7
Redmire 101 E5
Redmoor 5 C5
Rednal 60 B3
Redpath 121 F8
Redpoint 149 B12
Red Rail 36 B2
Red Rock 86 D3
Red Roses 32 C3
Red Row 117 E8
Redruth 3 B5
Red Street 74 D5
Redvales 87 D6
Red Wharf Bay . . 82 C5
Redwick Newport . 35 F8
. . . . S Glos . . . 36 F2
Redworth 101 B7
Reed 54 F4
Reedham 69 D7
Reedness 89 B8
Reeds Beck 78 C5
Reepham Lincs . . . 78 B3
. . . . Norf 81 E6
Reeth 101 E5
Regaby 84 C4
Regoul 151 F11
Reiff 156 H2
Reigate 28 D3
Reighton 97 B7
Reinigeadal 154 G7
Reiss 158 E5
Rejerrah 4 D2

Releath 3 C5
Relubbus 2 C4
Relugas 151 G12
Remenham 39 F7
Remenham Hill . . 39 F7
Remony 132 E4
Rempstone 64 B2
Rendcomb 37 D7
Rendham 57 C7
Rendlesham 57 D7
Renfrew 118 C5
Renhold 53 D8
Renishaw 76 B4
Rennington 117 C8
Renton 118 B3
Renwick 109 E5
Repps 69 C7
Repton 63 B7
Reraig 149 F13
Rescobie 135 D5
Resipole 147 E10
Resolis 151 E9
Resolven 34 D2
Reston 122 C4
Reswallie 135 D5
Retew 4 D4
Retford 89 F8
Rettendon 42 E3
Rettendon Place . 42 E3
Revesby 79 C5
Revesby Bridge . . 79 C6
Rew 10 E4
Rew Street 15 E5
Reydon 57 B8
Reydon Smear . . . 57 B8
Reymerston 68 D3
Reynalton 32 D1
Reynoldston 33 E5
Rezare 5 B8
Rhaeadr Gwy
  = Rhayader 47 C8
Rhandirmwyn . . . 47 E6
Rhayader
  = Rhaeadr Gwy . . 47 C8
Rhedyn 70 D3
Rhemore 147 F8
Rhencullen 84 C3
Rhes-y-cae 73 B5
Rhewl Denb 72 C5
. . . . Denb 73 F5
Rhian 157 H8
Rhicarn 156 G3
Rhiconich 156 D5
Rhicullen 151 D9
Rhidorroch
  House 150 B4
Rhifail 157 E10
Rhigos 34 D3
Rhilochan 157 J10
Rhiroy 150 C4
Rhisga = Risca . . . 35 E6
Rhiw 70 E3
Rhiwabon
  = Ruabon 73 E7
Rhiwbina 35 F5
Rhiwbryfdir 71 C7
Rhiwderin 35 F6
Rhiwlas Gwyn . . . 72 F3
. . . . Gwyn 83 E5
. . . . Powys . . . 73 F5
Rhodes 87 D6
Rhodesia 77 B5
Rhodes Minnis . . 31 E5
Rhodiad 44 C2
Rhondda 34 E3
Rhonehouse or
  Kelton Hill . . . 106 D4
Rhoose = Y Rhws . 22 C2
Rhôs Carms 46 F2
. . . . Neath 33 D8
Rhosaman 33 C8
Rhosbeirio 82 B3
Rhoscefnhir 82 D5
Rhoscolyn 82 D2
Rhoscrowther . . . 44 E4
Rhosesmor 73 C6
Rhos-fawr 70 D4
Rhosgadfan 82 F5
Rhosgoch 82 C4
Rhos-goch 48 E3
Rhos-hill 45 E3
Rhoshirwaun 70 E2
Rhoslan 71 C5
Rhoslefain 58 D2
Rhosllanerchrugog 73 E6
Rhosmaen 33 B7
Rhosmeirch 82 D4
Rhosneigr 82 D3
Rhosnesni 73 D7
Rhos-on-Sea 83 C8
Rhossili 33 F5
Rhosrobin 73 D7
Rhosson 44 C2
Rhostryfan 82 F4
Rhostyllen 73 E7
Rhosybol 82 C4
Rhos-y-brithdir . . 59 B8
Rhos-y-garth 46 B5
Rhos-y-gwaliau . . 72 F3
Rhos-y-llan 70 D3
Rhos-y-Madoc . . . 73 E7
Rhos-y-meirch . . 48 C4
Rhu Argyll 145 E11
. . . . Argyll . . . 145 G7
Rhuallt 72 B4
Rhuddall Heath . . 74 C2
Rhuddlan Ceredig . 46 E3
. . . . Denb 72 B4
Rhue 150 B3
Rhulen 48 E3
Rhunahaorine . . 143 D8
Rhuthun
  = Ruthin 72 D5
Rhyd Gwyn 71 C7
Rhyd-Ddu 83 F5
Rhydfudr 46 C4
Rhydlewis 46 E2
Rhydlios 70 D2
Rhydlydan 83 F8
Rhyd-moel-ddu . . 48 B2
Rhydness 48 E3
Rhydowen 46 E3

Rhyd-Rosser 46 C4
Rhydspence 48 F4
Rhydtalog 73 D6
Rhyd-uchaf 72 F3
Rhyd-wen 58 C4
Rhydwyn 82 C3
Rhyd-y-clafdy 70 D4
Rhydycroesau 73 F6
Rhydyfelin Ceredig 46 B4
  Rhondda 34 F4
Rhyd-y-foel 72 B3
Rhyd-y-fro 33 D8
Rhyd-y-gwin 33 D7
Rhydymain 58 B5
Rhyd-y-meirch 35 D7
Rhyd-y-meudwy 72 D5
Rhydymwyn 73 C6
Rhyd-y-pandy 33 D7
Rhyd-yr-onen 58 D3
Rhyd-y-sarn 71 C7
Rhyl = *Y Rhyl* 72 A4
Rhymney
  = *Rhymni* 35 D5
Rhymni
  = *Rhymney* 35 D5
Rhynd Fife 129 B6
  Perth 128 B3
Rhynie Aberds 140 B3
  Highld 151 D11
Ribbesford 50 B2
Ribblehead 93 B7
Ribbleton 93 F5
Ribchester 93 F6
Ribigill 157 D8
Riby 91 D5
Riby Cross Roads 91 D5
Riccall 96 F2
Riccarton 118 F4
Richards Castle 49 C6
Richings Park 27 B8
Richmond London 28 B2
  N Yorks 101 D6
Rickarton 141 F7
Rickinghall 56 B4
Rickleton 111 D5
Rickling 55 F5
Rickmansworth 40 E3
Riddings Cumb 108 B4
  Derbys 76 D4
Riddlecombe 9 C8
Riddlesden 94 E3
Riddrie 119 C6
Ridge Dorset 13 F7
  Hants 14 C4
  Wilts 24 F4
Ridgebourne 48 C2
Ridge Green 28 E4
Ridgehill 23 C7
Ridge Lane 63 E6
Ridgeway Cross 50 E2
Ridgewell 55 E8
Ridgewood 17 C8
Ridgmont 53 F7
Riding Mill 110 C3
Ridleywood 73 D8
Ridlington Norf 69 A6
  Rutland 64 D5
Ridsdale 116 F5
Riechip 133 E7
Riemore 133 E7
Rienachait 156 F3
Rievaulx 102 F3
Rift House 111 F7
Rigg 108 C2
Riggend 119 B7
Rigsby 79 B7
Rigside 119 F8
Riley Green 86 B4
Rileyhill 62 C5
Rilla Mill 5 B7
Rillington 96 B4
Rimington 93 E8
Rimpton 12 B4
Rimswell 91 B7
Rinaston 44 C4
Ringasta 160 M5
Ringford 106 D3
Ringinglow 88 F3
Ringland 68 C4
Ringles Cross 17 B8
Ringmer 17 C8
Ringmore 6 E4
Ringorm 152 D2
Ring's End 66 D3
Ringsfield 69 F7
Ringsfield Corner 69 F7
Ringshall Herts 40 C2
  Suff 56 D4
Ringshall Stocks 56 D4
Ringstead N Nhants 53 B7
  Norf 80 C3
Ringwood 14 D2
Ringwould 31 E7
Rinmore 140 C3
Rinnigill 159 J4
Rinsey 2 D4
Riof 154 D6
Ripe 18 D2
Ripley Derbys 76 D3
  Hants 14 E2
  N Yorks 95 C5
  Sur 27 D8
Riplingham 97 F5
Ripon 95 B6
Rippingale 65 B7
Ripple Kent 31 E7
  Worcs 50 F3
Ripponden 87 C8
Rireavach 150 B3
Risabus 142 D4
Risbury 49 D7
Risby 55 C8
Risca = *Rhisga* 35 E6
Rise 97 E7
Riseden 18 B3
Risegate 66 B2
Riseholme 78 B2
Riseley Bedford 53 C8
  Wokingham 26 C5
Rishangles 57 C5
Rishton 93 F7
Rishworth 87 C8
Rising Bridge 87 B5
Risley Derbys 76 F4
  Warr 86 E4
Risplith 94 C5
Rispond 156 C7
Rivar 25 C8
Rivenhall End 42 C4
River Bank 55 C6
Riverhead 29 D8
Rivington 86 C4
Roachill 10 B3
Roade 53 D5
Road Green 69 E5
Roadhead 108 B5
Roadmeetings 119 E8
Roadside 158 D3
Roadside of
  Catterline 135 B8
Roadside of
  Kinneff 135 B8
Roadwater 22 F2
Roag 149 D7
Roa Island 92 C2
Roath 22 B3
Roberton Borders 115 C7
  S Lanark 114 B2
Robertsbridge 18 C4
Roberttown 88 B2
Robeston Cross 44 E3
Robeston Wathen 32 C1
Robin Hood 88 B4
Robin Hood's
  Bay 103 D7
Roborough Devon 6 C3
  Devon 9 C7
Roby 86 E2
Roby Mill 86 D3
Rocester 75 F8
Roch 44 C3
Rochdale 87 C6
Roche 4 C4
Rochester Medway 29 C8
  Northumb 116 E4
Rochford 42 E4
Roch Gate 44 C3
Rock Corn 4 B4
  Northumb 117 B8
  Worcs 50 B2
  W Sus 16 C5
Rockbeare 10 E5
Rockbourne 14 C2
Rockcliffe Cumb 108 C3
  Dumfries 107 D5
Rock Ferry 85 F4
Rockfield Highld 151 C12
  Mon 36 C1
Rockford 14 D2
Rockhampton 36 E3
Rockingham 65 E5
Rockland All
  Saints 68 E2
Rockland St Mary 69 D6
Rockland St Peter 68 E2
Rockley 25 B6
Rockwell End 39 F7
Rockwell Green 11 B6
Rodborough 37 D5
Rodbourne Swindon 37 F8
  Wilts 37 F6
Rodbourne Cheney 37 F8
Rodd 48 C5
Roddam 117 B6
Rodden 12 F4
Rode 24 D3
Rodeheath 75 C5
Rode Heath 74 D5
Roden 61 C5
Rodhuish 22 F2
Rodington 61 C5
Rodley Glos 36 C4
  W Yorks 94 F5
Rodmarton 37 E6
Rodmell 17 D8
Rodmersham 30 C3
Rodney Stoke 23 D6
Rodsley 76 E2
Rodway 22 F4
Rodwell 12 G4
Roecliffe 95 C6
Roe Green 54 F4
Roehampton 28 B3
Roesound 160 G5
Roffey 28 F2
Rogart 157 J10
Rogart Station 157 J10
Rogate 16 B2
Rogerstone 35 F6
Roghadal 154 J5
Rogiet 36 F1
Rogue's Alley 66 D3
Roke 39 E6
Roker 111 D7
Rollesby 69 C7
Rolleston Leics 64 D4
  Notts 77 D7
Rolleston-on-
  Dove 63 B6
Rolston 97 E8
Rolvenden 18 B5
Rolvenden Layne 19 B5
Romaldkirk 100 B4
Romanby 102 E1
Romannobridge 120 E4
Romansleigh 10 B2
Romford 41 F8
Romiley 87 E7
Romsey 14 B4
Romsey Town 55 D5
Romsley Shrops 61 F7
  Worcs 50 B4
Ronague 84 E2
Rookhope 110 E2
Rookley 15 F6
Rooks Bridge 23 D5
Roos 97 F8
Roosebeck 92 C2
Rootham's Green 54 D2
Rootpark 120 D2
Ropley 26 F4
Ropley Dean 26 F4
Ropsley 78 F2
Rora 153 C10
Rorandle 141 C5
Rorrington 60 D3
Roscroggan 3 B5
Rose 4 D2
Roseacre Kent 29 D8
  Lancs 92 F4
Rose Ash 10 B2
Rosebank 119 E8
Rosebrough 117 B7
Rosebush 32 B1
Rosecare 8 E3
Rosedale Abbey 103 E5
Roseden 117 B6
Rosefield 151 F1
Rose Green 16 E3
Rose Grove [illegible]
Rosehall 156 J7
Rosehaugh Mains 151 F9
Rosehearty 153 B9
Rosehill 74 F3
Rose Hill E Sus 17 C8
  Lancs 93 F8
  Suff 57 E5
Roseisle 152 B1
Roselands 18 E3
Rosemarket 44 E4
Rosemarkie 151 F10
Rosemary Lane 11 C6
Rosemount 134 E1
Rosenannon 4 C4
Rosewell 121 C5
Roseworth 102 B2
Roseworthy 2 C5
Rosgill 99 C7
Roshven 147 D10
Roskhill 149 D7
Roskill House 151 F9
Rosley 108 E3
Roslin 121 C5
Rosliston 63 C6
Rosneath 145 E11
Ross Dumfries 106 E3
  Northumb 123 F7
  Perth 127 B6
Rossett 73 D7
Rossett Green 95 D6
Rossie Ochill 128 C2
Rossie Priory 134 F2
Rossington 89 E7
Rosskeen 151 E9
Rossland 118 B4
Ross-on-Wye 36 B3
Roster 158 G4
Rostherne 86 F5
Rosthwaite 98 C4
Roston 75 E8
Rosyth 128 F3
Rothbury 117 D6
Rotherby 64 C3
Rotherfield 18 C2
Rotherfield Greys 39 F7
Rotherfield
  Peppard 39 F7
Rotherham 88 E5
Rothersthorpe 52 D5
Rotherwick 26 D5
Rothes 152 D2
Rothesay 145 G9
Rothiebrisbane 153 E7
Rothienorman 153 E7
Rothiesholm 159 F7
Rothley Leics 64 C2
  Northumb 117 F6
Rothley Shield
  East 117 E6
Rothmaise 153 E6
Rothwell Lincs 91 E5
  N Nhants 64 F5
  W Yorks 88 B4
Rothwell Haigh 88 B4
Rotsea 97 D6
Rottal 134 C3
Rotten End 57 C7
Rottingdean 17 D7
Rottington 98 C1
Roud 15 F6
Rougham Norf 80 E4
  Suff 56 C3
Rougham Green 56 C3
Roughburn 137 F6
Rough Close 75 F6
Rough Common 30 D5
Roughlee 93 E8
Roughley 62 E5
Roughsike 108 B5
Roughton Lincs 78 C5
  Norf 81 D8
  Shrops 61 E7
Roughton Moor 78 C5
Roundhay 95 F6
Roundstonefoot 114 D4
Roundstreet
  Common 16 B4
Roundway 24 C5
Rousdon 11 E7
Rous Lench 50 D5
Routenburn 118 C1
Routh 97 E6
Row Corn 5 B5
  W&F 99 F6
Rowanburn 108 B4
Rowardennan 126 E2
Rowde 24 C4
Rowen 83 D7
Rowfoot 109 C6
Row Heath 43 C7
Rowhedge 43 B6
Rowhook 28 F2
Rowington 51 C7
Rowland 76 B2
Rowlands Castle 15 C8
Rowlands Gill 110 D4
Rowledge 27 E6
Rowlestone 35 B7
Rowley E Yorks 97 F5
  Shrops 60 D3
Rowley Hill 88 C2
Rowley Regis 62 F3
Rowly 27 E8
Rowney Green 50 B5
Rownhams 14 C4
Rowrah 98 C2
Rowsham 39 C8
Rowsley 76 C2
Rowstock 38 F4
Rowston 78 D3
Rowton Ches W 73 C8
  Shrops 60 C3
  Telford 61 C6
Roxburgh 122 F3
Roxby N Lincs 90 C3
  N Yorks 103 C5
Roxton 54 D2
Roxwell 42 D2
Royal Leamington
  Spa 51 C8
Royal Oak Darl 101 B7
  Lancs 86 D2
Royal Tunbridge
  Wells 18 B2
Royal Wootton
  Bassett 37 F7
Roybridge 137 F5
Roydhouse 88 C3
[illegible]
  Norf 68 F3
  Norf 80 E3
Roydon Hamlet 41 D7
Royston Herts 54 E4
  S Yorks 88 C4
Royton 87 D7
Rozel 17 I3
Ruabon = *Rhiwabon* 73 E7
Ruaig 146 G3
Ruan Lanihorne 3 B7
Ruan Minor 3 E6
Ruarach 136 B2
Ruardean 36 C3
Ruardean
  Woodside 36 C3
Rubery 50 B4
Ruckcroft 108 E5
Ruckhall 49 F6
Ruckinge 19 B7
Ruckland 79 B6
Ruckley 60 D5
Rudbaxton 44 C4
Rudby 102 D2
Ruddington 77 F5
Rudford 36 B4
Rudge Shrops 62 E2
  Som 24 D3
Rudgeway 36 F3
Rudgwick 27 F8
Rudhall 36 B3
Rudheath 74 B3
Rudley Green 42 D4
Rudry 35 F5
Rudston 97 C6
Rudyard 75 D6
Rufford 86 C2
Rufforth 95 D8
Rugby 52 B3
Rugeley 62 C4
Ruglen 112 D2
Ruilick 151 G8
Ruishton 11 B7
Ruisigearraidh 154 J4
Ruislip 40 F3
Ruislip Common 40 F3
Rumbling Bridge 128 E2
Rumburgh 69 F6
Rumford 4 B3
Rumney 22 B4
Runcorn 86 F3
Runcton 16 D2
Runcton Holme 67 D6
Rundlestone 6 B3
Runfold 27 E6
Runhall 68 D3
Runham Norf 69 C7
  Norf 69 D8
Runnington 11 B6
Runsell Green 42 D3
Runswick Bay 103 C6
Runwell 42 E3
Ruscombe 27 B5
Rushall Hereford 49 F8
  Norf 68 F4
  Wilts 25 D6
  W Mid 62 D4
Rushbrooke 56 C2
Rushbury 60 E5
Rushden Herts 54 F4
  N Nhants 53 C7
Rushenden 30 B3
Rushford 68 F2
Rush Green 41 F8
Rush-head 153 D8
Rushlake Green 18 D3
Rushmere 69 F7
Rushmere St
  Andrew 57 E6
Rushmoor 27 E6
Rushock 50 B3
Rusholme 87 E6
Rushton Ches W 74 C2
  N Nhants 64 F5
  Shrops 61 D6
Rushton Spencer 75 C6
Rushwick 50 D3
Rushyford 101 B7
Ruskie 126 D5
Ruskington 78 D3
Rusland 99 F5
Rusper 28 F3
Ruspidge 36 C3
Russell's Water 39 F7
Russel's Green 57 B6
Rusthall 18 B2
Rustington 16 D4
Ruston 103 F7
Ruston Parva 97 C6
Ruswarp 103 D6
Rutherford 122 F2
Rutherglen 119 C6
Ruthernbridge 4 C5
Ruthin = *Rhuthun* 72 D5
Ruthrieston 141 D8
Ruthven Aberds 152 D5
  Angus 134 E2
  Highld 138 E3
  Highld 151 H11
Ruthven House 134 E3
Ruthvoes 4 C4
Ruthwell 107 C7
Ruyton-XI-Towns 60 B3
Ryal 110 B3
Ryal Fold 86 B4
Ryall 12 E2
Ryarsh 29 D7
Rydal 99 D5
Ryde 15 E6
Rye 19 C6
Ryecroft Gate 75 C6
Rye Foreign 19 C5
Rye Harbour 19 D6
Ryehill 91 B6
Rye Park 41 C6
Rye Street 50 F2
Ryhall 65 C7
Ryhill 88 C4
Ryhope 111 D7
Rylstone 94 D2
Ryme Intrinseca 12 C3
Ryther 95 F8
Ryton Glos 50 F2
  N Yorks 96 B3
  Shrops 61 D7
  T&W 110 C4
Ryton-on-
  Dunsmore 51 B8

S

Sabden 93 F7
Sacombe 41 C6
Sacriston 110 E5
Sadberge 101 C8
Saddell 143 E8
Saddington 64 E3
Saddle Bow 67 C6
Saddlescombe 17 C6
Sadgill 99 D6
Saffron Walden 55 F6
Sageston 32 D1
Saham Hills 68 D2
Saham Toney 68 D2
Saighdinis 148 B3
Saighton 73 C8
St Abbs 122 C5
St Abb's Haven 122 C5
St Agnes Corn 4 D2
  Scilly 2 F3
St Albans 40 D4
St Allen 4 D3
St Andrews 129 C7
St Andrew's
  Major 22 B3
St Anne 16 I1
St Annes 85 B4
St Ann's 114 E3
St Ann's Chapel
  Corn 6 B2
  Devon 6 E4
St Anthony-in-
  Meneage 3 D6
St Anthony's Hill 18 E3
St Arvans 36 E2
St Asaph
  = *Llanelwy* 72 B4
St Athan 22 C2
St Aubin 17 I3
St Austell 4 D5
St Bees 98 C1
St Blazey 5 D5
St Boswells 121 F8
St Brelade 17 I3
St Breock 4 B4
St Breward 5 B5
St Briavels 36 D2
St Bride's 44 D3
St Brides Major 21 B7
St Bride's
  Netherwent 35 F8
St Brides-
  super-Ely 22 B2
St Brides
  Wentlooge 35 F6
St Budeaux 6 D2
St Buryan 2 D3
St Catherine 24 B2
St Catherine's 125 E7
St Clears
  = *Sanclêr* 32 C3
St Cleer 5 C7
St Clement 3 B7
St Clements 17 I3
St Clether 8 F4
St Colmac 145 G9
St Columb Major 4 C4
St Columb Minor 4 C3
St Columb Road 4 D4
St Combs 153 B10
St Cross South
  Elmham 69 F5
St Cyrus 135 C7
St David's 127 B8
St David's
  = *Tyddewi* 44 C2
St Day 3 B6
St Dennis 4 D4
St Devereux 49 F6
St Dogmaels 45 E3
St Dogwells 44 C4
St Dominick 6 C2
St Donat's 21 C8
St Edith's 24 C4
St Endellion 4 B4
St Enoder 4 D3
St Erme 4 D3
St Erney 5 D8
St Erth 2 C4
St Ervan 4 B3
St Eval 4 C3
St Ewe 3 B8
St Fagans 22 B3
St Fergus 153 C10
St Fillans 127 B5
St Florence 32 D1
St Genny's 8 E3
St George 72 B3
St George's 22 B2
St Germans 5 D8
St Giles 78 B2
St Giles in the
  Wood 9 C7
St Giles on the
  Heath 9 E5
St Harmon 47 B8
St Helena 63 D6
St Helen
  Auckland 101 B6
St Helens IoW 15 F7
  Mers 86 E3
St Helen's 18 D5
St Helier Jersey 17 I3
  London 28 C3
St Hilary Corn 2 C4
  V Glam 22 B2
Saint Hill 28 F4
St Illtyd 35 D6
St Ippollytts 40 B4
St Ishmael's 44 E3
St Issey 4 B4
St Ive 5 C8
St Ives Cambs 54 B4
  Corn 2 B4
  Dorset 14 D2
St James South
  Elmham 69 F6
St Jidgey 4 C4
St John 6 D2
St John's IoM 84 D2
  Jersey 17 I3
  Sur 27 D7
  Worcs 50 D3
St John's Chapel 109 F8
St John's Fen End 66 C5
St John's Highway 66 C5
St John's Town of
  Dalry 113 F6
St Judes 84 C3
St Just 2 C2
St Just in
  Roseland 3 C7
St Katherine's 153 E7
St Keverne 3 D6
St Kew 4 B5
St Kew Highway 4 B5
St Keyne 5 C7
St Lawrence Corn 4 C5
  Essex 43 D5
  IoW 15 G6
St Leonards Dorset 14 D2
  E Sus 18 E4
  S Lanark 119 D6
St Leonard's 40 D2
St Levan 2 D2
St Lythans 22 B3
St Mabyn 4 B5
St Madoes 128 B3
St Margarets 41 C6
St Margaret's 49 F5
St Margaret's at
  Cliffe 31 E7
St Margaret's
  Hope 159 J5
St Margaret South
  Elmham 69 F6
St Mark's 84 E2
St Martin 5 D7
St Martins Corn 3 D6
  Perth 134 F1
St Martin's Jersey 17 I3
  Shrops 73 F7
St Mary Bourne 26 D2
St Mary Church 22 B2
St Mary Cray 29 C5
St Mary Hill 21 B8
St Mary Hoo 30 B2
St Mary in the
  Marsh 19 C7
St Mary's Jersey 17 I3
  Orkney 159 H5
St Mary's Bay 19 C7
St Maughans 36 C1
St Mawes 3 C7
St Mawgan 4 C3
St Mellion 5 C8
St Mellons 35 F6
St Merryn 4 B3
St Mewan 4 D4
St Michael
  Caerhays 3 B8
St Michael
  Penkevil 3 B7
St Michaels 49 C7
St Michael's 19 B5
St Michael's on
  Wyre 92 E4
St Michael South
  Elmham 69 F6
St Minver 4 B4
St Monans 129 D7
St Neot 5 C6
St Neots 54 C2
St Newlyn East 4 D3
St Nicholas Pembs 44 B3
  V Glam 22 B2
St Nicholas at
  Wade 31 C6
St Ninians 127 E6
St Osyth 43 C7
St Osyth Heath 43 C7
St Ouens 17 I3
St Owens Cross 36 B2
St Paul's Cray 29 C5
St Paul's Walden 40 B4
St Peter Port 16 I2
St Peter's Jersey 17 I3
  Kent 31 C7
St Petrox 44 F4
St Pinnock 5 C7
St Quivox 112 B3
St Ruan 3 E6
St Sampson 16 I2
St Stephen 4 D4
St Stephens Corn 6 D2
  Herts 40 D4
St Stephen's 8 F5
St Teath 8 F2
St Thomas 10 E4
St Tudy 5 B5
St Twynnells 44 F4
St Veep 5 D6
St Vigeans 135 E6
St Wenn 4 C4
St Weonards 36 B1
Salcombe 6 F5
Salcombe Regis 11 F6
Salcott 43 C5
Sale 87 E5
Saleby 79 B7
Sale Green 50 D4
Salehurst 18 C4
Salem Carms 33 B7
  Ceredig 58 F3
Salen Argyll 147 G8
  Highld 147 E9
Salesbury 93 F6
Salford C Beds 53 F7
  Gtr Man 87 E6
  Oxon 38 B2
Salford Priors 51 D5
Salfords 28 E3
Salhouse 69 C6
Saline 128 E2
Salisbury 14 B2
Sallachan 130 C3
Sallachy Highld 150 H2
  Highld 157 J8
Salle 81 E7
Salmonby 79 B6
Salmond's Muir 135 F5
Salperton 37 B7
Salph End 53 D8
Salsburgh 119 C8
Salt 62 B3
Saltaire 94 F4
Saltash 6 D2
Saltburn 151 E10
Saltburn-by-
  the-Sea 102 B4
Saltby 65 B5
Saltcoats Cumb 98 E2
  N Ayrs 118 E2
Saltdean 17 D7
Salt End 91 B5
Salter 93 C6
Salterforth 93 E8
Salterswall 74 C3
Saltfleet 91 E8
Saltfleetby All
  Saints 91 E8
Saltfleetby St
  Clements 91 E8
Saltfleetby St
  Peter 91 F8
Saltford 23 C8
Salthouse 81 C6
Saltmarshe 89 B8
Saltney 73 C7
Salton 96 B3
Saltwick 110 B4
Saltwood 19 B8
Salum 146 G3
Salvington 16 D5
Salwarpe 50 C3
Salwayash 12 E2
Sambourne 51 C5
Sambrook 61 B7
Samhla 148 B2
Samlesbury 93 F5
Samlesbury
  Bottoms 86 B4
Sampford Arundel 11 C6
Sampford Brett 22 E2
Sampford
  Courtenay 9 D8
Sampford Peverell 10 C5
Sampford Spiney 6 B3
Sampool Bridge 99 F6
Samuelston 121 B7
Sanachan 149 D13
Sanaigmore 142 A3
Sanclêr
  = *St Clears* 32 C3
Sancreed 2 D3
Sancton 96 F5
Sand Highld 150 B2
  Shetland 160 J5
Sandaig 149 H12
Sandale 108 E2
Sandal Magna 88 C4
Sandbach 74 C4
Sandbank 145 E10
Sandbanks 13 F8
Sandend 152 B5
Sanderstead 28 C4
Sandfields 37 B6
Sandford Devon 10 D3
  Dorset 13 F7
  IoW 15 F6
  N Som 23 D6
  Shrops 74 F2
  S Lanark 119 E7
  W&F 100 C2
Sandfordhill 153 D11
Sandford on
  Thames 39 D5
Sandford Orcas 12 B4
Sandford St
  Martin 38 B4
Sandgate 19 B8
Sandgreen 106 D2
Sandhaven 153 B9
Sandhead 104 E4
Sandhills 27 F7
Sandhoe 110 C2
Sand Hole 96 F4
Sandholme E Yorks 96 F4
  Lincs 79 F6
Sandhurst Brack 27 C6
  Glos 37 B5
  Kent 18 C4
Sandhurst Cross 18 C4
Sandhutton 102 F1
Sand Hutton 96 D2
Sandiacre 76 F4
Sandilands Lincs 91 F9
  S Lanark 119 F8
Sandiway 74 B3
Sandleheath 14 C2
Sandling 29 D8
Sandlow Green 74 C4
Sandness 160 H3
Sandon Essex 42 D3
  Herts 54 F4
  Staffs 75 F6
Sandown 15 F6
Sandplace 5 D7
Sandridge Herts 40 C4
  Wilts 24 C4
Sandringham 67 B6
Sandsend 103 C6
Sandside House 157 C12
Sandsound 160 J5
Sandtoft 89 D8
Sandway 30 D2
Sandwell 62 F4
Sandwich 31 D7
Sandwick Orkney 159 K5
  Shetland 160 L6
  W&F 99 C6
Sandwith 98 C1
Sandy Carms 33 D5
  C Beds 54 E2
Sandy Bank 79 D5
Sandycroft 73 C7
Sandyford
  Dumfries 114 E5
  Stoke 75 D5
Sandygate 84 C3
Sandy Haven 44 E3
Sandyhills 107 D5
Sandylands 92 C4
Sandy Lane Wilts 24 C4
  Wrex 73 E7
Sandypark 10 F2
Sandysike 108 C3
Sangobeg 156 C7
Sangomore 156 C7
Sanna 146 E7
Sanndabhaig
  W Isles 148 D3
  W Isles 155 D9
Sannox 143 D11
Sanquhar 113 D7
Santon 90 C3
Santon Bridge 98 D3
Santon Downham 67 F8
Sapcote 63 E8
Sapey Common 50 C2
Sapiston 56 B3
Sapley 54 B3
Sapperton Glos 37 D6
  Lincs 78 F3
Saracen's Head 66 B3
Sarclet 158 F5
[illegible]
Sarn Bridgend 34 F3
  Powys 60 E2
Sarnau Carms 32 C4
  Ceredig 46 D2
  Gwyn 72 F3
  Powys 48 F2
  Powys 60 C2
Sarn Bach 70 E4
Sarnesfield 49 D5
Sarn Meyllteyrn 70 D3
Saron Carms 33 C7
  Carms 46 F2
  Denb 72 C4
  Gwyn 82 E5
  Gwyn 82 F4
Sarratt 40 E3
Sarre 31 C6
Sarsden 38 B2
Sarsgrum 156 C6
Satley 110 E4
Satron 100 E4
Satterleigh 9 B8
Satterthwaite 99 E5
Satwell 39 F7
Sauchen 141 C5
Saucher 134 F1
Sauchie 127 E7
Sauchieburn 135 C6
Saughall 73 B7
Saughtree 115 E8
Saul 36 D4
Saundby 89 F8
Saundersfoot 32 D2
Saunderton 39 D7
Saunton 20 F3
Sausthorpe 79 C6
Saval 157 J8
Savary 147 G9
Savile Park 87 B8
Sawbridge 52 C3
Sawbridgeworth 41 C7
Sawdon 103 F7
Sawley Derbys 76 F4
  Lancs 93 E7
  N Yorks 94 C5
Sawston 55 E5
Sawtry 65 F8
Saxby Leics 64 C5
  Lincs 90 F4
Saxby All Saints 90 C3
Saxelbye 64 B4
Saxham Street 56 C4
Saxilby 77 B8
Saxlingham 81 D6
Saxlingham Green 68 E5
Saxlingham
  Nethergate 68 E5
Saxlingham
  Thorpe 68 E5
Saxmundham 57 C7
Saxondale 77 F6
Saxon Street 55 D7
Saxtead 57 C6
Saxtead Green 57 C6
Saxthorpe 81 D7
Saxton 95 F7
Sayers Common 17 C6
Scackleton 96 B2
Scadabhagh 154 H6
Scaftworth 89 E7
Scagglethorpe 96 B4
Scaitcliffe 87 B5
Scalasaig 144 D2
Scalby E Yorks 90 B2
  N Yorks 103 E8
Scaldwell 53 B5
Scaleby 108 C4
Scaleby Hill 108 C4
Scale Houses 109 E5
Scales Lancs 92 F4
  W&F 92 B2
  W&F 99 B5
Scalford 64 B4
Scaling 103 C5
Scallastle 124 B2
Scalloway 160 K6
Scalpay 154 H7
Scalpay House 149 F11
Scalpsie 145 H9
Scamadale 147 B10
Scamblesby 79 B5
Scamodale 130 B2
Scampston 96 B4
Scampton 78 B2
Scapa 159 H5
Scapegoat Hill 87 C8
Scar 159 D7
Scarborough 103 F8
Scarcliffe 76 C4
Scarcroft 95 E6
Scarcroft Hill 95 E6
Scardroy 150 F5
Scarff 160 E4
Scarfskerry 158 C4
Scargill 101 C5
Scarinish 146 G3
Scarisbrick 85 C4
Scarning 68 C2
Scarrington 77 E7
Scartho 91 D6
Scarwell 159 F3
Scatness 160 M5
Scatraig 151 H10
Scawby 90 D3
Scawsby 89 D6
Scawton 102 F3
Scayne's Hill 17 B7
Scethrog 35 B5
Scholar Green 74 D5
Scholes W Yorks 88 B2
  W Yorks 88 D2
  W Yorks 95 F6
School Green 74 C3
Scleddau 44 B4
Scofton 89 F7
Scole 56 B5
Scolpaig 148 A2
Scone 128 B3
Sconser 149 E10
Scoonie 129 D5
Scoor 146 K7
Scopwick 78 D3
Scoraig 150 B3
Scorborough 97 E6
Scorrier 3 B6
Scorton Lancs 92 E5
Scorton *continued*
  N Yorks 101 D7
Sco Ruston 81 E8
Scotbheinn 148 C3
Scotby 108 D4
Scotch Corner 101 D7
Scotforth 92 D4
Scothern 78 B3
Scotland Gate 117 F8
Scotlandwell 128 D3
Scotsburn 151 D10
Scotscalder
  Station 158 E2
Scotscraig 129 B6
Scots' Gap 117 F6
Scotston Aberds 135 B7
  Perth 133 E6
Scotstoun 118 C5
Scotstown 130 C2
Scotswood 110 C4
Scottas 149 H12
Scotter 90 D2
Scotterthorpe 90 D2
Scottlethorpe 65 B7
Scotton Lincs 90 E2
  N Yorks 95 D6
  N Yorks 101 E6
Scottow 81 E8
Scoughall 129 F8
Scoulag 145 H10
Scoulton 68 D2
Scourie 156 E4
Scourie More 156 E4
Scousburgh 160 M5
Scrabster 158 C2
Scrafield 79 C6
Scrainwood 117 D5
Scrane End 79 E6
Scraptoft 64 D3
Scratby 69 C8
Scrayingham 96 C3
Scredington 78 E3
Scremby 79 C7
Scremerston 123 E6
Screveton 77 E7
Scrivelsby 79 C5
Scriven 95 D6
Scrooby 89 E7
Scropton 75 F8
Scrub Hill 78 D5
Scruton 101 E7
Sculcoates 97 F6
Sculthorpe 80 D4
Scunthorpe 90 C2
Scurlage 33 F5
Seaborough 12 D2
Seacombe 85 E4
Seacroft Lincs 79 C8
  W Yorks 95 F6
Seadyke 79 F6
Seafield S Ayrs 112 B3
  W Loth 120 C3
Seaford 17 E8
Seaforth 85 E4
Seagrave 64 C3
Seaham 111 E7
Seahouses 123 F8
Seal 29 D6
Sealand 73 C7
Seale 27 E6
Seamer N Yorks 102 C2
  N Yorks 103 F8
Seamill 118 E2
Sea Palling 69 B7
Searby 90 D4
Seasalter 30 C4
Seascale 98 D2
Seathorne 79 C8
Seathwaite Cumb 98 C4
  W&F 98 E4
Seatoller 98 C4
Seaton Corn 5 D8
  Cumb 107 F7
  Devon 11 F7
  Durham 111 D6
  E Yorks 97 E7
  Northumb 111 B6
  Rutland 65 E6
Seaton Burn 110 B5
Seaton Carew 102 B3
Seaton Delaval 111 B6
Seaton Ross 96 E3
Seaton Sluice 111 B6
Seatown Aberds 152 B5
  Dorset 12 E2
Seave Green 102 D3
Seaview 15 E7
Seaville 107 D8
Seavington St
  Mary 12 C2
Seavington St
  Michael 12 C2
Sebergham 108 E3
Seckington 63 D6
Second Coast 150 B2
Sedbergh 100 E1
Sedbury 36 E2
Sedbusk 100 E3
Sedgeberrow 50 F5
Sedgebrook 77 F8
Sedgefield 102 B1
Sedgeford 80 D3
Sedgehill 13 B6
Sedgley 62 E3
Sedgwick 99 F7
Sedlescombe 18 D4
Sedlescombe
  Street 18 D4
Seend 24 C4
Seend Cleeve 24 C4
Seer Green 40 E2
Seething 69 E6
Sefton 85 D4
Seghill 111 B5
Seifton 60 F4
Seighford 62 B2
Seilebost 154 H5
Seion 82 E5
Seisdon 62 E2
Seisiadar 155 D10
Selattyn 73 F6
Selborne 26 F5
Selby 96 F2
Selham 16 B3
Selhurst 28 C4
Selkirk 115 B7

Sellack 36 B2
Sellafirth 160 D7
Sellibister 159 D8
Sellindge 19 B7
Sellindge Lees 19 B8
Selling 30 D4
Sells Green 24 C4
Selly Oak 62 F4
Selmeston 18 E2
Selsdon 28 C4
Selsey 16 E2
Selsfield Common . 28 F4
Selsted 31 E6
Selston 76 D4
Selworthy 21 E8
Semblister 160 H5
Semer 56 E3
Semington 24 C3
Semley 13 B6
Send 27 D8
Send Marsh 27 D8
Senghenydd 35 E5
Sennen 2 D2
Sennen Cove 2 D2
Sennybridge
  = Pont Senni . . 34 B3
Serlby 89 F7
Sessay 95 B7
Setchey 67 C6
Setley 14 D4
Setter Shetland . 160 E6
  Shetland. 160 H5
  Shetland. 160 J7
Settiscarth 159 G4
Settle 93 C8
Settrington 96 B4
Sevenhampton . . . 37 B7
Seven Kings 41 F7
Sevenoaks 29 D6
Sevenoaks Weald . . 29 E6
Seven Sisters 34 D2
Severn Beach 36 F2
Severnhampton . . . 38 E2
Severn Stoke 50 E3
Sevington 30 E4
Sewards End 55 F6
Sewardstone 41 E6
Sewardstonebury . . 41 E6
Sewerby 97 C7
Seworgan 3 C6
Sewstern 65 B5
Sezincote 51 F6
Sgarasta Mhor . . 154 H5
Sgiogarstaigh . . 155 A10
Shabbington 39 D6
Shackerstone 63 D7
Shackleford 27 E7
Shade 87 B7
Shadforth 111 E6
Shadingfield 69 F7
Shadoxhurst 19 B6
Shadsworth 86 B5
Shadwell Norf . . . 68 F2
  W Yorks. 95 F6
Shaftesbury 13 B6
Shafton 88 C4
Shalbourne 25 C8
Shalcombe 14 F4
Shalden 26 E4
Shaldon 7 B7
Shalfleet 14 F5
Shalford Essex . . . 42 B3
  Sur 27 E8
Shalford Green . . . 42 B3
Shallowford 21 E6
Shalmsford Street . 30 D4
Shalstone 52 F4
Shamley Green . . . 27 E8
Shandon 145 E11
Shandwick 151 D11
Shangton 64 E4
Shankhouse 111 B5
Shanklin 15 F6
Shanquhar 152 E5
Shanzie 134 D2
Shap 99 C7
Shapwick Dorset . . 13 D7
  Som 23 F6
Shardlow 76 F4
Shareshill 62 D3
Sharlston 88 C4
Sharlston
  Common 88 C4
Sharnbrook 53 D7
Sharnford 63 E8
Sharoe Green 92 F5
Sharow 95 B6
Sharpenhoe 53 F8
Sharperton 117 D5
Sharpness 36 D3
Sharp Street 69 B6
Sharpthorne 28 F4
Sharrington 81 D6
Shatterford 61 F7
Shaugh Prior 6 C3
Shavington 74 D4
Shaw Gtr Man . . . 87 D7
  W Berks. 26 C2
  Wilts 24 C3
Shawbury 61 B5
Shawdon Hall . . . 117 C6
Shawell 64 F2
Shawford 15 B5
Shawforth 87 B6
Shaw Green 86 C3
Shawhead 107 B5
Shaw Mills 95 C5
Shawton 119 E6
Shawtonhill 119 E6
Shear Cross 24 E3
Shearington 107 C7
Shearsby 64 E3
Shebbear 9 D6
Shebdon 61 B7
Shebster 157 C13
Sheddens 119 D5
Shedfield 15 C6
Sheen 75 C8
Sheepscar 95 F6
Sheepscombe 37 C5
Sheepstor 6 C3
Sheepwash 9 D6
Sheepway 23 B6
Sheepy Magna . . . 63 D7
Sheepy Parva 63 D7

Sheering 41 C8
Sheerness 30 B3
Sheet 15 B8
Sheffield 88 F4
Sheffield Bottom . . 26 C4
Sheffield Green . . . 17 B8
Shefford 54 F2
Shefford
  Woodlands 25 B8
Sheigra 156 C4
Sheinton 61 D6
Shelderton 49 B6
Sheldon Derbys . . . 75 C8
  Devon 11 D6
  W Mid 63 F5
Sheldwich 30 D4
Shelf 88 B2
Shelfanger 68 F4
Shelfield Warks . . . 51 C6
  W Mid 62 D4
Shelford 77 E6
Shellacres 122 E4
Shelley Essex 42 D1
  Suff 56 F4
  W Yorks. 88 C3
Shellingford 38 E3
Shellow Bowells . . 42 D2
Shelsley
  Beauchamp. . . . 50 C2
Shelsley Walsh . . . 50 C2
Shelthorpe 64 C2
Shelton Bedford . . 53 C8
  Norf 68 E5
  Notts 77 E7
  Shrops 60 C4
Shelton Green . . . 68 E5
Shelve 60 E3
Shelwick 49 E7
Shenfield 42 E2
Shenington 51 E8
Shenley 40 D4
Shenley Brook End 53 F6
Shenleybury 40 D4
Shenley Church
  End 53 F6
Shenmore 49 F5
Shennanton 105 C7
Shenstone Staffs . . 62 D5
  Worcs 50 B3
Shenton 63 D7
Shenval Highld . . 137 B7
  Moray. 139 B8
Shepall 41 B5
Shepeau Stow . . . 66 C3
Shephall 41 B5
Shepherd's Green . . 39 F7
Shepherd's Port . . . 80 D2
Shepherdswell 31 E6
Shepley 88 D2
Shepperdine 36 E3
Shepperton 27 C8
Shepreth 54 E4
Shepshed 63 C8
Shepton
  Beauchamp. . . . 12 C2
Shepton Mallet . . . 23 E8
Shepton Montague 23 F8
Shepway 29 D8
Sheraton 111 F7
Sherborne Dorset . 12 C4
  Glos 38 C1
Sherborne St
  John 26 D4
Sherbourne 51 C7
Sherburn Durham . 111 E6
  N Yorks. 97 B5
Sherburn Hill . . . 111 E6
Sherburn in Elmet . 95 F7
Shere 27 E8
Shereford 80 E4
Sherfield English . . 14 B3
Sherfield on
  Loddon 26 D4
Sherford 7 E5
Sheriffhales 61 C7
Sheriff Hutton . . . 96 C2
Sheringham 81 C7
Sherington 53 E6
Shernal Green . . . 50 C4
Shernborne 80 D3
Sherrington 24 F4
Sherston 37 F5
Sherwood Green . . 9 B7
Shettleston 119 C6
Shevington 86 D3
Shevington Moor . . 86 C3
Shevington Vale . . 86 D3
Sheviock 5 D8
Shide 15 F5
Shiel Bridge 136 C2
Shieldaig Highld. . 149 A13
  Highld 149 C13
Shieldhill Dumfries 114 F3
  Falk 119 B8
  S Lanark. 120 E3
Shielfoot 147 E9
Shielhill Angus . . 134 D4
  Inverclyd. 118 B2
Shifford 38 D3
Shifnal 61 D7
Shildon 101 B7
Shillingford Devon . 10 B4
  Oxon 39 E5
Shillingford St
  George 10 F4
Shillingstone 13 C6
Shillington 54 F2
Shillmoor 116 D4
Shilton Oxon 38 D2
  Warks 63 F8
Shimpling Norf . . 68 F4
  Suff 56 D2
Shimpling Street . . 56 D2
Shiney Row 111 D6
Shinfield 26 C5
Shingham 67 D7
Shingle Street . . . 57 E7
Shinner's Bridge . . 7 C5
Shinness 157 H8
Shipbourne 29 D6
Shipdham 68 D2
Shipham 23 D6
Shiplake 27 B5
Shipley Derbys . . . 76 E4
  Northumb. . . . 117 C7
  Shrops 62 E2

Shipley continued
  W Sus 16 B5
  W Yorks. 94 F4
Shipley Shiels . . . 116 E3
Shipmeadow 69 F6
Shippea Hill
  Station 67 F6
Shippon 38 E4
Shipston-on-
  Stour 51 E7
Shipton Glos 37 C7
  N Yorks. 95 D8
  Shrops 61 E5
Shipton Bellinger . 25 E7
Shipton Gorge . . . 12 E2
Shipton Green . . . 16 D2
Shipton Moyne . . . 37 F5
Shipton on
  Cherwell 38 C4
Shipton Solers . . . 37 C7
Shiptonthorpe . . . 96 E4
Shipton-under-
  Wychwood 38 C2
Shirburn 39 E6
Shirdley Hill 85 C4
Shirebrook 76 C5
Shiregreen 88 E4
Shirehampton 23 B7
Shiremoor 111 B6
Shirenewton 36 E1
Shireoaks 89 F6
Shirkoak 19 B6
Shirland 76 D3
Shirley Derbys . . . 76 E2
  London 28 C4
  Soton 14 C5
  W Mid 51 B6
Shirl Heath 49 D6
Shirrell Heath 15 C6
Shirwell 20 F4
Shirwell Cross . . . 20 F4
Shiskine 143 F10
Shobdon 49 C6
Shobnall 63 B6
Shobrooke 10 D3
Shoby 64 C3
Shocklach 73 E8
Shocburyness . . . 43 F5
Sholden 31 D7
Sholing 14 C5
Shoot Hill 60 C4
Shop Corn 4 B3
  Corn. 8 C4
Shop Corner 57 F6
Shoreditch 41 F6
Shoreham 29 C6
Shoreham-by-Sea 17 D6
Shore Mill 151 E10
Shoresdean 123 E5
Shoreswood 122 E5
Shoreton 151 E9
Shorncote 37 E7
Shorne 29 B7
Shortacombe 9 F7
Shortgate 17 C8
Short Heath 62 D3
Shortlanesend . . . 3 B7
Shortlees 118 F4
Shortstown 53 E8
Shorwell 15 F5
Shoscombe 24 D2
Shotatton 60 B3
Shotesham 69 E5
Shotgate 42 E3
Shotley 57 F6
Shotley Bridge . . . 110 D3
Shotleyfield 110 D3
Shotley Gate 57 F6
Shottenden 30 D4
Shottermill 27 F6
Shottery 51 D6
Shotteswell 52 E2
Shottisham 57 E7
Shottle 76 E3
Shottlegate 76 E3
Shotton Durham . . 111 F7
  Flint 73 C7
  Northumb. . . . 122 F4
Shotton Colliery . . 111 E6
Shotts 119 C8
Shotwick 73 B7
Shouldham 67 D6
Shouldham
  Thorpe 67 D6
Shoulton 50 D3
Shover's Green . . . 18 B3
Shrawardine 60 C4
Shrawley 50 C3
Shrewley Common 51 C7
Shrewsbury 60 C4
Shrewton 25 E5
Shripney 16 D3
Shrivenham 38 F2
Shropham 68 E2
Shrub End 43 B5
Shucknall 49 E7
Shudy Camps . . . 55 E7
Shulishadermor . 149 D9
Shurdington 37 C6
Shurlock Row . . . 27 B6
Shurrery 157 D13
Shurrery Lodge . 157 D13
Shurton 22 E4
Shustoke 63 E6
Shute Devon 10 D3
  Devon. 11 E7
Shutford 51 E8
Shuthonger 50 F3
Shutlanger 52 D5
Shuttington 63 D6
Shuttlewood 76 B4
Siabost bho
  Dheas 154 C7
Siabost bho
  Thuath 154 C7
Siadar 155 B8
Siadar Iarach . . . 155 B8
Siadar Uarach . . 155 B8
Sibbaldbie 114 F4
Sibbertoft 64 F3
Sibdon Carwood . . 60 F4
Sibford Ferris . . . 51 F8
Sibford Gower . . . 51 F8
Sible Hedingham . 55 F8
Sibsey 79 D6
Sibson Cambs . . . 65 E7
  Leics 63 D7
Sibthorpe 77 E7
Sibton 57 C7

Sibton Green 57 B7
Sicklesmere 56 C2
Sicklinghall 95 E6
Sid 11 F6
Sidbury Devon . . . 11 E6
  Shrops 61 F6
Sidcot 23 D6
Sidcup 29 B5
Siddick 107 F7
Siddington Ches E . 74 B5
  Glos 37 E7
Sidemoor 50 B4
Sidestrand 81 D8
Sidford 11 E6
Sidlesham 16 E2
Sidley 18 E4
Sidlow 28 E3
Sidmouth 11 F6
Sigford 7 B5
Sigglesthorne . . . 97 E7
Sighthill 120 B4
Sigingstone 21 B8
Signet 38 C2
Silchester 26 C4
Sildinis 155 F7
Sileby 64 C2
Silecroft 98 F3
Silfield 68 E4
Silian 46 D4
Silkstone 88 D3
Silkstone
  Common 88 D3
Silk Willoughby . . 78 E3
Silloth 107 D8
Sills 116 D4
Sillyearn 152 C5
Siloh 47 F6
Silpho 103 E7
Silsden 94 E3
Silsoe 53 F8
Silverburn 120 C5
Silverdale Lancs . . 92 B4
  Staffs 74 E5
Silver End 42 C4
Silvergate 81 E7
Silverhill 18 D4
Silverley's Green . . 57 B6
Silverstone 52 E4
Silverton 10 D4
Silvington 49 B8
Silwick 160 J4
Simmondley 87 E8
Simonburn 109 B8
Simonsbath 21 F6
Simonstone 93 F7
Simprim 122 E4
Simpson 53 F6
Simpson Cross . . . 44 D3
Sinclair's Hill . . . 122 D4
Sinclairston 112 C4
Sinderby 101 F8
Sinderhope 109 D8
Sindlesham 27 C5
Singdean 115 D8
Singleborough . . . 53 F5
Singleton Lancs . . 92 F3
  W Sus 16 C2
Singlewell 29 B7
Sinkhurst Green . . 30 E2
Sinnahard 140 C3
Sinnington 103 F5
Sinton Green 50 C3
Sipson 27 B8
Sirhowy 35 C5
Sisland 69 E6
Sissinghurst 18 B4
Sisterpath 122 E3
Siston 23 B8
Sithney 2 D5
Sittingbourne . . . 30 C2
Six Ashes 61 F7
Sixhills 91 F5
Six Mile Bottom . . 55 D6
Sixpenny Handley 13 C7
Sizewell 57 C8
Skail 157 E10
Skaill Orkney . . . 159 G3
  Orkney. 159 H6
Skares 113 C5
Skateraw 122 B3
Skaw 160 G7
Skeabost 149 D9
Skeabrae 159 F3
Skeeby 101 D7
Skeffington 64 D4
Skeffling 91 C7
Skegby 76 C4
Skegness 79 C8
Skelberry 160 M5
Skelbo 151 B10
Skelbrooke 89 C6
Skeldyke 79 F6
Skellingthorpe . . . 78 B2
Skellister 160 H6
Skellow 89 C6
Skelmanthorpe . . 88 C3
Skelmersdale 86 D2
Skelmonae 153 E8
Skelmorlie 118 C1
Skelmuir 153 D9
Skelpick 157 D10
Skelton E Yorks . . 89 B8
  N Yorks. 101 D5
  Redcar 102 C4
  W&F. 108 F4
  York 95 D8
Skelton-on-Ure . . 95 C6
Skelwick 159 D5
Skelwith Bridge . . 99 D5
Skendleby 79 C7
Skene House . . . 141 D6
Skenfrith 36 B1
Skerne 97 D6
Skeroblingarry . . 143 F8
Skerray 157 C9
Skerton 92 C4
Sketchley 63 E8
Sketty 33 E7
Skewen 33 E8
Skewsby 96 B2
Skeyton 81 E8
Skiag Bridge . . . 156 G5
Skibo Castle . . . 151 C10
Skidbrooke 91 E8
Skidbrooke North
  End 91 E8
Skidby 97 F6

Skilgate 10 B4
Skillington 65 B5
Skinburness 107 D8
Skinflats 127 F8
Skinidin 148 D7
Skinnet 157 C8
Skinningrove 103 B5
Skipness 145 H7
Skippool 92 E3
Skipsea 97 D7
Skipsea Brough . . 97 D7
Skipton 94 D2
Skipton-on-Swale 95 B6
Skipwith 96 F2
Skirbeck 79 E6
Skirbeck Quarter . 79 E6
Skirlaugh 97 F7
Skirling 120 F3
Skirmett 39 F7
Skirpenbeck 96 D3
Skirwith 109 F6
Skirza 158 D5
Skulamus 149 F11
Skullomie 157 C9
Skyborry Green . . 48 B4
  Lincs. 90 D4
Skye of Curr . . . 139 B5
Skyreholme 94 C3
Slackhall 87 F8
Slackhead 152 B4
Slad 37 D5
Slade Devon 20 E4
  Pembs 44 D4
Slade Green 29 B6
Slaggyford 109 D6
Slaidburn 93 D7
Slaithwaite 87 C8
Slaley 110 D2
Slamannan 119 B8
Slapton Bucks . . . 40 B2
  Devon. 7 E6
  W Nhants. . . . 52 E4
Slatepit Dale 76 C3
Slattocks 87 D6
Slaugham 17 B6
Slaughterford . . . 24 B3
Slawston 64 E4
Sleaford Hants . . . 27 F6
  Lincs. 78 E3
Sleagill 99 C7
Sleapford 61 C6
Sledge Green 50 F3
Sledmere 96 C5
Sleightholme 100 C4
Sleights 103 D6
Slepe 13 E7
Slickly 158 D4
Sliddery 143 F10
Sligachan Hotel . 149 F9
Slimbridge 36 D4
Slindon Staffs . . . 74 F5
  W Sus 16 D3
Slinfold 28 F2
Sling 83 E6
Slingsby 96 B2
Slioch 152 E5
Slip End C Beds . . 40 C3
  Herts 54 F3
Slipton 53 B7
Slitting Mill 62 C4
Slochd 138 B4
Slockavullin 124 F4
Sloley 81 E8
Slochby 79 B7
Slough 27 B7
Slough Green 17 B6
Sluggan 138 B4
Slumbay 149 E13
Slyfield 27 D7
Slyne 92 C4
Smailholm 122 F2
Smallbridge 87 C7
Smallburgh 69 B6
Smallburn
  Aberds 153 D10
  E Ayrs. 113 B6
Small Dole 17 C6
Smalley 76 E4
Smallfield 28 E4
Small Hythe 19 B5
Smallridge 11 D8
Smannell 25 E8
Smardale 100 D2
Smarden 30 E2
Smarden Bell 30 E2
Smeatharpe 11 C6
Smeeth 19 B7
Smeeton Westerby 64 E3
Smercleit 148 G2
Smerral 158 G3
Smethwick 62 F4
Smirisary 147 D9
Smisby 63 C7
Smith End Green . 50 D2
Smithfield 108 C4
Smith Green 92 D4
Smithincott 11 C5
Smith's Green . . . 42 B1
Smithstown . . . 149 A12
Smithton 151 G10
Smithy Green . . . 74 B4
Smockington 63 F8
Smoogro 159 H4
Smythe's Green . . 43 C5
Snaigow House . . 133 E7
Snailbeach 60 D3
Snailwell 55 C7
Snainton 103 F7
Snaith 89 B7
Snape N Yorks . . . 101 F7
  Suff 57 D7
Snape Green 85 C4
Snarestone 63 D7
Snarford 90 F4
Snargate 19 C6
Snave 19 C7
Snead 60 E3
Sneath Common . . 68 F4
Sneaton 103 D6
Sneatonthorpe . . 103 D7
Snelland 90 F4
Snelston 75 E8
Snettisham 80 D2
Sniseabhal 148 E2
Snitter 117 D6
Snitterby 90 E3
Snitterfield 51 D7
Snitton 49 B7
Snodhill 48 E5
Snodland 29 C7
Snowden Hill 88 D3

Snowdown 31 D6
Snowshill 51 F5
Snydale 88 C5
Soar Anglesey . . . 82 D3
  Carms 33 B7
  Devon. 6 F5
Soar-y-Mynydd . . 47 D6
Soberton 15 C7
Soberton Heath . . 15 C7
Sockbridge 99 B7
Sockburn 101 D8
Soham 55 B6
Soham Cotes 55 B6
Solas 148 A3
Soldon Cross 8 C5
Soldridge 26 F4
Sole Street Kent . . 29 C7
  Kent 30 E4
Solihull 51 B6
Sollers Dilwyn . . . 49 D6
Sollers Hope 49 F8
Sollom 86 C2
Solva 44 C2
Somerby Leics . . . 64 C4
  Lincs. 90 D4
Somercotes 76 D4
Somerford 14 E2
Somerford Keynes . 37 E7
Somerley 16 E2
Somerleyton 69 E7
Somersal Herbert . 75 F8
Somersby 79 B6
Somersham Cambs 54 B4
  Suff 56 E4
Somerton Oxon . . 38 B4
  Som 12 B2
Sompting 17 D5
Sonning 27 B5
Sonning Common . 39 F7
Sonning Eye 27 B5
Sontley 73 E7
Sopley 14 E2
Sopwell 40 D4
Sopworth 37 F5
Sorbie 105 E8
Sordale 158 D3
Sorisdale 146 E5
Sorn 113 B5
Sornhill 118 F5
Sortat 158 D4
Sotby 78 B5
Sots Hole 78 C4
Sotterley 69 F7
Soudley 61 B7
Soughton 73 C6
Soulbury 40 B1
Soulby 100 C2
Souldern 52 F3
Souldrop 53 C7
Sound Ches E . . . 74 E3
  Shetland. 160 H5
  Shetland. 160 J6
Sound Heath 74 E3
Soundwell 23 B8
Sourhope 116 B4
Sourin 159 E5
Sourton 9 E7
Soutergate 98 F4
South Acre 67 C8
Southall 40 F4
South Allington . . 7 F5
South Alloa 127 E7
Southam Glos . . . 37 B6
  Warks 52 C2
South Ambersham 16 B3
Southampton 14 C5
South Anston 89 F6
South Ascot 27 C7
South
  Ballachulish . . 130 D4
South Balloch . . . 112 E3
South Bank 102 B3
South Barrow 12 B4
South Beach 70 D4
South Benfleet . . . 42 F3
South Bersted . . . 16 D3
Southborough . . . 29 E6
Southbourne BCP . 14 E2
  W Sus 15 D8
South Brent 6 C4
South Brewham . . 24 F2
South Broomhill . 117 E8
Southburgh 68 D2
South Burlingham 69 D6
Southburn 97 D5
South Cadbury . . . 12 B4
South Cairn 104 C3
South Carlton . . . 78 B2
South Cave 96 F5
South Cerney 37 E7
South Chard 11 D8
South Charlton . . 117 B7
South Cheriton . . 12 B4
Southchurch 43 F5
South Cliffe 96 F4
South Clifton 77 B8
South
  Cockerington . . 91 F7
South Cornelly . . . 34 F2
Southcott 25 D6
Southcourt 39 C8
South Cove 69 F7
South Creagan . . 130 E3
South Creake 80 D4
South Croston . . . 64 C3
South Croydon . . 28 C4
South Dalton 97 E5
South Darenth . . . 29 C6
Southdean 116 D2
Southdene 86 E2
South Duffield . . . 96 F2
South Elkington . . 91 F6
South Elmsall . . . 89 C5
Southend Argyll . 143 H7
  W Berks. 26 B3
  Wilts 25 B6
South End Bucks . . 40 B1
  N Lincs. 90 B5
  W&F. 92 C2
Southend-on-Sea . 42 F4
Southernden 30 E2
Southerndown . . . 21 B7
Southerness 107 D6
South Erradale . . 149 A12
Southery 67 E6
South Fambridge . 42 E4
South Fawley 38 F3
South Ferriby 90 B3

Southfield 111 B5
Southfleet 29 B7
South Garth 160 D7
South Garvan . . . 130 B3
Southgate Ceredig . 46 B4
  London 41 E5
  Norf 81 E7
  Swansea 33 F6
South Glendale . . 148 G2
South Godstone . . 28 E4
South Gorley 14 C2
South Green Essex . 42 E2
  Kent 30 C2
South-haa 160 E5
South Ham 26 D4
South
  Hanningfield . . 42 E3
South Harting . . . 15 C8
South Hatfield . . . 41 D5
South Hayling . . . 15 E8
South Hazelrigg . . 123 F6
South Heath 40 D2
South Heighton . . 17 D8
South Hetton . . . 111 E6
South Hiendley . . 88 C4
South Hill 5 B8
South Hinksey . . . 39 D5
South Hole 8 B4
South Holme 96 B2
South Holmwood . 28 E2
South Hornchurch . 41 F8
South Hykeham . . 78 C2
South Hylton . . . 111 D6
South Kelsey 90 E4
South Kessock . . 151 G9
South
  Killingholme . . 91 C5
South Kilvington . 102 F2
South Kilworth . . 64 F3
South Kirkby 88 C5
South Kirkton . . . 141 D6
South Kiscadale . 143 F11
South Kyme 78 E4
South Lancing . . . 17 D5
South Leigh 38 D3
South Leverton . . 89 F8
South Littleton . . 51 E5
South Lopham . . . 68 F3
South Luffenham . 65 D6
South Malling . . . 17 C8
South Marston . . . 38 F1
South Middleton . 117 B5
South Milford . . . 95 F7
South Milton 6 E5
South Mimms . . . 41 D5
South Molton . . . 10 B2
South Moreton . . 39 F5
South Mundham . . 16 D2
South Muskham . . 77 D7
South Newbald . . 96 F5
South Newington . 52 F2
South Newton . . . 25 F5
South Normanton 76 D4
South Norwood . . 28 C4
South Nutfield . . . 28 E4
South Ockendon . 42 F1
South Ormsby . . . 79 B6
South
  Otterington . . . 102 F1
South Owersby . . 90 E4
South Oxhey 40 E4
South Perrott 12 D2
South Petherton . . 12 C2
South Petherwin . . 8 F5
South Pickenham . 67 D8
South Pool 7 E5
Southport 85 C4
South Port 125 C6
Southpunds 160 L6
South Radworthy . 21 F6
South Rauceby . . 78 E3
South Raynham . . 80 E4
Southrepps 81 D8
South Reston 91 F8
Southrey 78 C4
Southrop 38 D1
Southrope 26 E4
South Runcton . . 67 D6
South Scarle 77 C8
Southsea 15 E7
South Shian 130 E3
South Shields . . . 111 C6
South Shore 92 F3
South Somercotes 91 E8
South Stainmore . 100 C3
South Stifford . . . 29 B7
Southstoke 24 C2
South Stoke Oxon . 39 F5
  W Sus 16 D4
South Street E Sus . 17 C7
  Kent 30 C5
  Kent 30 D4
  London 29 C5
South Tawton . . . 9 E8
South Thoresby . . 79 B7
South Tidworth . . 25 E7
Southtown Norf . . 69 D8
  Orkney. 159 J5
South Town 26 F4
South View 26 D4
Southwaite 108 E4
South Walsham . . 69 C6
Southwark 28 B4
South
  Warnborough . . 26 E5
Southwater 17 B5
Southwater Street . 17 B5
Southway 23 E7
South Weald 42 E1
Southwell Dorset . 12 G4
  Notts 77 D6
South Weston . . . 39 E7
South Wheatley
  Corn 8 E4
  Notts 89 F7
Southwick Hants . 15 D7
  Northants. . . . 65 E7

Southwick continued
  Wilts 24 D3
  W Sus 17 D6
South Widcombe . 23 D7
South Wigston . . . 64 E2
South Willingham . 91 F5
South Witham . . . 65 C6
Southwold 57 B9
South Wonston . . 26 F2
Southwood Norf . . 69 D6
  Som 23 F7
South Woodham
  Ferrers 42 E4
South Wootton . . 67 B6
South Wraxall . . . 24 C3
South Zeal 9 E8
Soval Lodge 155 E8
Sowber Gate . . . 102 F1
Sowerby N Yorks . 102 F2
  W Yorks. 87 B8
Sowerby Bridge . . 87 B8
Sowerby Row . . . 108 F3
Sowood 87 C8
Sowton 10 E4
Soyal 151 B8
Spacey Houses . . 95 D6
Spa Common 81 D8
Spadeadam Farm 109 B5
Spalding 66 B2
Spaldington 96 F3
Spaldwick 54 B2
Spalford 77 C8
Spanby 78 F3
Sparham 68 C3
Spark Bridge 99 F5
Sparkford 12 B4
Sparkhill 62 F4
Sparkwell 6 D3
Sparrow Green . . . 68 C2
Sparrowpit 87 F8
Sparsholt Hants . . 26 F2
  Oxon. 38 F3
Spartylea 109 E8
Spaunton 103 F5
Spaxton 22 F4
Spean Bridge . . . 136 F5
Spear Hill 16 C5
Speen Bucks 39 E8
  W Berks. 26 C2
Speeton 97 B7
Speke 86 F2
Speldhurst 29 E6
Spellbrook 41 C7
Spelsbury 38 B3
Spelter 34 E2
Spencers Wood . . 26 C5
Spennithorne . . . 101 F6
Spennymoor 111 F5
Spetchley 50 D3
Spetisbury 13 D7
Spexhall 69 F6
Spey Bay 152 B3
Speybridge 139 B6
Speyview 152 D2
Spilsby 79 C7
Spindlestone 123 F7
Spinkhill 76 B4
Spinningdale . . . 151 C9
Spirthill 24 B4
Spital Hill 89 E7
Spital in the Street 90 F3
Spithurst 17 C8
Spittal Dumfries . . 105 D7
  E Loth. 121 B7
  Highld 158 E3
  Northumb. . . . 123 D6
  Pembs 44 C4
  Stirling 126 F4
Spittalfield 133 E8
Spittal of
  Glenmuick . . . 140 F2
Spittal of
  Glenshee 133 B8
Spixworth 68 C5
Splayne's Green . . 17 B8
Spofforth 95 D6
Spondon 76 F4
Spon End 51 B8
Spon Green 73 C6
Spooner Row 68 E3
Sporle 67 C8
Spott 122 B2
Spratton 52 B5
Spreakley 27 E6
Spreyton 9 E8
Spridlington 90 F4
Springburn 119 C6
Springfield
  Dumfries 108 C3
  Essex 42 D3
  Fife. 128 C5
  Moray. 151 F13
  W Mid 62 F4
Springhill 62 D3
Springholm 106 C5
Springkell 108 B2
Springside 118 F3
Springthorpe 90 F2
Spring Vale 88 D3
Spring Valley 84 E3
Springwell 111 D5
Sproatley 97 F7
Sproston Green . . 74 C4
Sprotbrough 89 D6
Sproughton 56 E5
Sprouston 122 F3
Sprowston 68 C5
Sproxton Leics . . . 65 B5
  N Yorks. 102 F4
Spurstow 74 D2
Spynie 152 B2
Squires Gate 92 F3
Srannda 154 J5
Sronphadruig
  Lodge 132 B4
Stableford Shrops . 61 E7
  Staffs 74 F5
Stacey Bank 88 E3
Stackhouse 93 C8
Stackpole 44 F4
Staddiscombe . . . 6 D3
Staddlethorpe . . . 90 B2
Stadhampton . . . 39 E6
Stadhlaigearraidh
  . . . . . 148 E2
Staffin 149 B9
Stafford 62 B3

Stagsden 53 E7
Stainburn Cumb . . 98 B2
  N Yorks. 94 E5
Stainby 65 B6
Staincross 88 C4
Staindrop 101 B6
Staines-upon-
  Thames 27 B8
Stainfield Lincs . . 65 B7
  Lincs. 78 B4
Stainforth N Yorks 93 C8
  S Yorks. 89 C7
Staining 92 F3
Stainland 87 C8
Stainsacre 103 D7
Stainsby 76 C4
Stainton Durham . 101 C5
  Mbro 102 C2
  N Yorks. 101 E6
  S Yorks. 89 E6
  W&F. 99 B7
  W&F. 99 F7
Stainton by
  Langworth 78 B3
Staintondale . . . 103 E7
Stainton le Vale . . 91 E5
Stainton with
  Adgarley 92 B2
Stair Cumb 98 B4
  E Ayrs. 112 B4
Stairhaven 105 D6
Staithes 103 C5
Stakeford 117 F8
Stake Pool 92 E4
Stalbridge 12 C5
Stalbridge Weston 12 C5
Stalham 69 B6
Stalham Green . . . 69 B6
Stalisfield Green . . 30 D3
Stallingborough . . 91 C5
Stalling Busk . . . 100 F4
Stalmine 92 E3
Stalybridge 87 E7
Stambourne 55 F8
Stambourne Green 55 F8
Stamford 65 D7
Stamford Bridge
  Ches W 73 C8
  E Yorks. 96 D3
Stamfordham . . . 110 B3
Stanah 99 C5
Stanborough 41 C5
Stanbridge C Beds . 40 B2
  Dorset 13 D8
Stanbrook 50 E3
Stanbury 94 F3
Stand Gtr Man . . . 87 D5
  N Lanark 119 C7
Standburn 120 B2
Standeford 62 D3
Standen 30 E2
Standford 27 F6
Standingstone . . . 107 F7
Standish 86 C3
Standlake 38 D3
Standon Hants . . . 14 B5
  Herts 41 B6
  Staffs 74 F5
Stane 119 D8
Stanfield 80 E5
Stanford C Beds . . 54 E2
  Kent 19 B8
Stanford Bishop . . 49 D8
Stanford Bridge . . 50 C2
Stanford Dingley . 26 B3
Stanford in the
  Vale 38 E3
Stanford-le-Hope . 42 F2
Stanford on Avon . 52 B3
Stanford on Soar . 64 B2
Stanford Rivers . . 41 D8
Stanfree 76 B4
Stanghow 102 C4
Stanground 66 E2
Stanhoe 80 D4
Stanhope Borders 114 B4
  Durham 110 F2
Stanion 65 F6
Stanley Derbys . . . 76 E4
  Durham 110 D4
  Lancs. 86 D2
  Perth 133 F8
  Staffs 75 D6
  W Yorks. 88 B4
Stanley Common . 76 E4
Stanley Gate 86 D2
Stanley Hill 49 E8
Stanlow 73 B8
Stanmer 17 D7
Stanmore Hants . . 15 B5
  London 40 E4
  W Berks. 26 B2
Stannergate 134 F4
Stanningley 94 F5
Stannington
  Northumb. . . . 110 B5
  S Yorks. 88 F4
Stansbatch 48 C5
Stansfield 55 D8
Stanstead 56 E2
Stanstead Abbotts 41 C6
Stansted 29 C7
Stansted Airport . 42 B1
Stansted
  Mountfitchet . . 41 B8
Stanton Glos 51 F5
  Mon 35 B7
  Northumb. . . . 117 F7
  Staffs 75 E8
  Suff 56 B3
Stanton by Bridge . 63 B7
Stanton-by-Dale . 76 F4
Stanton Drew . . . 23 C7
Stanton
  Fitzwarren . . . 38 E1
Stanton Harcourt . 38 D4
Stanton Hill 76 C4
Stanton in Peak . . 76 C2
Stanton Lacy 49 B6
Stanton Long 61 E5
Stanton-on-the-
  Wolds 77 F6
Stanton Prior 23 C8
Stanton St
  Bernard 25 C5
Stanton St John . . 39 D5
Stanton St Quintin 24 B4
Stanton Street . . . 56 C3

Stanton under
  Bardon 63 C8
Stanton upon Hine
  Heath 61 B5
Stanton Wick 23 C8
Stanwardine in the
  Fields 60 B4
Stanwardine in the
  Wood 60 B4
Stanway Essex 43 B5
  Glos 51 F5
Stanway Green 57 B6
Stanwell 27 B8
Stanwell Moor 27 B8
Stanwick 53 B7
Stanwick-St-
  John 101 C6
Stanwix 108 D4
Stanydale 160 H4
Staoinebrig 148 E2
Stape 103 E5
Stapehill 13 D8
Stapeley 74 E3
Stapenhill 63 B6
Staple Kent 31 D6
  Som 22 E3
Staple Cross 18 C4
Staplefield 17 B6
Staple Fitzpaine . . 11 C7
Stapleford Cambs . . 55 D5
  Herts 41 C6
  Leics 64 C5
  Lincs 77 D8
  Notts 76 F4
  Wilts 25 F5
Stapleford Abbotts 41 E8
Stapleford Tawney . 41 E8
Staplegrove 11 B7
Staplehay 11 B7
Staplehurst 29 E8
Staplers 15 F6
Stapleton Bristol . . 23 B8
  Cumb 108 B5
  Hereford 48 C5
  Leics 63 E8
  N Yorks 101 C7
  Shrops 60 D4
  Som 12 B2
Stapley 11 C6
Staploe 54 C2
Staplow 49 E8
Star Anglesey 82 D5
  Fife 128 D5
  Pembs 45 F4
  Som 23 D6
Stara 159 F3
Starbeck 95 D6
Starbotton 94 B2
Starcross 10 F4
Stareton 51 B8
Starkholmes 76 D3
Starlings Green . . . 55 F5
Starston 68 F5
Startforth 101 C5
Startley 37 F6
Stathe 11 B8
Stathern 77 F7
Station Town 111 F7
Staughton Green . . 54 C2
Staughton
  Highway 54 C2
Staunton Glos 36 B4
  Glos 36 C2
Staunton in the
  Vale 77 E8
Staunton on
  Arrow 49 C5
Staunton on Wye . . 49 E5
Staveley Derbys . . . 76 B4
  N Yorks 95 C6
  W&F 99 E6
  W&F 99 F5
Staverton Devon . . . 7 C5
  Glos 37 B5
  Wilts 24 C3
  W Nhants 52 C3
Staverton Bridge . . 37 B5
Stawell 23 F5
Staxigoe 158 E5
Staxton 97 B6
Staylittle 59 E5
Staynall 92 E3
Staythorpe 77 D7
Stean 94 B3
Stearsby 96 B2
Steart 22 E4
Stebbing 42 B2
Stebbing Green . . . 42 B2
Stedham 16 B2
Steele Road 115 E8
Steen's Bridge 49 D7
Steep 15 B8
Steeple Dorset 13 F7
  Essex 43 D5
Steeple Ashton . . . 24 D4
Steeple Aston 38 B4
Steeple Barton . . . 38 B4
Steeple
  Bumpstead 55 E7
Steeple Claydon . . 39 B6
Steeple Gidding . . 65 F8
Steeple Langford . . 24 F5
Steeple Morden . . 54 E3
Steep Marsh 15 B8
Steeton 94 E3
Stein 148 C7
Steinmanhill 153 D7
Stelling Minnis . . . 30 E5
Stemster 158 D3
Stemster House . . 158 D3
Stenalees 4 D5
Stenhousemuir . . 127 F7
Stenigot 91 F6
Stenness 160 F4
Stenscholl 149 B9
Stenso 159 F4
Stenson 63 B7
Stenton E Loth. . . . 122 B2
  Fife 128 E4
Stenwith 77 F8
Stepaside 32 D2
Stepping Hill 87 F7
Steppingley 53 F8
Stepps 119 C6
Sterndale Moor . . . 75 C8
Sternfield 57 C7
Sterridge 20 E4
Stert 24 D5
Stetchworth 55 D7

Stevenage 41 B5
Stevenston 118 E2
Steventon Hants . . 26 E3
  Oxon. 38 E4
Stevington 53 D7
Stewartby 53 E8
Stewarton Argyll . . 143 G2
  E Ayrs. 118 E4
Stewkley 40 B1
Stewton 91 F7
Steyne Cross 15 F7
Steyning 17 C5
Steynton 44 E4
Stibb 8 C4
Stibbard 81 E5
Stibb Cross 9 C6
Stibb Green 25 C7
Stibbington 65 E7
Stichill 122 F3
Sticker 4 D4
Stickford 79 D6
Sticklepath 9 E8
Stickney 79 D6
Stiffkey 81 C5
Stifford's Bridge . . 50 E2
Stillingfleet 95 E8
Stillington N Yorks . 95 C8
  Stockton 102 B1
Stilton 65 F8
Stinchcombe 36 E4
Stinsford 12 E5
Stirchley 61 D7
Stirkoke House . . . 158 E5
Stirling Aberds . . . 153 D11
  Stirling 127 E6
Stisted 42 B3
Stithians 3 C6
Stittenham 151 D9
Stivichall 51 B8
Stixwould 78 C4
Stoak 73 B8
Stobieside 119 F6
Stobo 120 F4
Stoborough 13 F7
Stoborough Green . 13 F7
Stobshiel 121 C7
Stobswood 117 E8
Stock 42 E2
Stockbridge 25 F8
Stockbury 30 C2
Stockcross 26 C2
Stockdalewath . . . 108 E3
Stockerston 64 E5
Stock Green 50 D4
Stockheath 15 D8
Stockiemuir 126 F4
Stockingford 63 E7
Stocking Pelham . . 41 B7
Stockland 11 D7
Stockland Bristol . . 22 E4
Stockleigh English 10 D3
Stockleigh
  Pomeroy 10 D3
Stockley 24 C5
Stocklinch 11 C8
Stockport 87 E6
Stocksbridge 88 E3
Stocksfield 110 C3
Stockton Hereford . . 49 C7
  Norf 69 E6
  Shrops 60 D2
  Shrops 61 E7
  Warks 52 C2
  Wilts 24 F4
Stockton Heath . . . 86 F4
Stockton-on-
  Tees 102 C2
Stockton on Teme . 50 C2
Stockton on the
  Forest 96 D2
Stock Wood 50 D5
Stodmarsh 31 C6
Stody 81 D6
Stoer 156 G3
Stoford Som 12 C3
  Wilts 25 F5
Stogumber 22 F2
Stogursey 22 E4
Stoke Devon 8 B4
  Hants 15 D8
  Hants 26 D2
  Medway 30 B2
  Suff 57 E5
Stoke Abbott 12 D2
Stoke Albany 64 F5
Stoke Ash 56 B5
Stoke Bardolph . . . 77 E6
Stoke Bliss 49 C8
Stoke Bruerne 52 E5
Stoke by Clare 55 E8
Stoke-by-Nayland 56 F3
Stoke Canon 10 E4
Stoke Charity 26 F2
Stoke Climsland . . .5 B8
Stoke D'Abernon . . 28 D2
Stoke Doyle 65 F7
Stoke Dry 65 E5
Stoke Farthing . . . 13 B8
Stoke Ferry 67 E7
Stoke Fleming 7 E6
Stokeford 13 F6
Stoke Gabriel 7 D6
Stoke Gifford 23 B8
Stoke Golding 63 E7
Stoke Goldington . 53 E6
Stoke Green 40 F2
Stokeham 77 B7
Stoke Hammond . . 40 B1
Stoke Heath 61 B6
Stoke Holy Cross . . 68 D5
Stokeinteignhead . .7 B7
Stoke Lacy 49 E8
Stoke Lyne 39 B5
Stoke Mandeville . . 39 C8
Stokenchurch 39 E7
Stoke Newington . . 41 F6
Stokenham 7 E6
Stoke on Tern 61 B6
Stoke-on-Trent . . . 75 E5
Stoke Orchard 37 B6
Stoke Poges 40 F2
Stoke Prior
  Hereford 49 D7
  Worcs 50 C4
Stoke Rivers 20 F5
Stoke Rochford . . . 65 B6
Stoke Row 39 F6
Stoke St Gregory . . 11 B8
Stoke St Mary 11 B7

Stoke St Michael . . 23 E8
Stoke St
  Milborough 61 F5
Stokesay 60 F4
Stokesby 69 C7
Stokesley 102 D3
Stoke sub
  Hamdon 12 C2
Stoke Talmage . . . 39 E6
Stoke Trister 12 B5
Stoke Wake 13 D5
Stolford 22 E4
Stondon Massey . . 42 D1
Stone Bucks. 39 C7
  Glos 36 E3
  Kent 19 C6
  Kent 29 B6
  Staffs 75 F6
  S Yorks 89 F6
  Worcs 50 B3
Stone Allerton 23 D6
Ston Easton 23 D8
Stone Bridge
  Corner 66 D2
Stonebroom 76 D4
Stone Chair 88 B2
Stone Cross E Sus . . 18 E3
  Kent 31 D7
Stone-edge Batch . 23 B6
Stoneferry 97 F7
Stonefield 119 D6
Stonegate E Sus . . . 18 C3
  N Yorks. 103 D5
Stonegrave 96 B2
Stonehaugh 109 B7
Stonehaven 141 F7
Stonehouse Glos . . 37 D5
  Northumb. 109 D6
  S Lanark 119 E7
Stone House 100 F2
Stoneleigh 51 B8
Stonely 54 C2
Stonesby 64 B5
Stonesfield 38 C3
Stone's Green 43 B7
Stone Street Kent . . 29 D6
  Suff 56 F3
  Suff 69 F6
Stonethwaite 98 C4
Stoneybreck 160 N8
Stoneyburn 120 C2
Stoney Cross 14 C3
Stoneygate
  Aberds 153 E10
  Leicester 64 D3
Stoneyhills 43 E5
Stoneykirk 104 D4
Stoney Middleton . 76 B2
Stoney Stanton . . . 63 E8
Stoney Stoke 24 F2
Stoney Stratton . . . 23 F8
Stoney Stretton . . . 60 D3
Stoneywood
  Aberdeen 141 C7
  Falk 127 F6
Stonganess 160 C7
Stonham Aspal . . . 56 D5
Stonnall 62 D4
Stonor 39 F7
Stonton Wyville . . . 64 E4
Stony Cross 50 E2
Stonyfield 151 D9
Stony Stratford . . . 53 E5
Stoodleigh 10 C4
Stopes 88 F3
Stopham 16 C4
Stopsley 40 B4
Stores Corner 57 E7
Storeton 85 F4
Stornoway 155 D9
Storridge 50 E2
Storrington 16 C4
Storrs 99 E5
Storth 99 F6
Storwood 96 E3
Stotfield 152 A2
Stotfold 54 F3
Stottesdon 61 F6
Stoughton Leics . . . 64 D3
  Sur 27 D7
  W Sus 16 C2
Stoul 147 B10
Stoulton 50 E4
Stourbridge 62 F3
Stourpaine 13 D6
Stourport on
  Severn 50 B3
Stour Provost 13 B5
Stour Row 13 B6
Stourton Staffs 62 F2
  Warks 51 F7
  Wilts 24 F2
Stourton Caundle . 12 C5
Stove Orkney 159 E7
  Shetland 160 L6
Stoven 69 F7
Stow Borders 121 E7
  Lincs. 78 F3
  Lincs. 90 F2
Stow Bardolph . . . 67 D6
Stow Bedon 68 E2
Stowbridge 67 D6
Stow cum Quy 55 C6
Stowe 48 B5
Stowe-by-
  Chartley 62 B4
Stowe Green 36 D2
Stowell 12 B4
Stowford 9 F6
Stowlangtoft 56 C3
Stow Longa 54 B2
Stow Maries 42 E4
Stowmarket 56 D4
Stow-on-the-
  Wold 38 B1
Stowting 30 E5
Stowupland 56 D4
Straad 145 G2
Strachan 141 E5
Stradbroke 57 B6
Stradishall 55 D8
Stradsett 67 D6
Stragglethorpe . . . 78 D2
Straid 112 E1
Straith 113 F8
Straiton Edin 121 C5
  S Ayrs. 112 D3
Straloch Aberds . . 141 B7

Straloch continued
  Perth 133 C7
Stramshall 75 F7
Strang 84 E3
Stranraer 104 C4
Stratfield
  Mortimer 26 C4
Stratfield Saye . . . 26 C4
Stratfield Turgis . . 26 D4
Stratford 41 F6
Stratford St
  Andrew 57 C7
Stratford St Mary . . 56 F4
Stratford Sub
  Castle 25 F6
Stratford Tony . . . 13 B8
Stratford-upon-
  Avon 51 D6
Strath Highld 149 A12
  Highld 158 E4
Strathan Highld . . 136 E2
  Highld 156 G3
  Highld 157 C8
Strathaven 119 E7
Strathblane 119 B5
Strathcanaird . . . 156 J4
Strathcarron 150 G2
Strathcoil 124 B2
Strathdon 140 C2
Strathellie 153 B10
Strathkinness . . . 129 C6
Strathmashie
  House 137 E8
Strathmiglo 128 C4
Strathmore
  Lodge 158 F3
Strathpeffer 150 F7
Strathrannoch . . . 150 D6
Strathtay. 133 D6
Strathvaich
  Lodge 150 D6
Strathwhillan . . . 143 E11
Strathy 157 C11
Strathyre 126 C4
Stratton Corn 8 D4
  Dorset 12 E4
  Glos 37 D7
Stratton Audley . . . 39 B6
Stratton on the
  Fosse. 23 D8
Stratton St
  Margaret 38 F1
Stratton St
  Michael 68 E5
Stratton Strawless 81 E8
Stravithie 129 C7
Streat 17 C7
Streatham 28 B4
Streatley C Beds . . . 40 B3
  W Berks. 39 F5
Street Lancs 92 D5
  N Yorks. 103 D5
  Som 23 F6
Street Dinas 73 F7
Street End Kent . . . 30 D5
  W Sus 16 E2
Street Gate 110 D5
Streethay 62 C5
Streetlam 101 E8
Streetly 62 E4
Street Lydan 73 F8
Streetly End 55 E7
Strefford 60 F4
Strelley 76 E5
Strensall 96 C2
Stretcholt 22 E4
Strete 7 E6
Stretford 87 E6
Strethall 55 F5
Stretham 55 B6
Strettington 16 D2
Stretton ChesW . . 73 D8
  Derbys 76 C3
  Rutland 65 C6
  Staffs 62 C2
  Staffs 63 B6
  Warr. 86 F4
Stretton
  Grandison 49 E8
Stretton-on-
  Dunsmore 52 B2
Stretton-on-Fosse 51 F7
Stretton Sugwas . . 49 E6
Stretton under
  Fosse. 63 F8
Stretton
  Westwood 61 E5
Strichen 153 C9
Strines 87 F7
Stringston 22 E3
Strixton 53 C7
Stroat 36 E2
Stromeferry 149 E13
Stromemore 149 E13
Stromness 159 H3
Stronaba 136 F5
Stronachlachar . . 126 C3
Stronchreggan . . . 130 B4
Stronchrubie 156 H5
Strone Argyll 145 E10
  Highld 136 F4
  Highld 137 B8
  Invclyd 118 B2
Stronmilchan 125 C7
Strontian 130 C2
Strood 29 C8
Strood Green Sur . . 28 E3
  W Sus 16 B4
  W Sus 28 F2
Stroud Glos 37 D5
  Hants 15 B8
Stroud Green 42 E4
Stroxton 78 F2
Struan Highld 149 E8
  Perth 133 C5
Strubby 91 F8
Strumpshaw 69 D6
Strutherhill 119 E7
Struy 150 H6
Stryt-issa 73 E6
Stuartfield 153 D9
Stubbington 15 D6
Stubbins 87 C5
Stubbs Cross 19 B6
Stubbs Green 69 E6
Stubb's Green 69 E5
Stubhampton 13 C7
Stub Place 98 E2
Stubton 77 E8

Stuckgowan 126 D2
Stuckton 14 C2
Stud Green 27 B6
Studham 40 C3
Studland 13 F8
Studley Warks. . . . 51 C5
  Wilts 24 B4
Studley Roger 95 B5
Stump Cross 55 E6
Stuntney 55 B6
Sturbridge 74 F5
Sturmer 55 E7
Sturminster
  Marshall 13 D7
Sturminster
  Newton 13 C5
Sturry 31 C5
Sturton 90 D3
Sturton by Stow . . 90 F2
Sturton le Steeple . 89 F8
Stuston 56 B5
Stutton N Yorks . . . 95 E7
  Suff 57 F5
Styal 87 F6
Styrrup 89 E7
Suainebost 155 A10
Suardail 155 D9
Succoth Aberds . . 152 E4
  Argyll 125 E8
Suckley 50 D2
Suckquoy 159 K5
Sudborough 65 F6
Sudbourne 57 D8
  Mon 36 F2
Sudbrooke 78 B3
Sudbury Derbys . . . 75 F8
  London 40 F4
  Suff 56 E2
Suddie 151 F9
Sudgrove 37 D6
Suffield Norf 81 D8
  N Yorks 103 E7
Sugnall 74 F4
Suladale 149 C8
Sulaisiadar 155 D10
Sulby 84 C3
Sulgrave 52 E3
Sulham 26 B4
Sulhamstead 26 C4
  Suff 57 B6
Sulland 159 D6
Sullington 16 C4
Sullom 160 F5
Sullom Voe Oil
  Terminal 160 F5
Sully 22 C3
Sumburgh 160 N6
Summer Bridge . . 94 C5
Summercourt 4 D3
Summerfield 80 D3
Summergangs 97 F7
Summer-house . . 101 C7
Summerleaze 35 F8
Summersdale 16 D2
Summerseat 87 C5
Summertown 39 D5
Summit 87 D7
Sunbury-on-
  Thames 28 C2
Sundaywell 113 F8
Sunderland Argyll . 142 B3
  Cumb 107 F8
  T&W. 111 D6
Sunderland
  Bridge. 111 F5
Sundhope 115 B6
Sundon Park 40 B3
Sundridge 29 D5
Sunipol 146 F6
Sunk Island 91 C6
Sunningdale 27 C7
Sunninghill 27 C7
Sunningwell 38 D4
Sunniside Durham . 110 F4
  T&W. 110 D5
Sunnyhurst 86 B4
Sunnylaw 127 E6
Sunnyside 28 F4
Sunton 25 D7
Surbiton 28 C2
Surby 84 E2
Surfleet 66 B2
Surfleet Seas End . 66 B2
Surlingham 69 D6
Sustead 81 D7
Sutcombe 8 C5
Suton 68 E3
Sutors of
  Cromarty 151 E11
Sutterby 79 B6
Sutterton 79 F5
Sutton Cambs 54 B5
  C Beds 54 E3
  Kent 31 E7
  London 28 C3
  Mers 86 E3
  Norf 69 B6
  Notts 77 F7
  N Yorks 89 B5
  Oxon. 38 D4
  Pboro 65 E7
  Shrops 61 F7
  Shrops 74 F3
  Som 23 F8
  Staffs 61 B7
  Suff 57 E7
  S Yorks 89 C6
  W Sus 16 C3
Sutton at Hone . . . 29 B6
Sutton Bassett . . . 64 E4
Sutton Benger . . . 24 B4
Sutton Bonington . 64 B2
Sutton Bridge 66 B4
Sutton Cheney . . . 63 D8
Sutton Coldfield . . 62 E5
Sutton Courtenay . 39 E5
Sutton Crosses . . . 66 B4
Sutton Grange . . . 95 B5
Sutton Green 27 D8
Sutton Howgrave . 95 B6
Sutton in Ashfield . 76 D4
Sutton-in-Craven . 94 E3
Sutton Ings 97 F7
Sutton in the Elms . 64 E2
Sutton Lane Ends . 75 B6
Sutton Leach 86 E3

Sutton Maddock . . 61 D7
Sutton Mallet 23 F5
Sutton Mandeville . 13 B7
Sutton Manor 86 E3
Sutton Montis 12 B4
Sutton on Hull 97 F7
Sutton on Sea 91 F9
Sutton-on-
  the-Forest. 95 C8
Sutton on the Hill . 76 F3
Sutton on Trent . . . 77 C7
Sutton St Edmund . 66 C3
Sutton St James . . 66 C3
Sutton St Nicholas . 49 E7
Sutton Scarsdale . . 76 C4
Sutton Scotney . . . 26 F2
Sutton under
  Brailes 51 F8
Sutton-under-
  Whitestonecliffe 102 F2
Sutton upon
  Derwent 96 E3
Sutton Valence . . . 30 E2
Sutton Veny 24 E3
Sutton Waldron . . . 13 C6
Sutton Weaver . . . 74 B2
Sutton Wick 23 D7
Swaby 79 B6
Swadlincote 63 C7
Swaffham 67 D8
Swaffham Bulbeck 55 C6
Swaffham Prior . . . 55 C6
Swafield 81 D8
Swainby 102 D2
Swainshill 49 E6
Swainsthorpe 68 D5
Swainswick 24 C2
Swalcliffe 51 F8
Swalecliffe 30 C5
Swallow 91 D5
Swallowcliffe 13 B7
Swallowfield 26 C5
Swallownest 89 F5
Swallows Cross . . . 42 E2
Swanage 13 G8
Swanbister 159 H4
Swanbourne 39 B8
Swan Green
  Ches W 74 B4
  Suff 57 B6
Swanland 90 B3
Swanley 29 C6
Swanley Village . . 29 C6
Swanmore 15 C6
Swannington Leics . 63 C8
  Norf 68 C4
Swanscombe 29 B7
Swansea
  = Abertawe 33 E7
Swanton Abbott . . 81 E8
Swanton Morley . . 68 C3
Swanton Novers . . 81 D6
Swanton Street . . . 30 D2
Swanwick Derbys . . 76 D4
  Hants 15 D6
Swarby 78 E3
Swardeston 68 D5
Swarister 160 E7
Swarkestone 63 B7
Swarland 117 D7
Swarland Estate . 117 D7
Swarthmoor 92 B2
Swathwick 76 C3
Swaton 78 F4
Swavesey 54 C4
Sway 14 E3
Swayfield 65 B6
Swaythling 14 C5
Sweet Green 49 C8
Sweetham 10 E3
Sweethouse 5 C5
Swefling 57 C7
Swepstone 63 C7
Swerford 51 F8
Swettenham 74 C5
Swetton 94 B4
Swffryd 35 E6
Swiftsden 18 C4
Swilland 57 D5
Swillington 95 F6
Swimbridge 9 B8
Swimbridge
  Newland 20 F5
Swinbrook 38 C2
Swinderby 77 C8
Swindon Glos 37 B6
  Staffs 62 E2
  Swindon. 38 F1
Swine 97 F7
Swinefleet 89 B8
Swineshead
  Bedford 53 C8
  Lincs. 78 E5
Swineshead
  Bridge. 78 E5
Swiney 158 G4
Swinford Leics . . . 52 B3
  Oxon. 38 D4
Swingate 76 E5
Swingfield Minnis . 31 E6
Swingfield Street . . 31 E6
Swinhoe 117 B8
Swinhope 91 E6
Swining 160 G6
Swinithwaite 101 F5
Swinnow Moor . . . 94 F5
Swinscoe 75 E8
Swinside Hall . . . 116 C3
Swinstead 65 B7
Swinton Borders . . 122 E4
  Gtr Man 87 D5
  N Yorks 94 B4
  N Yorks 96 B3
  S Yorks 88 E5
Swintonmill 122 E4
Swithland 64 C2
Swordale 151 E8
Swordland 147 B10
Swordly 157 C10
Sworton Heath . . . 86 F4
Swydffynnon 47 C5
Swynnerton 75 F5
Swyre 12 F3
Sychtyn 59 D6
Syde 37 C6
Sydenham London . 28 B4
  Oxon. 39 D7
Sydenham
  Damerel 6 B2

Syderstone 80 D4
Sydling St
  Nicholas 12 E4
Sydmonton 26 D2
Syerston 77 E7
Syke 87 C6
Sykehouse 89 C7
Sykes 93 D6
Syleham 57 B6
Sylen 33 D6
Symbister 160 G7
Symington S Ayrs . 118 F3
  S Lanark 120 F2
Symondsbury 12 E2
Symonds Yat 36 C2
Synod Inn 46 D3
Syre 157 E9
Syreford 37 B7
Syresham 52 E4
Syston Leics 64 C3
  Lincs. 78 E2
Sytchampton 50 C3
Sywell 53 C6

T

Taagan 150 E3
Tàbost 155 A10
Tabost 155 F8
Tackley 38 B4
Tacleit 154 D6
Tacolneston 68 E4
Tadcaster 95 E7
Taddington 75 B8
Taddiport 9 C6
Tadley 26 C4
Tadlow 54 E3
Tadmarton 51 F8
Tadworth 28 D3
Tafarnau-bach . . . 35 C5
Tafarn-y-gelyn . . . 73 C5
Taff's Well 35 F5
Tafolwern 59 D5
Tai 83 E7
Taibach 34 F1
Tai-bach 59 B8
Taigh a
  Ghearraidh . . . 148 A2
Tai-mawr 72 E3
Tain Highld 151 C10
  Highld 158 D4
Tainant 73 E6
Tainlon 82 F4
Tairbeart
  = Tarbert 154 G6
Tai'r-Bull 34 B3
Tairgwaith 33 C8
Tai-Ucha 72 D4
Takeley 42 B1
Takeley Street . . . 41 B8
Talachddu 48 F2
Talacre 85 F2
Talardd 59 B5
Talaton 11 E5
Talbenny 44 D3
Talbot Green 34 F4
Talbot Village 13 E8
Tale 11 D5
Talerddig 59 D6
Talgarreg 46 D3
Talgarth 48 F3
Taliesin 58 E3
Talisker 149 E8
Talke 74 D5
Talkin 109 D5
Talladale 150 D2
Talla Linnfoots . . 114 B4
Tallarn Green 73 E8
Tallentire 107 F8
Talley 46 F5
Tallington 65 D7
Talmine 157 C8
Talog 32 B4
Talsarn 34 B1
Tal-sarn 46 D4
Talsarnau 71 D7
Talskiddy 4 C4
Talwrn Anglesey . . 82 D4
  Wrex 73 E6
Tal-y-bont Ceredig . 58 F3
  Conwy 83 D7
  Gwyn 71 E6
  Gwyn 83 D6
Tal-y-cafn 83 D7
Talygarn 34 F4
Talyllyn 58 D4
Tal-y-llyn 58 D4
Talysarn 82 F4
Talywain 35 D6
Tal-y-wern 58 D5
Tame Bridge 102 D3
Tamerton Foliot . . .6 C2
Tamworth 63 D6
Tandem 88 C2
Tanden 19 B6
Tandridge 28 D4
Tanerdy 33 B5
Tanfield 110 D4
Tanfield Lea 110 D4
Tangasdal 148 J1
Tangiers 44 D4
Tangley 25 D8
Tanglwst 46 F2
Tangmere 16 D3
Tangwick 160 F4
Tan Hinon 59 F5
Tankersley 88 D4
Tankerton 30 C5
Tan-lan Conwy . . . 83 E7
  Gwyn 71 C7
Tannach 158 F5
Tannachie 141 F6
Tannadice 134 D4
Tannington 57 C6
Tansley 76 D3
Tansley Knoll 76 C3
Tansor 65 E7
Tantobie 110 D4
Tanton 102 C3
Tanworth-in-
  Arden 51 B6
Tan-y-bwlch 71 C7
Tan-y-fron 72 C3
Tan-y-graig
  Anglesey 82 D5
  Gwyn 70 D4
Tan-y-groes 45 E4

Tan-y-pistyll 59 B7
Tan-yr-allt 82 F4
Tanygrisiau 71 C7
Tan-y-groes 45 E4
Taobh a Chaolais . 148 G2
Taobh a' Ghlinne . 155 F5
Taobh a Thuath Loch
  Aineort 148 F2
Taobh a Tuath Loch
  Baghasdail . . . 148 G2
Taobh Tuath 154 J4
Taplow 40 F2
Tapton 76 B3
Tarbat House . . . 151 D10
Tarbert Argyll . . . 143 C7
  Argyll 144 E5
  Argyll 145 G7
Tarbert
  = Tairbeart . . . 154 G6
Tarbet Argyll 126 D2
  Highld 147 B10
  Highld 156 E4
Tarbock Green . . . 86 F2
Tarbolton 112 B4
Tarbrax 120 D3
Tardebigge 50 C5
Tarfside 134 B4
Tarland 140 D3
Tarleton 86 B2
Tarlogie 151 C10
Tarlscough 86 C2
Tarlton 37 E6
Tarnbrook 93 D5
Tarporley 74 C2
Tarr 22 F3
Tarrant Crawford . 13 D7
Tarrant Gunville . . 13 C7
Tarrant Hinton . . . 13 C7
Tarrant Keyneston . 13 D7
Tarrant
  Launceston . . . 13 D7
Tarrant Monkton . 13 D7
Tarrant Rawston . . 13 D7
Tarrant Rushton . . 13 D7
Tarrel 151 C11
Tarring Neville . . . 17 D8
Tarrington 49 E8
Tarsappie 128 B3
Tarskavaig 149 H10
Tarves 153 E8
Tarvie Highld 150 F7
  Perth 133 C7
Tarvin 73 C8
Tasburgh 68 E5
Tasley 61 E6
Taston 38 B3
Tatenhill 63 B6
Tathall End 53 E6
Tatham 93 C6
Tathwell 91 F7
Tatling End 40 F3
Tatsfield 28 D5
Tattenhall 73 D8
Tattenhoe 53 F6
Tatterford 80 E4
Tattersett 80 D4
Tattershall 78 D5
Tattershall Bridge . 78 D4
Tattershall Thorpe 78 D5
Tattingstone 56 F5
Tatworth 11 D8
Taunton 11 B7
Taverham 68 C4
Tavernspite 32 C2
Tavistock 6 B2
Taw Green 9 E8
Tawstock 9 B7
Taxal 75 B7
Tay Bridge 129 B6
Tayinloan 143 D7
Taymouth Castle . 132 E4
Taynish 144 E6
Taynton Glos 36 B4
  Oxon. 38 C2
Taynuilt 125 B6
Tayport 129 B6
Tayvallich 144 E6
Tealby 91 E5
Tealing 134 F4
Teangue 149 H11
Teanna Mhachair . 148 B2
Tebay 99 D8
Tebworth 40 B2
Tedburn St Mary . . 10 E3
Teddington Glos . . 50 F4
  London 28 B2
Tedstone
  Delamere 49 D8
Tedstone Wafre . . 49 D8
Teeton 52 B4
Teffont Evias 24 F4
Teffont Magna . . . 24 F4
Tegryn 45 F4
Teigh 65 C5
Teigncombe 9 F8
Teigngrace 7 B6
Teignmouth 7 B7
Telford 61 D6
Telham 18 D4
Tellisford 24 D3
Telscombe 17 D8
Telscombe Cliffs . . 17 D7
Templand 114 F3
Temple Corn 5 B6
  Glasgow 118 C5
  Midloth. 121 D6
Temple Balsall . . . 51 B7
Temple Bar Carms . 33 C6
  Ceredig 46 D4
Temple Cloud 23 D8
Temple Combe . . . 12 B5
Temple Ewell 31 E6
Temple Grafton . . 51 D6
Temple Guiting . . . 37 B7
Templehall 128 E4
Temple
  Herdewyke 51 D8
Temple Hirst 89 B7
Temple
  Normanton . . . 76 C4
Temple Sowerby . . 99 B8
Templeton Devon . 10 C3
  Pembs 32 C2
Templeton Bridge . 10 C3
Templetown 110 D4
Tempsford 54 D2
Tenbury Wells . . . 49 C7
Tenby = Dinbych-y-
  Pysgod 32 D2
Tendring 43 B7

Tendring Green . . . 43 D7
Ten Mile Bank . . . 67 E6
Tenston 159 G3
Tenterden 19 B5
Terling 42 C3
Ternhill 74 F3
Terregles Banks . . 107 B6
Terrick 39 D8
Terrington 96 B2
Terrington St
  Clement 66 C5
Terrington St
  John 66 C5
Teston 29 D8
Testwood 14 C4
Tetbury 37 E5
Tetbury Upton. . . . 37 E5
Tetchill 73 F7
Tetcott 8 E5
Tetford 79 B6
Tetney 91 D7
Tetney Lock 91 D7
Tetsworth 39 D6
Tettenhall 62 E2
Teuchan 153 E10
Teversal 76 C4
Teversham 55 D5
Teviothead 115 D7
Tewel 141 F7
Tewin 41 C5
Tewkesbury 50 F3
Teynham 30 C3
Thackthwaite 98 B3
Thainston 135 B6
Thakeham 16 C5
Thame 39 D7
Thames Ditton . . . 28 C2
Thames Haven . . . 42 F3
Thamesmead 41 F7
Thanington 30 D5
Tharston 68 E4
Thatcham 26 C3
Thatto Heath 86 E3
Thaxted 55 F7
The Aird 149 C9
Theakston 101 F8
Thealby 90 C2
Theale Som 23 E6
  W Berks. 26 B4
The Arms 67 E8
Thearne 97 F6
The Bage 48 E4
The Balloch 127 C7
The Barony 159 F3
Theberton 57 C8
The Bog. 60 E3
The Bourne 27 E6
The Braes 149 E10
The Broad 49 C6
The Butts 24 E2
The Camp Glos . . . 37 D6
  Herts 40 D4
The Chequer 73 E8
The City 39 E7
The Common 25 F7
The Craigs 150 B7
The Cronk 84 C3
Theddingworth . . . 64 F3
Theddlethorpe All
  Saints 91 F8
Theddlethorpe St
  Helen 91 F8
The Dell 69 E7
The Den 118 D3
The Eals 116 F3
The Eaves 36 D3
The Flatt 109 B5
The Four Alls 74 F3
The Garths 160 B8
The Green Cumb . . 98 F3
  Wilts 24 F3
The Grove 107 B6
The Hall 160 D8
The Haven 27 F8
The Heath Norf. . . 81 E7
  Suff 56 F5
The Hill 98 F3
The Howe IoM 84 F1
  W&F 99 F6
The Hundred 49 C7
Thelbridge Barton . 10 C2
The Lee 40 D2
The Lhen 84 B3
Thelnetham 56 B4
Thelveton 68 F4
Thelwall 86 F4
The Marsh Powys. . 60 E3
  Wilts 37 F7
Themelthorpe 81 E6
The Middles 110 D5
The Moor 18 C4
The Mumbles
  = Y Mwmbwls. . . 33 F7
The Murray 119 D6
The Neuk 141 E6
Thenford 52 E3
The Oval 24 C2
The Pole of Itlaw . 153 C6
The Quarry 36 E4
Therfield 54 F4
The Rhos 32 C1
The Rock 61 D6
The Ryde 41 D5
The Sands 27 E6
The Stocks 19 C5
Thetford Lincs . . . 65 C8
  Norf 67 F8
The Throat 27 C6
The Vauld 49 E7
The Wyke 61 D7
Theydon Bois 41 E7
Thickwood 24 B3
Thimbleby Lincs. . . 78 C5
  N Yorks 102 E2
Thingwall 85 F3
Thirdpart 118 E1
Thirlby 102 F2
Thirlestane 121 E8
Thirn 101 F7
Thirsk 102 F2
Thirtleby 97 F7
Thistleton Lancs . . 92 F4
  Rutland 65 C6
Thistley Green . . . 55 B7
Thixendale 96 C4

Thockrington ... 110 B2
Tholomas Drove ... 66 D3
Tholthorpe ... 95 C7
Thomas Chapel ... 32 D2
Thomas Close ... 108 E4
Thomastown ... 152 E5
Thompson ... 68 E2
Thomshill ... 152 C2
Thong ... 29 B7
Thongsbridge ... 88 D2
Thoralby ... 101 F5
Thoresway ... 91 E5
Thorganby Lincs ... 91 E6
  N Yorks ... 96 E2
Thorgill ... 103 E5
Thorington ... 57 B8
Thorington Street ... 56 F4
Thorlby ... 94 D2
Thorley ... 41 C7
Thorley Street
  Herts ... 41 C7
  IoW ... 14 F4
Thormanby ... 95 B7
Thornaby-on-
  Tees ... 102 C2
Thornage ... 81 D6
Thornborough
  Bucks ... 52 F5
  N Yorks ... 95 B5
Thornbury Devon ... 9 D6
  Hereford ... 49 D8
  S Glos ... 36 E3
  W Yorks ... 94 F4
Thornby ... 52 B4
Thorncliffe ... 75 D7
Thorncombe
  Dorset ... 11 D8
  Dorset ... 13 D6
Thorncombe
  Street ... 27 E8
Thorncote Green ... 54 E2
Thorncross ... 14 F5
Thorndon ... 56 C5
Thorndon Cross ... 9 E7
Thorne ... 89 C7
Thorner ... 95 E6
Thorne St
  Margaret ... 11 B5
Thorney Notts ... 77 B8
  Pboro ... 66 D2
Thorney Crofts ... 91 B6
Thorney Green ... 56 C4
Thorney Hill ... 14 E2
Thorney Toll ... 66 D3
Thornfalcon ... 11 B7
Thorngumbald ... 91 B6
Thornham ... 80 C3
Thornham Magna ... 56 B5
Thornham Parva ... 56 B5
Thornhaugh ... 65 D7
Thornhill Cardiff ... 35 F5
  Cumb ... 98 D2
  Derbys ... 88 F2
  Dumfries ... 113 E8
  Soton ... 15 C5
  Stirling ... 127 E5
  W Yorks ... 88 C3
Thornhill Edge ... 88 C3
Thornhill Lees ... 88 C3
Thornholme ... 97 C7
Thornley Durham ... 110 F4
  Durham ... 111 F6
Thornliebank ... 118 D5
Thorns ... 55 D8
Thornsett ... 87 F8
Thorns Green ... 87 F5
Thornthwaite
  Cumb ... 98 B4
  N Yorks ... 94 D4
Thornton Angus ... 134 E3
  Bucks ... 53 F5
  E Yorks ... 96 E3
  Fife ... 128 E4
  Lancs ... 92 E3
  Leics ... 63 D8
  Lincs ... 78 C5
  Mbro ... 102 C2
  Mers ... 85 D4
  Northumb ... 123 E5
  Pembs ... 44 E4
  W Yorks ... 94 F4
Thornton Curtis ... 90 C4
Thornton-hall ... 119 D5
Thornton Heath ... 28 C4
Thornton Hough ... 85 F4
Thornton in
  Craven ... 94 E2
Thornton-le-
  Beans ... 102 E1
Thornton-le-Clay ... 96 C2
Thornton-le-
  Dale ... 103 F6
Thornton le Moor ... 90 E4
Thornton-le-
  Moor ... 102 F1
Thornton-le-
  Moors ... 73 B8
Thornton-le-
  Street ... 102 F2
Thorntonloch ... 122 B3
Thorntonpark ... 122 E5
Thornton Rust ... 100 F4
Thornton
  Steward ... 101 F6
Thornton Watlass 101 F7
Thornwood
  Common ... 41 D7
Thornydykes ... 122 E2
Thoroton ... 77 E7
Thorp Arch ... 95 E7
Thorpe Derbys ... 75 D8
  E Yorks ... 97 E5
  Lincs ... 91 F8
  Norf ... 69 E7
  Notts ... 77 E7
  N Yorks ... 94 C3
  Sur ... 27 C8
Thorpe Abbotts ... 57 B5
Thorpe Acre ... 64 B2
Thorpe Arnold ... 64 B4
Thorpe Audlin ... 89 C5
Thorpe Bassett ... 96 B4
Thorpe Bay ... 43 F5
Thorpe by Water ... 65 E5
Thorpe Common ... 57 F6

Thorpe
  Constantine ... 63 D6
Thorpe Culvert ... 79 C7
Thorpe End ... 69 C5
Thorpe Fendykes ... 79 C7
Thorpe Green
  Essex ... 43 B7
  Suff ... 56 D3
Thorpe Hesley ... 88 E4
Thorpe in Balne ... 89 C6
Thorpe in the
  Fallows ... 90 F3
Thorpe Langton ... 64 E4
Thorpe Larches ... 102 B1
Thorpe-le-Soken ... 43 B7
Thorpe le Street ... 96 E4
Thorpe Malsor ... 53 B6
Thorpe Mandeville 52 E3
Thorpe Market ... 81 D8
Thorpe Marriot ... 68 C4
Thorpe Morieux ... 56 D3
Thorpeness ... 57 D8
Thorpe on the Hill ... 78 C2
Thorpe St Andrew ... 69 D5
Thorpe St Peter ... 79 C7
Thorpe Salvin ... 89 F6
Thorpe Satchville ... 64 C4
Thorpe Thewles ... 102 B2
Thorpe Tilney ... 78 D4
Thorpe
  Underwood ... 95 D7
Thorpe Waterville ... 65 F7
Thorpe Willoughby 95 F8
Thorrington ... 43 C6
Thorverton ... 10 D4
Thrandeston ... 56 B5
Thrapston ... 53 B7
Thrashbush ... 119 C7
Threapland Cumb ... 107 F8
  N Yorks ... 94 C2
Threapwood
  Ches W ... 73 E8
  Staffs ... 75 E7
Three Ashes ... 36 B2
Three Bridges ... 28 F3
Three Burrows ... 3 B6
Three Chimneys ... 18 B5
Three Cocks ... 48 F3
Three Crosses ... 33 E6
Three Cups
  Corner ... 18 C3
Threehammer
  Common ... 69 C6
Three Holes ... 66 D5
Threekingham ... 78 F3
Three Leg Cross ... 18 B3
Three Legged
  Cross ... 13 D8
Threemile Cross ... 26 C5
Threemilestone ... 3 B6
Threemiletown ... 120 B3
Three Oaks ... 18 D5
Threlkeld ... 99 B5
Threshfield ... 94 C2
Thrigby ... 69 C7
Thringarth ... 100 B4
Thringstone ... 63 C8
Thrintoft ... 101 E8
Thriplow ... 54 E5
Throckenholt ... 66 D3
Throcking ... 54 F4
Throckley ... 110 C4
Throckmorton ... 50 E4
Throphill ... 117 F7
Thropton ... 117 D6
Throwleigh ... 9 E8
Throwley ... 30 D3
Thrumpton ... 76 F5
Thrunton ... 117 C6
Thrupp Glos ... 37 D5
  Oxon ... 38 C4
Thrushelton ... 9 F6
Thrussington ... 64 C3
Thruxton Hants ... 25 E7
  Hereford ... 49 F6
Thrybergh ... 89 E5
Thulston ... 76 F4
Thundergay ... 143 D9
Thundersley ... 42 F3
Thundridge ... 41 C6
Thurcaston ... 64 C2
Thurcroft ... 89 F5
Thurgarton Norf ... 81 D7
  Notts ... 77 E6
Thurgoland ... 88 D3
Thurlaston Leics ... 64 E2
  Warks ... 52 B2
Thurlbear ... 11 B7
Thurlby Lincs ... 65 C8
  Lincs ... 78 C2
Thurleigh ... 53 D8
Thurlestone ... 6 E4
Thurloxton ... 22 F4
Thurlstone ... 88 D3
Thurlton ... 69 E7
Thurlwood ... 74 D5
Thurmaston ... 64 D3
Thurnby ... 64 D3
Thurne ... 69 C7
Thurnham Kent ... 30 D2
  Lancs ... 92 D4
Thurning Norf ... 81 E6
  N Nhants ... 65 F7
Thurnscoe ... 89 D5
Thurnscoe East ... 89 D5
Thursby ... 108 D3
Thursford ... 81 D5
Thursley ... 27 F7
Thurso ... 158 D3
Thurso East ... 158 D3
Thurstaston ... 85 F3
Thurston ... 56 C3
Thurstonfield ... 108 D3
Thurstonland ... 88 C2
Thurton ... 69 D6
Thurvaston ... 76 F2
Thuxton ... 68 D3
Thwaite N Yorks ... 100 E3
  Suff ... 56 C5
Thwaites ... 94 E3
Thwaite St Mary ... 69 E6
Thwaites Brow ... 94 E3
Thwing ... 97 B6
Tibbermore ... 128 B2
Tibberton Glos ... 36 B4
  Telford ... 61 B6
  Worcs ... 50 D4

Tibenham ... 68 F4
Tibshelf ... 76 C4
Tibthorpe ... 97 D5
Ticehurst ... 18 B3
Tichborne ... 26 F3
Tickencote ... 65 D6
Tickenham ... 23 B6
Tickhill ... 89 E6
Ticklerton ... 60 E4
Ticknall ... 63 B7
Tickton ... 97 E6
Tidcombe ... 25 D7
Tiddington Oxon ... 39 D6
  Warks ... 51 D7
Tidebrook ... 18 C3
Tideford ... 5 D8
Tideford Cross ... 5 C8
Tidenham ... 36 E2
Tideswell ... 75 B8
Tidmarsh ... 26 B4
Tidmington ... 51 F7
Tidpit ... 13 C8
Tidworth ... 25 E7
Tiers Cross ... 44 D4
Tiffield ... 52 D4
Tifty ... 153 D7
Tigerton ... 135 C5
Tigh-na-Blair ... 127 C6
Tighnabruaich ... 145 F8
Tighnafiline ... 155 J13
Tigley ... 7 C5
Tilbrook ... 53 C8
Tilbury ... 29 B7
Tilbury Juxta Clare 55 E8
Tile Cross ... 63 F5
Tile Hill ... 51 B7
Tilehurst ... 26 B4
Tilford ... 27 E6
Tilgate ... 28 F3
Tilgate Forest Row 28 F3
Tillathrowie ... 152 E4
Tilley ... 60 B5
Tillicoultry ... 127 E8
Tillingham ... 43 D5
Tillington Hereford ... 49 E6
  W Sus ... 16 B3
Tillington
  Common ... 49 E6
Tillyarblet ... 135 C5
Tillybirloch ... 141 D5
Tillycorthie ... 141 B8
Tillydrone ... 140 E5
Tillyfour ... 140 C4
Tillyfourie ... 140 C5
Tillygarmond ... 140 E5
Tillygreig ... 141 B7
Tillykerrie ... 141 B7
Tilmanstone ... 31 D7
Tilney All Saints ... 67 C5
Tilney High End ... 67 C5
Tilney St
  Lawrence ... 66 C5
Tilshead ... 24 E5
Tilstock ... 74 F2
Tilston ... 73 D8
Tilstone Fearnall ... 74 C2
Tilsworth ... 40 B2
Tilton on the Hill ... 64 D4
Timberland ... 78 D4
Timbersbrook ... 75 C5
Timberscombe ... 21 E8
Timble ... 94 D4
Timperley ... 87 F5
Timsbury Bath ... 23 D8
  Hants ... 14 B4
Timsgearraidh ... 154 D5
Timworth Green ... 56 C2
Tincleton ... 13 E5
Tindale ... 109 D6
Tingewick ... 52 F4
Tingley ... 88 B3
Tingrith ... 53 F8
Tingwall ... 159 F4
Tinhay ... 9 F5
Tinshill ... 95 F5
Tinsley ... 88 E5
Tintagel ... 8 F2
Tintern Parva ... 12 C3
Tintinhull ... 12 C3
Tintwistle ... 87 E8
Tinwald ... 114 F3
Tinwell ... 65 D7
Tipperty ... 141 B8
Tipsend ... 66 E5
Tiptoe ... 14 E3
Tipton ... 62 E3
Tipton St John ... 11 E5
Tiptree ... 42 C4
Tirabad ... 47 E7
Tiraghoil ... 146 J6
Tirley ... 37 B5
Tirphil ... 35 D5
Tir-y-dail ... 33 C7
Tisbury ... 13 B7
Tisman's Common 27 F8
Tissington ... 75 D8
Titchberry ... 8 B4
Titchfield ... 15 D6
Titchmarsh ... 53 B8
Titchwell ... 80 C3
Tithby ... 77 F6
Titley ... 48 C5
Titlington ... 117 C7
Titsey ... 28 D5
Tittensor ... 75 F5
Tittleshall ... 80 E4
Tiverton Ches W ... 74 C2
  Devon ... 10 C4
Tivetshall St
  Margaret ... 68 F4
Tivetshall St Mary ... 68 F4
Tividale ... 62 E3
Tivy Dale ... 88 D3
Tixall ... 62 B3
Tixover ... 65 D6
Toab Orkney ... 159 H6
  Shetland ... 160 M5
Toadmoor ... 76 D3
Tobermory ... 147 F8
Toberonochy ... 124 E3
Tobha Mor ... 148 E2
Tobhtarol ... 154 D6
Tobson ... 154 D6
Tocher ... 153 E6
Tockenham ... 24 B5
Tockenham Wick ... 37 F7
Tockholes ... 86 B4
Tockington ... 36 F3
Tockwith ... 95 D7

Todber ... 13 B6
Todding ... 49 B6
Toddington C Beds ... 40 B3
  Glos ... 50 F5
Todenham ... 51 F7
Todhills ... 108 C3
Todlachie ... 141 C5
Todmorden ... 87 B7
Todrig ... 115 C2
Todwick ... 89 F5
Toft Cambs ... 54 D4
  Lincs ... 65 C7
Toft Hill Durham ... 101 B6
  Lincs ... 78 C5
Toft Monks ... 69 E7
Toft next Newton ... 90 F4
Toftrees ... 80 E4
Tofts ... 158 D5
Toftwood ... 68 C2
Togston ... 117 D8
Tokavaig ... 149 G11
Tokers Green ... 26 B5
Tolastadh a
  Chaolais ... 154 D6
Tolastadh bho
  Thuath ... 155 C10
Toll Bar ... 89 D6
Tollard Royal ... 13 C7
Tollbar End ... 51 B8
Toll End ... 62 E3
Toller Fratrum ... 12 E3
Toller Porcorum ... 12 E3
Tollerton Notts ... 77 F6
  N Yorks ... 95 C8
Tollesbury ... 43 C5
Tolleshunt D'Arcy ... 43 C5
Tolleshunt Major ... 43 C5
Toll of Birness ... 153 E10
Tolm ... 155 D9
Tolpuddle ... 13 E5
Tolvah ... 138 E4
Tolworth ... 28 C2
Tomatin ... 138 B4
Tombreck ... 151 H9
Tomchrasky ... 137 C5
Tomdoun ... 136 D4
Tomich Highld ... 137 B6
  Highld ... 151 D9
Tomich House ... 151 G8
Tomintoul Aberds ... 139 E7
  Moray ... 139 C7
Tomnaven ... 152 E4
Tomnavoulin ... 139 B8
Tonbridge ... 29 E6
Tondu ... 34 F2
Tonfanau ... 58 D2
Tong Shrops ... 61 D7
  W Yorks ... 94 F5
Tonge ... 63 B8
Tongham ... 27 E6
Tongland ... 106 D3
Tong Norton ... 61 D7
Tongue ... 157 D8
Tongue End ... 65 C8
Tongwynlais ... 35 F5
Tonna ... 34 E1
Ton-Pentre ... 34 E3
Tonwell ... 41 C6
Tonypandy ... 34 E3
Tonyrefail ... 34 F4
Toot Baldon ... 39 D5
Toothill ... 14 C4
Toot Hill ... 41 D8
Topcliffe ... 95 B7
Topcroft ... 69 E5
Topcroft Street ... 69 E5
Top of Hebers ... 87 D6
Toppesfield ... 55 F8
Toppings ... 86 C5
Topsham ... 10 F4
Torbay ... 7 D7
Torbeg ... 143 F10
Torboll Farm ... 151 B10
Torbryan ... 7 C6
Torcross ... 7 E6
Tore ... 151 F9
Torinturk ... 145 G7
Torksey ... 77 B8
Torlum ... 148 C2
Torlundy ... 131 B5
Tormarton ... 24 B2
Tormisdale ... 142 C2
Tormitchell ... 112 E2
Tormore ... 143 E9
Tornagrain ... 151 G10
Tornahaish ... 139 D8
Tornaveen ... 140 D5
Torness ... 137 B8
Toronto ... 110 F4
Torpenhow ... 108 F2
Torphichen ... 120 B2
Torphins ... 140 D5
Torpoint ... 6 D2
Torquay ... 7 C7
Torquhan ... 121 E7
Torran Argyll ... 124 E4
  Highld ... 149 D10
  Highld ... 151 D10
Torrance ... 119 B6
Torrans ... 146 J7
Torranyard ... 118 E3
Torre ... 7 C7
Torridon ... 150 F2
Torridon House ... 149 C13
Torrin ... 149 F10
Torrisdale ... 157 C9
Torrisdale-
  Square ... 143 E8
Torrish ... 157 H12
Torrisholme ... 92 C4
Torroble ... 157 J8
Torry Aberdeen ... 141 D8
  Aberds ... 152 E4
Torryburn ... 128 F2
Torterston ... 153 D10
Torthorwald ... 107 B7
Tortington ... 16 D4
Tortworth ... 36 E4
Torvaig ... 149 D9
Torver ... 98 E4
Torwood ... 127 F7
Torworth ... 89 F7
Tosberry ... 8 B4
Toscaig ... 149 E12
Toseland ... 54 C3
Tosside ... 93 D7
Tostock ... 56 C3

Totaig Highld ... 148 C7
  Highld ... 149 F13
Tote ... 149 D9
Totegan ... 157 C11
Tothill ... 91 F8
Totland ... 14 F4
Totnes ... 7 C6
Toton ... 76 F5
Totronald ... 146 F4
Totscore ... 149 B8
Tottenham ... 41 E6
Tottenhill ... 67 C6
Tottenhill Row ... 67 C6
Totteridge ... 41 E5
Totternhoe ... 40 B2
Tottington ... 87 C5
Totton ... 14 C4
Touchen End ... 27 B6
Tournaig ... 155 J13
Toux ... 153 C9
Tovil ... 29 D8
Toward ... 145 G10
Towcester ... 52 E4
Towednack ... 2 C3
Tower End ... 67 C6
Towersey ... 39 D7
Towie Aberds ... 140 C3
  Aberds ... 153 B8
Towiemore ... 152 D3
Tow Law ... 110 F4
Townend ... 118 B4
Town End Cambs ... 66 E4
  W&F ... 99 F6
Towngate ... 65 C8
Townhead
  Dumfries ... 106 E3
  S Ayrs ... 112 D2
  S Yorks ... 88 D2
  W&F ... 108 F5
Townhead of
  Greenlaw ... 106 C4
Townhill ... 128 F3
Town Row ... 18 B2
Townsend Bucks ... 39 D7
  Herts ... 40 D4
Townshend ... 2 C4
Town Yetholm ... 116 B4
Towthorpe ... 96 D2
Towton ... 95 F7
Towyn ... 72 B3
Toynton All Saints 79 C6
Toynton Fen Side ... 79 C6
Toynton St Peter ... 79 C7
Toy's Hill ... 29 D5
Trabboch ... 112 B4
Traboe ... 3 D6
Tradespark
  Highld ... 151 F11
  Orkney ... 159 H5
Trafford Park ... 87 E5
Trallong ... 34 B3
Tranent ... 121 B7
Tranmere ... 85 F4
Trantlebeg ... 157 D11
Trantlemore ... 157 D11
Tranwell ... 117 F7
Trapp ... 33 C7
Traprain ... 121 B8
Traquair ... 121 F6
Trawden ... 94 F2
Trawscoed ... 47 B5
Trawsfynydd ... 71 D8
Trealaw ... 34 E4
Treales ... 92 F4
Trearddur ... 82 D2
Treaslane ... 149 C8
Trebanog ... 34 E4
Trebanos ... 33 D8
Trebartha ... 5 B7
Trebarwith ... 8 F2
Trebetherick ... 4 B4
Treborough ... 22 F2
Trebudannon ... 4 C3
Trebullett ... 5 B8
Treburley ... 5 B8
Trebyan ... 5 C5
Trecastle ... 34 B2
Trecenydd ... 35 F5
Trecwn ... 44 B4
Trecynon ... 34 D3
Tredavoe ... 2 D3
Treddiog ... 44 C3
Tredegar ... 35 D5
Tredegar =Newydd
  New Tredegar ... 35 D5
Tredington Glos ... 37 B6
  Warks ... 51 E7
Tredinnick ... 4 B4
Tredomen ... 48 F3
Tredunnock ... 35 E7
Tredustan ... 48 F3
Treen ... 2 D2
Treeton ... 88 F5
Trefaldwyn
  =Montgomery ... 60 D2
Trefasser ... 44 B3
Trefdraeth ... 82 D4
Trefdraeth
  =Newport ... 45 F2
Trefecca ... 48 F3
Trefechan ... 58 F2
Trefeglwys ... 59 E6
Trefenter ... 46 C5
Treffgarne ... 44 C4
Treffynnon
  =Holywell ... 73 B5
Trefgarn Owen ... 44 C3
Trefi ... 44 B3
Trefil ... 35 C5
Treflach ... 60 B2
Trefnanney ... 60 C2
Trefnant ... 72 B4
Trefonen ... 60 B2
Trefor Anglesey ... 82 C3
  Gwyn ... 70 C4
Treforest ... 34 F4
Trefriw ... 83 E7
Tref-y-Clawdd
  =Knighton ... 48 B4
Trefynwy
  =Monmouth ... 36 C2
Tregadillett ... 8 F5
Tregaian ... 82 D4
Tregare ... 35 C8
Tregaron ... 47 D5
Tregarth ... 83 E6
Tregeare ... 8 F4

Tregeiriog ... 73 F5
Tregele ... 82 B3
Tregidden ... 3 D6
Treglemais ... 44 C3
Tregole ... 8 E3
Tregonetha ... 4 C4
Tregony ... 3 B8
Tregoss ... 4 C4
Tregoyd ... 48 F4
Tregroes ... 46 E3
Tregurrian ... 4 C3
Tregynon ... 59 E7
Trehafod ... 34 E4
Treharris ... 34 E4
Treherbert ... 34 E3
Trekenner ... 5 B8
Treknow ... 8 F2
Trelan ... 3 E6
Trelash ... 8 E3
Trelassick ... 4 D3
Trelawnyd ... 72 B4
Trelech ... 45 F4
Treleddyd-fawr ... 44 C2
Trelewis ... 35 E5
Treligga ... 8 F2
Trelights ... 4 B4
Trelill ... 4 B5
Trelissick ... 3 C7
Trellech ... 36 D2
Trelleck Grange ... 36 D1
Trelogan ... 85 F2
Trelystan ... 60 D2
Tremadog ... 71 C6
Tremail ... 8 F3
Tremain ... 45 E4
Tremaine ... 8 F4
Tremar ... 5 C7
Trematon ... 5 D8
Tremeirchion ... 72 B4
Trenance ... 4 C3
Trenarren ... 3 B9
Trench ... 61 C6
Treneglos ... 8 F4
Trenewan ... 5 D6
Trent ... 12 C3
Trentham ... 75 F5
Trentishoe ... 20 E5
Trent Vale ... 75 E5
Treoes ... 21 B8
Treorchy =Treorci ... 34 E3
Treorci =Treorchy ... 34 E3
Tre'r-ddôl ... 58 E3
Tresaith ... 45 D4
Trescowe ... 2 D4
Tresham ... 36 E4
Tresillian ... 3 B7
Tresinwen ... 44 A4
Treskinnick Cross ... 8 E4
Tresmeer ... 8 F4
Tresparrett ... 8 E3
Tresparrett Posts ... 8 E3
Tressait ... 133 C5
Tresta Shetland ... 160 D8
  Shetland ... 160 H5
Treswell ... 77 B7
Tretfire ... 35 E8
Tre-Taliesin ... 58 E3
Trethosa ... 4 D4
Trethurgy ... 4 D5
Tretio ... 44 C2
Tretire ... 36 B2
Tretower ... 35 B5
Treuddyn ... 73 D6
Trevalga ... 8 F2
Trevalyn ... 73 D7
Trevanson ... 4 B4
Trevarren ... 4 C4
Trevarrian ... 4 C3
Trevarrick ... 3 B8
Trevaughan ... 32 B4
Tre-vaughan ... 32 B4
Trevellas ... 4 D2
Treverva ... 3 C6
Trevethin ... 35 D6
Trevigro ... 5 C8
Treviscoe ... 4 D4
Trevone ... 4 B3
Trewarmett ... 8 F2
Trewassa ... 8 F3
Trewellard ... 2 C2
Trewen ... 8 F4
Trewennack ... 3 D5
Trewern ... 60 C2
Trewethern ... 4 B5
Trewidland ... 5 D7
Trewint Corn ... 8 E3
  Corn ... 8 F4
Trewithian ... 3 C7
Trewoofe ... 2 D3
Trewoon ... 4 D4
Treworga ... 3 B7
Treworlas ... 3 C7
Tre-wyn ... 35 B7
Treyarnon ... 4 B3
Treyford ... 16 C2
Trezaise ... 4 D4
Triangle ... 87 B8
Trickett's Cross ... 13 D8
Triffleton ... 44 C4
Trimdon ... 111 F6
Trimdon Colliery ... 111 F6
Trimdon Grange ... 111 F6
Trimingham ... 81 D8
Trimley Lower
  Street ... 57 F6
Trimley St Martin ... 57 F6
Trimley St Mary ... 57 F6
Trimpley ... 50 B2
Trimsaran ... 33 D5
Trimstone ... 20 E3
Trinafour ... 132 C4
Trinant ... 35 D6
Tring ... 40 C2
Tring Wharf ... 40 C2
Trinity Angus ... 135 C6
  Jersey ... 17 I3
Trisant ... 47 B6
Trislaig ... 130 B4
Trispen ... 4 D3
Tritlington ... 117 E8
Trochry ... 133 E6
Trodigal ... 143 F7
Troed-rhiwdalar ... 47 D8
Troedyraur ... 46 E2
Troedyrhiw ... 34 D4

Tromode ... 84 E3
Trondavoe ... 160 F5
Troon Corn ... 3 C5
  S Ayrs ... 118 F3
Trosaraidh ... 148 G2
Trossachs Hotel ... 126 D4
Troston ... 56 B2
Trottiscliffe ... 29 C7
Trotton ... 16 B2
Troutbeck W&F ... 99 B5
Troutbeck Bridge ... 99 D6
Trow Green ... 36 D2
Trowbridge ... 24 D3
Trowell ... 76 F4
Trowle Common ... 24 D3
Trowley Bottom ... 40 C3
Trows ... 122 F2
Trowse Newton ... 68 D5
Trudoxhill ... 24 E2
Trull ... 11 B7
Trumaisgearraidh 148 A3
Trumpan ... 148 B7
Trumpet ... 49 F8
Trumpington ... 54 D5
Trunch ... 81 D8
Trunnah ... 92 E3
Truro ... 3 B7
Trusham ... 10 F3
Trusley ... 76 F2
Trusthorpe ... 91 F9
Trysull ... 62 E2
Tubney ... 38 E4
Tuckenhay ... 7 D6
Tuckhill ... 61 F7
Tuckingmill ... 3 B5
Tuddenham ... 55 B8
Tuddenham
  St Martin ... 57 E5
Tudeley ... 29 E7
Tudhoe ... 111 F5
Tudorville ... 36 B2
Tudweiliog ... 70 D3
Tuesley ... 27 E7
Tuffley ... 37 C5
Tufton Hants ... 26 E2
  Pembs ... 32 B1
Tugby ... 64 D4
Tugford ... 61 F5
Tullibardine ... 127 C8
Tullibody ... 127 E7
Tullich Argyll ... 125 D6
  Highld ... 138 B2
Tullich Muir ... 151 D10
Tulliemet ... 133 D6
Tulloch Aberds ... 135 B7
  Aberds ... 153 E8
  Perth ... 128 B2
Tulloch Castle ... 151 E8
Tullochgorm ... 125 F5
Tulloes ... 135 E5
Tullybannocher ... 127 B6
Tullybelton ... 133 F7
Tullyfergus ... 134 E2
Tullymurdoch ... 134 D1
Tullynessle ... 140 C4
Tumble ... 33 C6
Tumby
  Woodside ... 79 D5
Tummel Bridge ... 132 D4
Tunga ... 155 D9
Tunstall E Yorks ... 97 F9
  Kent ... 30 C2
  Lancs ... 93 B6
  Norf ... 69 D7
  N Yorks ... 101 E7
  Stoke ... 75 D5
  Suff ... 57 D7
  T&W ... 111 D6
Tunstead Derbys ... 75 B8
  Gtr Man ... 87 D8
  Norf ... 81 E8
Tunworth ... 26 E4
Tupsley ... 49 E7
Tupton ... 76 C3
Turgis Green ... 26 D4
Turin ... 135 D5
Turkdean ... 37 C8
Tur Langton ... 64 E4
Turleigh ... 24 C3
Turn ... 87 C6
Turnastone ... 49 F5
Turnberry ... 112 D2
Turnditch ... 76 E2
Turners Hill ... 28 F4
Turners Puddle ... 13 E6
Turnford ... 41 D6
Turnhouse ... 120 B4
Turnworth ... 13 D6
Turriff ... 153 C7
Turton Bottoms ... 86 C5
Turves ... 66 E3
Turvey ... 53 D7
Turville ... 39 E7
Turville Heath ... 39 E7
Turweston ... 52 F4
Tushielaw ... 115 C6
Tutbury ... 63 B6
Tutnall ... 50 B4
Tutshill ... 36 E2
Tuttington ... 81 E8
Tutts Clump ... 26 B3
Tuxford ... 77 B7
Twatt Orkney ... 159 F3
  Shetland ... 160 H5
Twechar ... 119 B7
Tweedmouth ... 123 D5
Tweedsmuir ... 114 B3
Twelve Heads ... 3 B6
Twemlow Green ... 74 C4
Twenty ... 65 B8
Twerton ... 24 C2
Twickenham ... 28 B2
Twigworth ... 37 B5
Twineham ... 17 C6
Twinhoe ... 24 D2
Twinstead ... 56 F2
Twinstead Green ... 56 F2
Twiss Green ... 86 E4
Twiston ... 93 E8
Twitchen Devon ... 21 F6
  Shrops ... 49 B5
Two Bridges ... 6 B4
Two Dales ... 76 C2
Two Mills ... 73 B7
Twycross ... 63 D7
Twyford Bucks ... 39 B6
  Derbys ... 63 B7
  Hants ... 15 B5

Twyford *continued*
  Leics ... 64 C4
  Lincs ... 65 B6
  Norf ... 81 E6
  Wokingham ... 27 B5
Twyford Common ... 49 F7
Twyn-y-Sheriff ... 35 D8
Twynholm ... 106 D3
Twyning ... 50 F3
Twyning Green ... 50 F4
Twynllanan ... 34 B1
Twynmynydd ... 33 C7
Twywell ... 53 B7
Tyberton ... 49 F5
Tyburn ... 62 E5
Tycroes ... 33 C7
Tycrwyn ... 59 C8
Tyddewi
  =St David's ... 44 C2
Tydd Gote ... 66 C4
Tydd St Giles ... 66 C4
Tydd St Mary ... 66 C4
Tyddyn-mawr ... 71 C6
Ty-draw ... 83 F8
Tye Green Essex ... 41 D7
  Essex ... 42 B3
  Essex ... 55 F6
Tyldesley ... 86 D4
Tyler Hill ... 30 C5
Tylers Green ... 40 E2
Tylorstown ... 34 E4
Tylwch ... 59 F6
Ty-mawr ... 82 C4
Ty Mawr ... 46 E4
Ty Mawr Cwm ... 72 D3
Ty-nant Conwy ... 72 E3
  Gwyn ... 59 B6
Tyncelyn ... 46 C5
Tyndrum ... 131 F7
Tyneham ... 13 F6
Tynehead ... 121 D6
Tynemouth ... 111 C6
Tyne Tunnel ... 111 C6
Tynewydd ... 34 E3
Tyninghame ... 122 B2
Tynron ... 113 E8
Tyn-y-celyn ... 73 F5
Tyn-y-coed ... 60 B2
Tyn-y-fedwen ... 72 F5
Tyn-y-ffridd ... 72 F5
Tynygongl ... 82 C5
Tyn-y-graig ... 48 D2
Ty'n-y-groes ... 83 D7
Ty'n-y-maes ... 83 E6
Ty'n-y-pwll ... 82 C4
Ty'n-yr-eithin ... 47 C5
Tyr-felin-isaf ... 83 E8
Tyrie ... 153 B9
Tyringham ... 53 E6
Tythecott ... 9 C6
Tythegston ... 21 B7
Tytherington
  Ches E ... 75 B6
  S Glos ... 36 F3
  Som ... 24 E2
  Wilts ... 24 E4
Tytherleigh ... 11 D8
Tywardreath ... 5 D5
Tywyn Conwy ... 83 D7
  Gwyn ... 58 D2

U

Uachdar ... 148 C2
Uags ... 149 E12
Ubbeston Green ... 57 B7
Ubley ... 23 D7
Uckerby ... 101 D7
Uckfield ... 17 B8
Uckington ... 37 B6
Uddingston ... 119 C6
Uddington ... 119 F8
Udimore ... 19 D5
Udny Green ... 141 B7
Udny Station ... 141 B8
Udston ... 119 D6
Udstonhead ... 119 E7
Uffcott ... 25 B6
Uffculme ... 11 C5
Uffington Lincs ... 65 D7
  Oxon ... 38 F3
  Shrops ... 60 C5
Ufford Pboro ... 65 D7
  Suff ... 57 D6
Ufton ... 51 C8
Ufton Nervet ... 26 C4
Ugadale ... 143 F8
Ugborough ... 6 D4
Uggeshall ... 69 F7
Ugglebarnby ... 103 D6
Ughill ... 88 E3
Ugley ... 41 B8
Ugley Green ... 41 B8
Ugthorpe ... 103 C5
Uidh ... 148 J1
Uig Argyll ... 145 E10
  Highld ... 148 C6
  Highld ... 149 B8
Uigen ... 154 D5
Uigshader ... 149 D9
Uisken ... 146 K6
Ulbster ... 158 F5
Ulcombe ... 30 E2
Uldale ... 108 F2
Uley ... 36 E4
Ulgham ... 117 E8
Ullapool ... 150 B4
Ullenhall ... 51 C6
Ullenwood ... 37 C6
Ulleskelf ... 95 E8
Ullesthorpe ... 64 F2
Ulley ... 89 F5
Ullingswick ... 49 E7
Ullinish ... 149 E8
Ullock ... 98 B2
Ulnes Walton ... 86 C3
Ulpha ... 98 E3
Ulrome ... 97 D7
Ulsta ... 160 E6
Ulva House ... 146 H7
Ulverston ... 92 B2

Ulwell ... 13 F8
Umberleigh ... 9 B8
Unapool ... 156 F5
Unasary ... 148 F2
Underbarrow ... 99 E6
Undercliffe ... 94 F4
Underriver ... 29 D6
Underwood ... 76 D4
Undy ... 35 F8
Unifirth ... 160 H4
Union Cottage ... 141 E7
Union Mills ... 84 E3
Union Street ... 18 B4
Unstone ... 76 B3
Unstone Green ... 76 B3
Unthank W&F ... 108 F4
  W&F ... 109 E5
Unthank End ... 108 F4
Upavon ... 25 D6
Up Cerne ... 12 D4
Upchurch ... 30 C2
Upcott ... 48 D5
Upend ... 55 D7
Up Exe ... 10 D4
Upgate ... 68 C4
Uphall ... 120 B3
Uphall Station ... 120 B3
Upham Devon ... 10 D3
  Hants ... 15 B6
Uphampton ... 50 C3
Up Hatherley ... 37 B6
Uphill ... 22 D5
Up Holland ... 86 D3
Uplawmoor ... 118 D4
Upleadon ... 36 B4
Upleatham ... 102 C4
Uplees ... 30 C3
Uploders ... 12 E3
Uplowman ... 10 C5
Uplyme ... 11 E8
Up Marden ... 15 C8
Upminster ... 42 F1
Up Nately ... 26 D4
Upnor ... 29 B8
Upottery ... 11 D7
Upper Affcot ... 60 F4
Upper
  Ardchronie ... 151 C9
Upper Arley ... 61 F7
Upper Arncott ... 39 C6
Upper Astrop ... 52 F2
Upper Badcall ... 156 E4
Upper Basildon ... 26 B3
Upper Beeding ... 17 C5
Upper Benefield ... 65 F6
Upper Bighouse ... 157 D11
Upper
  Boddington ... 52 D2
Upper Borth ... 58 F3
Upper Boyndlie ... 153 B9
Upper Brailes ... 51 F8
Upper Breakish ... 149 F11
Upper Broadheath 50 D3
Upper Broughton ... 64 B3
Upper Bucklebury 26 C3
Upper
  Burnhaugh ... 141 E7
Upperby ... 108 D4
Upper Caldecote ... 54 E2
Upper Catesby ... 52 D3
Upper Chapel ... 48 E2
Upper Church
  Village ... 34 F4
Upper Chute ... 25 D7
Upper Clatford ... 25 E8
Upper Clynnog ... 71 C5
Upper
  Cumberworth ... 88 D3
Upper Cwmbran ... 35 E6
Upper Dallachy ... 152 B3
Upper Dean ... 53 C8
Upper Denby ... 88 D3
Upper Denton ... 109 C6
Upper Derraint ... 151 H13
Upper Dicker ... 18 E2
Upper Dovercourt ... 57 F6
Upper Druimfin ... 147 F8
Upper Dunsforth ... 95 C7
Upper Eathie ... 151 E10
Upper Elkstone ... 75 D7
Upper End ... 75 B7
Upper Farringdon ... 26 F5
Upper Framilode ... 36 C4
Upper
  Glenfintaig ... 137 F5
Upper Gornal ... 62 E3
Upper Gravenhurst 54 F2
Upper Green Mon ... 35 C7
  W Berks ... 25 C8
Upper Grove
  Common ... 36 B2
Upper Hackney ... 76 C2
Upper Hale ... 27 E6
Upper Halistra ... 148 C7
Upper Halling ... 29 C7
Upper Hambleton ... 65 D6
Upper Hardres
  Court ... 31 D5
Upper Hartfield ... 29 F5
Upper Haugh ... 88 E5
Upper Heath ... 61 F5
Upper Hellesdon ... 68 C5
Upper Helmsley ... 96 D2
Upper Hergest ... 48 D4
Upper Heyford
  Oxon ... 38 B4
  W Nhants ... 52 D4
Upper Hill ... 49 D6
Upper Hopton ... 88 C2
Upper
  Horsebridge ... 18 D2
Upper Hulme ... 75 C7
Upper Inglesham 38 E2
Upper
  Inverbrough ... 151 H11
Upper Killay ... 33 E6
Upper
  Knockando ... 152 D1
Upper Lambourn 38 F3
Upper Leigh ... 75 F7
Upper Lenie ... 137 B8
Upper Lochton ... 141 E5
Upper Longdon ... 62 C4
Upper Lybster ... 158 G4
Upper Lydbrook ... 36 C3
Upper Maes-coed 48 F5
Upper Midway ... 63 B6

Uppermill...87 D7

V

Upper Milvaig...148 D6
Upper Minety...37 F7
Upper Mitton...50 B2
Upper North Dean...39 E8
Upper Obney...133 F7
Upper Ollach...149 E10
Upper Padley...76 B2
Upper Pollicott...39 C7
Upper Poppleton...95 D8
Upper Quinton...51 E6
Upper Ratley...14 B4
Upper Rissington...38 C2
Upper Rochford...49 C8
Upper Sandaig...149 G12
Upper Sanday...159 H6
Upper Sapey...49 C8
Upper Saxondale...77 F6
Upper Seagry...37 F6
Upper Shelton...53 E7
Upper Sheringham...81 C7
Upper Skelmorlie...118 C2
Upper Slaughter...38 B1
Upper Soudley...36 C3
Uppersound...160 J6
Upper Stondon...54 F2
Upper Stowe...52 D4
Upper Stratton...38 F1
Upper Street Hants. 14 C2
  Norf...69 C6
  Suff...56 F5
Upper Strensham...50 F4
Upper Sundon...40 B3
Upper Swell...38 B1
Upper Tean...75 F7
Upperthong...88 D2
Upperthorpe...89 D8
Upper Tillyrie...128 D3
Upperton...16 B3
Upper Tooting...28 B3
Upper Tote...149 C10
Uppertown
  Derbys...76 C3
  Highld...158 C5
  Orkney...159 J5
Upper Town...23 C7
Upper Treverward...48 B4
Upper Tysoe...51 E8
Upper Upham...25 B7
Upper Wardington 52 E2
Upper Weald...53 F5
Upper Weedon...52 D4
Upper Wield...26 F4
Upper Winchendon...39 C7
Upper Witton...62 E4
Upper Woodend...141 C5
Upper Woodford...25 F6
Upper Wootton...26 D3
Upper Wyche...50 E2
Uppingham...65 E5
Uppington...61 D6
Upsall...102 F2
Upshire...41 D7
Up Somborne...25 F8
Upstreet...31 C6
Up Sydling...12 D4
Upthorpe...56 B3
Upton Cambs...54 B2
  Ches W...73 C8
  Corn...8 D4
  Dorset...12 F5
  Dorset...13 E7
  Hants...14 C4
  Hants...25 D8
  Leics...63 E7
  Lincs...90 F2
  Mers...85 F3
  Norf...69 C6
  Notts...77 B7
  Oxon...39 F5
  Pboro...65 D8
  Slough...27 B7
  Som...10 B4
  W Nhants...52 C5
  W Yorks...89 C5
Upton Bishop...36 B3
Upton Cheyney...23 C8
Upton Cressett...61 E6
Upton Cross...5 B7
Upton Grey...26 E4
Upton Hellions...10 D3
Upton Lovell...24 E4
Upton Magna...61 C5
Upton Noble...24 F2
Upton Pyne...10 E4
Upton St Leonard's...37 C5
Upton Scudamore 24 E3
Upton Snodsbury...50 D4
Upton upon Severn...50 E3
Upton Warren...50 C4
Upwaltham...16 C3
Upware...55 B6
Upwell...66 D4
Upwey...12 F4
Upwood...66 F2
Uradale...160 K6
Urafirth...160 F5
Urchfont...24 D5
Urdimarsh...49 E7
Ure...160 F4
Ure Bank...95 B6
Urgha...154 H6
Urishay Common...48 F5
Urlay Nook...102 C1
Urmston...87 E5
Urpeth...110 D5
Urquhart Highld...151 F8
  Moray...152 B2
Urra...102 D3
Urray...151 F8
Ushaw Moor...110 E5
Usk = Brynbuga...35 D7
Usselby...90 E4
Usworth...111 D6
Utkinton...74 C2
Utley...94 E3
Uton...10 E3
Utterby...91 E7
Uttoxeter...75 F7
Uwchmynydd...70 E2
Uxbridge...40 F3
Uyeasound...160 C7
Uzmaston...44 D4

Valley...83 D3
Vallatown
  S Ayrs...112 B2
  E Ayrs...113 D2
Vallands Park...17 C8
Valley...83 D3
Valleyfield...106 D3
Valley Truckle...8 F2
Valsgarth...160 B8
Valtos...149 B10
Van...59 F6
Vange...42 F3
Varteg...35 D6
Vatten...149 D7
Vaul...146 G3
Vaynor...34 C4
Veensgarth...160 J6
Velindre...48 F3
Vellow...22 F2
Veness...159 F6
Venn Green...9 C5
Vennington...60 D3
Venn Ottery...11 E5
Venny Tedburn...10 E3
Ventnor...15 G6
Vernham Dean...25 D8
Vernham Street...25 D8
Vernolds Common...60 F4
Verwood...13 D8
Veryan...3 C8
Vicarage...11 F5
Vickerstown...92 C1
Victoria Corn...4 C4
  S Yorks...88 D2
Vidlin...160 G6
Viewpark...119 C7
Vigo Village...29 C7
Vinehall Street...18 C4
Vine's Cross...18 D2
Viney Hill...36 D3
Virginia Water...27 C8
Virginstow...9 E5
Vobster...24 E2
Voe Shetland...160 E5
  Shetland...160 G6
Vowchurch...49 F5
Voxter...160 F5
Voy...159 G3

W

Wackerfield...101 B6
Wacton...68 E4
Wadbister...160 J6
Wadborough...50 E4
Waddesdon...39 C7
Waddingham...90 E3
Waddington Lancs 93 E7
  Lincs...78 C2
Wadebridge...4 B4
Wadeford...11 C8
Wadenhoe...65 F7
Wadesmill...41 C6
Wadhurst...18 B3
Wadsley...88 E4
Wadsley Bridge...88 E4
Wadworth...89 E6
Waen Denb...72 C3
  Denb...72 C5
Waen Fach...60 C2
Waen Goleugoed...72 B4
Wag...157 G13
Wainfleet All Saints...79 D7
Wainfleet Bank...79 D7
Wainfleet St Mary...79 D8
Wainfleet Tofts...79 D7
Wainhouse Corner...8 E3
Wainscott...29 B8
Wainstalls...87 B8
Waitby...100 D2
Waithe...91 D6
Wakefield...88 B4
Wake Lady Green...102 E4
Wakerley...65 E6
Wakes Colne...42 B4
Walberswick...57 B8
Walberton...16 D3
Walbottle...110 C4
Walcot Lincs...78 F3
  N Lincs...90 B2
  Shrops...60 F3
  Swindon...38 F1
  Telford...61 C5
  Warks...51 D7
Walcote Leics...64 F2
  Warks...51 D6
Walcot Green...68 F4
Walcott Lincs...78 D4
  Norf...69 A6
Walden...101 F5
Walden Head...100 F4
Walden Stubbs...89 C6
Waldersey...66 D4
Walderslade...29 C8
Walderton...15 C8
Walditch...12 E2
Waldley...75 F8
Waldridge...110 D5
Waldringfield...57 E6
Waldringfield Heath...57 E6
Waldron...18 D2
Wales...89 F5
Walesby Lincs...90 E5
  Notts...77 B6
Walford Hereford...36 B2
  Hereford...49 B5
  Shrops...60 B4
Walford Heath...60 C4
Walgherton...74 E3
Walgrave...53 B6
Walhampton...14 E4
Walkden...86 D5
Walker...111 C5
Walker Barn...75 B6
Walkeringham...89 E8
Walker Fold...93 E6
Walkerith...89 E8
Walkern...41 B5
Walker's Green...49 E7
Walkerville...101 E7
Walkford...14 E3
Walkhampton...6 C3
Walkington...97 F5
Walkley...88 E4
Walk Mill...93 F8
Wall Northumb...110 C2
  Staffs...62 D5

Wallaceton...113 F8
Wallacetown
  S Ayrs...112 B2
  E Ayrs...112 D2
Wallands Park...17 C8
Wallasey...85 E4
Wall Bank...60 E5
Wallcrouch...18 B3
Wall Heath...62 F2
Wallingford...39 F6
Wallington Hants. 15 D6
  Herts...54 F3
  London...28 C3
Wallis...32 B1
Walliswood...28 F2
Walls...160 J4
Wallsend...111 C5
Wallston...22 B3
Wall under Heywood...60 E5
Wallyford...121 B6
Walmer...31 D7
Walmer Bridge...86 B2
Walmersley...87 C6
Walmley...62 E5
Walpole...57 B7
Walpole Cross Keys...66 C5
Walpole Highway...66 C5
Walpole Marsh...66 C4
Walpole St Andrew...66 C5
Walpole St Peter...66 C5
Walsall...62 E4
Walsall Wood...62 D4
Walsden...87 B7
Walsgrave on Sowe...63 F7
Walsham le Willows...56 B3
Walshaw...87 C5
Walshford...95 D7
Walsoken...66 C4
Walston...120 E3
Walsworth...54 F3
Walters Ash...39 E8
Walterston...22 B2
Walterstone...35 B7
Waltham Kent...30 E5
  NE Lincs...91 D6
Waltham Abbey...41 D6
Waltham Chase...15 C6
Waltham Cross...41 D6
Waltham on the Wolds...64 B3
Waltham St Lawrence...27 B6
Walthamstow...41 F6
Walton Cumb...108 C5
  Derbys...76 C3
  Leics...64 F2
  Mers...85 E4
  M Keynes...53 F6
  Pboro...65 D8
  Powys...48 D4
  Som...23 F6
  Staffs...75 F5
  Suff...57 F6
  Telford...61 C5
  W Yorks...88 C4
  W Yorks...95 E7
Walton Cardiff...50 F4
Walton East...32 B1
Walton-in-Gordano...23 B6
Walton-le-Dale...86 B3
Walton-on-Thames...28 C2
Walton on the Hill Staffs...62 B3
  Sur...28 D3
Walton-on-the-Naze...43 B8
Walton on the Wolds...64 C2
Walton-on-Trent...63 C6
Walton West...44 D3
Walwen...73 B6
Walwick...110 B2
Walworth...101 C7
Walworth Gate...101 B7
Walwyn's Castle...44 D3
Wambrook...11 D7
Wanborough Sur...27 E7
  Swindon...38 F2
Wandsworth...28 B3
Wangford...57 B8
Wanlockhead...113 C8
Wansford E Yorks...97 D6
  Pboro...65 E7
Wanstead...41 F7
Wanstrow...24 E2
Wanswell...36 D3
Wantage...38 F3
Wapley...24 B2
Wappenbury...51 C8
Wappenham...52 E4
Warbleton...18 D3
Warblington...15 D8
Warborough...39 E5
Warboys...66 F3
Warbreck...92 F3
Warbstow...8 E4
Warburton...86 F5
Warcop...100 C2
Warden Kent...30 B4
  Northumb...110 C2
Ward End...62 F5
Ward Green...56 C4
Wardhill...159 F7
Wardington...52 E2
Wardlaw...115 C5
Wardle Ches E...74 D3
  Gtr Man...87 C7
Wardley...64 D5
Wardlow...75 B8
Wardy Hill...66 F4
Ware Herts...41 C6
  Kent...31 C6
Wareham...13 F7
Warehorne...19 B6
Warenford...117 B7
Waren Mill...123 F7
Warenton...123 F7
Wareside...41 C6
Waresley Cambs...54 D3
  Worcs...50 B3
Warfield...27 B6

Warfleet...7 D6
Wargrave...27 B5
Warham...80 C5
Warhill...87 E7
Wark Northumb...109 B8
  Northumb...122 F4
Warkleigh...9 B8
Warkton...53 B6
Warkworth
  N Nhants...117 D8
  W Nhants...52 E2
Warlaby...101 E8
Warland...87 B7
Warleggan...5 C6
Warlingham...28 D4
Warmfield...88 B4
Warmingham...74 C4
Warmington
  N Nhants...65 E7
  Warks...52 E2
Warminster...24 E3
Warmlake...30 D2
Warmley...23 B8
Warmley Tower...23 B8
Warmonds Hill...53 C7
Warmsworth...89 D6
Warmwell...13 F5
Warndon...50 D3
Warnford...15 B7
Warnham...28 F2
Warninglid...17 B6
Warren Ches E...75 B5
  Pembs...44 F4
Warren Heath...57 E6
Warren Row...39 F8
Warren Street...30 D3
Warrington
  M Keynes...53 D6
  Warr...86 F4
Warsash...15 D5
Warslow...75 D7
Warter...96 D4
Warthermarske...94 B5
Warthill...96 D2
Wartling...18 E3
Wartnaby...64 B4
Warton Lancs...86 B2
  Lancs...92 B4
  Northumb...117 D6
  Warks...63 D6
Warwick...51 C7
Warwick Bridge...108 D4
Warwick on Eden...108 D4
Wasbister...159 E4
Wasdale Head...98 D3
Washaway...4 C5
Washbourne...7 D5
Wash Common...26 C2
Washfield...10 C4
Washfold...101 D5
Washford...22 E2
Washford Pyne...10 C3
Washingborough...78 B3
Washington T&W 111 D6
  W Sus...16 C5
Wasing...26 C3
Waskerley...110 E3
Wasperton...51 D7
Wasps Nest...78 C3
Wass...95 B8
Watchet...22 E2
Watchfield Oxon...38 E2
  Som...22 E5
Watchgate...99 E7
Watchhill...107 E8
Watcombe...7 C7
Watendlath...98 C4
Water Devon...10 F2
  Lancs...87 B6
Waterbeach...55 C5
Waterbeck...108 B2
Waterden...80 D4
Water End E Yorks...96 F3
  Herts...40 C3
  Herts...41 D5
Waterfall...75 D7
Waterfoot E Renf...119 D5
  Lancs...87 B6
Waterford Hants...14 E4
  Herts...41 C6
Waterhead
  Dumfries...114 E4
  W&F...99 D5
Waterheads...120 D5
Waterhouses
  Durham...110 E4
  Staffs...75 D7
Wateringbury...29 D7
Waterloo BCP...13 E8
  Gtr Man...87 D7
  Highld...149 F11
  Mers...85 E4
  N Lanark...119 D8
  Norf...68 C5
  Perth...133 F7
  Shrops...74 F2
Waterloo Port...82 E4
Waterlooville...15 D7
Watermeetings...114 C2
Watermillock...99 B6
Water Newton...65 E8
Water Orton...63 E5
Waterperry...39 D6
Waterrow...11 B5
Watersfield...16 C4
Waterside Aberds...141 B9
  Blackburn...86 B5
  Cumb...108 E2
  E Ayrs...112 D4
  E Ayrs...118 E4
  E Dunb...119 B6
  E Renf...118 D5
Water's Nook...86 D4
Waterstock...39 D6
Waterston...44 E4
Water Stratford...52 F4
Waters Upton...61 C6
Water Yeat...98 F4
Watford Herts...40 E4
  W Nhants...52 C4
Watford Gap...62 D5
Wath N Yorks...94 C4
  N Yorks...95 B6
  N Yorks...96 B2
Wath Brow...98 C2
Wath upon Dearne...88 D5
Watlington Norf...67 C6
  Oxon...39 E6

Watnall...76 E5
Watten...158 E4
Wattisfield...56 B4
Wattisham...56 D4
Wattlesborough Heath...60 C3
Watton E Yorks...97 D6
  Norf...68 D2
Watton at Stone...41 C6
Wattston...119 B7
Wattstown...34 E4
Wattsville...35 E6
Wauchan...136 F2
Waulkmill Lodge 159 H4
Waun...59 D5
Waunarlwydd...33 E7
Waunclunda...47 F5
Waunfawr...82 F5
Waungron...33 D6
Waunlwyd...35 D5
Waun-y-clyn...33 D5
Wavendon...53 F7
Waverbridge...108 E2
Waverley S Yorks...88 F5
Waverton Ches W...73 C8
  Cumb...108 E2
Wavertree...85 F4
Wawne...97 F6
Waxham...69 B7
Waxholme...91 B7
Way...31 C7
Wayfield...29 C8
Wayford...12 D2
Waymills...74 E2
Wayne Green...35 C8
Way Village...10 C3
Wdig = Goodwick...44 B4
Weachyburn...153 C6
Weald...38 D3
Wealdstone...40 F4
Weardley...95 E5
Weare...23 D6
Weare Giffard...9 B6
Wearhead...109 F8
Weasdale...100 D1
Weasenham All Saints...80 E4
Weasenham St Peter...80 E4
Weatherhill...28 E4
Weaverham...74 B3
Weaverthorpe...97 B5
Webheath...50 C5
Wedderlairs...153 E8
Wedderlie...122 D2
Weddington...63 E7
Wedhampton...25 D5
Wedmore...23 E6
Wednesbury...62 E3
Wednesfield...62 D3
Weedon...39 C8
Weedon Bec...52 D4
Weedon Lois...52 E4
Weeford...62 D5
Week...10 C2
Weeke...26 F2
Weekley...65 F5
Week St Mary...8 E4
Weel...97 F6
Weeley...43 B7
Weeley Heath...43 B7
Weem...133 E5
Weeping Cross...62 B3
Weethley Gate...51 D5
Weeting...67 F7
Weeton E Yorks...91 B7
  Lancs...92 F3
  N Yorks...95 E5
Weetwood Hall...117 B6
Weir...87 B6
Weir Quay...6 C2
Welborne...68 D3
Welbourn...78 D2
Welburn N Yorks...96 C3
  N Yorks...102 F4
Welbury...102 D1
Welby...78 F2
Welches Dam...66 F4
Welcombe...8 C4
Weld Bank...86 C3
Weldon...117 E7
Welford W Berks...26 B2
  W Nhants...64 F3
Welford-on-Avon 51 D6
Welham Leics...64 E4
  Notts...89 F8
Welham Green...41 D5
Well Hants...27 E5
  Lincs...79 B7
  N Yorks...101 F7
Welland...50 E2
Wellbank...134 F4
Welldale...107 C8
Well End...40 F1
Wellesbourne...51 D7
Well Heads...94 F3
Well Hill...29 C5
Welling...29 B5
Wellingborough...53 C6
Wellingham...80 E4
Wellingore...78 D2
Wellington Cumb...98 D2
  Hereford...49 E6
  Som...11 B6
  Telford...61 C6
Wellington Heath. 50 E2
Wellington Hill...95 F6
Wellow Bath...24 D2
  IoW...14 F4
  Notts...77 C6
Wellpond Green...41 B7
Wells...23 E7
Wellsborough...63 D7
Wells Green...74 D3
Wells-next-the-Sea...80 C5
Wellwood...128 F2
Welney...66 E5
Welshampton...73 F8
Welsh Bicknor...36 C2
Welsh End...74 F2
Welsh Frankton...73 F7
Welsh Hook...44 C4
Welsh Newton...36 C1
Welshpool = Y Trallwng...60 D2
Welsh St Donats...22 B2
Welton Cumb...108 E3

Welton continued
  E Yorks...90 B3
  Lincs...78 B3
  W Nhants...52 C3
  W Sus...16 C2
Welton Hill...90 F4
Welton le Marsh...79 C7
Welton le Wold...91 F6
Welwick...91 B7
Welwyn...41 C5
Welwyn Garden City...41 C5
Wem...60 B5
Wembdon...22 F4
Wembley...40 F4
Wembury...6 E3
Wembworthy...9 D8
Wemyss Bay...118 C1
Wenallt Ceredig...47 B5
  Gwyn...72 E3
Wendens Ambo...55 F6
Wendlebury...39 C5
Wendling...68 C2
Wendover...40 D1
Wendron...3 C5
Wendy...54 E4
Wenfordbridge...5 B5
Wenhaston...57 B8
Wennington Cambs. 54 B3
  Lancs...93 B6
  London...41 F8
Wensley Derbys...76 C2
  N Yorks...101 F5
Wentbridge...89 C5
Wentnor...60 E3
Wentworth Cambs...55 B5
  S Yorks...88 E4
Wenvoe...22 B3
Weobley...49 D6
Weobley Marsh...49 D6
Wereham...67 D6
Wergs...62 D2
Wern Powys...59 C6
  Powys...60 C2
Wernffrwd...33 E6
Wernyrheolydd...35 C7
Werrington Corn...8 F5
  Pboro...65 D8
  Staffs...75 E6
Wervin...73 B8
Wesham...92 F4
Wessington...76 D3
Westacott...20 F4
West Acre...67 C7
West Adderbury...52 F2
West Allerdean...123 E5
West Alvington...6 E5
West Amesbury...25 E6
West Anstey...10 B3
West Ashby...79 B5
West Ashling...15 D8
West Ashton...24 D3
West Auckland...101 B6
West Ayton...103 F7
West Bagborough...22 F3
West Barkwith...91 F5
West Barnby...103 C6
West Barns...122 B2
West Barsham...80 D5
West Bay...12 E2
West Beckham...81 D7
West Bedfont...27 B8
West Benhar...119 C8
Westbere...31 C5
West Bergholt...43 B5
West Bexington...12 F3
West Bilney...67 C7
West Blatchington...17 D6
Westborough...77 E8
Westbourne BCP...13 E8
  Suff...56 E5
  W Sus...15 D8
West Bowling...94 F4
West Bradford...93 E7
West Bradley...23 F7
West Bretton...88 C3
West Bridgford...77 F5
West Bromwich...62 E4
Westbrook...26 B2
West Buckland
  Devon...21 F5
  Som...11 B6
West Burrafirth...160 H4
West Burton
  N Yorks...101 F5
  W Sus...16 C3
Westbury Bucks...52 F4
  Shrops...60 D3
  Wilts...24 D3
Westbury Leigh...24 D3
Westbury-on-Severn...36 C4
Westbury on Trym 23 B7
Westbury-sub-Mendip...23 E7
West Butterwick...90 D2
West Byfleet...27 C8
West Caister...69 C8
West Calder...120 C3
West Camel...12 B3
West Challow...38 F3
West Chelborough 12 D3
West Chevington...117 E8
West Chiltington...16 C4
West Chiltington Common...16 C4
West Chinnock...12 C2
West Chisenbury...25 D6
West Clandon...27 D8
West Cliffe...31 E7
Westcliff-on-Sea...42 F4
West Clyne...157 J11
West Clyth...158 G4
West Coker...12 C3
Westcombe...23 E8
West Compton
  Dorset...12 E3
  Som...23 E7
Westcote...38 B2
Westcott Bucks...39 C7
  Devon...10 D5
  Sur...28 E2
Westcott Barton...38 B4
West Cowick...89 B7
West Cranmore...23 E8
West Cross...33 F7
West Cullery...141 D6
West Curry...8 E4
West Curthwaite...108 E3

West Darlochan...143 F7
Westdean...18 F2
West Dean Bedford...53 D7
  E Yorks...96 F5
  Hants...15 C5
  Wilts...14 B3
West Deeping...65 D8
West Derby...85 E4
West Dereham...67 D6
West Didsbury...87 E6
West Ditchburn...117 B7
West Down...20 E4
West Drayton
  London...27 B8
  Notts...77 B7
West Ella...90 B4
West End Bedford...53 D7
  E Yorks...96 F5
  E Yorks...97 F7
  Hants...15 C5
  Lancs...86 B5
  Norf...68 D2
  Norf...69 C8
  N Som...23 C6
  N Yorks...94 D4
  Oxon...38 D4
  S Lanark...120 E2
  Suff...69 F7
  Sur...27 C7
  S Yorks...89 D7
  Wilts...13 B7
  Wilts...24 B4
  W Sus...17 C6
West End Green...26 C4
Wester Aberchalder...137 B8
Wester Balgedie...128 D3
Wester Culbeuchly...153 B6
Westerdale Highld. 158 E3
  N Yorks...102 D4
Wester Dechmont...120 C3
Wester Denoon...134 E3
Westerfield
  Shetland...160 H5
  Suff...57 E5
Wester Fintray...141 C7
Westergate...16 D3
Wester Gruinards 151 B8
Westerham...28 D5
Westerhope...110 C4
Wester Lealty...151 D9
Westerleigh...23 B9
Wester Milton...151 F12
Wester Newburn.129 D6
Wester Quarff...160 K6
Wester Skeld...160 J4
Westerton Angus...135 D6
  Durham...110 F5
  W Sus...16 D2
Westerwick...160 J4
West Farleigh...29 D8
West Felton...60 B3
West Fenton...129 F6
West Ferry...134 F4
Westfield Cumb...98 B1
  E Sus...18 D5
  Hereford...50 E2
  Highld...158 D2
  N Lanark...119 B7
  Norf...68 D2
  W Loth...120 B2
Westfields...134 D3
Westfields of Rattray...134 E1
West Firle...17 D8
Westgate Durham...110 F2
  N Lincs...89 D8
  Norf...80 C4
  Norf...81 C5
Westgate on Sea...31 B7
West Ginge...38 F4
West Grafton...25 C7
West Green...26 D5
West Greenskares...153 B7
West Grimstead...14 B3
West Grinstead...17 B5
West Haddlesey...89 B6
West Haddon...52 B4
West Hagbourne...39 F5
West Hagley...62 F3
Westhall Aberds...141 B5
  Suff...69 F7
West Hall...109 C5
West Hallam...76 E4
West Halton...90 B3
Westham Dorset...12 G4
  E Sus...18 E3
  Som...23 E6
West Ham...41 F7
Westhampnett...16 D2
West Handley...76 B3
West Hanney...38 E4
West Hanningfield 42 E3
West Hardwick...88 C5
West Harnham...14 B2
West Harptree...23 D7
West Hatch...11 B7
Westhay...23 E6
Westhead...86 D2
West Head...67 D5
West Heath Ches E...74 D5
  Hants...26 D3
  Hants...27 D6
West Helmsdale.157 H13
West Hendred...38 F4
West Heslerton...96 B5
Westhide...49 E7
Westhill Aberds...141 D7
  Highld...151 G10
West Hill Devon...11 E5
  E Yorks...97 C7
  N Som...23 B6
West Hoathly...28 F4
West Holme...13 F6
Westhope Hereford...49 D6
  Shrops...60 F4
West Horndon...42 F2
Westhorpe Lincs...78 F5
  Suff...56 C4
West Horrington...23 E7
West Horsley...27 D8
West Horton...123 F6
West Hougham...31 E6
Westhoughton...86 D4
West Houlland...160 H4
Westhouse...93 B6
Westhouses...76 D4
West Overton...25 C6

Westhumble...28 D2
West Huntington...96 D2
West Hythe...19 B8
West Ilsley...38 F4
Westing...160 C7
West Itchenor...15 D8
West Keal...79 C6
West Kennett...25 C6
West Kilbride...118 E2
West Kingsdown...29 C6
West Kington...24 B3
West Kinharrachie...153 E9
West Kirby...85 F3
West Knapton...96 B4
West Knighton...12 F5
West Knoyle...24 F3
West Kyloe...123 E6
Westlake...6 D4
West Lambrook...12 C2
West Langdon...31 E7
West Langwell...157 J9
West Lavington
  Wilts...24 D5
  W Sus...16 B2
West Layton...101 D6
West Lea...111 E7
West Leake...64 B2
West Learmouth.122 F4
Westleigh Devon...9 B6
  Devon...11 C5
  Gtr Man...86 D4
West Leigh...9 D8
Westleton...57 C8
West Lexham...67 C8
Westley Shrops...60 D3
  Suff...56 C2
Westley Waterless 55 D7
West Lilling...96 C2
Westlington...39 C7
West Linton...120 D4
West Liss...15 B8
West Littleton...24 B2
West Looe...5 D7
West Luccombe...21 E7
West Lulworth...13 F6
West Lutton...96 C5
West Lydford...23 F7
West Lyng...11 B8
West Lynn...67 B6
West Malling...29 D7
West Malvern...50 E2
West Marden...15 C8
West Marina...18 E4
West Markham...77 B7
Westmarsh...31 C6
West Marsh...91 C6
West Marton...93 D8
West Meon...15 B7
West Mersea...43 C6
Westmeston...17 C7
Westmill...41 B6
West Milton...12 E3
West Minster...30 B3
Westminster...28 B4
West Molesey...28 C2
West Monkton...11 B7
West Moors...13 D8
West Morriston...122 E2
Westmuir...134 D3
West Muir...135 C5
Westness...159 F4
West Ness...96 B2
West Newham...110 B3
Westnewton Cumb 107 E8
  Northumb...122 F5
West Newton
  E Yorks...97 F7
  Norf...67 B6
West Norwood...28 B4
Westoe...111 C6
West Ogwell...7 B6
Weston Bath...24 C2
  Ches E...74 D4
  Devon...11 F6
  Dorset...12 G4
  Halton...86 F3
  Hants...15 B8
  Herts...54 F3
  Lincs...66 B2
  N Yorks...94 E4
  Shrops...60 B5
  Shrops...61 E5
  Staffs...62 B3
  W Berks...25 B8
  W Nhants...52 E3
Weston Beggard...49 E7
Westonbirt...37 F5
Weston by Welland...64 E4
Weston Colville...55 D7
Westoncommon...60 B4
Weston Coyney...75 E6
Weston Favell...53 C5
Weston Green
  Cambs...55 D7
  Norf...68 C4
Weston Heath...61 C7
Weston Hills...66 B2
Westoning...53 F8
Weston-in-Gordano...23 B6
Weston Jones...61 B7
Weston Longville...68 C4
Weston Lullingfields...60 B4
Weston-on-the-Green...39 C5
Weston-on-Trent...63 B8
Weston Patrick...26 E4
Weston Rhyn...73 F6
Weston-sub-Edge 51 E6
Weston-super-Mare...22 C5
Weston Turville...40 C1
Weston under Lizard...62 C2
Weston under Penyard...36 B3
Weston under Wetherley...51 C8
Weston Underwood
  Derbys...76 E2
  M Keynes...53 D6
Westonzoyland...23 F5
West Orchard...13 C6
West Overton...25 C6

Westow...96 C3
West Park...111 F7
West Parley...13 E8
West Peckham...29 D7
West Pelton...110 D5
West Pennard...23 F7
West Pentire...4 C2
West Perry...54 C2
Westport Argyll...143 F7
  Som...11 C8
West Putford...9 C5
West Quantoxhead 22 E3
West Rainton...111 E6
West Rasen...90 F4
West Raynham...80 E4
West Retford...89 F7
Westrigg...120 C2
West Rounton...102 D2
West Row...55 B7
West Rudham...80 E4
West Runton...81 C7
Westruther...122 E2
Westry...66 E3
West Saltoun...121 C7
West Sandwick...160 E6
West Scrafton...101 F5
West Sleekburn...117 F8
West Somerton...69 C7
West Stafford...12 F5
West Stockwith...89 E8
West Stoke...16 D2
West Stonesdale...100 D3
West Stoughton...23 E6
West Stour...13 B5
West Stourmouth...31 C6
West Stow...56 B2
West Stowell...25 C6
West Strathan...157 C8
West Stratton...26 E3
West Street...30 D3
West Tanfield...95 B5
West Taphouse...5 C6
West Tarbert...145 G7
West Thirston...117 E7
West Thorney...15 D8
West Thurrock...29 B6
West Tilbury...29 B7
West Tisted...15 B7
West Tofts Norf...67 E8
  Perth...133 F8
West Torrington...90 F5
West Town Hants...15 E8
  N Som...23 C6
West Tytherley...14 B3
West Tytherton...24 B4
Westville...76 E5
West Walton...66 C4
West Walton Highway...66 C4
Westward...108 E2
Westward Ho!...9 B6
Westwell Kent...30 E3
  Oxon...38 D2
Westwell Leacon...30 E3
West Wellow...14 C3
West Wemyss...128 E5
Westwick Cambs...54 C5
  Durham...101 C5
  Norf...81 E8
West Wick...23 C5
West Wickham
  Cambs...55 E7
  London...28 C4
West Williamston...32 D1
West Willoughby...78 E2
West Winch...67 C6
West Winterslow...25 F7
West Wittering...15 E8
West Witton...101 F5
Westwood Devon...10 E5
  Wilts...24 D3
West Woodburn...116 F4
West Woodhay...25 C8
West Woodlands...24 E2
Westwoodside...89 E8
West Worldham...26 F5
West Worlington...10 C2
West Worthing...16 D5
West Wratting...55 D7
West Wycombe...39 E8
West Wylam...110 C4
West Yell...160 E6
Wetheral...108 D4
Wetherby...95 E7
Wetherden...56 C4
Wetheringsett...56 C5
Wethersfield...55 F8
Wethersta...160 G5
Wetherup Street...56 C5
Wetley Rocks...75 E6
Wettenhall...74 C3
Wetton...75 D8
Wetwang...96 D5
Wetwood...74 F4
Wexcombe...25 D7
Wexham Street...40 F2
Weybourne...81 C7
Weybread...68 F5
Weybridge...27 C8
Weycroft...11 E8
Weydale...158 D3
Weyhill...25 E8
Weymouth...12 G4
Whaddon Bucks...53 F6
  Cambs...54 E4
  Glos...37 C5
  Wilts...14 B2
Whale...99 B7
Whaley...76 B5
Whaley Bridge...87 F7
Whaley Thorns...76 B5
Whaligoe...158 F5
Whalley...93 F7
Whalton...117 F7
Wham...93 C7
Whaplode...66 B3
Whaplode Drove...66 C3
Whaplode St Catherine...66 B3
Wharfe...93 C7
Wharles...92 F4
Wharncliffe Side...88 E3
Wharram le Street. 96 C4
Wharton...74 C3
Wharton Green...74 C3
Whashton...101 D6

Whatcombe . . . 13 D6
Whatcote . . . 51 E8
Whatfield . . . 56 E4
Whatley Som. . . 11 D8
  Som . . . 24 E2
Whatlington . . . 18 D4
Whatstandwell . . . 76 D3
Whatton . . . 77 F7
Whauphill . . . 105 E8
Whaw . . . 100 D4
Wheatacre . . . 69 E7
Wheatcroft . . . 76 D3
Wheathampstead . . . 41 C5
Wheathill . . . 61 F6
Wheatley Devon . . . 10 E4
  Hants . . . 27 E5
  Oxon . . . 39 D5
  S Yorks. . . . 89 D6
  W Yorks . . . 87 B8
Wheatley Hill . . . 111 F6
Wheaton Aston . . . 62 C2
Wheddon Cross . . . 21 F8
Wheedlemont . . . 140 B3
Wheelerstreet . . . 27 E7
Wheelock . . . 74 D4
Wheelock Heath . . . 74 D4
Wheelton . . . 86 B4
Wheen . . . 134 B3
Wheldrake . . . 96 E2
Whelford . . . 38 E1
Whelpley Hill . . . 40 D2
Whempstead . . . 41 B6
Whenby . . . 96 C2
Whepstead . . . 56 D2
Wherstead . . . 57 E5
Wherwell . . . 25 E8
Wheston . . . 75 B8
Whetsted . . . 29 E7
Whetstone . . . 64 E2
Whicham . . . 98 F3
Whichford . . . 51 F8
Whickham . . . 110 C5
Whiddon Down . . . 9 E8
Whigstreet . . . 134 E4
Whilton . . . 52 C4
Whimble . . . 9 D5
Whim Farm . . . 120 C5
Whimple . . . 10 E5
Whimpwell Green . . . 69 B6
Whinburgh . . . 68 D3
Whinnieliggate . . . 106 D4
Whinnyfold . . . 153 E10
Whippingham . . . 15 E6
Whipsnade . . . 40 C3
Whipton . . . 10 E4
Whirlow . . . 88 F4
Whisby . . . 78 C2
Whissendine . . . 64 C5
Whissonsett . . . 80 E5
Whistlefield
  Argyll . . . 145 D10
  Argyll . . . 145 D11
Whistley Green . . . 27 B5
Whiston Mers. . . 86 E2
  Staffs . . . 62 C2
  Staffs . . . 75 E7
  S Yorks . . . 88 F5
  W Nhants . . . 53 C6
Whitbeck . . . 98 F3
Whitbourne . . . 50 D2
Whitburn T&W . . . 111 C7
  W Loth . . . 120 C2
Whitburn
  Colliery . . . 111 C7
Whitby Ches W . . . 73 B7
  N Yorks. . . . 103 C6
Whitbyheath . . . 73 B7
Whitchurch Bath . . . 23 C8
  Bucks . . . 39 B7
  Cardiff . . . 35 F5
  Devon . . . 6 B2
  Hants . . . 26 E2
  Hereford . . . 36 C2
  Oxon. . . . 26 B4
  Pembs . . . 44 C2
  Shrops . . . 74 E2
Whitchurch
  Canonicorum . . . 11 E8
Whitchurch Hill . . . 26 B4
Whitcombe . . . 12 F5
Whitcott Keysett . . . 60 F2
Whiteacre . . . 152 D2
Whiteacre Heath . . . 63 E6
Whitebridge . . . 137 C7
Whitebrook . . . 36 D2
Whiteburn . . . 121 E8
Whitecairn . . . 105 D6
Whitecairns . . . 141 C8
Whitecastle . . . 120 E3
Whitechapel . . . 93 E5
Whitecleat . . . 159 H6
White Coppice . . . 86 C4
Whitecraig . . . 121 B6
Whitecroft . . . 36 D3
Whitecross Corn . . . 4 B4
  Falk . . . 120 B2
  Staffs . . . 62 B2
Whiteface. . . . 151 C10
Whitefarland . . . 143 D9
Whitefaulds . . . 112 D2
Whitefield Gtr Man . 87 D6
  Perth . . . 134 F1
Whiteford . . . 141 B6
Whitegate . . . 74 C3
Whitehall Blackburn 86 B4
  W Sus . . . 16 B5
Whitehall Village . 159 F7
Whiteham . . . 98 C1
Whitehill . . . 27 F5
Whitehills Aberds . 153 B6
  S Lanark. . . . 119 D6
Whitehough . . . 87 F8
Whitehouse
  Aberds . . . 140 C5
  Argyll . . . 145 G7
Whiteinch . . . 118 C5
Whitekirk . . . 129 F7
White Lackington . 12 E5
White Ladies
  Aston . . . 50 D4
Whitelaw . . . 119 E6
Whiteleas . . . 111 C6
Whiteley Bank . . . 15 F6
Whiteley Green . . . 75 B6
Whiteley Village . 27 C8
White Lund . . . 92 C4

Whitemans Green . 17 B7
White Mill. . . . 33 B5
Whitemire . . . 151 F12
Whitemoor . . . 4 D4
Whitenap . . . 14 B4
Whiteoak Green . . 38 C3
Whiteparish . . . 14 B3
White Pit . . . 79 B6
White Post . . . 77 D6
Whiterashes . . . 141 B7
White Rocks . . . 35 B8
White Roding . . . 42 C1
Whiterow . . . 158 F5
Whiteshill . . . 37 D5
Whiteside
  Northumb. . . . 109 C7
  W Loth . . . 120 C2
Whitesmith . . . 18 D2
Whitestaunton . . . 11 C7
Whitestone Devon. . 10 E3
  Devon. . . . 20 E3
  Warks . . . 63 F7
Whitestones . . . 153 C8
Whitestreet Green . 56 F3
Whitewall Corner . 96 B3
White Waltham. . . 27 B6
Whiteway Glos. . . 37 C6
  Glos. . . . 37 E5
Whitewell Aberds . 153 B9
  Lancs. . . . 93 E6
Whitewell Bottom . 87 B6
Whiteworks . . . 6 B4
Whitfield Kent . . . 31 E7
  Northumb. . . . 109 D7
  S Glos . . . 36 F3
  W Nhants. . . . 52 F4
Whitford Devon . . 11 E7
  Flint . . . 72 B5
Whitgift. . . . 90 B2
Whitgreave . . . 62 B2
Whithorn . . . 105 E8
Whiting Bay . . . 143 F11
Whitkirk . . . 95 F6
Whitland . . . 32 C2
Whitletts. . . . 112 B3
Whitley N Yorks . . 89 B6
  Reading . . . 26 B5
  Wilts . . . 24 C3
Whitley Bay . . . 111 B6
Whitley Chapel . . 110 D2
Whitley Lower. . . 88 C3
Whitley Row . . . 29 D5
Whitlock's End . . 51 B6
Whitminster . . . 36 D4
Whitmore . . . 74 E5
Whitnage . . . 10 C5
Whitnash . . . 51 C8
Whitrigg Cumb. . . 108 D2
  Cumb. . . . 108 F2
Whitsbury . . . 14 C2
Whitsome . . . 122 D4
Whitson . . . 35 F7
Whitstable . . . 30 C5
Whitstone . . . 8 E4
Whittingham . . . 117 C6
Whittingslow . . . 60 F4
Whittington Glos. . 37 B7
  Lancs. . . . 93 B6
  Norf . . . 67 E7
  Shrops . . . 73 F7
  Staffs . . . 62 F2
  Staffs . . . 63 D5
  Worcs . . . 50 D3
Whittlebury . . . 52 E4
Whittle-le-Woods . 86 B3
Whittlesey . . . 66 E2
Whittlesford . . . 55 E5
Whittlestone Head 86 C5
Whitton Borders. . 116 B3
  N Lincs. . . . 90 B3
  Northumb. . . . 117 D6
  Powys . . . 48 C4
  Shrops . . . 49 B7
  Stockton. . . . 102 B1
  Suff . . . 56 E5
Whittonditch . . . 25 B7
Whittonstall. . . . 110 D3
Whitway . . . 26 D2
Whitwell Derbys . . 76 B5
  Herts . . . 40 B4
  IoW . . . 15 G6
  N Yorks. . . . 101 E7
  Rutland . . . 65 D6
Whitwell-on-the-
  Hill. . . . 96 C3
Whitwell Street . . 81 E7
Whitwick . . . 63 C8
Whitwood. . . . 88 B5
Whitworth . . . 87 C6
Whixall . . . 74 F2
Whixley . . . 95 D7
Whoberley . . . 51 B8
Whorlton Durham . 101 C6
  N Yorks. . . . 102 D2
Whygate . . . 109 B7
Whyle . . . 49 C7
Whyteleafe . . . 28 D4
Wibdon . . . 36 E2
Wibsey . . . 88 A2
Wibtoft . . . 63 F8
Wichenford . . . 50 C2
Wichling . . . 30 D3
Wick BCP . . . 14 E2
  Devon. . . . 11 D6
  Highld . . . 158 E5
  S Glos . . . 24 B2
  Shetland. . . . 160 K6
  V Glam . . . 21 B8
  Wilts . . . 14 B2
  Worcs . . . 50 E4
  W Sus . . . 16 D4

Wickham Market . . 57 D7
Wickhampton . . . 69 D7
Wickham St Paul . 56 F2
Wickham Skeith . . 56 C4
Wickham Street
  Suff . . . 55 D8
  Suff . . . 56 C4
Wick Hill. . . . 27 C5
Wicklewood. . . . 68 D3
Wickmere. . . . 81 D7
Wick St Lawrence . 23 C5
Wickwar . . . 36 F4
Widdington . . . 55 F6
Widdrington . . . 117 E8
Widdrington
  Station . . . 117 E8
Widecombe in the
  Moor. . . . 6 B5
Widegates . . . 5 D7
Widemouth Bay . . 8 D4
Wide Open . . . 110 B5
Widewall . . . 159 J5
Widford Essex. . . 42 D3
  Herts . . . 41 C7
Widham . . . 37 F7
Widmer End. . . . 40 E1
Widmerpool . . . 64 B3
Widnes . . . 86 F3
Wigan . . . 86 D3
Wiggaton . . . 11 E6
Wiggenhall St
  Germans . . . 67 C5
Wiggenhall St Mary
  Magdalen . . . 67 C5
Wiggenhall St Mary
  the Virgin . . . 67 C5
Wigginton Herts . . 40 C2
  Oxon. . . . 51 F8
  Staffs . . . 63 D6
  York . . . 95 D8
Wigglesworth . . . 93 D8
Wiggonby . . . 108 D2
Wiggonholt . . . 16 C4
Wighill . . . 95 E7
Wighton . . . 80 D5
Wigley . . . 14 C4
Wigmore Hereford . 49 C6
  Medway . . . 30 C2
Wigsley . . . 77 B8
Wigsthorpe . . . 65 F7
Wigston . . . 64 E3
Wigthorpe . . . 89 F6
Wigtoft . . . 79 F5
Wigton . . . 108 E2
Wigtown . . . 105 D8
Wigtwizzle . . . 88 E3
Wike . . . 95 E6
Wike Well End . . 89 C7
Wilbarston . . . 64 F5
Wilberfoss . . . 96 D3
Wilberlee . . . 87 C8
Wilburton . . . 55 B5
Wilby N Nhants . . 53 C6
  Norf . . . 68 F3
  Suff . . . 57 B6
Wilcot . . . 25 C6
Wilcott . . . 60 C3
Wilcrick . . . 35 F8
Wilday Green. . . 76 B3
Wildboarclough . . 75 C6
Wilden Bedford. . 53 D8
  Worcs . . . 50 B3
Wildhern. . . . 25 D8
Wildhill . . . 41 D5
Wildmoor . . . 50 B4
Wildsworth . . . 90 E2
Wilford . . . 77 F5
Wilkesley . . . 74 E3
Wilkhaven . . . 151 C12
Wilkieston . . . 120 C4
Willand . . . 10 C5
Willaston Ches E . 74 D3
  Ches W . . . 73 B7
Willen . . . 53 E6
Willenhall W Mid . 51 B8
  W Mid . . . 62 E3
Willerby E Yorks . 97 F6
  N Yorks. . . . 97 B6
Willersey . . . 51 F6
Willersley . . . 48 E5
Willesborough . . 30 E4
Willesborough
  Lees. . . . 30 E4
Willesden . . . 41 F5
Willett . . . 22 F3
Willey Shrops . . 61 E6
  Warks . . . 63 F8
Willey Green . . . 27 D7
Williamscott . . 52 E2
William. . . . 54 F3
Willingale . . . 42 D1
Willingdon . . . 18 E2
Willingham . . . 54 B5
Willingham by
  Stow . . . 90 F2
Willington Bedford . 54 E2
  Derbys . . . 63 B6
  Durham . . . 110 F4
  T&W. . . . 111 C6
  Warks . . . 51 F7
Willington Corner . 74 C2
Willisham Tye . . 56 D4
Willitoft. . . . 96 F3
Williton . . . 22 E2
Willoughbridge . . 74 E4
Willoughby Lincs . 79 B7
Willoughby-on-the-
  Wolds . . . 64 B3
Willoughby
  Waterleys . . . 64 E2
Willoughton . . . 90 E3
Willows Green . . 42 C3
Willsbridge . . . 23 B8
Willsworthy . . . 9 F7

Wilsom . . . 26 F5
Wilson . . . 63 B8
Wilsontown . . . 120 D2
Wilstead . . . 53 E8
Wilsthorpe . . . 65 C7
Wilstone . . . 40 C2
Wilton Borders . . 115 C7
  Cumb. . . . 98 C2
  N Yorks. . . . 103 F6
  Redcar . . . 102 C3
  Wilts . . . 25 C7
  Wilts . . . 25 F5
Wimbish . . . 55 F6
Wimbish Green. . . 55 F7
Wimblebury . . . 62 C4
Wimbledon . . . 28 B3
Wimblington . . . 66 E4
Wimborne Minster 13 E8
Wimborne St Giles 13 C8
Wimbotsham . . . 67 D6
Wimpson . . . 14 C4
Wimpstone . . . 51 E7
Wincanton . . . 12 B5
Wincham . . . 74 B3
Winchburgh . . . 120 B3
Winchcombe . . . 37 B7
Winchelsea . . . 19 D6
Winchelsea Beach. 19 D6
Winchester . . . 15 B5
Winchet Hill . . . 29 E8
Winchfield . . . 27 D5
Winchmore Hill
  Bucks . . . 40 E2
  London . . . 41 E6
Wincle . . . 75 C6
Wincobank. . . . 88 E4
Windermere . . . 99 E6
Winderton . . . 51 E8
Windhill . . . 151 G8
Windhouse . . . 160 D6
Windlehurst . . . 87 F7
Windlesham . . . 27 C7
Windley . . . 76 E3
Windmill Hill
  E Sus . . . 18 D3
  Som . . . 11 C8
Windrush . . . 38 C1
Windsor N Lincs . . 89 C8
  Windsor . . . 27 B7
Windsoredge . . . 37 D5
Windygates . . . 128 D5
Windyknowe . . . 120 C2
Windywalls . . . 122 F3
Wineham . . . 17 B6
Winestead . . . 91 B6
Winewall . . . 94 E2
Winfarthing . . . 68 F4
Winford IoW . . . 15 F6
  N Som . . . 23 C7
Winforton . . . 48 E4
Winfrith
  Newburgh . . . 13 F6
Wing Bucks . . . 40 B1
  Rutland . . . 65 D5
Wingate . . . 111 F7
Wingates Gtr Man . 86 D4
  Northumb. . . . 117 E7
Wingerworth . . . 76 C3
Wingfield C Beds . 40 B2
  Suff . . . 57 B6
  Wilts . . . 24 D3
Wingham . . . 31 D6
Wingmore . . . 31 E5
Wingrave . . . 40 C1
Winkburn . . . 77 D7
Winkfield . . . 27 B7
Winkfield Row . . 27 B6
Winkhill . . . 75 D7
Winklebury . . . 26 D4
Winkleigh . . . 9 D8
Winksley . . . 95 B5
Winkton . . . 14 E2
Winlaton . . . 110 C4
Winless . . . 158 E5
Winmarleigh . . . 92 E4
Winnal . . . 49 F6
Winnall . . . 15 B5
Winnersh . . . 27 B5
Winscales . . . 98 B2
Winscombe . . . 23 D6
Winsford Ches W . 74 C3
  Som . . . 21 F8
Winsham . . . 11 D8
Winshill . . . 63 B6
Winskill . . . 109 F5
Winslade . . . 26 E4
Winsley . . . 24 C3
Winslow . . . 39 B7
Winson . . . 37 D7
Winson Green . . 62 F4
Winsor . . . 14 C4
Winster Derbys . . 76 C2
  W&F. . . . 99 E6
Winston Durham . 101 C6
  Suff . . . 57 C5
Winstone . . . 37 D6
Winston Green . . 57 C5
Winswell . . . 9 C6
Winterborne
  Clenston . . . 13 D6
Winterborne
  Herringston . . 12 F4
Winterborne
  Houghton . . . 13 D6
Winterborne
  Kingston . . . 13 E6
Winterborne
  Monkton . . . 12 F4
Winterborne
  Stickland . . . 13 D6
Winterborne
  Whitechurch . . 13 D6
Winterborne
  Zelston . . . 13 E6

Winterbourne
  Monkton . . . 25 B6
Winterbourne
  Steepleton . . . 12 F4
Winterbourne
  Stoke. . . . 25 E5
Winter Gardens . 42 F3
Winteringham . . 90 B3
Winterley . . . 74 D4
Wintersett . . . 88 C4
Wintershill . . . 15 C6
Winterton . . . 90 C3
Winterton-on-Sea 69 C7
Winthorpe Lincs . 79 C8
  Notts . . . 77 D8
Winton BCP . . . 13 E8
  N Yorks. . . . 102 E2
  Wilts . . . 25 D6
Wintringham . . 96 B4
Winwick Cambs . 65 F8
  Warr. . . . 86 E4
  W Nhants. . . . 52 B4
Wirksworth . . . 76 D2
Wirksworth Moor . 76 D3
Wirswall . . . 74 E2
Wisbech . . . 66 D4
Wisbech St Mary . 66 D4
Wisborough Green 16 B4
Wiseton . . . 89 F7
Wishaw N Lanark . 119 D7
  Warks . . . 63 E5
Wisley . . . 27 D8
Wispington . . . 78 B5
Wissenden . . . 30 E3
Wissett . . . 57 B7
Wistanstow . . . 60 F4
Wistanswick . . . 61 B6
Wistaston . . . 74 D3
Wistaston Green . 74 D3
Wiston Pembs. . . 32 C1
  S Ayrs . . . 112 B3
  W Sus . . . 16 C5
Wistow Cambs . . 66 F2
  N Yorks. . . . 95 F8
Wiswell . . . 93 F7
Witcham . . . 66 F4
Witchampton . . 13 D7
Witchford . . . 55 B6
Witham . . . 42 C4
Witham Friary. . 24 E2
Witham on the Hill 65 C7
Withcall . . . 91 F6
Withdean . . . 17 D7
Witherenden Hill . 18 C3
Witheridge . . . 10 C3
Witherley . . . 63 E7
Withern . . . 91 F8
Withernsea . . . 91 B7
Withernwick . . 97 E7
Withersdale Street 69 F5
Withersfield . . 55 E7
Witherslack . . 99 F6
Withiel. . . . 4 C4
Withiel Florey . . 21 F8
Withington Glos . 37 C7
  Gtr Man . . . 87 E6
  Hereford . . . 49 E7
  Shrops . . . 61 C5
  Staffs . . . 75 F7
Withington Green . 74 B5
Withleigh . . . 10 C4
Withnell . . . 86 B4
Withybrook . . . 63 F8
Withycombe . . 22 E2
Withycombe
  Raleigh . . . 10 F5
Withyham . . . 29 F5
Withypool . . . 21 F7
Witley . . . 27 F7
Witnesham . . . 57 D5
Witney . . . 38 C3
Wittering . . . 65 D7
Wittersham . . . 19 C5
Witton Angus . . 135 B5
  Worcs . . . 50 C3
Witton Bridge . . 69 A6
Witton Gilbert. . 110 E5
Witton-le-Wear . 110 F4
Witton Park . . 110 F4
Wiveliscombe . . 11 B5
Wivelrod. . . . 26 F4
Wivelsfield . . . 17 B7
Wivelsfield Green . 17 B7
Wivenhoe . . . 43 B6
Wivenhoe Cross . 43 B6
Wiveton . . . 81 C6
Wix . . . 43 B7
Wixford . . . 51 D5
Wixhill . . . 61 B5
Wixoe . . . 55 E8
Woburn . . . 53 F7
Woburn Sands . . 53 F7
Wokefield Park . . 26 C4
Woking . . . 27 D8
Wokingham . . . 27 C6
Wolborough . . 7 B6
Woldingham . . 28 D4
Wold Newton
  E Yorks . . . 97 B6
  NE Lincs. . . . 91 E6
Wolfclyde . . . 120 F3
Wolferton . . . 67 B6
Wolfhill . . . 134 F1
Wolf's Castle . . 44 C4
Wolfsdale . . . 44 C4
Woll . . . 115 B7
Wollaston
  N Nhants . . . 53 C7
  Shrops . . . 60 C3
Wollaton . . . 76 F5
Wollerton . . . 74 F3
Wollescote . . . 62 F3
Wolsingham . . 110 F3
Wolstanton . . 75 E5
Wolston . . . 52 B2
Wolvercote . . 38 D4
Wolverhampton . 62 E3
Wolverley Shrops . 73 F8
  Worcs . . . 50 B3
Wolverton Hants . 26 D3
  M Keynes . . . 53 E6
  Warks . . . 51 C7
Wolverton
  Common . . . 26 D3
Wolvesnewton . . 36 E1
Wolvey . . . 63 F8
Wolviston . . . 102 B2
Wombleton . . . 102 F4
Wombourne . . 62 E2

Wombwell . . . 88 D4
Womenswold . . 31 D6
Womersley . . . 89 C6
Wonastow . . . 36 C1
Wonersh . . . 27 E8
Wonson . . . 9 F8
Wooburn . . . 40 F2
Wooburn Green . 40 F2
Woodacott . . . 9 D5
Woodale . . . 94 B3
Woodbank . . . 143 G7
Woodbastwick . . 69 C6
Woodbeck . . . 77 B7
Woodborough
  Notts . . . 77 E6
  Wilts . . . 25 D6
Woodbridge Dorset 13 C5
  Suff . . . 57 E6
Woodbury
  Salterton . . . 10 F5
Woodchester . . 37 D5
Woodchurch Kent . 19 B6
  Mers . . . 85 F3
Woodcombe . . 21 E8
Woodcote . . . 39 F6
Woodcott . . . 26 D2
Woodcroft . . . 36 E2
Woodcutts . . . 13 C7
Wood Dalling . . 81 E6
Woodditton . . . 55 D7
Woodeaton . . . 39 C5
Woodend Cumb . 98 E3
  W Nhants. . . . 52 E4
  W Sus . . . 16 D2
Wood End Herts . . 41 B6
  Warks . . . 51 B6
  Warks . . . 63 D6
Wood Enderby . . 79 C5
Woodend Green . 52 F4
Woodfalls . . . 14 B2
Woodfield Oxon . . 39 B5
  S Ayrs . . . 112 B3
Wood Field. . . 28 D2
Woodford Corn. . 8 C4
  Devon. . . . 7 E5
  Glos . . . 36 E3
  Gtr Man . . . 87 F6
  London . . . 41 E7
  N Nhants. . . . 53 B7
Woodford Halse . 52 D3
Woodgate Norf . . 68 C3
  W Mid . . . 62 F3
  Worcs . . . 50 C4
  W Sus . . . 16 D3
Woodgreen . . . 14 C2
Wood Green . . 41 E6
Woodhall Herts . . 41 C5
  Inclyd. . . . 118 B3
  N Yorks. . . . 100 E4
Woodhall Spa . . 78 C4
Woodham . . . 27 C8
Woodham Ferrers . 42 E3
Woodham
  Mortimer . . . 42 D4
Woodham Walter . 42 D4
Woodhaven . . 129 B6
Wood Hayes . . 62 D3
Woodhead . . . 153 E7
Woodhey . . . 87 C5
Woodhill . . . 61 F7
Woodhorn . . . 117 F8
Woodhouse Leics . 64 C2
  N Lincs. . . . 89 D8
  S Yorks. . . . 88 F5
  W Yorks. . . . 88 B4
  W Yorks . . . 95 F5
Woodhouse Eaves . 64 C2
Woodhouselee . . 120 C5
Woodhouselees . . 108 B3
Woodhouse Park . 87 F6
Woodhouses . . 63 C5
Woodhurst . . . 54 B4
Woodingdean . . 17 D7
Woodkirk . . . 88 B3
Woodland Devon . 7 C5
  Durham . . . 101 B5
Woodlands Aberds 141 E6
  Dorset . . . 13 D8
  Hants . . . 14 C4
  Highld . . . 151 E8
  N Yorks. . . . 95 D6
  S Yorks. . . . 89 D6
Woodlands St
  Mary . . . 25 B8
Woodlane . . . 62 B5
Wood Lanes . . 87 F7
Woodleigh . . . 6 E5
Woodlesford . . 88 B4
Woodley Gtr Man . 87 E7
  Wokingham . . . 27 B5
Woodmancote Glos 36 E4
  Glos . . . 37 D7
  Glos . . . 37 D7
  W Sus . . . 15 D8
  W Sus . . . 17 C7
Woodmancott . . 26 E3
Woodmansey . . 97 F6
Woodmansterne . 28 D3
Woodminton . . 13 B8
Woodnesborough . 31 D7
Woodnewton . . 65 E7
Woodnook . . . 78 F2
Wood Norton . . 81 E6
Woodplumpton . 92 F5
Woodrising . . 68 D2
Woodseaves Shrops 74 F3
  Staffs . . . 61 B7
Woodsend . . . 25 B7
Woodsetts . . . 89 F6
Woodsford . . 13 E6
Wood's Green . 18 B3
Woodside
  Aberdeen . . . 141 D8
  Aberds . . . 153 D10
  Brack . . . 27 B7
  Fife. . . . 129 D6
  Hants . . . 14 E4
  Herts . . . 41 D5
  Perth . . . 134 F2

Woodthorpe continued
  Leics. . . . 64 C2
  Lincs. . . . 91 F8
  York . . . 95 E8
Woodton . . . 69 E5
Woodtown . . . 9 B6
Woodvale . . . 85 C4
Woodville . . . 63 C7
Wood Walton . . 66 F2
Woodyates. . . 13 C8
Woofferton . . . 49 C7
Wookey . . . 23 E7
Wookey Hole . . 23 E7
Wool. . . . 13 F6
Woolacombe . . 20 E3
Woolage Green . 31 E6
Woolaston . . . 36 E2
Woolavington . . 22 E5
Woolbeding. . . 16 B2
Wooldale . . . 88 D2
Wooler . . . 117 B5
Woolfardisworthy
  Devon. . . . 8 B5
  Devon. . . . 10 D3
Woolfords
  Cottages . . . 120 D3
Woolhampton . . 26 C3
Woolhope . . . 49 F8
Woolhope
  Cockshoot . . . 49 F8
Woolland . . . 13 D5
Woollaton . . . 9 C6
Woolley Bath. . . 24 C2
  Cambs. . . . 54 B2
  Corn . . . 8 C4
  Derbys . . . 76 C3
  W Yorks . . . 88 C4
Woolmere Green . 50 C4
Woolmer Green . 41 C5
Woolpit . . . 56 C3
Woolscott . . . 52 C2
Woolsington . . 110 C4
Woolstanwood . . 74 D3
Woolstaston . . 60 E4
Woolsthorpe Lincs . 65 B6
  Lincs. . . . 77 F8
Woolston Devon . . 6 E5
  Shrops . . . 60 B3
  Shrops . . . 60 F3
  Soton . . . 14 C5
  Warr. . . . 86 F4
Woolstone
  M Keynes . . . 53 F6
  Oxon. . . . 38 F2
Woolton . . . 86 F2
Woolton Hill . . 26 C2
Woolverstone . . 57 F5
Woolverton . . 24 D2
Woolwich . . . 28 B5
Woolwich Ferry . 28 B5
Woonton . . . 49 D5
Wooperton. . . 117 B6
Woore . . . 74 E4
Wootten Green . 57 B6
Wootton Bedford . 53 E8
  Hants . . . 14 E3
  Hereford . . . 48 D5
  Kent . . . 31 E6
  N Lincs. . . . 90 C4
  Oxon. . . . 38 C4
  Oxon. . . . 38 D4
  Shrops . . . 49 B6
  Shrops . . . 60 B3
  Staffs . . . 62 B2
  Staffs . . . 75 E8
  W Nhants. . . . 53 D5
Wootton Bridge . 15 E6
Wootton Common 15 E6
Wootton
  Courtenay . . . 21 E8
Wootton Fitzpaine . 11 E8
Wootton Rivers . 25 C6
Wootton St
  Lawrence . . . 26 D3
Wootton Wawen . 51 C6
Worcester . . . 50 D3
Worcester Park . 28 C3
Wordsley . . . 62 F2
Wordwell . . . 56 B2
Work . . . 159 G5
Workington . . 98 B1
Worksop . . . 77 B5
Worlaby . . . 90 C4
World's End . . 26 B2
Worle . . . 23 C5
Worleston . . . 74 D3
Worlingham . . 69 F7
Worlington . . 55 B7
Worlingworth . . 57 C6
Wormald Green . 95 C6
Wormbridge . . 49 F6
Wormegay . . . 67 C6
Wormelow Tump . 49 F6
Wormhill. . . . 75 B8
Wormingford . . 56 F3
Worminghall . . 39 D6
Wormington . . 50 F5
Worminster . . 23 E7
Wormit . . . 129 B5
Wormleighton . . 52 D2
Wormley Herts . . 41 D6
  Sur . . . 27 F7
Wormley West
  End . . . 41 D6
Wormshill . . . 30 D2
Wormsley . . . 49 E6
Worplesdon . . 27 D7
Worrall . . . 88 E4
Worsbrough . . 88 D4
Worsbrough
  Common . . . 88 D4
Worsley . . . 86 D5
Worstead . . . 69 B6
Worsthorne . . 93 F8
Worston . . . 93 E7
Worswell . . . 6 E3
Worth Kent . . . 31 D7
  W Sus . . . 28 F4
Wortham . . . 56 B4
Worthen . . . 60 D3
Worthenbury . . 73 E8
Worthing Norf . . 68 C2
  W Sus . . . 16 D5
Worthington . . 63 B8
Wortley S Yorks . . 88 E4
  W Yorks . . . 95 F5
Worton N Yorks . . 100 E4

Worton continued
  Wilts . . . 24 D4
Wortwell . . . 69 F5
Wotherton . . . 60 D2
Wotter . . . 6 C3
Wotton . . . 28 E2
Wotton-under-
  Edge . . . 36 E4
Wotton
  Underwood . . 39 C6
Woughton on the
  Green . . . 53 F6
Wouldham . . . 29 C8
Wrabness . . . 57 F5
Wrafton . . . 20 F3
Wragby Lincs . . 78 B4
  W Yorks . . . 88 C5
Wragholme . . 91 E7
Wramplingham . 68 D4
Wrangbrook . . 89 C5
Wrangham . . . 153 E6
Wrangle . . . 79 D7
Wrangle Bank . . 79 D7
Wrangle Lowgate . 79 D7
Wrangway . . . 11 C6
Wrantage . . . 11 B8
Wrawby . . . 90 D4
Wraxall Dorset . . 12 D3
  Som . . . 23 B6
  Som . . . 23 F8
Wray . . . 93 C6
Wraysbury . . . 27 B8
Wrayton . . . 93 B6
Wrea Green . . 92 F3
Wreay Cumb . . 108 E4
  W&F. . . . 99 B6
Wrecclesham . . 27 E6
Wrecsam
  = Wrexham . . . 73 D7
Wrekenton . . . 111 D5
Wrelton . . . 103 F5
Wrenbury . . . 74 E2
Wrench Green . . 103 F7
Wreningham . . 68 E4
Wrentham . . . 69 F7
Wrenthorpe . . 88 B4
Wrentnall . . . 60 D4
Wressle E Yorks . . 96 F3
  N Lincs. . . . 90 D3
Wrestlingworth . 54 E3
Wretham . . . 68 F2
Wretton . . . 67 E6
Wrexham
  = Wrecsam . . . 73 D7
Wrexham Industrial
  Estate . . . 73 E7
Wribbenhall . . 50 B2
Wrightington Bar . 86 C3
Wrinehill . . . 74 E4
Wrington . . . 23 C6
Writhlington . . 24 D2
Writtle . . . 42 D2
Wrockwardine . . 61 C6
Wroot . . . 89 D8
Wrotham . . . 29 D7
Wrotham Heath . 29 D7
Wroughton . . 37 F8
Wroxall IoW . . 15 G6
  Warks . . . 51 B7
Wroxeter . . . 61 D5
Wroxham . . . 69 C6
Wroxton . . . 52 E2
Wyaston . . . 75 E8
Wyberton . . . 79 E6
Wyboston . . . 54 D2
Wybunbury . . 74 E4
Wychbold . . . 50 C4
Wych Cross . . 28 F5
Wyck . . . 27 F5
Wyck Rissington . 38 B1
Wycoller . . . 94 F2
Wycomb . . . 64 B4
Wycombe Marsh . 40 E1
Wyddial . . . 54 F4
Wye . . . 30 E4
Wyesham . . . 36 C2
Wyfordby . . . 64 C4
Wyke Dorset . . 13 B5
  Shrops . . . 61 D6
  Sur . . . 27 D7
  W Yorks . . . 88 B2
Wykeham N Yorks . 96 B4
  N Yorks. . . . 103 F7
Wyken . . . 63 F7
Wyke Regis . . 12 G4
Wykey . . . 60 B3
Wylam . . . 110 C4
Wylde Green . . 62 E5
Wyllie . . . 35 E5
Wylye . . . 24 F5
Wymering . . 15 D7
Wymeswold . . 64 B3
Wymington . . 53 C7
Wymondham Leics 65 C5
  Norf . . . 68 D4
Wyndham . . . 34 E3
Wynford Eagle . 12 E3
Wyng . . . 159 J4
Wynyard Village . 102 B2
Wyre Piddle . . 50 E4
Wysall . . . 64 B3
Wythall . . . 51 B5
Wytham . . . 38 D4
Wythburn . . . 99 C5
Wythenshawe . . 87 F6
Wythop Mill . . 98 B3
Wyton . . . 54 B3
Wyverstone . . 56 C4
Wyverstone Street. 56 C4
Wyville . . . 65 B5
Wyvis Lodge . . 150 D7

Yarkhill . . . 49 E8
Yarlet . . . 62 B3
Yarlington . . . 12 B4
Yarlside . . . 92 C2
Yarm. . . . 102 C2
Yarmouth . . . 14 F4
Yarnbrook . . . 24 D3
Yarnfield . . . 75 F5
Yarnscombe . . 9 B7
Yarnton . . . 38 C4
Yarpole . . . 49 C6
Yarrow . . . 115 B6
Yarrow Feus . . 115 B6
Yarsop . . . 49 E6
Yarwell . . . 65 E7
Yate . . . 36 F4
Yateley . . . 27 C6
Yatesbury . . . 25 B5
Yattendon . . 26 B3
Yatton Hereford . 49 C6
  N Som . . . 23 C6
Yatton Keynell . . 24 B3
Yaverland . . . 15 F7
Yaxham . . . 68 C3
Yaxley Cambs. . . 65 E8
  Suff . . . 56 B5
Yazor . . . 49 E6
Y Bala = Bala . . 72 F3
Y Barri = Barry . . 22 C3
Y Bont-Faen
  = Cowbridge. . 21 B8
Y Drenewydd
  = Newtown . . 59 E8
Yeading . . . 40 F4
Yeadon . . . 94 E5
Yealand Conyers . 92 B5
Yealand
  Redmayne . . 92 B5
Yealmpton . . . 6 D3
Yearby . . . 102 B4
Yearsley . . . 95 B8
Yeaton . . . 60 C4
Yeaveley . . . 75 E8
Yedingham . . 96 B4
Yeldon . . . 53 C8
Yelford . . . 38 D3
Yelland . . . 20 F3
Yelling . . . 54 C3
Yelvertoft . . 52 B3
Yelverton Devon . 6 C3
  Norf . . . 69 D5
Yenston . . . 12 B5
Yeoford . . . 10 E2
Yeolmbridge . . 8 F5
Yeo Mill . . . 10 B3
Yeovil . . . 12 C3
Yeovil Marsh . . 12 C3
Yeovilton . . . 12 B3
Yerbeston . . . 32 D1
Yesnaby. . . . 159 G3
Yetlington . . 117 D6
Yetminster . . 12 C3
Yettington . . . 11 F5
Yetts o'Muckhart 128 D2
Y Felinheli . . . 82 E5
Y Fenni
  = Abergavenny . 35 C6
Y Fflint = Flint . . 73 B6
Y Ffôr . . . 70 D4
Y-Ffrith . . . 72 A4
Y Gelli Gandryll
  = Hay-on-Wye . 48 E4
Yieldshields . . 119 D8
Yiewsley . . . 40 F3
Y Mwmbwls
  = The Mumbles . 33 F7
Ynysboeth . . 34 E4
Ynysddu . . . 35 E5
Ynysgyfflog . . 58 C3
Ynyshir . . . 34 E4
Ynyslas . . . 58 E3
Ynys-meudwy . . 33 D8
Ynystawe . . . 33 D7
Ynysybwl . . . 34 E4
Yockenthwaite . 94 B2
Yockleton . . . 60 C3
Yokefleet . . . 90 B2
Yoker . . . 118 C5
Yonder Bognie . 152 D5
York . . . 95 D8
Yorkletts . . . 30 C4
Yorkley . . . 36 D3
York Town . . 27 C6
Yorton . . . 60 B5
Youlgreave . . 76 C2
Youlstone . . . 8 C4
Youlthorpe . . 96 D3
Youlton . . . 95 C7
Young's End . . 42 C3
Young Wood . . 78 B4
Yoxall . . . 62 C5
Yoxford . . . 57 C7
Y Pîl = Pyle . . 34 F2
Yr Hôb = Hope . 73 D7
Y Rhws = Rhoose. 22 C2
Y Rhyl = Rhyl . . 72 A4
Yr Wyddgrug
  = Mold. . . . 73 C6
Ysbyty-Cynfyn . 47 B6
Ysbyty Ifan . . 72 E2
Ysbyty Ystwyth . 47 B6
Ysceifiog . . . 73 B5
Yspitty . . . 33 E6
Ystalyfera . . . 34 D1
Ystrad . . . 34 E3
Ystrad Aeron . . 46 D4
Ystradfellte . . 34 C3
Ystradffin . . . 47 E6
Ystradgynlais . . 34 C1
Ystradmeurig . . 47 C6
Ystrad-mynach . 35 E5
Ystradowen Carms 33 C8
  V Glam . . . 22 B2
Ystumtuen . . 47 B6
Ythanbank . . 153 E9
Ythsie . . . 153 E8

Z

Zeal Monachorum. 10 D2
Zeals . . . 24 F2
Zelah . . . 4 D3
Zennor . . . 2 C3